Cataclysm 1914

Historical Materialism Book Series

The Historical Materialism Book Series is a major publishing initiative of the radical left. The capitalist crisis of the twenty-first century has been met by a resurgence of interest in critical Marxist theory. At the same time, the publishing institutions committed to Marxism have contracted markedly since the high point of the 1970s. The Historical Materialism Book Series is dedicated to addressing this situation by making available important works of Marxist theory. The aim of the series is to publish important theoretical contributions as the basis for vigorous intellectual debate and exchange on the left.

The peer-reviewed series publishes original monographs, translated texts, and reprints of classics across the bounds of academic disciplinary agendas and across the divisions of the left. The series is particularly concerned to encourage the internationalization of Marxist debate and aims to translate significant studies from beyond the English-speaking world.

For a full list of titles in the Historical Materialism Book Series available in paperback from Haymarket Books, visit:
www.haymarketbooks.org/category/hm-series

Cataclysm 1914

The First World War and the Making of Modern World Politics

Edited by
Alexander Anievas

Haymarket Books
Chicago, IL

First published in 2015 by Brill Academic Publishers, The Netherlands

Published in paperback in 2016 by
Haymarket Books
P.O. Box 180165
Chicago, IL 60618
773-583-7884
www.haymarketbooks.org

ISBN: 978-1-60846-634-4

Trade distribution:
In the US, Consortium Book Sales, www.cbsd.com
In Canada, Publishers Group Canada, www.pgcbooks.ca
In the UK, Turnaround Publisher Services, www.turnaround-uk.com
In all other countries, Publishers Group Worldwide, www.pgw.com

Cover design by Jamie Kerry of Belle Étoile Studios and Ragina Johnson.

This book was published with the generous support of
Lannan Foundation and the Wallace Global Fund.

Entered into digital printing March, 2022.

Library of Congress Cataloging-in-Publication data is available.

This book is dedicated to Raphael Anievas and Bill Cooper – my two first great teachers who instilled in me the desire to learn and teach.

∵

Contents

PART 2

Reconfigurations: Revolution and Culture after 1914

Acknowledgements

This collection was very much a collective effort and I thank all the contributors for their great assistance in helping this volume see the light of day. I must also thank the editors of the Historical Materialism book series for their general enthusiasm for the project and patience in waiting for its completion. I believe it was Josef Ansorge who first aired the idea that I should edit some sort of collection on the First World War for the 100th anniversary, so many thanks to him for giving me the idea in the first place. On a more personal note, I would be remiss not to acknowledge the loving support of my wife, Linda Szilas, throughout the development of the project. I must also thank my parents, family and friends for all their support throughout the years. I've decided to dedicate this book to my uncle, Raphael Anievas, and former tutor, Bill Cooper, as it was their examples as teachers, along with the many hours we spent discussing history, politics and various other subjects, that sowed in me the desire to learn, get political and eventually teach. So, to both of them I owe a great debt. Finally, I would also like to acknowledge the generous funding and support provided by the Leverhulme Trust.

List of Contributors

Alexander Anievas

is an Early Career Leverhulme Fellow at the Department of Politics and International Studies, University of Cambridge. He is the author of *Capital, the State, and War: Class Conflict and Geopolitics in the Thirty Years' Crisis, 1914–1945* (University of Michigan Press, 2014) and editor of *Marxism and World Politics: Contesting Global Capitalism* (Routledge, 2010). He is currently working on a manuscript (with Kerem Nisancioglu) rethinking the intersocietal origins of capitalism and the 'rise of the West' entitled *How the West Came to Rule: The Geopolitical Origins of Capitalism* (Pluto, 2015, forthcoming). He is a member of the editorial collective, *Historical Materialism: Research in Critical Marxist Theory.*

Shelley Baranowski

is Distinguished Professor of History Emerita at the University of Akron (USA). She is the author of four books, the most recent of which are *Nazi Empire: German Imperialism and Colonialism from Bismarck to Hitler* (Cambridge, 2011) and *Strength through Joy: Consumerism and Mass Tourism in the Third Reich* (Cambridge, 2004). She is currently working on a comparative and transnational study of Axis empires.

Neil Davidson

lectures in Sociology with the School of Political and Social Science at the University of Glasgow. He is the author of *The Origins of Scottish Nationhood* (2000), *Discovering the Scottish Revolution* (2003), for which he was awarded the Deutscher Memorial Prize, *How Revolutionary were the Bourgeois Revolutions?* (2012) and *Holding Fast to an Image of the Past* (2014). Davidson has also co-edited and contributed to *Alasdair MacIntyre's Engagement with Marxism* (2008), *Neoliberal Scotland* (2010) and *The Longue Durée of the Far Right* (2014).

Geoff Eley

is Karl Pohrt Distinguished University Professor of Contemporary History at the University of Michigan. He works on modern German and European history, fascism, film and history, and historiography. His earliest works were *Reshaping the German Right: Radical Nationalism and Political Change after Bismarck* (1980, 1991) and *The Peculiarities of German History* (1980, 1984) with David Blackbourn. More recent books include *Forging Democracy* (2002),

A Crooked Line: From Cultural History to the History of Society (2005), and (with Keith Nield) *The Future of Class in History* (2007). He is co-editor of *German Colonialism in a Global Age* (2014). *Nazism as Fascism: Violence, Ideology, and the Ground of Consent in Germany, 1930–1945* appeared in 2013. He is writing a general history of Europe in the twentieth century and a new study of the German Right, *Genealogies of Nazism: Conservatives, Radical Nationalists, Fascists in Germany, 1860–1945.*

Sandra Halperin
is Professor of International Relations and Co-Director of the Centre for Global and Transnational Politics at Royal Holloway, University of London. Her research focuses on global development, the historical sociology of global relations, the causes and conditions of war and peace, and Middle East politics. Her publications include: *In the Mirror of the Third World: Capitalist Development in Modern Europe*, Cornell University Press, 1997; *Global Civil Society and Its Limits* (co-edited with Gordon Laxer), Palgrave/Macmillan, 2003; *War and Social Change in Modern Europe: The Great Transformation Revisited*, Cambridge University Press, 2004; *Re-Envisioning Global Development*, Routledge, 2013; and articles on contemporary Middle East politics, Islam, nationalism, ethnic conflict, state-building, historical sociology, and globalisation.

Esther Leslie
is Professor of Political Aesthetics at Birkbeck, University of London. Her first book was *Walter Benjamin: Overpowering Conformism* (Pluto, 2000). She has also authored a biography of Benjamin (Reaktion, 2007). In 2002 she published *Hollywood Flatlands: Animation, Critical Theory, and the Avant Garde* (Verso). A subsequent book, *Synthetic Worlds: Art, Nature and the Chemical Industry* (Reaktion, 2005), investigated the industrial manufacture of colour and its impact on conceptions of nature and aesthetics. *Derelicts: Thought Worms from the Wreckage* explores the imbrication of war with the theory and practice of interwar German Marxists and avant gardists (Unkant, 2013). Her current research is on the aesthetics and politics of liquid crystals. She runs a website together with Ben Watson, www.militantesthetix.co.uk

Lars T. Lih
lives and works in Montreal, Quebec. He is an Adjunct Professor at the Schulich School of Music, McGill University, but writes on Russian and socialist history on his own time. His publications include *Bread and Authority in Russia, 1914–1921* (1990), *Lenin Rediscovered* (2006), and *Lenin* (2011).

Domenico Losurdo
is Professor of Philosophy at the University of Urbino, Italy. He is the author of many books in Italian, German, French and Spanish. His English language book publications include *Hegel and the Freedom of Moderns* (Durham, NC: Duke University Press, 2001), *Heidegger and the Ideology of War* (New York, NY: Humanity Books, 2004), *Liberalism: A Counter-History* (London: Verso, 2011) and the forthcoming *War and Revolution: Rethinking the Twentieth Century* (London: Verso, 2014). Moreover, a lengthy volume, *Nietzsche, il ribelle aristocratico: Biografia intellettuale e bilancio critico*, is currently being translated by Brill.

Wendy Matsumura
is Assistant Professor of History at Furman University where she teaches modern Japanese history. Her manuscript, *The Limits of Okinawa: Japanese Capitalism, Living Labor and Theorizations of Okinawan Community* is forthcoming from Duke University Press. She is currently investigating the reconfiguration of the Japanese Empire in the 1930s by tracing flows of migrant labour between colonial and metropolitan spaces.

Peter D. Thomas
lectures in the History of Political Thought at Brunel University, London. He is the author of *The Gramscian Moment: Philosophy, Hegemony and Marxism* (Leiden: Brill, 2009), and co-editor of *Encountering Althusser: Politics and Materialism in Contemporary Radical Thought* (New York, NY: Bloomsbury, 2012), and *In Marx's Laboratory: Critical Interpretations of the Grundrisse* (Leiden: Brill, 2013). He serves on the Editorial Board of *Historical Materialism: Research in Critical Marxist Theory*.

Adam Tooze
is the Barton M. Biggs Professor of History at Yale, where he also directs International Security Studies. He is the author of *Statistics and the German State 1900–1945: The Making of Modern Economic Knowledge* (Cambridge: CUP 2001), *Wages of Destruction: The Making and Breaking of the Nazi Economy* (London: Penguin, 2006) and *The Deluge: The Great War and the Remaking of the Global Order 1916–1931* (London: Penguin, 2014). New projects include books on 'War in Germany from the Thirty Years War to the War on Terror', 'The Great Recession as History' and a transnational account of the peasant question in the mid-twentieth century.

Alberto Toscano
is Reader in Critical Theory in the Department of Sociology, Goldsmiths, University of London. He is the author of *Fanaticism: On the Uses of an Idea*, *The Theatre of Production*, and, with Jeff Kinkle, of *Cartographies of the Absolute*. He sits on the editorial board of *Historical Materialism* and edits The Italian List for Seagull Books.

Enzo Traverso
was born in Italy in 1957. He obtained his PhD at the Ecole des Hautes Etudes en Sciences Sociales of Paris in 1989 and taught political science at the University of Picardy, France, for almost twenty years. Since 2013, he is the Susan and Barton Winokur Professor in the Humanities at Cornell University. He is the author of a dozen books, among which include *Understanding the Nazi Genocide* (London: Pluto Press, 1999), *The Origins of Nazi Violence* (New York, NY: The New Press, 2003) and *Fire and Blood: The European Civil War 1914–1945* (London: Verso, forthcoming 2015).

The First World War and the Making of Modern World Politics

Alexander Anievas

Introduction

The centenary anniversary of the First World War provides a unique opportunity to reconsider this critical juncture in the (re)construction of modern world politics as a space of imperial conflict, empire building and revolutionary contestation. It offers a moment of pedagogical reflection for the left on the successes and failures of revolutionary strategies and tactics (in thought and action), the conditions that produced them, and the reactionary politics that sought to counter them. With these goals in mind, *Cataclysm 1914* brings together a number of leftist scholars from a variety of different fields to explore the many aspects of the origins, trajectories and consequences of the First World War. The collection thus aims not only to examine the war itself, but to visualise 1914 as the *moment fatidique* rupturing, redefining, and reconstituting the modern epoch of world politics in its multiple and variegated instantiations.

In this short introductory chapter, I want to lay out some of the key themes of the collection, whilst offering some historical background as to the transformative impact of the First World War on Marxist thought and praxis. For 'it was the war itself', R. Craig Nation writes, 'that became the crucible within which the conceptual paradigms and underlying assumptions that would come to dominate twentieth century socialist and communist thought were forged'.[1]

The Problem of the International

Though Marx and Engels wrote extensively on matters of world politics broadly defined,[2] nowhere did they systematically consider the place of international relations in their theoretical systems. In his original plan for the critique of political economy, Marx projected writing six books, the last three of which would have taken up matters dealing with the state, international trade, and

1 Nation 1989, p. 24.

2 According to Rosenberg 1994, Marx and Engels' works on war, diplomacy and colonialism approximated eight hundred pages. For a judicious review of Marx and Engels' writings on international relations see Kandal 1989.

the world market.[3] As Marx never completed this undertaking, subsequent generations of Marxists were left with the task of providing a more sustained theoretical engagement with the issues of international relations, imperialism and war. Thus, as Nation notes, while 'the internationalist inspiration of Marx's social theory was striking, its prescriptions for managing the practical dilemmas of international relations outside the "realm of freedom" remained unclear'.[4]

Indeed, there remained some ambiguity in Marx and Engels' writings on colonialism, imperialism and war, and the political stand revolutionary socialists should take towards these issues. For while Marx and Engels clearly criticised the barbarities of European colonialism, they also pointed to the 'civilising' and developmental effects that the introduction of capitalism could have on target countries. In the *Communist Manifesto*, they famously described how the bourgeoisie would draw 'all, even the most barbarian, nations into civilisation', creating a 'world after its own image'.[5] Moreover, in analysing the effects of British rule in India, Marx recognised the destructive impact that British rule had on the existing social relations in India. Yet the ultimate end point would be, he argued, a world in which India industrialised on a pattern approximating the European experience. As he put it:

> England has to fulfil a double mission in India: one destructive, the other regenerating – the annihilation of old Asiatic society, and the laying of the material foundations of Western society in Asia ... They destroyed [Hindoo civilisation] by breaking up native communities, by uprooting the native community and by levelling all that was great and elevated in the native society. The historic pages of their rule in India report hardly anything but that destruction. The work of regeneration hardly transpires through a heap of ruins. Nevertheless it has begun.[6]

While Marx would eventually change his position on the role of colonialism in developing other nations, as well as dropping his earlier unilinear notions of socio-historical development,[7] many subsequent Marxists took his earlier writings as a model for interpreting twentieth-century world politics. Indeed, as Richard Day and Daniel Gaido point out in their meticulous survey of early

3 K. Marx, letter to Friedrich Engels, 2 April 1858, in Marx and Engels 1975–2005, Vol. 40, p. 298.
4 Nation 1989, p. 9.
5 Marx and Engels 2002 [1848], p. 11.
6 Marx 1853, p. 217.
7 See, for example, Stedman-Jones 2007; Anderson 2010.

Marxist writings on imperialism, '[u]ntil Marxists could formulate more comprehensive theories, the first inclination of many was to fall back on the view that capitalism's worldwide expansion would carry "civilisation" to backward peoples'.[8] In the debates within the Second International during the two decades before the First World War, this interpretation of the 'civilising mission' of capital actually led some Marxists (notably, Eduard Bernstein and August Bebel) to advocate for the adoption of a socialist policy of colonialism while also calling for the differentiation between 'offensive' and 'defensive' wars, in which the latter would find the support of socialist parties in the defending nations.[9]

Though the first distinctly Marxist works on imperialism and colonialism emerged at the turn of the twentieth century, particularly in the writings of Max Beer and Paul Lévi, the first sustained theoretical engagement with these questions was only furnished by Otto Bauer and Rudolf Hilferding, two Austro-Marxists writing nearly a decade later.[10] These works conceptualised imperialism as an emerging world system with its own unique political and economic imperatives, as imperialist policies came to be seen as a response to capitalism's crisis tendencies.[11] These themes were most systematically developed in Hilferding's landmark 1908 study *Finance Capital: A Study of the Latest Phase of Capitalist Development*, arguably the first book-length theoretical treatment of imperialism from a Marxist standpoint. The work had a major impact on Marxist debates at the time, forming the foundational bedrock of Lenin and Bukharin's later studies on imperialism written during the war.[12]

For Hilferding, like Lenin and Bukharin, imperialism was not simply a policy but an economic necessity of capitalism in its 'latest' phase. This phase was characterised, above all, by the emergence of a powerful fraction of finance capital that had resulted from the increasing concentration and

---

8 Day and Gaido 2011, p. 5.

9 See the discussion of the Stuttgart and Essen Congresses in 1907 in Day and Gaido 2011, pp. 29–38.

10 Day and Gaido 2011, p. 16.

11 See especially Hilferding 2011 [1907]; Hilferding 1985 [1908]; Bauer 2011a [1908]; Bauer 2011b [1910].

12 The other major Marxist work on imperialism during the pre-war period was Rosa Luxemburg's *The Accumulation of Capital* (1913). Though Luxemburg's work has been highly influential for subsequent generations of Marxists, at the time of its publication the work was almost universally criticised for having misinterpreted Marx's reproduction scheme. It was thus far less influential in the contemporary Marxist debates on imperialism than Hilferding's work. For discussions see Brewer 1990, pp. 58–72 and Day and Gaido 2011, pp. 69–76.

centralisation of capital in turn leading to the fusion of banking and industrial groupings. With this 'unification of capital' under the mastery of finance capital, eliminating any vestiges of free competition by the large monopolistic combinations, the entire relationship of the capitalist class to state power was transformed. The state now became 'a means of competition for finance capital on the world market'. And as 'finance capital demands unlimited power politics ... the demand for an expansionist policy revolutionises the whole world view of the bourgeoisie, which ceases to be peace-loving and humanitarian'.[13] Thus emerged an era of sharp economic and geopolitical competition inexorably leading to war.

As we can see, by the eve of the First World War Marxists had come to a much more sophisticated understanding of the relationship between capitalism, imperialism and war. However, finding common ground for a concrete political strategy in the event of war proved elusive. Those left revolutionaries who argued for using the likely outbreak of war to mobilise the working class into revolutionary action were continually opposed by the dominant centrist currents within the Second International, who tended toward pursuing socialism through parliamentary reforms. Hence, while nearly all socialists were committed to *some* form of internationalism based upon the premises of classical Marxism, they remained 'fundamentally divided over the issues of war and imperialism' even though in the decades before the war such divisions were 'patched over by vague pronouncements' of abstract international solidarity. The result was that the unanimously accepted resolutions of the Stuttgart, Copenhagen, and Basel congresses on war and imperialism were 'most notable for their failure to specify effective means of resistance to a danger that all acknowledged to be clear and present'.[14] As Karl Kautsky later reflected at the end of the First World War: 'It's astonishing that nobody, during that meeting [the International Socialist Bureau, 29–30 July 1914], put the question: what do we do in case of war? Which position should the socialist parties take in this war?' (Quoted in Traverso, 'European Intellectuals and the First World War', p. 204).

The 'New Era of War and Revolution'

For nearly two decades before the outbreak of the First World War, Marxists within Europe had been debating the evolving nature of capitalist imperialism and its inextricable connection to geopolitical rivalry and war. Time and time again, social democrats had warned of the impending dangers of global war, though they never adequately worked out a coherent political strategy in the

13 Hilferding 1985 [1908], pp. 301, 331, 335.

14 Nation 1989, p. 20.

event of such a war. Thus, whilst the outbreak of military conflict in Europe on 28 July 1914 came as a shock to many state managers and politicians of the time, social democrats *should* have been the least likely section of the population to be surprised. Yet, as we know, the war caught even the most prescient of socialists completely off guard. But it was the subsequent decision by Germany's Social Democratic Party (SPD), by far and away the largest and most politically important socialist party in Europe, to vote in favour of the government's requested emergency war appropriations on 4 August that came as an even greater shock to socialists. As Trotsky later recalled, when the issue of *Vorwärts* containing the report of the 4 August Reichstag debate arrived in Switzerland, Lenin thought it was a fake published by the German General Staff.[15] As the Russian socialist activist, Angelica Balabanov, later reflected: 'Never had the powerlessness of the International come so clearly and tragically to the fore'.[16]

The war thus not only signalled the emergence of a new epoch in world politics, but also a new age in socialist politics as the Second International effectively collapsed in the eyes of many of its hitherto most strident defenders and, within three years of the outbreak of the war, a socialist-inspired revolution would occur in the most unlikely of places: Tsarist Russia. Consequently, as the Dutch Marxist Anton Pannekoek proclaimed, 'The Second International is dead'.[17] While the socialist parties of the neutral countries continued to speak out against the continuation of the conflict, organised socialist opposition among the belligerent powers was nearly invisible. This of course did not stop a significant minority of left revolutionaries from criticising the 'leaders' of the Second International for their betrayal while continually agitating against the war, as some of the chapters in this book examine.

For Lenin and other fellow Bolsheviks, the war demonstrated the abject bankruptcy of the centrist currents within the Second International, and of Kautsky in particular. Yet, according to Lars T. Lih's provocative analysis below, the betrayal of the 'leaders' of the Second International did not signal Lenin's rejection of the 'Marxism of the Second International' or a renunciation of Kautsky's earlier writings, but instead just the opposite: a reaffirmation of what he took to be the 'pre-war consensus of revolutionary Social Democracy' in his own 'rhetoric of aggressive unoriginality in the years 1914–16'. During this period, Lenin was at pains to demonstrate the *essential continuity* between the Bolshevik programme of the time and the pre-war consensus of revolutionary Marxism as demonstrated, in particular, by Kautsky's pre-war analysis of

15 Day and Gaido 2011, p. 79.
16 Quoted in Nation 1989, p. 21.
17 Pannekoek 2011 [1914], p. 788.

a 'new era of war and revolution' characterised first and foremost by a *global* system of revolutionary interaction which found its practical expression in the Basel Manifesto of 1912 (see Lih, '"The New Era of War and Revolution"', p. 367). 'As Lenin saw it', Lih writes, 'the Manifesto was a solemn commitment by Europe's Social Democratic parties to use the outbreak of war to engage in revolutionary action or at least work in that direction. Not to honour this commitment was to be a betrayal of everything that Social Democracy stood for' (Lih, '"The New Era of War and Revolution"', p. 379).

Against the 'Hegelist' interpretation of Lenin's politics of the period, which argues for the central importance of Lenin's re-reading of Hegel's *Science of Logic* in the formulation of Lenin's innovative political programme during the war, Lih's chapter contends that Marxists and historians need to fundamentally rethink Lenin's political position towards the war in terms of his reiteration of Kautsky's pre-war analysis of the 'new era of war and revolution'. Lenin's political programme during the war thus represented much less of a fundamental departure from the Marxism and politics of the Second International, but rather its striking continuation in purified form, as he understood it.

If Lenin's political programme during the years between 1914 and 1916 was one of 'aggressive unoriginality', what was arguably original was his later pronouncement, after the success of the Bolshevik Revolution of November 1917, that Russia would immediately begin the transition to socialism. The idea that Russia, then regarded as one of the most 'backward' polities in Europe, was ripe for a proletarian rather than bourgeois revolution inaugurating a transition to socialism was virtually unthinkable to contemporary Marxists of the pre-war period, with the notable exception of Trotsky. What converted Lenin and other Russian revolutionaries to Trotsky's conclusion was the crisis brought about by Russia's involvement in the First World War, as Neil Davidson meticulously details in his chapter on Marxist thinking on revolution during the pre-war period.

In his chapter, Davidson provides a detailed analysis of what the leading Marxist intellectuals of the Second International thought of the revolutionary prospects in Russia and Eastern Europe before February 1917, before going on to explore the distinctiveness of the Russian experience which followed, and the singularity of the revolutionary outcome there when compared with the rest of the continent, to which the conflict was central. In doing so, Davidson offers a reconceptualisation of the concept of 'bourgeois revolution' in terms of its effects in establishing territorially-demarcated autonomous sites of capital accumulation, while providing a periodisation of the unique temporalities of bourgeois revolutions over the course of capitalist development. From this perspective, Davidson illustrates the changing forms bourgeois revolutions took vis-à-vis the evolving structure of capitalism in its world development, and the differential agencies which pursued these revolutions as the bourgeoisie generally ceased to function as a leading revolutionary force, particularly in the post-1848 period, as most Marxists came to recognise by the turn of the twentieth century. It was within this context, Davidson claims, that Marx and Engels's concept of 'permanent revolution' re-entered the Marxist vernacular. The concept was most generally used in describing the means by which the working class would have to carry out the *bourgeois* revolution in Russia. This position, shared by the majority of the centre and left of the Second International, denied any contradiction between working-class agency and bourgeois outcome in the making of a revolution in Russia. However, it stopped short of envisioning the possibility of the Russian proletariat, in alliance with the peasant majority, making a distinctly *socialist* revolution in Russia. Trotsky was alone in arguing for this scenario in the pre-war period, as he came to develop his own unique interpretation of the 'permanent revolution' developed over the course of the Russian Revolution of 1905. 'The very demonstration of working-class creativity and power demonstrated by the soviet and the general strike', Davidson writes in regards to the 1905 Revolution, 'seems to have confirmed in Trotsky the view that it could indeed advance toward socialism, but only under one condition, the identification of which represents his most original contribution to these discussions: the international dimension' (Davidson, 'The First World War, Classical Marxism and the End of the Bourgeois Revolution in Europe', p. 331).

It was indeed this *international* dimension of capitalist development, which Trotsky came to theoretically comprehend through the concept of 'uneven and combined development', that rendered the repetition of historical stages obsolete and thus provided the historical and sociological foundations for Russia's telescoping of the bourgeois and socialist revolutions into a single, uninterrupted process. As Trotsky put it:

> So far as its direct and indirect tasks are concerned, the Russian revolution is a 'bourgeois' revolution because it sets out to liberate bourgeois society from the chains and fetters of absolutism and feudal ownership. But the principal driving force of the Russian revolution is the proletariat, and that is why, so far as its method is concerned, it is a proletarian revolution. Many pedants, who insist on determining the historical role of the proletariat by means of arithmetical or statistical calculations, or establishing it by means of formal historical analogies, have shown themselves incapable of digesting this contradiction. They see the bourgeoisie as the providence-sent leader of the Russian revolution. They try to wrap the

> proletariat – which, in fact, marched at the head of events at all stages of the revolutionary rising [1905] – in the swaddling-clothes of their own theoretical immaturity. For such pedants, the history of one capitalist nation repeats the history of another, with, of course, certain more or less important divergences. Today they fail to see the unified process of world capitalist development which swallows up all the countries that lie in its path and which creates, out of the national and general exigencies of capitalism, an amalgam whose nature cannot be understood by the application of historical clichés, but only by materialist analysis.[18]

In these ways, Trotsky thus conceived the potentials of a socialist revolution occurring in Russia as a result of the international development of capitalism to which the trajectory of the revolution was intrinsically bound. With the theory of uneven and combined development and its strategic corollary, the 'permanent revolution', Trotsky arguably offered one of the single most important innovations in Marxist thought – ranking in significance with Lenin's rethinking of the revolutionary party – since Marx and Engels's time, providing what Michael Löwy has described as a fundamentally 'new understanding of human history' comprising 'a general theory of the socio-economic dynamics of the historical process'.[19]

Trotsky's strategy of permanent revolution is further explored in Peter Thomas's chapter where he examines the relationship of the category to Antonio Gramsci's concept of 'passive revolution', developed after the First World War. Against scholars who have claimed Gramsci and Trotsky's writings formed antipodal opposites, Thomas invites us to rethink Gramsci's passive revolution and Trotsky's permanent revolution together from the perspective of Marx and Engels's 'revolution in permanence'. This allows us to posit, as Thomas shows, a 'corrective' to each of their respective theories; or, rather, to make explicit elements that each theory constitutively leaves unthought as their respective *conditions of possibility*. As Thomas puts it,

---

18 Trotsky 1972a, p. 66 as quoted in Davidson, 'The First World War, Classical Marxism and the End of the Bourgeois Revolution in Europe, pp. 333–4.

19 Löwy 1981, p. 87. In recent years, Trotsky's theory of uneven and combined development has been the subject of enormous scholarly attention, particularly in the disciplines of International Relations, Historical Sociology, Geography and Literature, where the theory's insights have been further teased out and refined. For a list of recent contributions to these debates, particularly within International Relations, see: <www.unevenandcombineddevelopment.wordpress.com>.

> thinking these concepts together, in terms both of their response to the socio-economic and political consequences of the First World War, and in terms of their shared attempt to inherit and transform key elements of previous Marxist concepts of revolution, allows us to discern certain common elements in their novel formulations, at the same time as it highlights the different strategic consequences that flow from them (Thomas, 'Uneven Developments, Combined', p. 282).

As Thomas's chapter shows, Gramsci's theory of passive revolution in its extended usage sought to capture, as a criterion of historical research, the generalised *Sonderweg* of capitalist modernity, whereby societies undergoing 'bourgeois revolutions' were 'characterised by transformations of the political forms of a society that nevertheless failed to place in question their economic contents' (Thomas, 'Uneven Developments, Combined', p. 292). In its most general usage, passive revolution thereby came to represent the 'pacifying and incorporating nature' assumed by bourgeois hegemony in the epoch of imperialism, not only in the western European heartlands, but also with determinant effects upon the colonial periphery. This involved a 'molecular' process of transformation, 'progressively modify[ing] the pre-existing composition of forces' in the ruling classes' 'gradual but continuous absorption' of its '"antithesis"' (the proletariat).[20] Against this 'logic' of passive revolution overwhelming all of modernity, Gramsci sought to identify an institutional antithesis to it which he sought to capture in the notion of the 'Modern Prince'. As Thomas has explained elsewhere, Gramsci's 'Modern Prince' can be conceived as the concrete reconfiguration of the principle of political organisation as the necessary and dialectical complement to the theory of passive revolution thereby representing an actualisation of the revolution in permanence; that is, the formation of an independent political programme of the subaltern classes that constitutes the 'permanence' – in the Machiavellian sense of 'enduring' – of the political mobilisation of the masses.[21] In these ways, the theory of passive revolution finds its dialectical antithesis in Trotsky's 'permanent revolution' itself institutionalised in Gramsci's proscribed Modern Prince.

These changing conceptions of the revolutionary process in the Global South and North after both the decisive moments of 1914 and 1917 are explored in Domenico Losurdo's chapter. In it, Losurdo examines the underlying factors leading to the rise of communist movements within and particularly outside

20 Gramsci 1971, pp. 58, 109.

21 Thomas 2009.

of Europe in the years after the October Revolution. As he demonstrates, the revolution begun in October 1917 against the capitalist-imperialist system had provoked in these two regions, two unique forms of class struggle that were simultaneously different and complementary. What was at stake in the epoch of capitalist imperialism were thus two distinct yet intertwined struggles for recognition: the first concerning the protagonists of the working class and popular masses who refused to be 'raw material' at the disposition of the ruling classes; while the protagonists of the second were whole nations attempting to shake off the oppression, humiliation and dehumanisation inherent to colonial rule.

Detailing the strategic problems and dilemmas presented to revolutionaries attempting to build socialism in the aftermath of the First World War, often under conditions of severe political and economic 'backwardness', Losurdo examines the variegated struggles against internal and external inequalities while demonstrating the myriad ways by which the class struggle often took on national forms in the 'race in the East'. This race witnessed revolutionary socialist states seeking to bridge the gap between themselves and the more advanced capitalist nations as they sought to leave behind the economic and social fragilities of the ancien régimes in an often hostile and threatening geopolitical environment.

Thus, as Losurdo's chapter demonstrates, 1914 and 1917 were decisive moments in the transformation and refoundation of revolutionary socialist thinking in both the 'West' and 'East'. Though the October Revolution had a very different impact on the developmental trajectories of Marxist thought and revolutionary socialist strategy in the Global North and South, many of the strategic dilemmas and paradoxes that emerged with it remain as vital as ever for Marxists in both regions of the world. In 'the West', Losurdo argues, Marxism will not be able to regain its own vitality as a concrete project of emancipation without surpassing the counterposition to the so-called 'Oriental Marxism' of 'the East'.

While Losurdo, Lih and Thomas provide compelling analyses of the transformed world-historical conditions and resulting dilemmas confronting socialist revolutionaries in the aftermath of the First World War, Alberto Toscano's chapter offers a riveting examination of W.E.B. Du Bois's path-breaking theoretical investigation of the imperialist war's origins. As the likes of Luxemburg, Lenin and Bukharin were penning their seminal accounts of the origins of the First World War, which they saw as a fundamental consequence of the emergence of a world-wide system of capitalist imperialism, the foremost black Marxist intellectual and social theorist in the United States, Du Bois, was formulating his own distinct analysis of the war – one which rooted its origins in the racialised colonial rivalries in Africa. As Du Bois saw it, the fundamental issue of twentieth-century world politics, intersecting with and cutting across the inter-imperial rivalries leading to the First World War, was that of the 'global colour line'. As Du Bois put it more than ten years before the outbreak of the First World War: 'The problem of the twentieth century is the problem of the colour-line – the relation of the darker to the lighter races of men in Asia and Africa, in America and the islands of the sea'.[22] It was this 'present Problem of Problems' – namely, the global structure of the exploitation of labour – that needed to be re-envisioned with respect to the 'dark colonial shadow' cast by the European empires.[23]

As Toscano's chapter illustrates, for Du Bois, it was this exploitation and denigration of black and other forms of 'non-white' labour that played such a crucial role in the material and ideological apparatuses of European imperialism. Indeed, as Toscano notes, Du Bois's thesis in the 'African Roots of War', the most famous of his articles pertaining to the origins of the First World War, foregrounds the distinctly 'racial coordinates' of capitalist ideology, 'delineating something like *the global wages of whiteness*' (Toscano, ' "America's Belgium" ', p. 237). For Du Bois, the First World War thus represented a 'return onto (white) European soil of... the systematic violence and repression that had thereto taken place on the other side of the geographical colour line – in the colonies, among "the savages" '. This 'boomerang effect of imperialism', as Toscano calls it, would be later taken up as a 'founding tenet of much anti-colonial critique' while finding echoes in the works of Karl Korsch and Hannah Arendt, among others (Toscano, ' "America's Belgium" ', pp. 237–8). In these ways and more, Du Bois highlighted – perhaps more than any other Marxist figure of his time – the critical significance of race and racism as fundamental organising principles of the international politics of the epoch whilst illuminating a number of themes that would be subsequently picked up and elaborated upon by various critical scholars.[24] Hence, as with many of his radical socialist contemporaries, Du Bois's works reveal the tremendous transformative significance of the 1914 calamity, demonstrating, in particular, the racial foundations of its inception and consequences.

Of course, 1914 was not just a defining moment for Marxist thought and the international socialist movement, but also for European society and culture

22 Du Bois 1961 [1903], p. 23.

23 Du Bois 1925, p. 423.

24 The enduring significance of Du Bois's analysis of race, racism and imperialism, with particular reference to its contemporary relevance for International Relations theory, is further examined in Anievas, Manchanda and Shilliam 2015.

more generally. In his contribution, Enzo Traverso looks at both European intellectuals' seeming unawareness of the impending catastrophe and their subsequent reactions to it. Visualising the cataclysm of 1914 as representing both a 'historical break' and concatenation of existing (often latent) socio-historical tendencies, Traverso traces some of the ideological antecedents to the logic of 'total war' that would come to engulf Europe with such devastating consequences. In particular, he demonstrates the important role of Europe's colonial adventures and the Franco-Prussian War – especially the experience of the Paris Commune of 1871 – during the late nineteenth century in providing the ideological foundations for the subsequent demonisation and racialisation of the enemy carried out during the First World War – a theme, as noted, prefigured in the works of Du Bois. As Traverso puts it,

> In 1914, the enemy was external, but it was charged with all the elements of negative otherness that, all over the second half of the nineteenth century, distinguished the dangerous classes as well as the lower races, compelling the nation to protect itself through social repression in Europe and wars of extermination in the colonies (Traverso, 'European Intellectuals and the First World War', pp. 207–8).

The near hysterical fears of such internal and external 'enemies' catalysed by the Great War, would also become a staple of later fascist and Nazi ideologies which spread through the interwar years. These also took inspiration from the colonial wars of extermination and other late nineteenth-century wars (again, particularly, the Franco-Prussian War of 1870–1) which witnessed the first deployments of modern technologies on the battlefield. This in turn led to a peculiar fusion of a 'romantic revolt against modernity and an irrational cult of technology' which became a key premise of the so-called 'conservative revolution' of the interwar years and expressed in the *aestheticised politics* of avant-garde futurism prefiguring a fundamental aspect of fascist culture (Traverso, 'European Intellectuals and the First World War', p. 209).

Indeed, as Esther Leslie well demonstrates in her chapter 'Art after War', the experience of the First World War was for many artists absolutely crucial in formulating this *aestheticisation of politics*, as Walter Benjamin called it. As Benjamin wrote in *The Work of Art in the Age of its Technological Reproducibility*,

> Humankind, which once, in Homer, was an object of contemplation for the Olympian gods, has now become one for itself. Its self-alienation has reached the point where it can experience its own annihilation as a

> supreme aesthetic pleasure. Such is the aestheticising of politics, as practiced by fascism. Communism replies by politicising art.[25]

In her chapter, Leslie examines how the events of 1914–18 not only altered the terrain of the landscapes where the fighting occurred, but also the metaphorical terrain of experience and the medium of its expression, language, particularly through an analysis of the writings of Walter Benjamin. For Leslie, Benjamin not only diagnosed the shifts in experience and language resulting directly from the war, but also developed, on the basis of this, a strategy for becoming contemporary in our thinking, our political outlook and our cultural activity, illuminating 'the political and critical stakes of these reconfigurations, whereby the physical destruction of war makes necessary the conceptual elaboration of the world in its totality' (Leslie, 'Art after War', p. 216). Her chapter thus offers an analysis of the ways by which the war generated the destruction of things and thought and their reconfiguration in startlingly new forms.

On Origins and Effects

While the classical Marxist theories of imperialism, and notably Lenin and Bukharin's, were explicitly developed as a means to explain the emergence of inter-imperial rivalries leading to 1914, such Marxist theories and their contemporary successors are more notable by their very absence in recent historiographical debates on the origins of the war. Indeed, as Alexander Anievas notes in his chapter, it is no exaggeration to say that the closest thing to a strong 'consensus' contemporary historians of the war have reached is that the classical Marxist theories have little if anything to offer in understanding the origins of 1914. Redressing this unfortunate state of affairs, the first few chapters of this collection offer much needed re-examinations of some of the key political and economic factors leading to global war.

In his chapter 'Germany, the Fischer Controversy, and the Context of War', Geoff Eley offers an illuminating and wide-ranging survey of current developments in the historiography of the war's origins in light of Fritz Fischer's 'historiographical revolution' of the 1960s, focusing in particular on the course and dynamics of German imperial expansionism in the run-up to the war. In it, he emphasises the *interconnected* dynamism of the domestic and international spheres in seeking to avoid the pitfalls of privileging either an 'internalist' [*Primat der Innenpolitik*] or 'externalist' [*Primat der Außenpolitik*] mode of explanation that has characterised so much of the war's historiography, whilst demonstrating the complex relays of influence and determination

25 Benjamin 2008, p. 42 as quoted in Leslie, 'Art after War', p. 235.

(economically, politically, discursively) that drove the expansionism of the Wilhelmine period, by land or by sea, restlessly forward. In doing so, Eley well explicates the wider material and ideational global coordinates of empire thinking under the *Kaiserreich* which, as he argues, shows 'the degree to which, even *before* the Empire itself was founded in 1867–71, Germany's necessary future was being mapped onto a world scale' (Eley, 'Germany, the Fischer Controversy, and the Context of War', p. 31). In an era of empire-states carving out mutually exclusive spheres of interest in their attempts at mastering the world market, 'empire talk' became the default language of international politics in German policy-making circles in the years preceding the war. In far-right circles at home, particularly among Pan-German visions of a 'Greater Germany', these 'world imperial' frames of reference made a point of explicitly holding 'European and extra-European logics of imperial policymaking together, binding the prospects for colonial expansion overseas to the securing of Germany's dominance inside the continent at home' (Eley, 'Germany, the Fischer Controversy, and the Context of War', p. 38). It was such 'empire talk' that had created, as Eley claims, not just a climate of thought, but a sociopolitical environment of organised and active imperialist articulations, that came to establish a powerfully structured setting for the 1914 crisis when it occurred. In these ways, as Eley forcefully argues, 'a particular climate of political discussion, speculative thought, and visionary ideology coalesced during the pre-1914 decade into an entire discursive landscape of ideas and practices that disposed toward the coming of war' that, when faced with the domestic political deadlock of the 1912–14 period which saw the stunning electoral victory of the SPD and the annihilation of the political right, 'created the conditions for an extremely threatening radicalisation' (Eley, 'Germany, the Fischer Controversy, and the Context of War', pp. 43–4).

In her chapter 'War, Defeat, and the Urgency of *Lebensraum*', Shelley Baranowski takes some of these themes further in exploring two key dimensions of German imperialism – one maritime, one continental – from the prewar era to the Second World War. In doing so, Baranowski re-examines some of the continuities and breaks in German foreign policy over the course of the first half of the twentieth century as the second dimension (continental expansionism) came to take precedence over the first. A guiding theme of German expansionism of this period was, as Baranowski shows, the perceived necessity for 'living space' [*Lebensraum*]. 'From unification in 1871 to the end of the Third Reich', Baranowski writes, 'the need to complete the Bismarckian achievement to embrace all ethnic Germans and make Germany invulnerable to foreign depredations was a key element in German imperialism' (Baranowski, 'War, Defeat, and the Urgency of *Lebensraum*', p. 64).

In a wide-ranging historical analysis of the changing fortunes of the German polity from the pre-war period through the interwar years, Baranowski thereby demonstrates the many continuities in the aims and direction of German expansionism despite the transformative impact of the First World War. In the immediate aftermath of the war and peace settlement, almost universally perceived by Germans as unduly harsh, she shows how 'the containment of the revolution at home overlapped with the continuation of imperialism in the East where despite the armistice, the German wartime occupation, the memory of Brest-Litovsk, and anti-bolshevism conspired to sustain dreams of living space' (Baranowski, 'War, Defeat, and the Urgency of *Lebensraum*', p. 51). While American loans poured into the Weimar Republic during the 1920s, these revisionist expansionist aims of German policymakers were at least partially subdued. However, once the American-backed financial order collapsed and the effects of the Great Depression became widespread, a series of right-wing Weimar governments after 1930 encouraged aggressive revisionism and autarkic expansionism, culminating in the Nazi seizure of power in 1933.

In analysing the Nazi phenomenon and its renewed drive toward *Lebensraum* in the East, Baranowski traces the multifaceted ideological developments and tendencies of the Weimar Republic which came to underpin the radical nationalism of the far-right coalescing around the Nazi regime. She examines in particular how a heterogeneous mix of social forces, drawn from the lower-middle and middle classes, became radicalised by defeat, revolution, and hyperinflation and ended up embracing the banner of extreme nationalism, imperialism and anti-Marxism. From the perspective of these radical German nationalists, the East came to be seen as a 'vast space for exploitation and ethnic revitalisation after the trauma of defeat and foreign domination', promising what Germany needed most in the biologically determined competition for survival (Baranowski, 'War, Defeat, and the Urgency of *Lebensraum*', p. 55). Once firmly in power, the Nazi regime thus quickly set out to pursue a foreign policy aimed at capturing this 'necessary' *Lebensraum* in the East whilst eliminating its domestic 'enemies'. While again drawing out both the continuities and changes in German expansionism from the pre-war to post-war periods, Baranowski illustrates how Hitler's visions of continental *Lebensraum* mirrored the shift among Pan-Germans that began before World War I, but which assumed new urgency in light of the war experience as Imperial Germany's maritime empire rendered it vulnerable to the Entente's blockade. These long-held aims of *Lebensraum* in the East fused with the Nazi's radically racist *Weltanschauung* in destabilising and explosive ways, eventually leading the Nazi regime to the seemingly irrational decision to risk a global war on multiple fronts. As Baranowski puts it: 'In the Nazi *Weltanschauung*, after the apocalyptic struggles of the First World War and its aftermath, only an apocalyptic second war made "sense" ' (Baranowski, 'War, Defeat, and the Urgency of *Lebensraum*', p. 64).

Eley and Baranowski's chapters provide major contributions to the historiographical literatures on the underlying dynamics of German expansionism both before and after the war while offering significant insights into the more general origins of the First World War. In Adam Tooze and Alexander Anievas's subsequent chapters, an exploration into the origins of the war is further developed by widening the analysis beyond the specific case of Germany to a political economic examination of both the *longue durée* of the nineteenth century and the July 1914 conjuncture. As Tooze notes, questions of political economy in producing the July Crisis have been largely excised from the recent historiographical literatures after the 'fall' of the theories of imperialism. Moreover, recent economic histories of the 'first globalisation' have largely worked with a presumption of innocence with regard to 1914, treating World War I as a strictly *exogenous shock*. Yet, political scientists have been less shy. Liberal peace theories claim, for example, that there is a close connection between international economic integration and international politics, but that it is one of peace not war.

Drawing on these literatures, among others, Tooze's chapter thus seeks to rethink the connections between military-security issues and political economy in the run up to the First World War. In doing so, Tooze challenges both realist conceptions of a discretely constituted international system dictated by an anarchic logic of balance of power politics and liberal peace theory's arguments regarding the strong causal connection between liberal democracies and peace. Drawing on the alternative perspective of uneven and combined development and by giving due weight to the self-reflexive character of modernity, his chapter shows not only how globalisation may have actually contributed to the tensions that precipitated World War I, but how liberal peace theory itself is not innocent in regards to the origins of the war. Liberalism's hierarchical assumptions about political and economic modernity and military aggression were in fact operative in this historical moment and thereby helped to further exacerbate geopolitical tensions enabling the outbreak of the war.

In particular, Tooze examines how the growth of capitalist development over the nineteenth and early twentieth centuries – developments usually referred to under the rubric of 'globalisation' – made military elites in Europe less secure and more trigger-happy. 'Globalisation', Tooze writes, impacted military elites 'not only by means of the political currents it stirred up or by means of the coalitions it made possible, but by directly affecting the terms on which the state could appropriate resources' (Tooze, 'Capitalist Peace or Capitalist

War?', p. 74). From this perspective, Tooze captures the causal factors leading to the July Crisis emerging from 'the dynamic interconnectedness of a system of states undergoing transformation at different speeds and under different international and domestic pressures' or what Trotsky referred to as 'uneven and combined development' (Tooze, 'Capitalist Peace or Capitalist War?', p. 70). In these ways and more, Tooze also demonstrates how the notion of a liberal peace is not simply a political science hypothesis but a *political project* to be imposed by force if necessary.

The notion of uneven and combined development is also at the forefront of Anievas's chapter 'Marxist Theory and the Origins of the First World War', where he seeks to redeploy the concept as a theory of interstate rivalry and war. Demonstrating the analytical stalemate of the 'Long Debate' over the origins of the 1914 war, with its persistent oscillation between *Primat der Aussenpolitik* ('primacy of foreign policy') or *Primat der Innenpolitik* ('primary of domestic policy') perspectives, Anievas seeks to organically unite 'geopolitical' and 'sociological' modes of explanation into a single theory of the war's causes. Doing so, he draws on Trotsky's concept of uneven and combined development, which uniquely interpolates an international dimension of causality into its theoretical premises, while grounding it in a firm conception of the rhythms and dynamics of socio-historical development re-conceived as a *strategically interdependent* and *interactive whole*.

From this theoretical perspective, Anievas identifies three distinct but overlapping spatio-temporal vectors of unevenness whose progressive entwinement had increasingly significant consequences on the nature and course of European geopolitics over the Long Nineteenth Century feeding into both the general (structural) and proximate (conjunctural) causes of the 1914–18 war. These three vectors of unevenness include: (1) a 'West-East' plane of unevenness capturing the spatial-temporal ordering of industrialisations taking place across Europe and beyond over the 1789–1914 period; (2) a 'Transatlantic' vector representing the contradictory interlocking of the North American and European economies and the multiple cultural-linguistic, socio-economic and political links connecting the British Empire with its original white settler colonies; and (3) a 'North-South' constellation interlinking and differentiating the multi-ethnic empires from Central Eastern Europe to the Asia-Pacific into a dynamic of asymmetrical interdependency with the capitalist-industrial powers.

From the intersection of these different vectors, Anievas then traces the relations and alliances between state managers, politicians and specific factions of the capitalist class as they sought to mediate these social-international pressures, emanating from the uneven and combined character of development, into concrete strategies designed to preserve their domestic social standing and respond to the broader global context within which they were embedded. From this perspective, Anievas thus demonstrates the spatial and temporal specificities of the 1914 crisis, which witnessed German and Austrian policy-makers' use of the July Crisis in the Balkans as the opportunity to launch a 'preventive war' against the Russia menace abroad and destabilising social forces at home before the strategic 'window of opportunity' closed. In the conclusion, he then considers the theoretical implications of 'the international' for Marxist theory more generally.

With Wendy Matsumura's chapter, 'The Expansion of the Japanese Empire and the Rise of the Global Agrarian Question after the First World War', the focus shifts from the origins of the First World War to its effects, as Matsumura examines the opportunities presented by the 1914 cataclysm to Japan's ruling classes in expanding their political and economic reach, particularly in Southeast Asia. The experience of the First World War marked, as Matsumura demonstrates, a striking reorganisation of Japan's international trade relations indicative of a broader structural transformation of Japanese capitalism and the expansion of its agrarian question into a *global* problem. Initially, Japan's entry into the war spawned a major economic boom, particularly for Japan's largest monopoly capitals, whose vertical integration intensified due to their expanded lending operations abroad. This boom was spurred on by speculative fever across industries which was itself the result of Japan's transition from an importer to major exporter of military supplies, manufactured goods and foodstuffs to the warring countries of Europe and their colonies or spheres of interest in Asia and Africa. The overall upshot of these economic developments was the dominant position achieved by monopoly capital, particularly among the heavy and chemical industries, within the Japanese economy as a whole. In these ways, economic historians have generally considered the First World War an 'epochal moment for Japanese capitalism' (Matsumura, 'The Expansion of the Japanese Empire and the Rise of the Global Agrarian Question after the First World War', p. 149). Yet, with these structural transformations of the Japanese economy came a dramatic expansion of industrial production and concentration of capital during the war resulting in what the Marxist economist Uno Kōzō identified as the 'global agrarian question'.

Matsumura's chapter thus re-examines these transformations in Japan's domestic economic structure and their relationship to the reconfiguration of the Empire as a whole through a critical reading of Uno Kōzō's works on the emergence of a global agrarian question after the First World War. Taking Uno's point that any investigation of Japanese capitalism after the war requires a consideration of shifts in global capitalism, Matsumura's chapter analyses transformations in one of the Japanese Empire's most important and global commodities – sugar. As she demonstrates, an elucidation of post-war developments in the Japanese sugar industry reveals a heightened interconnectedness of metropolitan, colonial and regional markets, labour flows and production processes controlled by vertically integrated combines which made it increasingly difficult to distinguish between these spaces in terms of the roles they played for the reproduction of capitalism.

In her chapter, 'War and Social Revolution', Sandra Halperin provides an analysis of the origins and consequences of the First World War in terms of the interconnected dynamics of 'internal repression and external expansion' characterising the pre-1914 system of globalising production and exchange as a whole. As she demonstrates, in the decades leading up to the 1914 crisis, these two central elements of the ancien régime states, both within and outside of Europe, were rapidly coming into conflict as the Long Depression (1873–96) and rising global 'red tide' increased pressures within, and rivalries and conflicts among, the European imperial powers, eventually leading to a 'multilateral war in Europe' (Halperin, 'War and Social Revolution', p. 185). A consequence of the war was, Halperin claims, nothing less than a social revolution, as the mass mobilisation of labour for armies (the *lévee en masse*) and industry exponentially increased social tensions in Europe. By shifting the balance of class forces within and throughout Europe, the First World War thus made possible the transformation of European societies that emerged after the Second World War.

In these ways, Halperin writes, the 'First World War represents a great divide in modern European history' ('War and Social Revolution', p. 194). The Second World War emerged from essentially the same socio-economic and political conditions that had engendered the First World War. The result of the former was nothing less than the wholesale transformation of the European political order which, following the Great Depression of 1929, underwent another round of mass mobilisation and industrial expansion for a second World War that ended up 'forc[ing] governments into a political accommodation of working-class demands that made a restoration of the pre-war system impossible' (Halperin, 'War and Social Revolution', p. 194). The social democratic and Keynesian 'welfare' compromises of the post-WWII order brought a 'more balanced and internally oriented development' that, according to Halperin, divided the world into those areas that for a time adopted a relatively more nationally-embedded capitalism (as in 'the West') and, nearly everywhere else, where the structures characteristic of the pre-war order were consolidated and reproduced (as in the Global South). It was from this newly transformed (geo)political landscape that the imaginary of 'developed' and 'developing' worlds emerged.

In these ways and more, Halperin, among many of the other contributors, demonstrates the profound ways in which 1914 fundamentally transformed 'modern' world politics. From the reconfiguration of revolutionary consciousness resulting from the Bolshevik Revolution of 1917; to the splits within the international socialist-cum-communist movements emerging thereafter; to the rise of anti-colonial struggles in the Global South; to the start of the early 'Cold War'[26] inaugurated by the Allied intervention into the Russian Civil War in 1918; to the institutionalisation of international organisations such as the International Labour Organisation and the League of Nations, prefiguring the United Nations; to the tectonic geopolitical shift to US hegemony hastened by the 1914–18 conflict, the First World War and its immediate consequences set the fundamental geopolitical, ideological and world economic conditions and parameters for the post-WWII epoch of modern world politics lasting up until the fall of the Soviet Union in 1991, if not to this day. For these reasons and many more, the study of the First World War remains as important as ever, particularly for those seeking a more just and equitable world order.

---

26 On the significance of this 'early Cold War' for the geopolitics of the interwar years see Anievas 2014.

PART 1

Kladderadatsch! Capitalism, Empire, and Imperialism in the Making and Aftermath of World War I

∵

CHAPTER 1

Germany, the Fischer Controversy, and the Context of War: Rethinking German Imperialism, 1880–1914

Geoff Eley[1]

Introduction

'The lamps are going out all over Europe', the British Foreign Secretary, Sir Edward Grey, remembered thinking at dusk on 3 August 1914, as Europe's armies moved into position. 'We shall not see them lit again in our lifetime'.[2] Many of the responsible statesmen during the July Crisis shared these forebodings. Theobald von Bethmann Hollweg, the Chancellor of Germany, saw 'a doom greater than human power hanging over Europe and our own people'.[3] In his final meeting with the British Ambassador Sir Edward Goschen on 4 August, in which Goschen eventually burst into tears, Bethmann Hollweg called the war a 'crime' and 'an unlimited world catastrophe'.[4] Yet, in speaking of the prospects of war the year before, Bethmann used more heroic and optimistic tones.

> One thing will remain true: the victor, as long as the world has existed, has always been that nation [*Volk*] alone which has put itself in the position of standing there with its last man when the iron dice of its fate are cast, which has faced up to the enemy with the full force of its national character [*des Volkstums*].[5]

Also on 4 August, Erich von Falkenhayn, Minister of War and soon to become Chief of the General Staff, called the outbreak of the war 'beautiful', 'even if we perish because of it'.[6]

---

1 The thinking in this essay is heavily indebted to conversations with, among others, Jennifer Jenkins, Bradley Naranch, Hartmut Pogge von Strandmann, and Dennis Sweeney. It was prompted by reflection on the long-running influence of Fischer 1967.

2 Grey of Fallodon 1925, p. 20.

3 Riezler 1972, p. 192.

4 Jarausch 1973, pp. 176–7.

5 Bethmann Hollweg, April 7, 1913, cited in Düllfer 2003, p. 139.

6 Afflerbach 1996, p. 170.

A key motif of the larger historiography of the July Crisis has always been this back and forth between inevitabilism and agency – between the unmasterable logic of processes already set into motion on the one hand and human responsibility on the other, between a sense of being buffeted by powerful necessities and the existential rush of embracing a momentous future. While steering willingly towards the conflict, in fact, Europe's decision-makers felt pulled by larger impersonal forces. These ranged from the gathering strength of organised nationalist opinion to the unstoppable momentum of mobilisation plans once the alliance systems were activated, from the intensified economic rivalries of the Great Powers and accelerating arms race to the widely heralded clash of world empires. The tensions in European society around such questions rose ever higher during the pre-war decade. But sharply differing conclusions could be drawn. While strong pacifist and internationalist currents flourished, many approached war's possibility with excitement. One French writer in 1912 extolled the 'wild poetry' of going to war through which 'all is made new'. Two years before, the German expressionist poet Georg Heim confided these feelings to his diary: 'It is always the same, so boring, boring, boring. There happens nothing, nothing, nothing ... If something would only happen just for once ... Or if someone would only start a war, unjust or not. This peace is as foul, oily, and slimy as cheap polish on old furniture'. The Bavarian general Konstantin von Gebsattel told his fellow Pan-German, Heinrich Claß: 'I long for war the redeemer'.[7]

For civilians and soldiers alike, this was partly a matter of warfare's novelty. The peacefulness of the nineteenth century can easily be exaggerated.[8] In the minds of Western Europeans many actual wars were banished to a periphery they self-servingly dismissed as barbarous and uncivilised, as not really 'Europe' at all, whether in the recurring violence of the Ottoman Empire's slow retreat from the Balkans or in the disastrous Crimean War of 1854–6. The military exploits of European powers were also displaced to colonial arenas overseas, where bloody wars of conquest and pacification were repeatedly fought. But inside Europe itself recent military episodes were confined either to civil and revolutionary disorders or to wars of brief duration, like those for Italian and German unification between 1859 and 1871. Without any sobering experience to the contrary, therefore, prospects of war seemed invigorating, heroic, an unleashing of energies, a discharging of pent-up frustrations, the true metal's

7 Abel Bonnard 1912, cited in Joll 1992, p. 217; Georg Heim 1910, and Konstanin von Gebsattel 1913, both cited in Lohalm 1970, p. 29. See also Enzo Traverso's contribution to this volume detailing European intellectuals' musings on war before and after 1914.

8 For what follows, see Halperin 2003, pp. 119–44.

test. In the pressure cooker atmosphere after 1905, while Great Power tensions escalated, nationalist opinion aggressively radicalised, and civil conflicts slid into violence, thoughts of war increasingly came as a release.

Seeking to understand the place and meanings of the anticipated continental war inside pre-war Europe's social, cultural, and political imaginaries remains one of the biggest of the outstanding historiographical tasks left by the Fischer Controversy. Despite the new rush of publications prompted by the approaching centenary, for example, much startlingly new knowledge about the immediate outbreak of the conflict seems unlikely. For some time now, analysis of the mechanics of the July Crisis itself seems to have reached some reasonable closure.[9] Ever since Hans Koch's anthology of 1972, Volker Berghahn's *Germany and the Approach of War* in 1973, and John Moses's *Politics of Illusion* in 1975, each decade has seen its crop of updatings. Most recently, we have had Annika Mombauer's summation of *Controversies and Consensus*, the comprehensive country-by-country anthology of Richard Hamilton and Holger Herwig, and Mark Hewitson's magisterial *Germany and the Causes of the First World War*.[10] Hewitson's careful weighing of the vast monographic scholarship in particular makes the earlier revisionisms of Gregor Schöllgen and Klaus Hildebrand look increasingly unconvincing and threadbare. Emphasis on 'the exposed geostrategic position of the Reich' as the structural key to an essentially defensive set of military and diplomatic exigencies and compulsions – the claim that Germany was a 'nation-state against history and geography', in Michael Stürmer's formulation – seems an extraordinarily partial take on the full range and complexity of the determinations acting on the making of German policy, whether during the July Crisis *per se*, in the long conjuncture of Wilhelmine expansionism opened by the proclamation of *Weltpolitik* in 1896, or in the politics of war aims during 1914–18.[11] Here, Hartmut Pogge's brilliant 1988 essay on 'Germany and the Coming of War' is still hardly to be bettered.[12]

Primat der Innenpolitik

In contrast, the project of relating the purposes and presuppositions of the decision-makers in the July Crisis to a critical and concrete history of the prevailing popular culture, ideological mood, and everyday climate of commonplace ideas of the time remains highly unfinished. Beginning to map

9 However, see the following new contributions: Clark 2012; McMeekin 2013; Schmidt 2009.

10 Koch 1972; Berghahn 1993; Moses 1975; Mombauer 2002; Hamilton and Herwig 2003; Hewitson, 2004.

11 See especially Schöllgen 1990, 1992, and 1998; Hildebrand 2008; Stürmer 1990, pp. 63–72.

12 Pogge von Strandmann 1988a, pp. 86–123.

this discursive landscape was one of the major accomplishments of Fischer's second book, *War of Illusions*, although largely confined to the wealth of newspaper, magazine, and pamphlet literature mined by his students Dirk Stegmann and Klaus Wernecke.[13] In 1968, at the height of the Fischer Controversy itself, James Joll had delivered his inaugural lecture at the LSE on the subject of *The Unspoken Assumptions*, in which he wished to deepen discussion of the July Crisis from this point of view.[14] He suggested that the reactions of the responsible statesmen would only really make sense if we examined the attitudes and assumptions underlying their behaviour. That might mean everything from family socialisation and educational backgrounds to particular generational experiences and knowledge of philosophy and the arts. It must certainly mean examining the issue mentioned above, namely, the growing acceptance among right-wing publics in Germany during the pre-war decade of the necessity and desirability of war, what Wolfgang Mommsen called in the title of an important 1981 essay, 'The *Topos* of Inevitable War'.[15] It remains surprising how few studies of this kind we still possess. One might cite Peter Winzen's study of the influences acting upon Bülow's conception of 'world power', or Geoffrey Field's biography of Houston Stewart Chamberlain, or even Roger Chickering's life of Karl Lamprecht.[16] One might also cite Thomas Weber's account of elite education in Heidelberg and Oxford before 1914.[17]

One possible direction for such work lies in tracking the intellectual formation of key individuals or networks whose ideas and influence the war years brought to fruition, whose careers produce a coherence that spans the rupture of 1914, or provide genealogies for the decisive departures that came in wartime. The literatures on Walter Rathenau are an obvious case in point (it was no accident that it was James Joll who in 1960 pioneered an interest in Rathenau in his *Three Intellectuals in Politics*).[18] The latest research on the Pan-Germans would also allow this argument to be made.[19] Other examples might be a figure like Paul Rohrbach, whose variegated activities have become part of

13 Fischer 1974; Stegmann 1970; Wernecke 1970.
14 Joll 1978.
15 Mommsen 1981, pp. 23–45.
16 Winzen 1977; Field 1981; Chickering 1993.
17 Weber 2008.
18 Joll 1961, pp. 59–129. Most recently: Volkov 2012. Indispensable is Pogge von Strandmann 1985.
19 Critical here will be Dennis Sweeney's forthcoming study of the Pan-German League. In the meantime, see Sweeney 2014 [forthcoming]. Also: Frech 2009; Leicht 2012.

the architecture of a wide range of recent monographs, or Arthur Dix, whose 'World Political Discussion Evenings' during the winter of 1913–14 open a fascinating window onto the climate of imperialist projection on the very eve of the war.[20] Another fruitful direction might be to focus on particular generational histories, such as that of the 'unification youth generation' – those born in the 1860s, too late to serve in the wars of unification, but whose political maturity was then acquired inside the newly created nation-state setting, with its patriotic heroics, progressivist directionality, and exultantly expanding nationalist horizon.[21] That generation's political imagination was cast decisively in the languages of national consolidation. Its members came of age in the crucible of the 1870s and 1880s, as a defining succession of major nationalist drives – those of the *Kulturkampf*, Anti-Socialist Law, and colonialism – sought to solidify and sharpen the new nation's cultural solidarities, while pushing its presence outwards into the wider global arena. For these freshly formed adult nationalist convictions, the fall of Bismarck in 1890 and the adoption of Caprivi's 'New Course' came as a deeply felt ideological shock.

Under the aegis of the concept of 'social imperialism', Fischer's work inspired an especially strong linkage between Germany's world policy and the domestic political arena. Advanced initially by Hans-Ulrich Wehler for Bismarck's colonial policy in the 1880s, this idea was adopted with alacrity by historians of the *Kaiserreich* more generally, drawing particular inspiration from the work of Eckart Kehr, a brilliant early twentieth-century historian whose work was properly discovered in the 1960s.[22] Using the interconnectedness of *Weltpolitik*, the big navy policy, and high tariffs in the years 1897–1902 as his main case, Kehr found the key to Germany's expansionist foreign policy in the dominance of a particular coalition of interests – 'iron and rye', heavy industry and big-estate agriculture – that consistently shaped official policy. This became the basis for an overarching claim about the *Primat der Innenpolitik* ('primacy of domestic policy') as a defining principle of government, supplying Wehler and other critics of older-style political history with a materialist

---

20 Behm and Kuczynski 1970, pp. 69–100. For Rohrbach, see Mogk 1972; Bieber 1972; Vom Bruch 1982, esp. pp. 73–5; Van Laak 2004, pp. 184–94; Meyer 1955, pp. 95–9.

21 I have adapted this concept from that of the 'war youth generation' applied to those born between 1902 and 1912 who were themselves too young to have served in World War I, as distinct from their predecessors born in the 1890s who shared directly in the 'front experience' idealised by Ernst Jünger. The argument goes back to Peukert 1991, pp. 14–18, while the idea was first popularised by Gründel 1932, pp. 31–42. See also Wildt 2009, pp. 21–121.

22 See Kehr 1973 and 1977.

slogan against the fetishised autonomies of diplomacy and statecraft.[23] Volker Berghahn's grand thesis about the social imperialist purposes of the 'Tirpitz plan' was a prime example, explaining *Weltpolitik* and the naval arms race by these socio-economic coordinates of Wilhelmine politics as Kehr had defined them.[24] In Berghahn's argument the compulsions of Germany's world position became joined to a reading of the 'social question' in a time of breakneck industrial transformation. Obsessed with the fear of revolution, Wilhelmine elites wagered the chances for social cohesion on the prosperity promised by Germany's national strength in the world economy. A key part of the common template for nationalist thinking thus became a belief in the fateful necessity of Germany's foreign expansion – encompassing everything from colonial policy to the arms race and the big navy, export drives and trading policy, the competitiveness of the German economy in world markets, questions of migration and maintenance of ties with Germans overseas, German diplomacy and the wider realms of *Weltpolitik*, and of course the final brinkmanship of the July Crisis and Germany's unfolding aims during the First World War.

At a distance of four decades from the Fischer Controversy, this interpretive model of German expansionism has somewhat receded. While not reverting to the old 'pre-Fischerian' *Primat der Außenpolitik*, or that extreme emphasis on the exigencies of the international system registered by Schöllgen and others after the Controversy itself had settled, more recent works have certainly developed a far more decentred perspective on the war that comes closer to some variant of the 'primacy of foreign affairs'. Indeed, the entire back and forth between 'internalist' [*Primat der Innenpolitik*] and 'externalist' [*Primat der Außenpolitik*] modes of explanation has to remain a key axis of historiographical debate, even if we seek ways of breaking the unhelpful terms of this binary down. The entire thrust of my own argument is to stress precisely the *interconnected* dynamism of each of these arenas, whose complex relays of influence and determination (economically, politically, discursively) drove the expansionism of the Wilhelmine period, by land or by sea, restlessly forward. Fruitful guidance in this regard may be found in recent scholarship in

23 For Kehr this was both a particular reading of how German politics was structured under the *Kaiserreich* and a general methodological-theoretical standpoint. See Kehr 1977; Sheehan 1968, pp. 166–74.

24 Berghahn 1971, and 1976, pp. 61–88.

International Relations, where classical Marxist concepts of uneven and combined development have suggested ways forward.[25]

In the post-Fischer German historiography in the years after the immediate Controversy had died down, interest shifted markedly away from the interest-driven conception of how the *Primat der Innenpolitik* actually worked – often described during the 1970s as 'political social history' [*politische Sozialgeschichte*].[26] Whereas historians like Fischer and Wehler used the formula of the *Primat der Innenpolitik* to approach all aspects of foreign policy as integrally and functionally related to the conduct of politics inside Germany itself, the intervening growth of social history tended to move discussion away from those questions. As the enthusiasm for social and cultural history unfolded, so the interest in foreign policy fell away, a decoupling that leaves behind a very different historiographical landscape from the one we had before. The continuity thesis spawned by the Fischer Controversy took its cachet primarily from foreign policy and the similarities linking the war aims programme of the First World War to the later imperialism of the Nazis. The argument of Fischer's second book on the domestic origins of the war-producing crisis between 1911 and 1914 was also about the pressures driving Germany into foreign adventures. The continuity argument focused at the outset on Germany's grab for 'world power', in other words. In those discussions of the 1960s and 1970s, it was the compulsion toward 'empire' above all that defined the postulated continuity.[27]

Conceptually speaking, the biggest contrast between the 1970s and now is certainly to be found in the conceptual work that 'social imperialism' was expected to perform. For Wehler this had been *the* pivotal concept. It signified a 'defensive ideology' against the 'disruptive effects of industrialisation on the social and economic structure of Germany', one that enabled 'the diversion outwards of internal tensions and forces of change in order to preserve the social and political status quo'.[28] It supplied a vital 'technique of rule' for holding back 'the advancing forces of parliamentarisation and democratisation'. It allowed German foreign policymakers to convert popular nationalism into a 'long-term integrative factor which helped stabilise an anachronistic

25 See here Anievas 2013; Green 2012; Rosenberg 2013. For the move by historians toward 'de-centering', see especially Mulligan 2010, and Clark 2012.

26 For excellent commentary developed at the time, see Iggers 1985, pp. 1–48.

27 See especially Fischer 1975, and 1986.

28 See Wehler 1969, p. 115.

social and power structure'.[29] In one of his more recent iterations, '[i]t was only beneath this perspective that Wilhelmine *"Weltpolitik"* revealed its real meaning, its deeper driving force'. By 1914 that obduracy against reform translated into a permanently embedded pattern of politics, '[o]nly this technique of rule seemed to make it possible to continue blocking the reformist modernisation of the social and political constitution in the necessary degree'. Such recourse was also systemically imposed by the flawed and divisive nature of the Imperial-German polity:

> The 'imperial nation' was a class society dangerously riven with contradictions between a semi-constitutional authoritarian state, traditional power elites, and state-oriented bourgeoisie on the one side, and the gradually forward moving forces of democratisation and parliamentarisation on the other side. It had been clear from 1884 at the latest that mobilising a 'pro-Empire' imperialism could counter that divisiveness to great effect. In such a light and within the horizons of experience of the 'Berlin policy-makers', there was no superior alternative to a social imperialist policy of containment that enjoyed any comparable prospect of success.[30]

This line of argument was always developed with the continuity thesis in mind. Beginning in the Bismarckian period and then continuing through the later 1890s and early 1900s with growing recklessness and escalating results, a fateful pattern was being laid down for the future, one that became powerfully entrenched in the anti-democratic thinking of the German elites. This pattern had direct bearing on the origins of Nazism:

> If this single line of development is pursued – the social imperialist resistance to the emancipation process in industrial society in Germany – then in historical terms we may draw a connecting line from Bismarck, through Miquel, Bülow, and Tirpitz, right down to the extreme social imperialism of National Socialism, which once again sought to block domestic progress and divert attention from the absence of freedom at home by breaking out to the East.

29 Wehler 1972, pp. 89, 87, 88.

30 Wehler 1995, p. 1139.

'If there is a continuity in German imperialism', Wehler stated in no uncertain terms, then it consists in 'the primacy of social imperialism from Bismarck to Hitler'.[31]

Much of the historiographical radicalism inspired by the Fischer Controversy came from this insistence that the imperialist drives in each of the world wars displayed an equivalence in this way: successive waves of foreign expansionism were each driven in some degree by the persistence of a particular constellation of dominant class interests and associated anti-democratic politics. The resulting political logic was common to the wider politics of the German right, whether among the governmental allies of Bülow, Tirpitz, and the rest, or among the radical nationalist campaigners of the pressure groups. For the Nazi period, the analogue to this 'Fischerite' approach to the July Crisis then became Tim Mason's interpretation of the outbreak of the Second World War, which was a more pointed version of a more widely shared view that the essential principle of the Third Reich's social system was the drive for war.[32]

Whether or not such hard causal dependence of foreign policymaking on anti-democratic calculations by dominant societal elites can be shown, the wider global coordinates of thinking about German nationhood and German national interests under the *Kaiserreich* – pervasively, axiomatically, urgently – have become ever harder to ignore. Key recent works show the degree to which, even *before* the Empire itself was founded in 1867–71, Germany's necessary future was being mapped onto a world scale. In that 'pre-state' era, much wider fields of relations overseas already linked the populations of German-speaking Europe to sundry non-European worlds, whose tangible meanings were increasingly processed inside an avowedly *national* framework of aspiration. The bearers of 'Germandom' elsewhere – German migrants to the south of Brazil, German merchants in Chile and Venezuela, German commercial representatives in the Ottoman Empire, German travellers in central Africa, German missionaries in southern Africa – were the forerunners of a national-state project yet to be realised on the European continent itself. German patriots

31 See Wehler 1970a, pp. 161, 131.

32 For example Mason 1971, p. 218: 'National Socialism appears as a radically new variant of the social imperialism of Bismarck and Wilhelm II ... foreign expansion would legitimise not an inherited political and social system but an entirely new one'. See also Mason 1995, pp. 212–31, 295–322; Mason 1993, pp. 294–330; Mason 1989, pp. 205–40. A sense of the widely held and more diffuse view of the Third Reich as 'a regime inherently geared to war' can be gleaned from Noakes and Pridham 1988, pp. 750–5 (here p. 751); Kershaw 2000, pp. 134–60. See also Knox 1984, pp. 1–57; Knox 1996, pp. 113–33, and Knox 2000.

learned from their counterparts elsewhere in that regard too, for the existing imperial powers were already treating their own scattered overseas outposts as the heterogeneous attachments of sovereignty in that globalised sense. In a global setting of distributed nationhood, sovereignty could no longer be contained by its historic European base.[33] Indeed, by the later nineteenth century *nationhood* in Europe was fast becoming *imperial*.[34]

Between the 1840s and 1870s, Germany's emergent national intelligentsia – writers, journalists, travellers, academics, economists, businessmen, lobbyists, political activists – used the visionary landscape of a putative colonial imaginary to do much of the ideological work of elaborating a programme for what they assumed a future national government could be expected to do. To secure its popular legitimacy, that government should be capable of defending Germany's interests on the world stage of international competition, as well as sustaining the influence of German culture overseas and creating a framework of ties strong enough to retain the affiliations of the migrants who were leaving the German-speaking lands in such prodigiously disquieting numbers. But this mid-century discourse was also no mere preamble or back-story for the later main narrative of the Bismarckian colonial policy of the mid-1880s: it was a vital and integral part of the main story itself. 'Germany' was being realised transnationally in advance of the creation of the national state. Even

33 The concurrent trajectories of political thinking about the empire in Britain, particularly the idea of a 'Greater Britain' in its pertinence for a new era of intensified global economic and strategic competition, strikingly paralleled German anxieties about the rivalries of world empires. Driven by a comparable dialectic between fears of democracy and challenges to Britain's global supremacy, the advocates of a Greater Britain imagined some form of imperial union linking Britain itself to the white settler colonies of Australia, New Zealand, Canada, and southern Africa. As Duncan Bell shows, this projecting of a 'vast "Anglo-Saxon" political community' of dispersed global Britishness 'ranged from the fantastically ambitious – creating a globe-spanning nation-state – to the practical and mundane – reinforcing existing ties between the colonies and Britain'. Such ideas drew on a rich reservoir of received visions of how an imperial polity might be organised, ranging across Greece, Rome, and the Americas, while mobilising emergent attitudes towards 'the state, race, space, nationality, and empire'. See the jacket description of Bell 2007. Bell's book complements Pitts 2005, which shows the earlier nineteenth-century realignments of liberal thought in Britain and France around an affirmative vision of imperial expansion embracing the conquest of non-European peoples.

34 For statements of this argument, see Grant, Levine, and Trentmann 2007, esp. pp. 1–15; Stoler 2006, pp. 125–46; Stoler, McGranahan, and Perdue 2007, pp. 3–42. See also Bright and Geyer 2002, pp. 63–99; Smith 2003.

before Bismarck's wars of unification, the globally conceived 'boundaries of Germanness' were already being fashioned into place.[35]

Empire Talk

This construction of a German national imaginary that was expansive and far-flung rather than confined to contiguous German-speaking Europe itself – one that encompassed German interests, influences, and populations in the world at large rather than simply the heartlands of German nationality inside Europe, while looking past the core territories of 1871 to the dispersed topography of German settlement further to the east – had some major consequences for the shaping of politics under the *Kaiserreich*. In aggressively elaborating their maximalist ideology of German expansionism, for example, radical nationalists were fired by an impassioned dismay concerning all the ways in which unification seemed incomplete.[36] Almost from the very beginning, the Empire's nationalist sufficiency was brought into dispute, as diverse patriotisms lamented this or that area where the new state had fallen short, not least in the greater-German aspirations that embraced Austria. Certainly the *Kaiserreich* barely approximated to the idealised unity of lands, language, institutions, high-cultural traditions, and customary heritage that nationalist discourse wanted to presume. Both the existence of linguistically-defined German populations beyond the borders of 1871 and the dispersal of German speakers to settlements overseas easily encouraged ethno-cultural assumptions about German nationhood that were necessarily irredentist and diasporic. By the end of the Empire's first decade, moreover, the dynamics of European colonial expansion were already giving further edge to these unrequited nationalist hopes. As classic works by Wehler, Klaus Bade, and others showed, the early construction of a wider global imaginary for Germany's realisation as a

35 See Naranch 2006; Fitzpatrick 2008; O'Donnell, Bridenthal, and Reagin 2005; Conrad 2010.

36 I move here to focus more specifically on the outlook of a radical nationalist tendency within German politics, which had the greatest affinities with National Liberalism in party-political terms, but whose particular formation far exceeded the latter as it took shape between the later 1880s and final pre-war years. Most coherently borne by the Pan-German League, it was formed more broadly within the world of the *nationale Verbände* (nationalist associations and campaigning organisations), among whom the Navy League was by far the largest and most significant. See Eley 1991. I am revisiting the subject in a new book, *Genealogies of Nazism: Conservatives, Radical Nationalists, Fascists in Germany, 1860–1945*.

self-determining nation now became re-processed into a powerful consensus behind the new state's need for colonies.[37]

Under the intensifying imperialist rivalries of the last quarter of the nineteenth century, that consensus became further articulated to the nervousness about the mutually confining and necessarily adversarial competition among the globe's 'great world empires'. Here the so-called 'Scramble for Africa' and other instances of the new imperialism were only the spectacular manifestations of a broader 'transformation in the character and intensity of global integration', which brought the great powers into ever-more fraught competition for control over resources, markets, communications, spheres of influence, and worldwide geopolitical space.[38] The neo-mercantilist conviction that a nation's global competitiveness had become the vital condition not only of great power standing, but also of the expanding prosperity needed for social peace, acquired ever greater impetus after the 1880s across German-speaking Europe, suffusing the public realms of business, journalism, academic life, and politics. In its discursive architecture this thinking had become the common sense of German foreign policymaking by the turn of the century, combining hard-headed geopolitical calculation, economic projections, and much visionary social and political thought.

Such 'empire talk' explicitly forged connections across the presumptively interlinked priorities of several distinct domains in the life of the nation. Most obvious was the sphere of foreign policy and international conflict *per se*, increasingly defined after the proclamation of *Weltpolitik* in the late 1890s by the arms drive and a diplomacy of forceful interventions. Just beyond was the burgeoning discourse of national efficiency in the economy. Harnessed to projections of future growth, this area encompassed everything deemed necessary to secure Germany's competitiveness in the world economy, including the aggressive deployment of tariffs, bilateral trading treaties, and state-aided export offensives.[39] Then came the entire domain of social welfare, likewise conceived increasingly under the sign of national efficiency. While any particular public intervention or legislative act of social policy only ever emerged from complicated interactions among economic, socio-political,

---

37 A key emblematic text in that regard was Friedrich Fabri's *Bedarf Deutschland der Colonien?*, originally published in 1879 and passing rapidly through three editions in the next five years. See Fabri 1998. See especially Wehler 1969, pp. 112–93; Bade 1975, pp. 67–79, 80–135; also Pogge von Strandmann 1988b, pp. 105–20; Bade 1988, pp. 121–47.

38 Kramer 2006, p. 3.

39 Wehler 1969, pp. 112–42, pp. 423–53, remains the best overall guide, together with Spohn 1977. See also Torp 2005; Conrad 2010, pp. 27–76.

ethico-religious, institutional, and short-term political influences and motivations, sometimes strategically conceived and woven together, but as often discretely undertaken for reasons of expediency, most major initiatives were at some level consciously framed to further the cause of social cohesion and political stability.[40] Between the 1880s and the First World War the urgency of world-political advocacy developed symbiotically across each of these domains.[41]

Running through this discourse from the start was a belief in the existence of three 'world empires', namely the British, the U.S., and the Russian (sometimes the French was added as a fourth), against whose global dominance (economically, demographically, geo-strategically) Germany would require comparable resources in order to compete. Through the successful resolution of the struggle for German unification and French military defeat, it was argued, Germany had already prised open this global constellation of the British, Russian, and U.S. 'world nations', and the urgency of further securing Germany's claims to parity had now grown severe. As Paul Rohrbach succinctly put this: 'The fourth nation – that is ourselves'.[42] Indeed, a fundamental qualification for great power status under the new circumstances of intensifying world economic rivalry, which brought into question not just a society's future prosperity but its very survival, would be Germany's ability to assemble an equivalent basis for 'world imperial' expansion. That basis was usually conceptualised as some version of *Mitteleuropa* (Central Europe), extending (as Fischer put it) 'from Spitzbergen to the Persian Gulf'.[43]

With the outbreak of war in 1914 the Chancellor Bethmann Hollweg embraced this idea in the form of a customs union between Germany and Austria-Hungary together with the smaller economies of northern Europe and perhaps Italy, which Belgium and France would then be compelled to join. Crystallising from earlier discussions with the electrical industrialist Walter Rathenau and the banker Arthur von Gwinner and built into his September Programme, Bethmann's projections for *Mitteleuropa* hardwired his thinking

---

40 See here Eley 1986, pp. 154–67; Grimmer-Solem 2003a, pp. 89–168, pp. 171–245; Grimmer-Solem 2003b, pp. 107–22; Sheehan 1966.

41 This full range and complexity of these influences on the spread of 'empire talk' between the 1880s and 1914, summarised schematically here, seldom informs the scholarship on foreign policymaking. After its opening discussions of Serbia and to a lesser extent Austria-Hungary, for example, even the treatments in Clark 2012 remain confined largely to the first of these aforementioned domains.

42 Rohrbach 1916, quoted in Fischer 1967, p. 160.

43 Fischer 1967, p. 160.

about war aims. The outlines emerge clearly from this description by his main ally in the government, Interior Secretary Clemens von Delbrück:

> Where hitherto we have tried to protect our national production by high duties and tariff treaties with all European states, in future the free play of forces is to reign in most respects throughout the great area *from the Pyrenees to Memel, from the Black Sea to the North Sea, from the Mediterranean to the Baltic* ... [W]e are no longer fighting for the mastery in the internal market but for *mastery in the world market* and it is only a Europe which forms a single customs unit that can meet with sufficient power the over-mighty productive resources of the transatlantic world; we ought to thank God that the war is causing us, and enabling us, to abandon an economic system which is already beginning to pass the zenith of its success.[44]

This characteristic imagery of the globalised struggle for existence among rival 'world nations' or 'world empires' had become the default language of international politics in German policymaking circles in the preceding years.[45] It was always structured around the dialectics of prosperity and survival. *This* was how powerful nations – expanding economies, prosperous societies, dynamic cultures, strategically dominant great powers – *had* to develop if they were not to sink into stagnation, poverty, decadence, and marginality. The necessary terms of success under the prevailing rivalries of the world system *required* such a logic. As Rohrbach said in *Der Deutsche Gedanke in der Welt* in 1912, '[f]or

---

44 Fischer 1967, p. 248. See this similar statement by the Under-Secretary at the Ministry of Agriculture, Friedrich von Falkenhausen: 'To match the great, closed economic bodies of the United States, the British, and the Russian Empires with an equally solid economic bloc representing all European states, or at least those of Central Europe [*Mitteleuropa*] under German leadership, with a twofold purpose: (1) of assuring the members of this whole, and particularly Germany, the mastery of the European market, and (2) of being able to lead the entire economic strength of allied Europe into the field, as a unified force, in the struggle with those world powers over the conditions of the admission of each to the markets of the others'. Fischer 1967, p. 250.

45 Delbrück's assistant von Schoenebeck repeated the argument: 'Difficulties of procedure should not make us forget the "great final aim" of creating a great Central European economic unit to enable us to hold our place in the economic struggle for existence of the peoples and to save us from shrinking into economic impotence against the ever-increasing solidarity and power of the economic World Powers, Great Britain with her colonies, the United States, Russia, and Japan with China'. Fischer 1967, p. 251, and, more generally, pp. 247–56; see also Pogge von Strandmann 1985, pp. 183–91.

us there can be no standing still or stopping, not even a temporary renunciation of the expansion of our sphere of life; our choice is either to decline again ... or to struggle for a place alongside the Anglo-Saxons ... Our growth is a process of elemental natural force'.[46] That was partly what Max Weber meant in 1895 when he worried caustically that the unification of Germany was starting to seem like a 'costly' and frivolous 'youthful prank', which 'would have been better left undone if it was meant to be the end and not the starting point of a German policy of world power'.[47] Moreover, just as Germany's unification had required war, so too might its future survival. Here is Rohrbach again in 1913:

> *Whether we shall obtain the necessary territorial elbow room to develop as a world power or not* without use of the old recipe of 'blood and iron' is anything but certain ... Our situation as a nation today is comparable to that before the wars of 1866 and 1870 which it was necessary to fight to settle the national crisis. At that time it was Germany's political unification which was at stake, today it is Germany's admittance to the circle of World Nations or its exclusion from it.[48]

The Pan-German Contribution

A vital area of contention among radical nationalists before 1914 concerned the most effective direction for Germany's interests *inside* this commonly agreed and by then well-established 'world imperial' frame of reference. Was this, to use the title of a keynote debate at the 1905 Pan-German Congress between Theodor Reismann-Grone and Eduard von Liebert, to be 'Overseas Policy or Continental Policy?' [*Überseepolitik oder Festlandspolitik?*].[49] That

---

46 Fischer 1967, p. 264.

47 Fischer 1967, p. 459.

48 Fischer 1967, p. 264.

49 See Reismann-Grone and von Liebert 1905. As a twenty-eight year old, Theodor Reismann-Grone (1863–1949) had been a charter signatory of the Pan-Germans' founding manifesto in 1891 and remained a leading voice until he broke with the leadership around Heinrich Claß during World War I. Appointed in 1891 General Secretary of the Ruhr Mineowners's Association, he resigned after several years to devote himself fully to the *Rheinisch-Westfälische Zeitung*, which he made into an organ of pro-industrial, overtly radical nationalist opinion. An early associate of Hitler during the 1920s, he ended his political career after 1933 as first National-Socialist Mayor of Essen. A career officer of bourgeois provenance, Eduard von Liebert (1850–1934) served in the Russian section of the General Staff, developed an interest in colonial questions, and in 1897 became

public exchange staged a far more elaborate review of Pan-German perspectives already in train since the turn of the century, which made a point of explicitly *refusing* any such contradiction between landward expansionism and *Weltpolitik*. Under the terms of that inner-League discussion Germany's imperialist future was ambitiously reconceived as a new type of complex macropolity or 'imperial formation', whose spatial reach would go far beyond direct colonial annexation of the conventional kind. Instead it would embrace not only what Ann Stoler has called 'blurred genres of rule and partial sovereignties', but also varying modalities of cultural influence and economic penetration, whether inside Europe or in the wider extra-European world.[50] Within a federated European structure linked to variegated forms of global dominion, this empire was intended to realise the goal of gathering in those far-flung and heterogeneous outposts of displaced and alienated 'Germandom' – whether these were 'overseas' or 'continental' – already imagined before 1871 to belong with the community of the nation. The Pan-German project would combine gradated sovereignties arranged around a dominant German core with a machinery of integrated economic planning. It would also be linked to grandiose biopolitical programmes of social engineering and large-scale population transfers.

Pan-German visions of a 'Greater Germany' made a point of explicitly holding these European and extra-European logics of imperial policymaking together, binding the prospects for colonial expansion overseas to the securing of Germany's dominance inside the continent at home. If the resulting co-prosperity zone, a 'Greater German Federation', would have to include far more 'racially' or nationally mixed or heterogeneous populations, it would still be 'exclusively ruled' by the ethnic Germans.[51] The implications of these ideas were extraordinarily far-reaching, both for the populations and territories into which Germany was meant to expand and for the character of politics at home. In Pan-German thinking, the process of European empire-making also presumed an active social policy inside Germany itself, one that was profoundly

---

Governor of German East Africa, before being ennobled and retired in 1900–1. In 1904 he emerged as head of the Imperial League Against Social Democracy founded in the aftermath of the SPD's success in the 1903 elections. In 1907 he was elected to the Reichstag as a Free Conservative. An early supporter of the Pan-Germans, he joined the League's national leadership in the final years before 1914. He ended his political career in the late 1920s and early 1930s as a Reichstag deputy for the NSDAP. See Eley 1991, pp. 54–7, pp. 108–11, pp. 229–35; Frech 2009; von Liebert 1925.

50 Stoler 2006; also Stoler, McGranahan and Purdue 2007, pp. 8–13.

51 Hasse 1895, p. 47.

technocratic and hostile to democracy. As Dennis Sweeney argues, it was the racialised logic of this emergent biopolitical programme for the management of populations, intensifying on the eve of the First World War, that allowed a recognisably fascist conception of the *Volkskörper* (national body) to first gradually coalesce.[52]

This Pan-German vision was the most radical and forthright of the efforts at imagining, programmatically and consistently, how Germany might take its place among the vaunted 'world empires'. But as international tensions began escalating in the run-up to 1914 and the arms race intensified, others found the simultaneity of overseas and landward expansionism much harder to sustain. The government in particular found itself constrained to choose one set of operative priorities over the other. The abrupt reversion in 1911–12 to the more orthodox primacy of an armaments policy based on the army, after the long dominance of the big navy policy ushered in by the proclamation of *Weltpolitik* in 1896, provides the most obvious context for this. The debacle of the Second Moroccan Crisis during the summer of 1911, the government's policymaking disarray, and the associated 'breakthrough of the national opposition' combined with the growing difficulties of Germany's international trading position and the recession of 1913–14 to tarnish the appeal of overseas colonialism and bring the project of *Mitteleuropa* strongly back to the fore. Wartime and its constraints then necessarily privileged those ideas to the practical exclusion of extra-European goals, with the vital exception of the projected drive through the Balkans, Near East, and the Caucasus along the direction of 'Berlin-Baghdad'.[53]

A broad, heterogeneous consensus was able to coalesce around these ideas of German expansionism between the 1880s and 1914, one that began under Bismarck around the importance of colonies and protected markets overseas, galvanised first by the impact of the post-1873 depression, disruptions of the business cycle, and the international turn to protection, then by the steady pressure of emigrationist anxieties and worries about the 'social question' and stability of the social order.[54] If Wehler made a compelling case in these terms for the existence of his ideological consensus in the late 1870s and early 1880s, there were three subsequent spurts before 1914 through which this cumulative common sense became further broadened and solidified: *first*, during

52 See Sweeney 2014.

53 Volker R. Berghahn calls this a 'Retreat to the European Continent'. See Berghahn 1993, pp. 136–55, with the preceding discussion, pp. 97–135. For greater detail, see Fischer 1974, pp. 71–159, pp. 291–329, pp. 355–69, pp. 439–58.

54 See Wehler 1969, pp. 112–93.

the early Wilhelmine years in the mid-1890s; *next*, linking the First Moroccan Crisis and the so-called 'Hottentot elections' in 1903–7; and *finally*, after the Second Moroccan or Agadir Crisis in 1911–14. Each was marked by an intensive concentration of public discussion across the press, associations, universities, and wider publicistic activity, intersecting with the business and government worlds, while finding powerful resonance among the parties and in the Reichstag. If each was then followed by a relative lull, the political climate had nonetheless been dangerously ratcheted forward.[55]

Inside this consensus were some important fissures, the most serious involving the presence of an increasingly noisy and virulent radical nationalism, or so-called 'national opposition', which first emerged in the more radical wing of the colonial movement of the 1880s before regrouping into the Pan-German League during 1890–4. Enjoying something of a boost from the enthusiasm for navy and *Weltpolitik* in 1896–1900, these Pan-Germans then fell afoul of government disapproval during their pro-Boer campaigning in 1900–2, losing much of their public credibility and retreating to a less overtly political ground of journalism, 'science', and intellectual critique. While taking stock of their political options in a searching internal debate of 1904–5, they now concentrated on various strategies of secondary influence, whose vehicles included the Prussian state's East-Elbian apparatus of anti-Polish activities, the Imperial League Against Social Democracy, and especially the Navy League, which was the largest of the various nationalist pressure groups, with its 325,000 individ-

55 In the *initial* phase marked by Wehler's 'ideological consensus', the enormous surge of support for colonialism was matched by conventional strategic and diplomatic concern for stabilising the new Germany's geopolitical security in central Europe, by among other things the Dual Alliance of 1879 with Austria-Hungary. The *second* major spurt came in the mid-1890s with the end of the depression, Wilhelm II's announcement of *Weltpolitik*, and new interest in the navy. The new assertiveness behind German overseas interests was again matched by the drive for a politically secured central European trading region, focused via the Caprivi commercial treaties of 1892–4. The most sustained effort at holding these goals together occurred with the Pan-German League's foundation in 1890–1. The *third* phase was sparked by the 1902 tariffs, a standard of living crisis behind the Socialist electoral landslide of 1903, and recovery from the recession of 1900–2. While *Weltpolitik* continued apace (notably, in the First Moroccan Crisis of 1905–6 and the radicalising of naval agitation), the key step was the *Mitteleuropäischer Wirtschaftsverein* (Central European Economic Association) founded in 1904, again with strong Pan-German presence. It was now that the oscillation between 'world policy' and 'continental policy' began to be named. Finally, a *fourth* phase immediately preceded 1914, introduced by the watershed of the Second Moroccan Crisis in 1911 and the reversion to a military, rather than a naval, arms drive. The resulting intensification of public discourse was at the heart of Fischer's *War of Illusions*, see Fischer 1974.

ual and 675,000 corporately affiliated members by 1907–8. When a distinctively radical nationalist tendency captured the Navy League during 1903–8, Pan-Germans saw their chance, astutely collaborating with Major-General August Keim, its vigorous and charismatic leader. When Keim and his main supporters withdrew in protest against pressure from the Imperial Navy Office during 1908, the Pan-Germans gave them a political home. Almost immediately afterward, in November 1908, the government fell into one of its severest crises when Wilhelm II's embarrassing indiscretions to the British *Daily Telegraph* provoked public uproar amid a generalised crisis of confidence across the press and Reichstag. Though the Kaiser and his government formally survived the resulting turmoil, the Pan-Germans had placed themselves at the front of the criticisms from the right. As the national opposition began to harden its identity in contention with the Chancellorship of Bethmann Hollweg after the summer of 1909, Pan-Germans increasingly delivered the guiding political perspectives, particularly after the debacle of the 1912 elections, when the mainstream right could muster barely 60 seats against the SPD's 110.[56]

The Crisis Itself: Sleepwalking into War?

These arguments have direct relevance for how we should judge Germany's role in the outbreak of war. In his magisterial new account of the July Crisis, Christopher Clark has tried to dispense with the old 'blame game', or those familiar 'prosecutorial narratives' that seek to assign primary responsibility for the outbreak of war, including above all the 'Fischerian' thesis of Germany's aggression. In Clark's view, such an approach implies misguided notions of consciously planned agency and intentional coherence, simplistically binarised conceptions of 'right' and 'wrong', and a misplaced desire to make some imperialisms less destructive and ethically culpable than others: 'The outbreak of war in 1914 is not an Agatha Christie drama at the end of which we will discover the culprit standing over a corpse in the conservatory with a smoking pistol'.[57] He proposes instead that we begin from the convoluted multipolar intricacies of the decision-making process activated in July, which involved 'five autonomous players of equal importance – Germany, Austria-Hungary, France, Russia, and Britain – six if we add Italy, plus various other strategically significant and equally autonomous sovereign actors, such as the Ottoman

56 For the character and importance of this radical nationalism, see Eley 1991, also footnote 36 above.

57 Clark 2012, pp. 560–561.

Empire and the states of the Balkans, a region of high political tension and instability in the years before the outbreak of war. Nor were each of the governments concerned unified or even especially well-coordinated, but contended on the contrary with internal rivalries, indiscipline, and idiosyncrasies that made their reactions to the unfolding of the events anything but transparent or easily intelligible.

Relative to Fischer, Clark then shifts the narrative weight of the account *away* from the purposeful aggression of the Central Powers ('grab for world power', showdown with Serbia) and *toward* the Entente's provocations: a generous reading of Austrian behaviour on the one hand; and a highly jaundiced treatment of Serb nationalism (and especially the Black Hand), French belligerence, Russian aggression, and British passivity on the other. In what he calls 'the Balkan inception scenario', France and Russia ('at different paces and for different reasons') had 'constructed a geopolitical trigger along the Austro-Serbian frontier'. Once the Sarajevo assassination happened, in this account, Russia then set the pace, stiffening Serbian resolve and forcing the speed of mobilisation. Thus, events in the Balkans, especially the wars of 1912–13, had 'recalibrated the relationships among the greater and lesser powers in dangerous ways', through which French policy now licensed Russian intransigence: 'Russia and France thereby tied the fortunes of two of the world's greatest powers in highly asymmetrical fashion to the uncertain destiny of a turbulent and intermittently violent state'.[58]

This leaves German behaviour in the July Crisis far more reactive than in most of the other post-Fischer accounts. At one level, Clark presents all of the decision-making in July–August as far more confused and partially informed than we have easily assumed, so that the outcome is made to result from an aggregation of discretely generated governmental dilemmas, each with its own complicated field of national-imperial purposes and barely manageable domestic political dynamics, feeding into a complexly entangled sequence of miscalculations.[59] But in making the Balkans so firmly into his primary explanatory ground, while fixing the terms of the crisis and its temporality so strictly to the situational dynamics of what happened in July–August *per se*, he radically displaces the longer-standing histories stressed in this essay. At one level,

58 This is necessarily a stripped-down rendition of an immensely erudite, complex, and finely nuanced account. See Clark 2012, pp. 558–9.

59 This is the force of Clark's title. But though an arresting metaphor, 'sleepwalking' underestimates the relationship of the decision-making to consciously elaborated policies and purposes, recoverable and coherent understandings, explicit assumptions, and long-standing calculations.

he does capture their operative importance: 'All the key actors in our story filtered the world through narratives that were built from pieces of experience glued together with fears, projections, and interests masquerading as maxims'. Yet, this description of the decision-making process ('the stories they told themselves and each other about what they thought they were doing and why they were doing it') is distinguished sharply from everything outside the situational cauldron of the crisis itself (as 'the objective factors acting on the decision-makers'). Yet, as I have tried to show, 'empire talk' had created a climate not just of thought, but of organised and active articulations, continual transmissions from the practical worlds of the economy and politics, whose effects created a powerfully structured setting for the crisis when it occurred. All of this should not be bracketed into a series of background elements or 'objective factors', mainly severed from the multi-accented script that 'the many voices of European foreign policy' wrote for themselves in the immediately war-preceding years.[60]

In other words, the sheer breadth of underlying agreement around the urgency of Germany's need as a nation to compete effectively in a world economy and international system already ordered around aggressively secured imperial interests (the 'world nations' of Britain, Russia, and the USA) itself needs a salient place in the account. At the same time, even as this consensual recognition – from Weber through Bethmann Hollweg to the Pan-Germans – enabled German policy to keep on moving forward, it also encouraged, by its very breadth, a kind of fissiparity, a field of divergent and often bitterly held opinions about how exactly Germany's interests were best to be served. Indeed, the strength of the consensus that developed by stages between the 1880s and 1914 – everything encompassed in the obsession with Germany's global destiny, the rivalries of the great 'world nations', the conditions of societal health into the future, the dialectics of prosperity and survival – concealed potentially deep disagreements, the most important of which now set Bethmann Hollweg's government against an implacable front of foes on the right. Here, there were two vital fault-lines. One was a matter of degree: radical nationalist projections of *Mitteleuropa*, especially in Pan-German notations, were much earlier, sharper, and more elaborate, in every way more extreme. But the resulting conflicts inspired a second, more damaging divergence. Constantly riled by the government's slowness and lack of vigour, radical nationalists sharpened their complaints into an uncompromising stance of 'national opposition'. Still

60 See Clark 2012, p. 558. 'The Many Voices of European Foreign Policy' is the title of the chapter (pp. 168–241) where the book's structural analysis is principally to be found, focusing on the country-by-country systems and patterns of governance.

more, they angrily berated those Conservatives and National Liberals who still endorsed the government's point of view, taking that moderation as lack of commitment, lack of imagination, lack of knowledge and understanding, and lack of general political wherewithal. From conflicts over the substance, speed, and directions of foreign policy, this radical right intensified their complaints into a critique of political methods and the associated political forms. Attacks on particular policies of the government turned into questioning the legitimacy of the Imperial government *per se*. The resulting oppositional politics began to precipitate a populist set of departures in a long process of radicalisation. Taking the years between 1908–9 and 1918 as a whole, this foreign-political context inspired a field of disagreements that supplied the impetus for the German right's longer-term transformation.

In this way, a particular climate of political discussion, speculative thought, and visionary ideology coalesced during the pre-1914 decade into an entire discursive landscape of ideas and practices that disposed toward the coming of war. By 1913–14, a domestic political configuration was being assembled whose terms indirectly conduced to such a decision. As another of Fischer's students, Peter-Christian Witt, argued, and was compellingly reinforced by Niall Ferguson's article on 'Public Finance and National Security' almost twenty years ago, the fiscal entailments of the intensifying arms race were leading German politics into a dangerous impasse. Government's unwillingness to breach the fiscal immunities still enjoyed by the landed interests effectively applied the brakes to the army's intended maximal expansion, thereby backing the military leadership further into the 'sooner rather than later' mentality.[61] Concurrently, the resistance of military traditionalists against Erich Ludendorff's 1912 call for general conscription, basically out of fears of dilution, had a similar effect. But beyond each of these impedances lay the startling catastrophe of the right's dismal showing in the 1912 elections, which reduced its parliamentary strength to a mere rump of 72 seats.[62] That, in my view, created the conditions for an extremely threatening radicalisation. In these terms the arguments of Fischer, his students, and a number of contemporaries still stand.[63] This is how Berghahn poses the question:

61 Witt 1970, Ferguson 1994.

62 To the fifty-seven seats of the Conservatives and Free Conservatives could be added another fifteen of assorted Antisemites, militant agrarians, and *Mittelstand* deputies.

63 In addition to Stegman 1970, Wernecke 1970, and Witt 1970, see also Saul 1974, esp. pp. 382–94.

> By 1913/14 that system had reached an impasse. The modernity and richness of the country's organizational and cultural life notwithstanding and, indeed, perhaps because of it, in the end Wilhelmine politics was marked by bloc-formation and paralysis at home and abroad and finally by a *Flucht nach vorn* (flight forward) on the part of the political leadership that was fast losing control, but still had enough constitutional powers to take the step into a major war. It is the evolution of this outcome and the political culture that made it possible that still requires further study.[64]

It is not necessary to accept any simplistic version of the *Primat der Innenpolitik* or an overly straightforward and literal notion of the *Flucht nach vorn* in order to argue that a domestic political crisis established some of the ground from which the decision for war could unfurl.

Conclusion

If we play these arguments forward into the war itself, both the salience of the divisions between a governmentalist and a more radical right and the hardening of linkages between foreign and domestic goals become all the more clear. The drive to create a guaranteed basis for Germany's global power – the condition of its claim to world imperial standing – now aligned an aggressively annexationist camp against those who preferred more informal mechanisms of dominance constructed through tariffs, trading reciprocities, market federation, and other forms of more or less forcible economic integration. But if the seaward expansionism associated since the 1880s and 1890s with colonialism and *Weltpolitik* now went effectively into recession, the ulterior world-political purposes of *Mitteleuropa* and the competing perspectives of a land-based empire built in the east at the expense of a defeated Russia remained no less evident. During 1917–18, especially with the opportunities promised by the Treaty of Brest-Litovsk, the latter now opened toward a distinctively world-political horizon of its own, namely, that of a German imperial macro-polity extending through southern Russia and the Ottoman Empire to the Caucasus, Mesopotamia, Persia, and beyond. Projected continentally, rather than overseas, this was a prospect imagined no less globally in its relationship to the empire talk discussed earlier in this essay. In a vital way, not least in relation

64 Berghahn 1993, p. 9.

to the future histories of the 1940s, this Central Asian imaginary [*Mittelasien?*] now effectively trumped *Mitteleuropa*.[65]

These decisively world political or global dimensions of German policy, which had arrived inescapably between the 1880s and 1900s and came back again with a vengeance after the 1920s, were not as self-evidently present in the diplomatic exchanges and high-political deliberations of July–August 1914, although they became quickly palpable again almost immediately afterward in Bethmann Hollweg's September Programme and the other contexts where war aims were being worked out. The force of my argument in this essay is that virtually any serious thinker seeking to strategise Germany's viable future as a great power – a category indistinguishable by the late nineteenth century from normative ideas of a successful national economy or predictions of a prosperous and cohesive society – would of necessity approach that question by considering German interests in the far larger setting of a wider-than-European-world. This was true almost irrespective of particular political persuasion. As a basic appraisal of the underlying exigencies of the world economy and international system, which imposed definite constraints and priorities for any country seeking to maximise the welfare of its population, it enlisted liberals no less than conservatives, Social Democrats no less than Pan-Germans, though the programmatic conclusions could clearly be very different.[66] This common understanding of what were deemed to be inescapable facts did much to enable that particular breadth of readiness in July 1914 which wagered Germany's future on the incalculable risk of a continental and tendentially global war.

---

65 I owe this formulation to many conversations with Jennifer Jenkins, who is developing the argument in full in her forthcoming book, *Weltpolitik on the Persian Frontier: Germany and Iran, 1857–1953*. See also Jenkins 2013.

66 For fascinating insight into socialist thinking about these questions before 1914, see Fletcher 1984; Bley 1975; Schröder 1975 and 1979; Hyrkkänen 1986; Salvadori 1979, pp. 169–203; Geary 1987, pp. 46–59; Nettl 1966, pp. 519–30.

CHAPTER 2

War, Defeat, and the Urgency of *Lebensraum*: German Imperialism from the Second Empire to the Third Reich

Shelley Baranowski

Introduction

In August 1914, Imperial Germany declared war on France, the Russian Empire, and Great Britain, convinced that defeating its neighbours at that moment would eliminate its long-term strategic disadvantage. Despite a century-long debate as to which belligerent was most responsible for the outbreak of World War I, the competition and paranoia among the European powers leading up to the war makes it difficult to blame a single party for a global catastrophe. Arguing against the still prevalent view that Germany was most responsible, Christopher Clark argues compellingly that the explosive nationalism in the Balkans so intensified the rivalries among the great powers that each was willing to risk war.[1] Yet Germany's emergence as an economic and military great power in the decades after unification, and its desire for an enlarged empire as testimony to that fact, no doubt contributed to a more competitive continental and global rivalry. That rivalry in turn spawned the dread of encirclement by enemies that the German attack in 1914 sought to remedy.

The imperialism of the *Kaiserreich* consisted of two distinct but overlapping dimensions, the first maritime, the second continental. The need for commercial and trading interests for markets, raw materials, and labour was a prime motivation in the first case, in addition to the particular objectives of cultural emissaries such as missionaries and geographers. The second embraced desires both for an informal continental empire [*Mitteleuropa*] that Germany would dominate economically, and for territorial expansion into Eastern Europe. Until the Kaiser removed the 'Iron Chancellor' Otto von Bismarck in 1890, continental expansion was not in play because Bismarck did not want to endanger the gains of unification by antagonising Germany's neighbours. Yet by the first decade of the twentieth century, expansion gained more traction.

1 Clark 2012.

Militant nationalist pressure groups, most notably the Pan-German League, which because of its connections occupied the centre of the radical nationalist movement, obsessed over Germany's population deficit in comparison with Slavs. Although the Pan-Germans continued to promote overseas colonialism, they now advocated living space in the East to provide land for German settlers, who otherwise would have emigrated to the Americas.[2] Despite the diverse threads of German imperialism, a common theme united them. In addition to creating a world power, empire would triumph over a history of division among Germans and vulnerability to foreign intervention.[3]

Since the end of the Second World War, historians have struggled to identify the roots of the Nazi catastrophe, especially since the early 1960s when the Hamburg scholar Fritz Fischer linked the imperialist war plans of the Second Empire and those of the Third Reich.[4] Teleological notions of continuity associated with Fischer and his successors have fallen out of favour as historians have narrowed their focus to the First World War as decisive in radicalising German expansionism.[5] Nevertheless, the rediscovery of German imperialism and colonialism before World War I as topics for scholarly discussion has once more put the continuity question on the table. Jürgen Zimmerer's attempt to link the genocidal violence of the Herero War in German South West Africa from 1904 to 1907 with that of the Third Reich indicates that the desire for a broader optic through which to examine the Third Reich remains palpable.[6] The historical connections between National Socialism and the more distant past deserve attention, especially the dream of an enlarged empire that would embrace all Germans. If dreams of continental living space during the *Kaiserreich* were less potent than they became after the Great War, the racist biopolitics of the Pan-German League envisioned the elimination of the

---

2 See the argument of the Pan-German leader Heinrich Claß 1914, p. 440, who looked to the Medieval German settlements in the East as his model. As Liulevicius 2009, p. 3 notes, defining the geographical boundaries of the 'East' has eluded precision, but it potentially included Poland, the Baltic lands, Ukraine, Russia, the Czech lands and the Balkans, as well as the eastern Prussian provinces of Imperial Germany.

3 There is a large literature on German imperialism. For a superb summary and analysis of recent scholarship, see Conrad, 2008.

4 Fischer 1961 and 1969.

5 See Alexander Anievas's essay in this volume, 'Marxist Theory and the Origins of the First World War', for a thoroughgoing critique of the scholarship and a sophisticated theoretical 'way out' of the difficulties embedded in previous explanations for the war's outbreak.

6 See Zimmerer 2003, pp. 1098–119; 2004, pp. 49–76; 2004, pp. 10–43; and his most recent book, 2011. The revisiting of continuities in German history extends as well to the important exploration of nationalism and anti-semitism by Helmut Walser Smith 2008.

genetically 'inferior' and the removal of 'aliens', namely Jews and Poles, in a manner that prefigured the National Socialists.[7]

Regardless, World War I was transformative. The war and its consequences redefined German politics and reshaped German imperialist priorities. They added urgency to the racial-biological imperatives that emerged among pre-war radical nationalists and over the long term opened new opportunities for expansion in a weakened and unstable post-war order. Three outcomes of the war enabled the survival of imperialist aspirations into the post-war period, which the National Socialists ultimately exploited: the self-imposed limitations of the German Revolution of 1918; the implications of the Versailles Treaty specifically and the post-war peace settlement generally; and the perceived crisis of German ethnicity that strengthened the radical nationalist critique of Wilhelmine imperialism.

The Revolution of 1918 and the Unrequited Imperial Imagination

The German Revolution, which began in late October 1918 with the sailors' mutiny at the naval base in Kiel, stemmed from the desperation in the German armed forces after the failed spring offensive on the Western Front and the collapse of Germany's allies. The powerful army Quartermaster General Erich Ludendorff gambled that installing a new government consisting of a new chancellor, Prince Max von Baden, and the dominant parties in the Reichstag, the Majority Social Democrats, the Center, and the Progressives, would negotiate an armistice and buy time to regroup for a 'final struggle' in the west. In addition, Ludendorff hoped to exploit the Allies' revulsion at the Bolshevik Revolution of the previous November so that Germany would keep the huge territorial gains that it wrested from the Soviet Union at Brest-Litovsk in March 1918.[8] Yet mounting popular resistance to the war's privations brought the collapse of Prince Max's government, the abdication of the Kaiser, and renewed pressure to sue for peace.[9]

The Allied armistice agreement of November 1918 mandated the withdrawal of Germany's army from west of the Rhine and the surrender of its weapons, the renunciation of the Treaty of Brest-Litovsk, and the capitulation of

7 See Walkenhorst 2007, 80–165. See Geoff Eley's assessment of Wilhelmine radical nationalism 2013, pp. 136–40, and especially Eley's essay, 'Germany, the Fischer Controversy, and the Context of War', in this volume.

8 On the *Endkampf*, see Hull 2005, pp. 309–19.

9 On this episode, see Geyer 2001, pp. 459–527.

its fleet. To ensure that Germany complied, the Allied blockade remained in force. Like most Germans, the Majority Socialist-led Council of People's Deputies formed after the collapse of Prince Max's coalition, hoped for a moderate peace based on President Woodrow Wilson's Fourteen Points. Instead it had to accede to unexpectedly harsh terms to end the hostilities and confront the spread of revolution at home. In response to the workers' and soldiers' councils that sprung up after the Kiel mutiny and the pressure for more radical change from the SPD's secessionists, the Independent Social Democrats and the Spartacists, the Council's Majority Socialist leaders, Friedrich Ebert and Philipp Scheidemann, moved to restore order. Thus, Ebert concluded an agreement with the army to secure the latter's loyalty and an orderly demobilisation in return for suppressing the councils and maintaining the integrity of the officer corps. Although demoralised and uncertain of the loyalty of its own troops, the army command, backed up by radical nationalists organised into right-wing paramilitary Freikorps units, retained enough influence to narrow the lens through which the German public viewed the defeat. Germany had not lost on the battlefield at all. Rather, Marxists, pacifists, liberals, and Jews had 'stabbed' Germany in the back by capitulating to the Entente.

The Weimar Republic, which formally came into being in June 1919, brought liberal democracy to Germany after elections in January 1919 yielded a government composed of Majority Socialists, Catholics, and Progressives. Its constitution guaranteed the civil and political equality of men and women. It contained extensive social rights that ranged from collective bargaining and factory committees that enhanced the power of labour to the protection of women, children, and the unemployed.[10] Nonetheless the refusal of the dominant coalition party, the Majority Socialists, to socialise the means of production and unseat Imperial Germany's political and military elites, has generated continuous debate as to whether the Republic would have survived had such initiatives been carried out.[11] In fact, the odds were stacked in favour of caution from the beginning. Although the Independent Socialists participated briefly on the Council of People's Deputies, the schism within the SPD left the gradualist majority with the opportunity to advance its own goals. In addition, the opposition to socialisation from the other parties of the 'Weimar coalition', the Progressives and Center Party (indeed the early 1919 elections amounted to an endorsement of reformism rather than further revolution), reinforced the Majority Socialists' inclinations to pursue socialism through electoral and parliamentary means. In the interim, Ebert and Scheidemann wanted

10 Weitz 2007, pp. 32–3.

11 For a recent summary and analysis of this discussion, see Hagen 2012, pp. 233–40.

desperately to contain the popular revolution, and they succeeded with the help of counterrevolutionaries who loathed them only slightly less than the radical left at home and Bolsheviks abroad. On top of that, neither the council nor the Weimar coalition contested the legitimacy of the imperialist ambitions that fuelled the military during the war and the paramilitaries afterward, nor did they challenge the myth of a Germany undefeated on the battlefield.

Indeed, the containment of the revolution at home overlapped with the continuation of imperialism in the East where despite the armistice, the German wartime occupation, the memory of Brest-Litovsk, and anti-bolshevism conspired to sustain dreams of living space. In early 1919, roughly the same time that Gustav Noske, the Majority Socialist in charge of military affairs, authorised the formation of paramilitary Freikorps units to assist the army in quelling the Spartacists, Freikorps units in the Baltic region waged war against Bolshevik forces with the approval of the government in Berlin, and the indulgence of the Allies. Unhappy that the Paris peace negotiations abandoned the Fourteen Points as the basis for a permanent settlement while Germany had to cede territories that it occupied at the armistice, Noske used the Freikorps as a bargaining chip.[12] Yet the Freikorps went well beyond their prescribed role as pawns. They imagined themselves as crusaders in the tradition of the Teutonic Knights, the modern-day colonisers of the 'wild East', and as the heroic bulwark against Bolshevism. Had not the Allies finally forced them to withdraw, the free booters would have reaped their reward, a huge expanse without borders open to them for conquest and settlement.[13] As it stood, the conclusion of the Paris Peace Conference in June 1919, which imposed terms seen as punitive, provided returning Freikorpsmen with another task as the shock troops behind the counterrevolutionary Kapp Putsch in March of the following year. Although this and other putsch attempts failed during the tumultuous early years of the Republic, paramilitary violence whether in the Baltic, along Germany's borders against foreigners, or in its cities against leftists, had long-term consequences that survived its early defeats: the radicalisation of countless young men and the durability of expansionist aspirations.

The Post-War Peace Settlement: Punishment and Opportunity

The hostile reception from most Germans to the Treaty of Versailles is well-known. The loss of 13 percent of Germany's pre-war territory and 10 percent of

12 See Noske's memoir 1920, pp. 175–85.

13 Liulevicius 2000, pp. 227–46; Theweleit 1977 and 1979.

its population, the demilitarisation of the Rhineland, the seizure of its overseas empire, the drastic reduction in the size of its military, restrictions on its foreign trade, and the assessment of reparations amounted (in German eyes) to Germany's expulsion from the ranks of the great powers.[14] Moreover, the French occupation of the Rhineland, which included French Arab and African troops, seemed to subvert the 'natural' colonial order of white over black, and the return of an unhappy past before unification when foreign meddling in the affairs of German states was common.[15] Although it is easy to overstate the effectiveness of the Versailles Treaty's enforcement mechanisms, the constraints on Germany's room to manoeuvre were real enough, an obvious example being the French and Belgian occupation of the Ruhr industrial region in early 1923 to force the German government to pay reparations. To give a less obvious example: The Locarno Treaty of 1925, negotiated by Weimar's leading statesman Gustav Stresemann, signified the recovery of German sovereignty and led to its membership in the League of Nations one year later. It normalised relations between Germany and the Entente and left Germany's eastern borders open to future negotiation. It also let stand the Rapallo Treaty of 1922 between Germany and the Soviet Union, which included a secret clause allowing the German military to train on Soviet territory. Despite those achievements, Locarno also meant painful compromises: Germany had to guarantee the permanence of its western borders and accept the loss of Alsace and Lorraine.[16]

Over time, however, the Paris peace settlement betrayed its vulnerabilities, especially in the post-imperial 'shatter zone', which extended from Central Europe to the shrunken borders of the Soviet Union. The instability there offered the greatest potential for a German resurgence. Working from the contradictory principles of national self-determination and anti-communism, the peacemakers created new nation states as successors to the collapsed empires that would be cohesive enough to satisfy nationalist demands for independence but strong enough to contain the Soviet Union. Yet, class and ethnic conflicts, discord among the new nations over borders, and congenital economic weakness challenged the successor states sufficiently to provide a tempting target for Germany's economic, political, and territorial extension.[17] To be sure, German imperialist aspirations endured, notably in the army and industry, but

14 Marks 2013, challenges this still widely-held view that Versailles was excessively harsh, a view that essentially replicates the German interpretation of the treaty since 1919.

15 Mass 2006, pp. 76–120, 198–9; Lebzelter 1985, pp. 37–58; Poley 2005, pp. 151–247.

16 Mommsen 1996, pp. 203–7.

17 Rothschild and Wingfield 2000, pp. 1–21.

they remained on the back burner as long as American loans and investment flooded into Germany and Stresemann's pragmatism prevailed. However, the effects of the Great Depression and right-wing Weimar governments after 1930 encouraged aggressive revisionism and autarkic expansionism. Coupled with the loss of American financial support and the Allies' declining willingness to punish violations of Versailles, the genie was let out of the bottle. Hitler's successful challenges to the peace settlement after 1933 testified to the Reich's effort to break free of the Anglo-American dominated global economy through bi-lateral trade agreements with the nations of Southeastern Europe, to economic weakness and social conflict in Britain and France, and to the reluctance of the British especially to engage the Soviet Union in a renewed 'encirclement' against Germany.[18] Yet the Entente's reluctance to shore up the post-war European order and its economic support for Eastern Europe was evident well before the Nazi takeover.

New Imperialist Priorities and 'Stranded' German Minorities

During the stabilisation era, revisionism – or the demand that Germany's 1914 borders be restored – was the answer to the Versailles opprobrium. In line with Stresemann's approach, it was the best that could be achieved under the circumstances and it accorded with the expectations of many Germans for whom 'Germany' continued to mean the Bismarckian Reich.[19] Yet as the escapades of the Freikorps revealed, the war and its aftermath, beginning with the German occupation of Poland and the Baltic regions between 1915 and 1919, had encouraged less inhibited visions of Germany's geographical expanse. To be sure, German conduct in Poland followed conservative and patriarchal principles of direct rule. The military encouraged cultural autonomy and enough political participation to lay the groundwork for a future client state and buffer against Russia.[20] Yet the occupation of the *Ober Ost* under Ludendorff's command followed a different model. Although conditions were harsh in Poland, the *Ober Ost* became the setting for a more ambitious agenda, in which its commander Erich Ludendorff pursued the complete exploitation and mobilisation of labour and resources. He envisioned a future utopia that protected Germany against enemy blockades by modernising the land for the benefit of its German overlords, and it soon included plans to 'cleanse' the soil by removing the native

18 Tooze 2006, pp. 85–90.
19 For this argument, see Chu 2012, pp. 49–56.
20 Chu, Kauffman, and Meng 2013, p. 323.

population. The military extended the Ludendorff model to Estonia, Latvia, and most of the Ukraine, after the Treaty of Brest-Litovsk awarded those territories to Germany.[21] Such schemes were not confined to the military. They replicated late pre-war and early wartime Pan-German social engineering designs (in fact, Ludendorff maintained close ties to the Pan-Germans), which focused on Eastern Europe as the core of an expanded, autarkic German empire made prosperous through German settlements.[22] And they appeared once more in the annexationist platform of the radical nationalist and aggressively populist Fatherland Party late in the war.[23] Taken together, increasingly racist and social Darwinian assumptions about the struggle for survival among peoples and the biological need for living space at the expense of the Slavs underwrote the compulsion to autarky. Thus, wartime imperialism in the East implicitly challenged Wilhelmine assumptions about maritime colonialism as the primary route to global power. Total war and the British control of the oceans required a foundation for economic growth and German settlement that an overseas empire would not provide. That would be in Europe itself.

The political reconstruction of Eastern Europe reinforced the shift in imperialist priorities. The creation of new nation-states threatened the status of over 8.5 million ethnic Germans scattered from Poland to Czechoslovakia and to the Balkans and Romania, in addition to the Germans in the much weakened Austrian rump state.[24] With the exception of Austrians, Germans elsewhere were recast as 'minorities' but provided with constitutional guarantees of civil rights and equality under the law. Regardless, economic competition, cultural resentments, and conflict over political representation rendered the position of ethnic Germans increasingly precarious, and in the case of former German territories annexed to Poland, ethnic Germans emigrated in droves.[25] Many Germans spent little time concerning themselves with Germans outside Germany, the exception being former citizens whose immigration aroused as much resentment as pity.[26] Yet Germans 'stranded' abroad drew the attention of numerous well-connected imperialists, such as Paul Rohrbach and the Pan-German leader Heinrich Claß, and advocates of expanded living space such as the geographer Karl Haushofer. Their predicament also engaged scholars

21 Liulevicius 2000, pp. 54–112 and 51–226.

22 For a detailed discussion of Pan-German imperialism, see Walkenhorst 2007, pp. 166–303; and Hofmeister 2012, pp. 78–100.

23 Breundel 2003, pp. 149–50; Hagenlücke 1997, pp. 248–71 and 388–411.

24 Göktürk, Gramling, and Kaes 2007, p. 7.

25 Oltmar 2005, p. 99; Blanke 1993, p. 32.

26 Föllmer 2005, pp. 202–31.

across disciplines, who pursued the study of the East [*Ostforschung*]. Although in the early and mid-twenties the political implications of their work were ambiguous, many *Ostforscher* supported revision at minimum and at maximum *völkisch* expansionism by the onset of the Depression.[27] The desire to regain Germany's overseas territories by no means disappeared. Former settlers, colonial officials, and nationalist organisations lobbied persistently for the return of Germany's maritime empire, with many proposing investment in infrastructure and public health to assure an efficient indigenous labour force.[28] Nevertheless, from the perspective of many German nationalists, the East promised what Germany needed most in the biologically determined competition for survival, a vast space for exploitation and ethnic revitalisation after the trauma of defeat and foreign domination.

The social diversification of radical nationalists in post-war Germany, indeed the migration of radical nationalism from academic and journalistic debate to outright violence, followed directly from the perception of ethnic endangerment. Before 1914 the industrial, commercial and professional middle classes carried the banner of imperialism and anti-Marxism.[29] Now a more heterogeneous mix drawn from the lower-middle as well as the middle classes moved front and center, radicalised by defeat, revolution, and hyperinflation. University students, who might otherwise have become solid *Bildungsbürger* after receiving their degrees, stood out among the newly militant. Alienated by their declining job prospects because of economic crisis and embittered by the defeat, many flocked to paramilitary units to do battle against the Poles in Upper Silesia, the French in the Rhineland, and Socialists and Communists at home.[30] For them, armed combat was not just more effective than talk; it was in fact redemptive, the triumph over Germany's humiliation. Even former pillars of the Second Empire, landed estate owners and especially the Junker nobility, became angry and marginalised in the new order, another indication of radical nationalism's diversity. The ignominious abdication of the Kaiser, severe limitations on the size of the army and officer corps, which had been

---

27 On Claß, see Jochmann 1963, pp. 10–24. Claß wanted the annexation of Austria, the acquisition of the Baltic lands, western Hungary, and Alsace-Lorraine for German settlements, as well as the reincorporation of ethnic Germans elsewhere in the East in an enlarged Reich. See also Rohrbach's lengthy, well-illustrated book, 1926. See too Chu's finely-grained analysis of *Ostforschung* (Chu 2012, pp. 40–9). Although the views of scholars who pursued *Ostforschung* were fluid and hard to pin down, many became unambiguously expansionist by the late twenties.

28 See van Laak 2004, pp. 248–53; and Bullard 2012.

29 Jens-Uwe Guettel 2012 makes this especially clear.

30 See Wildt 2002, pp. 41–143.

a prime career choice, the Weimar constitution's elimination of aristocratic privileges, and the impoverishment of their estates led many to lead Freikorps units to fight striking farm workers, leftists, and Poles. They played key roles in the March 1920 Kapp Putsch, the failed attempt at overthrowing the Republic after the forced withdrawal of Freikorps units from the Baltic. In a departure from their pre-war position when Junkers especially displayed little enthusiasm for imperialism, their declining economic viability made them increasingly receptive to eastward expansion. After the Nazis came to power, the regime's determination to acquire 'living space' attracted many Junkers to their ranks. The expansion of the armed forces once again provided careers in the officer corps and the *Drang nach Osten* promised new lands for those who had lost their property to bankruptcy.[31]

The Exclusionary *Volksgemeinschaft*: National Socialism as a Post-War Phenomenon

Neither the collapse of the Weimar Republic nor the Nazi assumption to power was inevitable. By 1924, the Republic had contained counterrevolution, even if the sentiments that fuelled it had by no means evaporated. Despite the hyperinflation and sectoral weaknesses that persisted after stabilisation, it took the Great Depression to undermine the Republic's ability to deal effectively with economic crisis and mediate social conflict. After 1928, the last year of modest economic recovery, the Nazis grew into a formidable electoral machine that crowded out its closest competitors, especially the right-wing German National People's Party (DNVP). Yet up to that point, they had made little electoral headway despite having expanded the party's apparatus nationwide.

At its founding in 1919, the Nazi Party was but one of many counterrevolutionary movements seeking the overthrow of the Weimar Republic. Having originated in the Bavarian capital of Munich, a magnet for an array of putschist groups from Europe's post-imperial 'shatter zone', the party like so many others espoused virulent anti-Bolshevism, anti-liberalism, and especially anti-semitism inflamed by the apocalyptic fantasies of a global Jewish revolutionary conspiracy in *The Protocols of the Elders of Zion*. The 'Jew' personified the upheavals of war, the destruction of centuries-old land empires, and the spectre of Bolshevism. In addition to war veterans organised into paramilitary units, the counterrevolutionaries included men too young to have fought in the war but who were embittered by the result. In addition to fantasising

31 Malinowski 2004, pp. 198–202, 476–552.

about overthrowing the 'November Criminals' in Berlin, they participated in the violent suppression of the Munich Soviet in the spring of 1919.[32]

Adolf Hitler personified the transnational counterrevolutionary exchange. A decorated war veteran who fought with a Bavarian regiment on the Western Front,[33] his exposure to the tiny German Workers' Party came about while identifying right-wing groups for financial support from the military. As a subject of the Austro-Hungarian Empire, who abandoned what he later called the Slavic 'corpse of a state' to enlist in a German unit, Hitler became a fervent Pan-German in Vienna before the war. Despite his rejection of Austria-Hungary, Hitler disliked what he saw as Imperial Germany's commercialised overseas colonialism and its tepid attempts to Germanise the Polish-speaking regions of the eastern Prussian provinces. Instead, it should have expanded eastward at Russia's expense to secure the biological future of the *Volk*. In Hitler's view, Germany had to be reimagined as a racial entity. There could be no restoration of the Bismarckian Reich, even one from which 'aliens', Jews especially, would be expelled. Rather, the new Reich would include Russia west of the Urals. Hitler's imaginings of continental *Lebensraum* mirrored the shift among Pan-Germans that began before World War I, but they assumed new urgency in light of the war because Imperial Germany's maritime empire rendered it vulnerable to the Entente's blockade.[34]

Hitler also embodied the populism of post-war radical nationalism. Unlike the pre-war leaderships of Wilhelmine nationalist pressure groups, many of whom were drawn from the educated and propertied middle classes, he operated comfortably in a populist milieu. As the Nazi Party's paramilitary Storm Troops demonstrated, he was more willing to use violence against his political opponents.[35] Yet Hitler demonstrated another quality that would prove crucial in his eventual rise to power, his ability to temper his populism enough to attract the support of well-heeled conservatives, who appreciated his common touch and his anti-republicanism, even as they looked askance at the party's roughness. During the Nazi Party's early years in Munich, Hitler won

---

32 See Gerwarth 2008, pp. 175–209; and Kellogg 2005.

33 The circumstances surrounding Hitler's war decorations for valour were considerably less heroic than the Führer and his followers later made them out to be, according to Thomas Weber 2010.

34 Hitler 1971, pp. 126–56, and 2003, pp. 51–118.

35 The elitism of the Pan-Germans, despite their vehement *völkisch* nationalism, has emerged clearly in the burgeoning scholarship on them. See Frech 2009 and Leicht 2012; as well as Hering 2003, pp. 319–504 and Hofmeister 2012, pp. 305–22.

strong support from the local elite, which included the Beckstein family, the Wagner circle in Bayreuth, the steel magnate Fritz Thyssen, wealthy Russian émigrés, and a number of aristocrats whose financial support supplemented party member subscriptions and entrance fees to party meetings.[36] Despite the altered nature of politics under the Republic, which undoubtedly benefited the Nazis, the support of elites would prove critical to taking power.

The failure of the Munich Putsch in November 1923, which Hitler orchestrated in a coalition with other right-wing groups, sent Hitler to prison and his party into illegality. The defeat testified to Germany's weakness in the wake of hyperinflation, the occupation of the Ruhr to force the Weimar government to pay reparations, and the massive popular resistance to the French. Although the occupation sharply divided the Entente powers, the Reichswehr refused to back the putsch fearing further foreign intervention and territorial dismemberment. Together with the American-backed stabilisation that followed, the Entente's willingness to enforce the post-war settlement (or at least the fear that it would) was crucial to containing the radical right. The renegotiation of reparations payments through the Dawes Plan, which included a provision that suspended payments in times of economic downturn, and the influx of American investment stimulated a modest economic recovery that encouraged Weimar cabinets to pursue multilateral and peaceful approaches to revising the Versailles Treaty and regaining Germany's status as a great power.

By the end of the decade, however, economic catastrophe and sharpening political polarisation created favourable conditions for the resurgence of the nationalist right and autarkic imperialism as the solution to the Great Depression and social conflict. The question remains: why did Nazism become the primary beneficiary of the late Weimar crisis, especially since after its re-legalisation in 1925 and its decision to pursue the 'legal' route to power, it languished in the electoral wilderness? A number of explanations have arisen: Hitler's charisma, which unified the party and mitigated internal conflicts; the Nazi Party's ability to attract young, ambitious, and energetic talent from the 'uncompromising generation' born after 1900, imbued with hatred for the Republic and 'Jewish Marxism'; and the party's organisational depth and sophistication. Lastly, one cannot ignore Nazism's most distinguishing feature, the unusual diversity of its membership and electorate. The NSDAP drew disproportionately from shopkeepers, peasants, civil servants, and artisans, and performed especially well in Protestant small towns and rural regions in the north and east. Yet it also cut across the stubborn barriers of class, region, and religion to a greater extent than other parties with its promise to create a

36 See Kershaw 1998, pp. 186–91 and d'Almeida, 2007, pp. 30–46.

genuine *Volk* community.[37] Even though the Nazi movement never came close to obtaining a majority in the Reichstag, having reached its high watermark of 37.4 percent in the July 1932 national elections, its mass support gave it leverage with conservative brokers who orbited around the Reich President, Paul von Hindenberg. In sum, the Nazis bested their competitors in reflecting and embracing the transformations arising from the First World War, such that conservatives saw no other option but to appoint Hitler to the chancellorship.

The pattern that the NSDAP set in Munich of welcoming the support of elites while ensuring that they did not compromise the party's independence from them, continued after 1928 when the Nazis gained substantially in national elections, and after 1930 when parliamentary gridlock and three authoritarian governments in succession eroded Weimar democracy. In 1929 the party allied with conservatives in the campaign against the Young Plan, the second Allied attempt after the Dawes Plan to reschedule Germany's reparations payments. In 1931 it once again joined with the far-right German National People's Party (DNVP) and its Pan-German leader Alfred Hugenberg, nationalist pressure groups, and the paramilitary Stahlhelm to force the then Chancellor Heinrich Brüning from power. Having siphoned voters from the bourgeois right, especially the DNVP, Hitler sought to exploit his party's advantage, refusing to agree to a government in which he was not chancellor.[38] The reluctance of conservatives to accede to this resulted in mounting pressure from Nazi propaganda attacks against 'reactionaries' and from Hitler's own insistence that the torch be passed from the Pan-Germans with roots in the *Kaiserreich* to the Pan-Germans of the future. Thus, at a meeting in January 1932 with Ruhr industrialists, who if they despised the Weimar welfare state feared Nazi populism, Hitler reminded his audience of how much had changed, for 'millions of our German fellow countrymen' now flocked to the Nazi movement. They created 'something which is unique in German history. The bourgeois parties have had seventy years to work in; where, I ask you, is the organisation which could be compared with ours?' The Führer concluded by summarising what Nazism's 'idealism' had to offer, the energy to acquire *Lebensraum* and the development

37 On Hitler's charisma, see Kershaw 1987. Falter 1991 provides the most comprehensive analysis of Nazi voters. Recently, scholars have begun to question the significance of Hitler's charisma to the Nazi takeover. For an up-to-date analysis of the literature on the Nazi rise to power, see Ziemann and Szejnmann 2013, especially pp. 321–37.

38 On the tensions between the Nazis and the conservative right, see Jones 2006, pp. 483–94; and most recently Jackisch 2012, 159–79. See also Müller 2005, pp. 23–4.

of a 'great internal market', and the ruthlessness to suppress Germany's internal and external enemies and resurrect the German nation.[39]

In the end, conservatives consented to Hitler's terms. As the last pre-Nazi cabinet under General Kurt von Schleicher collapsed in another failed attempt to create a government with a parliamentary majority, Hindenburg formed a conservative-Nazi coalition with Hitler as chancellor. The Nazi Party's lacklustre performance in the November 1932 national elections briefly assured conservatives that the Nazis' momentum had slowed. Nevertheless, the electoral growth of the Communist Party and repeated Communist-Nazi street battles forced the hands of the Reich President and the coterie around him. The Reichswehr especially feared that without a Hitler chancellorship, which would put the SA at its disposal to crush the 'Marxists', it could not prevent a civil war and perhaps a revolution more radical than that of 1918. Ultimately, conservatives consoled themselves with the hope that Hitler would be aggressive enough to carry out the agendas that they and Nazis held in common; the destruction of the left, the creation of a dictatorship with broad popular support, and a foreign policy that guaranteed the resurgence of German power and the prospect of expansion. If worried about the Nazis' contempt for 'reactionaries', conservatives expected that the party would confine its violence to groups that both sides designated as 'enemies'. Even though conservatives tolerated and even endorsed Nazi measures after Hitler's appointment, Nazism became more radical than they bargained for.[40] The unrestrained violence that the Third Reich unleashed had no precedent, for it was its response to the humiliations of 1918. Violence was central to creating the *Volk* 'community' because the *Volk*'s enemies had grown too powerful to handle with kid gloves. Only their destruction would achieve the desired end.

From the outset, the Nazi regime put into practice what it saw as the positive legacies of World War I while dealing violently with the negative. To recapture the 'front experience', when in the face of a common danger German soldiers putatively put aside their class, regional, and religious differences in service to the nation, the Third Reich fetishised the militarised mobilisation of its population, especially the young. Numerous avenues of popular participation which enabled Germans to become Nazis – the Hitler Youth, the League of German Girls, the Labor Service, among others – sought to recapture a sense

---

39 'Address to the Industry Club', 27 January 1932, in Kaes, Jay, and Dimendberg 1994, pp. 138–41.

40 Although not suffering anywhere near the punishment endured by the left, Jews, and other 'community aliens', Nazi terror did not spare conservatives. See Beck 2008, especially pp. 114–73.

of collective obligation to the 'community' while overcoming corrosive liberal individualism and socialist class conflict.[41] The exclusion and elimination of 'community aliens' was the flipside of uniting the *Volk*. The violence applied to this task proceeded from the bottom up as well as from the top down, for it empowered many ordinary Germans, who participated in assaulting those who did not belong.[42] The regime's first initiative, the obliteration of the Socialists and Communists through emergency decrees, mass arrests, terror, and concentration camps incapacitated organised labour and laid the foundations for an expanded police state. The biopolitical, as opposed to political, dimension of purifying the *Volk*, the sterilisation and eventual elimination of the genetically unfit, the mentally and physically handicapped and social deviants, was scarcely less hesitant. Beginning with the Law for the Prevention of Hereditarily Diseased Offspring in July 1933, countless welfare workers, judges, and health care professionals implemented legislation designed to rid Germany of 'useless eaters'. Above all, the regime's increasingly systematic and anti-semitic measures, which deprived Jews of full citizenship, curtailed their interaction with Christian Germans, 'aryanised' their property, and subjected them to continuous physical assaults, might not have amounted to the Holocaust of wartime. Yet they marginalised and impoverished Jews sufficiently to lay the groundwork for their later deportation to ghettos and death camps in the East.[43] Taken together, the persecution of political, social, and racial 'enemies' was at least as important as rearmament and the expansion of the armed forces. The first assaulted 'enemies', who compromised the cohesiveness of the *Volk*. The second flouted Versailles in preparation for redrawing the map of Europe.

Among the institutions of the Third Reich, the SS best embodied Nazism's fusion of racism and imperialism.[44] From its modest beginnings in the late twenties as Hitler's bodyguards, the SS grew exponentially as a consequence of the terror, and especially after the Röhm Purge eliminated the SA, its major rival. In addition to assuming the management of the concentration camps, the Reichsführer SS, Heinrich Himmler, took command of the police in the German states and expanded the use of 'protective custody' without judicial

41 See Fritzsche 2008.

42 Wildt 2007, pp. 101–351.

43 Despite the very different perspectives, Michael Burleigh 2000, pp. 147–404; and Richard J. Evan 2004, pp. 309–90, and 2005 provide excellent overviews of the Nazi regime's multidirectional terror.

44 In addition to Wildt's study of the SS *Reichssicherheitshauptamt*, a spate of recent biographies on SS leaders are indispensable. See especially Longerich 2008, Herbert, 2001, and Gerwarth 2001.

review. With the outbreak of war in 1939, the SS assumed responsibility for the racial 'cleansing' of the East and the establishment of German settlements. The composition of the SS, young men of Aryan pedigree, military prowess, and educational attainment, merged militant racism with the efficiency of a highly developed economy and culture. Its recruits, most of them drawn from the 'uncompromising' generation, honed their counterrevolutionary enthusiasm at the universities while in the process earning doctorates. Carrying over the imperialist imagination of the Baltic Freikorps and envisioning themselves as modern-day Teutonic Knights, SS men saw the resources and settlement possibilities of the East as the fulfilment of Germany's imperial destiny.[45]

To be sure, anxiety permeated Nazi ambitions to acquire living space, reflecting deep-seated fears of annihilation by foreign enemies; anxiety that was also present in the imperialism of the *Kaiserreich*. Regardless, the Nazi regime exceeded the wildest imaginings of pre-war radical nationalists, testimony to the altered geopolitical conditions of the interwar period. In October 1939, Hitler laid out his vision of the 'new order' to the Reichstag. In an era in which the struggle among peoples had contributed to and profited from the collapse of multi-ethnic empires, he averred, traditional power politics among nations had absolutely no place. Only a new, purified ethnographic order would assure the security and economic prosperity of the German *Volk*.[46] After the Wehrmacht's stunning victory over France and the Low Countries in the spring of 1940, Hitler considered extending German control into central Africa and placing long-range bombers in West Africa to threaten the United States.[47] Yet the Luftwaffe's failure to knock Britain out of the war and the British refusal to yield their control of the oceans ruled out those plans. Regardless, the planning for Africa sought to raise the living standards of 'natives' so as to produce a reliable labour force under the eye of German overseers, which Nazis feared would lead to racial mixing.[48] The East was the regime's bedrock, and not just because of its rich mineral and food resources. As a site for German settlements it would increase and revitalise the *Volk* and with the exception of those required for labour, remove the indigenous population altogether.

At its height in early 1942, the Nazi empire extended from the Atlantic to the Urals in a vast continental imperium. The severity of the regime's occupation policies, although hardly benign anywhere, varied according to its assessment of the occupied's place in its racial hierarchy. In northern and western

---

45 See Burleigh 1997, pp. 22–4.

46 Wildt 2006.

47 Goda 1998.

48 Linne 2002, pp. 38–183.

Europe, the regime let the nation-state stand as the principal form of political organisation, despite the fantasies of some in the SS to consider ethnographic alternatives.[49] In the East, with due allowance for nuances in treatment, the regime considered Slavs as largely incapable of higher forms of government, which ruled out collaborative rule other than complete vassalage, as Hitler briefly considered for Poland before the German invasion. As it happened, the German attack amounted to an ideologically motivated total war to destroy the Polish nation, first by eliminating the Polish elite, second by reserving its western territories annexed to the Reich for German settlers, and deporting the Poles to the General Government.[50] The invasion of the Soviet Union in June 1941 was even worse. The Nazis' hatred of the Bolshevik Revolution magnified their hostility toward Slavs and accelerated the ruthless exploitation of resources, particularly food, and annihilation of peoples. Hitler's 'commissar order', which decreed the wanton execution of Soviet prisoners suspected of being Communist Party officials, the 'Hunger Plan', which envisioned the procurement of the Soviet food supply by starving the indigenous population, and the 'General Plan East', which projected the removal of some fifty million soviets for German settlement and rural development programmes, testified to a murderous utopianism that exceeded that of the *Ober Ost*.[51]

The Holocaust, the Third Reich's campaign to annihilate every Jew who fell into its grasp, outstripped even the extremes of Barbarossa. Compared to the Imperial German occupation of Poland in World War I, where for instrumentalist reasons the encouragement of cultural distinctiveness was commonplace and the treatment of Jews was relatively mild, the eliminationist anti-semitism of the Nazis was monstrous. Nazi anti-semitism blended a diverse array of threatening myths and images, some ancient and rooted in Christian anti-Judaism, others clearly modern. Its comprehensive and apocalyptic explanation for Germany's post-war vulnerabilities, implemented within the context of total war, made it genocidal. The Jew compounded 'his' responsibility for the upheavals of the First World War with 'his' role in the Second. 'He' personified the global capitalist economy dominated by American plutocrats who enchained Germany in 'interest slavery'. 'He' stood for the opposite of the

49 Mazower 2008, p. 111; Herbert 2001, pp. 295–8.

50 On the invasion of Poland as *Volkstumskampf*, see Rossino 2003, Rutherford 2007, and Böhler 2006. The regime's vicious occupation policies did not spare the territories controlled by the Soviet Union between 1939 and 1941 after the Reich took them over. On the occupation, see Heinemann 2003, especially pp. 187–303 and 357–415.

51 There are numerous works on Barbarossa and its consequences, but the following recent works are indispensable: Gerlach 1998 and 1999, Lower 2005, and Pohl, 2011.

harmonious *Volksgemeinschaft* that the Nazis yearned for, 'Marxism' at home and Bolshevism abroad. 'He' directed Nazi Germany's imperialist enemies, the United States, the Soviet Union, and the British Empire, who collectively challenged the Nazi quest for *Lebensraum*, which was essential to the survival of the *Volk*. The German-Jewish philologist and professor Victor Klemperer summarised it best: 'The Jew', he explained, had

> the bracketing effect of binding together all adversaries into a single enemy: the Jewish-Marxist *Weltanschauung*, the Jewish-Bolshevik philistinism, the Jewish-Capitalist system of exploitation, the keen Jewish-English, Jewish-American interest in seeing Germany destroyed: thus from 1933 every single hostility, regardless of its origin, can be traced back to one and the same enemy, Hitler's hidden maggot, the Jew, who in moments of high drama is referred to as 'Judah' or, with even greater pathos, '*Alljuda* {Universal Judah}'.[52]

The desperation inherent in Nazi anti-semitism, which grew more pronounced as the Third Reich's military reverses mounted, helps to explain the paradox of Nazi imperialism: its decision to wage war on multiple fronts, and the likelihood that the very same war would end in a catastrophic defeat. In the Nazi *Weltanschauung*, after the apocalyptic struggles of the First World War and its aftermath, only an apocalyptic second war made 'sense'.

From unification in 1871 to the end of the Third Reich, the need to complete the Bismarckian achievement to embrace all ethnic Germans and make Germany invulnerable to foreign depredations was a key element in German imperialism. Despite that continuity, expansion into the European East remained but an aspiration until World War I destroyed the Russian, Austro-Hungarian, and Ottoman Empires, and it competed with overseas empire-building. A precarious post-war order that weakened even the surviving great powers awakened the prospect of achieving *Lebensraum* in Europe; if not immediately, then after the onset of the Depression. The war's consequences, revolution, and a hated peace treaty that among other punishments confiscated the German 'blue water' empire, resulted in a populist and violent nationalism that gave priority to expansion within Europe. The most successful of the radical rightist movements, National Socialism, which effectively exploited the anti-republicanism of elites to take power, had no scruples about eliminating

52 Klemperer 2000, pp. 176–7. As Tooze 2006 argues, pp. 244–325, the regime's connection of the Jewish global conspiracy with the West, and especially the United States, intensified with the growing likelihood of war.

domestic 'enemies', who in its view presided over Germany's ruin. And it had no reservations about revamping the continent through ethnic cleansing and genocide according to the racist *Weltanschauung* of the Third Reich. Imperial Germany willingly risked war to escape a dilemma that its ambitions created, and its military during World War I hardly treated their conquered subjects with kid gloves. Yet on balance, the war's outcomes, which included the visions of empire that the war stimulated, spawned a new generation of German imperialists whose brutality and ruthlessness made pre-war German imperialists look tame by comparison.

CHAPTER 3

Capitalist Peace or Capitalist War? The July Crisis Revisited

Adam Tooze

Introduction

What is the frame within which we place the July Crisis in 1914 and everything that followed? Was it the derailment of an all-encompassing but brittle culture of masculine militarism? Was it a diplomatic debacle? Was it an expression of a pathological modernity? Was it Europe's colonial violence turned back on itself? Under the sign of some encompassing synthesis, was it many of these things, or all of them simultaneously? For those coming from a Marxist tradition, but by no means only for them, an idea of an 'age of imperialism' provided an encompassing historical backdrop against which to understand World War I. World War I was a clash of expansive nation states whose rivalry was fuelled by commercial and industrial interests and ultimately expressed certain essential insufficiencies within capitalism. The wide currency of imperialism theory right across the political spectrum began with the Boer War.[1] It would retain considerable plausibility even in mainstream liberal circles down to the mid-century. It is hard to credit today, but in 1945 it seemed reasonable for the United States government to put the corporate leadership of IG Farben and Krupp on trial not only for war crimes, for spoliation and slave labour, but for crimes against peace and conspiracy to launch aggressive war; in other words for the crimes of imperialism.

The idea of an age of imperialism came in many different shades.[2] Some were more holistic and deterministic than others. But they all had in common that they described the current moment of imperialism as something new. It was clearly the final stage in a Western drive to expansion that began in the early modern period, but it had taken on a radical new expansiveness and violence. This new era of imperialism was dated to the last decades of the nineteenth century, commonly to the scramble for Africa from the early 1880s. It extended by the late nineteenth century to literally every part of the globe.

1 Hobson 1902; Etherington 1984.

2 Wolfe 1997.

The global frontier was closing. And it was also a common perception amongst theorists of imperialism that this outward expansive drive was connected not just to the desire for conquest or political domination, but to deeper economic, social or cultural forces.

In 1959 the publication of William Appleman Williams's *Tragedy of American Diplomacy*, and in 1961 Fritz Fischer's *Griff nach der Weltmacht*, gave imperialism theory a new lease on life in the historical profession.[3] Amidst the general resurgence of imperialism-talk in the context of Vietnam and Third World struggles, Fritz Fischer's Germano-centric version of imperialism theory produced an extraordinary éclat. But as far as the July Crisis was concerned this was also the last great hurrah of imperialism theory. The critical onslaught against Fischer's one-sided interpretation of the outbreak of the war helped to discredit models of imperialism more generally. By the 1990s whether or not historians have ascribed responsibility for the July Crisis to Germany, the focus has shifted away from an economically founded logic to one based on political and military culture. Often this is associated with a stress on the July Crisis as an event determined by the 'provincial' logic of Central Europe rather than the wider forces of global struggle across Africa and Asia that were once invoked by way of reference to empire.

One reaction to the collapse of the imperialism paradigm amongst economic historians has been to infer that political economy is excused from any significant role in explaining the July Crisis. Since the 1990s in the orbit of the late Angus Maddison at the OECD and Jeffrey G. Williamson at the NBER, an innovative new literature on the global economy before 1914 has sprung up, written not under the sign of imperialism but under that of globalisation.[4] The shift in label is significant. In the new economic histories of globalisation there is what one might term a presumption of innocence with regard to 1914. The analysts of globalisation point to a variety of tensions that were unleashed by the global integration of markets for commodities and factors of production. But both the Maddison and Williamson circles treat the July Crisis in 1914 as an exogenous shock that interrupted globalisation. Indeed, the assumption that war and politics are antithetical to globalisation is axiomatic for this entire school. As Williamson and O'Rourke put it with characteristic frankness, in their calculations of market integration they assume that '[i]n the absence of transport costs, monopolies, wars, pirates, and other trade barriers, world

3 Williams 1959; Fischer 1961.

4 For the 'NBER' perspectives see O'Rourke and Williamson 1999; Bordo et al. 2003. For the OECD, Maddison 2001. An alternative Franco-American perspective is provided by Berger 2003.

commodity markets would be perfectly integrated' and globalisation, by their measure, would thus be complete.[5]

But this begs the question of causation. Are wars really exogenous with regard to the logic of global economic development? Whereas economic historians have on the whole been content to allow diplomatic and economic history to drift apart, and many cultural and political historians have been only too happy to reinforce this tendency, a substantial body of political scientists has taken the opposite tack. They have formulated a severe critique of the separation within their discipline between International Political Economy (IPE) and International Relations (IR), which they see as a regrettable effect of the Cold War.[6] It was no doubt true that under the conditions of the nuclear stalemate, strategy was radically insulated from economic and social conditions. But this was a special case. If one wishes to develop truly general accounts of political economy and international security this separation is disabling. In fact, markets, contracts, business relations, international trade, labour and capital market integration are all essential elements in the construction of international society. The quality of that international society in turn is crucial in deciding the question of how interests are formulated and negotiated with each other and whether conflicts will be resolved through violent or non-violent means. Under the sign of so-called bargaining theories of war, armed conflict is seen as an extension of political negotiation and argument by other means.[7] How likely a conflict is to become militarised depended on the type of societies involved and the nature of their relations, whether these were mediated by intense trade contacts, tight monetary relations, or whether the societies involved were dominated by powerful militaries with unaccountable sources of finance, or civilian-controlled security establishments.

Clearly this way of thinking poses a challenge to conventional realist IR theories. But if social, economic and political development are all in play in defining the field of international relations, what is the nature of that connection? In the wake of the cold war, under the sign of the 'end of history', it was liberal IR theorists who gave the most forthright answer. They turned the presumption of innocence that allowed political economy to become dissociated from accounts of modern conflict into something much stronger – an assertive prediction of a democratic, capitalist peace.[8] Drawing on a tradition that ascends from classical political thinkers of the eighteenth century, liberal peace

5 O'Rourke and Williamson 2004, p. 112.

6 Kirschner 1998 and Mastanduno 1998.

7 Well summarised in Reiter 2003.

8 For example Russett 1993.

theories can be divided into two interconnected but distinct currents. One branch, the political branch, declared that democracy was the crucial variable. Democracies did not fight wars with each other. A democratic world would thus be a world of perpetual peace, a world beyond military history. Advocates of the 'capitalist peace' took a different view.[9] For them it was the economic not the political institutions of liberalism that were decisive. Precisely what degree of trade and capital market integration, what level of monetary cooperation was necessary to secure peace was not easy to specify, but one threshold, at least, could be specified. No two countries hosting McDonald franchises had ever been engaged in armed conflict.[10]

Born in the eighteenth century as an ideal vision and revived in the aftermath of the Cold War as a social scientific hypothesis, the empirical evidence for the liberal peace hypothesis was drawn above all from the period after World War II. For the eighteenth century and much of the nineteenth century it is for obvious reasons hard to construct sufficiently large datasets to test the theory. There were not enough democracies. But the period before 1914 poses particular challenges for liberal peace theory. If there were few actually achieved democratic constitutions, the nineteenth century was nevertheless a great age of democratisation. It was also the first great age of a truly globalised capitalism. And yet the Long Nineteenth Century ended in 1914 in an apocalyptic war. How to address this puzzle?

One solution for the political scientists would simply be to dismiss the war as an outlier. The capitalist peace hypothesis is no more than a probabilistic statement. Perhaps 1914 is simply an anomalous case. Or perhaps the tendencies towards a capitalist peace were indeed operative, but simply in too weak a form for them to suppress the aggressive forces of the ancien régime.[11] But as the advocates of liberal peace theory themselves admit such evasions are self-defeating. The burst of globalisation between 1870 and 1914 was as significant as anything that occurred after 1970. And yet the conflict which began in 1914 was responsible for 83 percent of battlefield deaths between 1816 and 1918 and no less than 27 percent of battlefield deaths between 1816 and 1997. This is too important a case to simply dismiss as an anomaly. If the first dramatic wave of globalisation and democratisation was not enough to substantially moderate the forces of violence, or worse still, if globalisation actually contributed to the

9 Gartzke 2007.

10 When the NATO bombing of Serbia falsified the 'Golden Arches Theory of Conflict Prevention' an indignant nationalist mob promptly wrecked the Belgrade outlet of the franchise, see Friedman 2000, pp. 252–3.

11 Oneal and Russett 2001 and Rosecrance 1985.

tensions leading to war, then the liberal peace hypothesis is on shaky ground indeed.[12] To their credit the advocates of the liberal peace hypothesis have not dodged this challenge. What has ensued within political science is a fascinating debate in which, unlike in the disciplines of history or economic history, the question of the relationship between democratisation, capitalist development and the outbreak of World War I has been posed explicitly. Realists have argued that 1914 exposes the fundamental inadequacy of liberal IR theorising. Defenders of the liberal peace hypothesis have reacted with a variety of imaginative rationalisations and formalisations to account for the outbreak of war. Of late some of the economic historians most prominently associated with the new globalisation literature have finally begun to get to grips with the question of 1914.[13] But their reading of the political science literature has been half-hearted at best. If there is to be a more sustained and serious engagement it is crucial to explore more critically some of the basic premises common to both liberal and realist brands of IR theory, as well as to the economic history literature on which they have so productively drawn. Two points in particular merit critical attention.

Firstly, the result of evacuating the concept of imperialism has been to produce an image of globalisation which is surprisingly static and rooted in methodological nationalism. The world economy is viewed as a field divided into discrete national entities. The statistical measures on which recent accounts of globalisation are based, are unprecedentedly precise, but they are also extremely narrow in their relentless focus on market integration. They lack structure and they cannot capture more subtle patterns of interaction, of action and reaction, of rivalry and cooperation that marked the international system. Specifically, they cannot do justice to what analysts working in the tradition of Trotsky refer to as 'uneven and combined development'; i.e. the dynamic interconnectedness of a system of states undergoing transformation at different speeds and under different international and domestic pressures.[14]

Secondly, what the positivism of both political scientists and economic historians obscures is the reflexivity that is such an essential feature of turn-of-the-century modernity. This is ironic because the data, the concepts and institutions of modern macroeconomics, including the NBER, which has hosted so much of this literature, were in fact products of the World War I crisis, as was the academic discipline of International Relations. It is no

12 Rowe 2005, p. 409.

13 O'Rourke et al. have taken up the realist work of Rowe to point to the paradoxical relationship between globalisation and war, see Daudin, Morys and O'Rourke 2010.

14 For recent applications to the July Crisis, see Green 2012, Rosenberg 2013, and Anievas 2013.

coincidence that the data are all better after 1945 for it was then that the institutions of modern social science really began to reach maturity. Part of the difficulty in analysing the period before 1914 in these terms, is that we are turning the gaze of modern social science back to the moment of its own birth and before. Marxist theorists of ideology, one thinks particularly of Lukács, were quick to seize on the imbrication of the emerging 'bourgeois' social sciences with the social reality that they sought to capture in objective, quantified form.[15] Though Lukács was concerned principally with economics, sociology, and literary studies, Lenin, Trotsky and the Comintern made the peculiar shortcomings of liberal theories of internationalism of the Wilsonian variety into the butt of regular criticism from 1919 onwards.[16] The risk involved in this kind of critique of ideology are all too familiar. Critics do not take the ideologies they expose seriously enough, either in their specific content or in their importance as actual guides to action on the part of the operators of the system. But to take them seriously is essential, because as the state, big business and other large-scale organisations took on a greater and greater role, technical management became an ever-more defining aspect of the social and economic system, now explicitly and self-consciously conceived as such.

From the first critiques of reformism and new liberalism penned in the era of World War I, down to Foucault's dissections of neoliberal governmentality, Ulrich Beck's account of 'risk society' and Anthony Giddens's sociology of 'reflexive modernity', understanding the entanglement of power and knowledge would become crucial to the diagnosis of the twentieth-century condition.[17] Though such accounts of reflexive modernity were often concentrated on the economic, social or environmental sphere, there was no sphere in which self-reflexive autonomous state action was more important than in diplomacy and military strategy, what was between the early modern period and the twentieth century the preeminent sphere of autonomous state action. As Chris Clark's *Sleepwalkers* has recently reminded us, the July Crisis of 1914 was perhaps the quintessential modern crisis precisely in that it was a failure of self-reflexive control within a pluralistic, complex and extremely heterogeneous system.[18] As such, the search for a final causality is liable to exhaust itself in vain. If we follow Beck's account of risk society we may find it easier

---

15 Lukács 1971. Lih 2014 in this volume notes the importance of mutual observation for Kautsky's theory of the dawning of a new age of war and revolution.

16 See for instance Trotsky's devastating commentary on 1920s internationalism in Trotsky 1929.

17 Foucault 2003; Foucault 2008; Beck 1986; Giddens et al. 1994.

18 Clark 2012.

to admit that this undecidability is not a frustrating failure of the historical profession to make up its mind, but a characteristic feature of reflexive modernity.

What implications does this double redescription – the stress on combined and uneven development overlaid by layers of reflexivity – have for this essay on liberal peace theories and the July Crisis? As I will conclude by arguing in this chapter, one can construct a coherent account of the July Crisis in terms of liberal IR theory. But to do so we must sacrifice the innocence of 'liberal peace theory'. Not only should we acknowledge that liberal peace theory always implied its twin, namely a theory of liberal war, a justification of war against those lower down the civilisational gradient. But, we should also recognise that such theories were in fact active in the crisis of 1914, helping to exacerbate the crisis and to justify war. Indeed, the incredibly complex pattern of entanglement created by the condition of combined and uneven global development made it possible for these hierarchical theories to be deployed as justification by all sides. The result was to scramble thoroughly the terms of the IR debate. On the one hand, the war was justified on all sides as defensive and thus appeared to be a perfect illustration of the realist security dilemma. On the other hand, what was at stake in self-defence, why it mattered to defend oneself, was intelligible only in terms of narratives of historical development that derived not from the timeless world of realism, but from liberal conceptions of progressive history. If this is so, it brings us to the final question to be posed in this chapter. To encapsulate this all-encompassing, hyper self-reflexive, no holds barred competition for a place in the historical sun, is there, in fact, a better term, than the one coined by contemporaries and set aside too hastily at the beginning of our discussion, namely 'the age of imperialism'?

Globalisation and Its Discontents

The recent economic history of globalisation has avoided drawing direct connections from international competition to international geopolitical rivalry. However it has not denied the tensions and conflicts generated by the dramatic process of globalisation. Defining globalisation as market integration, it has traced with unprecedented precision the massive redistributive effects generated within the Atlantic world by mass migration and the emergence of markets for basic commodities such as grain. Taking its cue from the classic result of Stolper-Samuelson in international trade theory, it has shown how international trade levels the prices of factors across the world economy.[19] This has the

19 Stolper and Samuelson 1941.

effect of reducing the premium that can be commanded in receiving countries by owners of scarce commodities or factors of production and raising the premium that can be commanded by owners of factors where they are abundant. More concretely globalisation tended to raise the price of labour and capital in Europe through emigration and capital export. At the same time it reduced the premium they could command overseas. The result, as the GDP data generated by the authors working for the OECD suggested, was convergence.

Crusading liberals were of course tempted to tell this story as a triumph for free-trade reason over mercantilist and protectionist superstition. The struggle over the Corn Laws of the 1840s, the Cobden-Chevalier Treaty and the invention of Most Favoured Nation status all had their place in this heroic narrative. But what the work of the NBER authors shows is that the surge in trade integration was associated less with the politics of trade liberalisation than with the massive supply-side shock delivered by plunging transport costs.[20] This makes it easier to understand why the political consequences of globalisation were so ambiguous. It was as a result of a massive technological shock, not of conscious political decision that European society from the 1870s was integrated into a world economy as never before. This unleashed unprecedented shifts in basic hierarchies of value, notably in the relative value of land and labour, which in turn triggered a decisive backlash towards protectionism, a populist assault on the gold standard and nativist immigration restriction in the 'New World'.

Distinguishing de facto trade integration from the politics of free trade is the simplest route to explaining how the first globalisation might in fact have produced not peace and harmony, but international tensions in the early twentieth century.[21] Nor is this particularly novel. It is the route marked out decades ago in classic mid-century texts which themselves echoed the intellectual rearguard action mounted by free-trading liberals from the 1900s onwards. What the NBER and OECD economic historians have done is to give massive quantitative heft and precision to the narratives sketched by Karl Polanyi and Hans Rosenberg in their readings of the 1870s crisis.[22] Amidst trade integration heralded by boosters of globalisation, liberalism died, xenophobic nationalism flourished and power politics came back to the fore. The roots of modern antisemitism and populist nationalism are to be found in this period, which in turn opened the door to manipulative and aggressive elites who sought to master the challenges of democracy by building new coalitions around the politics of protection. In Rosenberg's words, the long period of traumatic adjustment to

---

20 O'Rourke and Williamson 1994.

21 Mcdonald and Sweeney 2007.

22 Rosenberg 1943; Polanyi 1944.

globalisation: '... helped to lay the foundation for the bolder and more aggressive and reckless political and economic imperialism of the Wilhelmian era, eager for expansion, taking its risks and bursting forth in spurts of self-assertion under the impetus of the prosperity of 1897–1914'.[23]

A more original account of the consequences of globalisation has been offered not by advocates of the liberal peace but by their chief realistic critic. Rowe argues that rather than juxtaposing politics and economics, state and civil society, imperialists and businessmen, the military themselves should be analysed as competitors in the market for resources. Globalisation impacted them not only by means of the political currents it stirred up, for and against militarism, but by directly affecting the terms on which the state could appropriate resources. The result is a more complex, pluralistic and convincing image of the pre-1914 world than that offered by the simple anti-liberal backlash story. European society did not simply yield to 'social imperialist' manipulation, the xenophobic backlash unleashed by globalisation was cross-cut by powerful countervailing forces of anti-militarism. And there was an economic counterpart to the resulting political tension.

In 1914 the peacetime strength of Europe's major armies amounted to eight percent of the male population of military age on the continent.[24] The military were thus a significant drag on the labour force. Much of this manpower was of course conscripted. But by increasing the price commanded by abundant resources (labour) on which the military state apparatus had traditionally relied, globalisation increased the opportunity cost of conscription. Furthermore, it enhanced the bargaining power of groups whose politics made them opponents of the military state. All the militaries of Europe faced an uphill battle by the early twentieth century to pay for armaments, to recruit the essential backbone of NCOs and to attract bourgeois talent into the ranks of the officer corps. Despite the prestige enjoyed by the Imperial German army before 1914, 20 percent of the junior officer positions were unfilled. Russia suffered the same problem. The French army was able to retain less than half the military graduates of the ecole polytechnique between 1907 and 1912. Meanwhile, as the global recovery from the recession of 1907 took hold, and trade boomed the naval purchasing offices suffered a huge surge in prices charged by dockyards for warships.[25]

---

23 Rosenberg 1943, p. 72.

24 See Tables 9 and 10 in Ferguson 1999.

25 Rowe 2005.

Viewed narrowly this confirms the basic supposition of the liberal peace hypothesis. In an increasingly bourgeois, commercialised and internationalised world it was indeed getting harder to be a soldier. The question however is whether or not this pacification contributed to stability and security in Europe. In 1994, Niall Ferguson, in what is perhaps his most influential contribution to historical scholarship, argued that the fiscal problems of the Imperial German state had made it not less, but more likely to start a war.[26] Germany's soldiers and diplomats who were deeply concerned about the shifting balance of power within the European state system were hugely frustrated by the delay of the Reichstag in voting them adequate funds. Having lost the naval arms race with Britain, facing pressure from France and Russia, they viewed the crisis in the Balkans in the summer of 1914 as a welcome opportunity to bring on the crisis that they believed to be inevitable in any case. Ferguson attributed those problems principally to the federal structure of the German state. But the point could be generalised to turn the liberal peace argument on its head. Rowe argues that precisely because it caused pacifying changes at the national level, globalisation made all the military elites of Europe less secure and more trigger happy. Liberal pacification weakened deterrence and undermined the credibility of alliance commitments.

As a particular case study, Rowe and colleagues examined the case of Britain. Britain may have outcompeted Germany in the naval arms race, but from 1911 the priority of British strategy was in fact moving towards land power. To back up France, Britain needed a significant expeditionary force. However, to introduce conscription was a political impossibility in Britain and the costs of a fully professional army of significant size would have been exorbitant. As it was, the British Army paid its enlisted men even less than unskilled agricultural labourers. Only when trade conditions were bad was recruiting easy. Otherwise, the army resorted to progressively lowering its physical standards. Whereas in 1861 the standard had been five feet 8 inches, by 1913 it had been reduced to five feet 3 inches. During the Boer War, the army took men as short as five feet. This was a physical indication of the competitive pressure to which a booming market economy exposed an all-volunteer army. In 1914, Britain's cash-starved strike force consisted of a derisory six divisions. Its first line of professional soldiers were underweight, underpaid and poorly led. At the crucial moment in the last days of July 1914, the Entente lacked the teeth to deter the Germans and their Schlieffen plan.[27]

26 Ferguson 1994.

27 Rowe, Bearce and McDonald 2002.

Uneven Development

Rowe thus performs a classic realist inversion: 'liberalism's internal constraints on military force in pre-war Europe ignited not virtuous circles, but vicious ones. Rather than assume that peace follows naturally from constraints against war', liberals, according to Rowe, needed to understand how 'states use violence to construct and sustain international order'. A historical change that weakened militarism might in fact help to weaken international order rather than strengthen it.[28] Rowe derived this tragic conclusion by superimposing on a generic model of capitalist development a generic model of the security dilemma. This can explain how capitalist growth in general could make the military elites in each nation less secure. The resulting view of the July Crisis sits well with a model of the outbreak of the war that sees it as a general systemic failure, a war of inadvertence unleashed when a spark was struck at Sarajevo into the 'powder keg' of the international system.[29] The first point of attack for defenders of the liberal peace theory is to challenge this undifferentiated model of the July Crisis.

It is no doubt true that Britain's lack of a major land army in 1914 meant that it was in no position to deter German aggression. But this 'cause' came at the end of a chain of causation that stretched back to Central Europe. In its simplest version this argument simply stops in Germany. It was the incomplete modernisation of Germany that was at the root of its dangerous behaviour in the summer of 1914.[30] And there is no doubt truth in this version of events. As the twentieth century opened, the conservative elite in Germany were under pressure. Since 1912 they faced a massive majority in the Reichstag made up of Socialists, Progressive Liberals and Christian Democrats, all of them former opponents of Bismarck. Though they were by far the largest military spenders in Western Europe and though the Reichstag did approve a momentous increase in spending in 1913, the German military despaired of keeping up with the Russians. In the Kaiser's circles, talk of an inevitable racial clash with the Slavs and a coming confrontation with Britain in the global arena was common place. More conciliatory and liberal visions of a possible 'world policy without war' were drowned out.

But aggressive though the German militarists may have been and though the Bismarckian constitution was tearing at the seams, it will not do to

---

28 Rowe 2005, p. 447.

29 For an analytic explication of this common place language see Goertz and Levy 2005.

30 For one of the earliest statements of this view see Veblen 1915.

overstress the atavism of the Wilhelmine regime.[31] If it is backwardness we are looking for to underpin a liberal narrative of the July Crisis, the argument is far more convincing if it is extended out beyond Anglo-German, Franco-German comparison. And this is after all warranted by the events of the July Crisis in which Germany's role was that of a facilitator rather than that of an immediate aggressor. If there is a chain of causation in the July Crisis it must be anchored not in Berlin, but in the entanglement of the beleaguered imperial regimes of Austria-Hungary and Russia in the violent affairs of the backward and impoverished Balkans. The chain of causation thus ascends the hierarchy of development, what Trotsky would call the 'hierarchy of backwardness'.[32] As Gartzke, the leading advocate of the capitalist war hypothesis has pointed out, once we look in detail at the series of international crises from the late nineteenth century two things become evident.[33] First, amidst the group of great powers that were in fact important players in the process of globalisation, with Germany in the forefront, diplomatic crises tended to be resolved peacefully. By contrast, amongst the Balkan states that were largely disconnected from world trade currents, violence was the norm. The mistake, therefore, lies in referring in undifferentiated terms to the period before 1914 as an age of globalisation and in treating the July Crisis of 1914 as a crisis of the whole system, as Rowe does. In fact, there was not one highly integrated Europe before 1914 but two sub-systems, one dynamic and integrated (UK, France, Italy, Germany), the other backward and only partially integrated into international trade flows (Bulgaria, Serbia, Austria-Hungary, Ottoman Empire), with Russia and Austria-Hungary occupying a mediating position in between.

This move towards identifying separate sub-systems within the international economy is extremely helpful. The first wave of research on globalisation prior to 1914 focused self-consciously on the Atlantic world as the hub of the new system. It is far from obvious that conclusions drawn from the literature on Atlantic globalisation can really be applied to crises in other regions, whether in Central and Eastern Europe or in East Asia. Gartzke and Lupu's data highlights the varying degrees of integration in Europe. Unfortunately, they lack data for Serbia. But if we take Bulgaria as a proxy for the Balkans as a whole, the levels of trade integration with Austria and Russia was clearly very low. This conclusion is entirely consistent with liberal theory. And though

31 For excellent summaries of the argument see, in this volume, Alexander Anievas, 'Marxist Theory and the Origins of the First World War'; and Geoff Eley, 'Germany, the Fischer Controversy, and the Context of War'.

32 Trotsky 1938.

33 Gartzke and Lupu 2012.

Gartzke and Lupu's dualistic distinction between an integrated and an unintegrated Europe is certainly helpful, one is tempted to say that we should go further. To lump Russia and Austria-Hungary in with the Balkans may be to create a new confusion. There were not two but three systems.[34] The Balkans belonged in a world of their own, a world in which modernisation showed its bloody borders.

The contribution that has dramatised Balkan backwardness most vividly is Clark's *Sleepwalkers*, which begins with a remarkable psychogram of Serbian political culture. Clark stresses the apocalyptic tendencies within Serbian nationalism. And in a bold interpretative move he roots this split political consciousness in social facts. For Clark, the Serbian nationalist covens were akin to AQ cells in modern-day Pakistan, or the Arab world. They were ultra-aggressive because they are experiencing what the leading economic historian of the Balkans Palairet has described as 'evolution without development'. For Clark, the particularly violent quality of Serbian nationalism is explicable in terms of a social and economic environment in which 'the development of modern consciousness was experienced not as an evolution from a previous way of understanding the world, but rather as a dissonant overlaying of modern attitudes on to a way of being that was still enchanted by traditional beliefs and values'.[35] It is testament to Clark's extraordinary skill as a reader of political culture and his artistry as a writer that he manages to make this kind of formulation compelling as an explanation of the basic catalyst of the July Crisis. In so doing, he reinstates an anthropologically enhanced vision of modernisation theory as the ground of the discussion.[36]

To drive this point home Clark draws a sharp distinction between Serbia and Vienna. Whereas Serbia was a peasant state, Vienna was, Clark emphasises, a laboratory of modernity. Certainly the pairwise comparison with Serbia serves to confirm Habsburg modernity. But if Vienna was a laboratory of modernity, it was also a laboratory of crisis. If rather than with Serbia, the Habsburg state is compared to the UK or France, the conventional ranking surely stands, certainly as far as the important indicators of the liberal peace hypothesis are concerned – democratisation and trade integration. Thanks to the trade wars since the turn of the century Vienna had little or nothing to lose in economic terms through a war with Serbia. Domestically, the Dual Monarchy's parliamentary

34 This call for a consideration of multiple levels of unevenness echoes Anievas 2014, who refers to three separate 'vectors of unevenness'.

35 Clark 2012, p. 32.

36 In constructing his remarkable portrait Clark draws on the cultural geography of Simic 1973 and the reflections of memoirist Mira Crouch. See Crouch 2008.

system was deadlocked and there was little love lost between the parliamentarians in Vienna and Hungary and those in Belgrade. It would come as no surprise to a liberal theorist to see tensions escalating.

But the true anchor of any liberal account of the outbreak of World War I, beyond Serbia and the Central Power, must be Russia.[37] Russia was the great menace to both Germany and Austria. It had a neutered parliamentary system. In its governing circles politicised nationalist protectionism was rampant.[38] Added to which, Russia's power was growing by the year, exerting huge pressure on all its potential enemies. In the summer of 1912, Jules Cambon of France noted after a conversation with Germany's Chancellor Bethmann Hollweg that, regarding Russia's recent advances,

> the chancellor expressed a feeling of admiration and astonishment so profound that it affects his policy. The grandeur of the country, its extent, its agricultural wealth, as much as the vigour of the population ... he compared the youth of Russia to that of America, and it seems to him that whereas (the youth) of Russia is saturated with futurity, America appears not to be adding any new element to the common patrimony of humanity.[39]

The French themselves were extremely optimistic about Russia's prospects. A year later French Foreign Minister Pichon received from Moscow a report commenting that

> there is something truly fantastic in preparation, ... I have the very clear impression that in the next thirty years, we are going to see in Russia a prodigious economic growth which will equal – if it does not surpass it – the colossal movement that took place in the United States during the last quarter of the 19th century.[40]

As bargaining theorists of war persuasively argue, major power shifts are the destabilising factor most likely to trigger war. And as McDonald has pointed out, it is not enough to focus on GDP growth alone. What is really crucial is the ability of states to actually harness that growth for the purposes of military

37 For the challenge posed by Russia for Marxist efforts to grasp the central dynamics of development before 1914, see Davidson 2014 and Lih 2014 in this volume.

38 McDonald and Sweeney 2007, pp. 401–2.

39 Quoted in Clark 2012, p. 326.

40 Quoted in Clark 2012, p. 312.

mobilisation.[41] What is truly destabilising for the international power structure is not, therefore, growth per se, but sudden shifts in the resources in the hands of particular states. Under conditions of private property ownership and parliamentary government, the capacity of states for sudden mobilisation is doubly constrained and thus sudden shifts in international power structure are less likely. It was this that made Tsarism so terrifying to its neighbours. Tsarism was an autocracy that did not have to struggle with the problems of parliamentary approval that made the arms race so hard to sustain for the Western powers. As the correspondent for *Le Temps* noted in November 1913, Russia's huge military effort

> is produced without creating the slightest trouble of inconvenience to the prosperity of the country ... Whereas in France, new military expenses posed a budgetary problem, Russia has no need to go in search of a new source of revenues. ... in this arms race, Russia is thus better placed than anyone to sustain the competition.[42]

It was this sense of menace from its Eastern neighbour that raised to a dangerous pitch the impatience of Germany's military and diplomatic elite with the slowness, obstructionism and progressive leanings of their national political system. In 1913 the Kaiser's government finally persuaded the Reichstag to agree to raise the size of the peacetime army from 736,000 to 890,000. But the immediate response was to trigger the passage of the French three-year conscription law and the promulgation of Russia's 'Great Programme', which raised its peacetime strength by 800,000 by 1917. By 1914 Russia's army strength was double that of Germany and 300,000 more than that of Germany and Austria combined, with a target by 1916 of 2 million.[43] Against this backdrop the Germans were convinced that by 1916–17 they would have lost whatever military advantage they still enjoyed. This implied to them two things. First, Russia would be unlikely to risk a war until it reached something closer to its full strength. So Germany could risk an aggressive punitive policy in Serbia. If this containment were to fail, then 1914 would be a better moment to fight a major war than 1916 or 1917.

The upshot is that once we move away from the generalities of a realist view of the international security situation to a specific reading of the chain of causation in 1914 we end up reinstating the hierarchy of liberal peace theory.

---

41 McDonald 2011.

42 Quoted in Clark 2012, p. 312.

43 Clark 2012, p. 331.

It was a clash between backward and brutal Serbian fanatics and an increasingly defunct Austrian regime that brought in the Tsarist autocracy, which in turn triggered Germany's beleaguered Kaiser and his anxious military into action. France and Britain moved last of all to a war footing. Before 1914, all powers may have been struggling to get to grips with the implications of globalisation for international security, but not all of them were equally bellicose or insecure. Those that seemed most anxious for a clash of arms were the least democratic and had the least to lose in any breakdown of global economic integration.

Unevenness Combined

But in resting their case on this reassertion of a developmental hierarchy, theorists of the liberal peace reveal their failure to recognise the implications of the entanglements of the international system. For it was an essential feature of the alliance system that exploded into war in August 1914 that it harnessed together countries at very dissimilar stages of development. What the liberal theory captures is the unevenness of international development. What it does not address are the mechanisms by which those differences were produced, or how they were brought into combination with one another. And yet the flow of resources across developmental gradients is essential to the liberal model of economic history. In the neoclassical growth model, convergence is the key term. The ultimate demonstration of the power of the liberal narrative before 1914, as from the 1970s onwards, is that it delivers convergence. Convergence in turn operates through the movement of factors and technological expertise across gradients of scarcity and income level. Some of this movement is driven by nothing more than price differentials and free-form market activity. But as the NBER authors amongst others are only too well aware, resources do not always move simply as neoclassical theory would predict. Foreign investment in particular tends to bundle with labour flows. And in the pre-1914 period capital flows also tended to be braided with strategic alliances.

The problem this poses for the defenders of the liberal peace hypothesis becomes obvious if we examine the work of one of the most sophisticated exponents of the bargaining theory of war, Patrick J. McDonald. As we have seen, for McDonald the fundamental trigger for war is a major power shift. This could be due to exogenous factors such as GDP growth. But these will be mediated by the mobilisation capacity of the state. This will depend in part on its relationship to holders of private property and their willingness to be taxed. But a state may also gain autonomy by laying its hands on 'free' resources, by nationalising assets, by imposing non-parliamentary taxes or monopolies, or by finding sources of easy credit. In his famous essay on perpetual peace, echoing a wide current of eighteenth-century thought, Immanuel Kant had called for state credit to be outlawed as a 'dangerous money power' and menace to peace.[44] By the late nineteenth century any such talk was utopian. Large-scale lending, including to governments, was a major part of international economy. McDonald, incorporates these 'free resources' provided by foreign borrowing into his bargaining model of the July Crisis.[45] The Tsar's easy access to foreign credit, along with his autocratic power, resources unfettered by parliamentary control, made him a terrifying strategic antagonist. But as McDonald has himself elsewhere acknowledged, reliance on foreign lending cannot simply be treated as a characteristic of the recipient country and thus as a correlate of autocratic fiscal autonomy. Such lending was in fact a defining feature of the international system as a whole. McDonald immediately goes on to point out that credit flows from both the Paris and Berlin capital markets were tied directly to the alliance mechanisms of the pre-1914 period. To his mind this contradicts the claim that capital markets pre-1914 were in fact liberal and governed by the profit-motive.[46]

The overlap between capital markets and strategic alliances is undeniable. Thanks in large part due to their imperial financial connections it was London and Paris that dominated the business of international lending.[47] Though Germany undoubtedly belonged to the rich country club, the capital markets of Berlin, Frankfurt and Hamburg did not compare to that of Paris, let alone London. Germany was involved in making loans to the Balkans and to Russia but its role was dwarfed by that of Paris. The Russian government was above all a recipient of French loans. The Balkan states played the field. Japan was above all a client of London.[48] This was not inter-governmental lending of the type that became common as a result of World War I and World War II. The funds came from private investors. But their strategic consequences were dramatic and not just in the Russian case. Loans taken by Japan and Serbia supercharged their aggression too. It was British loans that assisted the Japanese in crushing first the Chinese and then the Russians. The strategy was risky. The loans had to be repaid from the profits of war. In 1895 Japan received large reparations from China. Japan's yield from its spectacular military defeat of Russia

44 See Article 4 of Kant, *Perpetual Peace*.

45 McDonald 2011.

46 McDonald 2009, pp. 120–1.

47 Feis 1930.

48 Metzler 2006.

was less satisfactory. In 1906, the Portsmouth Treaty arbitrated by US President Teddy Roosevelt was a disaster from the Japanese point of view because it did not provide for substantial reparations. From then until 1914, Japan's balance of payments was heavily burdened by its obligations to London.

Russia's debacle at the hands of the Japanese left it more dependent than ever on France. The Tsarist regime received a gigantic loan in 1906 as it recovered from the twin disasters of defeat and revolution in 1905. After 1910, as Russia's rebuilding continued apace, the linkage between French funding and strategic objectives became more and more explicit. In 1911, Tsar Nicholas II's Chief of the General Staff had committed himself to attack Germany on Day 15 after mobilisation and when the French Prime Minister, Raymond Poincaré, visited Russia for talks in August 1912 Joffre picked out railway improvements as the single military item for the agenda. The key issue as far as Paris was concerned was that Russia should speed up its army's deployment by doubling and in some cases quadrupling the track that led from West to East Prussia and Galicia. This would dramatically increase the pressure Russia could exercise against Germany and the Dual Monarchy. The funds would be provided by French investors.[49] The outcome was the September 1912 agreement for 900 km of extra track. The impact on Germany of this leveraged Russian mobilisation was dramatic. General Moltke viewed the Franco-Russian loan of 1912 as the 'most sensitive strategic blow that France has dealt us since the war of 1870–71'.[50] The revised Schlieffen plan had been premised on the assumption that the Russian army in the aftermath of the 1905 debacle would be in no position to threaten East Prussia for weeks after the outbreak of a war. Germany could therefore safely concentrate the overwhelming majority of its forces in the West. Given the pace at which French money allowed the Russians to rebuild their railway system, by 1916–17 the Germans expected this most basic assumption of the Schlieffen plan to be invalid. It was a remarkably direct demonstration of the way in which financial leverage, translated into technical facts on the ground, could alter the basic parameters of military planning.

Foreign loans thus made a critical difference to the strategic posture of both Japan and Russia and these were both very large economies. In the Balkans, the effect was even more pronounced. Rich-country creditors could make loans so large that they transformed the financial situation of their debtors and effectively purchased their allegiance. Between 1906 and 1914, Serbia became massively dependent on a single creditor, France, which held three quarters of its debt. In 1914 in the wake of its success in the Balkan wars, Serbia

49 Clark 2012 pp. 223, 304–6.

50 Quoted in Stevenson 1999, p. 186.

contracted a loan with Paris that amounted to twice its entire state budget in 1912.[51]

Certainly it was not foreign credits alone that made Serbia or Russia or Japan aggressive. But foreign credits provided by the affluent centres of modernity had the effect of enhancing that aggressiveness sometimes to a spectacular degree. Furthermore they undermined the development of parliamentary budgetary controls, the bedrock of constitutional government, in the recipient countries, whilst at the same time raising the political stakes. Precisely because foreign loans came with decisive strategic entanglements, their effect on domestic politics in the recipient countries was often explosive. To give one particularly drastic example, strategic competition between France, Russia, Austria-Hungary and Germany completely scrambled Bulgarian politics by the summer of 1914.[52] The struggle over whether to accept loans from Germany or Russia along with the strategic commitments that went with the money tore the Bulgarian constitution to shreds. The correlation between political backwardness, economic underdevelopment and aggression that underpins the liberal peace model, should not be seen in isolation from the impact on fragile peripheral states of their entanglement in the high-powered network of strategic alliances and global finance spun by the great powers.

But the point to be made here is more general. If it is true that foreign lending did not make the recipients aggressive, it is also obviously true that not all foreign lending can be reduced to political motives, or, for that matter, that politically motivated action by market agents was necessarily inspired by governments. In 1904 and 1905, liberal bankers, some of Jewish origin, eagerly lent to the Japanese to fund their anti-Russian war. Whereas McDonald suggests that French lending to Russia was a creature of political influence and thus antithetical to liberalism, such 'downhill flows' of capital were precisely what liberal theory would predict. These are after all the drivers of convergence. The fact that lending helped to enhance growth in France's great ally and that this shifted the odds against Germany was in no way a contradiction of liberal assumptions. It was a sign of convergence achieved and fully in line with the optimistic historical assumption harboured by liberals that right would make might. What this involved, however, was harnessing the most and the least advanced economies together in dynamic and destabilising combinations.

51 Clark 2012, p. 357.

52 Tooze and Ivanov 2011.

Reflexivity

In a remarkable exercise in intellectual jiu-jitsu, Gartzke and Lupu attempt to turn even this point to the advantage of the liberal peace model.[53] If it is true that the forces of liberal pacification were working powerfully in Northwestern Europe, then, as realists like Rowe argue, the problems of commitment would be serious. How then could states that appeared constitutionally reluctant to launch war and were bound to suffer terrible economic losses if they did, commit to such self-harming behaviour in a sufficiently credible fashion to deter potential enemies? The answer was to tie themselves as irreversibly as possible to more backward states whose bellicosity was vouchsafed by their 'primitive' level of political and economic development. Alliances running across the developmental gradient thus become backhanded confirmation of the tensions generated by an underlying process of liberal pacification.

This is an intriguing effort to handle the problem of alliances within the terms of the liberal model. But what it downplays is the destabilising effect of the element of self-reflexivity that it incorporates into the model. This was already implied by Rowe's tragic vision of the unintended consequences of liberal pacification. But, if the logic of Gartzke and Lupu's rationalisation holds, this is taken to another level. A self-reflective response by military and diplomatic elites to the force of the liberal peace hypothesis becomes a structuring factor in the reorganisation of the international system resulting in alliances specifically designed to cut across the developmental gradient on which the defence of the liberal peace theory rests. One might imagine that these self-reflexive entanglements ought to be destabilising to the social scientific self-confidence of mainstream political science. As Clark has recently argued, as we look more and more closely into the decision-making processes during the July Crisis, what we mean by a 'cause' becomes increasingly opaque.[54] But for those not burdened by the same kind of objectivist presumptions, it is here that the story really begins to get interesting. For a whole range of complex, self-reflexive entanglements become apparent in the pre-war world.

A general staff officer or diplomat who was not himself committed to the cause of liberal progress but recognised its consequences for the world that he was trying to manipulate might well respond in the way that Gartzke suggests. An alliance with a trigger-happy second or third tier power would stand in for the domestic political will necessary to uphold deterrence. But those who were actually of a liberal disposition in France, or Britain or Germany

53 Gartzke and Lupu 2012.

54 Clark 2012, pp. xxi–xxix.

could not share this view. Such alliances of convenience required justification. On grounds of liberal political ethics, an alliance between the French republic and the autocratic and anti-semitic regime of Tsarist Russia was clearly to be regarded as odious. But furthermore, if as liberals insisted, the domestic constitution of a society was predictive of its likely international behaviour and its future prospects, then an alliance between a republic and an autocracy was questionable not merely on normative liberal, but on realist grounds as well. For a convinced liberal placing a wager on the survival of the Tsarist regime was a dubious bet at best. Tsarism's army was huge and it was convenient to be able to count on the Russian steamroller. But could Tsarism really be trusted as an ally? Might Tsarism not at some point seek a conservative accommodation with Imperial Germany? Furthermore, given liberals' understanding of history, was the Tsar's regime not doomed by its brittle political constitution and lack of internal sources of legitimacy? Following the defeat at the hands of the Japanese and the abortive revolution in Russia in 1905, Georges Clemenceau, an iconic figure of French radicalism before his entry into government in 1906, was particularly prominent in demanding that France should not bankroll the collapsing Tsarist autocracy.[55] From Russia itself came pleas from liberals calling on France to boycott the loan to the Tsar. Poincaré typically cast the problem in legal terms: How was Russia to re-establish its bona fides as a debtor after the crisis of 1905? If Russia was to receive any further credits it must provide guarantees of their legal basis. That would require a constitution, precisely what the Tsar was so unwilling to concede. Meanwhile, France's own democracy suffered damage as Russian-financed propaganda swilled through the dirty channels of the French press.[56] The most toxic product of this multi-sided argument was the notoriously anti-semitic *Protocols of the Elders of Zion*, a forgery generated by reactionary Russian political policemen stationed in Paris, who were desperate to persuade the Tsar that the French-financed capitalist modernisation of Russia was, indeed, a Jewish plot to subvert his autocratic regime.[57]

But the demands from French Republicans and Russian liberal radicals were, in fact, to no avail. The international system had its own compulsive logic that might be modified but could not so easily be overridden by political considerations, however important they might be. The consequences of Bismarck's revolution of 1866–71 could not be so easily escaped. By the 1890s the triumphant consolidation of the German nation state had created enormous pressure for

55 Long 1975 and Berelowitch 2007.

56 Long 1972.

57 Taguieff 2004.

the formation of a balancing power bloc anchored by France and Russia. This type of peacetime military bloc might be a novelty in international relations. It might be odious to French radicals. But Tsarism knew it was indispensable. By 1905 Russia was too important both as a debtor and as an ally to be amenable to pressure. With the French demanding that foreign borrowing be put on a secure legal basis and the Duma parliament uncooperative, the Tsarist regime simply responded by decree powers, arrogating to itself the right to enter into foreign loans.[58]

Desperate to escape this dependence on Russia, French radicals looked to the Entente with liberal Britain. Clemenceau indeed risked his entire political career in the early 1890s through his adventurous advocacy of an Anglo-French alliance, laying himself open to allegations that he was a hireling of British intelligence.[59] And certainly some British liberals, Lloyd George notable amongst them, understood the 1904 Entente with France as a way of ensuring that there would be no war between the two 'progressive powers' in Europe. But Britain's own concern for its imperial security was too pressing for it to be able to ignore the appeal of a détente with Russia. It was the hesitancy of the British commitment to France that combined with the Russian revival to push Paris back in the direction of Moscow. By 1912 the French republic was committing itself wholeheartedly not to regime change in Russia but to maximising its firepower.

The appeal of the 'liberal' British option was not confined to France. In Germany too, the idea of a cross-channel détente with Britain was attractive to those on the progressive wing of Wilhelmine politics. Amongst reformist social democrats there were even those who toyed with the idea of a Western democratic alliance against Russia, including both France and Britain. Eduard Bernstein reported that when he discussed the possibility of a Franco-German rapprochement with Jean Jaurès, the Frenchman had exclaimed that in that case France would lose all interest in the alliance with Russia and the 'foundations would have been laid for a truly democratic foreign policy'.[60] Beyond the ranks of the SPD, 'Liberal imperialists' speculated publicly about the possibility of satisfying Germany's desire for a presence on the world stage, without antagonising the British.[61] But in practice the Kaiser and his entourage, no doubt backed by a large segment of public opinion, could never reconcile themselves to the reality that they would forever play the role of a junior

58 McDonald 2009, p. 203.
59 Watson 1974.
60 Quoted in Fletcher 1983, p. 87.
61 Von Hagen 1955; Schoellgen 1980.

partner to the British Empire. Antagonism with Britain, however, implied an alliance system that bound Germany to the Habsburg Empire as its main ally. And this commitment was reaffirmed in 1908 by Chancellor Bülow's support for Austria's abrupt annexation of Bosnia-Herzegovina. This in the eyes of many liberal imperialists in Berlin was to prove a tragic mistake. Richard von Kühlmann, a leading advocate of détente with Britain, who would serve as Germany's Foreign Secretary during World War I and was driven out of office in the summer of 1918 as a result of clashes with Ludendorff and Hindenburg, would describe Berlin's dependence on Vienna as the true tragedy of German power.[62] From the vantage point of a liberal view of history, the true logic of World War I was a struggle over the inevitable dismantling of the Ottoman and Habsburg Empires. For a German liberal such as Kühlmann, for Berlin to have tied itself to the Habsburg Empire, a structure condemned by the nationality principle to historical oblivion, was a disaster. A true realism involved not sentimentality or blank cynicism but an understanding of history's inner logic. A new Bismarck would, Kühlmann believed, have joined Britain in a partnership to oversee the dismantling of both Habsburg and Ottoman Empires, whose crisis was instead to result in the self-destruction of European power.

It was in speculations of this type that the full implications of a liberal progressive view of history for international politics became visible. Tsarism was undeniably reactionary and its empire was crowded with oppressed national and ethnic minorities. But this expansionism could itself be read as the expression of the dynamic and vital force of the Russian nation. The Habsburg and Ottoman empires appeared to liberals by contrast as moribund minority regimes. The crisis of the Ottoman Empire was the root cause of the repeated tensions in Morocco and over control of Egypt and Mesopotamia. But thanks to the struggles of the early modern period the Ottoman Empire was eccentric to the great power system. Austria, by contrast, since the wars of succession of the eighteenth century, had been the anchor of the conservative legitimist order. It had survived 1848 by the skin of its teeth and was buffeted by Italian and German unification. After its humiliation at the hands of the Prussians in 1866, Berlin promptly committed itself to upholding the Empire. But it was a highly unstable solution. If the hallmark of the new era of international relations was intensified global competition, in Central Europe the counterpart to this shift was an end to the Austrophilia which had been at the core of European international relations since the eighteenth century. Once, sustaining the Habsburgs had been acknowledged as the common interest of all the powers. By contrast, one of defining features of European international

62 Kühlmann 1931.

relations from the 1890s onwards was that Vienna seemed to have forfeited its right to act as a self-interested major power. As Clark puts it, underpinning Entente diplomacy from 1904 onwards was 'a refusal – whether explicit or implicit – to grant Austria-Hungary the right to defend its close-range interests in the manner of a European power'.[63] Austria-Hungary was either doomed to disintegration or, even worse, to act as the pawn of the more modern, more dominant, more industrial and urban Germany. In the run up to 1914, as Clark points out, the Entente propagandists even managed to present Serbia as a legitimate contender for modernity as opposed to Vienna. These narratives 'served to legitimate the armed struggle of the Serbs, who appeared in them as the heralds of a pre-ordained modernity destined to sweep away the obsolete structures of the dual monarchy'.[64]

Given the manifest backwardness of Serbia this inverted role assignment is indicative for Clark of the fact that the Habsburg Monarchy had become the victim of a broader drama. The actors in 1914 were no longer willing to play the old game. They were in the grip of a new conception of international relations, understood as a drama of historical progress. It was this that forced the Austrian leadership into the annexation of 1908 and the decision for war in 1914. Vienna must do or die. But it was this same conception that made Austria's enemies unwilling to grant Vienna a new lease of life. In the stylised contrast drawn by Entente propagandists between Serbia and the Habsburg Empire, Clark detects a master narrative whose principal function was to shut down argument.

> [T]he most important function of such master narratives was surely that they enabled decision-makers to hide, even from themselves, their responsibility for the outcome of their actions. If the future was already mapped out, then politics no longer meant choosing among options, each of which implied a different future. The task was rather to align oneself with the impersonal, forward momentum of History.[65]

Social Darwinism was one way to cast this historical grand narrative, another was a liberal narrative of historical development. It was liberal notions of the rise of nationality that changed the terms of the debate in the Balkans and led the Entente to denounce the appropriation of Bosnia by Austria-Hungary that

---

63 Clark 2012, p. 356.

64 Clark 2012, p. 350.

65 Clark 2012, p. 350.

had been regarded as legitimate thirty years earlier at the Congress of Berlin of 1878.

This was the merciless logic of the liberal peace hypothesis operating in reverse. If it is true that advanced, tightly integrated capitalist democracies do not make war on each other, there is nothing in theory or the historical record to suggest that they will not make war on less developed societies. Indeed, precisely on the grounds of their hierarchical, developmentalist model of history it may be enjoined upon them to make war for the sake of progress. This was an abiding feature of liberal imperialist thinking. But it was also deep in the DNA of Marxism. At the time of the 1848 Revolutions and after, both Marx and Engels had preached the need for a revolutionary war against reactionary Russia.[66] And this was another route by which the liberal peace model entered into the politics of war in 1914.

Since the 1912 election, the SPD had emerged as the largest party in the Reichstag. As a socialist party it was committed to a Marxist interpretation of history and thus to the cause both of progress and internationalism. It was also, of course, a mass party enrolling millions of voters many of whom were proud German patriots, who saw in August 1914 a patriotic struggle and an occasion for national cross-class unity. Famously the party, like virtually all its other European counterparts, voted for war credits. But despite the abuse hurled at them by more radical internationalists, for the SPD, as for other European socialists, it was not naked patriotism that triumphed in 1914. What overrode their internationalism was their determination to defend a vision of progress cast within a national developmental frame. World War I was a progressive war for German social democracy in that it was through the war that domestic reform would be won. It was not by coincidence that it was during the war that the Weimar coalition between the SPD, progressive liberals and Christian Democrats was forged. It was that coalition that delivered the progressive constitution of the Weimar Republic. This was a democratic expression of the spirit of August 1914. It was the first incarnation of *Volksgemeinschaft* in democratic form. It was defensive in inspiration. An Anglophile like Bernstein deeply regretted the war in the West, but there was no question where he stood in August 1914. The cause of progress in Germany would not be helped by surrendering to the rapacious demands of the worst elements of Anglo-French imperialism. If the Tsar's brutal hordes were to march through Berlin, the setback to progress would be world historic.[67] But it was not merely a revisionist like Bernstein who took this view. Hugo Haase, the later founder of the USPD,

66 Engels 1884.

67 Fletcher 1983.

justified his support for the war on 4 August in strictly anti-Russian terms: 'The victory of Russian despotism, sullied with the blood of the best of its own people, would jeopardise much, if not everything, for our people and their future freedom. It is our duty to repel this danger and to safeguard the culture and independence of our country'.[68]

As Lars T. Lih has shown in this volume, Lenin himself employed a similar logic in developing his position on the war in 1914. In his September 1914 manifesto, Lenin declared the defeat of Tsarism the 'lesser evil'. Nor did Lenin shrink from making comparisons. In his letter to Shlyapnikov of 17 October, he wrote:

> for us *Russians*, from the point of view of the interests of the working masses and the working class of *Russia*, there cannot be the smallest doubt, absolutely any doubt, that the *lesser* evil would be now, at once the *defeat* of tsarism in this war. For tsarism is a hundred times worse than Kaiserism.[69]

Early in 1915 this line was reiterated in a resolution proposed to the conference of the exiled Bolshevik Party that echoed Marx and Engels in 1848. All revolutionaries should work for the overthrow of their governments and none should shrink from the prospect of national defeat in war. But for Russian revolutionaries this was essential, Lenin noted, because a

> victory for Russia will bring in its train a strengthening of reaction, both throughout the world and within the country, and will be accompanied by the complete enslavement of the peoples living in areas already seized. In view of this, we consider the defeat of Russia the lesser evil in all conditions.[70]

Lenin, of course, was at pains to distance himself from the logic of national defence that would seem to follow from his comment for German social democracy. Instead, he called on revolutionaries to raise the stakes by launching a civil war.[71] But, given the difficulties that Lenin had in formulating his own position, it is hardly surprising that the SPD chose a more obvious path. A German defeat at the hands of the Russian army would be a disaster. So long as the main aim was defence against the Tsarist menace they could be won over

68 Maehl 1952, p. 41.
69 Lenin 1976, Vol. 35, pp. 161–4.
70 Lenin 1974, pp. 158–164.
71 Lih 2014 in this volume.

for a defensive war. And this was well understood on the part of the Reich's leadership who by 1914 were convinced that they needed to bring the opposition party onside. The correlation between backwardness and aggression, exemplified by Tsarist Russia and seized upon so insistently by modern day academic exponents of the liberal peace hypothesis, thus became operative in the moment itself. To secure the solidity of the German home front it was absolutely crucial from the point of view of Bethmann Hollweg's grand strategy during the July Crisis that Russia must be seen to be the aggressor. Throughout the desperate final days of July, Berlin waited for the Tsar's order to mobilise before unleashing the Schlieffen Plan. As Bethmann Hollweg well understood, whatever Germany's own entanglements with Vienna, only if the expectations of a modernist vision of history were confirmed in this basic respect could the Kaiser's regime count on the support of the Social Democrats, who were in their vast majority devoted adherents of a stagist view of history that placed Russia far behind Imperial Germany. It is not by accident therefore that this correlation is waiting in the historical record to confirm the liberal peace theory. It was Russia's mobilisation on 30 July 1914 that served as a crucial justification for a defensive war, which by 1915 had become a war to liberate the oppressed nationalities from the Tsarist knout, first the Baltics and Poland then Ukraine and the Caucasus.

Conclusion: Imperialism and Post-Imperialism

In a remarkable recent article Paul Schroeder, the doyen of European diplomatic history, pushes back against the prevailing tide of historiographical opinion.[72] How are we to characterise the sea-change that had clearly come over the international system in the generation before 1914? The world that the modern political science literature takes for granted, of multi-dimensional, full spectrum international competition was not a state of nature. It had taken on a new comprehensive form in the late nineteenth century. There is still no better concept, Schroeder insists, to grasp this competition that embraced every dimension of state power – GDP growth, taxation, foreign loans – that made the constitution of Russia itself endogenous to grand strategic competition, than the concept of an 'age of imperialism'. Schroeder is not, of course, appealing for a return to Lenin. Even to many on the left, that seems like an increasingly implausible option.[73] But what Schroeder wishes to highlight is what it

72 Schroeder 2007.

73 Teschke and Lacher 2007.

was that Lenin, Kautsky and other theorists of the Second International were trying to analyse and rationalise; namely the widely shared awareness that great power competition had become radicalised, expanded in scope, and had taken on a new logic of life and death. The world had entered a 'new era of war and revolution'.[74] It was that situation, that same sense of do-or-die dynamism, that Clark seeks to capture with his invocation of a progressive historical imperative at work in the 1914 moment.

What is the link between imperialism and the notion of History that Clark invokes? This subtle point is explicated by Schroeder himself in the telling image he chooses to illustrate the difference between the classical game of great power politics and the age of imperialism. The classical game of great power politics, Schroeder suggests, was like a poker game played by highly armed powers but with a sense of common commitment to upholding the game. It was thus eventful, but repetitive, highly structured and to a degree timeless. There was no closure. Win or lose, the players remained the same. Imperialism, by contrast, was more like the brutal and notoriously ill-defined game of Monopoly. Under the new dispensation, the players' sole aim was accumulation up to and including the out-right elimination of the competition through bankruptcy. As Eric Hobsbawm also pointed out, one of the novelties of the situation before 1914 was that great power status and economic standing had come to be identified with the accumulation of capital and the terrifying aspect of capital accumulation was that it had no natural limit.[75]

The difference with regard to temporal dynamics is striking. Unlike an endlessly repeated poker round, as the game of Monopoly progresses, the piling up of resources and the elimination of players marks out an irreversible, 'historical' trajectory. Unselfconsciously Schroeder thus introduces into the discussion one of the most fundamental ideas suggested by Hannah Arendt in the critique of imperialism and capitalist modernity that she first developed in *The Origins of Totalitarianism*.[76] What she described was precisely the colonisation of the world of politics by the limitless voracious appetites of capital accumulation. And for her too this brought with it a new and fetishistic relationship to history.

Could this violent dynamic be contained? The advocates of imperialism theory à la Lenin or Luxemburg of course reject any such possibility, short of revolution. The expansionary aggressive logic was a product of capitalism's inner instability and insufficiency. This was a determinism deliberately

74 Lih 2014.

75 Hobsbawm 1987, pp. 318–19.

76 Arendt 1951; King and Stone 2007; and Benhabib 2010.

espoused and artfully constructed, all the better to set off the necessity of a revolutionary politics. Liberal internationalism for them was nothing more than a bourgeois façade. Arendt was no friend of Leninism, but her concept of political action was similarly voluntarist. And it is perhaps no coincidence therefore that she took over from Lenin and Luxemburg much of their deterministic logic when it came to thinking about the economic underpinnings of modern society. For her too a bleakly deterministic vision of economic logic serves all the better to highlight the volitional quality that is essential to truly political action. Admittedly, of course, Arendt was rather less precise than Lenin and rather less actively engaged in seeking the weakest link in the imperialist chain that might enable political action to be actually efficacious.

But whether in Lenin, Luxemburg or Arendt, the contrast between the violent mechanism of imperialist competition and freeing political action is etched in starkest black and white. For a more nuanced reading of the alternatives, it is liberal anti-imperialists such as Hobson that we must turn. Hobson was of course a major source for Lenin. But Hobson's own understanding of the economic logic of imperialism was far more open-ended than that of Lenin. And Hobson exerted an influence not just on the Bolshevik theorists. He also influenced revisionist German social democrats, notably Bernstein. Hobson himself evolved over the course of World War I towards an advocacy of world government.[77] Similarly, in Karl Kautsky's notion of ultra-imperialism, one of Lenin's polemical targets in his 1916 pamphlet, we see a Marxist reworking of the idea that a global capitalism might in fact provide the foundation for a new international order.[78] By 1918 that would be combined in Kautsky's case with an explicit commitment to democracy as an independent value of progressive politics and a precondition of peace under the auspices of the League of Nations.[79]

All of these authors espoused a vision of a 'democratic peace' not as an academic hypothesis, but as a political project. All of them were aware of the violent possibilities of the age of imperialism. All could see exits from that disaster short of cataclysmic war or revolution. All were frustrated by the contorted international politics of the July Crisis. By 1917, disillusioned by the failure of their pre-war politics, Bernstein and Kautsky both ended up in the USPD, and Hobson in the Union of Democratic Control. Liberalism was to triumph in World War I, but not in their sense as a formula of peace, but as a battle cry, carrying the Entente and a reluctant President Wilson to victory

77 Long 1996.

78 Holloway 1983.

79 Kautksy 1919 and Kautsky 1920.

over the Central Powers.[80] In truth, as we have seen, the only consistent way to incorporate the July Crisis of 1914 into liberal IR theory is to acknowledge the degree to which that war was not an accident, or a puzzle, but a clash driven by a progressive historical logic. At first it was understood as a war of defence. But as the losses mounted up it came to be seen by all sides as a war of fundamental transformation. Whether it be through the dismantling of the Tsarist Empire at the hands of the Central Powers, or through the destruction of the Habsburg and Ottoman Empires by the Entente, the world would be made right. It would in the term so essential to liberal pragmatists, be 'adjusted' to conform to a new model.[81] As it turned out, not one of the European coalitions was in fact powerful enough to bring about the 'adjustment' it had in mind, not one was powerful enough to impose its distinctive vision of historical progress. It would therefore be through the rise of the United States, first as a tie breaker and then as overwhelming hegemon, that the association claimed by liberal IR theory between capitalist democracy and great power peace would be instantiated as a dominant reality of international politics. It is no coincidence that the outbreak of new hostilities between 1937 and 1941 is so much more easily legible in terms of liberal theory than events during the July Crisis of 1914. Nor is it any coincidence that the data so strongly confirms the liberal peace theory after 1945. To think of the idea of a democratic capitalist peace as a hypothesis fit for testing is to misconstrue its relationship to historical reality. In the twentieth century, it was no longer a utopia or a hypothesis, but a project backed by massive power. What August 1914 made clear was just how much force this would require.[82]

80 For Wilson's reluctance see Tooze 2014.

81 For adjustment as a key term in Dewey's thinking see Hickman and Alexander 1998 and Rosenthal 1986.

82 For the question staked out in the fundamental debate between Wilson and Roosevelt over the future of American power, see Cooper 1983.

CHAPTER 4

Marxist Theory and the Origins of the First World War

Alexander Anievas[1]

Introduction

Despite the profound importance of the First World War in transforming Marxist thought and praxis – notably including the hugely significant works on imperialism produced by Luxemburg, Lenin, Bukharin and others – subsequent Marxists (at least within the English-speaking world) have paid very little attention to theorising the war's origins. The few studies that have addressed this issue in any systematic way have remained either situated within the original classical Marxist theories of imperialism[2] or have produced works of a more theoretically eclectic nature with as many family resemblances to neo-Marxism as liberalism.[3] This dearth of inquiries into the origins of the war may very well have to do with the long legacy cast by Lenin's theory of imperialism, and the orthodoxy this imposed on many subsequent generations of Marxists. Whatever the reasons may be, the time to reassess the contribution Marxist theory can make in explaining the war's genesis is long overdue. For, as examined below, while both the original Marxist theories of imperialism and later theories of 'social imperialism' focusing on the anachronistic pathologies of the German polity have illuminated significant processes and elements vital to any adequate theorisation of the war's causes, both sets of theories are hamstrung by particular methodological and theoretical deficiencies.

These theoretical problems cut to the heart of ongoing historiographical debates over the origins of the First World War in which, unfortunately, Marxist

---

1 This chapter draws on and further develops (particularly empirically) arguments first made in Anievas 2013. My thanks to Josef Ansorge for his comments on an earlier draft of this chapter. Usual disclaimers apply.

2 See, for example, Hobsbawm 1987; Callinicos 2009.

3 Most notably, those works associated with the *Sonderweg* ('Special Path') perspective and the Old Regime thesis, both of which are amenable to liberal iterations of the 'democratic peace thesis'. See, respectively, Wehler 1985 and Halperin 2004 and Mayer 1981.

theories have been entirely side-lined. This concerns the persistent division between whether a *Primat der Aussenpolitik* ('primacy of foreign policy') or *Primat der Innenpolitik* ('primary of domestic policy') perspective best explains the causes of the war.[4] The 'Long Debate' has then been left at something of an analytical stalemate. For, over the years, historiographical trends have tended to move back and forth between these two conflicting modes of explanation: the Versailles 'war guilt' charge blaming Germany as the primary cause for war was replaced by the 'comfortable consensus' of shared responsibility among the belligerents developed in the 1930s and particularly after the Second World War;[5] this was then overthrown by Fritz Fischer's 'historiographical revolution' re-identifying Germany as the main culprit which has now given some way to more 'global' and 'de-centered'[6] perspectives sharing some common ground with earlier 'primacy of foreign policy' approaches.[7] Indeed, one author has gone so far as to claim that '[b]y the early 1990s, the emerging consensus on the origins of the First World War was that even if Germany was primarily to blame, her motivations were primarily power-political and largely unrelated to any domestic impasse in 1914'.[8] While likely an overstatement regarding the supposed renewed hegemony of 'primacy of foreign policy' perspectives in the historiographical debates, the overall orientation of these debates remained centred around questions of domestic or international primacy.

While scholars have insisted on the need to integrate both domestic ('unit-level') and international ('system-level') factors in offering a more satisfactory explanation of the war,[9] there remain few – if any – substantive theoretical advances in providing such an explanation.[10] Instead, attempts at offering such an integrated theory have primarily taken the form of a 'mix and match' of different domestic and international determinations whereby internal and external factors are conceived as relating to one another as 'independent variables' incorporated at different, discretely-conceived 'levels of analysis'. The problem with such theoretical models is that the objects of their analyses (the

4 For recent overviews of these historiographical debates see Mombauer 2002; Hamilton and Herwig 2003; Joll and Martell 2007; Mulligan 2010.

5 See Mombauer 2002, pp. 105–18, 121–6.

6 Eley this volume.

7 Such recent works include Schöllgen, 1990; Mulligan 2010; Clarke 2012; Simms 2013, Chapter 5.

8 Simms 2003, p. 286.

9 Blackbourn 2003, p. 335.

10 The closest we have to such an integrated approach is Gordon 1974.

domestic and international) remain fundamentally *external* to one another. The relationship between the international and domestic is thus shorn of any theoretical basis in the same socio-historical process from which they emerged. They remain *analytically* and *ontologically distinct*; the objects of *separate theories* retaining only an external (if not contingent) association to one another thereby perpetuating the fundamental disjunction between 'geopolitical' and 'sociological' modes of explanations. Recent historiographical studies have of course continued to provide a wealth of much needed and highly innovative analyses of the war – particularly of late on the cultural, ideological, and linguistic aspects of the war.[11] Yet debates concerning the *causal* sources of the war still remain locked in such unhelpful dichotomies privileging either geopolitical or sociological-based explanations. What is to be done?

This chapter proposes a solution to this 'eternal divide' between sociological and geopolitical, domestic and international, forms of explanation – one firmly grounded in the classical Marxist tradition. It does so by drawing on and further developing Trotsky's concept of uneven and combined development which uniquely interpolates an 'international' dimension of causality as *interior* to socio-historical development itself. This then allows for the *organic* – rather than external – integration of geopolitical and sociological determinations into a single unified theory of socio-historical development and, by extension, interstate rivalry and war.

The chapter is developed in three movements. The first critically examines two of the main theories currently on offer in explaining the causes of the First World War, with a particular emphasis on the classical Marxist theory of imperialism as formulated by Lenin and Bukharin. It then moves to outline my proposed alternative theoretical framework drawing on the concept of uneven and combined development. The third and longest part of the chapter then proceeds to offer a theoretically-informed empirical analysis of the key structural tendencies and conjunctural trends leading to the outbreak of war in 1914. The conclusion in turn reflects on the challenge uneven and combined development poses to the basic theoretical premises of historical materialism more generally.

---

11 For an overview of some of these more recent studies, particularly in regards to German history, see Eley and Baranowski's contributions in this volume.

Theorising the Origins of the First World War: Review and Critique

The Sonderweg *of German Imperialism*

In 1961, the German diplomatic historian Fritz Fischer published *Griff nach der Weltmacht: die Kriegszielpolitik des Kaiserlichen Deutschland, 1914–18,*[12] irrevocably transforming debates on the origins of the war. Fischer's analysis exploded the hitherto reigning historiographical consensus that the great powers had unconsciously 'slithered into war', as Lloyd George had famously put it. Drawing on a wealth of archival materials (some previously undiscovered), Fischer laid blame for the war's outbreak squarely on the shoulders of Germany's antiquated ruling elites who sought to consolidate their fragile domestic position against attacks from both the left and right.[13] The 1914 conflict was thus conceived as a 'preventive war' consciously launched by German decision-makers in their attempt to eliminate both perceived internal and external enemies – notably, the Social Democratic challenge at home and the growing threat of Russian power abroad, respectively. Fischer's argument – later dubbed the 'Fischer thesis' – that German policymakers bore the main responsibility for the war's outbreak and that their motivations were primarily rooted in domestic socio-political concerns and developments, thus explicitly arguing for a *Primat der Innenpolitik* perspective, inaugurated 'one of the most heated historiographical debates of the twentieth century'[14] – one which continues to orient historiographical and theoretical discussions of the origins of the First World War to this day.[15]

The theoretical perspective underlying Fischer's empirical claims made in his original 1961 publication *Germany's Aims in the First World War* would be further fleshed out in subsequent works, particularly *The War of Illusions* (1975) and *From Kaiserreich to the Third Reich* (1986). The latter in particular sought to demonstrate the essential continuities in German foreign policymaking from the late nineteenth century to the Second World War, which, according to Fischer, derived from Germany's 'special path' [*Sonderweg*] of socio-political

---

12 'Grab for World Power: The War Aims of Imperial Germany, 1914–1918' later published in English under the less provocatively titled *Germany's Aims in the First World War*. Fischer 1967.

13 See especially Fischer 1975.

14 Mombauer 2013a, p. 231.

15 In addition to Geoff Eley's contribution to this volume, see the recent symposium in the *Journal of Contemporary History* (2013) devoted to the 'Fischer Controversy'.

development.[16] This notion of a *special path* of German development would come to be taken up and further refined by both liberal and neo-Marxist scholars, including some of Fischer's students and those associated with the 'Bielefeld School' of German history.[17] This sought to explain the fragility of Germany's domestic ruling order on the eve of the First World War and after as a result of the peculiarities of Prussian-German socio-political development over the 'Long Nineteenth Century', emphasising in particular the failure or incompleteness of an indigenous bourgeois revolution, thus essentially leaving intact the old ruling class alliance – 'the marriage of iron and rye', an anti-democratic coalition of heavy industrialists and agrarian Junkers cobbled together under the reign of Bismarck.

Hence, by the turn of the twentieth century, German society had experienced the economic transformations associated with any advanced capitalist society as Bismarck's state-led 'revolution from above' achieved an intensive process of industrialisation and urbanisation, embedding capitalist property relations throughout the *Reich*. Yet the Prussian-German state failed to undergo the normally associated political process of 'modernisation' as the state remained authoritarian and civil society 'underdeveloped'. The *Kaiserreich* was thus distinguished from other advanced European countries by a striking dissonance between a highly developed economic 'base' and an underdeveloped or 'backward' socio-political superstructure, facilitating the 'powerful persistence of pre-industrial, pre-capitalist traditions'.[18] This then explained the anti-democratic, illiberal, militaristic and authoritarian features of the peculiarly 'pre-modern' German state. Characteristic here was the 'political abdication' of a nascent German bourgeoisie[19] and, consequently, their subordination to the pre-industrial Junker class in the 'marriage of iron and rye'. It was precisely this ruling class – steeped in pre-capitalist mind-sets and value systems – that would lead Germany into war in 1914 and continue to dominate German political life right up until the Nazi defeat in 1945.[20]

From this perspective of the *Sonderweg* of German development, the country's drive toward imperialist expansionism and colonialism is viewed as a particularly virulent form of 'social imperialism'. In Wehler's conception, this served to defend the traditional structures of the Prussian-German state, shielding the socio-political status-quo from the consequences of rapid industrialisation and urbanisation, while diverting movements for parliamen-

16 Fischer 1986.

17 See especially, Geiss 1976; Kocka 1999; Wehler 1985.

18 Jürgen Kocka as quoted in Childers 1990, p. 332.

19 Wehler 1972, p. 77.

20 Fischer 1986; Wehler 1985.

tarisation and democratisation.[21] Social imperialism was thus actively promoted by the traditional ruling class with the help of a 'feudalised' bourgeoisie who were assimilated 'by the agrarian-feudal forces' in staving off social reform and other threats to the status-quo.[22] If one can trace a line of continuity running throughout German history from 1871 to 1945 then it was precisely this 'primacy of social imperialism from Bismarck to Hitler'.[23]

The origins of German imperialism are thereby conceived as *atavistic* in nature: rooted in the fundamentally *pre-modern* qualities of a state characterised by the persistence of anachronistic 'pre-capitalist' mentalities 'steeped in a feudal value system'.[24] The causes of the First World War are, then, viewed as the consequence of Germany's imperfect modernisation and failure to transform itself into a liberal-democratic polity; a *specific crisis* of Germany's fractured transition to capitalist modernity. If not entirely external to capitalism, the First World War is thus conceived as an *aberration* within it.

The methodological and theoretical difficulties of the *Sonderweg* approach to German history have been well documented and need not be repeated here in their entirety.[25] Instead, for the remainder of this section, I focus on the most important issues as specifically pertaining to theorising the origins of the First World War.

A fundamental problem with the *Sonderweg* thesis is its *static* comparative approach to German development. Simply put, to have an 'aberration' one must first have a norm from which contrastive comparisons can be made. The norm usually assumed is the British and French paths to modernity, where the former provides the model of 'normal' economic development, and the latter 'normal' political development. These two normative models are based upon these countries' successful 'bourgeois revolutions' which Germany did not ostensibly undergo.

Obscured from this static picture is a perspective that interconnects the time-space relations of capitalist development into a wider interactive totality of world development. The point is that the reasons why German development differed from those of previous states such as Britain and France are precisely explained by those earlier transitions. For 'once breakthroughs to ongoing capitalist economic development took place in various regions', Robert Brenner writes, 'these irrevocably transformed the conditions and character

21 Wehler, 1970b, p. 153.
22 Fischer 1986, p. 40; Wehler 1985, pp. 173–4.
23 Wehler 1972, p. 88.
24 Gessner 1977; Berghahn 1993, p. 54.
25 See especially Blackbourn and Eley 1984 and Evans 1985.

of analogous processes which were to occur subsequently elsewhere'.[26] The sequencing of bourgeois revolutions thus 'entered into the definition of their differences. *Their order was constitutive of their structure*'.[27]

The comparative model assumed by the *Sonderweg* obfuscates these constitutive interrelations between spatio-temporal variations of capitalist development, thus essentially providing a 'freeze-frame' view of German development abstracted from the developmental rhythms of world history. The *Sonderweg* approach essentially subsumes Germany's developmental trajectory under a liberal-inspired unilinear model of development whereby the German experience is judged an aberration. In maintaining this Enlightenment-inspired unilinear narrative of modernity, the origins of the First World War are then located outside the world-historical development of capitalism as a concrete lived reality. A German *Sonderweg*, determined by pre-modern remnants, is the 'Othering' mechanism through which capitalism is absolved of any responsibility for the war.

These above points directly tie to a second problem with the *Sonderweg* thesis: the unhelpful normative presuppositions linking the succession of democracy, modernisation and a progressive foreign policy, on the one hand, with capitalism and the political ascendancy of the bourgeoisie, on the other. To understand the complex relations between the German bourgeoisie and liberalism, their interests and actions should instead be situated within the context of the internal conflicts and external exigencies facing the German social formation as a whole. From this perspective, the authoritarian and expansionist tendencies of the German state should not be conceived as serving the *specific* interests of the Junker class and other traditional political elites. They were instead *symptomatic* of ruling-class strategies within late-industrialising states more generally. The key difference lay in the *form* these policies took, not the interests and agents they represented.

Under the imperatives of geopolitical competition over the nineteenth century, the German state was forced to industrialise as quickly as possible. As a consequence of this accelerated industrialisation, both the traditional ruling elites and the emerging bourgeoisie confronted the growing threat of a radicalised working-class movement. The majority of non-socialist *bürgerliche Parteien* were thus willing – and in most cases welcomed – the state-assisted industrialisation drive and 'revolution from above' inaugurated by Bismarck. To fend off and harness the popular discontent inevitably arising from it, the bourgeoisie were forced to co-opt popular peasant and petty-bourgeois forces, supporting – if not actively promoting – the anti-parliamentarian elements

26 Brenner 1985, p. 322.
27 Anderson 1992, p. 116.

and expansionist foreign policies of the German state. Indeed, the chief instrument of German authoritarianism, and a symbol of its ostensibly 'pre-modern' character – the infamous Prussian three-class franchise – was introduced and partly drafted by a commission which counted prominent liberals among its members.[28]

The identification of 'social imperialism' and German expansionism with the specific interests of the traditional conservative elites is therefore fundamentally misleading. *Pace* Wehler's influential account of social imperialism and reform as conflicting strategies, the two were more often viewed as complementary. Social imperialism held a much wider resonance across the political spectrum. There were both conservative and reformist conceptions of social imperialism, the latter of which can be found in Friedrich Naumann's 'policy of power abroad and reform at home'.[29] Narrowing the applicability of social imperialism to the particular interests of the Prussian-German conservative elite, the *Sonderweg* thesis thereby ignores this much wider spectrum of debate, with its differing conceptions of social imperialism. It thus overlooks the crucial role of the German bourgeois in promoting imperial expansion.[30] More problematically still, it fails to recognise the more general, *structural* nature of the crisis facing the German state. If feudal 'hang-overs' were the fundamental problem, then a more thoroughgoing modernisation process rooting out these pathologies from the social-political body would have sufficed. If, instead, the sources of the erratic (if not unusual) expansionist foreign policies of the *Kaiserreich* were symptoms of a deeper and wider *systemic* crisis, then such 'pathologies' would have been more difficult to eradicate.

The so-called 'flight into war' taken by the German ruling classes was not the result of Germany's lack of modernity, but rather its *over-stimulation* from both below and without. This was a consequence of the explosive, time-compressed character of Germany's industrialisation and national-state-formation processes, pressurised in time and space by the strategic interaction of a multiplicity of unevenly developing societies. In other words, German development must be situated within the broader dynamics of this *international* conjuncture. For once this is recognised, the so-called 'peculiarities' of German development were far from the aberration that the *Sonderweg* thesis proclaims, but rather one developmental trajectory among the many variegated patterns of uneven and combined development characteristic of the conjuncture as a whole.

---

28 Blackbourn and Eley 1984, pp. 19–20.

29 Eley 1986, p. 161.

30 See, for example, Berghahn 1993.

The recognition of this wider international terrain of German development in relation to the causes of 1914 points to one final difficulty of Fischer's approach. Despite the virtues of emphasising the substantive socio-political differences between Germany and the other great powers, of which there were certainly many, the *Sonderweg* nonetheless too narrowly associates the cause of war with an essentialising narrative of German 'misdevelopment'. As Fritz Fischer puts it: 'I look upon the July crisis from the angle that it developed specifically from the entire intellectual, political and economic position of the [German] Empire in Europe'.[31] While German policymakers' provocation to war in July 1914 seems clear, one must still focus on the more *general* and *systemic* origins of the war. Simply put, the German ruling classes were not the only ones prepared to risk war in a juncture of domestic crises and external pressures, as 1914 all too clearly demonstrated. This wider terrain of systemic inter-imperial rivalries is precisely what the classical Marxist theorists sought to capture, and to which we now turn.

The Geopolitics of Monopoly Capitalism

Writing in 1972, Roger Owen and Bob Sutcliffe could note that the classical Marxist theory of imperialism was one of the 'strongest branches' of Marxist thinking as it was treated with respect by Marxists and non-Marxists alike. 'Virtually all discussions of imperialism at the theoretical level', they wrote, 'assign importance to the Marxist theory ... as even its sharpest critics admit, [the theory] appears to have offered a stronger challenge to orthodox non-Marxist scholars than most branches of Marxism has yet succeeded in doing'.[32] Unfortunately, within the contemporary historiographical literature on the origins of the First World War, this is no longer the case. Indeed, it is tempting to say that the closest thing to a strong 'consensus' historians have reached is that the classical Marxist theories have little if anything to offer in understanding the origins of 1914.[33] Even amongst contemporary Marxists, the theory has fallen on hard times, as many dispute its historical and, more often, contemporary relevance as a theory of geopolitical rivalry and war.[34] Yet, unlike Fischer's *Sonderweg* approach, the classical Marxist theories do capture a very important part of the story left out by other perspectives: that is, a recognition of the genuinely world systemic dimension of the socio-economic developments leading to the First World War, firmly rooted in a theory of capitalist devel-

---

31 Fischer 1984, p. 183.

32 Owen and Sutcliffe 1972, p. 312.

33 See, for example, Gordon 1974, p. 206; McDonough 1997, pp. 36–7; Strachan 2001, p. 100; Hamilton and Herwig 2003; cf. Joll and Martel 2007.

34 See, among others, Gindin and Panitch 2004; Halperin 2004; Teschke and Lacher 2007.

opment. This is an indispensable ingredient – indeed, the necessary point of departure – for any satisfactory theoretical explanation of the war's origins so often overlooked in the standard diplomatic historical accounts. At the same time, however, the classical Marxist theories are beset by a number of theoretical deficiencies rendering them fundamentally problematic in explaining the war's origins.

Before examining these problems we need to first briefly lay out the main claims of these theories – and, in particular, Lenin and Bukharin's theory. At the most general level, we can view Lenin and Bukharin's theories of imperialism as constituting a single, unified theory of imperialism which conceived of 'inter-imperialist' rivalry and war as the organic consequences of the development of capitalism as a world system, specifically in its transition from the 'competitive' to 'monopoly' stage of capitalism occurring sometime around the turn of the twentieth century. This marked the beginning of a distinctly capitalist form of imperialism. A basic way of distinguishing the *differentia specifica* of this capitalist form, as conceptualised by Lenin and further developed by Bukharin, is to say that it signified the historical point when processes of territorial-military rivalry among states were subsumed under the generalised competition among 'many capitals'.[35] In this sense, geopolitical conflict was transformed into a *distinct species* of inter-capitalist competition: war became a continuation of economic competition by other means. The monopoly stage of capitalism was, in turn, conceptualised as resulting from two key tendencies of capitalism identified by Marx: the increasing concentration and centralisation of capital which, as Rudolf Hilferding so brilliantly demonstrated, led to the fusion of banking and industrial capitals into a single fraction of 'finance capital'.[36]

Important for our discussion here is that, although examining the 'domestic-level' transformations associated with the rise of this fraction of finance capital, Lenin and Bukharin both conceived of imperialism as a *world system irreducible to its national parts*.[37] Thus, contrary to the well-worn criticisms of Lenin's theory as 'reductionist' (meaning that his theory reduced systems to their units and was therefore an essentially 'inside-out' or 'internalist' account of imperialism and war),[38] Lenin and Bukharin's theory was in fact a *systemic* not

35 Callinicos 2007.

36 Hilferding [1908] 2006.

37 See esp. Lenin 1960, Volume 22, p. 272; Bukharin 1973, pp. 17–8.

38 A critique most famously put forward by Waltz 1979, and largely accepted within mainstream IR theory. The similar charge that Lenin's – and, by default, Bukharin's – theory was irredeemably 'economistic' or economically reductionist also does not hold (see Anievas 2014, Chapter 1).

unit-level theory. Yet, the very systemic nature of the theory is part of its problem. For, within Lenin's work at least, the causal connections between world systemic determinations and state action are murky at best. The crucial linkages and mediations between state and capital are never adequately worked out. But, it is important to remember that Lenin's pamphlet was intended as a 'popular outline' of already existing theories and ideas; it was not a refined piece of theoretical work. For this, one needs to turn to Bukharin's more theoretically rigorous *Imperialism and World Economy*, where the relations between state and capital are conceived as being fused into a single unit through the transformation of national economies into 'state-capitalist trusts'.[39]

Yet, this too comes with its own difficulties. For it was precisely Lenin and Bukharin's *upward conflation* of the international to the world-systemic level which renders their work so problematic. Three difficulties in particular arise from this move. First, the theory *assumes*, but does not explain, the existence of a multiplicity of territorial nation-states. The question of *why* inter-capitalist conflicts take a *territorial-military* form is thus left theoretically unaddressed. As David Harvey remarks:

> To convert the Marxian insights into a geopolitical framework, Lenin introduced the concept of the state which... remains the fundamental concept whereby territoriality is expressed. But in so doing, Lenin largely begged the question as to how or why the circulation of capital and the deployment of labor power should be national rather than global in their orientation and why the interests of either capitalists or laborers should or even could be expressed as national interests.[40]

This then leaves unresolved the 'problematic of the international'[41] facing any Marxist theory of interstate rivalry and war: that is, how to theoretically capture the distinct causal determinations and behavioural patterns emerging from the co-existence and interaction of societies. For irrespective of whether the particular Marxist approach in question conceptualises social systems as operating primarily at the domestic or world level – as exemplified by the *Sonderweg* thesis and classical Marxist theories of imperialism, respectively – the dilemma remains the same. By working outwards from a conception of a specific social structure (be it slavery, feudalism or capitalism), the theorisation of the geopolitical takes the form of a reimagining of domestic society

39 Bukharin 1973, Chapter 11.
40 Harvey 2001, p. 326.
41 Rosenberg 2000.

writ large: an extrapolation from analytical categories derived from a society conceived in the *ontological singular*.[42] This then vanishes what is arguably unique to any multistate system: a superordinating 'anarchical' structure irreducible to the historically variable types of societies constituting them. In this more fundamental sense, then, the classical Marxist theories of imperialism do reproduce the problems of internalist analyses – or, more precisely, they work with a kind of 'domestic analogy' fallacy.[43]

More recently, Marxist scholars seeking to revitalise the classical Marxist theories of imperialism to better account for geopolitics in a non-reductionist way have sought to reconceptualise imperialism as the historical fusion of two analytically distinct, and thus irreducible, 'logics' of geopolitical and economic completion, or territorial and capitalist logics of power.[44] While this avoids the problems of instrumentalism or economic reductionism, it nonetheless leaves 'the international' untouched as their conception of geopolitics remains theoretically external to their theories of social development. Even Alex Callinicos's more theoretically sophisticated account, which draws on a particular interpretation of Marx's method in theorising imperialism as the fusion of economic and geopolitical competition, is problematic. For Callinicos, Marx's method is viewed as one of non-deductive concretisation whereby, in moving from the abstract to the concrete, the analysis requires the introduction of new levels of determinations irreducible to those preceding it. This thereby conceptualises 'the international' as a 'set of determinations' over and above those existing at the domestic level. Yet, in deploying this method, the problem still persists: there remains no substantive theorisation of 'the international' as a distinct and causally consequential historical-sociological form.

Granting a distinct logic to geopolitics irreducible to any logic of capital accumulation and class conflict, Callinicos evokes the necessity of a 'realist moment'[45] in Marxist accounts of international relations, essentially giving the game away.[46] For the 'two logic' approach that he and Harvey ascribe to latches a proto-realist conception of the states system as an inherently anarchic and conflict prone field of social interaction onto a Marxist theory of capitalist development in a way that leaves the former theoretically unpenetrated,

42 On the problem of 'ontological singular' conceptions of societies see Rosenberg 2006.

43 Bull 1966.

44 See, respectively, Callinicos 2009 and Harvey 2003.

45 'Realist' refers here to realist theories of international relations, and not to realist philosophies of science.

46 Callinicos 2007, p. 542.

reified and thus external to the latter.[47] The geopolitical, on this view, retains a non-sociological content and standing, having little to no effect on the trajectory and forms of individual societies' development besides reinforcing and imposing capitalist social relations and logics of development on such societies. This perhaps explains why – despite the *empirical* recognition of all kinds of differences among the imperialist states and their 'models of expansionism'[48] – Callinicos (and Harvey) do not go much further than the original classical Marxist theories of imperialism in *theoretically* confronting the problem of interactive difference: that is, the ways in which the geopolitically-interconnected nature of social development rules out the repetition of historical stages thus producing a plurality of differentiated models of development.

In this way, the second problem with Lenin and Bukharin's theory emerges from the same source as the first. By subsuming the intersocietal dimension of historical development and reproduction to a world systemic level, Lenin and particularly Bukharin fall into the trap of unit homogenisation: that is, they work with an assumption that all imperialist states are essentially the same.[49] While Lenin *empirically* recognised differences between various imperialist states – for example, labelling French expansionism 'usury imperialism' – the fundamental features of 'monopoly capitalism' that he theoretically identified as the causal sources of imperialism were seen as operating within *all* the advanced capitalist states: Britain, France, Germany, the US, etc. Yet, these features only applied to the later-developing capitalist states, and particularly Germany, on which much of their evidence was based. These economies were generally characterised, as Lenin and Bukharin noted, by high levels of vertical-horizontal business integration (economies of scale), oligopolistic markets (cartels and trusts), large-scale banking-industrial combinations ('finance capital'), protectionist trade policies, export combinations, and statist forms of industrialisation. By contrast, the increasing tendency to export capital (over trade) postulated by Lenin and Bukharin was a main feature of earlier developers (specifically, Britain and France). Hence, the causal connections hypothesised by Lenin and Bukharin between finance capital and territorial expansionism simply do not hold.[50] To take the example of German development, the paradigm of Lenin and Bukharin's 'monopoly capitalism', the economy actually suffered from a *shortage* of money capital, not a sur-

47 For an excellent critique see Pozo-Martin 2007.

48 Arrighi 1978.

49 This problem of 'unit homogenisation' (the assumption that all states are essentially the same) equally applies to neorealist and Arno Mayer's 'Old Regime' explanations of the war. For a critical engagement with these two theories see Anievas 2014, Chapter 1.

50 Barratt Brown 1970, pp. 97–107; Brewer 1990, pp. 114–16.

plus. In the run up to 1914, this actually weakened the economic means at the *Wilhelmstraße*'s disposal to entice Russia into a political alliance against France (see below).[51]

Here, the significance of Lenin's thesis of 'uneven development' in the theory of imperialism needs to be noted since it is often conflated with Trotsky's more specific interpretation of unevenness. Although 'uneven development' between nation-states played a key explanatory role in Lenin's framework, it did so primarily as a cause for the persistence of inter-imperialist rivalries over any potential harmonisation of international capitalist interests (Kautsky's 'ultra-imperialist' thesis'). The possibility of unevenness and intersocietal interaction *generating* sociologically amalgamated and differentiated states (that is, forms of 'combined development') in turn conditioning and feeding back into the causes of inter-imperialist rivalries never entered into Lenin's framework.

The problem of unit homogenisation (imperialist states conceived as fundamentally identical) common to Lenin and Bukharin's theory relates to a third dilemma in explaining the First World War. Simply put, while the classical Marxist theories have much to say about the 'structural' or 'epochal' causes of wars, they provide little help in explaining concrete conjunctures of wars.[52] As James Joll and Gordon Martell put it, if the Marxist theory of imperialism was accurate 'it would provide the most comprehensive explanation of the outbreak of the First World War, though *it would still leave open the question why this particular war started at that particular time in the mounting crisis of capitalism*'. It would still require an explanation of the 1914 juncture 'in terms of specific decisions by particular individuals'.[53] In other words, what the classical Marxists lack is the ability to offer a theoretical analysis of the *specificities* of the immediate pre-war period differentiating it as a distinct, but not autonomous, temporality. This is in part a consequence of the problem of 'unit sameness' noted above, which identifies a single 'model of expansionism' and foreign policy behaviour common to all imperialist states. This chapter responds to that challenge.

The explanatory difficulties encountered by the homogenisation of political agents are demonstrated in Eric Hobsbawm's influential account of the origins

---

51 Fischer 1975.

52 With the very notable exception of Hobsbawm (1987, pp. 302–27), scholars drawing on the classical theories have offered little in the way of thorough historical analyses of the conjuncture of the First World War. Even the more historically sensitive works do not spend much time on the war's origins (see, most recently, Callinicos 2009, pp. 156–8).

53 Joll and Martel 2007, 146, 238, emphasis mine.

of the First World War.[54] This is arguably the best application of the 'Leninist' theory of imperialism explaining the 1914 conjuncture available in the English language. Hobsbawm's account interweaves sociological and historical factors into a rich and penetrating narrative, tracing the long-term causal forces leading the capitalist states to world conflagration. The destabilising role of the uneven and interactive character of capitalist industrialisation and its relation to economic crisis, revolutionary nationalism and domestic class conflict is not at all lost in Hobsbawm's historical narrative.[55] Yet when narrowing in to *theoretically explain* the causes of the July 1914 crisis the account runs into trouble.

Stopping to consider the historiographical debates, Hobsbawm rightly dismisses the 'war guilt' thesis identifying the *Kaiserreich* as the sole 'aggressor'. He throws doubt on the validity of the Fischerite 'social imperialism' thesis and chastises the proponents of this thesis for assigning 'responsibility' for the outbreak to German policymakers.[56] And while Hobsbawm is no doubt correct in questioning the analytical validity of the 'war guilt' issue, this unnecessarily leads him to *ontologically flatten* the differences between socio-political agents and the variations in state behaviour during the war juncture. In doing so, he then restates the 'slither into war' thesis. Claiming that no great power 'before 1914 wanted either a general European war or even ... a limited military conflict with another European power', Hobsbawm claims the war's origins must be sought in 'a progressively deteriorating international situation which increasingly escaped the control of governments'.[57] Yet Hobsbawm's historical account here is suspect: both Austrian and German policymakers *actively sought* such a war, as has now been well documented by historians.[58] As Herwig notes, while some of Fischer's views remain controversial, 'three-quarters' of his empirical arguments are now accepted by the majority of historians.[59] It is thus with no exaggeration that Pogge von Strandmann could argue in 1988 that 'the evidence that Germany and Austria started the war ... is even stronger than in the 1960s when Fritz Fischer published his analysis'.[60] Dissolving any specificity of the war juncture, Hobsbawm further writes: 'By 1914 *any* confrontation between the [alliance] blocs ... brought them to the verge of war ... *any*

54 Hobsbawm 1987. The following critique is informed by Rosenberg 2008, pp. 23–4.

55 See especially Hobsbawm 1987, Chapters 2, 3, 6, and 12.

56 Hobsbawm 1987, pp. 309–10, 323–5.

57 Hobsbawm 1987, pp. 310–11, 312.

58 See Mombauer 2002 and 2007.

59 Herwig 1991, p. 59.

60 Pogge von Strandmann 1988, p. 97.

incident, however random ... could lead to such a confrontation'.[61] This again is historically suspect as the time-space coordinates for the war's outbreak were in fact crucial, as examined below.

This sets the stage for Hobsbawm's alternative theorisation which locates the causal sources of the war in the inherently expansive, infinite aims of capital accumulation. The 'development of capitalism inevitably pushed the world in the direction of state rivalry, imperialist expansion, conflict and war' as the 'characteristic feature of capitalist accumulation was precisely that it had no limit'.[62] Though recognising that domestic troubles pushed at least one country (Austria-Hungary) to solving its internal crisis through war,[63] the role of interactively-generated socio-political differences are essentially erased in Hobsbawm's explanation of the war, which rests on this 'unlimited dynamism' of the capital accumulation process. While this is surely an indispensable part of any theorisation of the conflicts leading to war, socio-political unevenness still needs to be theoretically incorporated somewhere within the analysis. Further, much more explanatory weight must be given to the particularities of the 1914 spark: it was not just 'any incident' that fulfilled the time-space conditions that would lead to war, nor was it likely that all of the powers would equally instigate the conflict.

In better addressing these issues, the next section offers an alternative logic of explanation drawing on the theory of uneven and combined development. In particular, it illustrates how the multilinear and interactive nature of socio-historical development fed into the causal sources of geopolitical rivalry and war. In doing so, it offers a theoretical explanation of the origins of 1914 contextualised within the broad developmental tendencies of the Long Nineteenth Century (1789–1914) and their particular articulation during the immediate pre-war juncture.

---

61 Hobsbawm 1987, pp. 323–4. Hobsbawm's analysis of WWI is anything but unique within the Marxist literature. Illustrative of the many problems noted above, Robert Brenner writes (2006, p. 85) in regards to the causes of WWI, that 'the action of any state can easily set off responses by other states that detonate a chain reaction controllable by none of them. Chain reactions of this sort are the stuff of international history and, though not in contradiction with standard historical-materialist premises ... they are not fully illuminated by those premises, but require analysis in their own terms'. Not only is this account historically problematic, it again illustrates the untenable detachment of theory from history. The internationally constitutive character of capitalist development (producing the classic 'security dilemma' Brenner highlights) is merely *assumed* but in no way explained. Are conjunctures of war merely the object of history but not Marxist theory?

62 Hobsbawm 1987, pp. 316, 318.

63 Hobsbawm 1987, p. 323.

Uneven and Combined Development and the Origins of the First World War

Theory: Structure and Conjuncture

The above sections examined the most significant theoretical difficulties with existing (neo)Marxist explanations of the causes of the First World War. For these accounts, the problem of capturing the genuinely systemic nature of the crisis leading to the war whilst remaining sensitive to the socio-political differences among the actors involved proved the most difficult to resolve. Now we are confronted with the more difficult task of formulating an alternative, *positive* theorisation of the war's origins which addresses these issues. How might the theory of uneven and combined development contribute to this endeavour?[64] To answer this, we need to first detail exactly what requires explanation in order to judge whether this alternative perspective marks an advance upon existing approaches.

A satisfactory theory of the war's causes must fulfil, at a minimum, three criteria. It requires: first, an analysis of the central tendencies of the epoch setting and conditioning the international-domestic contexts leading to war; second, an account of how these structural tendencies related to and were articulated through different social formations in the immediate period leading to the war's outbreak; and, third, an elucidation of the structural specificities of the war juncture delimiting it from the broader epochal context of which it nonetheless formed a part. What is needed, in other words, is an explanation capturing the precise articulation of a universal crisis – itself emerging from the *general* structural tendencies of the era – with the *particularities* of the pre-war conjuncture differentiating it as a distinct, but in no sense autonomous, temporality.

This would address two important questions posed by the historian Gustav Schmidt in explaining why the July Crisis developed into a *world* war rather than remaining a localised or even European-wide conflict: that is, firstly, 'what is special about the conjunction of the July crisis, apart from the simple fact that an explosion was becoming more and more likely after a series of acts of brinkmanship?'; and, secondly, 'are the general explanations of the causes of the First World War satisfactory, if the structural elements of the crisis… did not result in the outbreak of war during any of the other Balkan crises'

64 See also Green 2012 and Rosenberg 2013, who provide accounts of the war's origins drawing on the theory of uneven and combined development and Tooze's contribution to this volume.

of 1908–13?[65] A satisfactory theorisation of the war would therefore need to account for why war did *not* break out under similar circumstances.

The concept of uneven and combined development, reworked as a theory of interstate conflict and war, can offer such a theorisation by capturing and explaining the differential forms of development (and state action) emerging from the internationally-mediated spread of industrial capitalism across the Long Nineteenth Century. It also provides an approach that is sensitive to the *interaction* of structural and conjunctural factors while avoiding the dual dilemmas of either a historically under-specified causality or a radically contingent historicism: that is, either subsuming the conjunctural phenomenon (in this case, war) under unmediated 'abstract' sociological laws or by treating it as a hermetically-sealed temporality constituted by contingently-determined, self-contained causes. In these ways, it can conceive the specificities of the conjuncture (1912–14) while nonetheless situating them within the broader context of epochal developments. So what are the main components of the theory of uneven and combined development?

At the most general level, the theory of uneven and combined development identifies three socio-international mechanisms of social interaction and development: the 'whip of external necessity' (the pressures generated by interstate competition), the 'privilege of historic backwardness' (the opportunities opened up to late-developing states to adopt the most advanced cutting-edge technologies from the leading states in the international system) and the 'contradictions of sociological amalgamation' (the time-compressed character of these developments, taking inorganic, spasmodic, and destabilising forms, and unhinging traditional social structures). Standing at the intersection of these mechanisms, we may then analyse the relations and alliances among state managers, politicians and specific segments of the capitalist class as they sought to mediate these social-international pressures into concrete strategies designed to preserve their domestic social standing and respond to the broader international and global context within which they were embedded.

From this general framework, we may then identify[66] three distinct but overlapping spatio-temporal vectors of unevenness whose progressive entwinement had increasingly significant consequences on the nature and course of European geopolitics over the Long Nineteenth Century feeding into both the general and proximate causes of the 1914–18 war. These three vectors of unevenness include: (1) a 'West-East' plane of unevenness capturing

65 Schmidt 1990, p. 97.

66 This formulation draws on Rosenberg 2008, pp. 25–6, albeit with a broader geographical scope.

the spatial-temporal ordering of industrialisations taking place across Europe and beyond over the 1789–1914 period; (2) a 'Transatlantic' vector representing the contradictory interlocking of the North American and European economies and the multiple cultural-linguistic, socio-economic and political links connecting the British Empire with its original white settler colonies; and (3) a 'North-South' constellation interlinking and differentiating the multi-ethnic empires from Central Eastern Europe to the Asia-Pacific into a dynamic of asymmetrical interdependency with the capitalist-industrial powers. For each vector, a specific pattern of interdependent and co-constitutive development can be identified – respectively, the variegated patterns of interconnected industrialisations; the emergence of a distinctive 'Anglo-Saxon' sphere; and the deepening international impediments to modern nation-state building resulting in partially 'blocked' forms of development. This gives each vector its own unique developmental inflection, permitting their demarcation as an *object of theorisation* rather than simply describing a series of arbitrary instantiations of socio-political differences.

The accumulation of socio-economic and (geo-)political contradictions emerging from these historical processes set the conditions leading to global conflagration in July 1914. The causal interlocking of the constellations of unevenness was the effect of the dramatic expansion of the world market and spread of capitalist relations over the course of the preceding century. 'If capitalist development and imperialism must bear responsibility' for the causes of war, then it was not so much a consequence of the limitless aims of capital accumulation,[67] as Hobsbawm suggests,[68] but rather the outcome of capitalism's transformation of the pre-existing conditions of unevenness, reconstituted upon firmly new socio-economic bases, into active causal determinations of 'combined' geopolitical and social development. The inherited anarchic structure of the international – forming part of the interactive nature of all socio-historical development – was in this sense both cause *and* effect of this capitalist transformation of the developmental process to which we now turn.

The Rise of Industrial Capitalism and Its 'Geo-Social' Consequences

The expansion of the world market and the accompanying industrialisation process over the course of the 1789–1914 period was largely a result of British development in all its *global-colonial* dimensions. That British capitalists could

67 In a different way, Adam Tooze in this volume also emphasises this 'terrifying aspect of capital accumulation' which had no 'natural limit' in explaining the origins of the July Crisis. See Tooze, 'Capitalist Peace or Capitalist War?', p. 93.

68 Hobsbawm 1987, p. 315.

develop international trade and production to such an unprecedented degree was the result of the preponderance of British military power, which benefited from the almost complete monopolisation of industrialisation it held for nearly half a century. Such were the 'privileges of priority' enjoyed by the early development of British capitalism.[69]

The unparalleled position of power Britain had attained by the early nineteenth century was, however, relatively fleeting. For the direct corollary of Britain's worldwide expansion of market relations, commodities, and foreign investments was that it enabled other states to acquire the means to industrialise their own economies in much more intensive concentrations of time than had the original purveyor. Later developing states no longer needed to start from scratch in their industrialisation drives, but could instead acquire and innovate upon the most advanced technologies and organisational forms pioneered by earlier developers.

Thus emerges the 'West-East' axis[70] of unevenness representing the classical Gerschenkronite sequencing of capitalist industrialisations: Britain (1780s), France (1830s), Germany (1850s), Russia (late 1880s), Japan (1890s), and Italy (late 1890s). This series of causally interwoven industrialisations was characterised by an interactive 'leapfrogging' process (Trotsky's 'skipping of stages' accrued by the 'privilege of historic backwardness') emanating from the 'whips of external necessity'. The effect was a succession of differentiated patterns of 'combined' social forms. The greater spatial and temporal distance travelled from the origin of industrial capitalism's inception, the more socio-political differences accumulated in an 'orderly system of graduated deviations'.[71]

The Prussian-German state held a distinctive position within this spatio-temporal sequencing of industrial revolutions. Unique among the European powers, it merged state-led, breakneck industrialisation and national state-formation into a single compressed 'stage' of development. Squeezed between the interval of earlier industrialisers such as Britain and France to the west and late-comers Russia and Japan to the east, German development was thus internationally pressurised in multiple directions at once.

This middling position of German industrialisation had significant geopolitical and sociological consequences for state development. To some extent, one might agree with David Calleo's suggestion that '[g]eography and history conspired to make Germany's rise late, rapid, vulnerable, and aggressive'.[72] The *Kaiserreich*'s belated arrival on the great power scene occurred after the world

69 See Trotsky 1973, Chapter 1.

70 Rosenberg 2008, p. 25.

71 Gerschenkron 1962, p. 44; cf. Weaver 1974; Trebilcock 1981.

72 Calleo 1978, p. 6.

was already partitioned among the great powers into colonies and informal spheres of influence. This made German expansionism appear particularly aggressive and prone to geopolitical counter-moves. A persistent disequilibrium thus emerged between Germany's spectacularly rising economic power and its relatively limited formal empire thereby fostering a simmering national sense of injustice and vague search for status recognition among policymakers and their conservative social bases, as demonstrated in Wilhelm's *Weltpolitik*. In these ways, the German experience represents a 'classical case of an *uneven and combined development*'.[73]

From the early nineteenth century, a pre-capitalist Prussian state was under severe international pressures (economic, ideological and military) emanating from industrial Britain and revolutionary France. This was exemplified by the 1848–9 revolution and near annihilation of Prussia at the battle of Jena.[74] Consequently, the monarchy embarked upon a series of agrarian reforms, institutionalising capitalist social relations in the countryside while strengthening the political hold of the aristocratic Junker class. It thereby left intact the essentially feudal-absolutist character of the Prussian state, but endowed it with a dynamically expansive economic structure. Having defeated Napoleonic France, Prussia was awarded the most economically developed and mineral-rich regions of Western Germany: the Rhine-Westphalia. This 'shifted the whole historical axis [of the] Prussian state' as it 'came to incorporate the natural heartland of German capitalism'.[75] Thereafter, the Junker class harnessed itself to the burgeoning industrial-capitalist forces of Western Germany. Imitating and borrowing technologies from abroad, the country also witnessed a dramatic acceleration of industrialisation granted by the 'privilege' of late development, itself *buttressed by* and *further strengthening* anti-liberal, authoritarian forms of political rule.[76]

This socio-economic 'dualism' of the Prussian-German state played itself out politically between the liberal bourgeoisie and conservative Junkers in the constitutional conflicts of the 1860s. Tendencies were, however, already laying the economic bases for their political rapprochement, eventuating in the *contradictory amalgam* of heavy industrial and Junker interests into a single hegemonic project (the famous 'marriage of iron and rye'). This provided the decisive socio-political foundation for Bismarck's 'revolution from above',

73 Anderson 1974, p. 234.

74 In addition to Anderson 1974, the following account of German development draws on Wehler 1985 and Blackbourn 2003.

75 Anderson 1974, pp. 272–3.

76 See Gerschenkron 1966; Gordon 1974; Wehler 1985; Berghahn 1993.

which sought to preserve the conservative-absolutist Prussian order while unifying the German nation under its hegemony. 'If revolution there is to be', Bismarck stated in 1866, 'let us rather undertake it than undergo it'.[77] This *political blueprint* for Germany's combined development came to dominate German politics and society, albeit in increasingly crisis-ridden ways, right down to the July Crisis.[78]

Bismarck's Constitution of 1871 encapsulated these conservative-authoritarian designs, maintaining the Monarchy while concentrating political power in an Imperial Chancellery that fused the offices of the Prussian Prime Minister and Minister of Foreign Affairs. Counting on overwhelmingly conservative support in the agrarian countryside to counter any creeping liberal reformism, Bismarck's strategy sought 'to overthrow parliamentarism ... by parliamentary means'.[79] Bismarck's constitutional hybrid of the 'most contemporary and archaic' made the Second Reich something of a political peculiarity in Europe. Though outwardly a trail-blazing model of progressive parliamentary democracy to be emulated throughout Europe, the federated governmental structure essentially devolved many of the old absolutist functions to the state level where reigning princely sovereignties were reconstituted on new foundations. At the same time, the Kaiser maintained exclusive prerogatives of war-making and the right to declare martial law in times of civil disorder. Reviewing this 'dual constitutional structure' of the new Empire, Seligmann and McLean note

> The Reich was declared to be a union of 25 separate states, with *sovereignty residing collectively in the state themselves*. As 22 of the states were monarchies, *this entrenched the idea of princely sovereignty into the very heart of the new nation* by avoiding a unitary structure and maintaining intact Germany's existing internal divisions, the constitution ensured that in practice a substantial proportion of government was conducted at the level of the sovereign federal states, whose existing constitutions were completely unaffected by the creation of the new Reich.[80]

German state sovereignty was thus internally differentiated, truncated and partially fragmented belaying any 'state qua state' assumption as found in both the classical Marxist and neo-realist IR theories. The *Kaiserreich* was defined by a *semi-parcelised* form of sovereignty fusing liberal-democratic and autocratic

77 Quoted in Gall 1986, vol. 1, p. 305.

78 See Fischer 1975; Geiss 1976; Eley 1980; Wehler 1985; Berghahn 1993.

79 Quoted in Wehler 1985, p. 53.

80 Seligmann and McLean 2000, p. 16, emphasis mine.

features in new and contradictory ways which, 'with its various disparate elements and conflicting authorities', made 'the political system of the Second Reich difficult to control'.[81]

The contradiction-ridden nature of German political order was clear from the start. Bismarck's state-sponsored programme of rapid industrialisation aimed at building a militarily powerful German state quickly undermined the socio-economic conditions upon which the *Kaiserreich* was founded. The conservative countryside, in which Bismarck laid his counter-parliamentary hopes, was drastically depleted during the 1890–1914 period. Massive urbanisation accompanied the explosive transformation of German society from a number of small, moderately 'backward' principalities into the most technologically advanced European capitalist state. A numerically diminished, but increasingly radicalised, conservative agrarian class thereby emerged in tandem with the precipitous rise of the largest, most well-organised and politically important working-class movement in the world.[82]

The sudden advent of the Social Democratic Party (SPD) and working-class radicalism developed into a significant challenge to the domestic status-quo, igniting near hysterical reactions within the ruling class – an ideologically inflected 'siege mentality'. In the December 1912 elections, the SPD gained over a third of the vote and 110 *Reichstag* seats. German Conservatives were mortified. As the conservative Chancellor Prince von Bülow (1900–9) would later report: 'Socialism, checked for six years in every part of the Empire ... was alive again' and 'constitut[ed] a serious menace to the future of the German nation'.[83] Consequently, imperialist agitation was increasingly used to ensure that bourgeois and conservative parties remain united against the 'socialist threat'. Yet, the reconstruction of the traditional *Sammlung* was moribund. Instead, between 1912 and 1914, the Reich had reached such a political deadlock 'that many Germans began to see war as a possible catalyst for stabilisation at home as well as abroad before time ran out'.[84]

Critical to explaining this cumulative process of socio-political destabilisation and corresponding *Weltpolitik*-orientation of German foreign policy was the severe economic dislocations resulting from the Long Depression of 1873–96. This was itself the consequence of the interconnected chain of industrialisations uniting the European and North American food economies (the 'Transatlantic vector') at a time when Continental European states were

81 Seligmann and McLean 2000, p. 20.

82 On the rise of the radical right see Eley 1980.

83 Bülow 1932, p. 85.

84 Beckett 2007, p. 26; see also Gordon 1974, pp. 198–9; Fischer 1975, pp. 230–6; Wehler 1985, pp. 192–233; Berghahn 1993, pp. 156–74.

abolishing protective tariffs between 1860 and 1877.[85] The Depression marked a crucial turning point in the restructuring of the rules of state reproduction within the world economy and states system, as it proved a key event undermining the fragile 'free trade' period of capitalist development. As Paul Bairoch has shown, the differential effects of the Depression on specific regions can be explained 'essentially in terms of the *different stages of economic development*' achieved by states at the time of their economic liberalisation. In other words, the differential effects of the Depression were rooted in the overall unevenness of the capitalist industrialisation process occurring in Europe and beyond. And again the Prussian-German state held a unique place in this interactively staggered process. For since Germany was the 'most liberal [commercially speaking] of the major European continental countries' at the onset of the Depression it was also the hardest hit.[86]

The Depression transformed the foundations of the Bismarckian order. Hitherto, free trade had formed the bedrock of the domestic coalition with the Liberals, providing outlets for the country's growing industries and commerce that Bismarck's laissez-faire policies fostered at home. As long as free trade prevailed, Germany could remain, in Bismarck's words, a 'satiated power'. But as Russian and American grain exports threatened German agriculture, the traditionally free-trade Junkers turned protectionist.[87] German industrialists in turn demanded the expansion of protected export markets and state contracts. The creation of a large-scale, modern navy satisfied these demands, cementing a strategic alliance between the German Admiralty and heavy industrialists. The protectionist cartel turn of the ruling industrial-Junker bloc resulting from the Depression was particularly significant as the agrarians threatened to veto naval expansionism unless the bourgeois parties repealed the reduced Caprivi tariffs of 1892.[88] There was, then, a direct link between Tirpitz's naval bills and increased agricultural protectionism, setting German expansionism on a 'collision course'[89] with Russia while increasingly antagonising British policymakers. This gave the heavy industrial-Junker bloc a new lease of life but at the cost of eventually destabilising the National Liberal Party, which increasingly divided between internationally-oriented light industries and conservative-protectionist heavy industries.[90]

85 Hobsbawm 1987, pp. 36–8; Bairoch 1989a, pp. 46–51.
86 Bairoch 1989a, pp. 48, 41.
87 Calleo 1978, pp. 13–15.
88 Berghahn 1993, pp. 39–40, 53–4.
89 Gordon 1974, p. 207.
90 See Eley 1980.

While the Junkers were committed to keeping out cheap Russian grain, industrialists sought to capture the Russian market. Yet, as Gordon notes, these 'two goals were irreconcilable, and the only way for the German government to try squaring them was by applying ever greater dosages of political pressure on Saint Petersburg'.[91] This was exemplified by the 1904 Russo-German commercial treaty, imposing severely disadvantageous terms on a temporarily weakened Tsarist regime, contributing to Russia's expansionist reorientation into the Balkans directly conflicting with Austro-Hungarian and German interests.

The (Geo)politics of German Combined Development: Towards 'Preventive War'

Returning to the specific *political* features of Germany's combined development, one of the major effects of the 1871 Constitution was the creation of a weakly centralised federal state unable to raise the adequate tax revenues from a Junker-dominated *Bundesstaat*. Since imperial budgets required parliamentary consent, Junker hegemony and the emerging power of the SPD in the *Reichstag*, meant increased armament expenditures came up against opposition from both sides of the political spectrum. Only by working with the SPD in 1913 was the liberal bourgeois fraction able to pass joint legislation on tax reforms and increased military expenditure. This acted to drive a wedge between the Bethmann Hollweg government and Conservatives, thereby further destabilising the already fragile political coalition but scarcely solving the structural dilemmas facing German public finances.[92]

While the Army Bill of 1913 constituted the largest increase in military manpower and expenditure in the history of the Reich, it fell far short of the 33 percent troop increase called for by the General Staff. Given the 1913 bill prompted similar spending measures by other European countries (most worryingly, Russia's 'Great Programme'), it only intensified anxieties within the military elite regarding their ability to raise the needed funds for further military increases, thus contributing to General Motlke and others' calls for a 'preventive war'.[93]

Indeed, German policymakers' continuing inability to meet dramatically rising tax revenues to finance the Reich's growing armaments was a major factor contributing to their decision to risk war 'sooner rather than later'. As Count

91 Gordon 1974, p. 206.

92 Heckart 1974, pp. 231–41; Ferguson 1994, pp. 158, 162–4.

93 Mombauer 2001, pp. 151–3.

Waldersee reported the opinions of Moltke and Conrad, the Austro-Hungarian Chief of the General Staff, in May 1914:

> They [Konrad and Moltke] were both agreed on the fact that at the moments things were still favourable for us [the Triple Alliance], that one should therefore not hesitate on a suitable occasion to proceed with vigour and, if necessary, to begin the war. With every passing year the chances were diminishing.[94]

State and military managers thus believed that by waiting a few years longer to launch a 'preventive war' against Russia, Germany would lose its competitive edge as the political deadlock over tax increases would continue. According to Ferguson, 'the domestically determined financial constraint on Germany's military capability was a – perhaps *the* – crucial factor in the calculations of the German General Staff in 1914'.[95] These factors combined with the abysmal showing of the political right in the 1912 elections, which reduced their parties to a mere 72 parliamentary seats, creating, as Geoff Eley puts it, 'the conditions for an extremely threatening radicalisation'.[96]

Further contributing to the decision for 'preventive war' was the unique socio-political physiognomy of the imperial army. As the mainstay of aristocratic power, the Prussian army offered the 'last bastion of the status-quo' fulfilling the 'dual function' of defending the monarchy against enemies from within and without.[97] Given the geographical position of Germany as a major land-power at the heart of continental Europe it would be expected, according to 'realist' logic, that military strategy would be tailored towards buttressing land armaments and manpower. However, until the army spending bills of 1912–13, the strategy pursued was exactly the opposite. As a percentage of gross national product (GNP), the 1890–1912 period saw naval armaments grow by leaps and bounds as army expenditures remained relatively stagnant.

94 Doc. 89, 31 May 1914, Waldersee to Kageneck in Mombauer 2013b, p. 137. Interestingly, it seems British policymakers were also aware of Germany's strategic dilemma, as Ambassador Buchanan wrote to Foreign Secretary Grey on 18 March 1914 that '[i]n the race for armaments Russia has more staying powers than Germany; and, as Germany is aware of that fact, *there is always the danger that she may be tempted to precipitate a conflict before Russia is fully prepared to meet it*' (Doc. 74 in Mombauer 2013b, p. 118, emphasis mine).

95 Ferguson 1999, p. 140.

96 Eley, 'Germany, the Fischer Controversy, and the Context of War', p. 44.

97 Berghahn 1993, pp. 26–8.

In fact, in terms of total defence expenditures as a percentage of net national product, German spending up until 1914 (that is, even after the army bills) consistently lagged behind France and Russia.[98] This was *despite* the identification of the growth of Russian power after 1908 as a clear and present danger to the European military balance of power as perceived by German military and civilian leaders. While obviously an exaggeration of the military situation, there was thus some truth to Moltke lamenting to Bethmann Hollweg that: 'Everyone prepares themselves for the big war that is widely expected sooner or later. Only Germany and her ally Austria do not participate in these preparations'.[99] The fear of a future Russian super-power was rife within German policymaking circles. Indeed, Wilhelm shared Chancellor Bethmann Hollweg's concerns regarding the extraordinary rise of Russian power, contemplating to his banker friend Max Warburg in June 1914 as to 'whether it would not be better to strike now [against Russia] than to wait'. More explicit, on 30 July 1914 the German diplomat Kanitz told the US ambassador to Turkey that 'Germany should go to war when they are prepared and not wait until Russia has completed her plan to have a peace footing of 2,400,000 men'.[100] What then explains Germany's seeming military unpreparedness for an eventual land war with Russia?

To explain the anomalies in the pace and direction of German armaments two interconnected factors need be taken into account. The first concerns the international economic interests of German capitalists, who favoured a larger navy for commercial purposes and generally supported the *Weltpolitik*-orientation of Admiral Tirpitz. The Naval Office worked closely with influential segments of the business community to these interrelated geopolitical and economic objectives.[101] At the same time, however, as a result of this rising power of the bourgeoisie within the German formation as a whole, army leaders sought to maintain the aristocratic constitution of the Prussian army.[102] There was then a second *class*-based factor arising from the specificities of Germany's combined development determining its military strategy.

---

98 See figures and tables in Ferguson 1994, pp. 148–55.

99 Doc 15, 2 December 1911, in Mombauer 2013b, p. 57.

100 Quotes in Seligmann and McLean 2000, p. 144. Original Kanitz quote can be found at <http://www.gomidas.org/gida/index_and_%20documents/MorgRecords_index_and_documents/docs/MorgenthauDiaries1914.pdf>. See further quotes by policymakers to this effect in Geiss 1967, pp. 65–8, Docs. 3, 4; Fischer 1975, pp. 172–4, 370–87; Berghahn 1993, pp. 164–7, 203; Ferguson 1994, pp. 144–5; Herrmann 1997, pp. 136–7, 213–15; Mombauer 2001, pp. 122, 145, 173–9, 189; and Copeland 2000, pp. 64, 69–70, 83–4.

101 See Berghahn 1993.

102 See Craig 1955; Förster 1999.

Fearing further contamination from the working and middle classes, from 1897 to 1912 the War Ministry repeatedly forewent any increases in manpower and expenditures as the navy was allowed to take priority. During this period, 'it was the leadership of the Army itself that had called a halt to expansion'.[103] Despite their efforts, however, the proportion of nobleman within the Prussian officer corps fell from 65 to 30 percent between 1865 and 1914. While aristocrats remained overrepresented in the army's highest ranks, by 1913 70 percent of the Great General Staff were 'commoners' by birth.[104]

In the debate over the army bills of 1912 and 1913, the peculiarly modern yet reactionary nature of the army's aristocratic *élan* came to the fore as General Heeringen's position against universal conscription and other institutional changes won out. Such reforms, he reasoned, would have jettisoned the army's 'permanent function as guarantor of domestic stability'. As General Wandel succinctly put it: 'If you continue with these armament demands, then you will drive the people to revolution'.[105] Revolution at that time was perhaps an overstatement. Those on the German right, including many military officials, tended to exaggerate the revolutionary threat of the SPD, viewing their victory in parliament in December 1912 elections as an ominous sign. They thus looked toward war as a possible means of reconstructing the domestic order in a conservative direction.[106] In response to their demands, Bethmann Hollweg actually thought a European conflict would instead promote the cause of social democracy. As he noted '[t]here are circles in the Reich who expect of a war an improvement in the domestic situation – in a Conservative direction'. By contrast Bethmann Hollweg thought that 'a World War with its incalculable consequences would strengthen tremendously the power of Social Democracy... and would topple many a throne'.[107] Bethmann Hollweg's prescient remarks went unheeded.

It was then the conflicts and threats to domestic stability coming from the political *right* – not the left, as often argued – that were the most immediate and pressing in 1914.[108] And if the launching of war in 1914 was not a direct means to avert revolution, the direction of German armaments nonetheless

103 Berghahn 1993, p. 16.
104 Stevenson 1996, p. 41; Craig 1955, pp. 232–8; Ferguson 1994, p. 155.
105 Quotes in Herwig 1994, pp. 263–4.
106 See quotes in Seligmann and McLean 2000, pp. 106–7.
107 Quoted in Geiss 1967, p. 47. A view shared by some Russian policymakers: see Doc. 72 in Mombauer 2013b, pp. 111–17.
108 See Seligmann and McLean 2000, pp. 105–7.

proved a vital *mediating link* between domestic and foreign policies.[109] As the worsening international environment after 1912 necessitated a substantial expansion of the army, risk of 'bourgeoisifying' the officer corps would, conservatives feared, inevitably sever the special bond between army and monarchy. 'All this raised doubts' within ruling circles 'as to their ability to overcome the growing military and strategic problems without resorting very soon to the extreme solution of a major war'.[110]

After the 1912 elections and subsequent fiscal crisis, German society had turned into a pressure-cooker. The political consequences growing out of these 'contradictions of sociological amalgamation' were taking their toll. As Berghahn puts it,

> By 1913/14 the German political system, under the impact of social, economic and cultural change, had reached an impasse. The modernity and richness of the country's organizational and cultural life notwithstanding and, indeed, perhaps because of it, in the end Wilhelmine politics was marked by bloc-formation and paralysis at home and abroad and finally by a *Flucht nach vorn* (flight forward) on the part of the political leadership that was fast losing control, but still had enough constitutional powers to take the step into major war.[111]

Even if the immediate decision for war in 1914 was not *directly* taken to avert the multiple domestic crises facing the German government, as some historians still hold,[112] it was no doubt a decisive factor setting the conditions under which German policymakers made the decision for war.[113]

In sum, the German state emerging from Bismarck's 1871 imperial constitution formed a contradictory amalgam of autocratic and representative institutions and principles – a 'combination of modern capitalism and medieval barbarism', as Trotsky characteristically called it.[114] These socio-political relations expressed the internationally pressurised and temporally condensed nature of the Empire's simultaneous traversal into an industrial-capitalist and modern national-state formation. German development thus drastically 'diverged' from those earlier roads to capitalist modernity set out by Britain

109 Stevenson 1996.
110 Mommsen 1981, pp. 29–30.
111 Berghahn 1993, p. 9.
112 For example, Hildebrand 1989 and Stürmer 1990.
113 As Eley also points out in his contribution.
114 Trotsky 1945, p. 79.

and France. Yet the alleged *Sonderweg* of German development may only be considered 'deviant' from a static comparative perspective; one abstracting from the spatio-temporally variegated but interactive history of capitalist development and thereby subsuming Germany's trajectory under an implicit unilinear stagism.[115] Accordingly, the German experience (authoritarian, illiberal and militaristic) is conceived as a *pathological anachronism* within the history of capitalism. Such an approach lacks appreciation of the ways in which the sequencing of capitalist transitions were central to the form subsequent 'bourgeois' revolutions took.

The putative 'peculiarities' of German development must be therefore conceived as one among many different forms of uneven and combined development characteristic of the *international conjuncture as a whole*. The destabilising effects of Germany's 'modernisation' were less a result of its incomplete or arrested character than a consequence of its *over-stimulation* from both within and without. This was an intensified 'combination of the basic features of the world process'; 'a social amalgam combining the local and general conditions of capitalism'[116] resulting from the particular spatio-temporal site of Germany's development within the interactive matrix of capitalist industrialisations.

As we have seen, the particular location of the German state within the interactively staggered (that is to say, uneven) process of capitalist industrialisation sweeping over Europe during the Long Nineteenth Century was crucial to the domestic contradictions besetting the German polity, the form of imperial expansionism it pursued and thus the origins of the First World War. The time-space relations of this industrialisation process also effected decisive strategic-military realignments as exemplified by the rapprochement between Republican France and autocratic Russia. That this long-held rivalry would be settled in the form of an alliance with Britain against Germany was all but unthinkable to most contemporaries.[117] Here, the exorbitant role of foreign finance in Russia's feverish industrialisation presents a particularly revealing illustration of the tight interrelations between the sequencing of industrialisations and alliance formations.

Like other late developers, Russia was starved of the massive resources required for an intensive state-led industrialisation centred on the militarily

---

115 See Blackbourn and Eley 1984.

116 Trotsky 1962, p. 23; 1969, p. 56.

117 But note the prescient remarks by Marx at the time of the Franco-Prussian conflict: 'If *Alsace* and *Lorraine* are taken, then *France* will later make war on *Germany in conjunction with Russia*'. Quoted in Joll and Martel 2007, p. 56.

crucial railway systems. Initially, German foreign loans satisfied Russia's money demands.[118] But as Germany's own accelerated industrialisation got under way, domestic resources became strained. No matter how much the *Wilhelmstraße* wanted to buttress its diplomacy by financial means, permanent shortages of financial capital thwarted such endeavours.[119] Thus, Russian state and business managers looked elsewhere. Fortunately for French policymakers – who were by this point anxiously searching for a reliable ally to counter German expansionism – Paris money markets had the capital 'surpluses' to spare. For a significant consequence of France's earlier, more gradual industrialisation was a higher rate of domestic savings.[120] Whatever other factors contributed to the formation of the Franco-Russian alliance, the staggered, interactive sequencing of their respective industrialisations proved crucial.[121]

Collapsing Empires and Rising Nationalisms: The 'Peripheral' Origins of 1914

The twin forces of modernity – nationalism and imperialism – form two sides of the same uneven and combined process of capitalist development. By the early twentieth century, the structured inequality of the world economy emerging from the uneven development between states proved a major source of friction among the great powers, a generative condition and rallying point of nationalist bourgeois forces budding within societies, and a means through which the developed capitalist metropoles enforced – individually or in competitive collaboration – their domination over the 'periphery'. The grafting of capitalist relations onto the social structures of the 'backward' countries and rapidly industrialising powers resulted in contradictory hybrids of different social systems, simultaneously unleashing centrifugal and centripetal tendencies uncoupling collective identities from their local and regional contexts and reconstituting them on national foundations. The interlacing dynamics of imperialism and revolutionary nationalism thus formed the basis of empire-building and reconstruction, as well as laying the conditions for their ultimate destruction. Two cases of the latter process of empire disintegration – Austro-Hungary and the Ottoman Empire – are particularly relevant to the discussion here, as their steady decline set the overall conditions leading to world conflict in 1914.

118 Geyer 1987, pp. 150–1; Trebilcock 1981, pp. 224–7.

119 Fischer 1975.

120 McGraw 1983, pp. 243–5; see Trebilcock 1981.

121 Rosenberg 2008, p. 25.

The 'North–South' vector of unevenness, as Rosenberg terms it,[122] interconnects the ancient multinational empires whose relative power was being progressively undermined by this overall process of capitalist industrialisation and nationalist effervescence. While the multinational formations of the Dual Monarchy and Ottoman Empire (like Dynastic China) were far from stagnant in the decades before the war, the *relative* disparities between these states and the western European powers were drastically increasing. The effects of this intersection of the West–East and North–South vectors were largely manifested through the series of wars, treaties, revolutions and diplomatic crises witnessed during the period following the start of the German wars of national unification and ending before the First Balkan War. This chain of causally interlinked events configured – and *re*configured – the patterns of military-strategic alliances that eventually went to war in 1914. It also fixed the geographical zone where any future world war would likely be ignited.

The emergence of the 'Eastern Question' from the late eighteenth century onwards constituted a particularly explosive element within European geopolitics as the advancing capitalist states struggled to come to grips with the myriad consequences of Ottoman decline first made plain by the Russo-Turkish War of 1768–74. The clichéd 'sick man' of Europe, like the later Dual Monarchy, was propped up by the great powers throughout the nineteenth century with the aim of maintaining the European military balance of power. If either empire fell, policymakers calculated, a geopolitical vacuum would emerge generating imperialist land grabs in the heart of the European landmass and strategically vital commercial sea-lanes in the Eastern Mediterranean. The result would be a massive rearrangement of the distribution of power, leaving Germany without its only reliable ally (Austria-Hungary), and opening the way for the swift application of Russian power in the Balkans and Straits – two prized areas long sought after by the Tsarist regime. It was precisely such a situation that the European powers (particularly Britain and Germany) long sought to avoid.[123]

The artificially prolonged decline of Ottoman power, interspersed with periods of internal renewal, was intrinsically connected to the phenomenal expansion of the world market and corresponding growth of European military strength. Throughout the nineteenth century, the Sublime Porte sought desperately to reform its internal structures to meet the threats posed by European states seeking to pry open Ottoman markets. The ability of the British and French empires to eventually impose a series of highly disadvantageous 'free trade' treaties on the Porte in the mid-nineteenth century was the result of an

122 Rosenberg 2008, p. 27.

123 Anderson 1966.

increasing military superiority deriving from the immense productive advantages emerging from their capitalist bases.[124] By contrast, Ottoman attempts to regularise administration and revenue clashed with the tax-farming and tribute-taking structures on which the Empire had hitherto relied.[125]

Unable to catch up and overtake the advanced industrialising states, the Ottoman formation suffered from a partially 'blocked development'. Escaping formal colonisation by the imperialist metropoles, the slowly crumbling Empire eventually fractured into a multiplicity of foreign-ruled and semi-autonomous areas, providing the opportunity for the Western powers to siphon off parts of Ottoman lands, while creating the conditions through which the 'Young Turks' seized power in 1908. The contrasting regional developments between an economically dynamic industrial-capitalism emerging in northwestern Europe (part of the 'West–East' vector) and the relatively stagnant tributary structures of the Porte ('North–South') was thus not only socio-economically uneven but geopolitically 'combined'.[126]

In addition, Ottoman development *sociologically* combined different 'stages' within the anterior structures of the Porte itself, as the interventions and pressures of capitalist states in the Middle East resulted in the superimposition of capitalist social relations onto the tributary structures of the Empire.[127] The Young Turks' aspiration to 'turn the foe into tutor' resulting from this process in turn fed back into the international political crises leading to World War I as the 'new regime in Istanbul, espousing a more assertive Turkish nationalism, became embroiled in the Balkan war, the direct prelude to August 1914'.[128] Trapped within the wider maelstrom of Eastern Mediterranean unevenness, the Ottoman formation, transformed through the geo-social ripple of capitalist industrialisation, thereby came to react back upon the international system in causally significant ways.

Further, the *timing* of the Empire's collapse was itself tied to changes in the international system, particularly the rise of German power and Britain's strategic readjustment away from the Ottoman Empire and towards Russia as a potential ally. There was then a specifically geopolitical component to the changing fortunes of the Ottoman Empire at the turn of the twentieth century, as demonstrated in the interconnected development of declining British sup-

---

124 Kasaba 1988, pp. 55–6.

125 Bromley 1994, pp. 50–1.

126 Bromley 1994, p. 61.

127 On the particular dynamics of this 'tributary-capitalist amalgam', see Nişancioğlu 2013, Chapter 6.

128 Halliday 1999, p. 197.

port for and increasing German influence in the Ottoman Empire. According to Kerem Nişancioğlu:

> As imperial competition between Germany and Britain grew (both within and without the Ottoman Empire), new strategic alignments emerged between former foes – Britain, France, and Russia – in order to balance against Germany. In this context, Britain's desire to maintain the Ottoman Empire came into conflict with its desire to appease its new allies ... Increasingly isolated internationally, the Ottoman Empire became exposed to latent internal and external pressures that had been building since the onset of the *Tanzimat*, and a period of massive territorial fragmentation ensued.[129]

This then set the stage for the inter-imperial scramble for previously Ottoman occupied lands, thereby setting the spatial coordinates for the 1914 'spark'. To fully understand these dynamics turning the Balkans into the 'powder keg' of Europe, attention must be turned to the two other great multinational Empires active in the region: Austria-Hungary and Russia.

The Making and Unmaking of the Dual Monarchy

A major outcome of the Austro-Prussian War was the *Ausgleich* [Compromise] of 1867 establishing the Dual Monarchy of Austria-Hungary. The *Ausgleich* was of decisive significance to the future direction of European geopolitics in central and southeastern Europe, particularly by institutionalising Prussian-Magyar hegemony within the Monarchy. This not only buttressed stronger economic-political relations with Germany, helping nurture the Dual Alliance of 1879, but also readjusted the Monarchy's policy towards the Balkans.

The ascendancy of Magyar power was symbiotically conditioned by the steady withdrawal of the Ottoman Empire from Europe, gradually enhancing the aggressiveness of the Hungarian landowning nobility. Extending their territorial possessions eastward, the class's overall economic importance grew in central and eastern Europe. Simultaneously, as the Habsburg Monarchy stumbled from one foreign disaster to another, its internal relations became ever more strained. Consequently, the dynasty was 'driven, logically and irresistibly, towards its hereditary foe' (the Hungarian aristocracy) which now became the only class capable of propping up the Empire's authority. The *Ausgleich* of 1867 formalised this tendency towards Magyar hegemony, shifting the 'geopolitical

129 Nişancioğlu 2013, pp. 207–8.

and economic axis of the Monarchy irrevocably ... eastward'.[130] Through these antecedent processes of interaction, the newly reconstituted Habsburg Empire was subjected to a novel set of pressures and influences, emerging from its deepening interaction in the uneven development of the Balkan region.

The crucial diplomatic event here was the Congress of Berlin in 1878, signalling the decisive retreat of Ottoman domination in the Balkans with the occupation of Bosnia and Herzegovina. Though officially remaining an Ottoman possession, the provinces inhabited by Croatian, Serbian and Muslim populations were now administrated by the Dual Monarchy. With this move, the Habsburgs thereby *internalised the powder magazines of the Balkans into the foundations of its own 'heteroclite' socio-political edifices*.[131] Austria-Hungary's incorporation of Bosnia and Herzegovina, its annexation 30 years later and the assassination of the Archduke at Sarajevo 'though separated by decades are inextricably linked'.[132] A further consequence of the Habsburg's eastward drive was the conclusion of the Dual Alliance of 1879 which undoubtedly contributed to closer Franco-Russian relations. Originally conceived as a defensive strategy by Bismarck, over time the Alliance turned into yet another factor destabilising international order.[133]

The exacerbation of tensions in central and eastern Europe was a consequence of the particularities of the Monarchy's combined development. Unlike Germany, the Habsburgs never achieved the twofold transformation into a fully capitalist and nationally-unified modern state. The political dualism of the new Monarchy was accompanied by a glaring economic asymmetry between the Austrian and Hungarian halves. Indeed, by the early twentieth century, internal regional economic disparities had actually increased. The sprawling Empire boasted the most modern industrial cities of the era, such as Vienna, Prague and Budapest, and contained highly industrialised regions in the Alpine and Bohemian lands. This contrasted starkly with the immense tracts of economically 'primitive', semi-feudal agrarian relations in the eastern and southeastern lands.[134] Formed at the interstices of the West–East and North–South vectors of unevenness, Austro-Hungarian development thus took on a unique hybridity of 'Western' and 'Eastern' forms. The Empire's 'heteroclite structures' expressed 'the composite nature of the territories over which it presided, and which it was never able in any lasting fashion to compress into

130 Anderson 1974, p. 325.
131 Anderson 1974, p. 299.
132 Williamson 1991, p. 59.
133 Joll and Martel 2007, pp. 54–5; Mulligan 2010, pp. 27–9.
134 See Good 1986.

a single political framework'. As the Magyar aristocracy was the chief obstacle to either a federal or unified royal state solution, the *Ausgleich* failed to resolve the nationalities problem. Instead, increasing the power of the most 'combative and feudal nobility left in Central Europe' only further aggravated the Monarchy's relations with the southern Slavs and Romanians.[135] Magyar hegemony was the 'grave-digger of the Monarchy' as witnessed by the Hungarian nobility's bellicose policy of Magyarisation which, according to R.W. Seton-Watson, 'led directly' to World War I.[136]

Perhaps more than in any other country of the pre-war era, the foreign policy of the Dual Monarchy was a function of the intractability of these internal problems. Since Magyar influence blocked all reforms aimed at quelling nationalist discontent, Vienna became convinced that controlling the Serbian 'Piedmont' was fundamental to state survival. The Monarchy thus became the 'one power which could not but stake its existence on the military gamble [of 1914] because it seemed doomed without it'.[137] Indeed, Austrian policymakers were all too aware of the continuing unmanageability of the Empire's internal problems and the need to show decisive resolve in the international arena lest the Monarchy's legitimacy be further challenged. Thus, shortly after Archduke Ferdinand's assassination in Sarajevo (28 June 1914), a 6 July memorandum by Berthold Molden noted that

> ... everywhere one finds doubts about the future of the monarchy, which is torn by conflicts internally and which is no longer respected by even her smallest neighbours ... it has long been the opinion that, in order to erase the impression of decline and disintegration, a striking deed, a punch of the fist would be necessary.[138]

Similarly, Leopold Baron von Andrian-Werburg, retrospectively commenting on Austria having started the war, stated his 'lively agreement with the basic idea that only a war could save Austria'.[139] It was with these domestic concerns in mind, along with the rising geopolitical threat of Russian power, that

135 Anderson 1974, pp. 299, 325.
136 Seton-Watson 1914, p. 109.
137 Hobsbawm 1987, p. 323.
138 Doc. 126 in Mombauer 2013b, p. 199. For similar themes of reversing the 'disintegration' of the Empire and 'loss of prestige' if Austria did not decisively eliminate the Serbian threat once and for all see Doc. 134: 'The Minutes of the Joint Council of Ministers for Common Affairs' (7 July 1914), in Mombauer 2013b, pp. 210–17.
139 Quoted in Mombauer 2013b, pp. 156–7.

Austrian policymakers were so receptive to Conrad, Moltke and others' persistent calls for a 'preventive war' sooner rather than later in the July Crisis. As Count Forgách reported to Tisza on 6 July 1914:

> Kaiser Wilhelm had it reported to Majesty that we could rely on the full support of Germany in a potential action. According to Kaiser Wilhelm's opinion we should now not wait any longer with an action against Serbia. We should not let this present favourable moment remain unused. Russia was today not ready for war and Germany stood on our side as a faithful ally.[140]

Indeed, since the Annexation crisis of 1908–9, cracks had also begun to surface in the international consensus propping up the Monarchy as subject nationalists began to look for foreign support (particularly Russian) for their claims to national autonomy. By that time, the constitutional dualism established by the *Ausgleich* was taking its toll on the Monarchy's ability to maintain itself as a formative military power.

Since the constitution of the Dual Monarchy mandated that parliament sanction most legislation, the only way the government could bypass the assembly was to pass legislation by decree. This made the Empire's common army a key institutional arena of factional disputes through which the Magyar minority could assert their independence from Vienna. Under these conditions, 'the army functioned as a barometer of separatist pressures in general'.[141] As Franz Josef was unwilling to risk making any move that could be interpreted as a *coup d'etat* by Vienna, domestic conflicts 'practically paralyzed' the Monarchy's military expansion until the Second Moroccan Crisis of 1911 finally galvanised the government into rapid rearmament. Yet, by that time it was too late. The military balance had already decisively tilted against the Dual Alliance in favour of the Franco-Russian Entente – though Austrian and German policymakers' still thought time was on their side.[142]

Between Revolution and War: Russian Imperialism and the European Balance of Power

The emergence of the 'Great Divergence' over the Long Nineteenth Century, signalling the formation of mutually constitutive 'core' and 'peripheral' regions of the rising capitalist world economy, witnessed a massive competitive gulf opening up between the ancient Chinese and Indian empires and a handful of

---

140 Doc. 131 in Mombauer 2013b, p. 208.

141 Herrmann 1997, p. 33.

142 Herrmann 1997, pp. 33–4, 173–4; Joll and Martel 2007, pp. 152–3.

rapidly industrialising 'Western' capitalist states. Though more geographically peripheral to European geopolitics, the slowly collapsing power of the Qing Dynasty in China, as well as the already colonised Indian landmass, were no less important in restructuring the direction and dynamics of inter-imperial rivalries. The Chinese Empire in particular formed the geo-strategic 'heartland' of the Asian-Pacific region, drawing the imperialist powers into a maelstrom of social upheaval with promises of its immense export-market potentials and investment opportunities. The orderly, managed decline of Imperial China was of profound importance to the capitalist metropoles.[143]

The effects of the power vacuum created by the deterioration of Qing rule was most consequential for Russian development, resulting in the unhinging of Europe's relative equilibrium of forces precipitating the continent's descent to war. As long as the crumbling Chinese Empire deflected Russian economic expansionism into Manchuria – Witte's policy of *pénétration pacifique* – it acted to at least partly alleviate European rivalries in the Balkans and Ottoman Empire. This relieved tensions between Austria-Hungary and Russia as demonstrated in their entente of 1897 pledging to secure the status quo in the Balkans. More generally, the 'Chinese Question' offered a momentary means of great power cooperation, as exemplified by the 'ultra-imperialist' experiments of the 'Open Door' and suppression of the Boxer Rebellion.[144]

At the same time, by drawing Russia into conflict with Japan over Manchuria, eventuating in the Tsarist regime's humiliating defeat and the revolution of 1905–7, the disintegrating Qing Dynasty effected a dramatic reconfiguration of the European strategic balance. As David Herrmann notes, the 'history of the balance of military power in Europe in the decade between 1904 and the outbreak of World War I was in large measure the story of Russia's prostration, its subsequent recovery, and the effects of this development upon the strategic situation'.[145] The 'geo-social' conflicts formed at the triangular intersection of the differentiated development of the Chinese, Russian and Japanese empires fundamentally augmented the geopolitical axis of European order. This Asia-Pacific 'periphery' of the North–South vector constitutes an important, if overlooked, factor unsettling the international system in the immediate pre-war years.

Here again we witness the immense significance of 'internal' factors (the 1905–7 revolutionary upheaval) having 'external' (geopolitical) consequences. Reframed from the perspective of Russia's uneven and combined development, the interrelations between the two spheres – the sociological (domestic) and

143 Mulligan 2010, p. 43.

144 Mulligan 2010, pp. 43–5.

145 Hermann 1997, p. 7.

geopolitical (international) – takes on new light. Rather than two discretely conceived 'levels of analysis' subsequently interacting with each other, one can begin to visualise their interconnectedness as a single theorisable whole. Here we may retrace just one thread of this multifaceted picture.

Under the 'external whip' of Russia's near constant contact with the more economically and militarily advanced Western powers, the Tsarist state was compelled to internalise the ready-made technologies, weapons and ideologies from 'the West' in the process of adapting them to its own 'less developed' social structure. Reaping the 'privilege of backwardness' Russia thereby came to make tiger-leaps in its own development, 'skipping a whole series of intermediate stages' leading to a 'peculiar combination' in the historic process. As with the stream of French money capital into Russia railways and armaments industries, the result was 'an amalgam of archaic with more contemporary forms': 'The most colossal state apparatus in the world making use of every achievement of modern technological progress in order to retard the historical progress of its own country'.[146] Indeed, the infusion of European armaments and finance was a severely contradictory process, simultaneously strengthening Tsarism whilst undermining its socio-economic and political foundations.

The 'combined' Russian social formation was characterised by islands of the most advanced capitalist relations and productive techniques enmeshed within a sea of feudal relations in potentially socially and geopolitically explosive ways: mass concentrations of cutting-edge technologies (particularly within the state-run military industries) imported from Western Europe, and a rapidly growing and ideologically radicalised proletarianised peasantry ('snatched from the plough and hurled into the factory furnace') existing alongside an unreformed absolutist monarchy and a dominant landowning aristocracy. Externally pressurised, time-compressed, and stage-skipping, Russia's development was 'no longer gradual and "organic" but assume[d] the form of terrible convulsions and drastic changes ...'[147] The result: the rapid rise of a highly class-conscious proletariat, joining together with a majority peasant class, capable of temporarily destabilising and nearly overthrowing Tsarist power in the midst of a war-induced domestic crisis. Such were the geopolitically 'overdetermined' sociological conditions leading to the war-revolution crisis of 1904–5 which, in turn, fed back into the structure of the international system.[148]

---

146 Trotsky 1969, p. 53.

147 Trotsky 1972b, p. 199.

148 For an excellent analysis of contemporary Marxists' views of the 1905 revolutionary crisis in Russia, and the changes this provoked in their conceptions of socialist revolution, see

Indeed, the disastrous defeat of Russia in the 1904–5 war signalled a collapse of its military clout resulting in an 'unstable equilibrium' in European land armaments from 1905 to 1908. The impotence of Tsarist power after 1905 was recognised within the policymaking circles of all the European great powers. Nowhere was this more clearly revealed than in Berlin and Vienna, which embarked upon a more assertive policy course in the Balkans. Russia's military weakness was, however, quickly followed by an extraordinarily rapid recovery of its industrial-military capacities. Russia's rearmament drive was largely catalysed by the regime's humiliation in the face of Habsburg intransigence during the Bosnian Annexation Crisis, itself set off by the Young Turk Rebellion of 1908. This marked a point of no return in Austro-Hungary's relations with Serbia and Russia. Unlike previous Austro-Hungarian aggressions in the Balkans, this time they were backed by German threats of war. Thus the 'unstable equilibrium' quickly collapsed as the newly accelerated arms race opened up a new phase of unease within Europe.[149]

The war-revolution crises of 1904–7 were also an important factor in the evolution of Russian–German rivalry. On the Russian side, the military defeat of 1905 marked a decisive *westward reorientation* in Russian foreign policy. Policymakers now sought to avoid further antagonising Japan over Manchuria and traditional British colonial interests in Persia, Afghanistan and India.[150] The new liberal-leaning Foreign Minister, Aleksandr Izvol'skii, was determined to resolve outstanding quarrels with them in the Far East and Inner Asia. This led to the conclusion of the 1907 Anglo-Russian agreement recognising their respective spheres of influence in Persia and similar agreements with Japan in July 1907 and 1910 that did much the same in the Pacific. Russian foreign policy now focused westward to the more 'traditional' focal points of Tsarist imperialism: gaining control over the economically vital Straits and securing influence in the Balkans.[151] By the early twentieth century, 37 percent of all Russian exports and over 90 percent of its critical grain exports travelled through the Straits at Constantinople. With Ottoman collapse looming, Russian

Davidson's chapter in this volume. As Davidson well demonstrates, Trotsky was the only Marxist among his contemporaries who envisioned the possibility of Russia's 'permanent revolution' entailing a *socialist* revolution rather than remaining within the bourgeois 'stage'. And it was precisely Trotsky's recognition of the internationally-constituted nature of Russia's combined social formation that provided the theoretical foundations for such a revolutionary conception.

149 Stevenson 2007, pp. 133–4; cf. Geyer 1987, pp. 255–72; Herrmann 1997, pp. 113–46.

150 Geyer 1987; McDonald 1992.

151 Geyer 1987.

policymakers became intensely worried that a rival power might come to dominate the Straits, thereby controlling this 'windpipe of the Russian economy'.[152] On the German side, state managers sought to exploit the opportunity of a momentarily prostrate Russian power bogged down in war and revolution by, first, pushing through the Commercial Treaty of July 1904 and, second, pressing economic claims in Central Africa. The latter sparked off the First Morocco Crisis of 1905. While designed by German policymakers to break up the *entente cordiale*, this event ended up only strengthening the Franco-Russian alliance while laying the first 'bridge between the Anglo-French Entente and Russia'.[153]

The nexus of relations between these three events – the 1904–5 war, the Russian Revolution of 1905–7 and First Moroccan Crisis of 1905 – also had a number of crucial long-term effects on German military strategy. First, it resulted in the General Staffs drawing up the infamous Schlieffen Plan for a two-front war against France and Russia. This proposed the concentration of superior German forces in the west in a knock-out campaign against the French, before turning to confront Russia in the east. The plan was based on calculations of Russia's *current* military-industrial power then in a condition of acute weakness. With the rapid recovery of Russian military capabilities and its completion of the western railway lines, however, the Schlieffen Plan's days were numbered – particularly after the 'Great Programme' announced in 1913.[154]

German strategists now calculated that the 'window of opportunity' to launch a successful two-front war would close *no later than 1916–17* thus setting the temporal coordinates for any future 'preventive war'. This incited growing demands within German military circles for the launching of a 'preventive war' before Germany's strategic advantage was overtaken. Such arguments were part of a broader consensus forming within Berlin and Vienna policymaking circles since 1912 that the military balance would soon swing against them. The time to increase armaments with the aim to strike was fast approaching.[155] In March 1914, the younger Moltke explained to Foreign Secretary Jagow that a war *had* to come soon or everything would be lost. As Jagow reported the conversation:

> Russia will have completed her armaments in 2 to 3 years ... In his view there was no alternative to waging a preventive war in order to defeat the enemy as long as we could still more or less pass the test. The chief

152 Stone 2007, p. 13.

153 Fischer 1975, p. 57; see Lieven 1983, pp. 29–31.

154 Herrmann 1997; Stevenson 1996.

155 See Copeland 2000; Herrmann 1997; Stevenson 1996.

> of the General Staff left it at my discretion to gear our policy to an early unleashing of a war.[156]

The tightly knit Schlieffen Plan was enticement for the General Staff to demand war before the circle of largely self-made enemies could arm in time to render it unviable. Despite the General Staff's continuing hopes, the plan was in fact already inoperable.

Since the First Moroccan Crisis, a *three-front* war had become increasingly likely as the debacle drove British policymakers further into the Franco-Russian camp, as revealed by the signing of the Anglo-Russian agreement of 1907. Already before German provocations at Tangiers, conditions had emerged for an eventual Anglo-Russian détente. Specifically, the Russian defeat of 1905 diminished St. Petersburg's ambitions in Central Asia, lessening the threat posed to British colonial interests in the region. The 1904–7 war-revolution imbroglios also reduced London's fears of Russian power providing 'the essential backdrop' to the Anglo-Russian agreement of 1907.[157] Though the issue of British participation in a future war on the side of France became a predominating question within German policymaking circles from then onwards, the Schlieffen Plan – as later altered by the younger Moltke – circumvented any chance of assuring British neutrality as it called for a first-strike offensive against France through Belgium.[158] Likewise, the 1905–7 Russian Revolution had crucial international socio-political effects: reverberating serially across the 'West–East' and 'North–South' planes, it causally interconnected with and hastened structurally analogous developmental dynamics within the different polities thrown up by the same international pressures of capitalist development. Of 'all the eruptions in the vast social earthquake zone of the globe', Hobsbawm writes, the 1905–7 Revolution had 'the greatest international repercussions'. For it 'almost certainly precipitated the Persian and Turkish revolutions, it probably accelerated the Chinese, and, by stimulating the Austrian emperor to introduce universal suffrage, it transformed, and made even more unstable, the troubled politics of the Habsburg Empire'.[159] Additionally, the 'knock-on' effects of the Russian Revolution fed into the series of crises in the Balkans immediately preceding the July–August 1914 diplomatic crisis.

---

156 Quoted in Berghahn 1993, pp. 181–2. Similarly, Moltke was reported to have expressed his desire that '[i]f only it [war] would finally boil over – we are ready and the sooner the better for us'. Doc. 93, 1 June 1914, in Mombauer 2013b, p. 116.

157 Lieven 1983, p. 31.

158 Gordon 1974.

159 Hobsbawm 1987, p. 300.

From Agadir to Sarajevo: Into the Conjunctural Abyss

At this point of the investigation, the moment is reached where deep structures and world-historical phenomena appear to recede into the background noise of the frenzied chaos and overwhelming detail of the diplomatic juncture. This is the realm of 'radical contingencies', where even the greatest of historically minded theorists proclaim 'cock-up, foul up' as a main cause of World War I.[160] Yet in the rush to eschew all modes of monocausal explanation – if not 'grand theory' altogether – scholars simply relinquish the task of theorising the socio-historical process as a single whole in all its richness and complexity. The following attempts to sketch how the framework developed above applies to examining the chain of events leading to the July Crisis. In so doing, it analyses the form of geopolitics as it appeared 'on the surface of society' in 'the ordinary consciousness' of the decision-making agents themselves.[161]

In any investigation of the pre-war juncture, the Second Moroccan Crisis (June–November 1911) plays a critical role. The crisis signifies the decisive *caesura* in the international relations of the pre-war period. What were its proximate causes? Why did it *not* result in a world war in 1911? And how did it nonetheless set off the chain of events leading to world war in July 1914?

The immediate background to the Moroccan Crisis was French colonialists' use of an indigenous revolt as the pretext for military intervention aimed at further expanding French economic interests in North Africa. The German Foreign Ministry in turn sought to score a diplomatic success against France with a view to weakening Germany's external enemies while strengthening the tottering ruling bloc against the SPD challenge in the forthcoming 1912 elections. In the short term, the diplomatic move had its intended effect. The '*Pather's* leap in Agadir' inspired a groundswell of domestic popular support, particularly among the conservative establishment.[162] But, its eventual failure was met by an outburst of nationalist fury further destabilising the heavy industrial-Junker bloc. Among the radical-nationalist right, the episode strengthened calls for launching a preventive war as a means to domestic unity – 'War as the only cure for our people'.[163] General Moltke in fact shared similar sentiments as he saw the Moroccan Crisis as a propitious opportunity to launch his cherished 'preventive war'. As he told his wife on 19 August 1911: 'If we once again emerge from this affair with our tail between our legs, if we cannot bring ourselves to make energetic demands which we would be ready

160 Mann 1993, pp. 740–802, esp. pp. 744–6, 766, 798.

161 Marx 1981, p. 117.

162 Fischer 1975, pp. 71–5.

163 Quoted in Eley 1980, p. 323; cf. Berghahn 1993; Mommsen 1981; Eley this volume.

to force through with the help of the sword, then I despair of the future of the German Reich'.[164]

At the same time, economic interests clamoured ever more loudly for decisive action as significant factions of capital perceived the raw materials and potential future markets of the African colonies as vital to the health of the German economy.[165] German state managers shared this identification of the 'national interest' with the perceived exigencies of the *Kaiserreich*'s expanding industrial economy. But, with the exception of Foreign Secretary Kiderlen-Wächter, they were *not* yet ready to risk the '*ultimate step*' (as he called it) of possible war with Britain over Morocco.[166] Why?

Much of their reluctance had to do with their fears that Germany still lacked the necessary naval armaments to adequately meet the British challenge and, further, that the 'masses' would not yet back war. Tirpitz repeatedly expressed such reservations, advising the chancellor and emperor 'to postpone this war which was probably unavoidable in the long run until after the completion of the canal'.[167] Ex-Chancellor Bülow's retrospective analysis was even more revealing:

> In 1911 the situation was much worse. Complications would have begun with Britain; France would have stayed passive, it would have forced us to attack and then there would have been no *casus foederis* for Austria ... whereas Russia was under an obligation to co-operate.[168]

The threat of British intervention and Austria-Hungary's abdication from its alliance role were principal issues. For most German policymakers, securing British neutrality in the case of a continental war was of the utmost importance.

During the July Crisis, Chancellor Bethmann Hollweg repeatedly sought to lock down such a pledge. Though remaining *hopeful* that Britain might remain neutral, in the end Bethmann Hollweg risked provoking a European war cognisant that its neutrality was unlikely as other German policymakers had been predicting for some time.[169] The chancellor's supposed 'calculated risk' was

164 Doc. 5 in Mombauer 2013b, pp. 46–7.

165 See Fischer 1975, pp. 80–1.

166 Quoted in Fischer 1975, p. 76.

167 Quoted in Fischer 1975, p. 85. And see Docs. 44 and 47 in Mombauer 2013b, pp. 85–7, 89.

168 Rathenau 1985, pp. 167–8.

169 See Copeland 2000, pp. 64–6, 111–16; Mommsen 1973, pp. 33, 37–9; Trachtenberg 1991, pp. 85–6. On the Kaiser and other German policymakers' predictions (if not always

largely the result of his belief that a European war was sooner or later inevitable and that Germany's chance of a decisive military success was steadily declining with every passing year given the incredible resurgence of Russian power since 1911 and specifically after the 'Great Programme' of 1913.[170] As Bethmann Hollweg warned on 7 July 1914: 'The future belongs to Russia which grows and grows and lies on us like an ever-heavier nightmare'.[171]

The necessity of the spark for war affecting the vital interests of the Dual Monarchy was made apparent by Austrian Prime Minister Aehrenthal's refusal to go to war on behalf of German colonial claims. As Bethmann Hollweg was already aware, if and when war came it was hoped that it would be against the Austro-Hungarians, so that they were not left to decide whether or not to fulfil their alliance obligations.[172] This is a particularly significant point. For it reveals the *specificity* of the 1914 'spark' involving Austro-Hungarian interests in the Balkans. It was not just *any* incident that could provoke a generalised world war, but only one directly involving Austro-Hungarian interests – meaning some issue relating to the 'Eastern Question' and thereby also inciting Russia. The outbreak of the Sarajevo Crisis some two years later thus offered the perfect opportunity to start a war as it fulfilled both the time (the 1912–16/17 'window of opportunity') and space (Balkans) conditions for the launching of what was perceived by Austrian and German policymakers as a likely successful strike against the Entente powers before the balance of power decisively tipped against them. The positions of German and Habsburg policymakers during the July Crisis were well summarised by Count Forgách in a private letter of 8 July:

> The Minister [Berchtold] is determined ... to use the horrible deed of Sarajevo for a military clearing-up of our impossible relationship with Serbia. The Austrian government, as well of course as the military and

---

consistent) that Britain would *not* remain neutral in the coming war see Docs. 36, 39, 51, 52, 54, 61, and 74 in Mombauer 2013b. On the immediate eve of war, however, many of these same policymakers still carried hope that Britain would remain neutral despite their earlier predictions.

170 Berghahn 1993; Fischer 1975, Chapter 9. It was perhaps for these reasons that Bethmann Hollweg supported the Dual Monarchy in their 'resolve' to deal with Serbia and pressured them to use the present opportunity to do so. As Szögyény reported to Berchtold on 6 July 1914: '... I ascertained that the Imperial Chancellor [Bethmann] like his Imperial Master considers immediate intervention on our part as the most radical and best solution for our difficulties on the Balkans. From an international point of view he considers the present moment as more favourable than a later one ...' Doc. 130 in Mombauer 2013b, p. 207.

171 Doc. 135 in Mombauer 2013b, p. 220.

172 See quotes in Fischer 1975, pp. 86–7.

> Biliński ... are in favour.... With Berlin we are in complete agreement. Kaiser & Reich-Chancellor etc. as decided as never before; they take on board complete cover against Russia, even at the risk of a world war which is not at all ruled out, they consider the moment as favourable & advise to strike as soon [as possible] without asking or consulting the other allies ...[173]

The Second Moroccan Crisis was also important for the effects it had on the spiralling arms race. The crisis offered the ideal opportunity for Tirpitz to introduce another naval bill, as well as new military demands for increases in the size of and spending on the army. Due to the already severe strains the military budget was having on the Reich's finances, the result was a rather modest, though still fiscally damaging, rise in German army spending and the scheduling of building three new battleships. But, most importantly from Tirpitz's perspective, the *Reichstag* moved forward the date of the fleet's battle-readiness.[174]

Then in 1913 came the crucial revelation of Russia's 'Great Programme' aimed at transforming the country into a military 'super power' greater than Germany in less than four years. Already at the so-called 'War Council' of 8 December 1912, following Britain's pledge to support France and Russia in a possible Balkan war, 'Moltke wanted to launch an immediate attack' as he now 'considered war unavoidable' and 'the sooner the better'.[175] The Kaiser and General Müller backed this injunction for immediate war. 'The army's position was quite clear: Germany could only lose her slight advantage over her enemies as time went on, because German army increases had led in turn to army increases in France and Russia'.[176] Tirpitz, on the other hand, claimed that the Navy was not ready, and the reconstruction of the Kiel Canal was not yet complete. Thus he argued that war be postponed for another 18 months.

Though calls for preparing the public for eventual war through a propaganda campaign were made, few concrete measures were taken. The principal significance of the December 1912 meeting lies instead with its convincing 'proof that at least by this date Germany's leaders were anticipating war in the near future and were quite ready to risk it when the moment seemed propitious, even if they were not planning for a particular war at a particular moment'.[177]

173 Doc. 140 in Mombauer 2013b, p. 224.
174 Herrmann 1997, 167–71; cf. Berghahn 1993, 115–35.
175 Muller's diary account of the meeting is reproduced in Röhl 1969, pp. 662–3, from which the quotes are taken.
176 Mombauer 2001, p. 140.
177 Joll and Martel 2007, p. 130.

Moltke's 'sooner the better' position for a preventive war against Russia was now appreciably strengthened by the Great Programme. The completion of Russia's strategic railways allowing for the Tsarist army's rapid mobilisation on Germany's eastern frontier now seemed destined, thereby undermining the foundations of the Moltke-Schlieffen Plan. In other words, the time for 'preventive war' had arrived and the Sarajevo Crisis of July-August 1914 would provide the opportunity to launch it.

So how do these events during the immediate pre-war conjuncture relate to the preceding analysis drawing on the theory of uneven and combined development? To re-trace just one thread of this interconnected picture: as we saw, Western European and Russian expansionism drove the disintegration of Ottoman rule in the Balkans. The ensuing Young Turks Revolt of 1908 in turn fed into the conditions resulting in the Bosnian Annexation Crisis of 1908–9 and Second Moroccan Crisis of 1911. The former irrevocably damaged Austro-Serbian relations, while Russian policymakers simultaneously became ever more determined in their resolve to avoid the domestic-international costs of yet another geopolitical humiliation – itself a major legacy of the earlier Russo-Japanese War that had reoriented Russian strategy westward in the first place. The Second Moroccan Crisis – largely the product of Germany's worsening domestic-international position, pushing it increasingly toward acts of diplomatic brinkmanship – then resulted in the Italian occupation of Tripoli, aggravating the Ottoman's precipitous decline and worsening Austro-Hungary's external/internal 'security dilemma' by setting off the two Balkan Wars. A further effect of the Moroccan Crisis was the dramatic acceleration of the European arms race into a classic action–reaction spiral as German rearmaments set-off Russia's 'Great Programme', which created the widespread perception among German policymakers that a 'preventive war' must be risked sooner rather than later. The concatenation of events producing this strategic 'window of opportunity' to be exploited by German and Austrian policymakers was thus the result of the intertwined nature of the socio-historical processes examined above. That is, the spatio-temporal unevenness of European development and the resulting forms of sociological combinations emerging over the Long Nineteenth were refracted through the immediate pre-war conjuncture with significant 'geo-social' consequences, thereby facilitating the conditions for the outbreak of the July Crisis and ultimately war. The conception of causality here is then necessarily 'multi-perspectival' or 'de-centred' – one that captures the 'synergistic interaction' of the different causal chains, whilst conceptualising the precise *links* connecting each chain along their differentiated sites within a single theorisable (uneven and combined) developmental logic of process.

Conclusion: Marxism and 'the International'

The preceding analysis has sought to provide a theoretical way out of the persistent separation of sociological and geopolitical modes of analysis continually besetting theoretical explanations of the origins of 1914. In doing so, it has drawn on Trotsky's concept of uneven and combined developed, reworked as a theory of interstate conflict and war, which theoretically fuses these two modes of analysis. This in turn requires a rethinking of historical materialism's fundamental theoretical premises as it incorporates a distinctly 'international' dimension of social development and reproduction into its core guiding 'general abstractions'. This can be seen to represent, in Lakatosian terms, a 'progressive problem-shift' *within* a historical materialist research programme, introducing and then 'stretching' an auxiliary theory *consistent* with the 'hard-core' premises of that programme.[178] Rather than protecting these hard-core premises by limiting their explanatory scope ('monster barring') or by identifying anomalies as exceptions or pathologies, the theory of uneven and combined development aims to *magnify* the explanatory power of the original research programme.[179] Thus, rather than replacing historical materialism's traditional focus on class conflict and modes of production, the theory of uneven and combined development directs our attention to the myriad ways in which both processes of class and state formation are inextricably bound to developments at the 'international' as well as domestic level, thus offering a synthesised theory of social development and reproduction that moves beyond the problematic 'eternal divide' between sociological and geopolitical theories. This then provides the kind of 'de-centred' analysis of the First World War demanded by more recent historiographical interpretations without slipping into the difficulties of multi-causality whereby different causal factors are conceived as relating to each other in wholly external ways. These points are particularly pertinent to any theoretical explanation of 1914 as domestic and international, sociological and geopolitical, factors causally intertwined with one another in producing a typically 'overdetermined' conjuncture only partially illuminated by theoretical frameworks focusing on one dimension of this social reality over another.

178 Lakatos 1970, pp. 133–4.

179 The implications of this progressive problem-shift are further teased out in Anievas 2014, Chapter 2.

CHAPTER 5

The Expansion of the Japanese Empire and the Rise of the Global Agrarian Question after the First World War

Wendy Matsumura

Introduction: Structural Transformation of the Japanese Economy and World War I

In the week leading up to Japan's entry into what was at the time a limited conflict between European powers, newspaper articles analysed the impact that a protracted conflict could have, particularly on Japanese trade with foreign nations. One such article was 'Keizaijō no Eikyō: Ōshu Karan to Honpō' [Economic Effects: Our Country and the European Tumult], published in two parts on 3 and 4 August 1914 in the *Chūgai Shōgyō Shimpō*, an economic daily with close ties to the Mitsui group, one of the largest concerns [*zaibatsu*] in the country whose interests ranged from finance, steel, mining, shipping and trading. The article expressed optimism about the expanded opportunities that Japanese shipping and commercial interests would enjoy if the conflict expanded into an international war.[1] It brushed aside worries that other articles expressed about the war's impact on capital and commodity imports from Europe and proclaimed the need for a shift in perspective amongst the country's producers and shippers who should be preparing themselves to handle the impending growth in exports to the warring countries. In addition to supplying to Europe, the article argued that war could break open the heavy walls that had long restricted Japanese exports to China. Japanese monopoly capital and its spokesmen eyed the conflict in its opening moments as an opportunity to gain a foothold in markets that had long been monopolised by European powers. The article concluded by emphasising that the opportunity could be seized even more definitively through direct entry into the conflict, as victory would ensure that routes and markets that were opened up would

1 The paper was originally known as *Chūgai Bukka Shimpō*, which the founder of the Mitsui Trading Company, Masuda Takashi, established in 1876. The paper was renamed the *Nihon Keizai Shimbun* immediately after Japan's surrender in World War II.

be protected after its conclusion.[2] Japan's own wars in the preceding decades had enabled the development of Mitsui into a full-fledged concern, and the *Chūgai Shōgyō Shimpō* wanted to make sure a new opportunity for growth would not be thwarted by those who insisted on non-involvement.[3] Mitsui and its fellow monopoly capitalists understood full well in 1914 what Lenin outlined in his *Imperialism: The Highest Stage of Capitalism* in 1916 – that in the age of 'modern monopolist capitalism' only the possession of colonies could guarantee the super-profits, supplies of raw materials and secure markets that were necessary for victory against the competition.[4] Japanese concerns like Mitsui, Mitsubishi, Sumitomo, Yasuda and Daiichi already enjoyed a dominant position in the economy by the eve of the war by establishing monopolies in finance, shipping, trade, steel, mining and railways after the financial panic of 1907, but found their desires for further expansion severely limited by the fact that European powers had already carved up the world into their own colonial possessions and spheres of influence. They felt most acutely Lenin's observation that repartitioning was the only way that they could continue their parasitic ways. The outbreak of war in Europe seemed a perfect opportunity to begin a re-division of the world to their advantage.

The Terauchi cabinet, which was also enthusiastic about the economic windfall that limited participation in the war could bring, commenced communications with the British Foreign Secretary Sir Edward Grey to negotiate entry into the conflict. Terauchi, who urged the hesitant Grey to invoke the 1902 Anglo-Japanese Alliance to formally request Japan's entry into the war, secured a rather tepid invitation following two weeks of persistent prodding. The arrangement that resulted required Terauchi to promise that upon entry, the Japanese military would not disrupt German possessions in the South Seas and would refrain from engaging in any acts of territorial aggrandisement in China.[5] His cabinet accepted these terms and declared war on Germany

2 The article's main concern was the United States, which the author believed was also poised to take advantage of the commercial and trade vacuum.

3 See Morikawa 1970 for more on *zaibatsu* formation in English. In Japanese, see Matsumoto 1979 and Yasuoka 1982.

4 See the section, 'Division of the World among the Great Powers' in Lenin 1968.

5 Japan entered the war by forcing the reluctant British to honour their hasty request for Japanese naval assistance in the East China Sea on 7 August 1918. By the time the British realised that they had miscalculated the German naval forces' capacity and intentions in the region, it was too late to withdraw the request. During the weeks between 9 August and Japan's formal declaration of war against Germany on 23 August 1914, the two governments negotiated and tried to come to an agreement that would be acceptable to each regarding the scope of involvement in the conflict. Peattie 1992 describes these negotiations and competing concerns in detail.

just a month after the young Bosnian Serb, Gavrilo Princip, assassinated the Archduke Franz Ferdinand and his wife in Sarajevo, nearly 10,000 kilometres away from Tokyo.[6] Japan's entry into World War I on 23 August expanded the roster of belligerent nations beyond Europe. For Mitsui and the other concerns, the violence that erupted in Sarajevo in the summer of 1914 provided the perfect opening for the realisation of their global aspirations.

Despite the repeated assurances it made to Grey and the British government that their navy would not enter German waters, the Terauchi cabinet immediately commenced preparations for the occupation of their new enemy's possessions in the South Pacific. The takeover was completed with little fanfare, bloodshed or panic by October of that year. Fearing that their claims on these islands would be fiercely protested once their allies could catch their breath to object, the new authorities quickly got down to the business of colonial rule.[7] By early 1915, a hundred Japanese arrived in the South Seas islands in order to supervise the work of indigenous labourers in the phosphate mines that they had taken over from the Germans.[8] Shipping interests, which had managed to carve out a small presence in the region from the early 1900s in intra-island transport and mail delivery, received a welcome boost from the Japanese government, which granted the Nippon Yusen Kaisha (NYK) a massive shipping company under the Mitsubishi group, and a lucrative government contract to handle shipping between the region and Japan in 1917.[9] Though full-fledged economic development projects in the occupied territories did not really start until Matsue Haruji, a sugar expert who had been instrumental in modernising Taiwan's industry, arrived in the Marianas in 1920, the newly established South Seas Government [*Nanyōchō*], and laid the groundwork for capitalist penetration of the islands during the war by surveying coastlines, conducting censuses, commencing public works projects and propagating Japanese language instruction amongst local populations.[10]

6 For a political history of the conflict see Stevenson 2010. Here, Stevenson uses the term cataclysm to refer to 1914 as the violent interruption of a century of increasing globalisation and economic interdependence that was not achieved again until the end of World War.

7 Peattie 1992, p. 64. Their first priority was establishing as strong a justification as they could for maintaining these islands as formal colonies after the war.

8 Peattie 1992, p. 67.

9 NYK took over this lucrative deal from the South Seas Trading Company (NBK) which itself had just received this exclusive contract in 1915. Peattie 1992, p. 121.

10 After working in the sugar industry in Japan, Matsue moved to Taiwan in 1910 and helped to found the Douliu Sugar Refinery. He moved on in 1915 to work for *Niitaka Seitō*, based in Chiayi in 1915, in the midst of the wartime sugar boom. According to Takagi Shigeki, by the

The South Seas islands and Germany's leased territories in the Shandong province, China, were the only regions that the Japanese military formally occupied during the war, but Japanese monopoly capital found other opportunities to expand its reach, particularly in Southeast Asia. As the Mitsui-backed paper had predicted in early August, the European conflict immediately resulted in a global shortage of both ships and cargo.[11] The 14 million square kilometres and 100 million people who were under the control of the four great colonial powers of Great Britain, Russia, France and Germany in 1914 needed supplies as well as markets for their goods.[12] Japan, which lagged far behind these four powers in the size and population of its colonies, looked to gain ground during the war.

As the traffic of European ships to Southeast Asia, East Asia and Africa slowed as fighting intensified, Japanese shipping interests filled the gap. Particularly important for future expansion was their acquisition of shipping routes to Java, a predominantly sugar-producing colony under Dutch control that supplied the majority of Japan's sugar imports until the late 1920s.[13] While only one company, the Nanyō Yūsen Kaisha (NYKA), had a route that connected Java and Japan in 1912, by the time the war neared its end, two major shipping companies, the Mitsui-backed Osaka Shōsen Kaisha (OSK) and the Mitsubishi-backed Nippon Yūsen Kaisha (NYK), entered the game, with OSK operating a route that connected Java and the northeastern city of Keelung in Taiwan and NYK commencing a Japan-Java-Calcutta-New York route.[14] The start of these new shipping routes enabled the expansion of the Japan-Java trade, particularly in the export of manufactured goods and the import of sugar for domestic consumption.[15] The effects were immediately visible. Between 1913 and

end of the decade Matsue was ready to move to the South Seas, seeing more opportunities for development there. Takagi 2008.

11 Shimizu 1988.

12 Lenin 1968, p. 75.

13 Knight 2010, p. 504.

14 Shimizu 1998, p. 6. Keelung was the first modern port built in Taiwan after occupation and India was a major importer of Java sugar.

15 This culminated in Japan's formal occupation of the Dutch East Indies in the early 1940s. It is worth noting though that Japan's position in Java's sugar industry was consolidated soon after World War I with the Suzuki Shōten of Kobe, a concern with major interests in sugar, steel and shipping, entering the island to procure sugar for its refineries on the mainland. Their entry was aided by the expansion of shipping routes outlined above and the retreat of European powers from the region. In addition to direct intervention, major Japanese and colonial banks strengthened their presence in Java by providing loans to the sugar-manufacturing cartel VJSP. See Knight 2010 for details.

1918, the value of Japanese commodities entering Java annually increased by 19 times from 5.5 to 104.8 million Dutch guilders. Imports also rose, though not as dramatically as exports, from 35.8 to 77.8 million in the same period but prefigured a dramatic rise mostly around sugar during the 1920s. We should note that the turn to Java for cheap supplies of sugar during World War I, even as production and monopolisation intensified in Taiwan (a formal colony) and Okinawa (a domestic periphery), reveals a structural reorganisation of Japan's international trade relations during and particularly after the war. This, in turn, is indicative of a structural transformation of Japanese capitalism and the expansion of its agrarian question into a global problem – something that will be explored in greater detail later in this piece.

As Western powers complained during the post-war treaty negotiations in Paris, the Japanese gained much while sacrificing little. The main beneficiaries of Japan's participation in World War I were the concerns, whose vertical integration became tighter than ever before due to their expanded lending operations abroad. In 1919, the number of joint stock companies – many of them vertically connected to these concerns as 'children' or 'grandchildren' companies – exceeded the number of limited partnership companies for the first time.[16] These interrelated phenomena indicate the high degree of control that a handful of capitalists and managers of capital achieved during the wartime boom.[17] This boom, which was spurred by speculative fever across industries, was the result of Japan's transition from an importer to major exporter of military supplies, manufactured goods and foodstuffs to the warring countries

16 Hayashi 1981, p. 116.

17 Marxist theorist Uno Kōzō, whose work on the agrarian question will be examined in detail in the following section, explains the historical significance of the emergence of joint stock companies to capitalism. He explained in his introductory remarks to the *Keizai Seisakuron* that this form enables a small number of large capitalists to utilise a colossal amount of social capital as their own: 'the so-called democratization of capital that mobilises the funds of even the owners of miniscule funds is nothing more than the method to realise the concentration of management by separating it from the concentration of ownership'. Uno 1974, p. 169. This process of the concentration of management or control over capital that is characteristic of a period dominated by finance capital eventually ends up realising the concentration of ownership. This ability is accelerated by the formation of concerns. As Lenin explained: 'The "democratization" of ownership of shares (some call it the democratization of capital), the strengthening of the role and significance of small scale production, etc., is in fact, one of the ways of increasing the power of the financial oligarchy'. Lenin 1968, p. 46.

of Europe and their colonies or spheres of interest in Asia and Africa.[18] These expanded commodity exports helped to transform Japan from a debtor nation that owed 1.1 billion yen to foreign countries in 1914 to a creditor that loaned 3.7 billion by 1920.[19]

It goes without saying that the wartime growth in capital and commodity exports was accompanied by vast transformations in the industrial sector at home. Manufacturing increased 4.4 times between 1914 and 1919, textiles production increased by 5.5 times and steel production increased by 5.9 times.[20] Most conspicuous was a structural transformation away from light industry to heavy chemical industries, whose proportion to total manufacturing in 1914 was 22 percent but ballooned to over 32 percent in 1919.[21] The dominant position that the heavy and chemical industries led by monopoly capital achieved during World War I is one of the reasons why economic historians consider this an epochal moment for Japanese capitalism.

The structural shifts in Japanese industry transformed the lives of workers and cultivators alike. First and foremost, the growth in industrial production led to a 30 percent increase in the populations of Japan's six main cities. While less than one percent of all factories employed more than 500 workers during the war, they employed over a quarter of the total working population.[22] This structural transformation and the failure of wages to keep pace with inflation spurred increased organisation and higher levels of unionisation amongst the urban working class. As Penelope Francks has argued, resentment toward the nouveau riche who profited from speculative activity grew amongst workers and exploded in the summer of 1918 as rice prices sharply escalated in Japanese cities following the government's purchase of large quantities to supply its troops in Siberia.[23] While there were only 50 recorded cases of strikes

---

18 The trade deficit was a major problem for Japan particularly after the Russo-Japanese war of 1904–5. The government tried to settle accounts by relying on gold exports and foreign capital imports from Britain, the US, France and Germany through government bonds. In 1914, right before the war, the amount of bonds issued was a staggering 1.5 billion yen, which required the government to issue even more bonds just to cover the interest payments, which totalled 48 million yen annually. This chronic deficit and debt was hindering the state's ability to take full advantage of their formal and informal colonies because it was not able to adequately fund the transport mechanisms and development of raw material sources. For more on these difficulties prior to World War I, see Yamazaki 1978.

19 Hayashi 1981, p. 115.

20 Yasui 1978, p. 49.

21 Yasui 1978, p. 49.

22 Hayashi 1981, p. 118.

23 Francks 2006, p. 176. For more on the Rice Riots in English, see Gordon 1988.

that involved 10,000 participants at the start of the war, by 1917 the numbers increased to 97 cases with over 57,000 participants. By the end of the war there were 497 recorded strikes that involved over 63,000 workers.[24]

The expansion of the heavy and chemical industries dominated by monopoly capital also greatly impacted social and economic relations in Japan's agrarian villages. Though agriculture lost its role as the predominant producer of national income by the war's end, it continued to employ the majority of the working population.[25] The Japanese government faced a dilemma as a 'food problem' developed due to shortages and rising prices of rice during the war. In response to the food problem in the cities, the state encouraged the development of commercial agriculture in Japan proper and in its formal colonies through subsidies and encouragement monies. This support led to the expansion of regional railways, refrigeration, banks and other measures to encourage cultivators to expand their activities into the production of vegetables, fruits, beef, poultry and dairy products to feed the hungry working population in the growing cities.[26] Commercial agriculture's growth had unintended consequences that only exacerbated labour unrest in the cities. As farming households transferred their energies to the production of lucrative cash crops they devoted less of their time and resources to the more labour-intensive and time-consuming cultivation of staple grains like rice, barley and millet that did not produce the same returns.[27] Decreased supplies of these staple grains as the industrial population expanded played a major role in the aforementioned Rice Riots that erupted throughout the nation around the time that armistice was signed with Germany.

In the countryside, class differentiation was accelerated by the rise of what Louise Young has called the nouveau riche farmer [*hyakushō narikin*] who made small fortunes by engaging in petty speculative activity, facilitating commercial agricultural development and using their profits to lend capital to their less prosperous neighbours at high interest rates. The rise of the nouveau riche farmer coincided with the expansion of the agricultural proletariat whose position during the boom years of the war actually declined because rising land prices forced more owner-cultivators to give up their lands, which in turn

24 Hayashi 1981, p. 121. The rise of labour conflicts and worker unrest witnessed in Japan after the war can be viewed within the broader developments Sandra Halperin describes in her chapter in this volume as the 'global Red Tide' engulfing much of the world in the aftermath of the war.

25 Morris-Suzuki 1991, p. 71.

26 Hayashi 1981, p. 123.

27 Hayashi 1981, p. 125.

enabled landlords to raise rents. Indebtedness, high rents and rising rice prices placed tenant farmers in an increasingly precarious position as monopoly capital secured its dominant position within the Japanese economy.[28]

Uno Kōzō and the Specificity of the Japanese Agrarian Question

When Japanese Marxist theorists debated the country's agrarian question [*nōgyō mondai*] from the mid-1930s, they specifically pointed to the inability of Japanese monopoly capital, despite the dominant position it carved out during the war and despite the class differentiation that accompanied its rise, to install capitalist relations of production in agriculture.[29] The feudality that remained in the countryside was an obstacle to capital's valorisation process but was also an important issue that Marxist theorists had to overcome if the peasantry who continued to comprise the majority of the working population of the country was to be radicalised for anti-capitalist struggle.[30] They debated both the nature of these feudal relations and the strategy required to create the necessary conditions for the unfolding of this struggle. These prewar debates concerning Japan's agrarian question were revived in the years immediately following Japan's surrender in World War II as Marxist theorists, including notably Uno Kōzō, contemplated the best response to the American Occupation authorities' impending agricultural land reforms.[31]

This section will focus on Uno's theorisation of the relationship between agriculture and capitalism. He explicitly identified World War I as the beginning of the appearance of a new agrarian question and argued that the structural transformations that expanded industrial production and the concentration of capital during the war created an agrarian question that was global in its

28 For more on the figure of the nouveau riche farmer during World War I, see Young 2013, Chapter 1.

29 In this way, their concerns were no different from those of Engels, Lenin, Kautsky, Luxemburg and others who problematised the backwardness of agriculture in relation to the emergence of revolutionary subjects.

30 Interwar Marxist debates on Japanese capitalism have been analysed in the English language by Hoston 1986; Harootunian 2000; Barshay 2007; Allinson and Anievas 2010; and Walker 2011. Studies in the Japanese language are too numerous to list here but Yamada Moritarō, Sakisaka Itsurō, Koike Motoyuki, Hasegawa Nyozekan and Hirano Yoshitarō were some of Uno's sparring partners. A comprehensive review of the interwar debate on the agrarian question can be found in Shōji 2012.

31 For more on the involvement of post-war Marxists in the Occupation forces' agricultural land reforms, see Gilmartin and Ladejinsky 1948 and Terada 2008.

scope and, therefore, all the more difficult to resolve. A resolution to Japan's agrarian question, defined as a national inflection of a general problem facing capitalism after World War I, required addressing the contradictions of Japanese capitalism from a global rather than national perspective.

Uno clarified the difference between this agrarian question and earlier manifestations of it in his July 1950 essay 'Sekai Keizairon no Hōhō to Mokuhyō' [Methods and Objectives of a Theory of Global Political Economy].[32] Conceding that the management of agriculture would always be a challenge for capital as long as it required the use of land as the primary means of production, Uno distinguished the agrarian question faced by countries like Britain and Germany prior to World War I from the one that all capitalist countries had to contend with following its conclusion. He explained that state representatives of capital in late nineteenth-century Britain or early twentieth-century Germany could temporarily resolve the contradictions that capitalist development unfolded in the agrarian sector through a variety of means including the conversion of weaker countries into suppliers of agriculture, the implementation of protective tariffs and the export of agricultural products to colonies, but emphasised that these were merely temporary fixes that by no means addressed the crux of the problem.[33]

The agrarian question was particularly pronounced in countries like Japan and the United States that greatly expanded industrial and agricultural production during World War I precisely because wartime demands significantly transformed the countryside. Europe's post-war recovery threatened the viability of these nations' economies because the substantial investments in constant capital they had made, particularly to develop commercial agriculture, made it extremely difficult to scale back production once the war ended.[34] The continuation of production at near wartime levels, combined with accelerated

---

32 Uno 1974c.

33 Uno 1974b, p. 12. Uno emphasised that despite its separate manifestations in predominantly industrial and agricultural countries, the global agrarian question must be understood as a problem for capitalism itself because it was the outward appearance of the internal contradictions of capitalism itself. What he meant by this was that its resolution could not be found in the further capitalisation of agriculture – the dissolution of agriculture and industry and further class differentiation within the agrarian villages – but required a 'fundamental resolution' of class relations. In this sense, he differed from both *Kōza* [Lectures] and *Rōnō* [Labour-Farmer] faction Marxists who believed that increased capitalist development would produce a proletariat in the city and countryside ready for revolution. For more on the agrarian question as fundamentally a question of capitalism, see Uno 1974b, p. 355.

34 For more on the spatial fix, see Harvey 2007.

production in Europe led to the flooding of industrial and agricultural commodities on the world market. Uno observed that capitalist states responded to overproduction and the intensification of worker and tenant disputes that followed the post-war recession by creating autarkic regional economies [*kōiki Keizai*] that established clear boundaries of inside and outside from the late 1920s.[35] The formation of these closed economic spaces – in many ways, a retreat from earlier policies emphasising liberalisation – counteracted many of the developments that World War I had brought to the agrarian villages. He contended that regional economies were responses to global overproduction but also, just as importantly, political responses of capitalist states to the rise of socialism. This political and ideological threat to capitalism compelled states to pursue policies of protection towards agriculture instead of allowing the national agricultural sector to collapse, letting the dissolution of agrarian villages continue unchecked or simply suppressing growing tenant radicalism with force. Uno argued that the protection of agriculture became absolutely necessary politically even if it did not benefit capital's reproduction process.[36] Citing the promotion of self-sufficiency in foodstuffs by those states dominated by monopoly capital in the 1930s, Uno reiterated the increasingly complex and global nature of the agrarian question after World War I.[37]

---

35 Germany was one of Uno's main examples. For more on the concept of the regional economy, refer to his 'Tōgyō Yori Mitaru Kōiki Keizairon', in Uno 1974b.

36 Uno 1974c, p. 39. As Uno hints in his supplementary remarks to the *Keizai Seisakuron*, the rise of socialism after 1917 was one of the reasons why these protectionist policies became politically necessary. Uno 1974a.

37 Enomoto Masatoshi, writing 15 years later, adds that this was in many ways the result of a political-economic problem that emerged as capitalism lost the conditions necessary for accumulation. He explained by distinguishing between the impact that World War I had on industrial and agricultural countries. First, for capitalist countries, it became increasingly difficult for them to expand their frontiers and thus they lost the conditions necessary for capital accumulation. In Luxemburgian terms, this was the loss of an 'outside' for capital as competition between capitalist countries for colonies intensified. As a result, these countries experienced mass unemployment and stagnation of accumulation. In order to respond to these domestic conditions that were conducive to class conflict, capitalist countries had no choice but to shift to protectionist policies that could help agrarian villages reabsorb the excess labour power of the cities. These protectionist policies had deep-reaching impacts on agricultural countries whose economic well-being depended on their ability to export agricultural produce. They were particularly hard hit following World War I, as they had been able to dramatically increase productivity in agriculture during the war in order to respond to expanded demand through technological investments. It goes without saying that buyers for these large quantities of agricultural products were difficult to find once capitalist countries enacted their protectionist policies.

Uno situated Japan's agrarian question within this global context but asserted that its specificity arose from the particular conditions under which its capitalist development unfolded. In *Nōgyō Mondai Joron* [Introduction to the Agrarian Question], Uno placed Japan within the camp of so-called late developing countries that had a high organic composition of capital in industry from their inception.[38] He explained that these historical conditions, in which the state imported capitalist technologies from abroad, played an instrumental role in promoting the development of finance capital, and encouraged the rapid formation of joint stock companies to jump-start the process of industrialisation, meant that agrarian villages did not have to completely dissolve for capitalist industry to develop. A high proportion of the population remained agricultural workers of various types because the centuries-long historical process of expropriation and enclosures were not required for the so-called primitive accumulation process.

In Japan's case, small-scale peasant management [*shōnō*] based on family labour power became the predominant form of social and economic relations in agrarian villages following the enactment of private property relations in 1873. As we have already seen, a significant degree of class differentiation and separation of industry and agriculture did take place between 1873 and World War I. However, political instability after the Bolshevik Revolution, the Rice Riots of 1918 and the growing radicalisation of tenant farmers in the early 1920s, forced the state to enact policies to protect and in some cases create the small owner-cultivator as a stabilising force in the countryside.[39]

With regards to the significance that the small peasantry had within capitalist society, Uno considered it an extreme example of a case that Marx presented in *Capital* Volume III, 'The Genesis of Capitalist Ground Rent': 'The peasant becomes a merchant and industrialist without the conditions in which he is able to produce his product as a commodity'.[40] Further, in much the same way that Lenin wrote about the peasant in capitalist society as constantly plagued by overwork and under-consumption, Uno clarified that the

These combined conditions culminated in the unfolding of a chronic global agricultural recession in the later part of the 1920s. World War I, which marked a significant turning point in the capitalisation of agricultural production for many so-called late-developing countries, was, for these reasons, understood as the origins of a global agrarian question that did not find a resolution even as Uno was theorising it during the immediate postwar period.

38 Uno 1974b, p. 14.

39 For a historiographical review of the literature concerning the state's creation of the *shōnō* and *shōnō* protectionist policies, see Mori 2002.

40 Marx 1993, p. 948.

Japanese small peasantry were constantly troubled by the fact that the price of their products was not governed by 'normal' capitalist regulations but was determined in a manner that was always disadvantageous to them. In order to reproduce themselves despite low prices that resulted from overproduction, the power of monopoly capital and competition from abroad, they supplemented their household budgets through excess labour. Their willingness to accept extremely difficult terms enabled landowners to collect extremely high rents. As a result of these high rents, cultivators competed with each other to become owners of their own scraps of land on which the surplus labour of their household could be completely expended.[41]

Within the broad category of the small peasantry, Uno paid particular attention to the figure of the *jikosaku nōka*, or farming households that owned part of the land they cultivated and paid rent on the rest. For him, a true understanding of Japan's agrarian question required an understanding of the historical significance of the consolidation of the *jikosaku nōka*'s dominant position within the agrarian villages after World War I. The persistence of this type of household that remained committed to agricultural production even amidst high rents, rising expenses and falling prices, and whose members dreamed of accumulating more land to cultivate, was all the proof that Uno needed to conclude that the rapid development of capitalism did not lead to or require the dissolution of the agrarian villages within a single country.

Uno clarified that as the penetration of capitalism into the agrarian villages accelerated after World War I, the *jikosaku nōka* continued to exhibit one of two tendencies: they either tried to acquire more land to convert themselves into parasitic landlords, or increase the amount of land that they borrowed in order to put all of their family's surplus labour to work.[42] The latter tendency became increasingly pronounced after their position in relation to large landowners *qua* moneylenders weakened during the war.[43] The protectionist policies toward agriculture that the state was forced to implement in response

41 Uno 1974b, p. 162.

42 Tama 1995.

43 As we stated earlier, the wartime boom also impacted the countryside. Some large landowners engaged in speculative activity and were able to use their freed up capital to transform themselves into moneylenders to their village communities. This in turn led to higher levels of indebtedness amongst small farming households who had to borrow in order to make improvements or, in the case of tenant farmers, to cover the rising costs of food.

to the post-boom immiseration of the countryside did not improve the lives of the *jikosaku nōka* but did slow their departure from agriculture.[44]

For Uno and other Marxist theorists, the predominance of the *jikosaku*-type peasantry, whose members were willing to work themselves to the point of exhaustion in order to increase their landholdings, constituted a stubborn obstacle to the penetration of revolutionary thought and action in the agrarian villages. In addition, their drive to survive as owner-cultivators instead of becoming tenant farmers or workers in the cities made it difficult for the left to envision the unfolding of the material conditions that they believed necessary for the organic emergence of revolutionary consciousness. Put differently, the resilience and drive for property on the part of the *jikosaku nōka* – their unwillingness to proletarianise themselves – meant that the creation of an urban or agricultural proletariat who owned nothing but their own labour power was thwarted to the detriment of revolutionary politics.[45]

The decidedly un-revolutionary character that Uno ascribed to this group comes forth most clearly in his evaluation of their utilisation of hired labour. Though Uno disagreed with the *Kōza* faction in defining the social relations of the agrarian villages as feudal, he agreed with their assessment that the *jikosaku nōka*, even when they hired workers, did not operate according to a capitalist logic because this was not done in order to realise surplus value.[46]

---

44 Those who could not make it in the villages turned outward to the colonies and beyond. They engaged in agricultural production in those regions as well.

45 Uno argues that this attitude manifests itself in the tenant disputes. He writes, 'so-called tenant disputes do not have an external, confrontational relationship founded on the separation of ownership and management'. Uno, 'Nōgyō no Kōsei', p. 458 (Unpublished work).

46 The *Kōza* faction thought it was a top-down process, while Uno argued that it came from below. There are a lot of similarities between Uno's theorisation of the relationship and that of Jairus Banaji. In his 1977 article 'Modes of Production in a Materialist Conception of History', Banaji dismissed the characterisation of the relations between small cultivators and capital as being non-capitalistic by arguing that the low price paid for their commodity actually conceals a hidden wage that is paid to the peasantry. He also pointed to advances – a key component of the reproduction of small cultivators – as another example of a capital relation that was concealed by the material form of a loan of money or goods to the cultivator. The main point that Banaji wanted to make is that these forms, which appeared to be remnants of a pre-capitalist past to observers of the countryside, actually concealed a capitalist logic that operated in the relations between capital and agriculture dominated by small cultivating households. He then continued by saying that the main problem of depressed prices and widespread use of advances – the result of capital's dominant position *vis-à-vis* agricultural production – was that the capitalist logic did not result in the creation of relative surplus value, but simply resulted in the pursuit

Rather, the operational decisions of these households were exclusively focused on the accumulation of assets, mostly in the form of land.[47]

From the distinction Uno made between capital and assets, we see that he understood that a 'true resolution' of the global agrarian question was not simply a matter of the installation of capitalist relations of production in agriculture by monopoly capital but required a transformation of subjectivities.[48] The strata that exemplified the feudality of Japan's agrarian villages, the *jikosaku*-type peasantry, could only become the protagonists of this resolution through their acquisition of a capitalist logic in which they too 'try to endlessly expand other people's labour power as capital'. That being said, only their departure from agriculture would signal that this transformation had been realised.[49]

As Tama Shinnosuke has argued, one of the curious aspects of Uno's theorisation of the Japanese agrarian question was that while he emphasised the need to account for the global scale of the problem and rejected the notion that a resolution could be found on a national or simply material level, his elaboration of its key features in the Japanese context focused almost exclusively on providing a typology of farming households and elaborating the nature of their productive activities.[50] Instead of linking shifts in global capitalism after World War I to the transformation of the relations of exploitation and production in Japan's agrarian villages and clarifying how the very meaning of the

---

of absolute surplus value in agriculture. In other words, the relationship did not lead to increased mechanisation or a higher organic composition of capital in agriculture, but simply resulted in a spatial expansion of the area over which capital exercised its control. Banaji called this a 'network of an ever-growing mass of peasant households' that maintained themselves through overwork and under-consumption. While emphasising the capitalist nature of the relations between capital and agriculture dominated by small cultivators, Banaji seems to assume what Uno argued – that the productive activities of such groups of peasants cannot be characterised as governed by a capitalist logic. See Banaji 2010.

47 Tama 1995, p. 86. Lenin, Kautsky, Chayanov and others also grappled with these questions of how to understand the decisions made by the small peasantry [*shōnō*] in agricultural production. It is possible that all are guilty of a type of stagism that may have been avoided in Marx's late works, but there is no time to grapple with this question here. See Banaji 1976.

48 Of course, he believed that a transformation of subjectivity required a material transformation of relations between agriculture and industry and a shift from the policies of agricultural self-sufficiency through the creation of the *kōiki keizai* (regional economy) that capitalist countries including Japan had been pursuing since the 1930s.

49 In Uno's writings it is unclear how the restructuring of the world into regional economies after World War I produced a reconceptualisation of the agrarian question in Japan.

50 Tama 1995, p. 81.

different categories of the peasantry changed as a result of a transformation of the organic composition of capital and the degree of embeddedness into the broader commodity-economy, Uno's writings seem to indicate his assumption of either an unchanging essence that each category possessed or unwavering laws that governed each type of small farming household's management activities since the installation of private property relations in 1873 provided the formal prerequisites for the development of Japanese capitalism for the first time in the nation's history.[51]

Taking Tama's observations as a starting point, the remainder of this piece will question the assumption from which Uno seems to begin, which is that *jikosaku*-type management in agriculture operated according to an unwavering and unchanging feudalistic logic by which farming households completely exhausted their available family labour in order to acquire wealth rather than capital.[52] In contrast to this characterisation, which places the single moment of decisive transformation for cultivators at the moment of the establishment of private property relations, this essay takes seriously the profound changes that World War I had on social and productive relations in the countryside. Concrete analysis of the changes that took place may require a re-evaluation of the notion that the interactions small cultivators – exemplified in the figure of the *jikosakunō* – had with capitalists who entered the countryside was characterised by forms of extra-economic compulsion because their productive activities were not yet governed by the logic of capitalist production. Rather, the entry of monopoly capital into Japan's agrarian villages transformed existing social relations, technical processes of production and the significance of productive activity itself.

Given these new conditions, it is necessary to keep open the possibility that the insistence on maintaining the status of *jikosaku nōka* was a mode of

51 Relying largely on a national census that was conducted in 1930, he examined the proportion of the working population engaged in agriculture (47.7 percent); the scale of ownership of arable lands (49.6 percent owned less than 5 *tan* of land, only 0.1 percent owned over 50 *chō* and 92.5 percent owned 3 *chō* or less, and of families that owned arable land, the average scale of ownership was 1 *chō* 2 *tan*); the average area of borrowed lands of farming families that also owned part of the land they cultivated; the proximity of rented lands to each other (the smaller the scale of tenancy, the more scattered the land was); the degree of self-sufficiency amongst the small peasantry; levels of engagement in subsidiary industries; and so on. By analysing the data provided by this census and additional studies from 1938 and 1941, Uno sought to clarify the key characteristics of Japanese farming households under monopoly capital.

52 Henry Bernstein would call this an outcome of the logic of subsistence characteristic of simple commodity production. See Bernstein 1977.

anti-capitalist struggle that seriously challenged monopoly capital's efforts to completely take hold of agriculture. This point will be considered through an examination of a series of non-selling alliances that small sugar producers in Okinawa, the southernmost prefecture of the Japanese nation-state that was annexed in 1879, organised at the height of the global sugar boom during World War I.[53] A close reading of these alliances reveal that at the very least, the absence of a capitalist logic governing the productive activity of small cultivators did not, as Uno argued in his works on the agrarian question, negate the possibility of the emergence of a revolutionary or anti-capitalist subjectivity.[54]

The Entry of Japanese Monopoly Capital into Okinawa's Sugar Industry

The Okinawa prefecture, the southernmost region of the Japanese nation-state, received the formal prerequisites for the enactment of capitalist relations of production through the completion of the land reorganisation project [*tochi seiri jigyō*] in 1903, 30 years after its equivalent was conducted in mainland Japan.[55] The completion of this project was a major event in the prefecture's young history as it clarified the boundaries of land ownership, classified lands according to their yield and function, and established private property relations on all islands. From the start, it was seen as a site of domestic sugar production that could help to alleviate the trade deficit, as sugar along with cotton comprised half of Japan's total imports in the late 1870s.

In addition to providing certificates of land ownership to individual households, land reorganisation was a comprehensive project of enclosure that converted communal lands into either state-owned or managed lands; lands

53 Living labour is understood by autonomists as the 'constituent side of surplus labour' and is the part of labour associated with the needs and desires of workers and producers. No matter how successful the indoctrination process by capital is, it conducts struggles over the wage and understands them as part of a broader struggle to 'communicate and constitute new social relations'. Working-class subjectivity emerges through constant struggles that are waged to increase the proportion of necessary labour time and function as both the condition and limit of the development of capitalism. As such, these struggles are immanent to the process of capitalist transformation. For more, see Read 2000.

54 This is the question that Marx addressed in his late works, particularly in his draft letters to Vera Zasulich. For more on this and for translations of these draft letters into English, see Shanin 1983.

55 This was Okinawa's equivalent of mainland Japan's 1873 land tax reforms.

owned by local municipalities; or lands owned by individual property-owners. By 1908 most of Okinawa's communal lands became publicly owned and individual farming households were formally deprived of access to forestlands and materials like firewood that had been vital components of their household economies in the past.[56] In his chapter on so-called primitive accumulation in *Capital* Volume I Marx showed that the process of enclosure was accompanied by the dissolution of the agrarian villages and understood it to be a policy that bourgeois states deployed in order to drive people out of their communities and into industry. In Japan and many other regions of the world, these processes did not take place simultaneously and agrarian villages remained intact despite losing access to their communal lands.[57]

Okinawa's conditions of incorporation into Japanese capitalism necessitated policies that strategically kept old administrative systems and tax collection methods intact for the first two decades of the prefecture's existence. As a result, many of its self-sufficient farming households that produced a mixture of their staple food, sweet potato and grains, cloth wovens and sugar, were converted into producers of brown sugar for mainland Japanese agrarian villages that could not afford the more expensive white sugar preferred by the urban middle-class market.[58] Next, we will examine some of the ways in which small farming households that lost access to communal lands during the first decade of the twentieth century responded to their further incorporation into

56 Access to forestlands was unofficially allowed but was subject to increased state supervision. The prefecture began to cut large quantities of lumber from Okinawa's forests to send to Taiwan in order to fuel its rapidly developing sugar industry. For policies regarding the division of these lands in mainland Japan around the same time, see Totman 2007.

57 For Marxists, the resolution of the 'agrarian question' was also necessary because the backwardness of agriculture and agrarian relations in the countryside was seen as an impediment to revolutionary struggle. Engels, Kautsky and Lenin dealt explicitly with the 'agrarian question' in this manner as both a theoretical and political issue. Marxist theoreticians in Japan and elsewhere labelled this phenomenon and the social, political and economic crises that emerged as a result of the 'agrarian question' and considered its resolution necessary before proper capitalist development could take place.

58 This was not limited to Okinawa. The changes that took place in mainland Japan in the first two decades after 1868 also worked through old systems and administrative units: see Kikekawa 1967. For an article that contrasts Okinawa and mainland Japan's administrative systems in this early Meiji period, see Uechi 2003. The category *shōnō* is difficult to define, but in Okinawa's case and in Chayanov's usage, it may refer to a family farm that is run by a farming household without the use of outside hired labour. In this sense, it may or may not differ from the way that *jisaku* is defined in mainland Japan – *jisaku* usually depends on hired labour, though in Okinawa's case, even *jisaku's* lands were small enough to not rely on hired labour.

the commodity-economy following the entry of mainland sugar companies backed by monopoly capital into the prefecture around World War I.

The Okinawa Seitō Kabushikigaisha was the first mainland sugar company to enter the prefecture.[59] It did so in 1911, four years after the start of prefecture-led efforts to promote mechanisation in the sugar industry.[60] Under the management of Okinawa Seitō, the Nishihara factory established by the prefecture in 1908 as a 100 ton/day operation was expanded by 2.5 times. It changed its name to Okitai Seitō following its entry into colonial Taiwan's sugar industry in November 1912. Following on their heels, the Tainansha, established by Suzuki Shōten, a powerful sugar merchant company turned concern based in Kobe, also set their sites on Okinawan sugar.[61] After beginning its operations in 1913 in Taiwan, the company entered Okinawa in August of 1917 in dramatic fashion, purchasing all three of Okitai Seitō's factories in December.[62]

In addition to the entry of these companies funded by large capital in the main island of Okinawa, Yaeyama – an archipelago comprised of 32 islands under the jurisdiction of Okinawa prefecture whose primary value to the Empire was its geographical proximity to Taiwan – also saw major transformations to its sugar industry.[63] Modern sugar production on Yaeyama's Ishigaki Island, Nagura village began in 1895 with the establishment of the Yaeyama Tōgyō Kabushikigaisha by local industrialist Nakagawa Toranosuke. The company had an impressive roster of investors that included entrepreneur Shibusawa

59 Its parent company was Abe Shōten, a sugar merchant company based in Yokohama that had expanded into manufacturing and refining.

60 The state's active promotion of industry began in the 1880s, but focused more on providing subsidies to encourage cultivation, not mechanisation. For more on the policy in the 1880s, see Mukai 1998.

61 Following its entry into Taiwan, the Suzuki Shōten was able to diversify its operations into industries like steel, shipping and commercial agriculture and quickly developed into a powerful *zaibatsu* with over 60 affiliate [*keiretsu*] companies and 560 million yen in capital. See Iritakenishi 1993, p. 83.

62 The Tainansha also purchased Okinawa Seitō, a company that had just been founded by Yano Keitarō, a well-known industrialist from the Kansai area. He established the company again in 1916 and built a 250-ton factory in Ginowan in central Okinawa. After that, he also purchased the 80-ton capacity communally-owned factory in Takamine village, located in the southern part of the main island, and expanded it into a 300-ton/day capacity factory. Once all of these mergers and purchases were completed, Suzuki Shōten's Tainansha operated as the only sugar manufacture capital in the Okinawa prefecture. See Mukai 1998, p. 307 and *Showa Seitō Kabushiki Gaisha 10 Nen Shi* 1937 for details. *Tainan Seitō Kabushiki Gaisha Hōkokusho* also provides detailed statistics about the Tainansha's operations. These records are available between 1918 and 1931.

63 The quasi-official Bank of Taiwan was a major financer of the Tainansha.

Eiichi but had to suspend its operations in 1902 after bad weather, malaria outbreaks and the lack of agricultural labourers plagued the operation.[64]

The outbreak of World War I brought mainland capital back into Yaeyama with a vengeance. Prior to its dramatic entry into Okinawa Island, Suzuki Shōten infiltrated Ishigaki in August 1916 by investing participation capital for the establishment of the Yaeyama Sangyō Kabushikigaisha.[65] In addition, its affiliate, the Tōyō Seitō Kabushikigaisha, entered Ishigaki's Ōhama village and established the Yaeyama factory in late 1917 after it consolidated its monopoly position in Taiwan.[66] As the history of Yaeyama's sugar industry reveals, Japanese large sugar capital leveraged the dominant position it was able to establish in colonial Taiwan through state encouragement during the early part of the decade to consolidate a monopoly position in Okinawa.[67] By the end of the war, these same concerns had laid the foundations for the development of the industry in the South Seas islands and had cultivated shipping routes in preparation for taking control of Java's sugar trade.[68] The aggressive entry of Japanese monopoly capital into the sugar industry during World War I in Okinawa and beyond was intimately linked to the severe reduction of European beet sugar output, which fell from 8.3 million tons during the 1912–13 season to 2.6 million tons in 1919–20 and did not fully recover until the late 1920s.[69] This contraction of European beet sugar production dramatically increased the price of sugar on the world market. In Okinawa's case, the price of brown sugar on the Naha market nearly quadrupled between 1910 and 1919.[70]

Iba Nantetsu, a poet from Ishigaki Island, wrote a piece called *Nangoku no Shirayuri* (*White Lilies of the South*) in 1927, a decade after the Tōyō Seitō established its Yaeyama factory. In it, he illuminated the embeddedness of sugar manufacturing in village-level social relations as a whole.[71] While it is necessary to exercise caution when reading Iba's romantic portrayal of Okinawa's peasantry, his depiction of the sugar-producing countryside in the interwar

64 Iritakenishi 1993, p. 73. They shifted their hopes to the burgeoning sugar industry in Taiwan after 1902.

65 In the meantime, it also entered Java and strengthened its presence in Taiwan.

66 Iritakenishi 1993, p. 83.

67 For state policies toward sugar in Taiwan, see Ka 1998 and Mazumdar 1998.

68 Knight 2010, p. 484.

69 James 1931, p. 482.

70 Mukai 1983.

71 The advantage of centrifugal sugar was that it could be refined into white sugar in mainland refineries. It was the preferred type of sugar compared to what was mainly produced in Okinawa, non-centrifugal sugar [*ganmitsutō*], where there is no separation of molasses and crystals in the manufacture process, or brown sugar.

period provides us with valuable insights into the everyday concerns of cultivators living and working within a complex web of relations, both old and new, within their villages. His description, written over a decade after the entry of large mainland capital into Ishigaki, reveals that small-scale brown sugar production was still very much part of the physical and social landscape of the island.

In a section titled 'Nōmin no Yorokobi' ['The Joy of the Peasantry'] Iba described a mesmerising, almost ecstatic scene of peasants who were engaged in the communal production of brown sugar. He began with a sketch of the sugar cultivating village during a normal season of harvest and manufacture: 'behind the pasture in spring that is like blue carpet laid out from corner to corner, young men and women become entangled ... the young girls' towels peeking out from the stalks'.[72] After remarking that the pure voices of young men and women singing folk melodies from behind the cane fields was 'irresistibly charming', Iba described the technical precision of these cultivators: 'how their hands move mechanically from years of experience ... passers-by stand still to watch, as the girls cut the cane without forgetting to sing their island folk songs'.[73] His description also highlighted the gendered division of labour that governed the process of manufacturing cane into brown sugar during the winter months after a long year of tending to the fields: 'The strong young men of the village wear blue vertical striped cotton shirts and white knit shirts with shorts. ... they cut down the swiftly grown cane with a thick sickle and transport them to the sugar huts'.[74] Of the young women of the village he wrote, '[t]hey wear simple cotton indigo-dye [*kasuri*] kimono and on top, a vermillion kimono cord the colour of flames ... They take the cane that the men transport and separate the leaves from the stalks. They bind just the mesocotyl into bunches approximately two *shaku* in diameter'.[75] While he did point out that there were occasional 'irreversible' accidents during the compressing process if kimono sleeves or hands got stuck in the gears, he described a well-oiled but thoroughly living machine that involved young men, women, children, cows and horses, all of whom soldiered through the arduous process of manufacturing that lasted all day and all night by singing folk songs and urging each other along.[76]

72 Iba 1927, p. 28.
73 Iba 1927, p. 30.
74 Iba 1927.
75 1 *shaku* = 30.3 cm. The quote is from Iba 1927, p. 30.
76 Iba 1927, p. 32.

Iba's work reminds us of the social character of production that entangled groups of ten or so farming families in small-scale credit and mutual labour exchange relations that by design could not be settled in a single season or even with a single transaction between two parties. Work shaped much of the collective entertainment and play that villagers enjoyed during the busy seasons, from songs that were performed during the planting, harvesting and transport of sugar; to the distribution of money to families within the collectives of neighbouring manufacturing families called *satō-gumi* after the sugar was sold; to the sharing of meals that were made with food that was purchased on a tab at the communal store. All of these activities remained part of a shared cycle of celebration that accompanied each season of strenuous labour long after the official conversion to the Gregorian calendar.[77] While such an explanation risks the romanticisation of communal life if taken completely at face value, Iba's work points to the dangers of underestimating the importance that this type of shared experience held for cultivators as they calculated the benefits and drawbacks to submitting cane to the nearby factory and provides us with a better understanding of why they did not convert themselves into the contract-abiding pure cane cultivators that the Tōyō Seitō, Tainansha and prefectural authorities desired.

The reaffirmation of these relations following large sugar capital's entry into the prefecture should not be read as evidence of small producers' feudality or inability to make rational economic decisions, but must be understood as calculated responses to the structural transformations in Okinawa's countryside resulting from the changing conditions of the global sugar industry. Their refusal to convert themselves into pure cane cultivators must be understood as conscious decisions that small producers made to reject pursuits that brought short-term increases but increased their vulnerability to external forces, rather than as futile revolutionary acts or reactionary attempts to maintain feudal ways of life.[78] One of the main outcomes of these acts of refusal was that

---

77 Tamura 1927 proves the continued existence of 'internal laws' that were enforced in Okinawa's villages. These ranged from regulations regarding public morals, like the prohibition of women going to other villages at night and men and women playing outside at night, to prohibitions against cutting down certain types of trees, dirtying communal wells, not keeping chickens in pens or taking cane from others without permission. For the full list from the Kadena region, see pp. 460–1.

78 In Scott's 2010 work, *The Art of Not Being Governed*, he writes about the way that communities self-consciously select crops that are amenable to a nomadic existence or those that can be left alone for some time, such as root vegetables. This point is useful for understanding why Okinawa's peasantry were reluctant to give up their cultivation of sweet potato and other crops to focus solely on growing cash crops. Their insistence upon

despite repeated injections of funds by the prefecture to increase production, the proportion of centrifugal sugar never exceeded 37 percent of total sugar production during the pre-war period and hovered around the 30 percent mark most years.[79] The reluctance of farming families to become pure cane cultivators for the modern mills was no doubt informed by the experiences that Okinawa's migrant workers had in the plantations and fields of Hawaii, the Philippines, New Caledonia, Brazil and Taiwan – all regions whose sugar industries were dominated by monopoly capital.[80]

The Eruption of Non-selling Alliances in the Midst of a Global Sugar Boom

In addition to the peasantry's reluctance to transform themselves into pure cane cultivators, mainland sugar capital and prefectural authorities were frustrated by the non-selling alliances that producers residing in carrying-in regions actively organised in order to secure more favourable terms for the cane that they did choose to submit to the centrifugal factories. The first of these was organised on Okinawa Island in late 1916 and was spurred by a disagreement over the price that sugar companies allocated as brown sugar production costs. The price at which sugar companies set these expenses – a crucial component in calculating the price that large factories paid cultivators for their cane – was determined by subtracting the figure designated as the total brown sugar manufacture production expense from the average price of grade two sugar on the Naha market during the 10 days prior to the designated

retaining the ability to produce a diverse array of crops can also be understood more fully by referring to Mintz 1989.

79 Kinjō 1985, p. 47. More specific figures on the different categories of yearly fluctuations in sugar production can be found in the *Okinawa Satō Dōgyō Kumiai Gairan* (1926), an account of the Sugar Production Association that was established in 1913. Most sugar producers on the main island were dues-paying members. According to their figures, the proportion of brown sugar output to *bunmitsutō* output per association member fell quite dramatically during the non-selling alliances, from 77 percent in 1917 to 73.5 percent in 1919 and 68 percent in 1921, despite subsidies granted by the prefecture to the companies.

80 See Aniya 1977 and Mukai 1988 for details on Okinawan immigration that began at the end of the nineteenth century. Between 1899 and 1941, Okinawa sent over 72,000 international emigrants to work primarily in the agricultural sector and a majority worked in sugar or other export agricultural industries. For conditions in these and other major sugar-producing regions around World War I, see Taylor 1978; Okihiro 1992; Larkin 1993; Ka 1998; Ayala 1999; McGillivray 2009; and Knight 2010.

date of submission. It was to the peasantry's advantage to negotiate the lowest possible figure while the company benefitted from publishing the highest cost, irrespective of whether or not cultivators actually spent this amount to manufacture brown sugar.

An article dated 25 December 1916 in the *Ryūkyū Shimpō* titled 'Gansha Baikyaku Mondai Kaiketsu' ['Resolution of the Dispute over the Sale of Cane'] reported the details of the negotiations between the alliance representatives and the Okitai Seitō, the specific target of the boycott. According to the article, alliance representatives held a meeting at Shinkyōji temple near Naha port where OSK-owned ships that monopolised the transport of Okinawan sugar to mainland Japan were docked in order to determine a response to the company's refusal to budge from the figure of 2.1 yen per barrel for brown sugar production expenses.[81] The alliance members decided that the highest figure they could accept was 1.7 yen per barrel, which was based on calculations made by the Sugar Production Association [Okinawa Satō Dōgyō Kumiai].[82] This meant that a 20 percent gap had to be bridged before the two sides could come to an agreement.

The company was simply unwilling to make this kind of concession. Instead of negotiating the brown sugar production expense it shifted tactics. It proposed a rebate system that offered peasants who submitted larger quantities of cane more favourable conditions.[83] Those who supplied 10 barrels or more received 0.3 yen per barrel; those supplying 50 barrels or more received 0.4 yen; and those who supplied all of their harvest regardless of quantity also received 0.4 yen back from the company.[84] This was the company's attempt to bridge the 0.4 yen per barrel gap that separated them from the alliance while simultaneously securing larger quantities of cane.[85]

Around the same time small producers near the 250-ton capacity Nishihara factory also owned by Okitai Seitō organised a similar non-selling alliance.

81 Kinjō 1983.

82 'Gansha Baikyaku Mondai', *Ryūkyū Shimpō* (15 February 1917) in *Okinawa Kenshi*, vol. 17, pp. 798–9.

83 'Seitōsha to Shasakumin', *Ryūkyū Shimpō* (12 January 1917), in *Okinawa Kenshi*, vol. 17, p. 803.

84 With regards to the production levels of cane cultivators in Okinawa, 80 percent of all sugar manufacturers produced less than 20 barrels of brown sugar per year. There were also quite a few who produced less than five barrels. See 'Satō Dōgyō Kumiai Sono Shin Ninmu', *Ryūkyū Shimpō* (18 November 1917) in *Okinawa Kenshi*, vol. 17, p. 803.

85 This was also likely an attempt to divide the cultivators, as those who were willing to submit a larger portion of their harvests to the company might favour this arrangement that rewarded them for bulk submissions.

Company representatives met with prefectural authorities when this boycott began and received from the latter an agreement for subsidies of 0.1 yen per barrel that would be granted to cultivators in addition to the company's own 'encouragement monies' to incentivise large submissions.[86] While the papers reported that the collective impact of government subsidies and the company's 'encouragement monies' were successful in convincing cultivators to dissolve their non-selling alliances, continued disputes in these regions following the takeover of the Okitai Seitō by the Tainansha indicates that these were merely temporary measures that did not resolve the core of the problem.[87]

The common thread that united these and other non-selling alliances and disputes that erupted during the interwar period between large sugar capital and Okinawa's small producers was that all were struggles that revolved around the valorisation of living labour. Large sugar capital, which attempted to realise stable procurements of cane by signing long-term contracts with the peasantry and providing incentives for large submissions, fought with small cultivators living in the carrying-in regions who understood that the conditions offered as 'conciliatory measures' such as longer contracts, rebates and remittances only indebted their futures to sugar brokers. These brokers travelled around the cane cultivating regions and offered small peasantry high interest loans in exchange for a guarantee of the bulk of their harvest and encouraged them to increase their submissions to make up for lower prices that the factories offered. Producers understood full well that completely embedding themselves into this system, designed to transform them into more efficient and focused cultivators of cane, would leave them with little time to devote to brown sugar manufacture and subsidiary industries like livestock raising and sweet potato cultivation.[88] They would become more dependent on the commodity

86 'Gansha Baikyaku Mondai Kaiketsu', p. 806.

87 Articles detailing other non-selling alliances during 1917 include: 'Ryōtō Gappei Kettei', *Ryūkyū Shimpō* (17 October 1917) in *Okinawa Kenshi*, vol. 17, p. 864; 'Baishū Hō Kaisei Riyū', *Ryūkyū Shimpō* (24 October 1917) in *Okinawa Kenshi*, vol. 17, p. 868; 'Genryō Baishū Hō', *Ryūkyū Shimpō* (24 October 1917) in *Okinawa Kenshi* 17, p. 871; and 'Shasakumin no Ikō', *Ryūkyū Shimpō* (13 November 1917) in *Okinawa Kenshi*, vol. 17, p. 879. Details are hazy but there were also non-selling alliances that were organised on Yaeyama's Ishigaki island by cultivators who submitted cane to the *Tōyō Seitō's* Yaeyama factory around the same time.

88 Pig raising was a crucial form of supplementary income. In addition, it was very important for new years' celebrations, soups throughout the year and for medicinal purposes. In many cases, more than one family owned one pig collectively. In addition, the cultivation of sweet potato played an important part in the overall household economy, as it was the staple food for members of the household. The skin of the sweet potato, in addition to leftovers and tofu, was used for the pig's feed. Finally, sweet potato could be used to

economy, even more vulnerable to price fluctuations and would end up giving their entire lives over to capital's realisation of surplus value. Their commitment to a single industry monopolised by large capital would ultimately strip them away from the social and economic protections provided by their existing networks of communal production and lending – mechanisms that granted them the possibility of self-valorisation.[89]

The desire to remain embedded in a village economy in which they performed agriculture as well as manufacturing indicates that while Okinawa's small producers may or may not have 'acted capitalistically', as Marxists who study peasant behaviour define it, they nonetheless understood the capitalist logic that governed decisions made by the Tainansha and responded in a way that would hurt it the most.[90] Whether the responses were governed by economic, social, rational or moral calculations is a complex matter that cannot be determined by the sources at our disposal. Still, a close examination of the carrying – in terms that they finally accepted and that ended the non-selling alliances can help to illuminate their motives and desires.

The disputes between cultivators and the companies that began in late 1916 continued until a truce was called in early January 1918. Representatives of the five villages that serviced the Tainansha's Nishihara factory decided to back down on the issue of the revised grade equivalents in exchange for extending the number of days after harvest in which cane could be submitted to the factory. The company had proposed 16 days but the representatives for the peasantry successfully extended it to 50. This was a key point for small producers because the securing of extra days addressed one of the main concerns that they had in these negotiations: flexibility that would protect their ability to

fuel the communal sugar manufacture of brown sugar. For these details, see Kinjō 1985, pp. 105–6 and *Okinawa Ken Kosaku ni Kansuru Chōsa* 1930, pp. 553–60 for a sample breakdown of a farming household in the Nakagami region.

89 See Read 2003 for more on the distinction between dead and living labour.

90 This is a point that Chayanov makes when he asserts that even in an environment clearly dominated by capitalism peasant agriculture followed a logic characteristic of the operational logic of family farms within that broader society. Faced with a 'diverse calculus of choices', he argues, they preferred a maximisation of total income rather than profit or marginal product. On this point, he and Uno agree. However, in contrast to Uno, he does not link this automatically to a drive for more land. For an explication of Chayanov's understanding of small producers' behaviour within a capitalist economy, see Shanin's essay 'Chayanov's Message: Illuminations, Miscomprehensions, and Contemporary "Development Theory"' that is included at the beginning of Chayanov 1986.

search for more advantageous conditions.[91] This extension would grant them more time to decide whether to sell to the factory or to manufacture the cane into brown sugar in their own sugar huts.[92] In addition to an extension of the number of days after harvest that cane could be sold to the factory, the peasant representatives negotiated a lower quota that tenants living in factory-managed farms had to sell to the company.[93]

Conclusion

Close examination of the way that Okinawa's sugar-producing small-farming families responded to the rapid influx of large sugar capital into the prefecture during the First World War reveals that despite the deep and wide arsenal of weapons that mainland concerns had at their disposal, the transformation of relations of production was by no means a smooth, or uncontested process.[94]

---

91 Chayanov points out that this quest for flexibility extended to keeping lands or means of production unused and ready for disposal. Chayanov 1986, p. 109. James Scott also argues something similar in *The Art of Not Being Governed.* There, he describes the way that communities pursue strategies of cultivation that protect them from the eye of the state. He writes: 'By pursuing a broad portfolio ... they spread their risks and ensure themselves a diverse and nutritious diet ...' He continues, '[p]articular crops have characteristics that make them more or less resistant to appropriation ... Roots and tubers after they ripen can be left safely in the ground for up to two years and dug up piecemeal as needed'. Scott 2010, p. 195. In Okinawa's case, the proportion of sweet potato cultivation to sugar production increased the poorer a household was.

92 As Mukai Kiyoshi argues, the peasantry would retain more control over the income they received from selling sugar if they manufactured it on their own because the contract with the company did not guarantee a price, and this could only be determined by the price at the Naha market the day that the cane was carried in.

93 'Gansha Baishū Rakuchaku', *Ryūkyū Shimpō* (11 January 1918) in *Okinawa Kenshi*, vol. 17, p. 917. This settlement was negotiated between the *Tainansha*'s Nishihara factory and Nishihara village's Arakawa Saburō and the head administrator [*kuchō*] of Yonabaru, Adaniya. The same article reported that the long-term goal of the cultivators' representatives was to eventually revive each village's sugar manufacture capacities and expand them so that they would be able to handle manufacturing all of the cane produced in their region through their own factory. While no new disputes were reported in 1918, 1919 saw non-selling alliances over 10–20 *chōbu* crossing two or three regions and a 400 worker strike in a sugar factory in Daitōjima in November over wages.

94 Scholars including Uno have noted that in certain historical conjunctures, capital does not require the installation of capitalist relations of production in agriculture. Though that is an important point to counter teleological notions of capitalist development, it

Conflicts that developed between Okinawa's sugar producers and these concerns forced the latter to come to the negotiating table with counteroffers numerous times. The small but determined non-selling alliances that erupted at the height of the wartime sugar boom reveal the small producers' reluctance to abandon the entire web of communal resources, social relations and supplementary activities that they had at their disposal in exchange for their transformation into raw material cultivators. This stance was based on both a refusal of sugar capital's attempts to create a cadre of indebted cultivators who could be counted on each season to submit set quantities of cane that could be manufactured and sold to feed the discerning tastes of middle-class consumers in mainland cities, and their affirmation of existing social relations that afforded them a certain degree of flexibility to pursue household interests on their own terms. Figures of farming household composition compiled by sugar expert Nakayoshi Chōkō reveal that even as the presence of large sugar factories strengthened after World War I, the proportion of tenant families to total farming families remained relatively steady between seven and nine percent. Combined with the declining proportion of farming households to all households in the prefecture from 81 percent prior to the entry of large mainland sugar capital in 1906 to 71 percent in 1921, we can conclude that families preferred to move out of agricultural production entirely rather than convert themselves into tenants who exclusively cultivated raw material cane.[95]

This can be seen in the way that agricultural household composition transformed in the Nakagami region of Okinawa island, the centre of Tainansha-led factory sugar production. There, the percentage of owner-farmer [*jisaku*] type farming families that owned land that they farmed with family labour increased from 61.25 percent in March 1914 to 68.6 percent in June 1917. The percentage of half-tenant [*jikosaku*] type farming families that owned some lands and borrowed some from others fell in contrast from 29.02 percent to 26.15 percent. These changes can be attributed to the peasantry's decision to turn to temporary migrant work and immigration instead of borrowing addi-

should be noted that in the period we are dealing with in Okinawa, concerns were actively trying to proletarianise at least a part of Okinawa's small producers. Their turn to Taiwan, the South Seas Islands and Java around this time was based on the belief that they could get away with more forceful tactics of expropriation in these regions than in Okinawa, which despite its own peripheralisation was formally part of the metropole.

95 See Nakayoshi 1928, pp. 53–86 for more figures. This article also examines the broader transformations in land ownership that took place in Okinawa following the final land redistribution that took place right before the start of the land reorganisation project.

tional plots of land to continue agricultural production.[96] Of course, many factors need to be taken into account to properly analyse these changes but it is important to note that despite these changes in the composition of farming households, the Tainansha continued to struggle to convert sugar manufacturers into pure cane cultivators. If additional income was needed, farming families preferred to send a family member outside of the village, prefecture or country over converting all family operations into supplying raw materials to the factory.[97]

Rather than reading this condition as a concrete manifestation of Uno's description of Japan's agrarian question as it unfolded after World War I – that is, as an example of the deeply rooted feudal thought, sentiments and customs amongst small peasants that led them to unrelentingly increase their assets through overwork, under-consumption and general exhaustion – we might read the continuation of these sub village-level mechanisms long after large sugar capital's entry into the prefecture as a reflection of the desire of small producers to remain embedded in communal forms of production, manufacturing and exchange precisely as the penetration of monopoly capital into their communities threatened to dismantle these existing mechanisms of support. If read this way, the peasants' reluctance to transform themselves into pure cane cultivators can be seen as a significant act of anti-capitalist refusal that obstructed the transformation of their work and lives into dead labour that would have remade them into alienated producers of raw materials or sellers of their labour power. Specifically, the struggles between mainland sugar capital and Okinawa's brown sugar producers reveals the need to understand these refusals as conscious decisions that small producers made to reject pursuits that brought short-term increases in income but heightened their vulnerability

96 For details of this move and the communities that formed in these new spaces, see Tomiyama 1990.

97 This was also the case with farming and fishing households in Yaeyama. Families began to move in significant numbers to Taiwan even though opportunities for work increased in Iriomote mining and in large sugar factories that arrived in Daitōjima in 1916. See Yanaihara 1929 and Okinawaken Yaeyama Shichō 1932 for contemporary accounts of these industries. With regards to sugar, the Yaeyama factory was built by the Tōyō Seitō Kabushikigaisha in 1917 and the area under cultivation increased dramatically by the following year. However, the factory suspended operations in 1921. Women in particular preferred to venture to Taipei to find work as maids and merchants in some cases because they saw Taiwan to be a more modern, attractive site of employment than their own hometowns. For more on the immigration of women from Yaeyama to Taiwan, see Kaneto 2007 and Matayoshi 1990. On the relationship between the development of industry in Yaeyama and immigration, see Miki 1996.

to external forces, rather than as reactionary attempts to maintain outmoded ways of life or holdouts purely designed to extract more money from the companies. The small successes that cane cultivators achieved in their disputes against large sugar capital backed by Japanese concerns transformed the realm of possibilities of belonging and action that they could imagine. The deeper impact of these struggles can be found in the radicalisation of the same agrarian village societies in the late 1920s and early 1930s as the prefectural economy approached crisis conditions.[98]

Finally, this understanding of the anti-capitalist struggle by small farming households in Okinawa's agrarian villages during World War I forces us to reject existing historiographical approaches that treat the prefecture's wartime experience as a black box during which no significant struggle was possible.[99] This perspective, which is also dominant in the way scholars understand the condition of Japan's agrarian villages during the total war period of the 1930s and the first half of the 1940s, assumes that small cultivators were particularly well-suited to be transformed into agents of Japanese fascism due to their

98 The post-boom agricultural crisis that ravaged Okinawa's countryside in the 1920s known as 'Sago Palm Hell' brought the demands of cultivators together with socialist and Marxist thinkers who began to organise in the prefecture in the beginning of the decade. The Social Science Research Incident, which took place between 1926 and 1928, was especially threatening to the company and the prefecture because it linked the activists and peasantry together for the first time and exposed the cooperation of the Tainansha and the prefecture to profit at the expense of ailing small producers. Two prominent Marxist activists, Yamada Kanji and Inoguchi, along with 20 or so teachers from Nakagami, organised the Social Science Research Group, which joined forces with the Okinawa Labour-Farmer [*Rōnō*] Party founded in February 1928 to establish a tighter coordination between thought, politics, and activism. A leaflet 'Tainansha e no Yokkyū' that was dated 27 December 1928 represented the merging of Marxist thought and activism with a longer tradition of peasant struggle against the exploitative practices of the company described in this chapter, and inspired widespread agitation in the prefecture. Approximately 60 copies of the secret leaflet were distributed among party leaders until they were discovered and banned by the authorities. It called for greater decision-making power by the peasantry and greater control over their product and rejected the Tainansha's assertion that the interests of capital and the peasantry were identical – something that the company used to justify its activities in Okinawa. For the full text, refer to *Okinawa Ken Kosaku ni Kansuru Chōsa* 1930.

99 It goes without saying that such a narrative of victimisation implicitly grants the state and capital almost exclusive control over the transformation of social, economic, political and cultural life and renders antagonisms in everyday life either ineffectual or non-existent.

innate conservatism.[100] Such a conclusion, intimately linked to the description that Uno and other Marxist theorists elaborated to analyse Japan's agrarian question, risks effacing the moments of anti-capitalist struggle that may not have crystallised into a single revolutionary moment but actively participated in drawing the contours of policies and relations that governed small farmers' everyday lives.[101]

---

100 For an example of this approach in the context of the Ōgimi village in the northern part of Okinawa, see Morita 1973.

101 Mori Takemaro in 'Nihon Fashizumu no Keisei to Nōson Keizai Kōsei Undō' expresses this position, stating that the reformist energies of the peasantry were absorbed into the right-wing fascist movement nationwide. For similar approaches, see Nagahara 1989, Saitō 1989, Yamazaki 1996 and Noda 1998. In Okinawa's case, the conclusion that follows is particularly violent: because of their longing to be considered 'truly Japanese' and due to the strength of their enduring primitive communal organisations, the prefecture's small producers were the most enthusiastic agents of Japanese fascism in the Empire. This has led to a strange discourse of 'betrayal' common to many writings about Okinawa's experience during the Battle of Okinawa and the immediate post-war period. This discourse, often produced by scholars who are quite critical of Japanese policies toward Okinawa as a whole, ends up in a sense affirming the policies of incorporation by operating from a logic that renders the state's betrayal all the more egregious because the people of Okinawa were such loyal adherents of the emperor-state ideology.

CHAPTER 6

War and Social Revolution: World War I and the 'Great Transformation'

Sandra Halperin

Introduction

This chapter revisits the 'great transformation' that began in Europe in 1914. It focuses, first, on the rising global 'red tide' in the years before 1914. It then shows how, in 1914, the mass mobilisation of labour for armies and industry exponentially increased social tensions in Europe. It argues that the war unleashed a social revolution that, by beginning to shift the balance of class power in Europe, made possible the transformation of European societies after World War II.

A number of parallels can be drawn between the war that began in 1914 and the earlier world war of 1793–1815. Both wars came after a long period of expansion (the 'Long Sixteenth Century', the 'Long Twentieth Century'), followed by periods of contraction and conflict.[1] In both cases, these conflicts culminated in an imperialist world war.[2] In both cases, social revolutionary currents were already underway before the war and were exacerbated by the mobilisation of mass armies. During the earlier war, the 'spectre of the international threat to property' from the French Revolutionary campaigns, together with slave and peasant revolts from within, combined to produce the 'Great Fear' across Eurasia and the Americas.[3] During the 1914 war, the Bolshevik Revolution and the crescendo of strikes and the groundswell of demonstrations and uprisings in support of it, instilled fear in wealthy classes around the world. The end

1 Halperin 1997, Chapter 2.

2 In the earlier war, France had declared its intention to acquire its 'natural frontiers' and had sought to acquire German and Italian lands, while landlocked countries, e.g., Austria, sought outlets to the sea.

3 The French Revolution unleashed slave revolts throughout the Caribbean empires of Britain, France, and Spain between 1791 and 1808. In 1791, a slave revolt on Saint Domingue (Haiti), France's richest colony, ignited a twelve-year revolution.

of both wars brought a period of restoration and reaction in Europe.[4] After 1815, the kings and aristocracies of Europe formed an *internationale*, a 'Concert of Europe' (concluded in 1815 among Great Britain, Russia, Austria, Prussia, and later France) for the purpose of suppressing revolutionary uprisings throughout the region.[5] After 1918, France, Britain, Czechoslovakia, Germany, and Poland (together with the United States and Japan) fought to overturn the Bolshevik Revolution in Russia and, throughout the world, the owning classes everywhere joined together to suppress dissident and revolutionary elements at home and abroad.[6] The difference between the two wars was that, in the latter case, the reconstruction and further consolidation of pre-war structures after 1918 led to a second war and a second mass mobilisation, and this forced concessions to labour which, by producing a relatively more broad-based and 'embedded' development, transformed European societies.

Before 1914, the globalising system of production and exchange was everywhere characterised by internal repression and external expansion through production for export. In the years leading up to the 1914–18 war in Europe, these two central features of states, both within and outside of Europe, were rapidly coming into conflict (Section I). By 1914, a global depression and a rising 'red tide', and increasing imperialist rivalry and conflict among European powers (Section II) combined to produce a multilateral war in Europe. World War I began a social revolution. After 1815, there had been few multilateral great power conflicts in Europe because Europe's monarchs and aristocracies feared that such conflicts would call into use the mass armies that, during and immediately after the Napoleonic Wars, had triggered revolutionary upheavals and threatened to destroy the social order. For one hundred years there had been no multilateral great power conflict in Europe.[7] But in 1914, European states were confronted with an existential threat that forced them, once again, to deploy the weapon of mass destruction introduced in the previous world war: the *lévee en masse*. The war forced European governments to mobilise the masses for war and for the expansion of industrial production needed to

4 A 'white terror' in France, and a long period of Ultra reaction; martial law provisions (in the Six Acts introduced in 1819) in Britain; the abrogation of Liberal constitutions and imposition of strict press and publication censorship (the Carlsbad Decrees) in Prussia; and, a conservative and clerical reaction in Piedmont.

5 English translation is in Hertslet 1891, I, p. 375, Article VI.

6 On some of these developments in Japan, for example, see Matsumura's chapter in this volume.

7 In the Crimean War, Russia conscripted large numbers of men; but the forces raised for that war did not constitute a *lévee en masse* on the scale of either the Napoleonic Wars or the war that began in 1914. Royle 1999, pp. 91–2.

support it – precisely what a century of external expansion had enabled them to avoid. The mass mobilisation in 1914 set in motion a social revolution that began in 1917 and, thereafter, swept through all of Europe (Section III). This and the continuing rise of a global 'red tide' led to World War II and, briefly, in Europe and a few other areas of the world, to a 'great transformation' and to the existence of 'three worlds' of development.

Expansion, Contraction, and Social Conflict, 1815–1914

Industrial Expansion in the Nineteenth Century[8]

During the nineteenth century, global economic expansion was fuelled largely by the production of goods and services for export to an expanding network of elites, ruling groups, and governments around the world. By expanding production largely for export, elites were able to accumulate wealth while at the same time limiting the scope of industrialisation and the growth of organised labour. The Great War and the revolutionary currents that had both unleashed and been released by it, had revealed the dangers of a trained and compact mass army. After the war, many analogies were drawn between the mass army of soldiers created in the Great War and the mass industrial army of workers needed for industrial capitalist production. This was the context in which elites in the nineteenth century and throughout the world undertook to mobilise labour for expanded production.

Maintaining the subordination of labour is always a key concern for elites, as evidenced by their great fear throughout history of slave revolts and peasant uprisings. But the temptation to reorganise production along the lines of industrial capitalism presented elites with a somewhat different dilemma: how to mobilise, train, and educate labour for industrial production while, at the same time, maintaining its subordination to capital. For Elites everywhere, the solution was to very slowly and selectively introduce mechanisation and use methods of production that deskilled workers and kept labour, as a whole, fragmented and poorly paid. However, while restricting the rapid rise of powerful new classes, this raised an additional problem: if the standard of consumption of the mass of the local population remained the same or was reduced, where would consumers be found for the products of expanded production? The overall pattern that emerged, therefore, was an expansion based on production principally for export to foreign ruling groups or areas of 'new'

8 This section is based on Halperin 2004 and 1997.

settlement abroad,[9] rather than on the growth and integration of local markets. This created the 'dualistic' economic expansion that came to characterise industrial capitalism, an expansion based, not on the development of mass purchasing power at home, but on its development among foreign groups and ruling bodies through loans and investment in infrastructure, railroads and armaments.

Beginning in the nineteenth century, goods and services were produced principally for an expanding network of elites, ruling groups, and governments in other countries. Britain expanded its shipbuilding, boiler-making, gun and ammunition industries, and built foreign railways, canals, and other public works – including banks, telegraphs, and other public services – owned or dependent upon governments. Its exports of capital provided purchasing power among foreign governments and elites for these goods and services, and funded the development and transport of food and raw mat erials exports to Europe, thus creating additional foreign purchasing power and demand for British goods. At the centre of this circuit was the City of London, which like the advanced sector of a 'dependent' third world economy worked to build strong linkages between British export industries and foreign economies, rather than to integrate various parts of the domestic economy.

On the eve of World War I, the dominant social, economic, and political system of Europe paralleled those which existed at the time in other regions and which exist still in many areas of the contemporary Global South. Its most effective elites were traditional and aristocratic, landowning and rent receiving, religious and oligarchic. Industry was penetrated by feudal forms of organisation, and characterised by monopolism, protectionism, cartelisation and corporatism, forming small islands within impoverished, backward agrarian economies. Political institutions had not significantly affected the character of popular representation; the great majority of adults were excluded from political participation. Economic expansion was external, rather than internal, and based on the enlargement of foreign markets rather than of domestic ones. Europe was still 'pre-eminently pre-industrial', as Arno Mayer has argued.[10] Except in England, agriculture was still the single largest and weightiest economic sector. Central Europe had not yet begun its industrial take-off; Eastern and Southern Europe had neither developed industrially nor moved

9 Between 1830 and 1914, about 50 million Europeans, 30 percent of Europe's population in 1830, immigrated to the Americas. The Americas provided markets for European products *overseas, rather than locally*, thus enabling Europeans to expand production without dangerously impacting social relations at home.

10 Mayer 1981, pp. 187, 301.

significantly into agricultural exports. In 1914, most of Europe was still rural, and most of rural Europe had not changed substantially since the Middle Ages. In fact, on the eve of World War I, Europe as a whole had achieved a level of economic well-being about equal with that of Latin America.[11]

Contraction: The Great Depression, 1873–96, and the Rising 'Red Tide'

During the decades between the Great Depression of 1873–96 and World War I, the nineteenth-century system of economic expansion began to unravel. Globally, depression and agricultural decline accelerated the rise of a global 'red tide' and, in Europe, the quest to escape the implications of those tensions brought about a sharp escalation of imperialist expansion.[12]

Contraction set in with a marked deterioration of agricultural conditions and a slowdown in world production and trade beginning in the 1870s, which exacerbated economic imbalances in Asia, Africa, Europe, and the Americas. Around the world, this produced a groundswell of social conflict. There was an explosive rise of violence in rural areas which proved increasingly difficult to keep in check by repression and emigration.

In the 1870s, growing land hunger in Europe gave rise to an unprecedented upsurge in agrarian agitation and protest. About 80 percent of the land in Britain was owned by some 7,000 persons,[13] and 87 percent of personal wealth (1911–13) was owned by the top five percent of the British population.[14] 25 percent of the land of Denmark and France was owned by less than four percent of the population. Over 40 percent of the land of southern and central Spain was controlled by less than one percent of the landowners.[15] The growing land hunger in Europe was reflected, not only by agrarian agitation and protest, but by the massive emigration which began in the final decades of the century. Between 1870 and 1914, 35 million Europeans left the region. 25 million left after 1890, most of whom were displaced peasants and agricultural labourers from Prussia's eastern agricultural regions, from southern Italy, the Austro-Hungarian Empire, and the Balkans.[16] In 1907, 0.2 percent of all farms in Prussia

---

11 See Halperin 1997, pp. 199–200, and *Statistical Appendix*, Tables 1–6.

12 On the effects of the Great Depression of the late nineteenth century on different European states and the great power rivalries precipitating the First World War more generally, see Anievas's chapter in this volume.

13 Romein 1978, p. 195.

14 Hobsbawm 1968, p. 274.

15 Goldstein 1983, p. 240.

16 Goldstein 1983, p. 246.

controlled 20 percent of the arable land.[17] 85 percent of the land of Italy was held by ten percent of landowners. In 1900, less than 1 percent of the population owned more than 40 percent of the land of Austria, Hungary, Romania, Germany and Poland.

A series of subsistence crises swept across Asia, Africa and Latin America: the Great Famine of 1876–9; a second wave in 1889–90; a third wave of crop failures across India, Australia, southern Russia, northern Africa, and Spain in 1896–97; followed, in 1902, by a wave of drought and famine, comparable in magnitude to the Great Famine of 1876–9 in India, northern China, Korea, Ethiopia, Java, Vietnam, the Philippines, northeast Brazil, and southern and eastern Africa.[18] Slow growth rates of agricultural production and foreign trade and declining wheat prices triggered a wave of agrarian unrest in the Ottoman Empire, from Syria to Algeria. In Egypt, a 'growing number of increasingly desperate landless peasants and service tenants' attacked moneylenders and landowners.[19]

The Rising Red Tide

In the urban areas of the global system, hungry and disenfranchised populations were fuelling a rising 'red tide' of radicals and socialists of various sorts, dissenters, trade unionists, and suppressed national minorities. It is often assumed that forms of labour in Europe and 'the West' were different than those found in other areas of the world. But throughout the nineteenth century, forms of coerced and semi-coerced labour appropriation associated with those found in the periphery persisted in Europe.[20]

Both in the 'core' and in the 'periphery', forms of labour (wage, coerced, and semi-coerced) were heterogeneous. Though forms of labour control in 'core' and 'peripheral' countries are often assumed to have been different, labour in Europe was subject to the same forms of collective coercion and surveillance associated with colonial and peripheral areas. In England, over thirty thousand troops were on permanent garrison duty in the 1830s. Local barracks and a state-controlled system of paramilitary and police forces were established beginning in the 1840s as part of an organisation headed by the Home Office, the local military command, and the local Home Office intelligence network.[21]

17 Puhle 1986, p. 84.
18 Davis 2001, p. 138.
19 Burke 1991, p. 33.
20 Halperin 2013, Portes et al. 1989; Sassen 1991; 1994; Stern 1988.
21 Foster 1974, Chapters 3 and 4.

European labour forces were larger than those in 'the periphery'. But while labour in the 'periphery' was numerically smaller, it was 'extremely influential', as Frederick Cooper points out, because 'the very narrowness of colonial commercial, mining, and industrial channels meant that a small group – in a position to use face-to-face relations to organise – could disrupt the entire import-export economy'.[22] It is also often assumed that labour was more effectively organised in Europe than elsewhere during the nineteenth century. But during that century, Europe's industrial expansion was largely carried out by atomised, low-wage and low-skilled labour forces. They were neither permanent nor full-time nor represented by national industrial unions.

Everywhere, dominant groups seeking to increase profits by expanding production confronted the problem of how to realise the value of a rising mountain of goods without a corresponding democratisation of consumption at home. How this problem was resolved varied across different societies, according to the type of goods each produced for sale and the relative power of capital and labour. However, similar capabilities, as well as a common system-wide context, tended to shape their interaction with labour in similar ways. Thus, during the nineteenth century, and throughout the world, the organisation of production and the direction of class formation and political change was broadly similar and gave rise to similar forms of conflict.

The experiences of weavers, artisans, miners and railwaymen in the Ottoman Empire and in Europe were not fundamentally different. In England, mechanised weaving and spinning caused a massive collapse of home-based crafts organised under the mercantile 'putting-out system'. But after 1815 some regions of the country were able to produce textile exports and this brought about the collapse of craft production elsewhere in Europe. By the 1830s, however, 'Alsatian and Swiss producers were almost on a par with Lancashire, and machines built by Escher Wyss of Switzerland were found to be superior in many ways to English ones'.[23] Weavers, however, were not the beneficiaries. There was a revolt of silk weavers in Lyon in 1834 in which 300 people were killed in six days of fighting.[24] There was an uprising in Prussian Silesia in June 1844 of about 5000 starving linen handloom weavers which resulted in thirty-five deaths.[25] Outside of Europe, weavers and other artisans 'suffered severely from a flood of cheap, machine-made goods coming from European factories'

22 Cooper 1994, p. 1534.
23 Komlos 2000, p. 309.
24 Goldstein 1983, p. 147.
25 Reichert 1969, p. 31.

after 1850.[26] Thousands of weavers in Damascus lost their jobs when relatively inexpensive Western European textiles flooded Ottoman markets. But by the end of the 1870s, Damascus' commercial textile sector had regained its earlier strength as a result of expanding rural demand for textiles, the cotton boom of the 1860s, appreciation for better quality, though slightly higher priced, local fabrics, and Ottoman fiscal policies encouraging local industries.[27] Factories in Japan, China and India soon began to produce cheaper and better goods than Europeans (and Americans) did.[28] Dyestuffs from India and the Caribbean replaced those of the Mediterranean; Chinese silk replaced Italian.[29]

Throughout the nineteenth century, and around the world, there were riots, insurrections, rebellions, revolutions, uprisings, violent strikes and demonstrations, and brutal repression. All of these expressed the basic antagonism between monopolists (large plantations, trading companies, and transnational corporations) and working populations seeking to reclaim more of the surplus-value they created. Similar forms of labour struggle, including Luddite, radical, trade-unionist, utopian-socialist, and democratic were found around the world. Machine-breaking (Luddism), a well-known practice in early nineteenth-century Europe, later occurred in the Ottoman Empire, Brazil and China.[30] In Asian centres of trade, population and production, a wage-labouring class emerged and, with it, trade unions and modern forms of labour struggle. Other collective action by workers – organised protests, strikes, the formation of labour movements – 'was part of the political and economic life of a number of Middle Eastern countries'.[31] The 1850s had seen the emergence of the strike as an offensive weapon for the improvement of wages and working conditions and, by the 1870s, strikes had replaced riots as 'the workers' preferred form of action'.[32]

The depression led to a sharp increase in strike activity in Europe in the 1880s. The rise in the number of strikes in Britain each year of that decade was indicative of the general trend.

---

26 Davis 1979, p. 38.

27 Vatter 1994, pp. 5–6.

28 McNeil 2008, p. 5.

29 Davis 1979, p. 38.

30 See, e.g. Quataert 1986; Meade 1989; Eng 1990.

31 Lockman 1994, p. xxviii.

32 Gillis 1982, p. 269. The gradual replacement of riots by strikes was noted by observers in the early 1870s. See, e.g. Potter 1870, pp. 34–5; and 1871, p. 535.

Strikes in the 1870s: Britain[33]

TABLE 6.1 *Strikes in the 1870s: Britain*

1870	30	1875	245
1871	98	1876	229
1872	342	1877	180
1873	365	1878	268
1874	286	1879	308

Violent strikes of miners and of transport and dock workers occurred throughout the 1880s and 1890s in Europe, Africa, and the Americas. Troops were required to put down rioting miners in Belgium in 1886, and an armed uprising of the mining population in 1893. In the 1890s there were also violent miners' strikes in Germany, and strikes in the United States and South Africa; and, in Britain, 300,000 mineworkers went on strike. In 1910–11, coal workers went on strike and conducted a national strike in 1912. Miners struck in Mexico in 1906 and in Chile in 1907.

Strikes of transport workers began in force in the 1880s in the United States, and in Europe, Asia, Africa, and the Middle East. In the United States, there was the Burlington Railroad Strike in 1888 and, in 1894, the Pullman Strike, which involved 125,000 workers on twenty-nine railroads, and which left 34 strikers dead and more than 50 wounded in clashes between strikers and some 12,000 federal troops and 5,000 federal marshals over the course of a week.[34] In Britain, there were dockers' strikes in 1898 and 1899; and, in 1911, a general strike involving 80,000 port workers took place in Southampton, Liverpool, Hull, Newport, Northeast coast, Humber, Leith, Manchester, Cardiff, and London, and was joined by striking railway workers, coal porters, lightermen and carters. The Great Anatolian Railway strike took place in September 1908 in the Ottoman Empire, and there were 104 strikes there in the last half of that year.[35] In 1900, tramworkers in Alexandria went on strike, and riots and revolutionary turmoil in Cairo and upper Egypt were violently repressed. Cairo tramworkers went on strike in October 1908, and there was an almost simultaneous strike of tram-

33 Bevan 1880, p. 37.

34 Schlager 2003, p. 94.

35 Quataert 1994, p. 27.

workers in Alexandria and Cairo in July and August 1911. In October 1910, railway workers throughout Egypt went on strike and cut the rail lines to Upper Egypt. A high level of labour violence also began in the plantation belt of the Dutch Indies in 1900. In addition, there was a series of massive general strikes in Argentina between 1902 and 1910, leading to violent confrontations between workers and the police and the imposition, by the national government, of a state of siege.[36]

Trade-union activity increased around the world with the upsurge of strikes. Between 1889 and 1900, the trade-union movement in Britain 'leaped to something like one and a half million members', and by 1914 it had grown to about four million.[37] European workers promoted trade unionism around the world. They formed unions in South Africa beginning in the 1880s and, by 1900, they were organised in Rhodesia, Mozambique, Algeria, and Egypt.[38] In the early years of the twentieth century, European railway workers formed trade unions in Rhodesia, Dahomey, the Ivory Coast, the Sudan, and Ethiopia; and European plantation employees formed a union in the Dutch Indies.

In the colonies, there were large populations of European paupers, which raised the prospect of European and non-European labour closing ranks against owners (and also called into question the status and authority of 'Europe's civilising mission'). In 1900, there was a vast population of lower-class Europeans in the French colonial communities in Northern Africa,[39] and tens of thousands of dangerously impoverished Eurasians ('Indos') and 'full-blooded' Europeans in the Netherlands Indies.[40] Poor whites made up nearly half the European population in India; some 6,000 of them in workhouses in 1900.[41] In the Netherlands Indies and British India, 'unfit whites' were simply sent home.[42] But in Johannesburg, where this was not the preferred option, urban planning was designed 'to eradicate inter-racial "slum-yards"' and increase the 'social distance between white and black miners'.[43] As 'part of the apparatus' to keep 'potentially subversive white colonials in line', colonial authorities promoted 'racist ideology, fear of the Other, preoccupation with

36 Rock 1975, p. 81.
37 Hobsbawm 1968, p. 165.
38 And, by 1910, also in Tunisia. Orr 1966, pp. 65–6.
39 Stoler 1998, p. 151.
40 *Encylopaedie van Nederlandsch-Indie* 1919, pp. 366–8; in Stoler 1998, pp. 150–1.
41 Arnold 1979, pp. 104, 122.
42 Stoler 1989, p. 151.
43 Van Onselen 1982, p. 39, in Stoler 1989, p. 138.

white prestige, and obsession with protecting European women from sexual assault by Asian and black males'.[44]

Despite the active opposition of colonial states and foreign companies to cooperation among European and indigenous workers (as well as inter-racial mixing among workers), European employees, found in all the large cities of the world, cooperated with indigenous workers in trade unions.[45] The union of European plantation employees formed in the Dutch Indies in 1909 [*Vakvereeniging voor Assistenten*] supported indigenous protests, railway strikes, and nationalist organisations;[46] and multiracial trade unions were formed in Java in the 1920s.[47] In 1908, a racially mixed tram workers' union was organised in Cairo. Europeans formed and led the first African or mixed trade unions in most of the African territories where there was a European working class.[48] Government workers in Egypt, South Africa, the French African territories, and the Belgian Congo, organised unions that were sometimes confined to Africans, sometimes to Europeans, but frequently had a mixed membership.[49]

The System Unravels

Throughout the nineteenth century, European powers had sought to capture and develop markets abroad, rather than expand production for mass local production. Throughout the century, this external expansion had made it possible for elites to increase production and profits without extensive redistribution and reform.

Throughout the century, European imperial agents had competed for clients and markets; but they did so through practices that during the course of the century assumed the character of an international regime. So while 'there were conflicts, frictions, and collisions at points where empires came geographically together and occasional armed skirmishes outside of Europe', there were also 'periodic conferences called to settle colonial issues, and countless bilateral treaties and agreements between colonial powers that defined borders on distant continents, transferred territories or populations, and codified the

44 These were not about white supremacy, but were aimed at European underlings in the colonies. Stoler 1989, p. 138.

45 Stoler 1989, p. 135. See, also, Comaroff 1985; 1986; Gordon and Meggitt 1985; Breman 1987; Callaway 1987; and Kennedy 1987.

46 Stoler 1989, p. 145.

47 Ingelson 1981, p. 55, cited in Stoler 1989, p. 138.

48 Orr 1966, p. 89.

49 Orr 1966, p. 78.

privileges and obligations of each colonial power with respect to the domains of others'.[50]

However, as more countries began to pursue externally-oriented economic expansion, opportunities to expand overseas quickly diminished. European imperialist activity abroad in the 1880s had produced 'a stupendous movement, without parallel in history'.[51] By the early twentieth century, the best markets had been formally annexed or informally established as spheres of influence; and as opportunities to expand overseas diminished, the expansionist aims of European powers began increasingly to focus on Europe itself. The scope of these expansionist ambitions was detailed in the set of treaties concluded by all the belligerents in the war that began in 1914, treaties which clearly expressed their hope of achieving vast extensions of their territories, both within and outside Europe, as a result of the war.[52]

With growing tensions at home, imperialist rivalries increased; and with Europe, itself, the target of the fiercest imperialist rivalries, the European balance of power collapsed. For the first time since 1815, a multilateral imperialist war *in Europe* forced governments and ruling elites to mobilise the masses, both for armies and industry. This is precisely what a century of imperialist expansion *overseas* had enabled them to avoid.

War and Social Revolution

In the years leading up to the 1914–18 war in Europe, the two central features of industrial production – internal repression and external expansion – were rapidly coming into conflict. Depression, a rising 'red tide', and increasing intra-elite imperialist rivalry combined to produce a multilateral war in Europe. Multilateral great power conflicts in Europe had been largely avoided for nearly a century because Europe's monarchs and aristocracies had feared that such conflicts would call into use the mass armies that, during and immediately after the Napoleonic Wars, had triggered revolutionary upheavals. But in 1914, European states confronted with an existential threat were forced, once again, to mobilise the masses for war and for the expansion of industrial production needed to support it. The mobilisation of increasingly politicised, radicalised, and organised masses to fight for a system that had, for decades,

---

50 Puchala and Hopkins 1983, p. 68.

51 Barraclough 1964, pp. 63–4. See Halperin 1997, Chapter 4.

52 Treaties setting out these intentions were published in the official journal of the Soviets, and in the *Manchester Guardian*. A good summary is found in Baker 1922, Vol. 1, Chapter 2.

generated increasingly divisive social conflict, set in motion a social revolution that began in 1917 and, thereafter, swept through all of Europe.

For all governments and ruling elites, war in 1914 came at a time of particularly intense domestic difficulties. The first half of 1914 had seen a marked rise in the intensity of both political and economic strikes in Russia, the threat of a massive confrontation between employers' organisations and labour unions in Germany, the assassination of the socialist leader, Jean Jaurès, in France; and the threat of civil war in Britain over the question of Irish home rule. In Britain, the National Transport Workers Federation had passed a resolution demanding a general strike 'in the event of national war being imminent'.[53] In Italy, a general strike was called in opposition to tax increases intended to pay for the looming war.[54] On the day war was declared, there were anti-war demonstrations in Moscow, St. Petersburg, and a number of Russia's other industrial centers. Reservists in the provinces demonstrated with red flags, revolutionary songs and cries of 'Down with the War!'[55] Even as they declared war, European governments were unsure whether workers would voluntarily join the war effort, or whether oppressive measures would be needed to induce them to participate.

But though governments everywhere in Europe succeeded in inducting their workers into national armies, throughout the war, labour struggles continued unabated and, in many places, increased both in number and intensity. In Britain, 10,000 miners in South Wales went on strike in 1915; and a rebellion began in Ireland in April 1916. In Germany, an average of 1,000 workers were on strike each month in 1915; in 1916, the average was 10,000.[56] In January 1917, a strike movement in St. Petersburg escalated and spread to other cities. The following month, when army units stationed in the cities refused to fire on the strikers, a coalition of the Constitutional-Democrat Party (the 'Cadets' or Liberal bourgeoisie) and the moderate Socialists secured the abdication of the Tsar and formed a provisional government. In October, the provisional government was removed and replaced with a Bolshevik government.

Throughout Europe, there were massive strikes and demonstrations involving millions of workers in solidarity with revolutionaries and workers in Russia. In Britain, a strike movement that spread to some 48 towns and involved some 200,000 workers threatened to paralyse the war industries. A great wave of strikes shook the munitions industry and the armed

53 National Transport Workers Federation, *Annual General Council Meeting*, 1913, p. 31.
54 Tipton and Aldrich 1987a, p. 115.
55 Hardach 1977, p. 219.
56 Hardach 1977, p. 183.

forces in France. In Germany, a million munitions workers went on strike in February to demand peace with Russia, and six companies of infantry were required to restore order in Hamburg after two days of rioting. In April 1917, between 200,000 and 300,000 workers went on strike, closing down more than 300 armament works in Berlin.[57] Strikes and rioting in industrial centres were similarly suppressed by the military in Spain. A general strike and insurrection in Turin, Italy involved some 50,000 workers in five days of street fighting, and led to hundreds of casualties.[58]

Violent uprisings continued into 1918. In October, there was open mutiny in Germany. Near Metz, a whole division of the territorial army refused to go back to the front, and thousands of soldiers did not return from their leave. A mutiny of sailors at Wilhelmshaven and other ports spread to Kiel, where most of the ships in the harbour hoisted the red flag, and dockyard workers struck in sympathy with the mutineers. The revolution spread to the ports along the coast of the Baltic and the North Sea. On 7 November, Kurt Eisner, the leader of the Independent Social Democratic Party (USPD), proclaimed a revolution in Munich, and the king and his family fled the city. Two days later, Phillip Scheidemann, a Social Democratic Party (SPD) member of the government, proclaimed the German Republic from the balcony of the parliament building in Berlin.[59]

Labour Unrest in Metropolitan Countries, before and during World War I

Many contemporary observers assumed, as have many accounts of this period, that working-class participation in the war effort represented a victory of nationalism over socialist solidarity.[60] But this decidedly was not the case. It seems reasonable to assume that when the working classes joined up with national armies, they did so to advance their own struggle for economic and

57 Carsten 1982, pp. 124–5.

58 Tilly et al. 1975.

59 Carsten 1982, pp. 215–26. Soon after, Karl Liebknecht, a leader of the Spartacus Group, proclaimed the 'German Socialist Republic' from the balcony of the royal palace.

60 See, e.g. Braunthal 1967, p. 355; Schumpeter 1950, p. 353; E.H. Carr 1945, pp. 20–1; and, for other works Doyle 1997, pp. 317–19, and esp. p. 318n9.

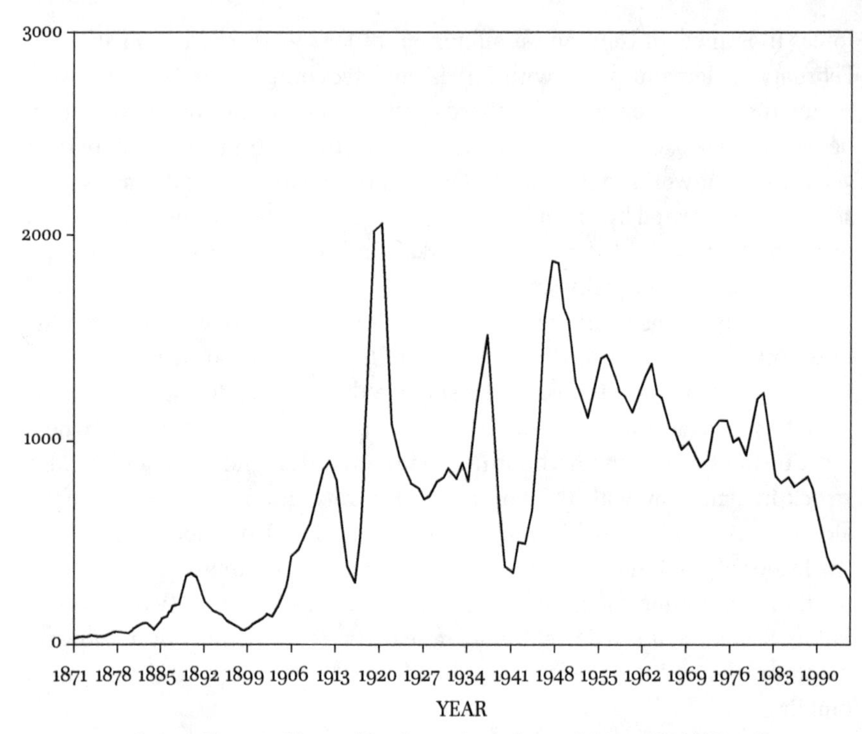

FIGURE 6.1 *Labour Unrest in Metropolitan Countries, before and during World War I. From Silver 2003, p. 127.*

political rights.[61] Workers had reason to believe that, through their patriotism and sacrifices, they might win the rights for which they had struggled for over a century. Their struggle continued, both during and after the war, and socialist solidarity continued to be an important means of advancing it.

The Revolutionary Post-War Years

Following World War I, Western states confronted newly organised and more powerful labour movements at home, as well as the Bolshevik Revolution abroad. By the end of World War I, labour's wartime mobilisation and participation had increased its relative power within European societies. Throughout Europe, the mobilisation of urban working classes and peasant masses to fight the war had produced stronger, larger, more united and better organised urban

61 Eric Hobsbawm has argued this view persuasively (1990, especially pp. 120–30). See, also Benson 1989, p. 162.

and rural labour movements. By 1920, Europe had 34 million trade unionists.[62] Skilled and unskilled workers, workers of different occupations, anarchists and socialists, Social Democrats and Communists, revolutionaries and reformists closed ranks.[63] In reaction to the explosive rise of trade-union membership, peasant organisation, socialist parties and socialist radicalism, all relatively privileged or well-to-do groups and elements in European societies united in a counter-revolutionary coalition. Attempts designed to block the rising 'red tide' by, among other things, actively aiding and abetting the re-armament and expansion of Germany as a bulwark against Bolshevism,[64] led directly to World War II. It was the demand for labour and need for its cooperation for a second European war that compelled a political accommodation with working-class movements.[65]

The Spectre of Revolution

The spectre of revolution haunted governments and ruling classes throughout the interwar years. At the conclusion of the war, troops from Czechoslovakia, Greece, Britain, the United States, France, Poland, Canada, Serbia, Romania, Italy, China, Finland, India, and Australia attempted to squash the Bolshevik menace through military means (1918–1920), until fear of social revolution at home impelled them to abandon this effort. Meanwhile, at the peace conferences the attention of the negotiators was riveted both on the Allied war against the Bolsheviks in Russia and on communist revolutions in Germany and Hungary. Decisions taken at the conference regarding Germany, Polish border disputes, political arrangements in the Baltic, and settlement of the 'Eastern Question', were shaped by concerns about the spread of Bolshevism from the Soviet Union and, ultimately, were designed to create a *cordon sanitaire* of new states between Germany and Russia.[66] At the same time, European leaders set up an International Labour Office in order to deter labour from

---

62 Ogg 1930, pp. 759–97. Trade-union membership doubled in Britain (from four to eight million; Geary 1981, pp. 151–5); in Italy, having doubled during the war, it nearly doubled again by 1920. By the autumn of 1919, the membership of the National Federation of Agrarian Workers had more than doubled to reach 475,000 militant members and a year later increased to almost 900,000 (Maier 1975, p. 47).

63 Cronin 1982, pp. 139, 121.

64 On this, see Halperin 2004, Chapter 7.

65 Fascism and the sacrifices entailed in defeating it effectively discredited the old right throughout Europe. Thus, even where workers were not mobilised for the war effort as, for instance, in France, the balance of political power after the war shifted in their favour.

66 Baker 1922, p. 64.

setting up a rival workers' peace conference.[67] It was labour's new power and the threat of social revolution that impelled European leaders to accede to the establishment of the League of Nations.

It was apparent that the war had been a watershed in the development of socialism and of organised labour as a political force. The war accomplished what the much feared *Internationale* had failed to do. The First International,[68] founded in 1864, had established regular contacts between labour leaders of different countries and, in many countries, inspired trade-union organisation and helped to formulate some of the ideas that later became the basis of the demands of organised labour. But the fear it instilled in European elites was exaggerated in relation to the organisation's actual strength. It was hardly 'the powerful, well administered, smoothly functioning organization' of legend.[69] The attempt to create working-class internationalism ultimately proved ineffective. The Second International (1889–1914) was much larger than its predecessor, but labour internationalism ultimately proved 'unable to move beyond the exchange of information and a reinforcement of national union identities'.[70] It failed to organise the unskilled majority of the working class; and the fact that capitalists were free to take their capital elsewhere made the conditions for forging labour solidarity internationally unfavourable.

By 1918, labour's wartime mobilisation and participation had increased its relative power within European societies. Left-wing parties and movements emerged throughout Europe, and trade-union membership skyrocketed as unskilled and agricultural labour and women joined unions for the first time. Skilled and unskilled labour, workers of different occupations, anarchists and socialists, Social Democrats and Communists, revolutionaries and reformists, closed ranks to produce a more-or-less continuous round of demonstrations, riots, violent strikes, and street fighting, as well as coups, rebellions and revolutions, which swept through France, Britain, Germany, Italy, Switzerland, East and Southeast Europe. Mass communist parties emerged in France, Germany and Italy; and Hungary briefly became a communist state. In 1919, a new revolutionary movement – the Third International – was formed under the auspices of Lenin and the Russian Bolsheviks. In Britain, '[t]he fear of serious

67 The League imposed upon all its members the obligations of becoming members of the ILO, and of performing the duties entailed by such membership. However, the ILO was a 'stabilising action' intended to induce the workers to content themselves with 'positive promises for the future' instead of 'achievement at the moment'. Zilliacus 1946, pp. 234–5.

68 The organisation was officially called the International Working Men's Association.

69 Collins and Abramsky 1965, pp. v–vi.

70 MacShane 1992, p. 47.

social unrest, even revolution' was 'widespread among the propertied classes' early that year;[71] when the red flag was raised on the town hall in Glasgow, the British War Cabinet feared that a Bolshevik revolution was being attempted.[72]

Around the world, the 'red tide' continued to rise. There had been only 49 labour unions in Japan in 1914, but by 1919 there were 187, with a total membership of 100,000. In Africa, transport unions were formed in the 1920s and 1930s in Gambia, Nigeria, and the Gold Coast, and during the 1940s in Kenya and Uganda, Tanganyika and Nyasaland, and Zanzibar.[73] There was an upsurge of trade-union organisation in France's African territories following the French People's Front agitation of 1936.[74] In the 1920s, the emerging trade-union movement in the Madras Presidency 'joined forces with the larger anti-colonial political struggle' opening up 'a whole new arena of urban radical action'.[75] In December 1925, leading trade unionists in Bombay formed the Bombay Textile Labour Union (BTLU), which began with a membership of about 5,000, but within a year had about 10,000 members.[76] In 1928, the communist-dominated Girni Kamgar Union (GKU) was formed and established its leadership over the mill workers. Throughout their colonial sphere, from Jamaica to Malaya, and especially in India, the British crushed labour unions and jailed trade unionists.[77]

Throughout the world, there was 'a rash of revolts, tribal unrest, nationalism, and Bolshevik intrigue'.[78] A wave of strikes and other labour disputes broke out in Japan at the end of World War I. A strike at the Ishikawajima shipyard in Tokyo lasted five weeks in October–November 1921. In 1919, an economic crisis in Argentina generated violent and numerous strikes and clashes. These culminated in the *Semana Trágica*, a week-long series of riots led by anarchists. In Colombia, the army massacred more than a thousand striking banana workers in 1928. In the second half of 1918, food riots and looting swept through the Madras Presidency. In the first months of 1924, a strike in the Bombay textile industry forced the great majority of its 82 textile mills to close.[79] Labour intensification and the threat of redundancy and unemployment precipitated

71 Wrigley 1990, p. 24.
72 Mayer 1967, Chapter 5.
73 Orr 1966, pp. 78–9.
74 Orr 1966, p. 68.
75 Chattopadhyay 2006, p. 166.
76 Sen 2000, p. 2565.
77 Thompson 2004, p. xiv.
78 Fisher 2009, p. 261.
79 Kooiman 1980, p. 1223.

a mammoth general strike in 1928 (26 April to 6 October) in the Bombay mill industry. Between 1929 and 1937, mills cut money wages by more than 20 percent and threw almost 52,000 workers out of employment.[80] During these years, the communists as well as the Congress socialists made considerable inroads into the mill areas, where their task was made easier by the savage wage cuts and retrenchment undertaken in textile industries during the Depression.[81] A three-month long strike involving 272,000 workers started in July 1929. A three-month strike that started in Bombay in February 1937 involved almost 220,000 workers (76 percent of the labour force).[82] In 1919, in Sierra Leone, government railway workers, employees of the Public Works Department, and some 2,400 African policemen came out on strike.[83] Miners went on strike in South Africa in 1922, and in the Zambian copper mines in 1935.

In Latin America, the first communist parties were founded in the wake of the Russian Revolution of 1917. The Mexican Communist Party, the first communist party outside Russia, was founded in 1919. A communist party was formed in Brazil in 1922 and the Partido Socialista del Perú (PSP) was founded in 1928. In the Middle East, there was an explosive growth of socialist and communist movements after the war, alongside increasing labour militancy. The Cairo tramwaymen were the first to go on strike, and were soon joined by the workers of the Egyptian State Railways, the Government Press, the Arsenal and government workshops, the Cairo light company, the Alexandria tramways, postal, port, lighthouse and customs workers, taxi and carriage drivers, the Hawamdiyya sugar refinery workers and others. Between 1919 and 1921, 81 strike actions took place in Egypt.[84] By 1922, there were 38 workers' associations in Cairo, 33 in Alexandria, and 28 in the Canal Zone. The Palestine Communist Party (PCP) was formed in 1921, a Lebanese Communist Party and a Syrian Communist Party emerged in the 1920s, and the Iraqi Communist Party (ICP) was founded in 1934.

Retrenchment and Counter-Revolution

After the war, the European response to the 'rising red tide' that had threatened the pre-war system of capital accumulation, as well as to the intense social conflict and revolutionary activism that had been unleashed by the mass mobilisation of 1914 and the Bolshevik Revolution, was fascist corporatism.

80 Goswami 1997, p. 571.
81 Goswami 1997, p. 568.
82 Goswami 1997, p. 60.
83 Orr 1966, p. 78.
84 Deeb 1976, p. 74.

As elites closed ranks to stem the rising red tide, European society became increasingly polarised between a newly-powerful left and a resurgent, ultra-conservative and militant right.[85] The struggle between left and right in Europe increasingly polarised international, as well as domestic, relations. British and French 'appeasement' policies reflected this polarisation, and led to World War II.[86] Having failed to defeat Bolshevism by military means, the rise of fascism offered a second line of attack. Britain and France made every effort 'to assist or condone' fascist Italy's attempts to strengthen itself in Africa and the Mediterranean, and Germany's quest to secure mastery of Central Europe.[87] This response not only failed to staunch revolutionary currents in Europe, but came perilously close to permitting a takeover of Europe by fascist Germany.

After a rapid and simultaneous price rise in most of the world during the 1920s, the 'great depression' hit all parts of the world at the same time in 1929. It spread through the tropical Far East, paralysing commerce and production. Mines and plantations were closed and abandoned, and many Europeans returned home. Commercial enterprises that continued to operate reduced costs by replacing European employees with natives or foreign orientals. The threat posed by large numbers of European paupers overseas continued, despite the profusion of relief agencies and community efforts; and by the 1930s, white pauperism had reached crisis proportions.[88]

The Depression eventually engulfed all of Europe except the Soviet Union. With unemployment and its repercussions increasingly posing a fundamental challenge to the existing order, governments set about restoring pre-war monopoly capitalism and shoring up its social structures. Pre-war trends towards increasing industrial concentration were carried forward in the corporatist structures which emerged throughout Europe. As a number of scholars have noted, these structures represented an attempt to recreate traditional, paternalistic, and rural ways of life and relations of authority characteristic of feudal society within the industrial sphere.[89] They recalled key features of feudal society: the fundamental antagonism between landlord and peasant, the exercise of power over the peasantry through economic exploitation and politico-legal coercion, and the ideological vision of an organic society of

85 Mayer 1959, p. 4.

86 See Halperin 1997, Chapter 7; and Anievas 2011.

87 Schuman 1942, p. 332. On the significance of attaining *Lebensraum* in Central Eastern Europe within interwar German policymaking circles, see Baranowski's contribution to this volume.

88 Stoler 1989, p. 152.

89 Elbow 1953.

orders.[90] Corporative institutions were established in Belgium, Holland, Italy, Norway and Sweden; and full-fledged corporatist regimes came to power in Germany, France, Austria, Portugal, Spain, and Poland. Corporatist structures everywhere were concerned with labour control, with containing the popular sector through electoral restrictions, limitations on the right to strike, and the corporatisation of unions. European governments suspended parliaments and outlawed opposition parties, censored the press and limited assemblies. In Italy (1922), Portugal (1926), the Baltic states (1926), Hungary (1919), Poland (1926), the Balkan countries (1923, 1926, 1929), Belgium (1926, 1935), Germany (1934), Austria (1934), the Netherlands (1935), Switzerland (1935), and Spain (1936), parliamentary democracy was destroyed.

Conclusion

The First World War represents a great divide in modern European history. Though revolutions in Europe in 1789, in the 1820s, 1830s and in 1848 had given a stronger position to industrialists and bankers, weakened the landlords' influence and, in places, partly replaced political personnel, they failed to bring about a thoroughgoing transformation of social structures. Except in Russia after 1917, the traditional social structure of Europe remained essentially intact up until 1945. The suffrage was expanded, and legislatures and local governments were reformed, but economic and social structures remained essentially the same.

After World War I, and despite the profound dislocations that had resulted from the war, leaders and ruling classes in all western European countries succeeded in re-establishing and maintaining the pre-war *status-quo*.[91] However, following the Great Depression, mass mobilisation for war and industrial expansion – again, for a massively destructive second European war – forced governments into a political accommodation with working-class demands that made a restoration of the pre-war system impossible. Economies were restructured on the basis of a social democratic compromise that required Social Democrats to accept private ownership of the means of production and capitalists to use the profits they realised from this to increase productive capacity and to allow labour to share in productivity gains. States adopted social

90 Elbow 1953, p. 183.

91 For a detailed discussion of these changes and of the post-World War restoration, see Halperin 1997, Chapters 5, 6, and 7.

democratic and Keynesian goals and policy instruments that, before the war, would never have been accepted by the wealthy classes. Wages rose with profits, making higher mass consumption possible for new mass consumer goods industries. This more balanced and internally-oriented development bought an end to intense social conflicts and the great movements of colonialism and imperialism. This was the context within which the imaginary of 'developed' and 'developing' world emerged.

It soon became a commonplace to attribute this division between 'developed' and 'developing' countries, not to recent and revolutionary transformations, but to a further evolution of processes that had purportedly defined the separation of 'the West' from 'the Rest' beginning in the sixteenth century. But it was only after 1945 that the set of conditions that defined the 'developed' countries emerged and produced, in those countries, phenomenal growth and a relatively broad-based prosperity. 'Developed' countries were those that had: (1) experienced a breakdown of their traditional social structures through land and other reforms, as a result of the world wars and their aftermath or the activities of external agents (all of Europe, Japan, Taiwan and South Korea); (2) earlier experienced a significant decline in the power of landowners as a result of one of the bloodiest wars in human history (the United States in the 1860s); or, (3) never had an entrenched landed elite (Australia, Canada, and New Zealand). We can say, then, that World War I began a social revolution that divided the world into those areas that, for a time, adopted a relatively more nationally-embedded capitalism and, nearly everywhere else, where the structures characteristic of the pre-war order were consolidated and reproduced.

After the end of World War II, the class structures of the states of both western and eastern Europe were radically changed. In almost all aspects of economic and social life, structural changes were 'greater than during the previous 200 years'.[92] These changes in class structures made possible the establishment of a new economic and political order in the region on the basis of interest groups, parties, unions, and other organisations linked to sectors of the economy that had been formerly excluded from power.

The role of the property elite in the economic field was limited by the development of state owned enterprises, the introduction of a capital-gains tax and the growth of managerial power.[93] Increasing job opportunities in the service sector swelled the ranks of the middle class. The expansion of the service sector, the development of new technologies, and the availability of

92 Bairoch 1993, p. 175.

93 Aron 1950, p. 129.

consumer products to large proportions of the population, also decreased the difference between the middle and working classes, and greater access to education opened up the path to middle-class status.[94] The blue-collar working class, those employed in mining, manufacturing, transport, building and artisanal trades, lost its primacy as the largest segment of the workforce in many European societies. By the 1980s, Romania was the only country in which the tertiary sector employed less than 30 percent of the active population.[95]

The provision of health care, education and other social services, the revival of trade unions and, following their nineteenth-century intentions, their provision of facilities and institutions for the working class,[96] improved the minimum standard of living for the working class. Lower-paid and less skilled workers gained through a narrowing of pay differentials. In Western Europe the average level of real earnings of industrial or manual workers in 1948 was almost a fifth higher than in 1938.[97] In the GDR real wages more than tripled in this period; in Bulgaria, Yugoslavia and Romania they rose by over 150 percent.[98] Lower paid workers also benefited from the lowering of housing rents and the greater security of employment compared with before the war.

During the nineteenth century and until the beginning of the 1950s, manufacturing productivity in Western Europe had increased at a rate almost twice as fast as that of agriculture. Since the 1950s the converse is true. Between 1850 and 1950, productivity increased annually by 1.8–2 percent in industry compared to 1.1–1.3 percent in agriculture. Between 1950 and 1990, this increase was 3.4–3.5 percent in industry and 5.4–5.6 percent in agriculture.[99]

This is important since before 1914 almost half of Western Europe's working population was employed in agriculture (including fishing and forestry). By 1955, the farming population represented only 24 percent of the total.[100]

94 Middle-class status generally implies work that is not manual labour, a minimal level of education, payment by salary rather than by hourly wages and a number of the comforts of consumer society.

95 Tipton and Aldrich 1987b, p. 173. By 1980, the tertiary sector accounted for at least 60 percent of employment in Belgium, Denmark, Norway, the Netherlands, Sweden and Switzerland, and at least 50 percent in Austria, Finland, France, Luxembourg, and the United Kingdom.

96 One major West German union, for example, owned the fourth largest bank in Germany, the largest insurance company, the largest property development firm and one of the three largest travel agencies. Tipton and Aldrich 1987b, p. 178.

97 Milward 1984, p. 486.

98 Aldcroft 1978, pp. 212–15.

99 Bairoch 1993, pp. 151, 175; see also Bairoch 1989b.

100 Laqueur 1992, p. 179.

Employment in agriculture declined dramatically in France (from 5.2 million in 1954 to 3.9 million in 1962), in West Germany (from 5.1 million in 1950 to 3.6 million in 1961). In Italy, agricultural employment fell from 8.3 million to 5.6 and industrial employment rose from 6.3 to 7.9 million between 1951 and 1961. During the 1960s, Spain began to follow along the same path. By the late 1970s, nowhere in Europe did agricultural workers account for a majority of the labour force, and only in Greece, Poland and Portugal did they make up a quarter of the workers. Most European countries had less than 10 percent of their workforce in agriculture.[101]

After 1945, western European economies were characterised by sustained growth and by a more equitable distribution of income.[102] In contrast to pre-war economic policies, post-war policies focused on expanding domestic markets through increased production, increasing and regulating domestic investment, and raising the level of working-class earnings and welfare. While there was a strong growth in the volume of exports, the expansion of domestic markets for domestic goods and services ensured that, until the 1960s, the proportion of resources devoted to exports declined. During the 1950s and 1960s, these policies produced unprecedented growth. Production grew much faster and with less interruption than in any previous period.[103] In most of western Europe, industrial production had surpassed pre-war levels by 1947.[104] Between 1850–1913, output per head in the most advanced countries of western Europe had grown by not more than 1.5–2 percent a year: between 1950 and 1973, it grew in those same countries by 3–4 percent per year.[105] Between 1950 and 1970, total output increased at 3.5 percent each year in Belgium, 4.2 percent in Switzerland and 5 percent in Austria and the Netherlands.[106]

Before World War II, the countries of eastern Europe were, in most cases, economically backwards relative to western Europe. Except for Czechoslovakia, every east European country was predominantly rural; industrial workers were a minority in Poland, Hungary, Romania, Yugoslavia, and Bulgaria. In the post-war period, these countries underwent a political and social revolution that

101 Tipton and Aldritch 1987b, pp. 114, 173.

102 There is near unanimity that, in Britain, income was distributed more equally. Before World War I (1911–13), the top 5 percent of the population owned 87 percent of personal wealth, the bottom 90 percent owned 8 percent; in 1960, the figures were 75 percent and 17 percent. Hobsbawm 1968, p. 274.

103 Schonfield 1965, p. 61.

104 Aldcroft 1978, p. 148.

105 Lewis 1978, p. 33.

106 Ricossa 1973, p. 291.

involved a complete change in the system of property relations and the emergence of the state as the main agent of economic activity. By the early 1950s, these countries were experiencing unprecedented and rapid economic growth and increasing affluence. In many countries, large estates were 'confiscated from the former owners without compensation and redistributed free among the peasants'.[107] Within one generation, rapid economic and especially industrial growth shifted a majority of labour and capital into non-agricultural activities.[108] Workers enjoyed health care, education and other social services, and lower housing rents and greater security of employment compared with before the war. In the GDR, real wages more than tripled in this period; in Bulgaria, Yugoslavia and Romania they rose by over 150 percent.[109]

After World War II, eastern Europe countries experienced the same structural changes as western European countries did and, like them, enjoyed an unprecedented period of rapid industrial development and increasing affluence in the 1950s and 1960s. Though there was no democracy in Eastern Europe, the social-structural changes that had been imposed from above eventually enabled it to achieve democracy by means of a 'velvet revolution'. This stands in stark contrast to the experience of many countries in the 'Third World', where the transition from authoritarianism to some sort of political pluralism has been only partial, and accompanied by much violence. There, the absence of the social-structural changes which occurred throughout Europe after World War II, and the Cold War crusade against communism, has worked effectively to block the growth of reformist and progressive elements and currents that, in Europe and elsewhere, supported and encouraged struggles for democracy and the democratisation of national politics. Thus, while the prospects for democracy continue to look fairly good in the former communist countries of Eastern Europe, they look fairly dim in 'Third World' regions where authoritarian regimes and ruling groups, with the support of Western powers, eliminated the social forces and conditions needed to produce and maintain democracy.

---

107 Aldroft 1978, p. 170.

108 Lampe and Jackson 1982, p. 576.

109 Aldcroft 1978, pp. 212–15.

PART 2

Reconfigurations: Revolution and Culture after 1914

CHAPTER 7

European Intellectuals and the First World War: Trauma and New Cleavages

Enzo Traverso

Introduction: Fractured Time

Very few events in the history of the modern world have had so deep an impact on European culture and, at the same time, have been so unpredictable, devastating and traumatising historical turns as the Great War. Of course, many observers had evoked the possibility of a new war and some lucid minds had also foreseen its continental dimensions, warning against the danger of a repetition of the fire that one century earlier the French Revolution and the Napoleonic Wars had set to the old world, changing its face. Many futuristic predictions had been formulated, but nobody could imagine a total war as well as the transformations it would have produced in the continent, concerning not only its social structures and political institutions but also its mentalities, cultures, behaviours, and perceptions. While Alexander Anievas's introduction to this collection touches on some of these issues, the cultural and intellectual transformation of Europe will be the focus of this chapter.

In 1919, writing in the wake of Oswald Spengler, Paul Valéry meditated upon the 'mortal character' of European civilisation, clearly highlighted by the 'extraordinary shiver' that had run through the spinal cord of Europe. He described himself like a new Hamlet contemplating a huge landscape of ruins spanning from Basel to Cologne, from the Somme to Alsace, inhabited by 'millions of ghosts' – the fallen soldiers of the Great War.[1] Europe was broken, its civilisation seemed vacillating and the world axis had slid toward the United States on the other side of the Atlantic Ocean. If we compare these observations on the war as a terrible Apocalypse of modernity with the enthusiasm and exaltation filling the newspapers and the most prestigious journals in the summer of 1914, we can grasp the enormous cleavage, the deep abyss separating the break up from the end of the world conflict. Criticism and rejection of war – a task supposedly belonging to the intellectual, a social figure appearing in Europe at the end of the nineteenth century, when it was symbolised by the defence of French Captain Dreyfus – did not precede but followed the war; it

1 Valéry 1957, p. 993.

was engendered by the vision of the wreckages of a continent that had lost its equilibrium and experienced its own self-destruction. In 1914, intellectuals perceived the war as a screen on which they could project their fantasies, values and ideals, rarely as the source of a moral rejection – except for the vituperation of the enemy – and almost never as a topic inspiring critical thought.[2]

In 1914, the Great War produced the traumatic fall of the 'Long Nineteenth Century' whose bases had been fixed in Vienna one century earlier. The conflicts perturbing this 'one hundred years peace' – according to the definition suggested by Karl Polanyi in *The Great Transformation*[3] – were local conflicts, like the Crimean War, the Risorgimento's wars against Austrian rule, the Austro-Prussian War of 1866–7, or the Franco-Prussian War of 1871 allowing Bismarck to achieve German unity. The Balkan Wars of 1912–13, on the other hand, had been perceived as the starting point of the dissolution of the Ottoman Empire rather than the announcement of a storm susceptible of destroying Europe, in spite of the fact that precisely there, in Sarajevo, the fuse of a general conflagration would be lit.

Karl Polanyi had indicated the pillars of the 'one hundred years peace' established in 1815: the balance-of-power system; the gold standard, i.e. a capitalist economy created by the industrial revolution and based on the principle (or the illusion) of socio-economic self-regulation through the market; and finally the state of law introducing the constitutional warranty of some fundamental liberties. With the exception of Tsarist Russia, which lacked the last element, all European states shared that foundational framework. The so-called 'European Concert' was based on a double equilibrium, both *mechanical*, because of the comparable strength of the states it concerned, and *organic*, because of the shared values inspiring them.[4] At the origins of this 'one hundred years peace' there was the feeling, deeply rooted in all the nations of the continent, of belonging to the same civilisation and of sharing its principles. Of course, such a civilisation defined itself in opposition to the colonial world, a space of otherness it needed in order to fixate its own image of superiority and ruling force, but also in order to legitimise its historical 'mission' of Progress. In the extra-European world, violence could be freely displayed without limits or rules. Within the old continent, nevertheless, throughout the nineteenth century, violence seemed mastered and 'humanised' by political institutions, and

2 Wohl 1979.

3 Polanyi 1957, Chap. 1. For a rethinking of Polanyi's 'Great Transformation' vis-à-vis the First World War and its aftermath, see Halperin's contribution to this volume.

4 Cf. Soutou 1998, pp. 117–36.

peace became a noble dream for all cultivated people. Torture had regressed almost everywhere, even in the Tsarist Empire, until its virtual disappearance. Peace was celebrated as a conquest, whereas wars were geographically circumscribed and shortened in duration. The concept of *Jus Publicum Europeum* – created in Westphalia in 1648 at the end of the Thirty Years' War – no longer appeared like a utopia but a reality truthfully mirrored by the alliances between the great powers. In such a political and mental framework, European culture seemed to remove the possibility of a war on a continental scale.

At the beginning of 1914, a representative of the British Foreign Office 'ascertained' that a new European war was extremely improbable. In his eyes, the emergence of a standardised diplomacy, embodied by a 'common type' of statesman managing international relations, constituted a powerful obstacle to a generalised war. 'In metaphorical terms', he highlighted, 'they speak the same language, share the same way of thinking and defend more or less the same points of view'. As the world's destiny was decided by an elite of men conforming to this 'common type', the possibility of a European war of annihilation like the colonial wars of conquest and extermination that had taken place in Africa, outside of the 'civilised' world, was excluded.[5] In April 1914, a few months before the start of the conflict, an editorial of the London *Times* reaffirmed the virtues of the 'European Concert'.

> The division of the Great Powers into two well-balanced groups with intimate relations between the members of each is … a twofold check upon inordinate ambitions or sudden outbreaks of race hatred. All sovereigns and statesmen – aye, and all nations – know that a war of group against group would be a measureless calamity. That knowledge brings with it a sense of responsibility which chastens and restrains the boldest and most reckless.[6]

Many intellectual and political currents shared this simple argument favouring quite naïve optimism. In the years preceding the Great War, different socialist parties launched a large pacifist campaign whose climax was the international conference of Basel in November 1912, dominated by charismatic leaders like Jean Jaurès, August Bebel and Victor Adler. In their opinion, the workers' movement would impede a world war or, if it did take place, they would have

5 Quoted in Joll and Martel 2007, p. 51.
6 Quoted in Joll and Martel 2007, pp. 53–4.

transformed it into a socialist revolution. The raw optimism of such solemn declarations, nevertheless, simply hid their scepticism about the possibility of a new war. All these principle assessments, indeed, were not followed by practical measures or by a plan of action in case of war. Kark Kautsky, the theoretician of the German Social Democratic Party and the director of *Neue Zeit*, the most important Marxist journal of the time, lucidly recognised at the end of the conflict the blindness of the International Socialist Bureau gathered on 29 and 30 July 1914: 'It's astonishing', he wrote, 'that nobody, during that meeting, put the question: what do we do in case of war? Which position should the socialist parties take in this war?'[7] In fact, in August 1914, almost all socialist parties were overwhelmed by the wave unfurling over the old world, and voted for war credits (defending a neutral position, the Italian Socialist Party was an exception).

Conservatives, on their own hand, did not show more lucidity. Fin-de-siècle cultural pessimism put into discussion the idea of Progress and interpreted modernity in terms of decadence, but it did not expect a new war. The industrial world announced catastrophes taking the form of mass society, democracy, demographic growth, physical and intellectual degeneration provoked by miscegenation, the revolt of the 'dangerous classes', and so on. Among many Cassandras describing apocalyptic scenarios for the future, however, almost none was able to foresee the millions of dead resulting from a total war. If they did, their prognoses were formulated in such abstract terms that its horror was neutralised, or even welcomed, as for many Social Darwinists and eugenicists who approved chemical weapons and approved a war in order to eliminate a surplus of population by selecting the fittest (putting forward the same arguments with which they had justified the famine in British India).[8] In 1911, Sir Reginald Clare Hart wished 'a pitiless war of extermination against lower individuals and nations', whereas Karl Pearson considered wars as a biological tool for making more virile the European nations.[9] But such theories did not produce any military project of aggression or annihilation; they simply revealed an intellectual predisposition toward the worst nationalist and racist fever of the following years. The optimism of Auguste Comte and Herbert Spencer, who had seen industrial society as a source of peace and progress, generally prevailed. Fertile in many fields, the European imagination wasn't prepared for the Great War. The intellectuals mirrored such blindness.

7 Quoted in Haupt 1970.

8 Cf. Davis 2001.

9 Quoted in Pick 1993, pp. 79–81.

Premises

The Great War merges, as a historical break, many tendencies accumulated in the previous decades, sometimes perceived and analysed but unpredictable in their explosive junction. At the turn of the century, many economists – both liberal and Marxist, from John Hobson to Rudolf Hilferding, to Rosa Luxemburg and Lenin – had emphasised the advent of financial and monopoly capital, resulting in a sharp competition for hegemony in the world market. Developing these intuitions, Trotsky described the Great War, in an essay of October 1914, as the expression of the historical crisis of the national states system. The growth of the productive forces clashed against this political framework and claimed world reorganisation beyond sovereignties and national egoisms. 'At the origins of the present war', he wrote, 'there is a revolt of the productive forces created by capitalism against their use on a national base. The entire planet, its continents and its oceans, the surface of the earth as well as the underground, constitute today the stage of the world economy, whose different parts are completely intertwined'. Thereafter, the Russian revolutionary added, 'the war of 1914 is the biggest historical convulsion of an economic system collapsing because of its own contradictions'.[10] Trotsky concluded his pamphlet heralding the idea of a federation of European socialist states.

Of course, the war had been necessary in order to formulate such a project. Before the conflict, the analysis of militarism did not prefigure total war, i.e. the submission of the civil society to a militarised state, the transformation of national economies into war economies, of culture and the media into propaganda tools. Rosa Luxemburg had devoted a chapter of *The Accumulation of Capital* (1913) to militarism, but she concluded her book by treating socialism as the natural issue of the insuperable contradictions of a world submitted to capitalism. The war pushed her to sketch a famous dilemma: socialism or barbarism.[11] Until 1914, barbarism appeared to socialist intellectuals as a very remote possibility, whereas a common mental habitus pushed them to consider socialism as a natural product of history, according to a teleological conception of progress. For classical Social Democrats, Walter Benjamin explained in his famous 'Thesis' of 1940, 'progress was regarded as irresistible, something that automatically pursued a straight or spiral course'.[12] The future belonged to socialism and a world war could not reverse this historical tendency.

10 Trotsky 1918.

11 Luxemburg 1969.

12 Benjamin 2007, p. 260.

Of course, the transformation of the armies through modern technology had already taken place during the American Civil War and the colonial wars, two historical experiences in which the new mechanical weapons had been tested. The European armies had used the machine guns in Africa, but the colonial 'small wars' did not modify the paradigms upon which the military elites based their conceptions of 'civilised' war. The surrealist scene that took place on the first day of the Somme Battle in 1916, with the British infantry advancing toward the German trenches, announced by the music of a bagpipe and by a jumping rugby balloon, retrospectively appears as terrible evidence of the abyss separating the modernisation of societies, whose result was total war, from the mental habitus of the military caste, the contradiction of a mass army led by a traditional, aristocratic elite.[13] The European economic and social body experienced a deep transformation within a cultural and institutional framework that revealed, according to Arno J. Mayer, the 'persistence of the Old Regime'.[14] The Great War put an end to this paradox.

Predictions

Among the very rare observers who intuited the consequences of a new war, we may mention two military experts. In 1888, in an extraordinarily premonitory article, Friedrich Engels warned against the risks of a new war that would inevitably take on a European dimension and throw the continent into an abyss of misery and decadence. In the eyes of Engels, the only possible example in order to imagine such a catastrophe was the Thirty Years' War. A new war, he wrote, will be 'a world war of an extent and violence hitherto unimagined'. In such a war, 'eight to ten million soldiers will be at each other's throats and in the process they will strip Europe barer than a swarm of locusts'. The destructions of the Thirty Years' War, he added, would have been 'compressed in three or four years' and 'extended over the entire continent'. It would engender starvation and mass diseases, throwing the economy into 'irreparable chaos' and 'universal bankruptcy'. People would experience the 'collapse of the old states' and dozens of crowned heads would be 'rolled into the gutters', where anyone would be able to 'pick them up'.[15] Ten years later, the Prussian general Helmut von Moltke formulated a similar prognosis, using more sober terms, in a speech at the Reichstag. Because of the power achieved by the armies, he said, not a

13 Cf. Diner 2008, Chapter 1.

14 Cf. Mayer 1981.

15 Engels 1971, pp. 350–1.

single state could prevail over the others, with the effect of transforming the war into a second Thirty Years' War even more devastating than the first one.[16] Yet, no one paid any attention to the catastrophic visions of a socialist and a general.

Leaving aside the military experts, some intuitions had been formulated in the academic sphere, especially after the Franco-Prussian War of 1870. One year later, two philologists, a German and a Frenchman, defending their national causes, started a dialogue on the crisis of Europe taking into account the cataclysmic effects of a general war inspired by the same Crusade spirit experienced during the dispute over the Alsace-Lorraine. In a letter to his colleague David-Friedrich Strauss in which he defended the French idea of the nation against the German one, the latter corrupted by a racial concept of *Volk*, Ernest Renan warned against the consequences of a European war proclaimed in the name of a 'superior race' that would inevitably destroy all 'shared idea[s] of civilization'. To conceive the division of humanity into separated races, he wrote, 'not only is a scientific fault, insofar as very few countries are founded on pure races, but inevitably produces extermination wars, "zoological" wars ... similar to the survival struggles of carnivores and rodents. It would be the end of that fruitful mixture, made of different and necessary elements, which is humanity'.[17]

The Napoleonic Wars had been fought in the name of universal values – on the one side, the principles of the French Revolution and, on the other side, those of the Old Regime – and the Revolutions of 1848 had appeared as a 'springtime of nations' gathering the continent far beyond its political frontiers. The Franco-Prussian War had already been a clash of nationalisms, but it did not present the features of a national Crusade like the war of 1914. The antecedents of demonisation and racialisation of the enemy carried on during the Great War could perhaps be found in an event occurring *inside* the Franco-Prussian War: the Paris Commune. During the bloody week that, in May 1871, concluded this revolutionary experience, a wave of violence took place against an internal enemy that was perceived as a foreign body inside the nation, depicted as a dangerous race, a source of moral and physical degeneration.[18] In 1914, the enemy was external, but it was charged with all the elements of negative otherness that, all over the second half of the nineteenth century, distinguished the dangerous classes as well as the 'lower' races, compelling the

---

16 Quoted in Howard 1993, p. 171. On the Thirty Years' War as a total war, cf. Chikering 1999, pp. 13–28.

17 Renan 1992, p. 157.

18 Tombs 1981.

nation to protect itself through social repression in Europe and wars of extermination in the colonies.

The Franco-Prussian War raised questions about the future of Europe even in the United Kingdom, merging in the following years with other worries about imperialism and mass society. In this context, George H. Wells wrote several science fiction novels – first of all *The War of the Worlds* (1898) – depicting a dark future of decadence.[19] He imagined the invasion of England by an army of aliens coming from Mars who tested in the British island their weapons of mass destruction: powerful machine guns, moving cannons prefiguring the tanks, chemical weapons and lethal bombs announcing both the gas attacks of Ypres and the atomic bombs of the Second World War, whereas the terrestrial epidemics defeating the aliens anticipated the fear of a bacteriological war.

The link between technology and modern war also intrigued Émile Zola. Echoing the Franco-Prussian War, his novel *The Human Beast* (1890) sketched a metaphor of technical progress as catastrophe, describing the crazy, blind run of a train whose locomotive had lost its driver. In a preparatory text, Zola imagined a train full of 'happy soldiers, singing patriotic songs, unaware of the danger', adding that this train symbolised France.[20] Zola wasn't alone in despising modern technology. With a realistic style analysing not an imagined future but a present tendency, Giovanni Papini – an avant-garde writer, later fascist, and finally holder of a peculiar form of Catholic conservatism – devoted to modern war a prophetic article titled 'Life Is Not Sacred'. Published by *Lacerba* in 1913, the same year in which the first car came out from the production lines of Detroit Ford plants, it stressed an unexpected homology between industrial production and industrial extermination. The new century, Papini observed, will not be happy; it will be a century of mechanical annihilation in which human life will irremediably lose its value. The taste of this article was a peculiar mixture of pre-fascist existentialism, eugenics and Weberian resignation in front of a modernity perceived as a world shaped by an inhuman and mechanical rationality. 'All the life of our time', he wrote,

> is organization of necessary massacres, visible and invisible. People trying to rebel in the name of life would be smashed by life itself. Industrial civilization, as well as the bellicose civilization, feeds itself on corpses: cannon fodder and machine fodder; blood in the battlefield and blood

19 Wells 1960.

20 Zola 1996; cf. also Pick 1993, p. 106.

> in the streets; blood in the tents and blood in the factory. Life floats only leaving behind it, like ballast, a part of itself.[21]

The eclectic and paradoxical fusion between a romantic revolt against modernity and an irrational cult of technology was the premise of the so-called 'conservative revolution' or what Jeffrey Herf terms the 'reactionary modernism' which spread far and wide in interwar Europe.[22] This tendency, however, was born before 1914, announced by some aesthetic avant-gardes like futurism. In his famous 'Manifesto' published by *Le Figaro* in 1909, Filippo Tommaso Marinetti invoked war as 'the world's only hygiene', conceiving it as a clash of technological forces. His aesthetic cult of the machine and velocity did not yet possess the existentialist accents that one finds in the essays of the later Jünger, but it clearly claimed an aggressive irrationalism announcing both 1914 nationalism and post-war fascism, to which futurists adhered in almost natural ways. In short, futurism *aestheticised politics* – as Walter Benjamin highlighted in the 1930s[23] – prefiguring a fundamental dimension of fascist culture. In 1914, futurists were interventionists and a year later, when Italy entered the war, they created a motorised battalion that ridiculously went to the front lines screaming 'Zang-Timb-Tuuum!'[24]

In spite of their political differences in the face of war, during the previous decade the aesthetic avant-gardes had expressed a deep historical break. Braque and Picasso's cubism decomposed the pictorial forms as Schönberg, Berg and Webern broke traditional harmonies putting the bases of atonal and dodecaphonic music. This is why the historian Modris Eckstein sees the first representation of Stravinsky's *Rite of Spring* at the Paris the Theatre of Champs-Elysées in 1913 as the starting point of a new time – many critics renamed it 'massacre of spring' – radically putting into question the traditional representation of the world: the eruption of a ferocious and wild primitivism rejecting the forms of civilisation, a vitalistic abandonment of musical conventions in the name of a rebellious subjectivity. The scandal raised by Stravinsky simply announced the end of the nineteenth century.[25] Nor is it astonishing that Belgian painter Fernand Léger saw the ruins of Verdun as the representation of a decomposed reality, broken into a thousand pieces. In his eyes, war transformed reality according to cubist lines. Fascinated by this devastated

---

21 Papini 1913, p. 208. On this text, cf. Isnenghi 1970, p. 94.

22 Herf 1984.

23 Benjamin 2007, p. 242. And see Leslie's chapter in this volume.

24 Cf. De Felice 1988.

25 Eksteins 1989, pp. 10–16.

landscape 'allowing all pictorial fantasies', he abandoned abstract art in order to create mechanical figures.[26]

Chauvinism

In 1914, the great majority of intellectuals were patriots, not to say chauvinists. In all European capitals, war declarations aroused collective enthusiasm, often reaching delirious dimensions. Nationalist fever suddenly conquered culture, contaminating minds almost without exceptions. In Paris, the *Union Sacrée* was unanimously celebrated, far beyond the circles of the Action Française that welcomed the conflict as the opportunity for revenge against Germany. Third Republic President Raymond Poincaré asked the members of the Académie Française to mobilise 'their pens' for contributing to the patriotic effort.[27] The voices of Barrès and Maurras merged with Dreyfusard intellectuals, whom they had hated just a few years before. Writers – from André Gide to Marcel Proust to Anatole France to Paul Claudel – as well as sociologists, philosophers and literary critics – from Émile Durkheim to Henri Bergson and Charles Péguy – viewed war as liberation. The 'Jacobin' historian of the French revolution, Albert Mathiez, claimed a new *levée en masse* like in 1792. In Belgium, medievalist historian Henri Pirenne broke his old friendship with his German colleague Karl Lamprecht because of his stance on the war.

Beyond the Rhine, in October 1914 the newspaper *Berliner Tagblatt* published a famous Manifesto in which ninety-three recognised scholars, among which were many Nobel prize-winners, defended the cause of German *Kultur* threatened by the new Barbarians. It included the signatures of personalities like the geographer Ernst Haeckel, the physician Max Planck, the historian Karl Lamprecht, the political scientist Friedrich Naumann and the psychologist Wilhelm Wundt.[28] Historian Ernst Troeltsch wished to 'transform words into bayonets';[29] philosopher Max Scheler considered war as 'the essence of life itself' and described combat as a cathartic experience revealing 'the mystery of rebirth', in which Germany accomplished the mission of 'regenerating the civilization'.[30] Poets composed lyrics for celebrating the glory of Germanic warriors, whereas the economist Werner Sombart opposed the heroic spirit

26 Cf. Dagen 1996, pp. 173–83.
27 Cf. Prochasson Rasmussen 1990; Hanna 1996.
28 Flasch 2000.
29 Quoted by Stromberg 1982, p. 137.
30 Scheler 1915, p. 65.

of the Germans [*Heldern*] to the merchant (and Jewish) spirit of the British [*Händler*].[31] Thomas Mann idealised the Hohenzollern Empire as the custodian of immortal *Kultur* against the corruptive tendencies of modern Western *Zivilisation*.

The 'ideas of 1914' aroused against the principles of 1789, the starting point of an era of peace and 'progress' that had weakened the souls and pushed humanity far from the noblest values of existence: courage, virility, spirit of sacrifice, struggle, and glory. In his *Reflections of a Non-Political Man* (1918), Thomas Mann affirmed his 'disgust' [*Ekel*] – an expression borrowed from Nietzsche – for the values of the Enlightenment. In his eyes, war was the extension through the gun of 'an ideological battle already fought in a purely spiritual sphere'.[32] In Austria, the chauvinist contagion did not exclude Sigmund Freud, proud of seeing his own sons leaving for the front lines. England was renewed with a political passion apparently lost from the times of Cromwell's Revolution, presently oriented against Germany. Writers, poets and dramatists like Thomas Hardy and G.K. Chesterton became propagandists of the anti-German crusade. All Italian nationalists – from the ex-socialist Benito Mussolini to the imperialist theoretician Enrico Corradini, from the futurist writer Filippo Tommaso Marinetti to the decadentist poet Gabriele D'Annunzio, from the revolutionary-unionist Filippo Corridoni to the socialist historian Gaetano Salvemini – wished the end of Italian neutrality and the beginning of a war against the Habsburg Empire in order to liberate the 'unredeemed' lands of Trento and Trieste.[33]

Even Russia did not remain uncontaminated by the nationalist virus in spite of the objective difficulties to support the Tsarist regime. Many opponents of the autocracy such as the anarchist Piotr Kropotkin and the Marxist Georgi Plekhanov, as well as the poets Alexander Blok, Sergei Esenin and Vladimir Mayakovski, denounced German 'barbarism'. In 1912, the Russian Marxist philosopher Plekhanov claimed the class struggle instead of the conflicts between peoples, but two years later he was deeply affected by the nationalist fever. 'So far as I am concerned', he wrote in a letter to the Russian socialist Angelica Balabanoff, 'if I were not old and sick I would join the army. To bayonet your German comrades would give me great pleasure'.[34] The futurist poet Vladimir Mayakovski, who in 1917 would join the Bolshevik Revolution, became, for a short moment, a fervent nationalist at the outbreak of the war, convinced that

31 Sombart 1915. See also Mitzman 1987, pp. 254–64.

32 Mann 1983.

33 Cf. Bobbio 1990, p. 129; Isnenghi 1970.

34 Baron 1963, p. 324.

only war could destroy the Old World and create the premises for its regeneration. He defended Russia as the homeland of poetry and wrote articles that were violently chauvinistic.[35]

In short, 1914 was both the climax and the end of a classic conception of war. Inherited from Antiquity and captured by the aphorism *pro patria mori* (dying for the fatherland), the myth of the heroic death had been rediscovered in the 'Long Nineteenth Century', at the time of the blossoming of nations as 'imagined communities'.[36] In August 1914, this ethical-political concept merged with a new sense of honour and found its accomplishment in the battlefields. It was with the memory of the nationalist fever of those days that, several decades later, Ernst Kantorowicz reconstructed the genealogy of medieval Europe, indicating the Great War as its terminus.[37] Max Weber, the theoretician of axiological neutrality of scientific knowledge, was probably the last great European scholar to conceptualise the myth of heroic death in his *Zwischenbetrachtung* (1915), written at the moment in which it afflicted millions of European soldiers. First of all, Weber emphasised the 'pathos' as well as the 'community feeling' that war created among the soldiers, pushing them to offer their own life, thus creating an 'unconditional community of sacrifice'. Defining war as a secularised crusade, he stressed the irresistible strength of such a feeling, 'in front of which nothing comparable can be offered by religion'. The pillar of such a warrior community was the sacralisation of death, by which the soldier's existence received its meaning. Irreducible to natural, ordinary passing away, death in the battlefield possessed an aura, a particular and sublime meaning, insofar as it corresponded with the 'calling' [*Beruf*] of the soldier. According to Weber, 'this extraordinary character of war's fraternity and death' was a modern phenomenon that 'combat shared with both sacred charisma and the experience of sacred community'.[38] In fact, the Great War destroyed the myth of heroic death, unveiling the horrors of technological massacre and mass anonymous death. Death in the no man's land was no longer the ransom for glory [*kleos*], according to the Homeric myth, but the unexpected experience of a human slaughter. The monuments to the 'unknown soldier' built everywhere in Europe after the conflict expressed a break with the romantic vision

35 Markov 1968, pp. 190–5.
36 Anderson 1983.
37 Kantorowicz 1951, pp. 472–92.
38 Weber 1995, pp. 377–8, and Weber 2004.

of death cultivated by nineteenth-century nationalism, transferring the notion of sacrifice from the level of individual heroism to that of collective holocaust.[39]

Even expressing a general eclipse of rationalism and critical thought, such a nationalist wave was not the result of a sudden and incomprehensible blinding. This aggressive and patriotic rhetoric – we can consider it a cultural seismograph of its historical time – gave a literary expression to the *nationalisation of the masses* whose origins dated back to the French Revolution. By this definition, George L. Mosse synthesised a conception – the sacralisation of the nation and the transformation of nationalism into a kind of *civil religion* made of rites, emblems, and symbols, including the cult of sacrifice and heroic death – that found its first political formulation with Jacobinism (the *levée en masse*), and subsequently the emergence of mass society and the democratisation of European nations.[40] This process reached its peak during the Great War.

Stefan Zweig, who observed the joyful and exalted Vienna demonstrations of summer 1914, when crowds merged in a unique and indissoluble body, vividly described this moment in which the nationalisation of the masses reached its climax. Remembering those days many years later, in the middle of a new war even more devastating than the previous one, he honestly recognised his incapacity, in spite of his scepticism in front of a 'fratricidal war' between European peoples, to remain indifferent to the blossoming of such a mystical experience of community. 'As never before', he wrote in *The World of Yesterday*,

> thousands and hundreds of thousands felt what they should have felt in peace time, that they belonged together. A city of two million, a country of nearly fifty million, in that hour felt that they were participating in world history, in a moment which would never recur, and that each one was called upon to cast his infinitesimal self into the glowing mass, there to be purified of all selfishness. All differences of class, rank, and language were flooded over at that moment by the rushing feeling of fraternity. Strangers spoke to one another in the streets, people who had avoided each other for years shook hands, and everywhere one saw excited faces. Each individual experienced an exaltation of his ego, he was no longer the isolated person of former times, he had been incorporated into the mass, he was part of the people, and his person, his hitherto unnoticed person, had been given meaning.[41]

---

39 Cf. Winter 1995; Koselleck 2002, pp. 285–326.

40 Mosse 1974.

41 Zweig 1964, p. 233.

Exceptions

The intellectuals able to resist such a nationalist wave were extremely few. In Vienna, Karl Kraus denounced war in a sharp piece of theatre like *The Last Days of Mankind*.[42] In London, Bertrand Russell was put in jail because of his anti-patriotic articles. In Paris, Romain Rolland published *Au-dessus de la mêlée* [*Above the Battle*], where he defined war as a 'slaughter' from which 'Europe will exit mutilated'.[43] In Turin, the young journalist and theatre critic, Antonio Gramsci, opposed war from the pages of *Avanti!*, the newspaper of the Socialist Party, invoking the union 'of all the humanity struck by the fury of war'. In Zurich, Dadaist Hugo Ball published a provocative anti-patriotic Manifesto. The reason of their opposition to war was basically ethical, an expression of the legacy of a humanistic Enlightenment that did not succumb to the law of nationalism. Different was the attitude of those who, like Lenin and the most radical current of Russian socialism, wished to 'transform the imperialist war into a civil war'. The most powerful pages against the massacre belonged to the intellectuals who, within the international socialist movement, protested against war credits. Rosa Luxemburg, a Polish-Jewish revolutionary who had immigrated to Berlin, did not experience the days of summer 1914 as an explosion of contagious happiness; she saw them rather as a wave of collective hysteria reminding her of the atmosphere of a pogrom. In those days, she wrote in *Juniusbrochure* (1914), 'a smell of ritual murder, a smell of Kishinev was in the air'. In her eyes, war revealed the true face of bourgeois society: 'violated, dishonoured, wading in blood, dripping filth'. Once the façade of ethics, peace, and the rule of law had fallen, it showed its violent face: 'the ravening beast, the witches' Sabbath of anarchy, a plague to culture and humanity. Thus it reveals itself in its true, its naked form'.[44]

Franz Kafka reacted with much more sober words, but the nationalist virus certainly did not contaminate him. On 6 August 1914, he wrote in his diary the following sentence: 'Patriotic demonstration … Such demonstrations are among the most disgusting phenomena accompanying war'.[45] It is not by chance that among the opponents to the war, especially the internationalist socialists like Rosa Luxemburg, Leon Trotsky, Gustav Landauer, Ernst Toller, and Karl Radek, the Jewish intellectuals were strongly represented. Social and political pariahs, they belonged to a minority put on the margins, often

42 Kraus 1974.
43 Rolland 1916.
44 Luxemburg 1969.
45 Kafka 1949.

excluded and hated, who remained outside this long process of the nationalisation of the masses. During the war, they were an exception, as well as in the post-war revolutions of Central and Eastern Europe – from Germany to Hungary to Russia – where they played a leading role. But the cultural and political landscape of the continent gradually changed in the years between the world wars. In the 1920s, two opposed camps replaced the monolithic nationalist stream of 1914: on the one hand, pacifism; on the other hand, nationalism. Since 1933, this cleavage has taken the form of an irreducible conflict between fascism and antifascism.[46] The intellectuals had to choose between them, becoming actors of an ideological and political war – we could speak of a *Weltanschauungskrieg* – in which the future of mankind was put into question. In such a battle, nobody could remain neutral, because neutrality meant impotency and cowardliness. This metamorphosis from nationalism to antifascism reached its peak in 1945. That was the epilogue of a process started in 1914: retrospectively, the Great War appears as a crucial turn in intellectual history.

46 See Traverso 2007.

CHAPTER 8

Art after War: Experience, Poverty and the Crystal Utopia

Esther Leslie

Introduction

This chapter considers how the First World War altered not just the terrain of the landscapes where the fighting occurred, but also the metaphorical terrain of experience and the medium of its expression, language. The Great War effectively shattered experience as it had been lived until that point. It did this through the intense deployments of shocking and explosive technologies. War is a watershed. This theme is addressed through a small number of writings by Walter Benjamin in the 1930s. This is not in order to compose an essay on the interpretation of Walter Benjamin solely, but rather to insist that he best articulates something that others express less definitively and more fatalistically. Benjamin not only diagnoses the apparent shifts in experience and language, which result directly from war, he also develops, on the basis of this, a strategy for becoming contemporary in our thinking, our political outlook and our cultural activity. Benjamin perceives and illuminates the political and critical stakes of these reconfigurations, whereby the physical destruction of war makes necessary the conceptual elaboration of the world in its totality. It is the experience of war that produces Benjamin as a revolutionary and critical thinker – along with others who also reach maturity in Central Europe, as the war begins. This chapter explores the ways in which the First World War generates the destruction (of things and thought) and the reconfiguration (of things and thought) in startlingly new ways.

Barbarism and Experience

In 1933 Walter Benjamin wrote 'Experience and Poverty'.[1] It was an essay reflecting on the ongoing effects of the First World War. He begins with an illustration of a time before the war when, apparently, wisdom was passed down

1 Benjamin 2005, pp. 731–6.

through the generations from mouth to ear. He relates a fable about how a father taught his sons the merits of hard work by fooling them into thinking that there was buried treasure in the vineyard by the house. The turning of soil in the vain search for gold results in a real treasure: a wonderful crop of fruit. Once, observes Benjamin, there was a world in which, in this way or another, the old passed down their wisdom to the young. This wisdom was borne of experience, which was passed on to the coming generation in the form of practical lessons, showing the young what might be taken forward from what had been learnt in a lifetime of trying. Such experience and its mode of communication meshed with the fairy and folk tale, themselves vectors of wisdom in a world in which yesterday was much like today. In re-telling the tale, Benjamin evokes a mode of communicating experience – storytelling – that is becoming outmoded and, in so doing, he estranges that mode, so that he might better outline the contours of the present.[2]

Benjamin goes on to report how the coming of the World War interrupted this handing on and down, in interrupting the modes of experience of the generation who came before and after war. It is as if the good and bountiful soil of the fable has become the sticky and destructive mud of the trenches, which will bear no fruit, but only moulder as a graveyard. 'Where do you hear words from the dying that last and that pass from one generation to the next like a precious ring?' asks Benjamin. Nowhere, he replies, and he goes on to explore why this is the case. It is not simply that experiences before the war are not consistent with those after, in a world that has changed. Rather, experience itself, as a way of relating to and with the world, is diminished.

> No, this much is clear. Experience has fallen in value, amid a generation which from 1914 to 1918 had to experience some of the most monstrous events in the history of the world.[3]

Experience has 'fallen in value'. Benjamin's metaphor stems from the world of economy, unsurprisingly, as he had annexed ideas of instability and disruption elsewhere to the event of the Great Inflation of the 1920s. In some writings associated with his study *One-Way Street* (1928), Benjamin recorded an extraordinarily swift inflation:

---

2 See 'The Storyteller: Observations on the Works of Nikolai Leskov', Benjamin 2002a, for further discussion of the origin in craft and the changing value of the story.

3 Benjamin 2005, p. 731.

> For this nation, a period of just seven years separates the introduction of the calculation with half-pfennigs (by the postal authorities in 1916) from the validity of the ten thousand mark note as the smallest currency unit in use (1923).[4]

In 1923, one dollar cost 31,700 marks on 1 May. On 1 July, it cost 160,400 and on 1 August it was 1,103,000. Prices doubled over the course of a few hours. For everyone, calculation was to the fore. In the post-war years, life as a calculated risk continued to be the order of the day, as existence was organised around the possibility of exchange and the pursuit of the best possible deal.

That experience that had fallen in value is linked by Benjamin directly to the trauma of the battlefield and the ways in which language that communicates experience proves itself inadequate.

> Wasn't it noticed at the time how many people returned from the front in silence? Not richer but poorer in communicable experience.[5]

Benjamin elaborates a discrepancy between experience and the words that would be expected to convey it. The experience of war took the words out of soldiers' mouths. Those who had fought experienced something that could not be spoken of, for there was no language that matched what they had gone through, if language is born of common experiences. Those who were too old to fight could not understand what the soldiers had suffered. And there was no experience amongst those who did not fight to tally with the language that the soldiers might have used to describe the horrors they had witnessed.

The word for experience in Benjamin's original German is *Erfahrung*, a particular notion of experience that is derived from the word *Fahren*, to travel, and which implies experience as gathered over time and through practice. Elsewhere, in writings on Charles Baudelaire, Benjamin set up a contrast between two German words for experience, in order to specify its changing character. There is experience as 'Erfahrung': '[i]t is experience [*Erfahrung*] that accompanies one to the far reaches of time, that fills and articulates time'.[6] But the notion of experience more suited to contemporary life is *Erlebnis*, which denotes something more like an adventure or the participation in a one-off event. It is *Erlebnis*, incidentally, that appears in the deluge of largely nationalistic memoirs a decade after the war. Benjamin acknowledges this in

4 Benjamin 1991d, p. 934.

5 Benjamin 2005, p. 731.

6 Benjamin 2003, p. 331.

the comment: 'what poured out from the flood of war books ten years later was anything but the experience that passes from mouth to ear'.[7] To name just three of these memoirs: Ernst Jünger's *Der Kampf als inneres Erlebnis*, 'The Fight as Internal Experience', from 1926;[8] Rüdiger Alberti's *Gott im Krieg. Erlebnisse an der Westfront*, 'God in War: Experiences on the Western Front', from 1930;[9] Gustav Praclik's *Unter Stahlhelm und Fliegerhaube: Fronterlebnisse eines Kriegsfreiwilligen, 1914–1918*, 'Under Steel Helmet and Flying Cap: Front Experiences of War Volunteers, 1914–1918', from 1936.[10]

Language is inadequate for conveying the character of contemporary war and post-war experience. Experience is too different and the words used to articulate what should be truisms of the time – the strategic nature of war, the stability of the economy, the continuities of physical well-being, the moral basis of existence – seem hollow, in the face of what has occurred in war.

> For never has experience been contradicted so thoroughly: strategic experience has been contravened by positional warfare; economic experience, by the inflation; physical experience, by hunger; moral experience, by the ruling powers.[11]

War smashed the expectations that had, at least roughly, pertained until then. That a life might be strategically plotted is overturned in the experience of a war of position in which soldiers are bogged down in the mud or buried in trenches, immobilised and endlessly struggling to hold the line or push forward centimetre by centimetre. All sides had expected and hoped for a quick and decisive battle and the war was sold as 'the war to end all wars'. But barbed wire made cheap and almost impenetrable fortifications. Mass armies provided mass fodder for digging in and for death.

Economic security was ruined in war, maintains Benjamin. The inflation began in the war years, because the German government launched a borrowing programme, hopeful of swift military victory and favourable repayment conditions. Victory never came, and defeat arrived slowly. The government printed ever more notes. Prices doubled in the war years. This quick-fix solution of mass reproducing notes continued after the war. From the war years, life appeared as worthless as did the paper money with its extending zeros.

7 Benjamin 2005, pp. 731–2.
8 Jünger 1926.
9 Alberti 1930.
10 Praclik 1936.
11 Benjamin 1991a, p. 214.

Inflation robbed the economy of any stability it might have possessed and made people feel that from minute to minute there was nothing to hold on to, nothing that might be trusted to hold the same value today as tomorrow.

Physical experience was altered in the hunger and misery for the many in war and its aftermath, as the bodily experience of satiety is not a given for so many. Any fantasy that the ruling classes were arbiters of morality was undermined in the bloodbaths of the battlefields, fought, according to all of the rulers, in the name of God and morality. In short, the modern world of the war and the post-war is a cold place. The poet Bertolt Brecht wrote in a poem, in 1922, of 'the windy world of chill distress' where friendliness lasts for but two or three moments.[12]

Benjamin concludes his adumbration of contemporary disappointed experience in this way:

> A generation that had gone to school in horse-drawn street-cars now stood in the open air, amid a landscape in which nothing was the same except the clouds and, at its center, in a forcefield of destructive torrents and explosions, the tiny, fragile human body.[13]

The sole continuity with the period before the war is the vulnerable human body standing exposed under the skies. It is as if, even after the peace is concluded, the combatant stands stranded, unprotected, on a field that does not revert from being a battlefield. The archetypal post-war figure is the soldier in a peacetime that is no less assaulting of his senses and his sense of life. That the clouds remained the same was perhaps too optimistic on Benjamin's part. New clouds were invented in the First World War, clouds of poisonous gas, used by all the warring nations: xylyl bromide, chlorine, phosgene, mustard gas. Indeed, in 1925, Benjamin wrote of these new clouds in urgent tones, for it was clear that their manufacture would only increase in the wars that were surely to come. 'The Weapons of Tomorrow: Chlorazetophenol, Diphenylamchorlizine and Dichlorlathyl-sulfide' names the poisonous substances that were being perfected in the new conglomerate IG Farben's laboratories.[14] As soon as they found more abbreviated forms, the strange 'tongue-breaking' words would become as much a part of the vocabulary, Benjamin notes, as the new words that fell from everyone's lips in the First World War: dugout, U-Boot, Dicke Berta und Tank. The chemical clouds had already, and would again in

12 Brecht 2003, p. 9.
13 Benjamin 2005, p. 732.
14 *Vossische Zeitung*, 1925, 303, pp. 1–2, reprinted in Benjamin 1991b, pp. 473–6.

the future, overcome the fragile body as much as any bullets and bombs, suffocating its breathing apparatus, blistering its skin. This fragile body, without a voice, exposed to a storm of metal, fire and the best fruits of the military laboratories, is the one that Benjamin sets at the heart of his political philosophy. It returns again in the essay 'Experience and Poverty' when he writes of the 'naked man of the contemporary world who lies screaming like a newborn babe in the dirty diapers of the present'.[15]

In a sense, this naked man who screams like a newborn baby describes Benjamin himself and others of his generation who came to a political awakening at the outbreak of war. Such awakening might be seen as a type of rebirth. For Benjamin, rebirth was not separate from death. A formative event for him was the double suicide, in August 1914, of two friends from the Youth Movement, in which he was very active, having taken on roles in its leadership.[16] In protest at the outbreak of war, nineteen-year-old Christoph Heinle committed suicide, by gassing, in the kitchen of the Berlin youth movement's meeting house, together with his girlfriend Rika Seligson. The influential pedagogue and adult mentor of the German Youth Movement, Gustav Wyneken, supported the war effort and delivered a public lecture entitled 'War and Youth' in Munich on 25 November 1914. Incensed by Wyneken's discourse on the 'ethical' experience afforded to youth by war, Benjamin severed all connection 'without reservation' and accused Wyneken of senselessly sacrificing youth to the very state that had persecuted him for his freethinking.[17] It was in this period that Benjamin came into contact with socialist ideas, for example, as propounded by Kurt Hiller. He read the first and only issue of Rosa Luxemburg's and Franz Mehring's journal *Die Internationale: Zeitschrift für Theorie und Praxis des Marxismus*, passed to him by his friend Gerhard Scholem, who had attended anti-war meetings staged by those sympathetic to a faction within the German Social Democratic Party, organised around Luxemburg and Karl Liebknecht – the International Group, nucleus of the future Communist Party of Germany.

Benjamin is born anew politically in the war – as were others of his generation. There is sentimental talk in Germany, as in England, of the war generation, the beautiful young officer men who went off to fight in a monstrous war. Such a generation is perceived as sacrificed. But there is another generation that comes to a political awakening through its opposition to the war, and for whom

---

15 Benjamin 1999c, p. 733.

16 See, for an example of the discussions and atmosphere in the Youth Movement in the months leading up to the war, Benjamin's letter to his friend Herbert Belmore, 15 May 1914, in Benjamin 1994, pp. 62–6.

17 Benjamin 1996a, p. 142.

their sense of how things not only must not stay the same, but also might be different, is confirmed by the events in Russia in 1917.

That Benjamin experiences the war as a breaking point – a point at which, for example, he has to cut himself off from the significant engagement with the Youth Movement – does not imply that he fully reinvents himself under the pressures of war. In the years prior to the war he had been developing critical, if idealist, ideas. That experience is a key term in 'Experience and Poverty' is no surprise, as he had considered experience as a critical philosophical concept in some of his earliest writing. In 1913, an essay titled 'Experience', written for the journal *Der Anfang* [The Beginning], was an attack on philistines who snort at spirit, ideals and compassion. Adults wear a mask called 'experience', but it is only a placeholder, 'expressionless, impenetrable and ever the same'. This is not the experience born of practice and communicated as wisdom, but rather another form of degraded *Erfahrung*. It is a mask of impassivity in the face of the dreams the older generation once shared and in which they lost faith. Adults use the notion of experience, the 'gospel of philistines', to smash down hope and novelty and a new future. Such a notion was, perhaps, what made war possible at all. Youth's brief moment, 'the childish intoxication before the long sobriety', is followed by adult years of experience, 'years of compromise, lack of ideas and lethargy'. Such adults find no meaning in the world, no 'inner relationship to anything other than the common and the already out-of-date'. But Benjamin and his comrades knew 'a different experience', 'the most beautiful, most untouchable, most immediate, because it can never be without spirit while we remain young'.[18] War cuts into this idealism and forces an awakening to political violence, but the key term of 'experience' remains guiding. In a note written around 1929 Walter Benjamin reflected on this article, noting how he had remained true to his initial thoughts, for the word 'experience' [*Erfahrung*] had continued to be 'a fundamental element' in much of his work.[19] In making experience so central a term in his thinking, Benjamin makes it a historical variable. Experience is something whose character and scope and ability to be communicated changes over time in accord with historical development. In this regard, Benjamin can be seen as a historical materialist of both objective and subjective life. But what might war-marked, post-combat experience be?

War is the context for the pulverisation of experience in the form of something passed down from mouth to ear. The rattle and roar of the battlefield is a technological deafening that blocks communication. In war, technology had proven itself to be the nemesis of human well-being. The soldier was reduced

18 Quotations from Benjamin 1996b, pp. 3–6.

19 See Benjamin 1991b, p. 902.

to the dual role of servant and victim of the machine. He might kill or be killed at a distance by shells or long-range artillery. The 'tremendous development of technology', states Benjamin, was not set at the service of human liberation, but rather furthered impoverishment.[20] Technology engendered poverty for humankind, because, in the hands of capitalists, it demoted humans (and nature), lording mechanically over the organisation of their social relations as an unmanageable fetish.

To fill in the space left behind by old-style experience's vacation comes a torrent of ideas that simply reverse the scientific, technocratic logic of the age. Benjamin cites yoga, astrology, and gnosis, amongst other examples.[21] These irrational belief systems attempt to make sense of a world that seems – and in some regard is – senseless. Benjamin finds no answer in these, nor in most of the culture that continues to be produced. 'What is the value of all of culture if it is divorced from experience?' he asks. Culture is cut adrift, floats above the brutal terrain of experience. Benjamin underlines this by mentioning disparagingly a longer history of culture's loss of integration in everyday life and the formation of values. He mentions 'the horrific mishmash of styles and ideologies' of the nineteenth century.[22] So poor is this culture and so unrelated to the needs and wants of those who inhabit the world that it becomes its flipside, barbarism.

The axis between culture and barbarism is one that Benjamin evokes at various points. Twice, in an essay on the Social Democrat Eduard Fuchs and in a series of theses on the concept of history, he wrote that there is no document of culture which is not at the same time a document of barbarism.[23] Culture rises to the top. For its production there is always something – someone – beneath reproducing life and conditions, characterised by Benjamin as 'the anonymous toil of others'. These toilers are, yet, denied the pleasure of culture and excluded from its ambit. Barbarism also taints the manner in which it is passed from hand to hand: dispossession and privatisation are its motifs. Culture comes to be the opposite of experience as wisdom, passed usefully from mouth to ear. Here there is only denial of access and sweat for the culturally-disenfranchised.

In the early 1930s, Benjamin's thinking explores barbarism not only as the other side of culture and civilised society. It becomes the basis for a cultural-political strategy. Perhaps the origins of this also lie in the First World War, for it seems that it is his explorations of the Austrian satirist Karl Kraus,

20 Benjamin 2005, p. 732.
21 Benjamin 2005, p. 732.
22 Benjamin 2005, p. 732.
23 Benjamin 2003, p. 392. See also, Benjamin, 2002a, p. 267.

whose main works exposed the nightmare of the First World War, that allow him to conceive barbarism tactically. Kraus ran a journal in Vienna called *Der Fackel* [The Torch] from 1899 to 1936.[24] Benjamin devoted an essay to him in 1931. Here he represented Kraus as an 'Unmensch', a non-human, who could bring about 'real humanism' by exposing the twistedness of the present. Kraus, notes Benjamin, identified how technologies had corrupted language in the 'empty phrase' churned out by the newspaper printing presses, 'journalism being clearly seen as the expression of the changed function of language in the world of high capitalism'.[25] Kraus cited the nonsense, clichés and jargon of journalists, politicians, ordinary citizens, and all who upheld the façades of empire, security and justice, in order to explain how the corruption of language related to the corruption of thinking and to corrupted actions, such as war. For Kraus, Benjamin wrote, 'justice and language remain founded in each other'.[26] In addition, Kraus had devised a practice that entered into that corrupted language and deformed it further in order to attempt to re-populate it with truthful utterances. Kraus often wrote his satirical commentaries by pasting an irritating newspaper clipping onto a piece of paper and encircling it by his comments. Sometimes the magazine would print contrasting news reports in parallel columns, in order to expose duplicity.[27] Lies and hypocrisy were exposed in ironic juxtaposition, and critique emerges. The outbreak of war had fuelled Kraus's wrath and wit. In November 1914 he wrote 'In These Great Times' (a mockable phrase from the press).

> In these great times which I knew when they were this small; which will become small again, provided they have time left for it; and which, because in the realm of organic growth no such transformation is possible, we had better call fat times and, truly, hard times as well; in these times in which things are happening that could not be imagined and in which what can no longer be imagined must happen, for if one could imagine it, it would not happen; in these serious times which have died laughing at the thought that they might become serious; which, surprised by their own tragedy, are reaching for diversion and, catching themselves redhanded, are groping for words; in these loud times which boom with the horrible symphony of actions which produce reports and of reports which cause actions: in these times you should not expect any

24 Benjamin 2005, pp. 433–58.
25 Benjamin 2005, p. 435.
26 Benjamin 2005, p. 444.
27 See Timms 1989, p. 45.

> words of my own from me – none but these words which barely manage to prevent silence from being misinterpreted.... In the realm of poverty of imagination where people die of spiritual famine without feeling spiritual hunger, where pens are dipped in blood and swords in ink, that which is not thought must be done, but that which is only thought is unutterable. Expect no words of my own from me. Nor would I be able to say anything new, for in the room in which one writes there is such noise, and at this time one should not determine whether it comes from animals, from children, or merely from mortars. He who encourages deeds with words desecrates words and deeds and is doubly despicable.... Let him who has something to say come forward and be silent![28]

The permanent postponement of the closing of the line plays with journalistic cliché and shows how saying nothing might play its part in killing a few million men. The call is for silence in the face of the chatter that ushers in war.

The following year Kraus began to compose an epic collage, *The Last Days of Mankind*, which he finished in 1921. It was made of spliced found and documentary materials.[29] Through more than two hundred scenes were scattered telegrams, reports from the army press office, newspaper small ads and headlines, conversations with friends, photographs, picture postcards, film sequences, popular wartime songs and waltzes. Kraus later acknowledged the peculiar process of turning documentary materials into a montaged artwork. It was so difficult to write a satire because reality itself was already a satire and needed only to be quoted by someone who could hear and see it as that. Kraus turned himself into a quoter. He wrote:

> The art of words consists in leaving off the quotation mark, in plagiarism of the suitable fact, in the grasp that turns its cutout into an artwork.[30]

In 1921, a piece titled 'Promotional Trips to Hell' underlined how simply quoting from a document – or absorbing it like a cannibal who seeks to absorb the potency of enemies – could expose the depths to which human culture had sunk as a result of war. The document in question was a Swiss newspaper advertisement for luxurious weekend trips to Verdun, a 'battlefield par excellence', complete with first-class train tickets, transportation in a 'comfortable automobile' and an 'ample breakfast'. Tourists learn that one and a half million

28 Extracts appear in Kraus 1990.

29 See Kraus 1990, pp. 89–93.

30 Kraus 1999, p. 237.

had to bleed to death in the very place where wine and coffee and everything else are included.

> You ride through destroyed villages to the fortress area of Vaux with its enormous cemeteries containing hundreds of thousands of fallen men.
> You receive in the best hotel in Verdun a luncheon with wine and coffee, gratuities included.

Kraus adds his own caustic observations.

> You receive unforgettable impressions of a world in which there is not a square centimeter of soil that has not been torn up by grenades and advertisements.

The trip, he concludes, was worth the war.

Positive Images

It is notable that in 'Experience and Poverty' Benjamin appears unimpressed by the visual art that is produced as a direct response to the battlefield and which comes subsequently to represent the Modernist moment in culture. Visual vocabularies were invented or augmented on the battlefields by the artists who joined the mobilisation. In part, these developed from the visual forms that had been coined in the years prior to war. It comes to seem as if art is a very sensitive gauge of historical tensions. In the visual idiom of German Expressionism, paintings anticipate the apocalypse that was about to befall the city and citizens, such as Ludwig Meidner's 'Ich und die Stadt' from 1913, with its toppling buildings and tortured figure, or Franz Marc's 'The Fate of the Animals', from the same year, in which the world appears as a turbulent domain where animals and trees are exposed and vulnerable. When Marc was sent a postcard reproduction of this painting while fighting at the front in 1915, he was shocked to discover that it seemed to him a premonition of war, 'at once horrible and stirring'.[31] Futurists in Italy had, in the years prior to the First World War, translated into painterly form a world infused by the elements that would come to play such a role in war. This involved an emphasis on new technologies and on abstract, non-human forces such as electricity or speed. Futurism began in 1908, driven by the poet Filippo Tomaso Marinetti, who authored several

---

31 Selz 1974, p. 267.

manifestos.[32] One, written in the months before the World War, in March 1914, proposed a new beauty of 'geometric and mechanical Splendour':

> In fact I observed in the battery of Sidi-Messri, in October, 1911, how the shining, aggressive flight of a cannon-shot, red hot in the sun and accelerated by fire, renders almost negligible the sight of human flesh that is flayed and dying.[33]

Marinetti delighted in the pyrotechnics of war, as did other soldier-artists after him, such as Ernst Jünger. Jünger was the officer-chronicler of the war, who drew Benjamin's ire in an essay written in 1930 titled 'Theories of German Fascism'.[34] In his various books and photo-essays, Jünger delighted in the dramatic tints of gas and fire, exploding fireworks and the metalised environment of the combat zone, which appeared to him not as a grey-brown sludge, but an intensified area of manoeuvres and jeopardy. An early memoir, from 1920, *In Stahlgewittern: Aus dem Tagebuch eines Stoßtruppführers* [In Storms of Steel: From the Diary of a Raiding Troop Leader], illustrates the forms of this new 'front-experience'. In the 'theatre of war' bullets flash and zing like fireworks, tracing their way through deep clouds of smoke and swirling purple and yellow gases. Steel flocks spike the blue sky, flares flicker up and explosions sting the air. In the final chapter of the book *The Great Slaughter*, Jünger describes a battle in March 1918. The battlefield is a place where

> Even the laws of nature seemed suspended. The air quivered, just as in the scorching days of summer and its flicker sent stationary objects dancing to and fro. Black shadow lines flitted through the clouds.[35]

This zone, where the laws of nature were abolished, had something of a factory about it, an immense turbine hall manufacturing fatalities and pain mechanically.

> The modern battlefield is like huge resting machinery, in which countless hidden eyes, ears and arms are unoccupied waiting for the minute on which it all depends. Then, as a fiery overture, a single red flare from one

32 For further reflections on this, see Enzo Traverso, 'European Intellectuals and the First World War', this volume.
33 Poggi and Wittman 2009, p. 177.
34 Benjamin 1999, pp. 312–21.
35 Jünger 1922, pp. 195–6.

> or other hole in the earth travels into the skies, and a thousand guns bellow simultaneously, and with one blow the work of destruction, driven by countless levers, begins its crushing operation.[36]

Jünger, like Marinetti, relished war. The experience of war formulated their aesthetic, as Benjamin would observe of Marinetti in his conclusion to the essay 'The Work of Art in the Age of Its Technological Reproducibility':

> 'Fiat ars, pereat mundus', says fascism, expecting from war, as Marinetti admits, the artistic gratification of a sense perception altered by technology.[37]

For the Futurists, war, or the militarised peacetime, was to deliver the new beauty of 'geometric and mechanical Splendour', along with other Futurist obsessions such as the cult of muscles and sport, controlled force, discipline, method – all soldierly virtues. In July 1915, Marinetti, Umberto Boccioni, Luigi Russolo, Sant'Elia and others joined the Volunteers Cyclists' Battalion. For them too, once at the front, expected experience did not always tally with actual life, given the poor equipment and the lack of training, but this did not lead necessarily to a break with the system that propounded violence, death and glory.

A generation of modern artists were called up on the outbreak of war. Fernand Léger became a stretcher-bearer, Oskar Kokoschka a cavalryman, Max Beckmann a military medical corpsman, André Derain an artilleryman, Otto Dix a machine-gunner. Roger de La Fresnaye, Henri Gaudier-Brzeska, August Macke, Boccioni and Marc fought and died during, or as a consequence of, the war. The artists who stemmed from or would make up the European avant-garde movements – German Expressionists, French Cubists, Italian Futurists and British Vorticists – rejected the rules which previously governed the painting of battle scenes, making of them allegorical scenes of heroic Realism. They sought new ways of depicting the muddy, smoky, noisy terrain of the battlefield, as well as its experience, which revolved around shock and speed. The explosion of a homogeneous visual field already initiated by industrialising societies intensified in wartime. Homogeneity was replaced by the heterogeneity of perceptual fields and a permanent possibility of fake, trick photography, false objects, mock-ups. Speed, flux, agility of vision, multiple viewpoints were characteristic of airborne military perspectives as well as its refractions in

---

36 Jünger 1922, pp. 87–8.

37 Benjamin 2008, p. 42.

avant-garde representations. Blind spots and new perspectives were brought suddenly and dramatically into view. The zones of war exploded into a shattered mirror-image, a nightmare realisation of Cubism, technologically staged and inescapable.

Artists devised new themes and methods suited to the monstrous new reality. But what seemed most noticeable was the threading of technology through experience. In May 1915, Léger wrote from the front at Argonne:

> This war is the perfect orchestration of every means of killing, both old and new. It is intelligent to its fingertips, which actually makes it damned annoying as there are no more surprises. We are controlled on either side by very talented people. It's as linear and as arid as a geometry problem. Such a large number of shells in such a short time over such a surface area, so many men per metre and in order at the specified time, it is all triggered off mechanically. It is pure abstraction, much purer even than Cubist Painting 'itself'. I can't deny my allegiance to this method.[38]

Gino Severini was unable to fight and languished ill in Paris, but still he painted his idea of war. One image from 1915, 'Cannon in Action', depicted a cannon: flame and clouds burst out of the barrel, as the surrounding landscape recoils. Curves curl up inscribed with words – penetration, noise and light, force, bboomm, charge, arithmetic perfection. The new language of war is conveyed, in some sort of way, but not undermined or mocked.

Positive Barbarians

Benjamin did not cite the work of these avant garde groupings as significant for the post-war reconstruction of experience. He, instead, has a different roster of cultural operators, who are able, on the basis of an appraisal of the energies of technology in war, to evoke the barbarism of the present. More than that, they forge it into an articulate encapsulation of the age, in order to reshape it towards revolutionary ends, such that war, and its horrors, might not occur again.

If barbarism is the truth of experience in the post-war moment, then, according to Benjamin, it should become the leit-motif for the culture that should communicate it. Freedom is born out of the spirit of alienation.

38 Léger 1990, p. 36.

Benjamin insists on the disruptive nature of thinking. He insists on not having a cool head, a calculating one, but rather advocates a sudden movement, getting the hands dirty in grasping or grabbing, as a mental equivalent to the wisdom borne of practical experience. Benjamin is interested in salvage, in extracting from the jaws of doom a better life, through a decisive and hard gesture, or at least a seemingly brutal one.[39] In 1931 he devised, in response to what he perceived as the brutality of capital, a brutish figure. The 'destructive character' was modelled on two friends, Brecht and Gustav Glück. It was a figure, who, 'because he sees ways everywhere', 'always stands at a crossroads'.[40] The 'destructive character' is a type without memory, opposed to repression in its political and psychic senses, who – causing havoc by cutting ways through, by liquidating situations – removes the traces which sentimentally bind us to the status quo; in order to make possible modes of behaving or misbehaving which are appropriate to the conditions of the world. The destructive character erases past traces, has abolished 'aura' and with it sentimentality about things, including his own self. The destructive character is the enemy of the comfort-seeking 'étui-person', who protects everything with velveteen cases.

> Some people hand things down to posterity by making them untouchable and thus conserving them; others pass on situations, by making them practicable and thus liquidating them. The latter are called destructive.[41]

Benjamin recognises that new models of association – ones appropriate to the character of experience in modernity – must emerge.

In 'Experience and Poverty' he coins a 'new, positive concept of barbarism'.[42] The positive barbarism has to 'start from scratch', 'make a new start', 'make a little go a long way', 'begin with a little and build up further, looking neither left nor right'.[43] In February 1933, Benjamin wrote a piece titled 'Live without Traces'. This tiny fragment presents a horror-vision of the over-stuffed bourgeois parlour alongside a plea for the potential lives to be led within shiny, translucent materials. These new lives will begin from scratch, junking the clutter of the past or acknowledging that it is destroyed, redundant or a clutter that impedes moving on.

---

39 See Benjamin 2002b, p. 473.
40 Benjamin 2005, p. 542.
41 Benjamin 2005, p. 542.
42 Benjamin 2005, p. 732.
43 Benjamin 2005, p. 732.

> Holding onto things has become the monopoly of a few powerful people, who, God knows, are no more human than the many; for the most part they are more barbaric, but not in the good way. Everyone else has to adapt, beginning anew and with few resources.[44]

It is not, notes Benjamin, 'artists' who emerge out of this war able to communicate the fault lines of existence, but rather 'constructors', such as Einstein who rebuilds a whole system of physics. Cubists likewise followed the mathematicians to build the world from stereometric forms and Paul Klee took engineers as his guides for his watercolours. (Perhaps Klee's engineering references came from his work on an airfield during the war, photographing crashes and touching up the paintwork on warplanes). Benjamin heralds a number of cultural workers who, for him, record honestly this newly devalued, technologised, impoverished experience: alongside Klee, there is Adolf Loos, Bertolt Brecht, and the utopians Paul Scheerbart and Mickey Mouse. In all of these the brutality and dynamism of contemporary technologised experience is used, abused, mocked and harnessed.

In 'Experience and Poverty', Benjamin indicates Mickey Mouse's capacity to personify utopian hopes for a technology-ravaged, yet technology-dependent populace.[45] Mickey Mouse's existence is full of miracles, and these miracles not only surpass technical wonders, but satirise them too. Mickey Mouse inhabits a world of wonders where things metamorphose at the drop of a hat, a cow becomes a musical box, a skirt a parachute, or a church steeple crunches itself up, so that the crazy plane may fly unimpeded with Mickey and Minnie Mouse on board. In Benjamin's analysis, Mickey Mouse is seen to fulfil the longing for a harmonious reconciliation of technology and nature, a co-operation, and that in an age when technological change threatens in all actuality to destabilise nature, and, moreover, destroy it. The benign union of technology and nature is relegated to the dream world of comics, photographs and cinema, where machinery indulges humans in darkened rooms or closeted parlours, for in reality, in industrial capitalism, technology and nature, or, in other words, machinery and humans, are so set against each other, torn apart or tearing each other apart.

Brecht reflects on the poverty of experience with his actors trained in his techniques of estrangement or alienation, on bare stages in exemplary fables. There were building designers too who made homes appropriate enough for the exigencies of the times: Adolf Loos with his unornamented buildings and

---

44 Benjamin 2005, p. 735.

45 Benjamin 2005, pp. 734–5.

Paul Scheerbart with his utopian fantasies of glass buildings and his science fictions that imagine how technologies transform people and fit them into the new homes. Scheerbart, one of Benjamin's favourite authors, was a writer of science fictions. Benjamin observes how through technologies, such as telescopes, humans are converted into 'lovable creatures'.[46] These newly born techno-humans speak a strange language, for they cannot partake of the old corrupted one. Arbitrary and constructed, it is one used to change reality not describe it. Benjamin compares Scheerbart's invented language to the language that is reinvented in the course of the Russian Revolution. In Scheerbart, the creatures of a better future live, he notes, in 'movable, adjustable, glass-covered dwellings', like mobile arcades and they are something like the new buildings that Loos and Le Corbusier are designing.

The reference to glass was significant, for Scheerbart wrote a manifesto in 1914 titled 'Glass Architecture'.[47] Scheerbart rebuffed the brickwork and clutter of the Victorian age and embraced the contemporary possibilities of glass, steel and concrete. His radiant homes, comprised mainly of windows, also made glass the purveyor of a new morality. Window glass is crystalline. Its crystalline character stands for absolute form, the perfection and completeness of materials. Its fragility becomes a moral trait: it breaks (rather than bending like metal). It is the converse of stone and brick. Those two are sturdy exteriors, impenetrable, blocking, like a shell or armour, keeping the world out. For Scheerbart, glass is more like a type of sensitive membrane, or like the retina of the eye: that which is looked through, the window, becomes the very mechanism of looking, the eye. Human and habitat share characteristics. It is as if in the imagining of a perfect future world there should be no difference between the structures we inhabit and ourselves. This is an alignment that utopia so often vaunts, and its implication is that the exploitation of nature, including ourselves as nature, and the impositions of technology are past.

Through a combination of light, colour and glass, as well as water, a natural ally of glass, modern living could be transformed. This is a utopia indeed, but one that teetered on realisation. Scheerbart's pamphlet was dedicated to Bruno Taut, who in the year of its publication had designed the brightly coloured Glass Pavilion at the Werkbund Exhibition in Cologne. Taut was the initiator of the 'Crystal Chain' or 'Glass Chain', a chain of letters, also known as 'the utopian correspondence' between architects and artists who imagined buildings of the future, irrespective of the practicality of their physical con-

---

46 Benjamin 2005, p. 733.

47 See the tract by Scheerbart 1972.

struction and in the context of social and spiritual revolution. Glass and crystal were endowed with spiritual, political qualities. And, importantly, an analogy was made between the orientation of the glass building to vision – to being seen through and into and from – and the visionary. The Glass Chain architect's language saw window-walls as points of access to the infinite spectacle of nature. Taut's Glass Pavilion was a fourteen-sided prismatic dome and glass block staircase which was in turn dedicated to Scheerbart and decorated with his slogans. Scheerbart's slogans included such lines as: 'COLOURED GLASS DESTROYS HATRED', 'WITHOUT A GLASS PALACE LIFE IS A BURDEN' and 'GLASS BRINGS US THE NEW ERA; BRICK CULTURE IS ONLY HARMING'.

The glassy utopia was conceived at the outbreak of war, a war that would shatter any of this crystal utopia into shards. Scheerbart notes hopefully: 'it remains to be wished that the new glass culture will not encounter too many enemies'. Such a fragile environment was imagined as the best accommodation for the fragile human body. It was a utopian dream, but it held a transparent window up to the time and highlighted the violence at work in it. The utopia of glass and crystal architecture born in the context of shattering war is more than just a fantastic effort to deny – or supersede – the realities of the day. The fragile architecture is precisely the vehicle of a new non-warring morality, which has to become political.

All these figures cited by Benjamin – Mickey Mouse, Brecht, Klee, Loos and Scheerbart – were presented as purveyors, in art, literature or drama, of an experience that properly acknowledged the moment and its barbarity following war. It is not that barbarism is to be remediated for its own sake. It is rather that only through an honest appraisal of the state of affairs might a genuine change come about. In the course of that, it may be that the fragile body finds a proper home in the fragile building – its crystal utopia of peace.

Conclusion: Battlefield and Technology

Walter Benjamin wakes up in the First World War. He wakes up, specifically, to the technology of the battlefield. This leads him to formulate his thinking in relation to the technology of the battlefield, monitoring its effects on human experience and sensibility. Equally, he flips the concern and constitutes technology itself as in a battlefield. That is to say, he explores how there is a battle to be waged over the uses and abuses of technology. If the technology that is threaded through modern existence is used productively in industry, but destructive socially, and certainly destructively in war, how might it be redeployed to productive social ends?

Benjamin writes in the final section of *One-Way Street*, 'To the Planetarium', of how humans have always sought to commingle with cosmic powers. The particular version of this seeking in his time relates to the immense forces of war and revolution. He captures, in grand language, the effects of the First World War on humanity and the landscape.

> Human multitudes, gases, electrical forces were hurled into the open country, high-frequency currents coursed through the landscape, new constellations rose in the sky, aerial space and ocean depths thundered with propellers, and everywhere sacrificial shafts were dug in Mother Earth. This immense wooing of the cosmos was enacted for the first time on a planetary scale – that is, in the spirit of technology. But because lust for profit of the ruling class sought satisfaction through it, technology betrayed man and turned the bridal bed into a bloodbath.[48]

Technology changes everything. It releases powers and forces in ways that appear, or indeed are, mythical, monstrous, immense. Technology effects a grand-scale communion with nature and natural forces. It reshapes the landscape. It changes the notion of distance and time. It alters the sensory environment. The ensnaring of this immense power within a capitalist framework limits the possibilities and directs it into massively destructive ends. Technology is not integrated in the world and with humans, and so becomes instead an oppressive force. The way out of this situation passes through a reorganisation of social relations. For Benjamin, the Russian Revolution is one effort at such reorganisation.

> In the nights of annihilation of the last war the frame of mankind was shaken by a feeling that resembled the bliss of the epileptic. And the revolts that followed it were the first attempt of mankind to bring the new body under its control.[49]

Technology – and technique, the social relations of technology – are a battlefield and Benjamin's ongoing interest is directed towards finding ways of democratising or – in his words – 'politicising' the uses of technology, including in art and culture. This is what stands behind the famous couplet from his essay 'The Work of Art in the Age of its Technological Reproducibility'.

---

48 Benjamin 1996b, p. 486.

49 Benjamin 1996b, p. 486.

> Humankind, which once, in Homer, was an object of contemplation for the Olympian gods, has now become one for itself. Its self-alienation has reached the point where it can experience its own annihilation as a supreme aesthetic pleasure. Such is the aestheticizing of politics, as practiced by fascism. Communism replies by politicizing art.[50]

One lesson Benjamin takes from the battlefield is that a critical art practice must acknowledge, incorporate and struggle with the technologies of the day, and not wish art back into some earlier age, before Cubism's break up of perspective and its mediation of modern complexity, chaos and relativism. There were those who desired of oil painting that it ignore the new vistas and modes of production and distribution inaugurated in photography, while novels should carry on in their forms of telling and consuming, as if cinema had never happened. Benjamin drew out the implications of his recognition of the deep experiential impact of the First World War, as did in their own ways the immediate post-war revolutionary experimenters who sought revolutionary forms for art – be they Dadaists, Constructivists, Productivists or Eccentrics. Beyond the formal experimentation of Cubism, Futurism, Suprematism and other pre-war avant garde groupings, these reflected on – or, more intensely, worked on and through – the developments and exigencies of technology, science, mass media and mass politics, turning their artworks thereby into a kind of battleground of class struggle. As the revolutionary impulses waned or were beaten back in the course of the 1920s, the dominant culture of the Communist movement forgot or ignored the lesson and preferred for the most part to revert to traditional forms of art-making and viewing, as exemplified in Socialist Realism, the cultural analogue of Stalinism.

---

50 Benjamin 2008, p. 42.

CHAPTER 9

'America's Belgium': W.E.B. Du Bois on Race, Class, and the Origins of World War I

Alberto Toscano

Is, then, this war the end of wars? Can it be the end so long as its prime cause, the despising and robbery of darker peoples, sits enthroned even in the souls of those who cry peace? So if Europe hugs this delusion, then this is not the end of world war – it is the beginning.

—DU BOIS, 'Of the Culture of White Folk' (1917)

What is the black man but America's Belgium, and how could America condemn in Germany that which she commits, just as brutally, within her borders?

—DU BOIS, *Darkwater* (1920)

Introduction

At the same time as the likes of Luxemburg and Lenin were setting down their seminal accounts of the origins of intra-European conflict in imperial plunder, the foremost black intellectual and social theorist in the United States, W.E.B. Du Bois – in a series of articles, addresses and editorials – declared that the roots of war were to be sought in Africa. This did not solely involve underscoring the predatory dynamics of competition and accumulation that pitted European capitals against one another. In Du Bois's eyes, the exploitation and denigration of black, and more broadly non-white, labour, played a critical role in the material and ideological apparatuses of European imperialism. It also vitiated at its root the US claim to provide democratic world leadership. As he would memorably summarise it in *Darkwater*:

> The present problem of problems is nothing more than democracy beating itself helplessly against the color bar, – purling, seeping, seething, foaming to burst through, ever and again overwhelming the emerging masses of white men in its rolling backwaters and held back by those

> who dream of future kingdoms of greed built on brown and black and yellow slavery.[1]

The thesis of white skin privilege, of a material and psychological wage to be extracted from 'whiteness',[2] was here projected out from the particular context of labour in the US – where the separation of black and white workers was the crucial factor in the rollback of 'Black Reconstruction' and the entrenchment of racial capitalism – onto a global scene. The thesis of the 'African Roots of War' – to cite the title of Du Bois's most famous article on the matter – can thus also be expanded into a contribution to the discussion of 'social imperialism' (a discussion in which Du Bois, like Lenin, is indebted to J.A. Hobson's 1902 *Imperialism*), one which foregrounds the racial coordinates of this particular form of capitalist ideology, delineating something like *the global wages of whiteness*.[3]

Ironically, it was precisely in order to defend the supremacy of white capital and labour that a prominent (and very mainstream) racist ideologue, Lothrop Stoddard, singled out Du Bois's text as a dire warning about the 'rising tide of colour' and the possible end of white supremacy. In this racial imaginary, World War I amounted to something like a 'white civil war'.[4] This was in a sense true from Du Bois's perspective too, albeit with a radically different valence: in a thesis that was later echoed by Karl Korsch and Hannah Arendt, and which was to become a founding tenet of much anti-colonial critique (most eloquently in Césaire's *Discourse on Colonialism*), the war represented the return onto (white) European soil of the systematic violence and repression that had thereto taken place on the other side of the geographical colour line – in the colonies, among 'the savages'. This was the boomerang effect of imperialism. In these ways, as the introduction to this volume suggests, Du Bois

1 Du Bois 1999, p. 33.

2 The literature on this question is considerable, but see especially Roediger 2007, building on the ground-breaking treatment in Du Bois 1998 [1935].

3 On social imperialism, see Semmel 1968; Eley 1976; and Mommsen 1980, pp. 93–9.

4 Stoddard 1920. A couple of sentences suffice to give the tenor of Stoddard's views (which were ubiquitous enough to make a cameo appearance in *The Great Gatsby*): 'The heart of the white world was divided against itself and, on the fateful 1st of August, 1914, the white race, forgetting ties of blood and culture, heedless of the growing pressure of the colored world without, locked in a battle to the death. An ominous cycle opened whose end no man can foresee' (p. 16). Stoddard had argued, as early as 1914, that the 'fundamental problem' of the twentieth century would be, not the colour line, but the '*conflict* of colour' – race war by another name. See Bush 2009, pp. 9–12. Du Bois debated Stoddard on the radio in 1927 and before a public audience in Chicago in 1929. See Lewis 2009, pp. 497–8, and Taylor 1981.

highlighted the crucial significance of race and racism as 'fundamental organising principles of the international politics of the epoch whilst illuminating a number of themes that would be subsequently picked up and elaborated upon by a number of critical scholars'.[5]

But Du Bois's standpoint was not that of an anti-colonial critic, perceiving from outside its perimeter the collapse of the civilisational hypocrisy of the 'West'. As his more autobiographical writings testified, especially in their thematising of the predicament of 'double consciousness', the colour line and its imperial repercussions cut right through him as a black American intellectual and social critic working in and against the 'white world'.

It was in the context of the US's entry into the war that Du Bois's most notorious intervention, his editorial 'Close Ranks', pressing African-Americans to suspend their 'special grievances' during the war effort, took place. Here we see a kind of racial counterpart to the class compromise, the *Burgfrieden* ('civil truce') that had torn the European workers' movement apart. The dubious background of the 'Close Ranks' article – Du Bois's attempt to gain an officership, his potential collaboration via the NAACP's Joel Springarn in an intelligence effort aimed at pre-empting 'black subversion' – has been amply explored in the literature.[6] Here, I instead want to bring into relief the 'tragic' (which is not to say inevitable) dimensions of Du Bois's stance.

The wager that social improvement and rights could be gained from the participation, in a non-subaltern capacity, of blacks in the US military effort, took place in the context of a further brutalisation of race relations – attacks on black soldiers, a spike in lynchings, which worsened further in the war's aftermath (the 'Red Summer' of 1919), and, among others, the East St. Louis race riots of 1917. The latter, which saw mobs of white workers murdering poor blacks (accused of 'scabbing'), was a brutal index of the nigh-on impossibility, in Du Bois's eyes, of building solidarity among white and black workers, and consequently of articulating any kind of progressive position about the war which didn't pass through the paradoxical position of a black patriotism.

The story of Du Bois's response to World War I – which in autobiographical retrospect, especially after his late rallying to communism, he would approach through a mix of disavowal, confusion and self-criticism[7] – is in many ways the story of the painful entanglement of two partially-overlapping colour lines:

---

5 Anievas, Introduction, this volume. For a further exploration and unpacking of Du Bois's 'international theory' see Anievas, Manchanda, and Shilliam 2015.

6 See Allen, Jr. 1979 and Ellis 1992, as well as the biographical account in Lewis 2009.

7 See Lewis 2009.

the one cutting through the US working class, the other dividing white and non-white labour globally. In their combination of epochal insight and political hesitation, Du Bois's interventions about the war provide a critical testing ground for thinking through the articulation between social imperialism and racial capitalism, allowing us to reflect on the complex and in multiple ways yet unlearned lessons that World War I offered to those trying to think the composition of the world working class and the obstacles to effective solidarity.

War along the Colour Line

In November 1914, only a few months after the outbreak of hostilities, Du Bois took to the pages of *The Crisis* – the NAACP's flagship journal which he had founded in 1910 and would edit until his resignation in 1934 – to place the conflict within the ambit of what he had for some time identified as the problem of the twentieth century. Addressing those who may have doubted that the subjugation of American blacks could be meaningfully connected to the European carnage, Du Bois urged a framing of both the war and US race relations in terms of the *global* question of race, understanding race prejudice – in the wake of Hobson – in its profound entanglement with capitalist imperialism.[8] Why should 'coloured persons' not make 'the mistake of supposing that the present war is far removed from the color problem of America', and of thinking that such 'local problems' can be momentarily set aside to focus on the world-changing events in Europe? Because, like the protracted tragedy that characterises the US black experience as it moves through slavery, the Civil War, the counter-revolution against Black Reconstruction and the continued oppression of the century's first decades, this too is 'one of the great disasters due to race and color prejudice'.[9] Or, as Du Bois would assert shortly thereafter,

> it is directly in this outer circle of races, and not in the inner European household, that the real causes of present European fighting are to be found.... The Balkans are convenient for occasions, but the ownership of

8 Du Bois had encountered Hobson in 1911 at the Universal Races Congress held in London. The common influence of Hobson's *Imperialism* is the most immediate reason for the analogies between Du Bois's essay 'The African Roots of War' and Lenin's *Imperialism*, noted, for instance, in Marable 2005, pp. 94–5. On Du Bois and Hobson, see Lewis 2009, pp. 291 and 328.

9 Du Bois 1914, p. 245.

> materials and men in the darker world is the real prize that is setting the nations of Europe at each other's throats.[10]

The articulation between the US and global colour lines will prove both analytically and politically daunting, but what allows one to vault the seeming chasm between the African-American struggle and the World War is imperialism, understood by Du Bois as a constitutively 'racial' phenomenon. A planetary gaze could de-provincialise the politics of race in the US, and link the black experience to the violence of exploitation and dispossession abroad:

> One has only to remember the forced labour in South Africa, the outrages in Congo, the cocoa slavery in Portuguese Africa, the land monopoly and peonage in Mexico, the exploitation of Chinese coolies and the rubber horror of the Amazon to realize what white imperialism is doing today in well-known cases, not to mention thousands of less-known instances.[11]

Accordingly, the cause of the war is to be located not primarily in Europe itself, but in the 'wild quest for imperial expansion among colored races'[12] affecting, to varying degrees, European states. This is an expansion which rests on the same ideological bases as the exploitation and suppression of African-Americans in the US.

It is in the context of a racial capitalist imperialism that, as Du Bois writes,

> a theory of the inferiority of the darker peoples and a contempt for their rights and aspirations have become all but universal in the greatest centers of modern culture. Here it was that American color prejudice and race hatred received in recent years unexpected aid and sympathy. Today civilized nations are fighting like mad dogs over the right to own and exploit darker peoples.[13]

And, as Du Bois forcefully denounced in the case of Haiti, victim of 'the outrage of uninvited American intervention',[14] the US was not entirely alien to such a fight.

---

10 Du Bois 1915a, pp. 370 and 366.
11 Du Bois 1914, p. 246.
12 Du Bois 1914, p. 245.
13 Du Bois 1914, p. 246.
14 Du Bois 1915b, p. 216.

Six months later, in the pages of the *Atlantic*, Du Bois published his most well-known statement on the racist and imperialist origins of the Great War. Though Du Bois alludes to Africa as the site of past empires' 'greatest crises', his outline of its generally disavowed centrality to world affairs puts the political economy of race front and centre. It is by attending to the immensely lucrative brutalisation of Africa and Africans at the hands of European powers that we can comprehend how 'the world began to invest in color prejudice', how the ' "color line" began to pay dividends'.[15] But behind this ideological and material exploitation of racial difference, Du Bois saw more than the instrumental legitimation of competition between national states and capitals.

Echoing aspects of Hobson's sociology of imperialism, Du Bois, while revealing an 'African' cause for the European conflict, also posited an endogenous dynamic for Europe's belligerent expansionism. The 'riddle' thrown up by the 'desperate flames of war' scorching Africa ever since the Berlin Conference was to be answered by 'economic changes in Europe'.[16] Or, more precisely, by the reaction of capital and the state to a social process – taking the names, sequentially, of Revolution, Democracy and the Socialisation of Wealth – which sees 'the dipping of more and grimier hands into the wealth-bag of the nation, until today only the ultrastubborn fail to see that democracy, in determining income, is the next inevitable step to Democracy in political power'.[17] This process, which Du Bois depicts in unconvincingly linear terms, is what drives a capital unable to super-exploit its 'own' working classes beyond its national borders, and pushes the state to promise or offer them a rising share of imperial spoils.

Whence the paradox of what Du Bois calls 'democratic despotism', which combines the tendency to increased political and economic democratisation with an intensification of exploitation and subjugation. The 'paradox' is not simply the purview of European imperialism, but defines the US polity itself, allowing 'the most rapid advance of democracy to go hand-in-hand in its very centers with increased aristocracy and hatred toward darker races, and which excuses and defends an inhumanity that does not shrink from the public burning of human beings'.[18] A global glance at the sociology of white supremacy thus reveals a solidarity between the strategies of state and capital across nations; a solidarity that can be captured in the notion of a racially-defined

15 Du Bois 1915a, p. 362.
16 Du Bois 1915a, p. 362.
17 Du Bois 1915a, pp. 362–3.
18 Du Bois 1915a, p. 363.

Herrenvolk democracy.[19] It is the violent drawing of the colour line through the working peoples of the world, and the circumscription of the democratising process by race, that, *in practice*, dispels the paradox:

> The white workingman has been asked to share the spoils of exploiting 'chinks and niggers'. It is no longer simply the merchant prince, or the aristocratic monopoly, or even the employing class, that is exploiting the world: It is the nation; a new democratic nation composed of united capital and labor. The laborers are not yet getting, to be sure, as large a share as they want or will get, and there are still at the bottom large and restless excluded classes. But the laborer's equity is recognized, and his just share is a matter of time, intelligence and skillful negotiation.[20]

As we will critically explore below, this iteration of Du Bois's account of 'racial prejudice as a prime cause of war'[21] rests very heavily on a presupposition about the material reality and indeed feasibility of a racial cross-class alliance, subscribing to, albeit from an antagonistic perspective, the wishes, more than the analyses, of the proponents of 'social imperialism'. In 'The African Roots of War', it is ultimately the racial and national compact between labour and capital, over and above the dynamics of imperial hyper-exploitation, which animates the conflict. Projecting on a global scale the critique of white hegemony in the socialist and labour movements that had already informed his resignation from the Socialist Party in 1912, Du Bois discerns the material bases for global conflict in these discriminatory covenants between capitalists and workers. He thus concludes that the war is 'the result of jealousies engendered by the recent rise of armed national associations of labour and capital'.[22]

How stable, we might ask, are such associations – in which we can see not just governments and armies, but the 'total mobilisation' of imperialist societies for war? Despite the aforementioned suggestion that social imperialism might prove feasible, Du Bois is also sensitive, following Hobson, to its internal shearing pressures. The war had exploded at a moment when 'the rising demands of the white laborer, not simply for wages but for conditions of work and a voice in the conduct of industry make industrial peace difficult'. Imperialist 'state socialism' is one tactic of appeasement, but it is generally accompanied by threats of capital flight and what in today's parlance would be referred to as

19 Fredrickson 1981; Losurdo 2011.

20 Du Bois 1915a, p. 363.

21 Du Bois 1915a, p. 368.

22 Du Bois 1915a, p. 366.

'social dumping'. Social imperialism along national-racial lines, 'the attempt to unite labor and capital in world-wide freebooting', appears as a more compelling and comprehensive strategy. But Du Bois seems to suggest that this too comes up against a limit, in the impossibility of including the whole of the (white) working class in the 'sacred space' of democratic despotism:

> Democracy in economic organization, while an acknowledged ideal, is today working itself out by admitting to a share in the spoils of capital only the aristocracy of labor – the more intelligent and shrewder and cannier workingmen. The ignorant, unskilled, and restless still form a large, threatening, and, to a growing extent, revolutionary group in advanced countries.[23]

It is stark racism, then, which comes to fill in the gap between the promise of spoils and the reality of continued exploitation. The felt experience by white workers that the social-imperialist compact cannot maintain its promise also explains why everywhere 'there leaps to articulate speech and ready action that singular assumption that if white men do not throttle coloured men, then China, India, and Africa will do to Europe what Europe has done and seeks to do to them'.[24] In this aggressive 'projective identification' with the racial enemy,[25] in racism as 'preventive counter-violence',[26] we can already glimpse the guilty consciousness of the paladins of civilisation in what concerns the repressed realities of their own barbarism.

This leitmotiv of civilisation shadows that of capital and labour in Du Bois's responses to the war. As he writes in a September 1916 editorial for *The Crisis*, with World War I (Western, European) 'civilization has met its Waterloo'.[27] The idea of civilisational crisis durably accompanied many of the intellectual responses to the war, both Western and non. Figures like Valéry or Hesse on the one side, and Tagore on the other, concurred in their recognition that 'the war had inverted the attributes of the dominant and revealed what the colonizers

23 Du Bois 1915a, p. 367.

24 Du Bois 1915a, p. 367.

25 Drawing on the psychoanalyst Melanie Klein, the US political theorist Robert Meister presents 'projective identification' as the psychic infrastructure of political violence. It accounts for how the dominator re-experiences his own aggression towards the dominated as a fear of the dominated's murderous hostility. For Meister, this constitutes the very 'basis of politics'. See Meister 2011, p. 148.

26 Balibar 2001, p. 16.

27 Du Bois 1916, p. 248.

had trumpeted as unprecedented virtues to be fatal vices'.[28] In Du Bois, the West's 'Waterloo' provides the occasion for a moral and aesthetic critique of the hegemonic figure of civilisation, which oscillates between racial vindication (the valorisation of black and African culture as an alternative)[29] and the announcement of a new humanism, in ways distantly echoed half a century later by Fanon, but which also remain strongly anchored in nineteenth-century imaginaries of progress (as testified by a view of the 'Orient' later abandoned by Du Bois):

> Music has always been ours; but with the disappearance of those effete ideals [of the white West] comes the assurance that the plantation song is more in unison with the 'harmony of the spheres' than Wagner's greatest triumph. Life, which in this cold Occident stretched in bleak, conventional lines before us, takes on a warm, golden hue that harks back to the heritage of Africa and the tropics. Brothers, the war has shown us the cruelty of the civilization of the West. History has taught us the futility of the civilization of the East. Let ours be the civilization of no *man*, but of *all men*. This is the truth that sets us free.[30]

More arresting than this vision of a civilisational *Aufhebung*, which arguably still remains constrained by Du Bois's 'Fabian' political imaginary,[31] and still awaits the black Marxist turn of *Black Reconstruction*, is the way in which the

---

28 Adas 2004, p. 89. On the post-World War I emergence of an Asian ideology of decolonisation and its critique of the Western ideal of civilisation, see Mishra 2012, especially chapter 4: '1919, "Changing the History of the World"'. As Adas himself notes: 'The sorry spectacle of the suicidal European cataclysm, and the shortages and hardships it inflicted on colonized areas, sparked widespread regional protest and resistance to Western domination that assumed genuinely global dimensions by the last years of the conflict' (p. 86). On the scope of Europe's civilisational trauma, as refracted through its intellectuals, see Enzo Traverso's illuminating essay in this volume, especially his attention to the intra-European dynamics of racialisation, as denounced by Ernest Renan. On the racial dimensions of *kriegsideologie*, see also the important discussion in Losurdo 2001.

29 Du Bois 1915a, but especially Du Bois 1999 [1920].

30 Du Bois 1916, p. 249.

31 Reed Jr. 1999. Though Reed's is a necessary counterweight to an excessively celebratory enlisting of Du Bois into the Black radical tradition, I think the writings of Marable, Robinson, Roediger and Olson, among others, as well as an attentive reading of the texts discussed in this essay, suggest serious qualification of Reed's grounding claim, to wit that Du Bois's work retains throughout 'the premises of the liberal collectivist paradigm' (p. 41).

conflict provides Du Bois with the occasion not only to explore the global scope of his argument about the wages of whiteness but to deepen his investigation of the 'souls of white folk'.[32] Beyond the surprise and *Schadenfreude* elicited by the 'sudden descent of Europe into hell', Du Bois, writing 'Of the Culture of White Folk' in the *Journal of Race Development* (a precursor of *Foreign Affairs*) in April 1917, notes that for 'darker peoples' the war is an occasion to reflect on 'the prophecy of our own souls', namely the insights into the violence and limitations of white Western civilisation afforded by 'double consciousness'. No one, Du Bois wryly notes, 'ever took himself and his own perfectness with such disconcerting seriousness as the white man'. And it is from the vantage point of the victims of this delusion of perfectness, those who 'pointed silently to [his] feet of clay', that the implosion of white Western civilisation's ego-ideal is the object of '*mild* amaze'.[33] 'Belgium' is here, as in 'The African Roots of War', the allegory for this reversibility in the white Western concept of civilisation. The victim *par excellence* of German militarism, Belgium is also the name for imperialism at its most predatory and barbaric. As Du Bois reminds his readers: 'What Belgium suffers now is not half, not even a tenth, of what she has done to black Congo since Stanley's great dream of 1880'. Yet while that vast 'rubber horror' was being perpetrated 'the fields of Belgium laughed, the cities were gay; art and science flourished; the groans that helped to nourish this civilization fell on deaf ears because the world roundabout was doing this same sort of thing elsewhere on its own account'.[34] For 'darker men' like Du Bois, obliged by the racial regime to see 'the Souls of White Folk stand singularly naked',[35] what appears to dominant opinion as an unexampled civilisational crisis is more aptly perceived as a moment of unveiling:

> This is not Europe gone mad; this is not aberration nor insanity; this *is* Europe; this seeming Terrible is the real soul of white culture – back of all culture – stripped and visible today. This is where the world has arrived – these dark and awful depths and not the shining and ineffable heights we boasted of. Here is whither the might and energy of modern humanity has really gone.[36]

---

32 Du Bois 1910.

33 Du Bois 1917a, p. 309 (emphasis mine). Much of this essay also concerns the broken promises of white Western Christianity, which I won't deal with here.

34 Du Bois 1917a, p. 311.

35 Du Bois 1910, p. 302.

36 Du Bois 1917a, pp. 311–12.

Though talk of soul may reinforce Marable's contention that Du Bois's account of imperialism remains an 'idealist interpretation',[37] Du Bois is quick to root European culture in the material achievements of prior civilisations, as well as in the spiritual rhetoric of the new imperialism – in particular German paeans to *Lebensraum*, which show how it is 'colonial aggrandizement which explains, and alone adequately explains the present war', in tandem with the 'theory of colonial expansion' according to which it is 'the duty of white Europe to divide up the darker world and administer it for Europe's good'.[38] But though Du Bois reiterates his conviction, first voiced in 1914, that the origins of the Great War are to be found in the imperialist dynamics of racism and colonisation, there is an important shift in emphasis.

Whereas 'The African Roots of War' had emphasised the social-imperialist cross-class alliance, 'Of the Culture of White Folk' – while not abandoning that thesis – puts the accent on the racialised hyper-exploitation of a non-white global proletariat. On the basis of a similar impasse as that described in the earlier piece, to wit that it is 'plain to modern white civilization that the subjection of the white working classes cannot much longer be maintained' and that, accordingly, the 'day of the very rich is drawing to a close', the imperialist countries have turned to a 'loophole': resource extraction and the 'exploitation of darker peoples' in domains where racial rule pushes aside any limit to 'inordinate profit'. This is how Du Bois depicts racial capitalism in his own letters of blood and fire:

> It is here that the Golden Hand still beckons: there are no labour unions or votes or questioning onlookers or inconvenient consciences. These men may be used down to the bone, and shot and maimed in 'punitive' expeditions when they revolt. In these dark lands 'industrial development' may repeat in exaggerated form every horror of the industrial history of Europe, from slavery and rape to disease and maiming, with only one test of success – dividends.[39]

---

37 Marable 2005, p. 94.

38 Du Bois 1917a, p. 313. Further regarding the significance of *Lebensraum* to German colonial expansionist designs both before and after 1914, see Baranowski's contribution to this volume.

39 Du Bois 1917a, p. 315. This is echoed three years later in *Darkwater*: 'All the industrial devilry, which civilization has been driving to the slums and backwaters, will have a voiceless continent to conceal it. If the slave cannot be taken from Africa, slavery can be taken to Africa'. Du Bois 1999 [1920], p. 36.

Imperial hyper-exploitation is indissociable here from racial theory, which has 'worked itself through the warp and woof of our daily thought with a thoroughness that few realize', and whose perpetuation has a disarmingly simple explanation: 'it pays'. Consequently, 'the world market most wildly and desperately sought today is the market where labor is cheapest and most helpless and profit most abundant. This labor is kept cheap and helpless because the white world despises "darkies" '.[40] Where 'The African Roots of War' sought the war's cause in 'jealousies engendered by the recent rise of armed national associations of labor and capital', that is, in the class sociology of the white metropolis, seeking safety valves in imperial depredation, 'Of the Culture of White Folk', in spite of its title, turns emphatically to the exploitation of the darker proletariat, to the 'vast quest of the dark world's wealth and toil':[41]

> Small wonder, then, in the practical world of things-that-be, there are jealousy and strife for the possession of the labor of dark millions, for the right to bleed and exploit the colonies of the world where this golden stream may be had, not always for the asking, but surely for the whipping and shooting. It is this competition for the labor of yellow, brown, and black folk that was the cause of the present World War.[42]

And it is on this backdrop that Du Bois – contemporaneously with his practical efforts to organise black support and participation in the US war effort, on which more below – sketches his strongest indictment of the United States's claim to intervene in the European conflict, as though it were unsullied by Europe's racial and imperial crimes:

> It is curious to see America, the United States, looking on herself as a sort of natural peacemaker in this terrible time. No nation is less fitted. For two or more centuries she has marched proudly in the van of human hatred. She makes bonfires of human flesh and laughs at them hideously. She makes the insulting of millions more than a matter of dislike – it becomes a great religion, a world war cry: Up white, down black; to your tents, O white folk, and world war with black and particolored mongrel beasts![43]

40 Du Bois 1917a, p. 318.

41 Du Bois 1917a, p. 316.

42 Du Bois 1917a, p. 315.

43 Du Bois 1917a, p. 319. It is worth noting that Du Bois places anti-black racism in the context of the United States' ambiguous relationship with ' "new" white people', with that 'white

Social Imperialism and the Aristocracy of White Labour

Though Du Bois's emphasis shifts in his writings on the origins of the war, whether he's singling out the democratic-despotic alliance of white labour and white capital or the hyper-exploitation of the darker proletariat, he consistently indicates the racial logics of worldwide capitalist exploitation as the causes of World War I. As his vocabulary indicates, he shared a common inspiration with Lenin, drawing on Hobson's path-breaking outline of the way in which the imperialist capitalist states strove to 'bribe [their] lower classes into acquiescence', while recognising that such bribes were principally directed at 'special classes of workers'.[44]

In 'Imperialism and the Split in Socialism', Lenin developed a sophisticated account of how 'social chauvinism' (his term for social imperialism as it specifically applies to the socialist labour movement) lay behind the fatal opportunism of Second International social democracy.[45] His diagnosis bears remarkable affinities to that of Du Bois, especially when he writes of how 'the exploitation of oppressed nations – which is inseparably connected with annexations – and especially the exploitation of colonies by a handful of "Great" Powers, increasingly transforms the "civilised" world into a parasite on the body of hundreds of millions in the uncivilised nations'. Though modern capitalist society lives off of unequal exchange with the proletariat, imperialism generates that paradoxical beast, the parasitical proletariat: 'A privileged upper stratum of the proletariat in the imperialist countries lives partly at the expense of hundreds of millions in the uncivilised nations'.[46] This conjuncture of imperialism is a chilling omen of an even more baleful possibility, a kind of super-parasitism whereby

ethnic' proletariat which is entreated to maintain itself above the colour line by repressing its darker brethren: America 'trains her immigrants to this despising of "niggers" from the day of their landing, and they carry and send the news back to the submerged classes in their fatherlands' (p. 320). It is difficult to ascertain the extent to which these 'remittances' of racial ideology were received by the European working classes.

44 Though Lenin also harkens back to Engels's analysis of the sociology of the British Empire, in particular to a letter to Marx of 7 October 1858, and a much later missive to Kautsky, referring to workers who 'gaily share the feast of England's monopoly of the world market and the colonies'. Lenin 1916, pp. 129–30.

45 On this category, see Boggio Éwanjé-Épée and Magliani-Belkacem 2013. For opposing appraisals of the theory of the labour aristocracy and its contemporary relevance, see Post 2010 and Cope 2012, as well as Neil Davidson's discussion in this volume.

46 Lenin 1916a, p. 125.

> a group of advanced industrial nations, whose upper classes drew vast tribute from Asia and Africa, with which they supported great tame masses of retainers, no longer engaged in the staple industries of agriculture and manufacture, but kept in the performance of personal or minor industrial services under the control of the new financial aristocracy.[47]

The alliance between opportunist social-chauvinist and the imperialist bourgeoisie is consolidated by the prospect of 'creating an imperialist Europe on the backs of Asia and Africa'.[48] And, as in Du Bois, there is an intimate bond between super-profits, hyper-exploitation and the formation of a labour aristocracy:

> The capitalists can devote a part (and not a small one, at that!) of these superprofits to bribe their own workers, to create something like an alliance (recall the celebrated 'alliances' described by the Webbs of English trade unions and employers) between the workers of the given nation and their capitalists against the other countries.[49]

The political struggle in the midst of the war is the struggle between two tendencies, both rooted in the contradictions of capitalist political economy, one – 'the tendency of the bourgeoisie and the opportunists' leading to the formation of leading nations into 'eternal parasites', the other – 'the tendency of the *masses*' – to revolution.

As Bukharin would argue a year later, it is false then to say that the working classes of the advanced nations have nothing to gain from colonial policies. On the contrary, the wages of workers in the imperialist countries can rise at the expense of the colonised:

> It is in the colonies that all the blood and the filth, all the horror and the shame of capitalism, all the cynicism, greed and bestiality of modern democracy are concentrated. The European workers, considered from the point of view of the moment, are the winners, because they receive increments to their wages due to 'industrial prosperity'. All the relative 'prosperity' of the European-American industry was conditioned by nothing but the fact that a safety valve was opened in the form of colonial policy. In this way the exploitation of 'third persons' (pre-capitalist

47 Lenin 1916a, p. 127.
48 Lenin 1916a, p. 128.
49 Lenin 1916a, p. 131. See also p. 132 on the question of the distribution of these super-profits.

> producers) and colonial labour led to a rise in the wages of European and American workers.[50]

Ten years prior, arguing against the (narrowly defeated) wing of the Second International that advocated for a socialist colonial policy, Lenin noted how, inasmuch as the European proletarian '*partly* finds himself in a position when it is *not* his labour, but the labour of the practically enslaved natives in the colonies, that maintains the whole of society', there is a 'material and economic basis for infecting the proletarian with colonial chauvinism'.[51] The Russian revolutionary leader later detailed this point further, by posing that there were three crucial differences in the conditions of workers in the oppressor and oppressed nations, or, to use Du Bois's terminology, in the white world and the darker world: first, the *economic* position of the proletariat in the imperialist nations made it possible *in part* for them to act as 'partners of *their own* bourgeoisie in plundering the workers (and the mass of the population) of the oppressed nations' (qualifying this, Lenin even speaks of 'crumbs' from superprofits); second, workers in oppressor nations can occupy a '*privileged* position in many spheres of political life'; third: 'Ideologically, or spiritually, the difference is that they are taught, at school and in life, disdain and contempt for the workers of the oppressed nations'. This leads Lenin to a crucial conclusion: 'Thus, all along the line there are differences in objective reality, i.e., "dualism" in the objective world that is independent of the will and consciousness of individuals'.[52]

Though for the Black American intellectual will and consciousness ('souls') were deeply implicated in these dynamics, it is fair to say that the name of this dualism for Du Bois was 'race'. As the passages above suggest, Lenin, like Bukharin and especially Rosa Luxemburg, was by no means oblivious to the function of race and racism in making both imperialist plunder and social-chauvinism possible. His annotated conspectus of Hobson's *Imperialism* has 'N.B.' noted in the margins of a passage that reads:

> the white *races, discarding labour in its more arduous forms*, LIVE AS A SORT OF WORLD ARISTOCRACY BY THE EXPLOITATION OF THE

---

50 Bukharin 1917, pp. 164–5. I owe this reference, and a number of insights that went into the composition of this chapter, to Robert Knox. Many thanks also to Brenna Bhandar and David Roediger for their comments.

51 Lenin 1907. See also Hobsbawm 1973, where this passage is quoted.

52 Lenin 1916b. Thanks again to Robert Knox for pointing me to this passage.

> 'LOWER RACES', while they hand over the policing of the world more and more *to members of these same races*.[53]

But Du Bois's vantage allowed him to develop, in ways that would only come to theoretical and historiographic fruition later, in the writing of *Black Reconstruction*, the crucial role of race in the development of social chauvinism. Though, as I've suggested, Du Bois can sometime take the *desideratum* of social-imperialist ideologues (a white pact between capital and labour) as a fact, or at least a strongly established tendency, he also provides us with a way of thinking what comes to fill the gap, or even chasm, between the ideological bribe and its material reality, and to explore the role of race in the tragedy of working-class disunity in the context of war.

To anticipate the terminology of *Black Reconstruction*, even when the *material* wages are limited (Lenin's crumbs, drawn on imperialism's super-profits) or not forthcoming, the *psychological* wages, including the function of racial privilege in politics and culture, can be formidably powerful. As David Roediger observes, though 'the wages of whiteness often turned out to be spurious', 'status and privileges conferred by race could be used to make up for alienating and exploitative class relationships'.[54] The imperial and settler-colonial project of the late nineteenth and early twentieth centuries was often founded on an ideal of intra-racial and trans-class 'egalitarianism', in which the populations of imperialist countries were addressed 'as *participants* in the adventure of empire'.[55]

Much controversy remains as to the political-economic ground of the social chauvinism thesis – on the size of the crumbs, so to speak. Yet even Hobsbawm, who notes (employing what is clearly a very restrictive criterion) that there is 'no good evidence that colonial conquest as such had much bearing on the employment or real incomes of most workers in the metropolitan countries', affirms that in the age of mass politics, 'empire made good ideological cement'.[56] Du Bois's responses to World War I help us to see, among other things, the preponderant role of race as an ingredient in that cement. Those responses, while seeking to open up Black American political consciousness to the colour line as a planetary issue, also emerged from Du Bois's often

---

53 Lenin 1968, p. 420.

54 Roediger 2007, p. 13.

55 Schwarz 2012, p. 67. There are important insights in this study of the cultural genesis of 'ethnic populism' in the context of the British Empire.

56 Hobsbawm 1987, pp. 69–70.

dispiriting experience of the racism or lack of solidarity in the socialist and labour movements.[57]

Where the key experience of social chauvinism for Lenin was the nationalist and imperialist implosion of the Second International, itself prepared by the 'colonial chauvinism' of some of its sectors, Du Bois's understanding of the racial dimensions of labour aristocracy were grounded in the wrenching experience of the exclusion and subjugation of black proletarians and poor at the hands of white workers and of their often segregated unions.[58] Reflecting on the pertinence of the theory of class struggle to the black American experience, Du Bois asked:

> How far ... does the dogma of the 'class struggle' apply to black folk in the United States today? Theoretically we are a part of the world proletariat in the sense that we are mainly an exploited class of cheap laborers; but practically we are not a part of the white proletariat and are not recognized by that proletariat to any great extent. We are the victims of their physical oppression, social ostracism, economic exclusion and personal hatred; and when in self-defense we seek sheer subsistence we are howled down as 'scabs'.[59]

In a *Crisis* editorial from March 1918, Du Bois underscored how the effort by white labour to maintain its privileges over black could be felt even in the everyday life of the NAACP's publication:

> I carry on the title page, for instance, of this magazine the union label, and yet I know, and everyone of my Negro readers knows, that the very fact that this label is there is an advertisement that no Negro's hand is engaged in the printing of this magazine, since the International

57 Davis 1986 provides an enlightening chronicle of the key role of anti-black and anti-immigrant racism in the stratification and 'unmaking' of the US working class, and consequently 'in preventing American workers from "seizing the time" in the pivotal turning points of class struggle', over this same period. See esp. Chapter 1: 'Why the US Working Class is Different'.

58 Though Cedric Robinson's characterisation of the (white) industrial working class in Du Bois as 'reactionary' seems too unnuanced. See Robinson 1983, p. 312, but also his insightful comments on the sources in nineteenth-century US race and labour history of Du Bois's endorsement of the 'labour aristocracy' thesis (p. 283).

59 Du Bois 1921a, p. 341.

> Typographic Union systematically and deliberately excludes every Negro that it dares from membership, no matter what his qualifications.[60]

Addressing the Ninth Annual Convention of the Intercollegiate Socialist Society, Du Bois, already under attack by white and black radicals alike for supporting the war effort, and the participation of blacks in the army, addressed the white left with bitter words. Not only had wartime seen a spike in lynchings, but in the East St Louis Riots of May and July 1917, white workers had lynched black men and women and torched their neighbourhoods – the black migrants from the South perceived there as a threat to unionised white labour.[61] The Houston or Camp Logan Riot of black soldiers responding to racist provocation had ended in the execution of nineteen of them, and in life sentences for forty-one. Racial dualism and white supremacy, in the context of the 'chronic oversupply of common labor', had led to a situation in which it was often at the hands of white workers that blacks suffered most. It is worth quoting at length Du Bois's peroration, as it gives the national context for his international analysis of the war's origins:

> The common laborer in the North is caught between the tyranny of exclusive trade unions and the underbidding of blacks. The result is murder and riot and unrest. Those who for a generation have been calling the black man a lazy, ignorant burden and incubus in the South have suddenly developed a determination not to allow the rest of the country to share that burden or pay Negroes higher wages. White northern laborers find killing Negroes a safe, lucrative employment which commends them to the American Federation of Labor. No discussion of labor problems arising out of the war can take place, then, without first facing the situation of the Negro laborer.[62]

Though the reasons behind Du Bois being 'disgusted with pacifists'[63] are complex – and some of them, as I'll touch on below, perhaps not so honourable – they stem in part from the conviction that even white socialists had not opposed colonial wars against the darker nations with sufficient

60 Du Bois 1918, p. 159.

61 As Du Bois would later quip: 'the black worker has small choice: to be lynched, to work for nothing in Georgia and Arkansas, or to be a scab in Pennsylvania'. Du Bois 1920, p. 161.

62 Du Bois 1917b, pp. 279–80.

63 Du Bois 1917b, p. 282.

vigour. That, until they proved otherwise by demonstrating effective solidarity with black workers, theirs would be 'a peace among white folk with the inevitable result that they will have more leisure to continue their despoiling of yellow, red, brown, and black folk', remaining attentive only to the 'successful revolution of white folk and not the unsuccessful revolution of black soldiers in Texas'.[64]

Though he would develop a more optimistic prospect for inter-racial proletarian unity in later years, the war and its impact on global and US race relations only consolidated Du Bois's perception of the co-option of the working classes of the white world into the project of racial imperialism.[65] As he wrote in 1921: 'I maintain that English working classes *are* exploiting India; that the English, French, and Belgian laborers *are* raping Africa; that the working classes of America *are* subjugating Santo Domingo and Haiti' – even if less directly, through wilful ignorance and political support for imperialist leaderships. Racial imperialism made of the white proletariat a 'co-worker in the miserable modern subjugation of over half the world'.[66] Here, and throughout his enduring polemic, engagement and eventual rallying to Marxist communism, Du Bois was, in Cedric Robinson's illuminating formulation 'concerned about the inability of the American Left ... to clearly identify the material force of racism as it related to the Left's struggle to destroy capitalism and replace it with socialism'.[67] Critical to his analysis of the 'material force of racism' was the violent policing and reproduction of the colour line across the working classes, within and without the United States. Echoing the language of the anti-war communist left, Du Bois saw in these forms of oppression internal to the working class the origins of 'Socialistic opportunism'.[68]

In 1933, in 'Marxism and the Negro Problem', Du Bois would assert the continued importance, in light of the enlisting of white workers in the suppression

64 Du Bois 1917b, p. 282. Aside from his organisational efforts, alongside Springarn, to promote a black officers' training camp, Du Bois wrote several pieces on the role of African-American and African soldiers in World War I, and stressed the lessons to be learned from their return to polities still rife with racism. See Du Bois 1919a, 1919b and 1919c.

65 Though mindful of how social imperialism presaged Hitler's own imperial project, I am using the term 'racial imperialism' here in the same semantic field as social chauvinism and social imperialism, and not in the more restricted sense proposed in Franz Neumann's *Behemoth*, itself a key source for Hannah Arendt's original formulation of what she later termed 'totalitarianism' as 'race-imperialism'. See Neumann 2009 and Arendt 1973.

66 Du Bois 1921b, pp, 346–7.

67 Robinson 1983, p. 280.

68 Du Bois 1913, p. 339.

of black proletarians, of the thesis of the aristocracy of labour. Considering how unions such as the AFL manifested a 'deliberate intention to keep Negroes and Mexicans and other elements of common labor in a lower proletariat as subservient to their interests as these are to the interests of capital', and of the ubiquitous employment of white workers to manage and repress the colonised proletariat from China to the West Indies, Du Bois couldn't but see the development of a 'petty bourgeoise within the American laboring class' as a crucial dimension in the reproduction of racial capitalism. It was only with *Black Reconstruction* that Du Bois truly laid the groundwork for combining his recognition of Marx's 'colossal genius' with a systematic inquiry into those formations of racial capitalism which thwarted proletarian unity across race and made it so that 'race antagonism and labor group rivalry' were 'undisturbed by world catastrophe'.[69]

Conclusion

Notwithstanding his unsparing dismissal, in 'Of the Culture of White Folk', of the United States' capacity to arbiter or intervene in the First World War, Du Bois would shortly thereafter come to pen a nigh-on infamous editorial in *The Crisis*, 'Close Ranks', where he would plead with his black readers – in a line excoriated by many of his critics, most effectively by the black communist intellectual Hubert Harrison[70] – to set aside their 'special grievances' and join the war effort. Du Bois had been involved by his fellow NAACP leader Joel Springarn, with whom he had strenuously been trying to promote a special training camp for black officers to counter the army's extreme racism, into a scheme that might have seen him join military intelligence as an officer. Springarn was already involved in a counter-espionage effort against '(1) Bolsheviki; I.W.W. Etc., (2) Negro subversion', and presented much of his work alongside Du Bois as 'counter-propaganda'.[71]

Some have seen in Du Bois's editorial, which proposed a kind of racial *Burgfrieden*, the result of 'extreme confusion and naivete', as 'the fragile ambivalence of Du Bois' own ideological formulations was pushed to the right

69 Du Bois 1933, pp. 287 and 293. For compelling contemporary reflections on Du Bois's contribution to a Marxian account of class, race and capital, see Roediger 2007, Taylor 2008 and Olson 2009.

70 See Perry 2009.

71 From a memorandum by Springarn included as appendix to Allen, Jr. 1979, p. 33.

under the weight of extreme political pressure';[72] others have discerned a more cynical move for self-advancement.[73] Many of Du Bois's black radical contemporaries took this as an opportunity to declare their erstwhile political beacon extinguished. And Du Bois himself, in his autobiographies, would look back on this moment with a mix of forgetfulness, regret and self-criticism.

Whatever one's ultimate judgment of this moment in Du Bois's political biography, it may also be worth reflecting on how (compounding the limits of Du Bois's own ideological formation) the 'double jeopardy' of the black US working class – exploited by capital, excluded or scapegoated by white labour – 'objectively' curtailed any real prospect, within the US and its racial class order, for the kind of revolutionary defeatism that animated the Zimmerwald Left in Europe. As Du Bois lamented in 1917:

> Even the broken reed on which we had rested the high hopes of eternal peace – the guild of the laborers – the front of the very movement for human justice on which we had builded most, even this flew like a straw before the breath of king and kaiser. Indeed, the flying had been foreshadowed when in Germany and America 'International' Socialists had all but read yellow and black men out of the kingdom of industrial justice. Subtly had they been bribed, but effectively: Were they not lordly whites and should they not share in the spoils of the rape?[74]

In the wake of the war, for Du Bois as for many of his black contemporaries, hope was to be placed not in proletarian unity in the US but in the rising of the darker nations and the anti-colonial movements for liberation and self-determination.[75] Yet Du Bois did not relent on the project of thinking through and practically transcending the racial logic of 'democratic despotism' – the 'race philosophy' and race politics which made 'labor unity or labor-consciousness impossible'.[76] It was in that monument of Black Marxist historiography that is *Black Reconstruction* that he would sow the seeds for

72 Allen, Jr. 1979, pp. 26 and 31.

73 See Ellis 1992, and less emphatically, Lewis 2009.

74 Du Bois 1917a, p. 317. Du Bois continues: 'High wages in the United States and England might be the skilfully manipulated result of slavery in Africa and peonage in Asia'.

75 The 'Hands of Ethiopia' chapter in the 1920 *Darkwater*, which reworks passages from 'The African Roots of War', is testament to this orientation, which can also be traced in Du Bois's subsequent political development. See Du Bois 1999 [1920], pp. 32–42.

76 Du Bois 1998, p. 680.

moving beyond the more mechanical formulation of the thesis of a white aristocracy of labour in 'The African Roots of War', exploring the tragedy of class *dis*unity and the complex interplay between the material and the psychological wages of whiteness. The dialectic of class struggle and the colour line, whose national and global facets World War I brought into such tragic relief, would continue to determine Du Bois's thought and action, as well as the later fortunes of Black Marxism and radical anti-racism.

CHAPTER 10

World War I, the October Revolution and Marxism's Reception in the West and East

Domenico Losurdo

Introduction

What underlying factors led to the ascendancy of the communist movement in 'the West' and 'East' that began to take shape in the wake of the October Revolution? The two paths differ significantly. Regarding the first, we can take as our starting point what already happened in Italy in the months before the advent of the Bolsheviks to power. Between February and October 1917 two delegates of the provisional government formed in Moscow visited Turin to make contact with an ally in the ongoing war. Even before their arrival, they made clear their hostility to the Bolsheviks. Nevertheless, when the two envoys of the Kerensky government made their appearance on the balcony of the Siccardi palace, a crowd of forty thousand workers waiting below cried: 'Long live Lenin!' The date was 13 August 1917. Ten days later barricades were erected to bolster the rejection of the war, with the result, however, that a little later in September, Turin was declared a war zone.[1]

It's part of a story that lends itself to many considerations. Nowadays it is politically correct to speak of October 1917 in Russia not as a revolution but as a coup, despite the fact that we see the protagonist of this alleged coup provoking a quasi-revolution thousands of miles away; while Lenin's name was already arousing passions even before the arrival of the Bolsheviks in power! It is clear, in Italy and throughout Europe, there was mounting outrage over the imperialist slaughter, what Rosa Luxemburg a year earlier had called the 'genocide' of World War I, and it is this outrage which stimulated adherence to the growing communist movement. To confirm this, we should mention the trajectory of a great intellectual such as Lukács, who later recalled: 'As for the war ... I can only say that I was ardently anti-war'.[2] The philosopher's correspondence of those years denounces the fury of the 'Moloch of militarism' that devours millions of lives, while conscription itself is described as 'the most abject slavery that has

1 Fiori 1966, pp. 128–9.

2 Lukács 1983, p. 53.

ever existed'.[3] Starting from the horror of the total mobilisation for the military code and firing squads, in his early unfinished essay on Dostoyevsky (1915), Lukács defines the state as 'organized tuberculosis', or as 'the organized immorality' that is expressed 'externally as will to power, war, conquest, vengeance'.[4] Already the prospect is raised of the revolutionary communist task.

The war and the measures related to the state of war gave rise to a moral revolt even before a political insurrection. Referring to his own evolution, Lukács observes: 'interest in ethics has led me to revolution'.[5] The more mature theoretical reflection emerges not surprisingly in a country that is driven by its leaders to the 'European slaughter',[6] despite the opposition of the broad masses of Catholic or socialist orientation, who were fully aware of the huge price in human lives that must be paid. We can appreciate the conclusion of Gramsci: always treated as a child and considered incapable of discernment on the political level, the masses can be safely sacrificed by the ruling class on the altar of its imperial designs. And, therefore, it was necessary that the 'working people' not remain in the condition of 'good prey for all' and mere 'human material' at the disposition of the elite, of 'raw material for the history of the privileged classes'.[7] The committed communist had to avoid a repeat of the immense tragedy consummated between 1914 and 1918.

In the East, the underlying motivations that stimulated adherence to the communist movement were considerably different. And we can readily understand the reasons for this diversity. The tragedy of the colonial peoples and what has been referred to as the 'crucifixion' of China had not waited until 1914 to occur. In this sense the dating of the 'short century', which according to Eric Hobsbawm takes as its starting point the traumatic experience of World War I, is clearly the result of a Eurocentric perspective.[8] Outside of Europe and the West, in the areas subjugated by these powers, the trauma had taken place long before. Stated differently, in the eyes of the colonial peoples the bourgeois state had proved long ago to be a 'tuberculosis', 'organized immorality' or 'Moloch'. And this emerged clearly from the contribution made by

3 Lukács 1984, pp. 366 and 360.

4 Quoted in Löwy 1992, p. 157.

5 Lukács 1983, p. 66; Lukács 1983, p. 66. For further analysis concerning the effects of the war on European intellectuals' political, moral and artistic thought, see Traverso and Leslie's contributions in this volume.

6 Gramsci 1984, p. 489.

7 Gramsci 1980, p. 175; Gramsci 1987, p. 520.

8 Hobsbawm 1994.

'the delegate of Indochina' (as defined by the conference stenographer) to the French Socialist Party's Congress of Tours on 26 December 1920:

> For half a century of French capitalism came to Indochina conquering us with the point of the bayonet, and in the name of capitalism, since then we have not only been shamefully harassed and exploited, but also horribly poisoned and martyred (and I stress the word poisoned, with opium, alcohol, etc.). It is impossible, in a few minutes, to show you all the atrocities committed by the bandits in the Indochinese capital. Prisons are more numerous than schools and are always open and frighteningly populated. Every native who is thought to have socialist ideas is imprisoned and sometimes put to death without trial. In Indochinese justice there are two weights and two measures. The Annamese do not have the same guarantees as Europeans and the Europeanized.[9]

Having uttered this terrible indictment, 'the delegate of Indochina' concludes: 'We see in adherence to the Third International, the formal promise that the Socialist Party will finally give the colonial problems the importance they deserve'.[10]

These are the years in which, without giving up on its own colonies (the Philippines) and the Monroe Doctrine for the control of Latin America, US foreign policy under President Wilson attempts to endow itself with an 'anti-colonialist' tone, waving the flag of national self-determination. However, when arriving in the United States looking for work, 'the delegate of Indochina' was horrified to witness a lynching, the slow torture of a black watched by a festive crowd of whites. Skipping the details, we come to the conclusion: 'On the ground, bathed in a stench of grease and smoke, a black head, mutilated, roasted, deformed, makes a horrible face and the setting sun seems to ask: "is this civilization?" '. To be thus oppressed, humiliated and dehumanised is the lot not only of the colonial peoples but also the populations of colonial origin, located in the very heart of the capitalist metropolis in the country that loves to vaunt itself as the oldest democracy in the world. The young Indochinese, who has now matured into a decisive revolutionary and communist, denounces the infamy of the system of white supremacy and the Ku Klux Klan in the 'Correspondance Internationale' (the French version of the organ of the Communist International). Ten years later he was back at home where

9 Quoted in Lacouture, 1967 pp. 36–7.

10 Quoted in Lacouture, 1967 pp. 36–7

he would take the name by which he would become known throughout the world: Ho Chi Minh.[11]

The reflection on the fate inflicted on African Americans by the country which loves to present itself as the oldest democracy in the world must have also played a role in the formation of Mao Zedong, as he 'knew something about the Negro question in America and unfavourably compared the treatment of negroes and American Indians with policies in the Soviet Union toward national minorities'.[12]

Two Struggles for Recognition

In 1960, nine years before his death, while the US was unleashing one of the most horrible colonial wars of the twentieth century in Indochina, Ho Chi Minh, on the occasion of his seventieth birthday, recalled his intellectual and political path: 'In the beginning the push to believe in Lenin and the Third International was patriotism, not communism'.[13] A cause of great emotion were primarily appeals and documents that supported and promoted the liberation struggle of the colonial peoples, emphasising their right to form independent national states: 'The thesis of Lenin [on the national and colonial question] aroused in me great emotion, great enthusiasm, great faith, and helped me to see the problems clearly. So great was my joy, that I cried'.[14] In his Testament, after calling his fellow citizens to 'patriotic struggle' and the commitment 'for the salvation of the fatherland', Ho Chi Minh traces this legacy on a personal level: 'Throughout my life, my body and soul have served my country; I have served the revolution, I have served the people'.[15]

One should now take a look at China where a revolution in 1911 led to the overthrow of the Manchu dynasty and the proclamation of the Chinese Republic. The first politician to occupy the office of president was Sun Yat-Sen. He, though not a Marxist, welcomed the rise of the Bolsheviks to power. The explanation of his position which he provided a few years later constituted a terrible indictment of colonialism and imperialism: 'The American Indians were already exterminated' and the 'curse' still hangs over other colonial peoples. Their situation is tragic; but now, 'suddenly one hundred and fifty million

11 Wade 1997, pp. 203–4.
12 Snow 1967, p. 85.
13 Quoted in Lacouture, 1967, pp. 39–40.
14 Quoted in Lacouture, 1967, pp. 39–40.
15 Ho Chi Minh 1969, pp. 75 and 78.

people of the Slavic race have risen to oppose imperialism, capitalism, and injustice in the interest of mankind'. And so, 'without anyone expecting him, a great hope for humanity is born: the Russian Revolution'; yes 'thanks to the Russian Revolution, all mankind is now animated by a great hope'. Of course, the response to this reaction was immediate: 'The powers attacked Lenin because they wanted to destroy a prophet of humanity'.[16]

Granted Sun Yat-Sen was neither a Marxist nor a communist, but only starting from this 'great hope', which he described with sometimes naïve though all the more effective language, can we understand the founding of the Communist Party of China (CCP) on 1 July 1921. Behind the stance of Sun Yat-Sen, as well as the founding of the CCP, are two events: in 25 July 1919, L.M. Karakhan, deputy People's Commissar for Foreign Affairs, declared that Soviet Russia was ready to give up all 'territorial and other advantages' acquired by the Tsarist Empire while actually calling into question as a whole, the 'unequal treaties' signed by China under the threat of gunboats and armies of invasion.[17] In the summer of that year, the Treaty of Versailles, ending the First World War, gave to Japan the Shandong concessions that Imperial Germany had once torn from the Beijing government. A huge wave of protest grew in China. This would become the Movement of May 4, from which more than a few leaders and activists of the Communist Party of China would emerge. Now that it was clear to all that the Western democracies, who had led the war against the Central Powers waving the flag of freedom and self-determination of peoples, had no difficulty in perpetuating the semi-colonial condition of China, the only hope would come from the country and the movement which had grown out of the October Revolution.

Later, while engaged in the war of national resistance against Japanese imperialism, which aimed 'to subjugate the whole of China and the Chinese to their colonial slaves', Mao recalled his first awakening (in the last years of the Manchu Dynasty) to the cause of revolution:

> In this period also I began to have a certain amount of political consciousness, especially after I read a pamphlet telling of the dismemberment of China ... After I read this I felt depressed about the future of my country and began to realize that it was the duty of all the people to help save it.[18]

16 Sun Yat-Sen 1976, pp. 65–8.

17 Carr 1953, p. 504.

18 Quoted in Snow 1967, p. 133.

Over ten years later, speaking on the immediate eve of the proclamation of the People's Republic, Mao recalled the history of his country. He recalled in particular the resistance against the great powers during the Opium Wars, the Taiping Rebellion 'against the Ching servants of imperialism', the war against Japan in 1894–5, 'the war against the aggression of the coalition forces of eight powers' (following the Boxer Rebellion), and, finally, the Revolution of 1911 against the Ching, lackeys of imperialism. 'Many struggles, many defeats. How can one explain the overthrow which eventually occurs?' As Mao went on to explain:

> For a long time, during this movement of resistance, that is, for more than seventy years, from the Opium War in 1840 until the eve of the May 4th Movement in 1919, the Chinese had no ideological weapons to defend themselves against imperialism. The old and immutable ideological weapons of feudalism were defeated, had to yield, and were declared out of order. In the absence of anything better, the Chinese were forced to arm themselves with ideological weapons and political formulas such as the theory of evolution, the theory of natural law and of the bourgeois republic, all borrowed from the arsenal of the revolutionary period of the bourgeoisie in the West, home of imperialism ... but all these ideological weapons, such as those of feudalism, proved to be very weak, and in turn had to yield, were withdrawn and declared out of order.
>
> The Russian Revolution of 1917 marks the awakening of the Chinese; they learn something new: Marxism-Leninism. In China, the Communist Party was born, and it is an event that inaugurates a new epoch ...
>
> Since they learned Marxism-Leninism, the Chinese have ceased to be intellectually passive and have taken the initiative. From that moment the period of the modern world history in which the Chinese and Chinese culture were looked upon with contempt ended.[19]

We are in the presence of an extraordinary text. Marxism-Leninism is the truth finally found after a long search; the ideological weapon capable of putting an end to the situation of oppression and 'contempt' imposed by colonialism and imperialism, the ideological weapon which ensures the victory of the revolution in China. And it is a pursuit which had already started with the Opium Wars, long before the formation of Marxism-Leninism, or even Marxism itself: in 1840 Marx was just a young university student. However, it is not Marxism which provokes the revolution in China, but rather the secular resistance of the Chinese people

19 Mao Zedong 1969–75, Vol. 4, pp. 469–70 and 472.

who, after a long and arduous search, succeed in achieving self-consciousness through the ideology that brings the revolution to victory. It is 16 September 1949. Five days later, Mao declares: 'We will no longer be a nation subject to insult and humiliation. We have stood up ... the era in which the Chinese people were considered uncivilized is now over'.[20]

While celebrating the redemption of a nation long subjected to 'contempt', 'insult and humiliation', Mao probably has in mind the sign exhibited in the French Concession in Shanghai during the nineteenth century: 'No dogs or Chinese allowed'. An historical cycle had come to end.

What aroused enthusiasm in the West was primarily the Leninist analysis and condemnation of imperialism as incorporating not just the synonym of wars and massacres, but also militarisation and total mobilisation, the 'military slavery' imposed on the population.[21] It is not only the war front which is characterised by regimentation, war codes and terror; even in the 'most advanced countries', the rears transform themselves into 'houses of military punishment for the workers'.[22] In the East, however, the Leninist analysis of imperialism has an immense echo, according to which 'a few elected nations base their own "wellbeing" and primacy on the plunder and domination of the rest of humanity',[23] while such 'model countries' attribute to themselves 'the exclusive privilege of state formation'.[24] Obviously there is no contradiction: we are dealing with two different prospective framings of the same social object, capitalism-imperialism, investigated in both cases from the analysis developed by Lenin. What is at stake in capitalism-imperialism are two struggles for recognition: the protagonists of the first are the working class and the popular masses who refuse to be 'raw material' at the disposal of the elite, while the protagonists of the second are whole nations attempting to shake off the oppression, humiliation and dehumanisation inherent in colonial rule.

The 'Money Economy' in the West and East

Read as a consequence of imperialist contention for the plunder of the colonies, the conquest of markets and raw materials as well as the hunt for profit and capitalist super-profits, and read sometimes in a moralising tone as the

20 Mao Zedong 1998, pp. 87–8.
21 Lenin 1955–70, Vol. 27, p. 393.
22 Lenin 1955–70, Vol. 25, p. 363.
23 Lenin 1955–70, Vol. 26, p. 403.
24 Lenin 1955–70, Vol. 20, p. 417.

product of the *auri sacri fames* rather than the consequence of a well-defined social system, the First World War in the West engenders a spiritual climate that finds expression in the works of prominent Western philosophers. In 1918, the young Bloch called the Soviets to put an end not only to 'every private economy' but also to the 'money economy' itself and, with it, the 'moral merchant who consecrates everything that is most evil in man'.[25]

Russia was among the main protagonists of the imperialist war, and even here, after the October Revolution, we see a vision that looks with disdain on the world economy as a whole and cries of scandal and betrayal at the introduction of the New Economic Policy (NEP). This view, not much different from that analysed in the West, was thus described by a Soviet communist in the 1940s:

> We were all young Communists who grew up believing that money had been taken away once and for all ... If money reappeared, wouldn't the rich reappear too? Were we not on a slippery slope bringing us back to capitalism?[26]

Only with great difficulty, and challenging the charges of treason, did Lenin and then Stalin begin to focus attention on the problem of the economic development of a backward country, one which came out prostrated by both the World War and the Civil War, while facing an international situation fraught with danger.

Well before the advent of the People's Republic, the spiritual climate that reigned in China was quite different in restricted areas already 'liberated' and governed by the Communist Party. The Kuomintang and the Nanjing government tried to force Communists to surrender by resorting to military force but also through encirclement and economic strangulation. In the course of his journey Edgar Snow observed: 'Trade between Red and White districts was prohibited by Nanking, but by using small mountain roads, and by oiling the palms of border guards, the Reds at times managed to carry on a fairly lively export business'.[27] Demonised in Russia and Europe as an expression of a greedy and rotten old world that must be broken down once and for all, the 'money economy' and trade are here synonymous instead with physical survival and the salvation of the revolutionary project called to build a new and better world. Once again we must avoid schematic juxtapositions: the situation is quite different,

25 Bloch 1971, p. 298.
26 Quoted in Figes 1997, p. 926.
27 Snow 1967, p. 233.

as is the context of the areas being compared; on the other hand, the sacred and legitimate protest against the economic system that had caused the carnage of the World War exceeds its initial naïve expression: in Soviet Russia War Communism would give way to the NEP, and, in publishing in 1923 the second edition of *Spirit of Utopia*, Bloch would see fit to delete the previously mentioned passages with messianic connotations.

Let's take a look at China during the 1930s: in the 'liberated' areas the concern to promote the development of the economy is so strong that various forms of ownership are promoted. As Snow observes:

> To guarantee success at these tasks it was necessary for the Reds, even from earliest days, to begin some kind of economic construction.
>
> Soviet economy in the North-west was a curious mixture of private capitalism, State capitalism, and primitive Socialism. Private enterprise and industry were permitted and encouraged, and private transaction in the land and its products was allowed, with restrictions. At the same time the State owned and exploited enterprises such as oil-wells, and coal-mines, and it traded in cattle, hides, salt, wool, cotton, paper, and other raw materials. But it did not establish a monopoly in these articles and in all of them private enterprises could, and to some extent did, compete.
>
> A third type of economy was created by the establishment of co-operatives, in which the Government and the masses participated as partners, competing not only with private capitalism, but also with State capitalism![28]

The contrast with the West was accentuated further in subsequent years. Especially after the rise of fascism and Nazism, in countries such as Italy, Germany and Japan, the fight for wages and better living conditions at the same time called into question the productive forces of the war effort and the war machine of the aggressors as examples of the revival of colonial expansionism. By contrast, in China, with the fury of large-scale Japanese invasion, we see what Mao defined in November 1938, as the 'identity between the national struggle and the class struggle'.[29] From this moment, the commitment to the production and development of the economy becomes, especially in the liberated areas controlled by the Communist Party, at the same time an integral part of the national class struggle. It is clear then why, even in the midst of the war effort, Mao called communist leaders to pay close attention to the

28 Snow 1967, p. 232.

29 Mao Zedong 1969–75, Vol. 2, p. 223.

economic dimension of the conflict.[30] And this emerges in particular from a directive of 1 October 1943:

> In the current conditions of war, all organizations, schools and army units should actively pursue the cultivation of vegetables, pig-keeping, collection of firewood, charcoal production, and must develop the craft and produce some of the cereals required for their livelihood ... The leaders of the Party, government and army at all levels, as well as their schools have to learn, systematically, the art of directing the masses in production. He who does not study carefully the problems of production is not a good leader.[31]

The founding of the People's Republic does not change this picture. In September 1949, on the eve of the immediate seizure of power, Mao Zedong invited us not to lose sight of Washington's desire for the great Asian country to be 'reduced to living on American flour', ending up 'becoming an American colony'.[32]

Far from dismissing the economic front, one integral part of the national and class struggle now tended to become the main front. Especially since shortly after China became the target of a deadly embargo which, according to explicit statements of representatives and partners of the Truman administration, sought to lead a country of 'desperate needs' into 'a catastrophic economic situation', 'to disaster' and 'collapse'. In the early 1960s, Walt W. Rostow, an official of the Kennedy administration, pointed out that, 'thanks to this policy, China's economic development has been delayed for at least dozens of years', while reports by the CIA emphasised 'the serious situation of agriculture in Communist China', now severely weakened by overwork and malnutrition.[33] The fact is that even if the United States had taken the place of Japan, the struggle for independence was not complete, and in this context the economic front continued to play a very important role.

When at the end of 1979, as the policy of reform and opening up began, the struggle took on a new configuration: the United States and more developed capitalist countries sought to make China a market for their high technology commodities as well as a dispenser of a subordinate low-cost labour force of low-cost goods with no real technological content. In turn, the Chinese leaders proposed and aimed to accelerate on the path of development, not only

30 Mao Zedong 1969–75, Vol. 3, p. 135.
31 Mao Zedong 1969–75, Vol. 3, p. 135.
32 Mao Zedong 1969–75, Vol. 4, p. 467.
33 Quoted in Losurdo 2008, p. 288.

economically but also in the scientific and technological domain, in order to break the Western monopoly of high technology that is the legacy of colonialism and imperialism, thereby dismantling the international division of labour which has allowed the United States and the West to control formerly independent neo-colonial countries.

Technology and Socialist Construction

But let's return to the 'delegate of Indochina' at the Congress of Tours in December 1920. We saw him travel long distances in the West. For what reason? An explanation is given by Truong Chinh, who would later found the Indochinese Communist Party with Ho Chi Minh in 1930. According to this witness, the future leader of Vietnam went to France in order to learn about the culture of that country 'as well as science and technology'.[34]

The Chinese revolutionaries approached things in the same way. For example, Sun Yat-Sen, who between 1896 and 1898 resided in Europe, 'became one of the most diligent frequenters of the library of the British Museum', the dear library well known to Marx. But for the future President of the Republic of China the motivation was not to study capitalism: 'The dominant interest of Sun remained the "secret" of the West, its technology in its various aspects, and especially in the military'.[35] Later, with the founding of the Communist Party of China, a considerable contribution was made by intellectuals who were living abroad in the 'Work and study' programme. Among them some were destined to play a major role: for example, Chou En-lai, Deng Xiaoping, and Chen Yi. They were located in Paris in the same period that saw the presence of Ho Chi Minh, which perhaps helped to put them 'in contact with the French Communists'.[36]

This movement was not entirely foreign even to Mao Zedong. Talking later with Edgar Snow, he referred to his final decision to cancel the trip to Europe: 'I felt I did not know enough about my own country and therefore I would have better spent my time in China'. But that does not mean indifference or hostility towards those who make a different choice. Recall the story told by Mao:

34 Truong Chinh 1969, p. 8.
35 Collotti Pischel 1973, pp. 99–100.
36 Collotti Pischel 1973, pp. 159–60.

> many students from Hunan were planning trips to France, to study under the 'work and learn' scheme, which France used to recruit young Chinese in her cause during the World War. Before leaving China these students planned to study French in Peiping, I helped organize the movement, and in the groups who went abroad were many students from the Hunan Normal School, most of whom were later to become famous radicals.[37]

There is a kind of division of labour here: if Mao remains at home to learn more about his country which is in fact a continent, other young revolutionaries go to France to learn about Western culture in order to help their compatriots. Common to one and the other was the conviction that, in order to achieve national redemption, China needed to critically assimilate the science and technology of advanced countries. The path of Chou En-lai is illuminating. After being one of the leaders of the May 4 student movement, for which he spent a year in prison, he left for France.[38] After provoking large street protests in China, the anti-colonial struggle made a momentary deviation towards one of the most advanced countries of the West, in order to assimilate science and technology.

This confidence in science and technology was not shared in the West. Writing during the war years, Bukharin, who in 1911 moved between Europe and the United States before returning to Russia in the summer of 1917, denounced the monstrous expansion of the state apparatus, which had occurred since the outbreak of the gigantic conflict: here was a 'new Leviathan, before which the imagination of Thomas Hobbes seems like child's play'. Now, everything was 'mobilised' and 'militarised', and this fate also involved the economy, culture, morality and religion. 'Medicine, chemistry and bacteriology, were not exempt either and were part of "the great technical machine", which had been turned into an "enormous death machine"'.[39]

No doubt, what we have before us is the first brilliant analysis of what will later be called 'totalitarianism', but one gets the impression that this analysis tends sometimes to connect strict science and technology, on the one hand, and capitalism and imperialism, on the other. And this view also emerges from an important book published in 1922, *History and Class Consciousness*, whose author seems to identify 'increasing mechanization' with 'reification'.[40] Even in this case, rather than actual contrast, it is necessary to speak of a

37 Quoted in Snow 1967, pp. 147–8.
38 Snow 1967, p. 60.
39 Bukharin 1984, pp. 140–1.
40 Lukács 1988, p. 179.

diversity of perspectives and tasks. In the West, science and technology are an integral part of the 'new Leviathan', they are used primarily by the capitalist bourgeoisie to increase the profits squeezed out of the salaried workforce, strengthening the 'technical machine' and 'machine of death' in the struggle for world hegemony. In the East, science and technology are essential for developing the resistance against the policies of subjugation and oppression carried out precisely by the 'new Leviathan'.

After all, the difference we are concerned with here is not between East and West, but between countries (mostly in conditions of economic and political backwardness) in which the communists have pledged to tread the uncharted territory of building a post-capitalist society, and the advanced capitalist countries in which the communists can only play the role of opposition and criticism. This is confirmed in the case of Lenin. In the years preceding the outbreak of the First World War, he denounced Taylorism as a 'scientific' system for squeezing the sweat of 'wage slaves'.[41] But even at this stage the great revolutionary leader was concerned with making the necessary distinctions: founded on 'competition', capitalism is forced to 'invent new ways to reduce production costs', but 'the rule of capital transforms all these media into even more tools to oppress the worker'.[42]

But it is in the following years, beginning with the needs for constructing the new society, that the distinction between science and the capitalist use of science became clearer and clearer to Lenin in relation to Taylorism:

> The Russian is a bad worker compared with people in advanced countries. It could not be otherwise under the tsarist regime and in view of the persistence of the hangover from serfdom. The task that the Soviet government must set the people in all its scope is – learn to work. The Taylor system, the last word of capitalism in this respect, like all capitalist progress, is a combination of the refined brutality of bourgeois exploitation and a number of the greatest scientific achievements in the field of analyzing mechanical motions during work, the elimination of superfluous and awkward motions, the elaboration of correct methods of work, the introduction of the best system of accounting and control, etc. The Soviet Republic must at all costs adopt all that is valuable in the achievements of science and technology in this field. The possibility of building socialism depends exactly upon our success in combining the Soviet

41 Lenin 1955–70, Vol. 18, p. 573.

42 Lenin 1955–70, Vol. 20, p. 141.

> power and the Soviet organization of administration with the up-to-date achievements of capitalism.[43]

Of course, among the Bolsheviks there were some who cried foul at the fact that this would reproduce the 'enslavement of the working class', entailing a return to capitalism, but equally hard was the riposte of Lenin, who saw in this attitude something 'outrageous and reactionary' and a 'threat to the revolution'.[44]

As is known, the Russian revolutionary leader did not like ambiguous wording and, in this case, Lenin stated with a clarity which was, perhaps even shocking, that only those who understood the importance of creating trusts were worthy of calling themselves communists. Given the fact that socialism presupposes 'the assimilation of the proletarian vanguard which has come to power, there must also be an assimilation and application of what has been created by the trust'.[45] For Soviet Russia it was absolutely necessary to learn the organisation and operation of modern industry, even if this meant studying in countries representing the most complete expression of imperialism. There is, indeed, a paradox here:

> the German now embodies apart from ferocious imperialism, the principles of discipline, organization, harmonious collaboration on the basis of modern mechanized inventory under the strictest control.
>
> And this is what we lack. It is just what we need to learn.[46]

We can summarise as follows: in the years preceding the outbreak of the First World War and the October Revolution, Bukharin and Lenin, exiled in the West and away from the tasks of state leadership, were in different ways close to 'Western Marxism'. Then, with an eye to the building of the new social order, they assumed (in different ways) positions similar to those expressed by the Vietnamese and Chinese communists from the needs and perspectives of the anti-colonial revolution. This is not surprising. Already the intervention of the coalition against Soviet Russia threatened the independence and very existence of the country and its ultimate reduction to a semi-colonial condition. Later, Hitler would conduct against the Soviet Union what has been described as 'the greatest colonial war in history'.[47]

43 Lenin 1955–70, Vol. 27, p. 231.
44 Lenin 1955–70, Vol. 27, p. 268.
45 Lenin 1955–70, Vol. 27, p. 318.
46 Lenin 1955–70, Vol. 27, pp. 142–3.
47 Olusoga and Erichsen 2011, p. 327.

The Fight against Inequality in the West and East

And so we come to the last point. A few years after the October Revolution, communist parties and organisations emerged in countries with very different levels of development: one thinks of Germany on the one hand, as well as Russia and the colonial and semi-colonial countries on the other. Disappointed by the failure to extend the anti-capitalist revolution further in the West among the industrially more advanced countries, the Bolsheviks in power soon realised that, on the basis of both their own ideal programme and the political and international situation that had arisen, they had the duty to fight not only against one but, rather, two different inequalities. On one level, there was the inequality ravaging a country that had not completely left behind the *ancien régime* and, therefore, where class differences tended to appear as differences of caste. On the other hand, this very backwardness enclosed the deep inequality that separated Soviet Russia, as a country engaged in the process of building a socialist society, from the more developed capitalist nations. This second type of inequality was certainly not experienced less painfully than the first. One therefore had to deal with the extreme social polarisation at work in Russia as well as on a global level. In the words of Lenin (January 1920):

> the working people must not forget that capitalism has divided nations into a small number of oppressor, Great-Power (imperialist), sovereign and privileged nations and an overwhelming majority of oppressed, dependent and semi-dependent, non-sovereign nations.[48]

Among this second group of nations was Soviet Russia, which first underwent drastic territorial amputations imposed by the Germany of Wilhelm II, while subsequently being forced to deal with the intervention of the Entente. Even after the consolidation of power and the Bolsheviks' stabilisation of the situation in the country, the international situation continued to be anything but reassuring. Immediately after the Treaty of Versailles, voices were being raised in the West, coming from many different backgrounds, some authoritative, evoking the peril of World War II. Lenin repeatedly warned against this danger. And this was one more reason for giving impetus to the struggle against the second type of inequality, which saw Russia lagging behind in the economic and technological sphere with respect to the more advanced countries. Unfortunately the revolution did not win in the more advanced countries:

48 Lenin 1955–70, Vol. 30, pp. 260–1.

> We must remember that at present all the highly developed technology and the highly developed industry belong to the capitalists, who are fighting us.
>
> We must remember that we must either strain every nerve in our daily effort, or we shall inevitably go under. Owing to the present circumstances the whole world is developing faster than we are. While developing, the capitalist world is directing all its forces against us. That is how the matter stands! That is why we must devote special attention to this struggle.[49]

The second type of inequality was also getting worse, and this would have had catastrophic consequences for Russia and Soviet power, eventually rendering meaningless any plan to fight against the first type of inequality. In this regard, Lenin never tired of insisting on the assimilation of science and technology produced by the West.

Hence, the two battles against two different types of inequality are intertwined: as well as having obvious military implications, technical and scientific development lays the foundation for the building of socialism, which presupposes the overcoming of backwardness. Yet, at the same time, the two struggles cannot go hand in hand: the limitation of one inequality can lead to the temporary worsening of the other. For a Communist Party coming to power in a backward country, the quickest way to catch up with the more advanced West is usually to focus on relatively more developed areas, where there are more favourable conditions for accelerated development. However, this strategy was always likely to widen the gap between different regions of Soviet Russia, tightening the first type of inequality. Conversely, the priority or exclusive focus on the latter would lead to the risk of slowing down the development of the productive forces (which is a basic objective of the socialist revolution) thereby deepening the country's backwardness compared to the great powers threatening its newly gained political independence.

In order to deal with the problem of overcoming underdevelopment immediately after the Peace of Brest-Litovsk, Lenin relied not on agriculture (extremely backward both in terms of social relations and technology), but on industry: here it was easier to 'increase national labor productivity'.[50] However, the further development of industrial areas could not but accentuate the advantage that they held over rural areas.

---

49 Lenin 1955–70, Vol. 33, p. 58.

50 Lenin 1955–70, Vol. 27, p. 219.

In October 1921, the Soviet leader noted that the new government was forced to 'remunerate bourgeois specialists at an exceptionally high rate'.[51] It was the price that had to be paid in order to begin to overcome the backwardness of Russia and thus reduce inequality in relation to the more developed countries. But the flipside of this egalitarian policy on the international level involved the escalation of internal inequalities; one could lay emphasis on the battle against them abandoning the help from the expensive 'specialists', but with the result of aggravating technological backwardness and economic inequality compared to potentially hostile countries.

Furthermore, in order to reduce this second type of inequality, efforts had to be made to attract foreign capital to Russia, thereby introducing 'installations equipped with state-of-the-art technology in order to progressively converge' with the modern forms of other countries 'and then sooner or later to join them, but taking into account the fact that foreign capital they seek to attract tends to pursue "unlimited profits"'.[52] Here again, these 'unlimited profits' of foreign capitalists contrasted heavily with the meagre wages of Russian workers.

In light of the problems, dilemmas and conflicts discussed here we can acquire a better understanding of the history (and tragedy) of another great revolution. The 'Great Leap Forward' in the 1950s of twentieth-century China, under the leadership of Mao Zedong, was an attempt to advance hand in hand the two struggles against the two inequalities. On the one hand, the mass mobilisation of men and women at work in building the economy demanded the use of collectivist practices in the production and delivery of services (laundries, canteens, etc.), and this gave the impression or the illusion of a mighty advance for the cause of equality within. On the other hand, this mobilisation of exceptional breadth was initiated in order to burn the bridges of China's economic development and thus inflict a decisive blow to the existing inequality in international relations. Similar considerations apply to the Cultural Revolution: denouncing the 'bourgeoisie' or 'privileged classes' who had infiltrated the Communist Party itself, it re-launched egalitarianism internally. Criticising 'the theory of the snail steps' attributed to the deposed president, Liu Shao-chi, the Cultural Revolution was intended to accelerate the prodigious development of the productive forces and bring the country in a very short time to the level of the most advanced capitalist countries, deleting or radically undermining the second type of inequality. But all this was based on the illusion that the accelerated economic construction could be promoted in the same way as the political battles carried out by the soldiers of

51 Lenin 1955–70, Vol. 33, p. 72.

52 Lenin 1955–70, Vol. 32, p. 166.

the Chinese Revolution; that is to say, relying on mobilisation and mass enthusiasm in the illusion that such mass enthusiasm could endure for a long time or indefinitely.

Because of the adverse and even hostile international environment, the result was a failure. This fact was the starting point of Deng Xiaoping, who, in a conversation of 10 October 1978, drew attention to the fact that China's technology 'gap' compared to more advanced countries was expanding. These were developing 'with tremendous speed', while China was likely to be further and further behind.[53] But if they had lagged behind the new technological revolution, they would have to see themselves as being in a position of weakness similar to their helpless predicament during the Opium Wars and aggressions of imperialism. If it had lagged behind, China would have caused enormous damage not only to itself but also to the cause of the emancipation of the Third World as a whole. It therefore imposed a policy of reform and openness: on the one hand, it was necessary to access the latest technology where, with the increasingly evident crisis of the Soviet Union, the West held a substantial monopoly, while, on the other hand, it was necessary to stimulate competition in China in order to develop the productive forces.

And the question that we have already seen in relation to Soviet Russia arises once again. A policy designed to overcome as quickly as possible the lag compared to more advanced countries could not but leverage the relatively more developed coastal regions that enjoyed a higher level of education, areas that were already equipped with basic infrastructure and that, due to their geographical location, were more easily able to trade with neighbouring countries and attract foreign capital. However, the immediate consequence of this policy was the worsening of the backwardness of the rural and interior of China compared to the coastal regions.

To these objections Deng Xiaoping replied that, of course, some regions of the country, and some sectors of the population would achieve prosperity first, but that this would encourage others to shake off poverty and backwardness: 'This will help the entire national economy to advance wave after wave and for the people of all our nationalities to become prosperous in a relatively short period of time'. 'In any case', added the Chinese leader in a polemic against the 'gang of four', 'there can be no poor socialism or poor communism. It is a contradiction in terms to speak of "poor communism"'.[54] Socialism and

53 Deng Xiaoping 1992–5, Vol. 2, p. 143.

54 Deng Xiaoping 1992–5, Vol. 3, p. 161.

communism have nothing to do with the egalitarian distribution of scarcity and poverty: first 'socialism means elimination of poverty' and the development of the productive forces.[55]

Behind this position one can discern to a certain extent the influence of the *Communist Manifesto*, according to which 'nothing is easier than to give Christian asceticism a Socialist coat of paint'. One should not think that this vision circulates only between openly religious milieus. Marx and Engels point out that the 'first movements of the proletariat' are often characterised by claims with the imprint of 'a universal asceticism and a rough egalitarianism'.[56]

We should add an important consideration. When the shortage reaches an extreme level, its egalitarian distribution is quite apparent and may actually tip over into its opposite. Faced with the danger of death by starvation, the piece of bread that provides survival to the most fortunate, no matter how modest and small, constitutes an absolute inequality, the absolute inequality that exists between life and death. This is what occurred in the tragic years of the People's Republic of China before the policy of reform and opening, both as a result of the catastrophic legacy handed down from plunder and imperialist oppression, but also from the merciless embargo imposed by the West, not to mention the serious mistakes made by the new political leadership.

So we can assert that the Great Leap Forward and the Cultural Revolution both ended with exacerbated inequalities. On the other hand, precisely because of having been able to drastically reduce the inequality (economic and technological) on the international stage, China is now in a better position, thanks to the economic and technological resources accumulated in the meantime, to address the issue of the struggle against domestic inequalities.

Unfortunately Western Marxists do not always appear to be sympathetic towards the need felt in countries undergoing socialist transformation to bridge the gap with respect to the advanced nations. Therefore, the race in the East to leave behind the ancient régime (characterised internally by economic backwardness and geopolitically by weakness) appears in the West as a march towards capitalism. Worse, when the race of Eastern countries ruled by a Communist party achieves some results, these appear to Western Marxists to establish a capitalistic system even more intolerable than the system prevailing in the West.

55 Deng Xiaoping 1992–5, Vol. 3, pp. 174 and 122.

56 Marx and Engels 1955–89, Vol. 4, pp. 484 and 489.

The Spin-off of 'Western Marxism' and 'Eastern Marxism'

So far I have talked about regional differences in the reading of Marx and the historical events that began with the First World War and, in particular, the October Revolution. At some point, these differences have ended up turning into a real confrontation. The condemnation of the spurious 'Eastern European Marxism' as opposed to authentic Marxism, that is to say its 'Western' version, acquired great acclaim, especially after the publication of a famous essay by Perry Anderson.[57] Today this opinion has become almost a commonplace within the 'Left' and is taken up, either explicitly or implicitly, by those who, in the aftermath of the 'End of History', constitute the new generation of 'Western Marxism' and are players or participants in what tends to be seen as a 'revival of Marx'.

For this reason, the history behind today's contrast between positive 'Western Marxism' and its 'Oriental' counterpart is often ignored. It's a problem that ultimately refers back to the controversy that developed in the international socialist movement in the aftermath of the October Revolution. In Italy, in two essays of 1919, the reformist leader Filippo Turati accused the Italian followers of Bolshevism of losing sight of 'our great superiority of civil evolution from the historical point of view' and for losing themselves in 'infatuation' for 'the oriental world *vis-à-vis* the western world and Europe'; they forget that the 'Soviet Russians' are to 'Western parliaments' what the 'barbaric hoards' were to the 'city'.[58] As it already appears in the heading of the first of two papers cited here ('Leninism and Marxism'), 'Leninism' denotes what will later be called 'Eastern Marxism' (unrefined by definition), while 'Marxism' is synonymous with what would later be presented, not without complacency, as 'Western Marxism' (always refined and authentic by definition).

The condemnation of the Orientalising 'Leninism' was expressed either from a liberal-democratic standpoint (in the name of freedom trampled upon by the Bolshevik terror), or from the position of revolutionary orthodoxy (in the name of true socialism, which could not in any way recognise the order that had emerged in Soviet Russia). Turati thus formulated his indictment: in Russia the new power

> is forced to turn to the other States and Europe calling on the bourgeoisie, engineers, technicians and paid middle class professionals, who are given money, capital, and are lavished with all sorts of concessions, which the country is offering as a pledge, because it cannot do without capitalism.[59]

57 Anderson 1976.

58 Turati 1979a, p. 332; Turati 1979b, p. 345.

59 Turati 1979b, p. 348.

Already a few months or weeks after October 1917, Kautsky declared in even harsher terms that what happened in Soviet Russia had nothing to do with socialism or Marxism. It was not just the 'loss of freedom'. The granting of land to the peasants consolidated 'the strength of the private ownership of land', 'private ownership of the means of production and the production of goods'. Not much different was the situation in industry, where 'those who were previously capitalists have now become proletarians, while intellectual proletarians have now become capitalists'. The necessary conclusion is as follows: 'In Russia, they are making the last of the bourgeois revolutions, not the first of the socialist revolutions'.[60]

And here we can recognise the underlying trend of today's 'Western Marxism' (or its heirs). In the eyes of Turati and Kautsky, Soviet Russia in 1919 was ultimately an 'authoritarian capitalism' devoid of democracy, to make use of a characterisation that has been made by Slavoj Žižek,[61] a characterisation that has not ceased to be relied upon since China emerged from the reforms of Deng Xiaoping. Immediately after the October Revolution, those who sought to justify Lenin invoked the argument according to which he could not relinquish the power acquired in the course of fighting the war. But Turati was not to be in any way impressed by this argument: the Bolshevik leader, he argued, 'should have vigorously rejected power'.[62] And this advice was not just meant for Russia. Even in Italy it was absurd to think seriously about the conquest of power: 'The liquidation of the war must be achieved by those who have desired it in the first place. We have to take advantage of the misery it left us for our critical and propaganda work as well as for our preparation'.[63] And again, we are led to think of 'Western Marxism', which in its reading of Marx tends to prioritise a critical reading of the present, while sometimes explicitly recommending the renunciation of power and a commitment to 'changing the world without taking power'.[64] The author quoted above can be considered the end point of the self-dissolution of 'Western Marxism'.

60 Kautsky 1977, pp. 95, 113, 120–1 and 100.
61 Žižek 2009, p. 131.
62 Turati 1979a, p. 333.
63 Turati 1979b, p. 347.
64 Holloway 2002.

Conclusion

As this chapter has shown, the First World War and the October Revolution had a very different impact on the development of Marxist thought and revolutionary socialist strategy in the West and East. The revolution against the capitalistic-imperialist system had provoked in these two regions two struggles for recognition and two forms of class struggle that are different and at the same time complementary. One should not lose sight of the fact that, without overcoming the division between so-called 'Western Marxism' and so-called 'Eastern Marxism', the former is no longer able to really criticise the existing order and thus stimulate the process of emancipation, while the latter is deprived of a theoretical and political contribution that could be most valuable today.

Translated by Gearóid Ó Colmáin

CHAPTER 11

Uneven Developments, Combined: The First World War and Marxist Theories of Revolution

Peter D. Thomas

Introduction

The First World War was a major formative moment in the development and refinement of Marxist theory and socialist strategy. Marxists found themselves unable to respond to the horrors of imperialist war with previously elaborated concepts; as a theoretical tradition, Marxism was profoundly transformed by the concrete political problems that were thrown up amidst the turmoil of the cataclysm that began in 1914.[1] In particular, the betrayals of the ostensibly 'revolutionary' Social Democratic movement prompted a profound rethinking of the concept of revolution itself, from Lenin's return to Hegel in the early years of the war, the intense debates among the Bolsheviks in the interregnum between February and October 1917, the long drawn out process of the tragically defeated German Revolution, to the foundation of the Third Communist International in 1919 and beyond.[2] A formulation from Lukács's homage to the recently deceased Lenin in 1924 succinctly captures the determining coordinates of this development: 'the actuality of the revolution', in its imminence and efficacy, retroacted upon the concept of revolution to produce a new understanding of the nature of, and possibilities for, socio-political transformation in the epoch of high imperialism.[3]

In this chapter, I examine the strategic political thought of two key Marxist figures of the period, Leon Trotsky and Antonio Gramsci, both of whom formulated novel Marxist theories in the interwar period, with their respective theories of permanent revolution and passive revolution. While Trotsky had already formulated the coordinates for his dialectically constitutive theories of permanent revolution and uneven and combined development in the crucible of the

1 As discussed in the introduction to this collection.

2 For an analysis of the impact of Lenin's reading of Hegel on his concept of revolution and Marxist theory more generally, see Anderson 2007, Balibar 2007 and Kouvelakis 2007a. See Lih's contribution to this volume for a powerful case against the 'Hegelist' interpretation.

3 Lukács 1970, p. 11.

war-generated Russian Revolution of 1905–7, it was not until after the outbreak of the First World War and, particularly, after the Bolshevik Revolution, that he thought to find both confirmation of the correctness of his theory, and a socialist strategy that might be appropriate to other similarly 'late-developing' societies. It was thus only in the changed conditions of international political space that emerged from the First World War that Trotsky was able to extend and to generalise his concepts, which had originally been focused primarily on the particular, 'exceptional' case of Tsarist Russia. In this sense, the First World War represents a watershed in Trotsky's political and theoretical development, and his fully elaborated concept of permanent revolution can only be understood in the context of the transformations that it produced.

For Antonio Gramsci, on the other hand, the war's effects on both capitalist development and the organisational forms of the internationalist socialist movement also entailed a rethinking of revolutionary theory and strategy.[4] Gramsci famously greeted the Bolshevik Revolution as a 'Revolution against *Capital*'. Breaking with the 'normal course of events', the Bolsheviks had responded to what Marx 'could not predict': 'the war in Europe', 'three years of unspeakable suffering and unspeakable hardship', a war which had aroused in Russia the unprecedented 'popular collective will' that had made the Revolution.[5] It was the defeat of the other revolutionary movements that emerged from the war years, however, that was decisive for Gramsci's rethinking of the concept of revolution, as it was also for the broader international communist movement.[6] With the rise of fascism in Italy and the generalised 'stabilisation' of international capitalism in the post-War period, Gramsci argued that there had been a transition from a 'war of movement' to a 'war of position'.[7] Following his imprisonment in the late 1920s, Gramsci worked in his *Prison Notebooks* to develop a distinctive concept of 'passive revolution' to describe the changed geopolitical and domestic conditions of revolutionary politics. As in the case of Trotsky, Gramsci's renovation of Marxist theories of revolution occurs within the coordinates established by the new state system and *tempo* of capitalist development that emerged from the First World War.

---

4 On the impact of the First World War on Gramsci's development from 'socialism to communism', see Rapone 2011.

5 Gramsci 1994, pp. 39–40.

6 Eley 2002, pp. 154–6.

7 Gramsci 1975, Q 101, § 9. Gramsci signalled the precise date as 1921 – the year of both the rise of fascism in Italy and the transition to the NEP in the Soviet Union.

The concepts of passive revolution and permanent revolution, just as the theories of Gramsci and Trotsky more generally, have sometimes been thought to represent fundamentally opposed orientations. As I will argue in this chapter, however, thinking these concepts together, in terms both of their response to the socio-economic and political consequences of the First World War, and of their shared attempt to inherit and transform key elements of previous Marxist concepts of revolution, allows us to discern certain common elements in their novel formulations, at the same time as it highlights the different strategic consequences that flow from them.

Permanent Revolution

Trotsky's theory of permanent revolution and its complement and theoretical precondition, the theory of uneven and combined development, was first sketched out in the course of the war-induced first Russian Revolution in a series of articles and analyses, culminating in *Results and Prospects* (1906).[8] It was also designed as an intervention into a debate then underway in the ranks of international Social Democracy, focused on the Russian experience, regarding the natures and temporal relations of 'bourgeois' (democratic) and 'proletarian' (socialist) revolutions.[9] However, it was only after the October Revolution of 1917, which Trotsky claimed constituted a 'vindication' of his original perspective on the Russian case, and, increasingly, under the pressure of polemics in the factional struggle that resulted in his exile from the Soviet Union and isolation in the international communist movement, that he moved to elaborate his theory into a more general strategic perspective, with particular relevance for other 'late-developing' societies. In the introduction to *The Permanent Revolution*, published in 1930 as a sequel to and defence of the earlier *Results and Prospects*, Trotsky provided the following succinct outline of the 'constituent elements of the theory of the permanent revolution':

8 See Trotsky 1969. In that text, however, Trotsky does not use the term 'permanent revolution' [*permanentnaya revolyutsiya*], but rather, its Russian 'ordinary language' equivalent, 'uninterrupted revolution' [*niepreryvnaya revolyutsiya*]. The two terms were often used synonymously in the Russian Marxist debates in this period. See Knei-Paz 1979, p. 152, and Day and Gaido 2009, p. 449.

9 See Day and Gaido 2009 for a compilation of the key contributions to this discussion. For a critical perspective on the ensuing debate, see Lih 2012.

> The permanent revolution, in the sense which Marx attached to this concept, means a revolution which makes no compromise with any single form of class rule, which does not stop at the democratic stage, which goes over to socialist measures and to war against reaction from without; that is, a revolution whose every successive stage is rooted in the preceding one and which can end only in the complete liquidation of class society.[10]

He further distinguished 'three lines of thought that are united in this theory'. First, it 'embraces the problem of the transition from the democratic revolution to the socialist' revolution.[11] In other words, the theory of permanent revolution rejects the historiosophical schema that has often been ascribed to Marxism, according to which there is a 'pattern of historical development', in which a bourgeois revolution establishes a 'democratic' form of government, which then becomes the foundation for the eventual transformation of form into content by the proletariat in the process of a socialist revolution, which would establish, finally, an 'authentic' democracy, or a socialist society. Trotsky's theory of permanent revolution, at least in its most developed form, is a theory that attempts to think the immanence of each revolution to the other, in a synchronic rather than diachronic fashion.

Second, permanent revolution signifies the process of continual transformation and renovation of society in the socialist revolution, as 'constant internal struggle', of 'revolutions in economy, technique, science, the family, morals and everyday life [that] develop in complex reciprocal action and do not allow society to achieve equilibrium'.[12] Necessarily, Trotsky argues, this process takes on a political (and not merely social) character, insofar as it develops through, or is enacted by, 'collisions' between various groups in the society.[13] Permanent revolution thus involves a continuous dialectical interaction between the social and the political, in which transformations on one 'terrain' are consolidated and in turn contested on the other.

Third, the theory of permanent revolution is premised upon the necessarily international character of the socialist revolution, which in turn presupposes the necessarily international character of the capitalist mode of production and its creation and extension of a world market. It 'flows', Trotsky argues, 'from the present state of the economy and the social structure of humanity', as

10 Trotsky 1969 pp. 130–1.
11 Trotsky 1969 p. 131.
12 Trotsky 1969 p. 132.
13 Trotsky 1969 p. 132.

a 'theoretical and political reflection of the character of the world economy'.[14] Permanent revolution, that is, is 'permanent' also because it is a revolutionary process that overflows the boundaries of individual countries. It therefore finds both its presupposition and conclusion in the notion of world revolution, itself determined by a maturation of the conflict of productive forces and relations of production in the global capitalist mode of production, as an increasingly articulated and internally differentiated totality. A 'national revolution', Trotsky states, 'is not [or rather, in an imperialist system of competing and mutually dependent states, as forms of organisation of markets, cannot be] a self-contained whole; it is only a link in the international chain. The international revolution constitutes a permanent process, despite temporary declines and ebbs'.[15]

Trotsky thus argued that the possibility of permanent revolution is founded upon socio-economic turmoil and transformations, but is only 'ratified', or 'historically confirmed', at the level of fundamental political transformations, which in turn redefine the socio-economic relations that are their necessary conditions. It involves simultaneously a 'permanence' or continuity of transformative relations at the level of state and governmental forms (bourgeois-democratic to socialist), at the level of the dialectical relation of the social and the political (social transformations giving rise to political struggles, and vice versa) and at the level of the national-international (the interlocking of discrete social formations in a global economico-political totality). In other words, permanent revolution is ultimately – or 'in the last instance' – an implicitly *political* theory of revolution (as opposed to an 'economic' or 'sociological' one), because it necessarily points towards a theory of organisation of the revolutionary forces that would be able to coordinate relations between revolutionary struggles in the history of a specific national formation, and their insertion in and overdetermination by an international mode of production and state system.[16]

---

14 Trotsky 1969, p. 133.

15 Trotsky 1969, p. 133.

16 I thus partially disagree with Knei-Paz when he argues that 'if what [Trotsky] believed about Russian workers was true, then the theory of permanent revolution had no need to take undue account of the organizational instrument which would set the mechanism of the revolution in motion – the workers themselves ... were the instrument, the agent and the vehicle, of social change' (1979, p. 172). Trotsky's fully developed theory does have clear organisational implications, in the necessity of a mediating instance between transformations in different sectors of society, though this arguably was not fully articulated in Trotsky's writings before 1930.

Uneven and Combined Development

Significantly, then, interpretations of the theory of permanent revolution have often focused overwhelmingly on the first and third of Trotsky's three 'lines of thought', exhibiting a relative neglect of the second. This is to say that there has been comparatively little attention dedicated to an analysis of its specificity as a 'political' process, in preference for a focus on the more strictly 'economic' theory that forms its presupposition, namely, the theory of 'uneven and combined development'. Indeed, the theories of uneven and combined development and of permanent revolution are often taken to be virtually synonymous, with the latter representing the logical conclusion of the former.[17] With the reconfiguration and extension of the capitalist world market in the period following what Arno Mayer has suggested was effectively a 'second thirty years war',[18] as national liberation movements and decolonisation movements gave way to the full integration of previously peripheral or excluded social formations into the circuits of Western capitalist accumulation, the relevance of a theory such as uneven and combined development that seeks to think the simultaneous international integration and distinction continuously produced and reproduced by the capitalist mode of production only increased. Arguably, it is the analytical fertility of this concept that constituted one of the main reasons for the appeal of Trotsky's thought in the post-World War II period, producing some remarkable theoretical syntheses.[19] Nor has the explanatory power of this theory waned in recent years; the last decade of Marxist theory at an international level has witnessed an ongoing debate that seeks to think the contemporary relevance of the theory of uneven and combined development as a prescient analysis of the fundamental dynamics of the capitalist mode of production that have returned to predominance in the latest round of globalisation.[20] Some of these discussions have even productively attempted to think the extent to which Gramsci also can be characterised as a theorist of the simultaneously uneven and combined nature of capitalist development, which actively produces the anachronisms

17 For an example of this tendency, see Dunn and Radice 2006. Despite the promise of the title (*100 Years of Permanent Revolution*), most of the contributions to the volume are instead focused primarily on the theory of uneven and combined development. For an attempt to think the political implications of the theory of uneven and combined development, focused on the status of 'the international', see Anievas's chapter in this volume.

18 See in particular Mayer 1981.

19 See, e.g., Mandel 1975. For critical reflections on the theory, see van der Linden 2007.

20 For representative examples, see Rosenberg 2005; Allinson and Anievas 2009; Davidson 2006.

that allow its instances of 'progress' to maintain their economic and political predominance.[21]

With some rare exceptions, however, the properly 'political' dimension of the theory of permanent revolution – that is, its status as a theory of transformative political practice, and its specific form as a revolution, in relation to the myriad of other forms of modern revolution – has remained relatively underdeveloped. Permanent revolution, that is, is thought to emerge almost 'organically' from the theory of uneven and combined development, in a well-known model of 'deriving' the political from the socio-economic, or of 'reducing' the former to a (more or less) automatic expression of the latter. In particular, the status of the revolution as 'permanent' for Trotsky has often been assumed to refer, simply and exhaustively, to the 'uninterrupted' or even 'continuous' nature of the revolution, as an immediate transition from the 'democratic' to the 'socialist' revolution.[22] As one of its most eloquent defenders, Michael Löwy, has argued, Trotsky's theory of permanent revolution involves 'the uninterrupted transition from the democratic to socialist revolution'; it was premised on the possibility of transforming the bourgeois-democratic revolution into a proletarian-socialist revolution by means of workers' protagonism in the revolutionary process.[23]

There are many of Trotsky's formulations, both in *Results and Prospects* and in *The Permanent Revolution*, which can be read in this optic. He argues, for instance, in fundamental agreement with the radical-democratic position championed by Marx and Engels in the *Manifesto of the Communist Party*, that '[d]emocracy ... is only a direct prelude to the socialist revolution. Each is bound to the other by an unbroken chain'. Thus, there is established between the democratic revolution and the socialist reconstruction of society a permanent state of revolutionary development.[24] The focus upon the uninterrupted nature of the permanent revolution clearly possesses great analytical strength in terms of understanding not only the types of revolutions that emerged directly out of the experiences of the First World War, such as the Russian Revolution and, in a

21 See, e.g., Morton 2007.

22 As already noted, permanent and uninterrupted were used synonymously in the original discussion in which Trotsky intervened, and this remained his usage. Beyond the claim of temporal immediacy and progression without pause through known stages, however, this identity of terms does not settle the question of the other qualities – structural, institutional and formal – that Trotsky (and other participants in the discussion) ascribed, implicitly or explicitly, to the uninterrupted/permanent revolution.

23 Löwy 1981, p. 1.

24 Trotsky 1969, p. 132.

different sense, the German Revolution. It would also seem to be an appropriate concept with which to comprehend the other revolutionary movements that, in the wake of October 1917, were determined by the changed geopolitical relations of force of the interwar and post-Second World War years. As Löwy argues in a popular presentation, understood as primarily a theory of the uninterrupted nature of the revolutionary process, Trotsky's theory of permanent revolution can be argued 'not only [to have] predicted the general strategy of the October revolution', but as also providing 'key insights into the other revolutionary processes which would take place later on, in China, Indochina, Cuba, etc'.[25]

There are, however, a number of historical and analytical difficulties with this 'classical' or 'traditional' reading of Trotsky's theory. First, it implicitly reduces the distance of Trotsky's theorisation from the typology of different revolutions as instances in a pre-determined sequence with which he, like Lenin (albeit for his own distinct reasons), was at such pains to break.[26] If 'permanent' is understood as only 'uninterrupted', the theory of permanent revolution would not in fact represent a radical break with 'stagist' theories of revolution, but rather, their 'telescoping' or even 'compression'.[27] It would posit a temporally determined linear sequence (or 'stages') of revolutions (from the 'bourgeois-democratic' to the 'proletarian-socialist'), precisely in order to deny it; that is, to advocate moving through quickly, or 'leaping over', a stage in order to attain to a more 'advanced' position in the linear sequence, or a 'higher' stage of development.[28] What is thereby lost is Trotsky's emphasis that permanent revolution represents a fundamental rejection of the notion of stages as such, in the definition of a qualitatively new type of revolution (neither

25 Löwy 2006.

26 Under the pressure of polemics waged in the factional struggle of the late 1920s, and in response to Radek's abandonment of Trotsky's position, Trotsky claimed in 1930 that Lenin's notion of a 'growing over' of the bourgeois revolution into the socialist revolution in 1917 represented the 'same idea' as that of an uninterrupted, permanent revolution. See Trotsky 1969, p. 136. Arguably, however, Lenin's conception of the distinctiveness of the situation of 'dual power' in the Russian revolutionary process in 1917 still involved a conception of stages that was incompatible with Trotsky's fully developed theory. See Lenin 1964, pp. 55–92.

27 Draper (1978, p. 175) uses the term 'telescoping' in relation to Engels's assessment of Germany in the *Vormärz*. Larsson (1970, p. 31) argues for a Marxist conception of 'compressed' development. Löwy (1981, p. 3) concedes that the texts of Marx and Engels contain both 'stagist' and 'permanentist' concepts of permanent revolution, with the latter constituting the decisive innovation that was taken up by Trotsky.

28 This is the argument of van Ree 2013. See, in particular, p. 546.

'bourgeois-democratic' nor even 'proletarian-socialist', if the latter is understood as necessarily founded upon the former), corresponding to the changed balance of class forces and political possibilities in the epoch of imperialism. Trotsky's argument is that the generalised possibility of permanent revolution involves a redefinition of the historical tasks of a process of fundamental socio-political transformation, and their likely agents. Democratic reforms instituted by a workers' government, for instance, are integrally linked to questions of property ownership at the level of what Hegel and Marx characterised as civil society in a way that bourgeois-democratic reforms limited to the Hegelian sphere of political society are not. Trotsky's proposal should therefore not be reduced to the equation 'permanent revolution = bourgeois revolution (political society) + proletarian revolution (civil society) in a short time span'. Rather, it should be comprehended as indicating the emergence of a qualitatively new type of revolution in the early twentieth century, irreducible to the sum of its supposed historical parts, which placed the division between civil and political societies itself in question.

Second, the analytic-descriptive strengths gained by a solely temporal understanding of permanent revolution might quickly turn into a profound weakness, when we come to consider its capacity for contemporary and future prediction and assessment. As a model of the 'temporal fusion' of the bourgeois and socialist revolutions, permanent revolution may help to analyse the many revolutions of the twentieth century that struggled against pre- or proto-bourgeois states, and in which the possibility of a direct transition to a socialist reconstruction of national social formations, on the basis of their presence in a fundamentally international capitalist system, was historically posed. The struggles for national liberation that were one of the major (even when indirect) consequences of the permanent mobilisation of the first half of the twentieth century are the most striking examples. It may even help us, today, to identify some of the challenges confronting contemporary movements in north Africa and the Arab world, among others, against authoritarian states, though a characterisation of them as prior to a properly 'bourgeois' revolution could only be maintained at the risk of an Orientalist flattening out of the real histories of revolution and counter-revolution in the twentieth century.[29] It is more difficult, however, to see how such a theory could help to coordinate revolutionary action in the contemporary all too bourgeois and formally democratic 'West', where no such transition is on the agenda. Permanent revolution

29 For representative attempts to analyse recent transformations in the Arab world in particular in relation to the concept of permanent revolution, see Bush 2011 and Michael-Matsas 2011.

would thus appear as relevant to a largely previous phase of the development of the capitalist mode of production and its state system, a historical aberration that emerged with the First World War and gradually lost its propulsive force in the wake of the Second.[30]

Third, and perhaps most problematically, a 'traditionalist' reading of the permanent revolution that focuses only on its temporal dimensions, conceived as the political reflection of the contradictions of uneven and combined development, fails to indicate what it would mean concretely, in terms of political forms and institutions, to make the revolution 'permanent'. Does not a call for 'uninterrupted', 'continuous' revolution without further qualification run the risk of falling into precisely the position that the young Marx, in *On the Jewish Question*, had criticised for its inability to grasp the dialectical relation between social transformation and its political coordination, comprehension and consolidation? Like many of their contemporaries, drawing upon traditions of revolutionary rhetoric deriving from the French Revolution and its legacies, Marx and Engels deployed, explicitly and arguably implicitly, a variety of concepts of permanent revolution in the 1840s, though without providing any single formulation or definition of it.[31] In particular, although the phrase itself does not appear there, the *Manifesto of the Communist Party* has seemed to many later scholars to provide a precedent for the notion of permanent revolution as a telescoping of bourgeois-democratic and proletarian-socialist/ communist revolutions into a unitary, short-term process.[32] At the time of the composition of *On the Jewish Question* (late 1843), however, Marx's discussion of permanent revolution drew attention to one of the immanent limits and

30 See Davidson 2010 and 2012, particularly pp. 621–9, and Davidson's chapter in this volume for critical reflections in this direction, with a distinctive conception of the historical status of 'bourgeois revolution'.

31 Explicit uses of the phrase 'permanent revolution' (and 'revolution in permanence') include, among others, passages in 'On the Jewish Question', *The Holy Family, The Class Struggles in France* and the March 1850 'Address' to the Communist League. See Marx and Engels 1975–2005, Vol. 3, pp. 155–6; Vol. 4, p. 123; Vol. 10, p. 127; Vol. 10, pp. 281, 287. The phrase was regularly invoked by other radicals in the years straddling 1848; see, e.g., Proudhon's 'Toast to the Revolution' of 14 October 1848 (Proudhon 1969, p. 158).

32 The claim for the 'implicit' presence of the concept in the *Manifesto*, as indeed in other texts by Marx and Engels of a later date, recalls a more general methodological challenge regarding anachronism and the relation between words and concepts in the history of political thought: namely, to what extent is it legitimate – and legitimate for what ends – to seek for the 'seeds' or 'component parts' of a theory or concept in texts composed before said theory or concept was explicitly formulated, particularly in texts in which the words or phrases themselves do not appear?

attendant risks of thinking revolutionary transformations in terms of a continuous, uninterrupted sequence. Reflecting on the contradictions of the process of radicalisation of the Jacobins, and the denouement of the Terror in particular, Marx noted that

> in periods when the political state as such is born violently out of civil society, when political liberation is the form in which men strive to achieve their liberation, the state can and must go as far as the *abolition of religion*, the *destruction* of religion. But it can do so only in the same way that it proceeds to the abolition of private property, to the maximum, to confiscation, to progressive taxation, just as it goes as far as the abolition of life, the *guillotine*... [I]t can achieve this only by coming into *violent* contradiction with its own conditions of life, only by declaring the revolution to be permanent.[33]

As Marx noted, this version of the 'permanence' of revolution (in truth, its fetishism, as end in itself) ends up exhausting itself, or devouring its own children, in the classical formulation. It is unable to think the necessity of the immanence of the forms of emancipatory politics to their socio-economic content. In order to avoid such 'terroristic' or even 'adventuristic' conclusions, it is necessary to think concretely the necessary political mediations that could sustain a process of uninterrupted revolution, in the 'constant internal struggle' and 'complex reciprocal action' between the socio-economic and political, as Trotsky had argued.[34] It was precisely such a theory of revolutionary organisation that Antonio Gramsci attempted to develop in his own distinctive reformulation of Marxist theories of revolution in the interwar period.

Passive Revolution

Gramsci's concept of 'passive revolution' was first sketched out in a series of successive drafts in the late 1920s and early 1930s in the texts that became known as the *Prison Notebooks*, written after his incarceration by the Fascists, but only published in the post-Second World War period. While the concept of 'hegemony' began to be discussed already in the 1950s, it was not until the late 1970s that the closely related concept of passive revolution, and its distinctiveness in comparison to other Marxist theories of revolution, began to be widely

33 Marx and Engels 1975–2005, Vol. 3, pp. 155–6.

34 Trotsky 1969, p. 132.

recognised.[35] A certain interpretation of the concept of passive revolution was central to the proposals of so-called Eurocommunism, exerting an influence upon the terms of debate of the 'crisis of Marxism' and the later transition to various post-Marxisms. In the UK in the 1980s, reformulated in the notion of 'regressive modernisation', it was deployed by Stuart Hall to describe the project of Thatcherism.[36] In Germany, the concept has played a prominent role in the theorisations of post-Fordism and neoliberalism by figures such as Wolfgang Fritz Haug, Mario Candeias and Jan Rehmann, among many others.[37] In recent Gramscian philological studies, particularly in Italy, Mexico and Brazil, the concept and its contemporary significance as an analysis of neoliberalism has been variously reconstructed or contested by scholars such as Frosini, Kanoussi and Coutinho.[38] More recently, the concept has also been deployed in debates regarding state formation and the international political economy, giving rise to conflicting interpretations regarding both the meaning of the concept and its relevance to the contemporary world.[39]

As the above abbreviated list of interpretations might suggest, however, there are many different versions of the theory of passive revolution, ranging from pessimistic, ultimately status-quo affirming, system theories, to perspectives that attempt to use it to identify possibilities for de-passifying mobilisation. Furthermore, precisely as interpretations, they were elaborated in very different historical periods from that of Gramsci's, and thus arguably were at least overdetermined by the political and theoretical debates and interests of those conjunctures, giving rise to their different emphases. What, then, was Gramsci's original formulation of this concept, in his historical context? As with all of Gramsci's concepts, it is necessary to study the development of this concept in what one of Gramsci's most attentive readers, Gianni Francioni, has described as the 'dialectical laboratory' of the *Prison Notebooks*.[40] Rather than a definitive statement or concluded analysis, Gramsci offered the outlines of a research project whose constitutive incompletion was centrally related to his strategic considerations in this period.

35 On the history of the reception of the concept of passive revolution, see Frosini 2007 and Liguori 2012.
36 Hall 1988.
37 Haug 2006; Candeias 2004; Rehmann 1998.
38 Frosini 2012; Kanoussi 2000; Coutinho 2012.
39 See the special issue of *Capital & Class* edited by Adam Morton (2010), which includes a range of historical and geographical contributions.
40 Francioni 1984.

In the early phases of his research, in late 1929 and 1930, Gramsci appropriated the concept of passive revolution from Vincenzo Cuoco, the historian of the failed Neapolitan Revolution of 1799. Gramsci transformed the concept, in the first instance, in order to provide an analysis of the distinctive features of the Italian *Risorgimento*, which he argued was characterised by a failure to construct a coherent hegemonic project. In this context, the term passive revolution was used to describe the 'historical fact of the absence of popular initiative in the development of Italian history', embodied in the role of the moderates in the *Risorgimento* in actively preventing popular initiative in an organised political form. In particular, Gramsci pointed to the lack of the radical-popular 'Jacobin moment' that had distinguished the experience of the French Revolution. The formation of the modern Italian nation state, according to Gramsci, had been a 'revolution without revolution', or in other terms, a 'royal conquest' and not 'popular movement'.[41] It was a transformation of political forms undertaken by elites, garbed in the rhetoric of previous revolutionary movements, but without the extensive involvement of subaltern classes that had led to the placing in question of social and economic relations in earlier transformations.

However, it soon became clear to Gramsci that the concept could have a more general significance as a criterion of historical research into periods and countries that had been similarly lacking in an impetus to modernity from below. Thus, in a second extension of the concept, undertaken from late 1930 onwards, Gramsci used it to describe the process of socio-political modernisation of other European nation states with experiences similar to those of Italy.[42] Foremost among these was Bismarckian Germany, similarly characterised by transformations of the political forms of a society that nevertheless failed to place in question their socio-economic contents. Here Gramsci's concept has undergone expansion by means of the identification of substantial similarities between the class content of these different national experiences, despite

41 The decisive note is Gramsci 1975, Q 1, § 44. Gramsci originally used the term 'revolution without revolution', adding 'passive revolution' at a later date in the margins. Elsewhere, he employed the term '"royal conquest" and not popular movement' (Q 3, §40). 'The historical fact of the absence of popular initiative in the development of Italian history, and the fact that "progress" would be verified as the reaction of the dominant classes to the sporadic and disorganic rebellion of the popular masses with "restorations" that comprehend some parts of the popular demands, thus "progressive restorations" or "revolutions-restorations" or even "passive revolutions"' (Q 8, § 25).

42 'The concept of passive revolution seems to me to be exact not only for Italy, but also for other countries that modernise the State by means of a series of reforms or national wars, without passing through the political revolution of the radical Jacobin type' (Q 4, § 57).

their apparent differences. Passive revolution, as in the first instance, continues to refer to a specific historical event or ensemble of events.

In yet a third moment, particularly in early 1932, Gramsci asked whether the concept of passive revolution might have a more general validity, as descriptive of an entire historical period in Europe as a whole: roughly, a period he characterised as the Restoration that followed upon the exhaustion of the energies that had driven the French Revolution, beginning in 1848 with the defeat of the Europe-wide workers' revolts, but intensifying after the defeat of the Paris Commune. In this version, passive revolution comes to signify the pacifying and incorporating nature assumed by bourgeois hegemony as such in the epoch of imperialism, extending across and beyond the First World War to the emergence of fascism, the 'current form' of passive revolution in the 1920s and 1930s. In 1932, Gramsci even extended his analysis of the passive revolution beyond its contemporary forms in the 'West' – of fascism and Americanism, or Fordism – to detect its nefarious hand at work even in the 'East', in the home of international revolution, the USSR itself.

The term 'revolution' in this third version still refers to the capacity of the ruling class still to deliver substantive and real historical gains, producing real social transformations that could be comprehended, formally at least, as progressive; the term 'passive' continues to denote the attempt to produce these transformations without the extensive involvement of subaltern classes *as* classes, but by means of molecular absorption of their leading elements into an already established hegemonic project (the mechanism of 'transformism', first in 'molecular' and then in corporative forms).[43] However, passive revolution, as a concept, no longer seems to refer primarily to a particular recognisable event. Rather, in this final usage, passive revolution has taken on a more general significance, as a logic of (a certain type) of modernisation.

The development of the concept of passive revolution would thus seem, according to the textual analysis thus far, to involve a gradual shift of emphasis from the substantive to the adjective. Beginning as a further development of the *Communist Manifesto*'s characterisation of the bourgeoisie as 'a most revolutionary class' – though in Gramsci's version placing greater emphasis upon the political forms and institutions of modernity, alongside and beyond Marx and Engels's analysis of the immense transformations in the world of production – Gramsci's concept would seem to conclude in a dystopian vision of modernity as continual degeneration, an 'iron cage' of 'rationalisation', in the Weberian sense. Passive revolution, that is, would seem to be a 'revolution' only in name, or rather, its exact antithesis. Rather than a theory of the

43 See, e.g., Gramsci 1975, Q 13, §7.

uninterrupted transformation of the existing state of affairs, as in Trotsky's concept, Gramsci's passive revolution would appear to describe a process of the uninterrupted consolidation and ossification of the ruling order. As a refined mechanism and political programme for the passification of popular initiatives, passive revolution would be the whimper rather than the bang with which the heroic modern age of revolutions arrives at its terminus.

Permanent Revolution in the *Prison Notebooks*

Such a dystopian reading, however, would neglect the complementary conceptual developments that Gramsci undertakes in relation to the concept of permanent revolution, conducted at the same time as and in parallel to his research on passive revolution. Crucially, these developments take place directly in relation to Trotsky's theory.[44] Famously, Gramsci discussed Trotsky's theory in a way that seems to indicate total rejection, giving rise to analyses that posit these theorists as committed to fundamentally opposed – 'Eastern' versus 'Western' – orientations.[45] Trotsky's theory of permanent revolution is variously characterised in the *Prison Notebooks* as a 'literary and intellectualistic label', possibly a mere 'political reflection of the theory of war of manoeuvre', 'cosmopolitan – i.e. superficially national and superficially Western or European', like French syndicalist and Rosa Luxemburg's theories of the Mass Strike, ultimately depending upon a suspect 'theory of spontaneity'.[46] Trotsky himself, in a number of other highly overdetermined passages in the *Prison Notebooks*, is singled out for a disparaging critique: 'in one way or another [he] can be considered the political theorist of frontal attack in a period in which it only leads to defeats'.[47] Finally, in the context of a discussion of the national-international nexus, the theory of permanent revolution is characterised as a reversion to, rather than break with, the evolutionary 'orthodoxy' (in truth, the perspective of the revisionist current around Bernstein) of the Second International:

---

44 It is significant that the first note in which Gramsci discusses the concept of hegemony in the *Prison Notebooks* (Q 1, § 44), and to which he later adds the concept of passive revolution, concludes with a discussion of the concept of permanent revolution and a critique of what Gramsci took to be Trotsky's version of it.

45 See, e.g., Saccarelli 2007.

46 Gramsci 1975, Q 7, § 16.

47 Gramsci 1975, Q 6, § 138.

> The theoretical weaknesses of this modern form of the old mechanicism are masked by the general theory of permanent revolution, which is nothing but a generic forecast presented as a dogma, and which demolishes itself, due to the fact that it is not actually manifested.[48]

As Frank Rosengarten has noted, much of Gramsci's polemic is not only unfair, but also at times close to a puzzling misattribution.[49] For it was precisely Trotsky who led the Third International's critique of 'theories of frontal attack in a period in which it only leads to defeats', particularly in relation to adventurism and revolutionary impatience in the German Revolution.[50] In many respects, the positions that Gramsci criticises are in fact the exact opposite of those upheld by Trotsky, nowhere more so than in terms of his non-mechanist conception of permanent revolution as the dialectical integration of the national and international in the specificity of a particular conjuncture.

The reasons for Gramsci's almost deliberate misreading of Trotsky's position are multiple and overdetermined. Previous political disagreements during Gramsci's period in Moscow may have played a role, as might the influence of the caricatures of Trotsky's theories that were current in the international communist movement in the late 1920s. The suggestion of Trotsky's impatience or adventurism might possibly have resulted from a conflation in Gramsci's mind of the positions of Trotsky and those of another early opponent of Stalin in the Communist International, the former head of the Italian Communist Party Bordiga, from whose intransigent ultra-leftist politics Gramsci had broken only after intense debates in Moscow at the 4th Congress (ironically, under the influence, among others, of Trotsky himself). Nevertheless, whatever the predominant reason, Gramsci's continuous rejection of Trotsky's notion of permanent revolution, as an untimely and utopian war of movement, would seem to leave little space for any reconciliation with the conceptual coordinates of his own theory of passive revolution, to which the theory of hegemony, as a complex and articulated war of position, was designed as a response.

Furthermore, in a number of instances, Gramsci seems to reject not merely Trotsky's theory of permanent revolution, but the notion of permanent revolution as such, including the concept employed by Marx and Engels. Describing the extension of the passive revolution on a European scale in the wake of the

48 Gramsci 1975, Q 14, § 68.

49 Rosengarten 1984–5.

50 See Bianchi 2008, particularly pp. 199–252, for an important attempt to rethink Gramsci's metaphors of war of position/war of movement in relation to Trotsky.

defeat of the Paris Commune and the consolidation of what he described as the bourgeois 'integral state', Gramsci argued that

> in the period after 1870, with the colonial expansion of Europe, all these elements change. The internal and international organisational relations of the State become more complex and massive, and the Forty-Eightist formula of the 'Permanent Revolution' is *expanded and superseded* in political science by the formula of 'civil hegemony'.[51]

In other notes, however, Gramsci suggests that the theory of hegemony he had developed, following Lenin, was itself in a certain sense a theory of 'permanent revolution', and thus an alternative to and indeed in competition with Trotsky's concept. This rivalry would in fact seem to constitute the fundamental theoretical (as opposed to personal or political) reasons that motivate his critique: Gramsci held that Trotsky, unlike Lenin, had misunderstood Marx and Engels's references to the permanence of the revolution in their historical context, and had consequently been unable to undertake a coherent 'actualisation' of the theory in the specific conditions of the post-First World War conjuncture. In early 1930, he argued that

> With respect to the 'Jacobin' slogan formulated in 1848–9 by Marx in relation to Germany, its complex fortunes are worth studying. Taken up again, systematised, developed, intellectualised by the Parvus-Bronstein group, it proved inert and ineffective in 1905, and subsequently. It had become an abstract thing, belonging in the scientist's cabinet. The tendency which opposed it in this literary form, and indeed did not use it on purpose, applied it in fact in a form which adhered to actual, concrete, living history, adapted to the time and the place; as something that sprang from all the pores of the particular society which had to be transformed; as the alliance of two social groups with the hegemony of the urban group.
>
> In one case, you had the Jacobin temperament without an adequate political content; in the second, a Jacobin temperament and content derived from the new historical relations, and not from a literary and intellectualistic label.[52]

---

51 Gramsci 1975, Q 13, § 7, my italics. *Superare*, here rendered as 'to supersede', is the standard Italian translation of Hegel's *aufheben*. Gramsci seems here to envisage a similar relation of preserving negation.

52 Gramsci 1975, Q 1, § 44.

In May 1932, he extended this argument, claiming that

> the greatest modern theoretician of the philosophy of praxis, on the terrain of political struggle and organisation and with a political terminology – in opposition to the various 'economistic' tendencies – revalued the front of cultural struggle and constructed the doctrine of hegemony as a complement to the theory of the State-as-force, and as the actual form of the Forty-Eightist doctrine of 'permanent revolution'.[53]

What did Gramsci understand by the 'Forty-Eightist' doctrine of permanent revolution? And in what sense could its 'actual form' be regarded as the 'doctrine of hegemony?'

The Revolution in Permanence

Like Marx and Engels themselves, Gramsci had critically reflected upon both the limitations and strengths of the Jacobin notion and practice of 'permanent revolution' and its inheritance by the 'men of 48'. As in Marx's critique in *On the Jewish Question*, the limitations of this concept seemed to consist for Gramsci in the notion of the escalation of a political process of transformation that did not take into account the necessity of mediating instances that could ground such a process in a real reorganisation of socio-economic relations at the level of civil society.[54] It was precisely such an understanding of the 'permanence' of the revolution that Gramsci held had been 'superseded' by the increasing complexity of social and political mediating instances in the 'trenches' of civil society after 1848. Furthermore, he thought to have found such a weakness also in what he characterised as Trotsky's 'abstract' theory. The strengths of the Jacobin example for Gramsci, on the other hand, resided in its elaboration of a structured political process that posed the question of the organisation of relations of force capable of transcending the given divisions of interests in a social formation – permanence understood not simply as continuous temporal development, but also as endurance, in an almost Machiavellian sense. It was this dimension of the 'Forty-Eightist' doctrine of permanent revolution

53 Gramsci 1975, Q10I, § 12. The 'greatest modern theoretician of the philosophy of praxis' is a reference to Lenin.

54 See in particular Q 1, §48, where Gramsci notes the class limits of the Jacobin programme, particularly in relation to the Le Chapelier law of 1791, limiting forms of popular political organisation.

that Gramsci argued had been inherited – 'expanded and superseded' – in the formula of 'civil hegemony', particularly as it was then later developed in the debates of the Bolsheviks both before and after the October Revolution.[55]

A precedent for this understanding can arguably also be found in the texts of Marx and Engels, in their reflections on the experience of 1848 and its aftermath. In that case, however, they do not use the phrase 'permanent revolution' in the same way as they had done in the years of the *Vormärz*, like many other radicals whose imaginations were fired by the thought of repeating, or restaging, the continuous transformations of the most radical years of the French Revolution. An almost indiscernible and seemingly inessential semantic difference signals the shift to a related, but nevertheless distinct, new concept: namely, the notion of 'the revolution in permanence', not as an historical description, but as a programmatic imperative.

In the work of Marx and Engels, the slogan of 'the revolution in permanence' represents simultaneously a rupture and a refoundation.[56] It breaks with the political perspective they had pursued in the lead up to the Revolutions of 1848; namely, the possibility of an (albeit temporary) alliance between the proletarians and the 'most revolutionary class', in the words of the *Manifesto*, of the bourgeoisie. According to this scenario, a class alliance of the democratic aspirations of a progressive bourgeoisie and the desires for socio-economic transformation of a nascent proletariat would engage in a struggle against the remnants of the absolutist state, proposing a rational programme of political modernisation. In the case of the 'late-developing' Germany in particular, a bourgeois-democratic revolution would be but the immediate prelude to a proletarian-communist revolution effecting a deep-going socio-economic transformation. It was this model of the 'telescoping' or 'compression' of two revolutions into one continuous process that, as we have seen, was taken up and further developed by Trotsky.

The experience of 1848 and its aftermath, however, convinced Marx and Engels that such an alliance was no longer viable. In Germany in particular, the bourgeoisie had compromised with the anti-democratic elements of the old order, making the previous stagist conception of a bourgeois 'prelude' to a proletarian revolution no longer tenable. At the most, democratic petty bourgeois

55 For a discussion of the varied uses of permanent revolution in Gramsci, with a focus on its political meaning for the entire *Prison Notebooks* project, see Frosini 2009, pp. 32–9 in particular.

56 For the most extensive philologically grounded analysis of the development of this concept in the late 1840s in Marx and Engels's work, see Draper 1978, pp. 169–263, 591–5, 599–612.

forces might be expected to stage a limited political revolution, which would close down, rather than open further, the possibility for more radical transformations. Marx and Engels responded by refounding their understanding of revolution on the terrain of an independent working-class political programme. Tentatively suggested throughout 1849, the decisive transition occurred in the 'Address of the Central Committee to the Communist League' in March of 1850. Much more than a 'sequel' to the *Manifesto of the Communist Party*, as it has sometimes been understood, this brief speech represents instead its post-revolutionary *Aufhebung*. Marx and Engels declared the need for the workers' movement

> to make the revolution permanent until all the more or less propertied classes have been driven from their ruling positions, until the proletariat has conquered state power and ... has progressed sufficiently far – not only in one country but in all the leading countries of the world – that competition between the proletarians of these countries ceases and at least the decisive forces of production are concentrated in the hands of the workers.[57]

They further specified the conjunctural dimensions of this analysis: in a period in which the revolutionary energies of 1848 were being dissipated or demobilised by a now much less revolutionary, if not reactionary, bourgeoisie and their petty bourgeois 'replacement', the workers' movement needed to resist any attempt to 'disband', 'dismiss' or 'retire' the revolution. In particular, at the sign of an upsurge in revolutionary struggle, the Communist League should advocate that

> the workers, as far as it is at all possible, must oppose bourgeois attempts at pacification and force the democrats to carry out their terrorist phrases. They must work to ensure that the immediate revolutionary excitement is not suddenly suppressed after the victory. On the contrary, it must be sustained as long as possible.[58]

Such a continuous or uninterrupted revolutionary process, however, could only be sustained if the workers' movement were organised independently around a series of policies corresponding to its class interests – in particular, a consistent attack upon private property in the means of production. Marx and

57 Marx and Engels 1975–2005, Vol. 10, p. 281.
58 Marx and Engels 1975–2005, Vol. 10, p. 286.

Engels could thus conclude that the 'battle-cry' of the proletariat should be: 'The Revolution in Permanence!'[59]

This performative strategy recalls one of the constant elements in the radicalisation of different waves of the 'long French Revolution': from the Tennis Court Oath of 1789 refusing to disperse the assembled Third Estate, to the declarations of the sectional assemblies throughout 1793 in particular that they would remain sitting 'in permanence', the phrase was used to signify the intention to remain constituted as a politically active public body, not reduced to the 'rights' of passive citizenship.[60] Indeed, the declaration of permanence itself constituted a political act, insofar as it claimed the right to public existence with no regard for an authorising figure or instance other than its own declaration. To remain 'in permanence' here connoted not simply a continuous temporal development, or lack of interruption: an imminence of the revolutionary process. Even more crucially, it pointed to a self-constituted institutional endurance of the assembled movement, which found its grounds of legitimacy in its own act of defiant assembly; the immanence of the revolutionary form to its content.

Marx and Engels's 'actualisation' of this performative strategy with their call for the 'revolution in permanence' in 1850 was thus not simply a repetition of their previously outlined theory of revolution as a compression of historical stages, or fusion of different types of revolution. Nor can it be reduced to a valiant last-ditch attempt to rally the exhausted revolutionary forces of the Forty-Eighters, with an exhortation to rise up 'once more unto the breach'. It was also, more fundamentally, the call for the enduring constitution of the working-class movement as an independent political force, organised around the independent political objectives corresponding to its class interests and simultaneously those of socio-political transformation itself. There is no indication that Marx and Engels ever abandoned this perspective, despite the political defeats and setbacks that soon followed in the early 1850s; on the contrary, its terms were deepened and developed in particular in relation to the events of the Paris Commune, and even retroacted upon later memories of their political positions in the early 1840s itself.[61] It was as an inheritance of such an understanding of the permanence of the revolution that Gramsci elaborated his concept of hegemony, and in particular, the specificity of working-class hegemonic politics embodied in his Machiavellian figure of the 'modern Prince', as

---

59 Marx and Engels 1975–2005, Vol. 10, p. 287.

60 See Sewell 1988.

61 For a pointed analysis of the role of permanent revolution in Marx's reflections on the Commune, in particular, see Kouvelakis 2007b.

a counter to the consolidated structural form of bourgeois hegemony of his time: the passive revolution.

Conclusion

Gramsci and Trotsky both responded to the challenges of the changed coordinates of the post-First World War conjuncture by elaborating novel conceptions of revolution. Significantly, both did so by attempting to ground their proposals in an interpretation of a central concept of revolution in the prior Marxist tradition: the permanent revolution, or the revolution in permanence. In the case of Trotsky, the result was a sophisticated theory that seemed to be able to account for the contours of revolutionary movements responding to the modernisation drives that marked the interwar years, and particularly the wave of anti-colonial and national liberation struggles after the Second World War. As in 1905 and again in 1917, it seemed that socio-economic and political modernisation might coincide and place the possibility of a direct transition to socialism firmly on the agenda. Gramsci's concept of passive revolution, on the other hand, provided a detailed account of the ruling class strategies deployed in order to prevent any such synchronisation of the political and socio-economic. As an analysis of European state formation in the late nineteenth century, it provided a powerful narrative to explain the conditions of possibility both for the emergence of the Fascist regime in Italy, and for the absorption of oppositional movements into the existing political order that marked social democracy in the interwar years. Yet both theories were marked by, if not consigned to, their times, in a way that places in doubt their continuing relevance today. As the international capitalist mode of production mutated again after the long post-Second World War boom, Trotsky's theory of permanent revolution, if not that of uneven and combined development, arguably began to lose some of both its strategic relevance, and analytic capacity to explain the political reasons for failures of revolutionary movements to remain 'in permanence'. Gramsci's theory of passive revolution, for its part, seems to have suffered an inverted fate: the more its analytical capacity to explain the political forms and foundations of bourgeois hegemony is emphasised, the more difficult it seems to think of the political practices that might be able to break out of such an 'iron cage'. It is perhaps in the dialectic between Trotsky and Gramsci's distinctive concepts, between the time and form, imminence and immanence, of the revolutionary movement, that similar attempts to actualise the strengths of Marxist theories of revolutions today might be able to begin.

CHAPTER 12

The First World War, Classical Marxism and the End of the Bourgeois Revolution in Europe

Neil Davidson

Introduction

At approximately 9.00 pm on 8 November 1917 (new style), Vladimir Illych Lenin rose in the meeting hall of the former Smolny Institute for Noble Girls and began his address to the Second All-Russian Congress of Soviets. Lenin's arresting opening line – 'we shall now proceed to construct the socialist order' – was only reported two years later by John Reed, and its content may have involved a certain amount of journalistic licence on his part.[1] Nevertheless, the startling central fact remains: Lenin was able to announce that Russia had begun the transition to socialism on the basis of a successful insurrection, an outcome that he had only concluded was possible six months earlier and of which it then took several months to persuade the overwhelming majority of Bolshevik Party members. Prior to Lenin's arrival at the Finland Station in April only Trotsky had seriously argued that the Russian Revolution could become a socialist rather than a bourgeois revolution, through the strategy of 'permanent revolution'.

What converted other Russian revolutionaries to Trotsky's conclusion, if not to his reasoning, was the crisis brought about by Russian involvement in the First World War. Russia was not of course the only Eastern European state in 1914 where the bourgeois revolution had still to be accomplished against an absolutist (Austro-Hungarian) or tributary (Ottoman) regime, and in which permanent revolution as Trotsky conceived it might have been possible. But those other countries never moved beyond bourgeois revolutions and that outcome effectively signalled the completion of the process in Europe, if we understand its eastern boundary to be the new Turkish state consolidated by 1923.

---

1 Reed, 1977, p. 129. Trotsky, who was not present, later commented: 'That initial statement which John Reed puts in the mouth of Lenin does not appear in any of the newspaper accounts. But it is wholly in the spirit of the orator. Reed could not have made it up'. Trotsky, 1977, p. 1168.

For some writers, Arno Mayer above all, it was the Second World War which in fact brought an end to the pre-bourgeois order in Europe. According to Mayer, until the conclusion of what he calls 'the Thirty Years' War of the general crisis of the twentieth century' [1914–45], Europe was still dominated by an order 'thoroughly pre-industrial and pre-bourgeois': 'The Great War was an expression of the decline and fall of the old order fighting to prolong its life rather than the explosive rise of industrial capitalism bent on imposing its primacy'. Mayer even extends his analysis to what had once seemed the obvious exceptions, writing that, '[n]either England nor France had become industrial-capitalist and bourgeois civil and political societies'.[2] During the thirty years between 1914 and 1945:

> The elites and institutions of Europe's embattled old regime were locked in a death struggle with those of a defiant new order: in the economic sphere merchant and manufactural capitalism against corporate and organized industrial capitalism; in civil society prescriptive ruling classes against university trained elites; in political society land-based notables and establishments against urban-based professional politicians; in cultural life the custodians of historicism against the champions of experimentation and modernism; and in science the guardians of established paradigms against the pioneers of the world's second great scientific and technological revolution.[3]

By the end of the Second World War the struggle was over: 'Throughout most of Europe the old regime was either decimated or cast off by 1945'.[4]

I want to dispute this conclusion. It was the 1914–18 War, rather than its successor, which sealed the fate of the old regimes. Even conservative historians are aware that the First World War involved a decisive shift in the nature of European state forms, although they tend to see this in purely political terms; Niall Fergusson, for example, writes that, 'the First World War turned out to be a turning point in the long-running conflict between monarchism and republicanism; a conflict which had its roots in eighteenth-century America and France, and indeed further back in seventeenth-century England'.[5] But why did the revolutions which occurred from October 1918 onwards not emulate the Russian experience, even though many – if not all – of the same conditions

2 Mayer 1981, pp. 3–4, 11.
3 Mayer 1981, p. 3.
4 Mayer 1990, p. 32.
5 Fergusson 1999, pp. 434–5.

were present? This chapter will examine what the leading Marxist thinkers of the Second International – in this context principally Lenin and Trotsky, but also Bauer, Kautsky, Luxemburg and Parvus – thought of the revolutionary prospects in Russia and Eastern Europe before February 1917, then explore the distinctiveness of the Russian experience which followed, and the singularity of the revolutionary outcome there compared with the rest of the continent, to which the War was central. To begin, however, we need a definition of bourgeois revolutions, and an outline of their chronology.[6]

Defining and Dating Bourgeois Revolution

I define a bourgeois revolution as a process by which a pre-capitalist state – whether feudal, absolutist, tributary or colonial – is destroyed, and a new nation state constructed in its place, capable of acting as a territorially-bounded centre of capital accumulation. This definition is therefore based on a specific outcome in relation to the state, which then either initiates or consolidates the transition to capitalism, depending where a particular case takes place in historical time and when it takes place in geographical space. It does not expect bourgeois revolutions to take a particular form, to be carried out by a social group or class fraction, or to involve other outcomes which may be important for any number of reasons – democracy, agrarian reform, national unification – but which have no necessary connection with capitalist development.

Prior to the 1917 Russian Revolution the bourgeois revolutions can be grouped into two major, sequential variations. The first and smallest group, comprising the Netherlands (1567–1648), England (1640–60/1689–90) and France (1789–1815) involved both actual bourgeois leadership and mass popular involvement, at least in the early stages; but even the members of this group need to be differentiated. The Dutch and English revolutions occurred where capitalist social relations of production were already highly developed internally, but where a world capitalist system was still only in the process of formation, even by the time both revolutions converged in 1688 with the Dutch 'invasion' of the British Isles. The same social relations were far less developed in France and elsewhere in Europe by 1789 – not least because of the success of the major continental absolutisms in preventing them growing beyond a certain controllable stage – but the world economy was now far more of a reality and the models existed in the Netherlands and Britain for aspirant bourgeois to emulate.

6 The discussion which follows is based on Davidson 2012, esp. chapters 15, 21 and 22.

France was the turning point, leaving a permanent fear among the European bourgeoisie about the consequences of mass insurgency which made any repetition more difficult to achieve, as the experience of 1848 in Germany was to demonstrate. These revolutions all involved important moments of 'revolution from below', although to simply describe them in this way is to pass over the way in which *all* bourgeois revolutions, including these, inescapably also involve moments 'from above', since they are ultimately about replacing one exploitative class with another.

Not all of the revolutions of 1848–9 were bourgeois in inspiration. Marx and Engels supported the Hungarian rising against the Hapsburgs, on the grounds that it would weaken absolutist dominance in Central and Eastern Europe; but in social terms it was reactionary, in the sense of reasserting the interests of the feudal nobility:

> The revolution that wracked Hungary halfway through the nineteenth-century was not a bourgeois revolution, but an effort to exchange Habsburg rule for liberal etatism under the control of the gentry. It changed the legal status both of the nobles, who no longer enjoyed seigniorial rights and were made technically equal to other citizens, and of the peasants, who no longer owed compulsory labour; but it did not abolish nobility as an honour, did not redistribute the land, and did not create a bourgeoisie.[7]

One unintended consequence of the reassertion of absolutist power in Central and Eastern Europe after the failures of 1848 was to accelerate a process of top-down reform. As Jerome Blum points out:

> It is difficult to imagine, much less to document, the thesis that bourgeois capitalists in Russia or Romania or Hungary, or in fact any of the servile lands, had sufficient influence to persuade governments to end the servile order, or that governments freed the peasants out of their concern for the needs of bourgeois capitalism. ... The final reforms that freed the peasants from their servility, and afforded them civil equality with the other strata in society, were the last great triumph of royal absolutism over nobility – and, in truth, its last great achievement.[8]

7 Stokes 1989, p. 225.

8 Blum 1978, pp. 372–3.

The short-lived revolutionary regimes of 1848–9 passed legislation that was never implemented, but 'when the absolutists gained control, as they quickly did, they carried out the revolution's agrarian reforms because these reforms suited their own interests'. What were these? One was 'reducing the power of the nobility' and the other 'enabled the throne to hold the loyalty and support of the peasantry': 'These men, advocates of the bureaucratic sovereign state, opposed the traditional order because it interfered with and impeded the welfare and power of the state'.[9] But in an environment in which capitalist market conditions increasingly prevailed, the slackening of feudal agrarian social relations could only result in adaptation to it. Eric Hobsbawm has described how in Bohemia and Hungary in the latter half of the nineteenth century, '[t]he large noble estates, sometimes helped by injections of finance from the compensation payments for the loss of labour services, transformed themselves into capitalist undertakings'.[10] This was a general trend after 1848, in Latin America and East Asia as much as Central Europe and it meant that landowners now came to have new expectations and requirements of the state. 'The landowners were trying to maximise profits by turning themselves into big local agrobusiness or efficient tax-collectors', writes Christopher Bayly, who mentions 'Prussian junkers, Mexican *hacendados*, and Javenese *regenten*' as examples. 'Entrepreneurial landed interests like this needed the government to put in roads, railways, and canals for them. Equally, the administrators needed the support of big landowners, provided they could be persuaded to reform sufficiently to head off peasant revolt and the hostility of urban dwellers'.[11]

But very few of the existing states had the structural capacity to make these provisions on the scale required. What made at least some fractions among the existing feudal ruling class opt for revolution was the need to respond to the immediate danger of defeat in war:

> The impetus towards these reforms had been the success of Great Britain and the failure of most of the continental countries in the middle of the century. In 1856, Russia had been humiliated in the Crimean War's outcome. Austria had been defeated in 1859 by the French and the Piedmontese, who established the kingdom of Italy in 1861. Prussia had been humiliated in 1850 by the Austrians. In the 1850s, most countries experienced financial confusion, and needed serious reforms and considerable loans to make good. But financiers would not give money unless

9 Blum 1978, p. 376.

10 Hobsbawm 1975, p. 188.

11 Bayly 2004, p. 298.

> there were reforms. One of these was that the running of the state should be entrusted, not to a Court and its hangers-on, but to experts, with the backing of law.[12]

The untransformed state therefore acted as a block to supporting capitalist expansion, restoring military capability, and achieving the financial stability necessary for either.

> To be a Great Power – and in Central Europe or Japan merely to survive – it was useful to have a central government wielding infrastructural coordination of its territories than confederal regimes could muster. Self-styled 'modernisers' everywhere regarded this as essential. Neither German nor Japanese confederations nor transnational dynasties could provide this. Their survival in war or anticipated war was in jeopardy, and so they fell.[13]

They fell, or at least some did; but who pushed them? The second variant of bourgeois revolution involved a group that was both larger and which occurred over a considerably shorter timescale than those of the first variant. Here, the period between 1848 and 1871, particularly the years after 1859, is decisive. The unifications of Italy, Germany and Canada, the re-unification of the US and the Japanese Meiji Restoration were, with the partial exceptions of the Italian guerrilla and role of the Black regiments in the American Civil War, 'revolutions from above' to a far greater extent than their predecessors were 'revolutions from below', the characteristic form being wars of territorial conquest and integration. Also characteristic of these revolutions was the ability of one territory – Piedmont, Prussia, the North, Upper Canada, Choushu-Satsuma – to act as the core of a new state, forcing, bribing or persuading other adjacent territories into submission. In Italy, Germany and Japan leadership was classically provided by sections of the existing feudal ruling class, aware of their declining geopolitical position and the threat from a growing working class. 'If revolution there is to be', said Bismarck in 1866, 'let us rather undertake it than undergo it'.[14] In Canada, intervention by the bureaucracy of the British colonial state was decisive. Only in the Northern side of the Civil War were local bourgeois politicians central and this case is virtually unique among all bourgeois revolutions in involving actual industrial capitalists among the leadership.

12 Stone 1983, pp. 17–18.

13 Mann 1993, p. 354.

14 Quoted in Gall 1986, p. 305.

The list of bourgeois revolutions down to 1871 only includes eight successful cases – nine if we also include the Scottish case (1692–1746) as a distinct process.[15] The majority of emergent nation states, in Europe at least, did not have to undergo even the decisive process from above typical of the later nineteenth-century bourgeois revolutions. Writing in 1891, one Portuguese republican writer, Joao Falcao, suggested that his nation had the possibility of alternative revolutionary paths, from above or below: 'There is only one remedy, and this remedy must come from the Revolution. Either Revolution made by the King or the revolution made by the people'.[16] In fact, neither was required. Instead, the global dominance of capitalist laws of motion, the need to compete with, or at least defend themselves against those states which had already undergone it, impelled those capable of doing so into a more-or-less prolonged pattern of cumulative structural change or accelerated reform without any single event carrying the main burden of decisive transformation. In some parts of Europe, principally in Scandinavia, this took place relatively peacefully. In others, such as the Iberian Peninsula, it was punctuated by a series of coups and insurrections which individually amounted to little, but cumulatively shaped the existing state into one structured by capitalist imperatives: in Spain these episodes mark the years 1808, 1820, 1834–43, 1854 and 1868, concluding with the fall of the monarchy in 1931; in neighbouring Portugal a series of parallel developments with an overlapping chronology can be traced from 1808, 1820, 1836 and 1846–47, culminating in the final overthrow of the local dynasty in 1910. 'The 1910 revolution did not usher in the millennium or a social revolution', one of its historians drily observes: 'The men who took power on October 5 were largely middle-class intellectuals and professional men, some of whom were ambitious for public office'.[17] In both cases, the possibility of socialist revolution had arisen decades before the final nails were tapped into the political coffins of their kings.

It was mainly smaller states which were able to transform in this extended way, however; for the surviving multinational empires this was impossible and the majority did not have personnel capable of forcing the issue from top-down. The Prussian Junkers and Japanese Samurai created or (in the case of the latter) recreated an Emperor in order to lend the legitimacy of tradition to

15 The complexities of the Scottish case are too great to detail here, but although chronologically occurring in the first period, it actually represents the earliest example of a 'bourgeois revolution from above'. See Davidson 2003 and, for summary of the argument, Davidson 2010a.

16 Quoted in Wheeler 1972, p. 175.

17 Wheeler 1972, p. 189.

their revolutionary achievement: the establishment of the empires themselves largely followed. In those states where emperors and their empires already existed, and had done so for centuries, as in those of the Ottomans, Romanovs and Hapsburgs, no such comparable level of ruling-class intelligence was at work. With the exception of Britain's Irish colony, which liberated most of its territory between 1916 and 1921, the location of the bourgeois revolutions after 1871 therefore shifted inexorably east and south of Europe, where the surviving pre-capitalist imperial states ruled over the main regions in which the bourgeois revolution was still to be accomplished. But if fractions of the existing ruling class were not capable of bringing these about from above, were there social forces capable of doing so from below? This was the problem with which Marxists in the Second International were faced in the years between its formation in 1889 and the outbreak of war in 1914. Of the three states concerned, Russia received their closest attention

Second International Marxism and the Problem of the 'Late' Bourgeois Revolutions

By the end of the nineteenth century it was generally accepted within the Second International that the bourgeoisie was no longer the revolutionary force it had been, even in 1848. Specifically, this meant that it would not play a revolutionary role in Russia, where the next great revolution was expected. In a speech to the founding congress of the Second International in 1889, Georgy Plekhanov said that, in relation to the overthrow of the autocracy: 'the revolutionary movement in Russia will triumph only as a working-class movement or else it will never triumph!'[18] The position was restated by Peter Struve in the 1898 Manifesto of the Russian Social-Democratic Worker's Party (RSDWP): 'The further east one goes in Europe, the meaner, more cowardly and politically weak the bourgeoisie becomes, and the greater are the cultural and political tasks that fall to the proletariat'. Struve was then at the beginning of a political descent that would see him move from 'Legal' Marxism to Liberalism to supporting the White counterrevolutionary movement in the Russian Civil War. Nevertheless, at this point, his conclusion was clear: 'The Russian proletariat will cast off the yoke of autocracy, so that it may continue the struggle with capitalism and the bourgeoisie with still greater energy until the complete victory of socialism'.[19] It was also generally accepted that a period of capitalist

18 Plekhanov 1961, p. 454.
19 Struve 1983, p. 224.

development would be necessary once the autocracy had been overthrown, in order to develop the productive forces to the point where socialism was achievable – a position that did not, of course, imply an uncritical attitude toward capitalism.

It was in the context of these general perspectives that the term 'permanent revolution' – first raised by Marx and Engels during the revolutions of 1848 and long since forgotten – now re-entered Marxist debates.[20] The first person to revive it seems to have been the Russian revolutionary David Ryazanov during his 1903 critique of the draft programme of *Iskra*, the paper of the RSDWP.[21] Within a year, however, it had once more become part of a general discourse of the centre and left wings of the Second International in Central and Eastern Europe, as a means of encapsulating how the working class would have to carry out the bourgeois revolution in Russia. Kautsky, Lenin, Luxemburg, Mehering, Plekhanov, Parvus, and Trotsky all held this perspective, with only Lenin refusing the actual term 'permanent revolution' and only Trotsky investing the term with a significantly different content. But even Lenin's refusal was semantic rather than substantive. During a discussion about the need to prepare for a forthcoming struggle between the rural proletariat and the peasant bourgeoisie, written during the revolution of 1905, Lenin wrote:

> For from the democratic revolution we shall at once, and precisely in accordance with the measure of our strength, the strength of the class-conscious and organized proletariat, begin to pass to the socialist revolution. We stand for uninterrupted revolution. We shall not stop half-way.[22]

Lenin's position was in fact a variant of the dominant position of the centre and left of the Second International, which, before 1905 at least, was also shared by the Mensheviks. It involved a continuum of views, the main difference between these views being the extent to which they regarded the peasantry as capable of independent activity, the nature of the relationship between the working class and the peasantry, and whether one or both of these classes would either seek to form a post-revolutionary government or abdicate immediately in favour of representatives of the bourgeoisie.

Some Marxists outside Russia were prepared to give the Russian bourgeoisie the benefit of the doubt. In an article first published in 1903 Kautsky wrote: 'To-day we can nowhere speak of a revolutionary bourgeoisie', adding,

20 Davidson 2012, pp. 144–8.

21 Ryazanov 2009, p. 131.

22 Lenin 1962c, pp. 237–8.

at the beginning of the revolution of 1905, 'with the possible exception of Russia'.[23] Kautsky was disabused of this notion during the 1905 Revolution, but within Russia itself, the Mensheviks now began to entertain precisely the illusions in the Russian bourgeoisie that the Russian movement and the Second International as a whole had previously rejected. At the beginning of 1905 their leader Julius Martov wrote: 'We have the right to expect that sober political calculation will prompt our bourgeois democracy to act in the same way in which, in the past century, bourgeois democracy acted in Western Europe, under the inspiration of revolutionary romanticism'.[24] Of course, the working class would be a participant in the bourgeois revolution, but only under bourgeois leadership. This meant that it could not undertake any forms of struggle that might cause the bourgeoisie to retreat from their mission – although the very fact that this was a concern should have spoken volumes about the reliability of the bourgeoisie as a revolutionary force. 'Social relations in Russia have not matured beyond the point of bourgeois revolution', said Pavel Axelrod. 'History impels workers and revolutionaries more and more strongly towards bourgeois revolutionism, making them involuntary political servants of the bourgeoisie, rather than in the direction of genuine socialist revolutionism and the tactical and organisational preparation of the proletariat for political rule'.[25] Their misplaced faith in the bourgeoisie, and the unwarranted assumption that the proletariat would exercise a self-denying ordinance, involved illusions that would ultimately lead the Mensheviks to substitute themselves for the former and attempt to restrain the latter.

Lenin was scathing, denouncing 'their doctrinaire and lifeless distortion of Marxism': 'They argue that the revolution is a bourgeois one and therefore ... we must retrace our steps in the same measure the bourgeoisie succeeds in obtaining concessions from Tsarism'. Later in the same article he mocked 'the magnificent principle: the revolution is a bourgeois revolution – therefore comrades, watch out lest the bourgeois recoil!'[26]

Lenin and the Bourgeois-Democratic Revolution

In Lenin's own case there is a problem of reconciling apparently contradictory positions in relation to his discussion of the Russian Revolution, at least until

23 Kautsky 2009b, p. 176.
24 Quoted in Deutscher 2003a, p. 99.
25 Axelrod 1976, p. 60.
26 Lenin 1962d, pp. 382–3.

April 1917, when he changed his assessment of its nature. Take for example these two passages on the nature of pre-revolutionary Russia, from adjoining pages of the same article. In the first Lenin argues that 'since the entire economic life of the country has already become bourgeois in all its main features, since the overwhelming majority of the population is in fact already living in bourgeois conditions of existence, the anti-revolutionary elements are naturally extremely few in number, constituting truly a mere "handful" as compared with the "people" '. On this account the Russian economy is essentially capitalist, but only a few paragraphs later he seems to backtrack from this position:

> True, in Russia capitalism is more highly developed at the present time than it was in Germany in 1848, to say nothing of France in 1789; but there is no doubt about the fact that in Russia purely capitalist antagonisms are very, very much overshadowed by the antagonisms between 'culture' and Asiatic barbarism, Europeanism and Tartarism, capitalism and feudalism; in other words, the demands that are being put first today are those the satisfaction of which will develop capitalism, cleanse it of the slag of feudalism and improve the conditions of life and struggle both for the proletariat and for the bourgeoisie.[27]

The inconsistency could be resolved if Lenin was in fact discussing two different aspects of Russian society, one being the dominant mode of production and the other the form of the state. There are certainly a number of historical examples, notably the United Netherlands and England, where bourgeois revolutions were made against foreign or native absolutist states in societies in which the transition to capitalism was all but complete. Russia was clearly nowhere near as advanced in capitalist terms as these forerunners; nevertheless as long as we understand that 'dominance' by the capitalist mode of production does not mean that the majority of social relations of production have to be capitalist – Lenin rightly did not believe this to be the case – we can still regard the Russian economy as a whole as subject to capitalist laws of motion.

How then did Lenin conceive of the nature of the Russian Revolution? Like everyone else on the Marxist left apart from Trotsky he argued that it could only be a bourgeois revolution, but his writings contain by far the most detailed arguments for this claim of anyone in his or the preceding generation of revolutionaries. Here is a passage written during the 1905 Revolution, which starts from the proposition that 'Marxists are absolutely convinced of the bourgeois character of the Russian revolution':

27 Lenin 1962e, pp. 75–6.

> What does this mean? It means that the democratic reforms in the political system and the social and economic reforms, which have become a necessity for Russia, do not in themselves imply the undermining of capitalism, the undermining of bourgeois rule; on the contrary, they will, for the first time, really clear the ground for a wide and rapid, European, and not Asiatic, development of capitalism; they will, for the first time, make it possible for the bourgeoisie to rule as a class.... The bourgeois revolution is precisely a revolution that most resolutely sweeps away the survivals of the past, the remnants of serfdom (which include not only autocracy but monarchy as well) and most fully guarantees the broadest, freest and most rapid development of capitalism. That is why a bourgeois revolution is in the highest degree advantageous to the proletariat. A bourgeois revolution is absolutely necessary in the interests of the proletariat. The more complete and determined, the more consistent the bourgeois revolution, the more assured will be the proletarian struggle against the bourgeoisie for Socialism.[28]

Who would lead these revolutions? In Lenin's own words: 'Does not the very concept "bourgeois revolution" imply that it can be accomplished only by the bourgeoisie?' As we have seen, he decisively rejected this implication and Menshevik attempts to base a strategy around it, arguing instead that the proletariat and peasantry would not only benefit from the success of a bourgeois revolution in Russia but would be responsible for making it:

> A liberation movement that is bourgeois in social and economic content is not such because of its motive forces. The motive force may be, not the bourgeoisie, but the proletariat and the peasantry. Why is this possible? Because the proletariat and the peasantry suffer even more than the bourgeoisie from the survivals of serfdom, because they are in greater need of freedom and the abolition of landlord oppression. For the bourgeoisie, on the contrary, complete victory constitutes a danger, since the proletariat will make use of full freedom against the bourgeoisie, and the fuller that freedom and the more completely the power of the landlords has been destroyed, the easier will it be for the proletariat to do so. Hence the bourgeoisie strives to put an end to the bourgeois revolution half-way from its destination, when freedom has been only half-won, by a deal with the old authorities and the landlords.[29]

28 Lenin 1962b, pp. 48–50.

29 Lenin 1962g, pp. 334–5.

Members of the bourgeoisie were unwilling to wage a decisive struggle against the autocracy and everything associated with it, not because they feared the actual strength of the regime, but rather because they feared the potential strength of the proletariat which, growing in conditions of untrammelled capitalist development and political freedom, would pose a far greater threat to their property than the Tsarist state. Kautsky, like the majority of the centre and left of the Second International, agreed with Lenin that revolutionary leadership could no longer be provided by the bourgeoisie, and for essentially the same reasons:

> The age of the bourgeois revolutions, i.e., of revolutions in which the bourgeoisie was the driving force, is over in Russia as well [as in Western Europe]. There too the proletariat is no longer an appendage and tool of the bourgeoisie, as it was in the bourgeois revolutions, but an independent class with independent revolutionary aims. But whenever the proletariat emerges in this way the bourgeoisie ceases to be a revolutionary class. The Russian bourgeoisie, insofar as it is liberal and has an independent policy at all, certainly hates absolutism but it hates revolution even more, and it hates absolutism because it sees it as the fundamental cause of revolution; and insofar as it asks for political liberty, it does so above all because it believes that it is the only way to bring an end to the revolution.[30]

Introducing this article to a Russian readership, Lenin was quick to assimilate Kautsky's position to his own: 'A bourgeois revolution, brought about by the proletariat and the peasantry in spite of the instability of the bourgeoisie – this fundamental principle of Bolshevik tactics is wholly confirmed by Kautsky'.[31] In fact, although tentative, the conclusions drawn by Kautsky as to the nature of the Russian Revolution are different from those of the Bolsheviks: 'The bourgeoisie therefore does not constitute one of the driving forces of the present revolutionary movement in Russia and to this extent we cannot call it a bourgeois one', he wrote. The assumption here is that bourgeois revolutions must be led by the bourgeoisie – a position that Kautsky had earlier rejected and that Lenin continued to reject. This is not, however, the most important difference. After confessing to being uncertain about the nature of the Russian Revolution, Kautsky eventually arrived at this formula:

30 Kautsky 2009e, p. 605.

31 Lenin 1962f, p. 411.

> We should most probably be fair to the Russian Revolution and the tasks that it sets us if we viewed it as neither a bourgeois revolution in the traditional sense nor a socialist one but as quite a unique process which is taking place on the borderline between bourgeois and socialist society, which requires the dissolution of the one while preparing for the creation of the other and which in any case brings all those who live in capitalist civilization a significant step forward in their development.[32]

The article from which these remarks are taken is one of a series written around the period of the 1905 Russian Revolution when Kautsky temporarily fell under the influence of Luxemburg – it is, in other words, a position associated with the height of his radicalism, not one prefiguring his later collapse into reformism. Indeed, those who remained politically aligned with Lenin after the collapse of the Second International, like Luxemburg herself, displayed similar uncertainties to those of Kautsky in defining the nature of the Russian Revolution:

> *In its content*, the present revolution in Russia goes far beyond previous revolutions, and, in its methods, it cannot simply follow either the old bourgeois revolutions or the previous – parliamentary – struggles of the modern proletariat. It has created a new method of struggle, which accords both with its proletarian character and with the combination of the struggle for democracy and the struggle against capital – namely, the revolutionary mass strike. In terms of content and methods, it is therefore a completely new type of revolution. Being formally bourgeois-democratic, but essentially proletarian-socialist, it is, in both content and method, *a transitional form* from the bourgeois revolutions of the past to the proletarian revolutions of the future, which will directly involve the dictatorship of the proletariat and the realization of socialism.[33]

Although he did not directly engage with Kautsky and Luxemburg on this issue, Lenin insisted that there was no necessary contradiction between working-class agency and bourgeois outcome, and consequently no difficulty in identifying the nature of the Russian Revolution:

> Bourgeois revolutions are possible, and have occurred, in which the commercial, or commercial and industrial, bourgeoisie played the part of the

32 Kautsky 2009, p. 607.

33 Luxemburg 2009, p. 526.

> chief motive force. The victory of such revolutions was possible as the victory of the appropriate section of the bourgeoisie over its adversaries (such as the privileged nobility or the absolute monarchy). In Russia things are different. The victory of the bourgeois revolution is impossible in our country *as the victory of the bourgeoisie*. This sounds paradoxical, but it is a fact. The preponderance of the peasant population, its terrible oppression by the semi-feudal big landowning system, the strength and class-consciousness of the proletariat already organized in a socialist party – all these circumstances impart to *our* bourgeois revolution a *specific* character. This peculiarity does not eliminate the bourgeois character of the revolution.[34]

Lenin situated these arguments within a longer-term historical context. He acknowledged that participation by the popular masses had been decisive in winning at least some of the earlier bourgeois revolutions, above all those in England and France, but that they had been unable to achieve their own objectives once the bourgeoisie or its representatives had been installed in power. The modern equivalent of these forces, the urban proletariat, was however in a position to do so, on account of its greater numeric strength, deeper implantation in the process of production, and higher cultural level: 'Consequently, the specific feature of the Russian bourgeois revolution is merely that instead of the plebeian element of the towns taking second place as it did in the sixteenth, seventeenth and eighteenth centuries, it is the proletariat which is taking first place in the twentieth century'.[35]

For Russian Marxists in particular, their forthcoming revolution had two key elements, which they summarised by describing it as bourgeois-*democratic* in nature – a compound term that had not appeared in the work of Marx or Engels, but by which they meant that the Russian Revolution would be both bourgeois in content (that is, it would establish the unimpeded development of capitalism) and that it would introduce democratic politics that the working class could use to further its own demands. The introduction of democracy as an objective in the bourgeois revolution introduced a certain conceptual instability to the concept that found expression in descriptions of the revolution that went from being *bourgeois* to *bourgeois-democratic* to *democratic*. Here is an example of this slippage from Lenin:

34 Lenin 1963a, pp. 56–7.

35 Lenin 1963b, pp. 377–8.

> This is a democratic revolution, i.e., one which is bourgeois as regards its social and economic content. This revolution is overthrowing the autocratic semi-feudal system, extricating the bourgeois system from it, and thereby putting into effect the demands of all the classes of bourgeois society – in this sense being a revolution of the whole people.[36]

Similarly, in the first manifesto of the Russian Social-Democratic Labour Party (RSDLP) to be issued after the outbreak of the First World War, Lenin wrote: 'Since Russia is most backward and has not yet completed its bourgeois revolution, it still remains the task of Social-Democrats in that country to achieve the three fundamental conditions for consistent democratic reform, viz., a democratic republic (with complete equality and self-determination for all nations), confiscation of the landed estates, and an eight-hour working day'.[37] The problem here is that democracy is a political concept that has no necessary connection to, still less equivalence with, 'bourgeois ... social and economic content'. Democracy may be desirable, even essential, for the proletariat to develop ideologically and organisationally to the point where it could challenge for power, but that is precisely why the bourgeoisie was hostile toward it. In fact, the necessity of democracy for the working class was true whether or not the bourgeois revolution had been achieved, as in Germany, or whether it had not, as in Russia. The German Empire was scarcely a model of parliamentary representation, and consequently elevating democracy to a necessary outcome of the bourgeois revolution would then cast doubt on whether it had been completed in Germany, or any of the other areas characterised by revolutions from above.

Lenin did not make this move and seems in fact to have had two alternative conceptions of the path to bourgeois revolution in Russia, based on the 'two types of bourgeois agrarian evolution' that had previously occurred in Europe and its overseas extensions. In the first, the 'Prussian' or reformist path that had been underway in Russia since the agrarian reform of 1861, the landowners of the great estates would gradually replace feudal methods of exploitation with those of capitalism, retaining feudal instruments of social control over their tenants (at least in the medium term), but ultimately transforming themselves into large capitalist landowners or farmers. In the second, the 'American' or revolutionary path, the landowners are overthrown, feudal or other precapitalist controls are removed and the estates redistributed among the previous

36 Lenin 1962e, p. 75.

37 Lenin 1964b, p. 33.

tenants, who now emerge as a new class of medium capitalist farmers.[38] The point here is less the accuracy of Lenin's distinction between the Prussian and American paths – in fact his discussion of the former is accurate, that of the latter considerably less so – than that these alternative paths to bourgeois revolution offered different sets of conditions for the proletariat and its peasant allies to conduct future struggles.

In arguing that the proletariat could be the agent of bourgeois revolution in Russia, he had returned to the paradox, which Marx and Engels had noted from the 1860s onward, that at least some of the objectives of the revolutions of 1848 had eventually been carried out by their opponents:

> If you want to consider the question 'historically', the example of any European country will show you that it was a series of governments ... that carried out the historical aims of the bourgeois revolution, that even the governments which defeated the revolution were nonetheless forced to carry out the historical aims of that defeated revolution.[39]

The proletariat would not therefore be the first class to carry out the bourgeois revolution in the absence of the bourgeoisie, a fact that had specific implications for Russia. In his reflections on the fiftieth anniversary of the 'peasant reform' of 1861, Lenin described it as 'a bourgeois reform carried out by feudal landowners' at the instigation of the greatest feudal landowner of all, Tsar Alexander II, who, like Bismarck, had 'to admit that it would be better to emancipate from above than to wait until he was overthrown from below'. Lenin identified three main reasons for these initiatives: to control the growth of capitalist relations of production stimulated by the increase in trade; to overcome military failure in the Crimean War through the expansion of arms manufacture; and to pacify an upsurge of peasant insurgency in the countryside. But even these reforms were only achieved through 'a struggle waged *within* the ruling class, a struggle waged for the most part *within the ranks of the landowner class*'.[40]

These arguments were liable to two different interpretations. One was that the Prussian path could begin the era of bourgeois revolution in Russia, but could not complete it, above all it could not achieve democracy; what Lenin called 'consummation' would therefore have to be the work of the proletariat and peasantry. As we have seen, this was the interpretation that dominated in

38 Lenin 1960, p. 239; Lenin 1962f, pp. 238–41.

39 Lenin 1962b, p. 42.

40 Lenin 1963a, pp. 120–2, 125.

Lenin's writings. The other was that the entire bourgeois revolution in Russia could be carried out by following the Prussian path – an interpretation that inevitably meant accepting that it need not involve democracy at all. Lenin was clear that the type of revolution from above that had unified Germany during the 1860s had begun during the same decade in Russia but nowhere near consummated. He was typically scathing about anyone who suggested otherwise, as in the following broadside from 1911 against the Menshevik Larin and his co-thinkers, who had raised the examples of Austria and Germany:

> Why are they so fond of these examples? ... because in these countries, after the 'unsuccessful' revolution of 1848, the bourgeois transformation was completed 'without any revolution'. That is the whole secret! That is what gladdens their hearts, for it seems to indicate that bourgeois change is possible without revolution!! And if that is the case, why should we Russians bother our heads about a revolution? Why not leave it to the landlords and factory owners to effect the bourgeois transformation of Russia 'without any revolution'! It was because the proletariat in Austria and Prussia was weak that it was unable to prevent the landed proprietors and the bourgeoisie from effecting the transformation regardless of the interests of the workers, in a form most prejudicial to the workers, retaining the monarchy, the privileges of the nobility, arbitrary rule in the countryside, and a host of other survivals of medievalism.... Why were 'crises' in Austria and in Prussia in the 1860s constitutional, and not revolutionary? Because there were a number of special circumstances which eased the position of the monarchy (the 'revolution from above' in Germany, her unification by 'blood and iron'); because the proletariat was at that time extremely weak and undeveloped in those countries, and the liberal bourgeoisie was distinguished by base cowardice and treachery, just as the Russian Cadets are in our day.... But that's the whole point – to the reformist the twaddle about the consummated bourgeois revolution ... is simply a verbal screen to cover up his renunciation of all revolution.[41]

Lenin's central point here is that the existing German and Austrian ruling classes were able to carry through bourgeois revolutions from above because of the weakness of the labour movement. Their equivalents in Russia, even assuming that they were interested in carrying through such a transformation, had not done so and could not do so without opening up the possibility of a working-class intervention that might destroy them – an intervention

41 Lenin 1963c, pp. 231, 234–5, 241.

that reformists like Larin were threatening to divert with their claims that the bourgeois revolution had already been accomplished. Consequently, as Lenin wrote in another article from the same period, 'you cannot transfer to Russia the German completion of the bourgeois revolution, the German history of a democracy that had spent itself, the German "revolution from above" of the 1860s, and the actually existing German legality'.[42] There are two questionable aspects to this argument.

One is the equation of Austrian and German development. Lenin repeated the point in his virtually contemporaneous debate with Luxemburg on the national question, where he addressed what he called 'the fundamental question of the completion of the bourgeois-democratic revolution': 'In Austria, the revolution began in 1848 and was over in 1867. Since then a more or less fully established bourgeois constitution has dominated, for nearly half a century, and on its basis a legal worker's party is legally functioning'.[43] This contrasts with the view expressed only two years earlier, in a statement on the First Balkan War issued in the name of the RSDLP Central Committee but drafted by Lenin, where we learn: 'In Easter Europe – the Balkans, Austria and Russia – alongside areas of highly developed capitalism, we find masses oppressed by feudalism, absolutism and thousands of medieval relics'. There are subsequent references to 'landowning serf-masters', 'piratical dynasties' and 'medieval oppression'.[44] This latter, more nuanced position is clearly nearer the truth. The former has unusual affinities with positions held by Otto Bauer, a thinker with quite different politics. Throughout his great if flawed work on 'the question of nationalities, Bauer assumes, like Lenin in his polemic with Luxemburg, that Austria can be abstracted from the structure of the Austro-Hungarian Empire within which it was situated, as if this had no consequences for the way in which revolutionary struggles were likely to develop, particularly in relation to their nationalist content. In Bauer's case this is due to his obsession with maintaining the structure of the Hapsburg Empire through the granting of 'autonomy' to the constituent national groups, leading him to one of the most wildly inaccurate predictions – from an extensive field – in the history of the Second International:

> If Austria disintegrates within the epoch of capitalist society, it will not be torn apart by the old, liberal principle of nationality. Rather, it will disintegrate only if capitalist expansionism is able to bring the national

42 Leni, 1963b, p. 187.

43 Lenin 1964a, p. 406.

44 Lenin 1984, p. 85.

> will to serve its cause. The collapse of Austria presupposes the triumph of imperialism in the German Empire, in Russia, in Italy.[45]

In fact, as Michael Mann writes, contrasting the German (1871) and Austro-Hungarian (1867) empires, in the former: 'The regime was strengthened. The bourgeoisie mobilised behind it, disparaging federalism as reactionary. The opposite was occurring in Austria, where modernising ideologies were snatched from centralising liberals by regional "nationalists"'.[46] Lenin's error here is more puzzling than Bauer's, given his far greater sensitivity to the nature of the state; the implications of it would only become apparent after October 1917.

The other aspect, of far more immediate relevance to Russia, emerges in the undertone of disquiet in Lenin's argument, which finds expression in the very ferocity of his polemic against Larin. There is a venerable right-wing argument that holds that Lenin thought the opportunity for revolution in Russia might be 'missed' if the ruling class was capable of delivering a series of concessions and reforms sufficient to demobilise the working class in the short to medium term, and that this accounted for his insistence on making the revolution, no matter how 'premature' it may have been in developmental terms.[47] There is an element of truth in this assessment, namely that Lenin generally saw politics in terms of alternatives – this is, after all, one of the ways in which his work is incompatible with any conception of historical inevitability. It does not mean, however, that the alternative to revolution was a more consistent and wide-ranging version of the reforms tentatively initiated by the regime after the defeat of the 1905 Revolution.

In fact, no Russian politician or state manager had the necessary strategic insight to carry through such a programme after the assassination of Peter Stolypin in 1911 effectively put an end to agrarian reform. The real alternative to revolution in Russia was more likely to have been a slow-motion version of the internal disintegration, territorial dismemberment, and quasi-colonisation that characterised China. But if there was, realistically, only one path to bourgeois revolution in Russia, Lenin did concede that there could be two elsewhere. A successful bourgeois revolution need not involve a peasant revolution, either because a peasantry no longer exists or because the bourgeoisie has been able

45 Bauer 2000, p. 403. Trotsky was therefore wrong to suggest in his autobiography that Bauer and the Austro-Marxists had no conception of the impact international relations might have on Austria-Hungary. See Trotsky 1975.

46 Mann 1993, p. 311.

47 See, for example, Ulam 1969, p. 350.

to bypass or sideline it in the process of seizing power from the absolutist state. A revolution that did involve the peasantry and the masses more generally was more likely to result in progressive social measures than one that did not, but their absence did not mean that a bourgeois revolution had failed to occur.[48] Lenin made this explicit in one of his last discussions of bourgeois revolutions as a general phenomenon:

> If we take the revolutions of the twentieth century as examples we shall, of course, have to admit that the Portuguese [1910] and the Turkish [1908] revolutions are both bourgeois revolutions. Neither of them, however, is a 'people's' revolution, since in neither does the mass of the people, their vast majority, come out actively, independently, with their own economic and political demands to any noticeable degree. By contrast, although the Russian bourgeois revolution of 1905–07 displayed no such 'brilliant' successes as at time fell to the Portuguese and Turkish revolutions, it was undoubtedly a 'real people's' revolution, since the mass of the people, their majority, the very lowest social groups, crushed by oppression and exploitation, rose independently and stamped on the entire course of the revolution the imprint of *their* own demands, *their* attempt to build in their own way a new society in place of the old society that was being destroyed.[49]

Portugal and Turkey, at opposite ends of Europe, were only the most 'Western' of a series of events that indicated that the revolutionary tradition was acquiring a new spatial focus:

> The epoch of bourgeois-democratic revolutions in Western, continental Europe embraces a fairly definite period, approximately between 1789 and 1871. This was precisely the period of national movements and the creation of national states. When this period drew to a close, Western Europe had been transformed into a settled system of bourgeois states, which, as a general rule, were nationally uniform states.[50]

48 Lenin 1962f, pp. 351–2.
49 Lenin 1964e, p. 421.
50 Lenin 1964a, p. 405.

These revolutions did not have immediate sequels for, by 1871: 'The West had finished with bourgeois revolutions. The East had not yet risen to them'.[51] Over thirty years would elapse before 'the East' would resume the sequence:

> In Eastern Europe and Asia the period of bourgeois-democratic revolutions did not begin until 1905. The revolutions in Russia, Persia, Turkey and China, the Balkan wars – such is the chain of world events of *our* period in our 'Orient'. And only a blind man could fail to see in this chain of events the awakening of a *whole series* of bourgeois-democratic national movements which strive to create nationally independent and nationally uniform states.[52]

Down to 1871 bourgeois revolutions therefore involved the consolidation and unification of states in those areas where capitalism had emerged earliest and was now the most developed. The second period involved those areas that were, with the partial exception of China, under the informal domination of those whose bourgeois revolutions had been consummated during the first. Now the bourgeois revolutions were increasingly concerned not with national unification but national liberation, often involving a movement in two directions: externally, for the declining tributary empires to put an end to Western interference; internally, for the subject peoples of these empires to free themselves from central control. In those countries for which the bourgeois revolution still lay in the future, capitalist development remained relatively progressive. It was for this reason that Lenin welcomed the victory over Russia of Japan, the only Eastern country to have consummated its revolutionary era between 1871 and the opening of the new period of bourgeois revolution in 1905.[53]

Russia occupied a contradictory role in the world system for Lenin. At one level it clearly belonged alongside China, Persia, and Turkey as one of the 'Asiatic' empires; but it also played a role as one of the European great powers, and to a far greater extent than Turkey, the only other country that belonged to both groups. Membership of the great powers was, however, an indication of military capacity rather than economic development, and so a bourgeois revolution was still necessary. Perhaps the greatest distinction that Lenin made between Russia and the other eastern areas was that in the latter he still expected the bourgeoisie to play a revolutionary role, writing in 1912:

---

51 Lenin 1963e, p. 583.

52 Lenin 1964a, p. 406.

53 Lenin 1962a, p. 52.

> What has decayed is the Western bourgeoisie, which is already confronted by its grave-digger, the proletariat. But in Asia there is *still* a bourgeoisie capable of championing sincere, militant, consistent democracy, a worthy comrade of France's great men of the Enlightenment and great leaders of the close of the eighteenth century. The chief representative, or the chief social bulwark, of this Asian bourgeoisie that is still capable of supporting a historically progressive cause, is the peasant. And side by side with him there already exists a liberal bourgeoisie whose leaders ... are above all capable of treachery: yesterday they feared the emperor, and cringed before him; then they betrayed him when they saw the strength, and sensed the victory, of the revolutionary democracy; and tomorrow they will betray the democrats to make a deal with some old or new 'constitutional' emperor.[54]

But these expectations extended beyond China. The following year he wrote, in more general terms: 'Everywhere in Asia a mighty democratic movement is growing, spreading and gaining in strength. The bourgeoisie there is as yet siding with the people against reaction'.[55] In this regard, as in so many others, there was a close correlation between Lenin and Luxemburg, who wrote:

> Revolution is an essential for the process of capitalist emancipation. The backward communities must shed their obsolete political organizations, relics of natural and simple commodity production, and create a modern state machinery adapted to the purposes of capitalist production. The revolutions in Turkey, Russia, and China fall under this heading. The last two, in particular, do not exclusively serve the immediate political requirements of capitalism; to some extent they carry over outmoded pre-capitalist claims while on the other hand they already embody new conflicts which run counter to the development of capital.[56]

Lenin's belief that the nascent bourgeoisies of the East were more capable of waging successful bourgeois revolutions than their post-1848 analogues in the West was over-optimistic. Nader Sohrabi has emphasised the influence of the French Revolution on the revolutions in the Russian (1905), Persian (1906) and Ottoman empires (1908), not merely in the ubiquity of 'La Marseillaise' as an anthem, but as a programme for establishing a constitutional regime. As this

---

54 Lenin 1963d, p. 165.

55 Lenin 1963f, p. 99.

56 Luxemburg 1963, p. 419.

suggests, however, with the partial exception of Russia, the example which these revolutionaries drew from France, was not that of the Jacobin Republic, but the failed project for a reformed monarchy which initiated the revolutionary process:

> The crucial contribution of the French Revolution was that it made available the revolutionary paradigm of constitutionalism, a paradigm that structured the relationship of the challengers with the old regimes. The revolutionaries, instead of demanding the complete and sudden overthrow of the old regimes, asked for the creation of an assembly by means of which they intended to render the traditional structures of rule ineffective. This path to power gave the constitutional revolutions an altogether different dynamic than revolutions that took place after the Russian Revolution of 1917.[57]

Nevertheless, in the colonial or semi-colonial world, from Russia eastward, bourgeois revolutions were still necessary for development, through whatever agency. On this last point Lenin was unshakeable, particularly in relation to his own nation: the bourgeois revolution in Russia could not be avoided or bypassed:

> The degree of Russia's economic development (an objective condition), and the degree of class consciousness and organization of the proletariat (a subjective condition inseparably bound up with the objective condition) make the immediate and complete emancipation of the working class impossible.... Whoever wants to reach socialism by any other path than that of political democracy, will inevitably arrive at conclusions that are absurd and reactionary both in the economic and political sense.[58]

Only one Marxist thinker among Lenin's contemporaries was prepared to consider the possibility that the Russian Revolution might lead not only to the overthrow of absolutism but to socialism, provided it was joined by the revolutionary movement in the advanced West: Trotsky. His original position on the nature of the Russian Revolution was impeccably orthodox.[59] Yet, in little over a year, Trotsky had moved to a position far beyond what Marx could possibly

57 Sohrani 1996, p. 1441.
58 Lenin 1962b, pp. 28–9.
59 Trotsky no publication date, p. 70.

have envisaged in 1850, or what his fellow-revolutionaries who had revived the term 'permanent revolution' actually envisaged in 1905. How?

Trotsky's Unique Version of Permanent Revolution

Trotsky's own writings suggest that he had formulated his version of permanent revolution before the general strike and formation of the St. Petersburg Soviet in October 1905. The first reference occurs in an article from November in which he actually uses Lenin's preferred term:

> Overcoming the mighty resistance of the autocratic state and the conscious inactivity of the bourgeoisie, the working class of Russia has developed into an organized fighting force without precedent. There is no stage of the bourgeois revolution at which this fighting force, driven forward by the steel logic of class interests, could be appeased. Uninterrupted revolution is becoming the law of self-preservation of the proletariat.[60]

Trotsky seems to have rapidly moved to his version of permanent revolution during the course of 1905. His initial position was essentially that common to the centre and left of the Second International, stressing the necessity for the proletariat to play the leading role in the Russian bourgeois revolution. If anything distinguished his position at this stage it was a particular emphasis on the centrality of the urban areas in the struggle, a key theme of 'Up to the Ninth of January', written toward the end of 1904: 'Above all else, we must clearly understand that the *main arena of events will be the city*'.[61] Decades later Trotsky claimed for tactical reasons that his conception of permanent revolution was the same as that used by Marx in 1850 and then by some of his contemporaries, particularly Mehering and Luxemburg. In fact, two other figures were most responsible for Trotsky's radicalisation of the concept and for rendering it quite different from that of anyone else in the Marxist tradition: Parvus and Kautsky.

Trotsky had a close intellectual and political partnership with Parvus during the latter half of 1904 and all through 1905. Parvus had recognised affinities with his own work in Trotsky's 'Up to the Ninth of January' and wrote a preface for the first edition, which appeared early in 1905. In particular, Trotsky seems to have been influenced by what, in comparison to his own work at this time,

60 Trotsky 2009c, p. 455.

61 Trotsky 2009a, p. 329.

was the far greater historical depth of Parvus's work, particularly in relation to the origins of the Russian state and, later, to the emergence of capitalism in Russia:

> ... during the pre-capitalist period in Russia the cities developed more along the lines of China than in accordance with the European pattern. They were administrative centres with a purely bureaucratic character and did not have the slightest political significance; in economic terms they were merely political bazaars for the surrounding gentry and peasantry. Their development had hardly progressed at all when it was interrupted by the capitalist process, which began to create cities in its own pattern, that is, factory cities and centres of world commerce. The result is that, in Russia, we have a capitalist bourgeoisie but not the intermediate bourgeoisie from whom political democracy in Western Europe emerged and upon whom it depended.[62]

The latter point concerning revolutionary agency was of extreme importance. Parvus rightly rejected the notion that large-scale capitalists themselves had ever been actively revolutionary, but saw that previously the lower levels of the bourgeoisie, those closest to the petty bourgeoisie, had acted as a revolutionary force. In addition to its fear of the working class, the weakness of the Russian bourgeoisie as a historical latecomer was that it did not have this more plebeian wing to act as a stimulus and support for its 'noneconomic' element. These consisted of either 'the liberal professions ... those strata that stand apart from the relations of production', or those groups that were only beginning to be classified in Germany as the New Middle Class – 'the technical and commercial personnel of capitalist industry and trade and the corresponding branches of industry such as insurance companies, banks, and so forth'. The former had been important as a component of revolutionary movements between 1789 and 1848, and the latter would become an equally important component of revolutionary movements later in the twentieth century; but in the contemporary Russian context, Parvus pointed to their fragmentation and vacillation: 'These diverse elements are incapable of producing their own class programme, with the result that their political sympathies and antipathies endlessly waver between the revolutionism of the proletariat and the conservatism of the capitalists'.[63]

62 Parvus 2009, p. 265.

63 Parvus 2009, p. 265.

But why was the Russian proletariat so prone to 'revolutionism'? Parvus offers the beginning of an explanation in his comments on the formation of 'factory cities and centres of world trade': 'The very same pattern that hindered the development of petty-bourgeois democracy served to benefit the class consciousness of the proletariat in Russia, namely, the weak development of the handicraft form of production. The proletariat was immediately concentrated in the factories'.[64] Until the end of his life Trotsky continued to pay homage to the influence that Parvus exercised over him during this period. But, as Trotsky wrote of Parvus's position during the 1905 Revolution:

> His prognosis indicated, therefore, not the transformation of the democratic revolution into the socialist revolution but only the establishment in Russia of a regime of worker's democracy of the Australian type, where on the basis of a farmers' system there arose for the first time a labour government which did not go beyond the framework of a bourgeois state.

Trotsky rejected this comparison (the only one available to Parvus at the time) on the grounds that Australia had developed within a capitalist framework from the start, that the government was based on a relatively privileged working class, and that neither of these conditions applied to Russia.[65]

Kautsky's theoretical influence on Trotsky's version of permanent revolution seems to have been through two texts, one published before Trotsky had begun the process of rethinking the concept, the other after Trotsky had completed it but before he published a detailed presentation of his conclusions: in the latter case Kautsky was mainly responsible for deepening the historical and sociological foundations of Trotsky's argument. In the first text, 'Revolutionary Questions', from November 1904, Kautsky argues the widely accepted case that a revolution in Western Europe would have a detonative effect in the eastern part of the continent:

> The political rule of the proletariat in Western Europe would offer to the proletariat of Eastern Europe the possibility of shortening the stages of its development and artificially introducing socialist arrangements by imitating the German example. Society as a whole cannot artificially leap over particular stages of development, but the backward development of some of its particular constituent parts can indeed be accelerated by the proximity of more advanced parts.

64 Parvus 2009, p. 268.
65 Trotsky 1973, pp. 68–9.

He then goes on to make the bolder and less conventional argument, in effect allowing that the spatial priority of influence might be reversed:

> They [the Eastern European nations] may even come to the foreground because they are not hindered by the ballast of traditions that the older nations have to drag along.... That *can* happen. But as we already said, we have gone beyond the field of discernible *necessity* and are at present considering only *possibilities*.[66]

The second text by Kautsky to have influenced Trotsky was an article of February 1906, 'The American Worker', where the former attempts to establish the circumstances in which a working class can emerge without being 'hindered' by 'tradition'. Here, Kautsky tried to establish, for the first time since the less developed remarks by Parvus the previous year, not only why the working class in Russia *is* politically militant but also why it is *more* politically militant than those areas of the West that are the most developed in capitalist terms. Kautsky then develops his argument with reference to the nature of the Russian absolutist state – again deepening the insights of Parvus. Russia had access to capital from the West where capitalists were looking for new areas of investment and provided the basis for a historically unprecedented process of industrialisation: 'This transformed a great part of the Russian proletarians from lumpen proletarians or indigent small peasants into wage-workers, from timid and servile beggars into decided revolutionary fighters. But this growth of a strong fighting proletariat was not paralleled by the growth of a similarly strong Russian capitalist class'. The proletariat has the possibility of uniting all the most vital national forces around it in the struggle against foreign-based capital and the absolutist state that protects it:

> In this way, the Russian workers are able to exert a strong political influence, and the struggle for liberation of the land from the strangling octopus of absolutism has become a duel between the Czar and the working class; a duel in which the peasants provide an indispensable assistance, but in which they can by no means play a leading role.[67]

The nature of the Russian state helped condition the nature of the working-class response, as did the nature of the American state, but in the opposite direction:

---

66 Kautsky 2009c, p. 219.

67 Kautsky 2009f, p. 624.

> The Russian worker developed in a state which united the barbarism of Asiatic despotism with the means of coercion developed by modern absolutism in the eighteenth century: it is within this framework that the capitalist mode of production developed in Russia. As soon as the proletariat began to move, it immediately came across almost insuperable obstacles in every direction, experienced in the most painful way the insanity of the political situation, learned to hate it, and felt compelled to fight against it. It was impossible to attempt to reform this situation; the only possible course was a complete revolution of the established order. Thus, the Russian worker developed as an instinctive revolutionary, who enthusiastically adopted conscious revolutionary thought because only it stated in a clearer and more precise way what he had already obscurely felt and suspected. And he found a broad stratum of intellectuals which, like him, suffered under existing conditions; like him, were mostly condemned to live a wretched existence; like him, could only exist in a constant struggle against the existing order of things; and, like him, could only hope of deliverance through complete revolution.[68]

Trotsky's appreciation of these texts was partly methodological, partly substantive. But Trotsky also relies on the same article to support his argument for why the working class was the dominant force in the Russian Revolution with the peasantry playing only a subordinate role.[69] Trotsky's expectations of the working class were not, however, derived solely from the theoretical insights gained from his Marxist teachers: at least as important was the practical influence of the 1905 Revolution itself. Unlike Lenin, Trotsky was deeply involved in the process almost from the beginning: the revolution began in January; Trotsky returned to Russia in February; Lenin did not return until November. Most importantly, from October Trotsky played a leading role as chair of the most striking organisational innovation produced by the working class during the revolution: the St. Petersburg Soviet. In his speech to the court following the defeat of the revolution, Trotsky described the Soviet as 'the organ of self-government of the revolutionary masses', 'a new historical power' hitherto unknown.[70] No one had expected this development – certainly not the Bolsheviks who were initially suspicious of the soviet as a body not subject to party control – and it was only later that the Paris Commune came to be seen as a historical precursor. Trotsky argues that Kautsky's case for the 'possibility'

68 Kautsky 2009f, pp. 642–3.

69 Trotsky 1969b; 65–6; Trotsky 1969c, pp. 33–4.

70 Trotsky 1972a, pp. 399–400.

of a revolution breaking out in Russia in advance of the West in 'Revolutionary Questions' had been rendered more likely by events:

> Later on, the Russian proletariat revealed a colossal strength, unexpected by the Russian Social-Democrats even in their most optimistic moods. The course of the Russian Revolution was decided, so far as its fundamental features were concerned. What two or three years ago was or seemed *possible*, approached to the *probable*, and everything points to the fact that it is on the brink of becoming *inevitable*.[71]

The very show of working-class creativity and power demonstrated by the soviet and the general strike seems to have confirmed in Trotsky the view that it could indeed advance toward socialism, but only under one condition, the identification of which represents his most original contribution to these discussions: the international dimension.

It is in this context that Trotsky's differences with Kautsky are most marked. Here, in an article written in December at the climax of the 1905 Revolution, the latter claimed that the growing interconnectedness of the world system would prevent external intervention in the Russian Revolution, in contrast with earlier bourgeois revolutions:

> During the seventeenth century, international intercourse was still so limited that the English Revolution remained a purely local event that found no echo in the remainder of Europe. It was not foreign wars but the long drawn-out civil war arising from the great power of resistance of the landed nobility that created the revolutionary military domination and finally led to the dictatorship of the victorious general, Cromwell. The end of the eighteenth century already found a more developed intercourse between European nations, and the French Revolution convulsed all Europe; but its liberating efforts found only a weak echo. The convulsion was a result of the war that in France led to the rise of a military regime and the empire of the victorious general, Napoleon. Now, at the beginning of the twentieth century, international relations have become so close that the beginning of the revolution in Russia was enough to awaken an enthusiastic response in the proletariat of the whole world, to quicken the tempo of the class struggle, and to shake the neighbouring empire of Austria to its foundations. As a consequence, any *coalition*

71 Trotsky 1969b, pp. 105–6.

> of European powers against the revolution, such as took place in 1793, is inconceivable.[72]

It is true that the Russian Revolution did not provoke external intervention, but only because there was no need, the power of the Tsarist state still being sufficient for the purpose of counterrevolution at this point; the experience of the Russian Revolution of 1917 was to demonstrate how extraordinarily complacent Kautsky was in relation to this threat. Here, the mechanistic aspects of his thought, his lack of dialectics, genuinely point toward his later collapse in a way that most of the passages from his work quoted in this chapter do not. Adopting his guise as arch-proponent of the inevitability of socialism, Kautsky assumes that working-class pressure against intervention would invariably be successful rather than involve a contest that, despite some successes for the labour movement (for example, the British 'Hands off Russia' campaign of 1919), the bourgeoisie won to the extent that they were able to intervene in the Russian Civil War. But there is a greater problem with Kautsky's formulation than excessive optimism. His entire perspective on 'the international' envisages a collection of national states in which an internal event in one, like a revolution, has an external effect on others by way of provoking opposition or support: there is no sense here that the international capitalist system has a collective reality of its own, or that individual revolutions are merely national manifestations of the general crisis of that system. Typically, Luxemburg had a far greater sense of how both bourgeois and proletarian revolutions since 1789 ('modern revolutions') were uncontainable within the framework of individual states:

> Nothing is more foolish and absurd than wanting to regard modern revolutions as national incidents, as events that display all their force only within the borders of the state in question and exert only a more or less weak influence on the 'neighbouring states' according to their 'internal situation'. Bourgeois society, capitalism, is an international, *world* form of human society. There are not as many bourgeois societies, as many capitalisms, as there are modern states or nations, but only *one* international bourgeois society, only *one* capitalism, and the apparently isolated, independent existence of particular states within their state frontiers, alongside the single and inseparable world economy, is only one of the contradictions of capitalism. That is why all the modern revolutions are also at bottom *international* revolutions. They are also one and the

72 Kautsky 2009d, p. 535.

> same violent bourgeois revolution, which took place in different acts over the whole of Europe between 1789 and 1848 and established modern bourgeois rule *on an international basis*.[73]

While this captures an important aspect of any revolution occurring in Russia and points east in the early twentieth century, Luxemburg still tends to retain the distinction between bourgeois and proletarian revolutions. It is this that Trotsky began to question, asking, 'Is it inevitable that the proletarian dictatorship should be shattered against the barriers of the bourgeois revolution, or is it possible that in the given *world-historical* conditions, it may discover before it the prospect of victory on breaking through those barriers?'[74] What were these world-historical conditions? The key issue is the outcome of a bourgeois revolution that occurs in the period when capitalist laws of motion already operate across the world economy as a whole: 'Imposing its own type of economy and its own relations on all countries, capitalism has transformed the entire world into a single economic and political organism'.[75] The consolidation of capitalism as a global system permeates every aspect of Trotsky's argument, beginning with his discussion of the nature of the Russian Revolution:

> So far as its direct and indirect tasks are concerned, the Russian revolution is a 'bourgeois' revolution because it sets out to liberate bourgeois society from the chains and fetters of absolutism and feudal ownership. But the principal driving force of the Russian revolution is the proletariat, and that is why, so far as its method is concerned, it is a proletarian revolution. Many pedants, who insist on determining the historical role of the proletariat by means of arithmetical or statistical calculations, or establishing it by means of formal historical analogies, have shown themselves incapable of digesting this contradiction. They see the bourgeoisie as the providence-sent leader of the Russian revolution. They try to wrap the proletariat – which, in fact, marched at the head of events at all stages of the revolutionary rising [1905] – in the swaddling-clothes of their own theoretical immaturity. For such pedants, the history of one capitalist nation repeats the history of another, with, of course, certain more or less important divergences. Today they fail to see the unified process of world capitalist development which swallows up all the countries that lie in its path and which creates, out of the national and general exigencies

73 Luxemburg 2009, p. 524.

74 Trotsky 1969b, p. 67.

75 Trotsky 2009b, p. 444; Trotsky 1969b, p. 107.

> of capitalism, an amalgam whose nature cannot be understood by the application of historical clichés, but only by materialist analysis.[76]

Trotsky occasionally came close to suggesting that the victory of the Russian Revolution on a socialist basis was preordained ('becoming *inevitable*'); but in more considered passages he rightly highlighted that this was dependent on what happened after the overthrow of the absolutist regime. If the political representatives of the proletariat took state power, should they then hand it over to representatives of the bourgeois classes that had been unable and unwilling to do so? He argued that such a self-denying ordinance should be rejected by socialists:

> To imagine that it is the business of Social-Democrats to enter a provisional government and lead it during the period of revolutionary-democratic reforms, fighting for them to have a most radical character, and relying for this purpose upon the organised proletariat – and then, after the democratic programme has been carried out, to leave the edifice they have constructed so as to make way for the bourgeois parties and themselves go into opposition, thus opening up a period of parliamentary politics, is to imagine the thing in a way that would compromise the very idea of a worker's government. This is not because it is inadmissible 'in principle' – putting the question in this abstract form is devoid of meaning – but because it is absolutely unreal, it is utopianism of the worst sort – a sort of revolutionary-philistine utopianism.[77]

For Trotsky, there were two reasons why a Social Democratic government would have to take more radical action than allowed for by the formula of 'bourgeois-democratic' revolution. One was the relationship between that government and the Russian working class. As he put it: 'Social Democrats cannot enter a revolutionary government, giving the workers in advance an undertaking not to *give way* on the minimum programme and at the same time promising the bourgeoisie not to *go beyond* it'.[78] To take the most obvious example: what attitude should a Social Democrat government take if workers began to take over factories, expropriate the owners, and run the enterprises themselves? Such actions would clearly be in breach of capitalist property relations – in other words, they would go beyond the supposedly bourgeois limits of the revolution. If the

76 Trotsky 1972a, p. 66.

77 Trotsky 1969b, p. 77.

78 Trotsky 1969b, p. 80.

government acted to restore the previous owners, it would be betraying its own supporters, thus weakening its social base and encouraging the bourgeoisie to resist any further attempts to dispossess them. '"Self-limitation" by a workers' government would mean nothing other than the betrayal of the interests of the unemployed and strikers – more, of the whole proletariat – in the name of the establishment of a republic'.[79] But if the government did not restore the former owners and instead supported working-class seizures of private property, then it would openly be declaring itself in conflict with capitalism. Such a conflict would not be confined to the native bourgeoisie, since so much of Russian capital was foreign in origin, although ruling-class solidarity against the threat of revolution would impel other states to intervene regardless of any actual investments their national capitals might have had in Russia.

The inevitability of intervention is the second reason why the Russian Revolution would be forced to move in a socialist direction.

> Should the Russian proletariat find itself in power, if only as the result of a temporary conjuncture of circumstances in our bourgeois revolution, it will encounter the organised hostility of world reaction, and on the other hand will find a readiness on the part of the world proletariat to give organised support. Left to its own resources, the working class of Russia will inevitably be crushed by the counter-revolution the moment the peasantry turns its back on it. It will have no alternative but to link the fate of its political rule, and, hence, the fate of the whole Russian revolution, with the fate of the socialist revolution in Europe. That colossal state-political power given it by a temporary conjuncture of circumstances in the Russian bourgeois revolution it will cast into the scales of the class struggle of the entire capitalist world.[80]

The Russian Revolution will both act as an inspiration to the global working class and exert a powerful claim on their solidarity, the most effective form of which would be other working-class revolutions in those states where the bourgeois revolution was already a matter of history. The implications of this argument (which Trotsky made more explicit in later writings) are that these revolutions would not only be undertaken in support of the Russian Revolution, but also because workers in other countries would also seek to replicate its socialist aims on their own behalf. Revolutions cannot be initiated acts of will, however, they require in addition a series of crises, the existence of

79 Trotsky 1972b, p. 333.
80 Trotsky 1969b, p. 115.

which outside of Russia was itself an indication of the way in which the world system formed a totality.

The final issue to be discussed by Trotsky was the fundamental one of Russia's socio-economic backwardness. This reality, emphasised most strongly among his contemporaries by Lenin, was the key factor in preventing any of them from accepting that socialism was possible in Russia, fixated as they were on Russia as an individual nation. Trotsky was aware of the problem that would face any Social Democratic government on the day after seizing power: 'The revolutionary authorities will be confronted with the objective problems of socialism, but the solution of these problems will, at a certain stage, be prevented by the country's economic backwardness. There is no way out from this contradiction within the framework of a national revolution'.[81] The solution therefore lay outside this framework, since 'the objective pre-requisites for a socialist revolution have already been created by the economic development of the advanced capitalist countries'.[82] The socialist revolution in the West was therefore necessary for the Russian Revolution to survive on a socialist basis, not only as a source of class solidarity in the struggle against counterrevolution – although this would be the most immediate requirement – but also as the mechanism that would make available to the new regime the financial, technological, and scientific resources that would enable it to overcome the inheritance of Tsarist backwardness. Without these twin supports the Russian Revolution would, at best, start and finish as a bourgeois revolution:

> If the proletariat is overthrown by a coalition of bourgeois classes, including the peasantry whom the proletariat itself has liberated, then the revolution will retain its limited bourgeois character. But if the proletariat succeeds in using all means to achieve its own political hegemony and thereby breaks out of the national confines of the Russian revolution, then that revolution could become the prologue to a world socialist revolution.[83]

Although one of the boldest innovations in historical materialism since the death of Marx himself – only Lenin's model of the revolutionary party really stands comparison – Trotsky's version of permanent revolution was essentially a strategic rather than a theoretical conception. His awareness of the international context in which the Russian Revolution would take place enabled him

81 Trotsky 1972a, p. 333.
82 Trotsky 1969b, p. 100.
83 Trotsky 1972a, pp. 303–4.

to envisage a different outcome than any of his peers; but he no more than they gave any detailed answer to the question of why the Russian working class displayed the militancy that would enable it to begin the process of international socialist revolution in these apparently unpropitious conditions. The nearest Trotsky came to providing an answer is in this passage from *1905*, in which he distils the work of Parvus and Kautsky into one aspect of what he called 'the peculiarities of Russian development':

> When English or French capital, the historical coagulate of many centuries, appears in the steppes of the Donets Basin, it cannot release the same social forces, relations, and passions which once went into its own formation. It does not repeat on the new territory the development which it has already completed, but starts from the point at which it has arrived on its own ground. Around the machines which it has transported across the seas and the customs barriers, it immediately, without any intermediate stages whatever, concentrates the masses of a new proletariat, and into this class it instils the revolutionary energy of all the past generations of the bourgeoisie – an energy which in Europe has by now become stagnant.[84]

It would be over twenty years before Trotsky provided the missing theoretical underpinning for his strategy of permanent revolution, in the form of the 'law' of uneven and combined development, the embryo of which can be seen in this passage.[85] As he left the subject toward the end of the first decade of the twentieth century, however, there was one aspect in which his conception of the bourgeois revolution was narrower and less developed than that of Lenin: in both form and content it is almost entirely based on the French Revolution. His discussion moves from the success of 1789 in France, through to the failure of 1848 in Germany, to the prevision of future success revealed by 1905 in Russia.[86] He did not consider at this stage the very different way in which the German, Italian, or Japanese revolutions were eventually accomplished in the 1860s. The point, of which Lenin was only too aware, was that there might be another route to bourgeois revolution than through the agency of the working class, if not in Russia, then perhaps in other backward areas. Would the fast-disintegrating Ottoman Empire be one of them?

---

84 Trotsky 1972a, p. 68.

85 For an application of the theory to the War itself, see Anievas, in this volume.

86 Trotsky 2009b, pp. 437–45; Trotsky 1969b, pp. 52–61.

Turkey: Exception in Europe?

If there was one part of Europe outside Russia where everyone agreed a bourgeois revolution was still required, it was Turkey, which in some respects was experiencing at a lower level of pressure what Trotsky would later call 'uneven and combined development', whereby less-developed societies adapt forms which had emerged 'organically' in the earlier and more-developed. In some cases adaptation is merely decorative, as the Balkan states formerly part of the Ottoman Empire:

> In the countries of the Near East, as of the Far East (and to some extent Russia too), one can observe in all spheres of life how ready-made European forms and ideas, or sometimes merely their names, are borrowed in order to give expression to the requirements of a very much earlier historical period. Political and ideological masquerades are the lot of all backward peoples.[87]

But in some cases the process of combination, starting with the economy, begins to work through society as a whole, as Trotsky noted in his journalism from the Balkans immediately prior to the First World War:

> Like all backward countries, Bulgaria is incapable of creating new political and cultural forms through a free struggle of its own inner forces; it is obliged to assimilate the ready-made cultural products that European civilisation has developed in the course of its history. Whether particular ruling groups wish it or not, Bulgaria is obliged, and urgently, to build railways and to re-equip the army, and that means obtaining loans; in order to introduce proper accounting for these, parliamentary forms are required; European political programmes are imitated, the proletarianising of the population is facilitated, and this means that social legislation has to be introduced.[88]

The key question was whether proleterianisation had occurred on a sufficient scale for the working class to organise independently from other classes, let alone challenge for power. What was the situation in the Ottoman Empire prior to the outbreak of war?

---

87 Trotsky 1980d, p. 83.

88 Trotsky 1980c, p. 49.

Luxemburg was the first Marxist to address this issue. In the late 1890s she observed that until the end of the eighteenth century, Turkey had been oppressive for the majority of the people, but stable. These conditions changed during the nineteenth century: 'Shaken by conflict with the strong, centralised states of Europe, but especially threatened by Russia, Turkey found itself compelled to introduce domestic reforms [that] abolished the feudal government, and in its place introduced a centralised bureaucracy, a standing army and a new financial system'. The cost of these reforms was paid in taxation and duties by the population, burdens that went toward maintaining a hybrid form of state:

> In a strange mixture of modern and medieval principles, it consists of an immense number of administrative authorities, courts and assemblies, which are bound to the capital city in an extremely centralised manner in their conduct; but at the same time all public positions are *de facto* venal, and are not paid by the central government, but are mostly financed by revenue from the local population – a kind of bureaucratic benefice.[89]

The effect was 'a terrible deterioration in the material conditions of the people':

> But what made them particularly unbearable was a quite modern feature that had become involved in the situation – namely, *insecurity*: the irregular tax system, the fluctuating relations of land ownership, but above all the money economy as a result of the transformation of tax in kind into tax in money and the development of foreign trade.[90]

As Luxemburg notes, these changes were 'in a certain respect, reminiscent of Russia'. But with one crucial difference: whereas in Russia the reforms of 1861 and after established the basis for capitalist development and industrialisation, 'in Turkey an economic transformation corresponding to the modern reforms was completely lacking'.[91]

During the following decade, Kautsky also compared Russia and Turkey, noting that in both cases the state grew militarily, bureaucratically and fiscally in order to compete in geopolitical terms with the Western European powers, but only by accruing a massive national debt. There was, however, a major difference between Turkey and Russia:

89 Luxemburg 2003, p. 38.
90 Luxemburg 2003, p. 39.
91 Luxemburg 2003, p 40.

> Turkey has become so helpless that it must inevitably submit to the dictate of foreigners. It exists as an independent state only thanks to the jealousy of the different powers, none of which can have the whole booty alone. They all agree, however, in plundering this unlucky land and forcing their own products onto it, thus hindering the development of any kind of local industry. As a result of this we see in the Turkish economy, as in the Russian, a progressive decay of agriculture and a growth in the number of proletarians, but in Turkey these proletarians can find no employment in capitalist industry.... But Russia was not as helpless as Turkey.[92]

Bauer was even more pessimistic about the future of Turkey than Kautsky. He noted elements of capitalist modernity like railways, but concluded:

> Turkey is condemned to decline because it has not developed into a modern state based on capitalist commodity production; however, the dissolution of Turkey is proceeding only very slowly because the slow rate of economic development there is only very slowly producing the forces capable of shattering the old state. The fact that there is no Turkish capitalism explains the curious phenomenon whereby Turkey cannot survive and yet is expiring so slowly.[93]

Bauer wrote this in 1907; the Turkish Revolution began the following year. Trotsky understood that this had occurred, despite the lack of capitalist development, because a significant social force within the Empire was interested precisely in achieving such development – the junior army officers of the Committee for Union and Progress (CUP):

> In Russia it was the proletariat that came forward as the chief fighter for the revolution. In Turkey, however... industry exists only in embryonic form, and so the proletariat is small in numbers and weak. The most highly educated elements of the Turkish intelligentsia, such as teachers, engineers, and so on, being able to find little scope for their talents in schools and factories, have become army officers. Many of them have studied in Western European countries and become familiar with the regime that exists there – only, on their return home, to come up against the ignorance and poverty of the Turkish soldier and the debased

92 Kautsky 2009f, p. 624.
93 Bauer 2000, p. 397.

> conditions of the state. This has filled them with bitterness; and so the officer corps has become the focus of discontent and rebelliousness.[94]

The absence of a working class of comparable size and strategic position to that of Russia meant that the revolution remained within bourgeois parameters:

> In the tasks before it (economic independence, unity of nation and state, political freedom), the Turkish revolution constitutes self-determination by the bourgeois nation and in this sense it belongs with the traditions of 1789–1848. But the army, led by its officers, functioned as the executive organ of the nation, and this at once gave events the planned character of military manoeuvres. It would, however, have been utter nonsense (and many people were guilty of this) to see in the events of last July a mere *pronunciamento* and to treat them as analogous to some military-dynastic coup d'etat in Serbia. The strength of the Turkish officers and the secret of their success lie not in any brilliantly organized 'plan' or devilishly cunning conspiracy, but in the active sympathy shown them by the advanced classes: the merchants, the craftsmen, the workers, sections of the officials and of the clergy and, finally, the countryside as embodied in the peasant army.[95]

Nevertheless, Trotsky emphasised popular support for the 'Young Turks', in the form of strikes by 'bakery workers, printers, weavers, tramway employees … tobacco workers … as well as port and railway workers', and how these had played a major role in the boycott of Austrian goods.[96] The Turkish Revolution, on the easternmost boundary of Europe, was the only revolution actually ongoing when war began in August 1914.

1914 and 1917 as Moments of Truth

The First World War was a moment of truth in two respects. For the Socialist and labour movement, as noted in Anievas's introduction, it proved the hollowness of the formal opposition to capitalism and war espoused by the vast majority of the Second International leadership and cadres: only in a handful of countries – all in Eastern Europe – did affiliated parties oppose the war and

94 Trotsky 1980a, p. 4.
95 Trotsky 1980b, p. 11.
96 Trotsky 1980b, p. 13.

refuse to support 'their' state. But for capitalism it also exposed the fault-lines of the system, the enormous social pressures brought by mass mobilisation and loss of life on an industrial scale threatened to break it at the weakest links, the most important of which was Russia.

The second Russian Revolution began on 23 February 1917, and quickly changed the entire debate on the future of the bourgeois revolution in Europe. Five days later the Tsarist regime fell, to be replaced by a Provisional Government dominated by bourgeois politicians. On 3 April, Lenin arrived at the Finland Station in St. Petersburg. Nothing he had written or said prior to that point fully prepared his fellow Bolsheviks, let alone the wider socialist movement, for the position that he now took. The last article that he wrote before leaving exile in Switzerland to return to Russia was notably cautious, emphasising the backwardness, not only of Russian economy and society, but also – perhaps more unexpectedly – of the Russian labour movement, and still referring to the revolution then underway as bourgeois-democratic in nature:

> Russia is a peasant country, one of the most backward of European countries. Socialism *cannot* triumph there *directly* and *immediately*. But the peasant character of the country, the vast reserve of land in the hands of the nobility, *may*, to judge from the experience of 1905, give tremendous sweep to the bourgeois-democratic revolution in Russia and *may* make our revolution the *prologue* to the world socialist revolution, a *step* toward it.[97]

Apart from the potential link between the Russian Revolution and the world socialist revolution, this was not the perspective from which Lenin addressed his listeners and readers after stepping out of the sealed train that had borne him through Germany. Instead, he called on the party to prepare for the overthrow of the Provisional Government and, in effect, for the socialist revolution. The Menshevik Nikolai Sukhanov recalled hearing Lenin's two-hour speech to a mainly Bolshevik audience on the night of 3 April:

> Of how ... his whole conception was to be reconciled with the elementary conceptions of Marxism (the only thing Lenin did not dissociate himself from in his speech) – not a syllable was said. Everything touching on what had hitherto been called scientific socialism Lenin ignored

97 Lenin 1964d, p. 371.

> just as completely as he destroyed the foundations of the current Social-Democratic programme and tactics.[98]

And it was not only Sukhanov who was astonished – so too were most Bolsheviks. At a meeting of all the Social Democratic factions the next day, he noted the reaction of the audience: 'They weren't only stunned: each new word of Lenin's filled them with indignation'.[99] In the days and weeks that followed, Lenin was variously accused of being out of touch with Russian realities, with having abandoned Marxism for anarchism or syndicalism, or of simply having lost his mind.

The dominant theme of Lenin's writings before 1917 was that a revolutionary alliance of the proletariat and peasantry would overthrow Tsarism, but that this revolution would be followed by a prolonged period of bourgeois democracy and capitalist economic development, after which a second, socialist revolution would be possible. The length of the intervening period would be impossible to determine in advance, since it would depend on the speed with which capitalist industrialisation proletarianised the peasantry and several other factors, but was certainly not coincident with the seven months between February and October. Why not? For the simple reason that none of the tasks that Lenin had identified as being the goals of the bourgeois revolution – agrarian reform, destruction of the Tsarist state, even a stable bourgeois democratic polity – were achieved by the February Revolution; they were only achieved or, in the case of the last, superseded, by the October Revolution. Lenin's final judgment on the short-lived bourgeois regime was delivered in a speech on the fourth anniversary of the October Revolution:

> The bourgeois-democratic content of the revolution means that the social relations (system, institutions) of the country are purged of medievalism, serfdom, feudalism. What were the chief manifestations, survivals, remnants of serfdom in Russia up to 1917? The monarchy, the system of social estates, landed proprietorship and land tenure, the status of women, religion, and national oppression. Take any one of these Augean stables, which, incidentally, were left largely uncleansed by all the more advanced states when they accomplished *their* bourgeois-democratic revolutions one hundred and twenty-five, two hundred and fifty and more years ago (1649 in England); take any of these Augean stables, and you will see that we have cleansed them thoroughly. In a matter of *ten*

98 Sukhanov 1984, pp. 284–5.

99 Sukhanov 1984, p. 286.

> *weeks*, from October 25 (November 7), 1917, to January 5, 1918, when the Constituent Assembly was dissolved, we accomplished a thousand times more in this respect than was accomplished by the bourgeois democrats and liberals (the Cadets) and by the petty-bourgeois democrats (the Mensheviks and the Socialist-Revolutionaries) *during the eight months* they were in power.[100]

Lenin's acceptance in practice of permanent revolution was based on a changed assessment of the nature of the Russian Revolution that brought him to the same conclusions as Trotsky, rather than because he was persuaded by Trotsky's theoretical work. A precondition for doing so was the study that Lenin undertook of Hegel following the outbreak of the First World War and the capitulation of the overwhelming majority of the Second International to social patriotism. Yet these notes – important in Lenin's development as a thinker as they undoubtedly are – remain at the level of philosophical abstraction. Lenin did not arrive at the notion of a 'leap' over the bourgeois-democratic stage or a 'break' in Russian development leading to socialism as a result of recovering the dialectical method alone: it also required the application of that method to the contemporary situation.[101]

One aspect of this was his analysis of imperialism – or rather the political implications of that analysis. In other words, the bourgeoisie had already passed the point at which it could be classified as progressive; consequently the revolution that bore its name would deliver no benefits to the proletariat or the oppressed – and Lenin's scathing comments on the fourth anniversary of October, quoted above, list in some detail precisely which benefits the Russian bourgeoisie had failed to deliver, even when presented with the gift of state power.

But the bourgeoisie was not the only class whose capacities were affected by the advent of imperialism as a stage in capitalist development: so too was the proletariat – or at least, the Western proletariat. What Lenin called 'opportunism' within the working-class movement had arisen first in Britain, then in all the nations that played an oppressive role within the imperialist system. According to Lenin, the bourgeoisie were able to use the super-profits from imperialism to 'bribe' trade-union officials and the upper strata of the working class into compromising with or openly capitulating to the system,

100 Lenin 1966b, pp. 52–4.

101 As these remarks suggest, I disagree with attempts to claim that Lenin's work in this period was primarily marked by continuity with his pre-war positions. See, for example, Lih, in this volume.

leading to the phenomena of opportunism, social patriotism, and reformism more generally.[102] As a proposition based solely on the supposed effects of imperialist bribery, this was dubious. What were the mechanisms through which these payments would be made? Moreover, the experience of the First World War was that the so-called labour aristocrats – the engineers of Berlin, Glasgow, and Turin, as much as Petrograd – led the great contemporary labour upheavals and later formed a major component of the industrial cadres who joined the communist parties in Europe.

If Lenin's explanation for the *existence* of reformism was flawed, his account of the *effect* of reformism in retarding socialist revolution in the West was, however, more realistic. In Russia, where the hold of reformism was weaker, workers could be won more easily to a revolutionary socialist perspective. As Lenin wrote in 1920, 'it was easy for Russia, in the specific and historically unique situation of 1917 to *start* the socialist revolution, but it will be more difficult for Russia than for the European countries to *continue* the revolution and bring it to its consummation'.[103]

In this respect there is at least a difference in emphasis between Trotsky and Lenin. For Trotsky, due to the peculiar nature of Russian capitalist development – not least the fact that it took place within the context of a repressive, undemocratic absolutist state – the working class tended to be more politically militant and theoretically advanced than its Western counterparts. For Lenin, the Russian working class simply had, so to speak, fewer opportunities for opportunism, given that the Russian bourgeoisie had less capacity for 'bribery'. Russian workers had then benefited from the brittleness of the Tsarist state, which, already under pressure from the war, had shattered relatively easily at the first manifestation of working-class and peasant resistance: the former were not necessarily better organised or more class conscious than their Western counterparts, they had been provided with an opening, in the form of a collapsing archaic state, that the latter had not. There were, however, two respects in which Lenin's reasons for arguing for a socialist outcome to the revolution were similar to those of Trotsky.

One was the nature of the institutions thrown up by the workers and soldiers themselves: the soviets or workers' councils. I argued above that Trotsky only completed his version of the conception of permanent revolution after experiencing the creativity and organisational élan demonstrated by the St. Petersburg Soviet at whose head he stood during the general strike; yet Trotsky wrote relatively little about the nature of soviet rule, then or subsequently,

102 Lenin 1964c, pp. 193–4, 301–2.

103 Lenin 1966a, pp. 320, 330.

even though he resumed his role as president of the Soviet of Workers' and Soldiers' Deputies during 1917. The soviets had a far more important role for Lenin. Lenin did not support the *policies* of the soviets in the early months of 1917, since these reflected their then reformist composition, itself an expression of what he regarded as the 'insufficient class consciousness' of the workers and soldiers at this point of the revolution. Instead he argued for the importance of the soviet *form* of government, which, given revolutionary class consciousness, could act as the democratic mechanism with which to overthrow and then replace the existing state. Typically, having arrived at these conclusions, Lenin sought theoretical justification in the writings of his Marxist teachers, and found that the critique of the state was present in the later writings of Marx and Engels, notably on the Paris Commune and the origins of the family, but that these insights had been ignored or dismissed by the guardians of Social Democratic orthodoxy, just as surely as they had ignored or dismissed the Hegelian dialectic. In effect, the soviet was the socialist solution to the problem of the state in general and the capitalist state in particular, which had previously only been glimpsed in embryonic form in the commune. Thus, in *The State and Revolution* he writes of 'the conversion of *all* citizens into workers and other employees of *one* huge "syndicate" – the whole state – and the complete subordination of the entire work of this syndicate to a genuinely democratic state, *the state of the Soviets of Worker's and Soldier's Deputies*'.[104]

The other way in which Lenin's thought was compatible with that of Trotsky was over the significance of the international setting in which the Russian Revolution had taken place. This too represented a shift in Lenin's thought. Although always insistent on the need for proletarian internationalism, he had not previously seen the Russian bourgeois revolution as being dependent on support from other revolutions. But, ever the realist, Lenin understood that a socialist revolution was a different matter: a bourgeois republic in Russia was acceptable to the global ruling class, a socialist republic was not. No matter how important the soviets were as examples of proletarian self-emancipation, they, and the revolution that rested upon them, would not survive the combination of internal bourgeois opposition and external imperialist intervention. A recurrent theme of Lenin's writings, from 25 October 1917 on, was that without revolutions in the West – whether caused by the wartime crisis, or undertaken in emulation of the Russian example or some mixture of the two – the Russian republic could not survive.[105] One example, taken from early in the revolution, will suffice here:

104 Lenin 1964e, p. 475.

105 Lenin's comments to this effect are legion but, for a selection, see Trotsky 1977, pp. 1227–38.

> We are far from having completed even the transitional period from capitalism to socialism. We have never cherished the hope that we could finish it without the aid of the international proletariat. We never had any illusions on that score.... The final victory of socialism in a single country is of course impossible.[106]

Where would revolutions capable of bringing aid to Russia be found?

The Consummation of the Bourgeois Revolution in Europe

Lenin and the Bolsheviks were not the only political actors who thought that the war would give rise to revolution; so too did the more intelligent members of the European ruling class. In the immediate pre-war period figures from what were to become the major combatants speculated on how prolonged hostilities could potentially lead to revolutions, above all in Russia.[107] The potential successors to the Russian Revolution began to take place in rapid succession from October 1918, following the collapse of the Bulgarian front. As Geoff Eley explains, the disintegration of the Austro-Hungarian Empire was central to this process:

> The first act was a series of 'national revolutions', erecting new republican sovereignties on the ruin of the Hapsburg monarchy: first Czechoslovakia (proclaimed on 28 October 1918), followed by Yugoslavia (29 October), 'German-Austria' (30 October), Hungary (31 October), Poland (28 October–14 November), and West Ukraine (Eastern Galicia), where the People's Republic was proclaimed on 31 October. These new states, except West Ukraine, which was annexed by Poland in July 1919, secured their constitutional legitimacy, not least via international recognition at the peace conference in Versailles. The chain of republican revolutions was concluded, moreover, with the toppling of the Hohenzolleren monarchy and the proclamation of a German Republic on 9 November 1918.

But as Eley adds: 'After Russia, there were no socialist revolutions in 1917–23, except the short-lived Hungarian Soviet'. There were, however, many 'revolutionary situations', above all resulting in 'popular militancy pushing

106 Lenin 1964g, pp. 464–5, 470.

107 Fergusson 1999, p. 28; Mayer, 1981, pp. 320, 327.

non-socialist regimes into pre-emptive reform, which was commonest of all in 1917–23'.[108]

Why did none of them repeat the Russian outcome? They were certainly all heading in a similar developmental direction, albeit at different speeds. Under pressure from the Western powers, not only Russia, but the other major feudal-absolutist or tributary states, Austria-Hungary and Turkey, were forced for reasons of military competition to introduce limited industrialisation and partial agrarian reform. Trotsky noted in 1924, 'the Great War, the result of the contradictions of world imperialism, drew into its maelstrom countries of *different* stages of development, but made the same *claims* on all the participants'.[109] The response to these 'claims' had the greatest impact on Russia, as Norman Stone, a historian whom no one could suspect of sympathy for Marxism, explains:

> ... economic chaos was frequently ascribed quite simply to backwardness: Russia was not advanced enough to stand the strain of war, and the effort to do so plunged her economy into chaos. But economic backwardness did not alone make for revolution, as the examples of Romania and Bulgaria showed; and in any case, Russia was backward in the same way as these countries, as was shown in her capacity to make war material in 1915–16. The economic chaos came more from a contest between old and new in the Russian economy. There was a crisis, not of decline and relapse into subsistence, but rather of growth.

And, as Stone points out, partly this was a growth in the size of the proletariat, above all in Petrograd:

> The huge mass of workers, some long-established, some newly brought into industry, were pushed together by inflation, which reduced differentials between old and new, skilled and unskilled, men and women. The growth of starvation and disease in the towns brought them together in a way that no amount of Bolshevik agitation could have done. All were agreed that capitalism had failed, and they became increasingly willing to listen to a Lenin who offered them hope. The First World War had not been the short outburst of patriotic sacrifice that men had expected.... In

108 Eley 2002, pp. 154, 156.

109 Trotsky 1972b, p. 199.

> the summer of 1917, virtually the whole of Russia went on strike. The Bolshevik Revolution was a fact before it happened.[110]

The actual degree of identity with the other imperial Central Europe lay in the relationship between the monarchy and the army: 'In Russia, Germany and Austria-Hungary, the army was central to the regime. The monarchs, their kinsmen, and their appointees were the government and the high command, and their courts and governments were dominated by military uniforms. If their armies failed, so did monarchical government'.[111] If the preceding argument about their different relationship to the bourgeois revolutions is correct, however, then even this apparent uniformity is actually illusionary.

The contrasting German and Austrian experiences are central here. The differences between them were not simply matters of degree, as has been argued, for example, by F.L. Carsten:

> In 1918 Germany – not Austria – was a highly advanced industrial country with a very antiquated political and social structure, the legacy of Bismarck and the period of unification.... Austria was behind Germany in her general and political development so that to her the same factors applied even more strongly.[112]

This greatly exaggerates the archaic nature of the German state; but even the greatest revolutionaries of the time failed to recognise the qualitative difference between it and Austria. Despite their emerging differences after the beginning of the German Revolution in November 1918, both Luxemburg and Liebknecht agreed that alternative revolutionary outcomes were possible: the former wrote that the elevation of a National Constituent Assembly over the workers' councils was 'shunting the revolution onto the rails of a bourgeois revolution'; the latter that the events of November were 'no more than the completion of the bourgeois revolution'.[113] Modern Marxists, like the French historian Pierre Broué, have arrived at similar conclusions, arguing that although Germany was 'an advanced capitalist country', it was still the site of 'an incomplete bourgeois revolution': 'Indeed, we may regard the first result of the November [1918] Revolution as the fulfilment of the bourgeois revolution which was aborted

110 Stone 1998, pp. 284, 301.

111 Mann 2012, p. 204.

112 Carsten 1972, pp. 334–5.

113 Luxemburg 1986, p. 80; Liebknecht, 1986, p. 84.

midway through the nineteenth century'.[114] But these verdicts rest on a mistaken understanding of what the completion of the bourgeois revolution means.

Like other post-bourgeois revolutionary states in Italy and Japan, Germany continued to be ruled by a monarch; but in terms of capitalist development, this is less significant than it at first appears. State managers took over the outer forms of the existing absolutist states, but internally transformed them into apparatuses capable of building an autonomous centre of capital accumulation. The dominance of capitalist economy did not mean that the bourgeoisie had to be in direct control of the state apparatus; all it required was that the apparatus functioned on its behalf, as Georg Lukács pointed out in 1923:

> The bourgeoisie had far less of an immediate control of the actual springs of power than had ruling classes in the past (such as the citizens of the Greek city-states or the nobility at the apogee of feudalism). On the one hand, the bourgeoisie had to rely much more strongly on its ability to make peace or achieve a compromise with the opposing classes that held power before it so as to use the power-apparatus they controlled for its own ends. On the other hand, it found itself compelled to place the actual exercise of force (the army, petty bureaucracy, etc.) in the hands of petty bourgeois, peasants, the members of subject nations, etc.[115]

Between 1870 and 1918, virtually all the great powers consciously emphasised the archaic, imperial role of their monarchies. Bayly has noted that these 'were useful to the political forces trying to mediate an increasingly complex society'. The role played by Kaiser Wilhelm II is typical in this respect:

> By astute manipulation of the press and acquiescence in the views of elected politicians, he could serve the interests of the new middle classes of Germany's industrial cities. As commander of the forces and descendant of Frederick the Great, he was the symbolic leader of the junkers of East Germany and of their brothers and sons in the imperial army. As emperor of Germany, he could pacify the interests of the states and regions, both Catholic and Protestant, that had seemed locked in battle at the time of Bismarck.

---

114 Broué 2005, pp. 2–5, 289.

115 Lukács 1971b, p. 307.

Bayly makes the obvious comparison with the Japanese emperor, but also another that is perhaps less obvious: 'The real parallel with late-imperial Germany was not imperial Russia ... it was Britain', where 'the royal ritual of coronations, parades, and state openings of Parliament became more elaborate and more beautifully choreographed as the century wore on'.[116]

This may look like the assertion of 'feudal' elements within the state, indicating an incomplete transition across Europe, including Britain, as it does for Mayer and likeminded thinkers. Tom Nairn, for example, claims that in the earlier case of the British state after 1688, 'an in-depth historical analysis shows that, while not directly comparable to the notorious relics of the 20th century, like the Hapsburg, Tsarist, or Prussian-German states, *it retains something in common with them*'. What is the basis of this commonality? 'Although not of course an absolutist state, the Anglo-British system remains a product of the general transition from absolutism to modern constitutionalism; it led the way out of the former, but never genuinely arrived at the latter'.[117] These arguments confuse form and content. In fact, the enhanced eminence of the British monarchy after 1870 was consciously engineered by the representatives of the capitalist ruling class for the same reasons and in much the same way as their equivalents did in imperial Germany and imperial Japan. There was only one respect in which Britain was exceptional: unlike the American president on the one hand or the German Kaiser on the other, its monarch wielded no real power.[118] In all these cases the pre-existing symbolism of the crown was imbued with a sense of national unity against two main challenges: internal class divisions and external imperial rivalry. The point was well made by Nikolai Bukharin, writing of the ideology of the imperialist powers in the First World War:

> These sentiments are not 'remnants of feudalism', as some observers suppose, these are not debris of the old that have survived in our times. This is an entirely new socio-political formation caused by the birth of finance capital. If the old feudal 'policy of blood and iron' was able to serve here, externally as a model, this was possible only because the moving springs of modern economic life drive capital along the road of aggressive politics and the militarization of all social life.[119]

116 Bayly 2004, pp. 426–30.
117 Nairn 1977, p. 49.
118 Cannadine 1983, pp. 120–50.
119 Bukharin 1972, p. 128.

And what was true for the rulers of these new states was also true of the nobility. One supporter of the Mayer thesis writes of 'a landowning elite [that] survived from the days of feudalism through the ages of absolutism and nationalism and into the twentieth century'.[120] The question, however, is whether they survived as representatives of the same socio-economic interests as they did in 'the days of feudalism'. Did the nobles represent feudal or capitalist landowning interests? If the latter, then, as in the case of England, whatever influences the nobility did possess should more properly be regarded as one of culture and style, rather than one that conflicted with the interests of the industrial or financial bourgeoisie. Heide Gerstenberger notes:

> If the 'bourgeois revolution' was achieved through a process of forced reform, the economic, cultural as well as political hegemony of those groups which occupied the ranks of the social hierarchy in societies of the *ancien régime* type could persist long after the capitalist form of exploitation had become dominant.[121]

As Hobsbawm explains, the economic orientation of the landlords was expressed with increasing ideological clarity:

> Never has there been a more overwhelming consensus among economists and indeed among intelligent politicians and administrators about the recipe for economic growth: economic liberalism. The remaining institutional barriers to the free movement of the factors of production, to free enterprise and to anything that could conceivably hamper its profitable operation, fell below a world-wide onslaught. What made this general raising of barriers so remarkable is that it was not confined to the states in which political liberalism was triumphant or even influential. If anything it was even more drastic in the restored absolutist monarchies and principalities of Europe than in England, France, and the Low Countries, because so much remained to be swept away there.[122]

Indeed, as Stone has written of this period, with the important exception of Russia, all the major states of Europe also had 'a large, educated, energetic middle class with enough money for its support to be essential to any state that wished to develop', but it was the state that acted as the main agent of

120 Halperin 1997, p. 23.
121 Gerstenberger 1992, p. 169.
122 Hobsbawm 1975, pp. 35–6.

development. Britain was also different, but not because the middle class was incapable of influencing the state:

> In Great Britain, that class existed so strongly, even in the eighteenth century, that liberal reforms were introduced piecemeal there, and often without formal involvement of parliament. Existing *ancien-régime* institutions, such as the old guilds or corporations, would be gradually adapted to suit a changing era. Thus, in form, England (more than Scotland) is the last of the *ancien régimes*; she did not even have a formal law to abolish serfdom.... In the 1860s, states, short of money, had to follow the British example by formal legislation.[123]

In other words, the extent to which Britain, or perhaps England, represented an *ancien régime* was an indication of its adaptive modernity, rather than the opposite. Britain could indeed be compared with Germany and Japan: all three were capitalist states that could be strongly contrasted with feudal absolutist Austria-Hungary or Russia, even down to the role of the emperor and empresses: 'Russia represented the opposite pole to Japan within the spectrum of authoritarian monarchy – no corporate regime strategy, much depending on the monarch himself'.[124]

Consequently, Trotsky was right to maintain that 'the German Revolution of 1918 ... was no democratic completion of the bourgeois revolution, it was a proletarian revolution decapitated by the Social Democrats; more correctly, it was a bourgeois counter-revolution, which was compelled to preserve pseudo-democratic forms after its victory over the proletariat'.[125] We might say that the German Revolution had the potential to be a *social* revolution – a socialist one – but ended as a *political* revolution, changing the nature of the regime while retaining the pre-existing capitalist state. The Austrian Revolution also had the potential to be a social revolution, but had the option of two different types – bourgeois and socialist – with the former quickly emerging as the actual outcome.

Had Germany emerged triumphant from the war, it is possible that it might have assimilated Austria-Hungary in ways which had already begun as the conflict progressed. Brendan Simms has argued that the agreement by Austria-Hungary to a unified high command under German leadership in 1916 meant

123 Stone 1983, pp. 18–19.
124 Mann 1988, p. 200.
125 Trotsky 1969d, p. 131.

that the former 'effectively ceased to exist as an independent state'.[126] This is something of an exaggeration, but in any case, the end came too quickly for Austria-Hungary to be transformed along German lines. The Hapsburg state simply collapsed. Lukács described the process in general terms five years later in *History and Class Consciousness*:

> The true revolutionary element is the economic transformation of the feudal system of production into a capitalist one so that it would be possible in theory for this process to take place *without a bourgeois revolution*, without political upheaval on the part of the revolutionary bourgeoisie. And in that case those parts of the feudal and absolutist superstructure that were not eliminated by 'revolutions from above' would collapse of their own accord when capitalism was already fully developed.[127]

In fact, the 'feudal and absolutist superstructures' rarely 'collapsed of their own accord', but they certainly collapsed. When the Hapsburg Empire disintegrated under the weight of military defeat, and nationalist and working-class pressure, Austro-Hungary fragmented into several different states that were already dominated by the capitalist mode of production to a greater (Austria, Czechoslovakia) or lesser (Hungary) extent. Take Czechoslovakia as an example; here a capitalist class existed ready to take over once the Hapsburg state fell:

> Strong parties, all committed to national democracy, provided the creators of the Czechoslovak state with the raw material of democracy. These parties existed because Czech economic development proceeded from a long history of proto-industry and industrialisation that created an alert middle-class able to take advantage of the relatively narrow niche assigned to it by the dominant landowning class and its emperor. Although the members of this landowning class participated heavily in the initial introduction of both proto-industry and industrialisation into the Czech lands, they did not undertake [Barrington] Moore's 'revolution from above'. By the time Czech industrialisation was accelerating rapidly in the last half of the nineteenth century, middle-class competitors were elbowing noble entrepreneurs aside. Furthermore, no modern state existed for the landed nobility to seize.[128]

126 Simms 2013, p. 303.

127 Lukács 1971a, p. 282.

128 Stokes 1989, p. 218.

Not all the component parts of the former Empire were as well developed in capitalist terms. Hungary itself was not; but as Lukács wrote the 'Blum Theses' of 1928 – his last significant political intervention – it was possible to recognise the survival of certain feudal relationships in Hungary without making any concessions to the notion that a further bourgeois revolution was required to remove them. 'The peculiarity of Hungarian development', he wrote, 'is that the feudal form of distribution of landed property remains unchanged alongside relatively highly developed and still-developing capitalism'. But the integration of feudal landowners and industrial capitalists meant that any expectation of the latter leading a bourgeois revolution was completely unrealistic:

> Here too, the H[ungarian] C[ommunist] P[arty] remains the only party which inscribes the consistent implementation of the demands of the bourgeois revolution on its banner: expropriation of the large landed-property owners without compensation, revolutionary occupation of the land, free land for the peasants! ... All party members must understand that what is at issue is a question which is fundamental to the transition from the bourgeois revolution to the revolution of the proletariat; they must understand that the power of large-scale landed property and large-scale capital cannot be destroyed except by this kind of revolution, and that the remnants of feudalism cannot be wiped out except through the elimination of capitalism.[129]

Shortly after Lukács delivered this assessment, Trotsky reviewed the entire progress of the bourgeois revolution in Europe from immediately prior to the outbreak of war:

> The Balkan war of 1912 marked the completion of the forming of national states in south-eastern Europe. The subsequent imperialist war completed incidentally the unfinished work of the national revolutions in Europe leading as it did to the dismemberment of Austria-Hungary, the establishment of an independent Poland, and of independent border states cut from the empire of the czars.[130]

The characteristic process of state formation taken by these revolutions had changed from that of earlier cases, both from above and below:

129 Lukács 1972, pp. 250–1.

130 Trotsky 1977, p. 889.

> Whereas in nationally homogeneous states the bourgeois revolutions developed powerful centripetal tendencies, rallying to the idea of overcoming particularism, as in France, or overcoming national disunion, as in Italy and Germany – in nationally heterogeneous states on the contrary, such as Turkey, Russia, Austria-Hungary, the belated bourgeois revolution released centrifugal forces. In spite of the apparent contrariness of these processes when expressed in mechanical terms, their historic function was the same. In both cases it was a question of using the national unity as a fundamental industrial reservoir. Germany had for this purpose to be united, Austria-Hungary to be divided.[131]

There were some exceptions. The formation of Yugoslavia bore some resemblance to the unifications of Germany and Italy, with Serbia playing an equivalent role to that of Prussia and Piedmont, but in most cases Trotsky's comments reflect a real shift in the form of bourgeois revolution. But the key point is that this was a retrospective judgement. Trotsky and the rest of the Bolshevik leadership had every reason to think that socialist rather than bourgeois revolutionary outcomes were in prospect. We can therefore return to the question with which we began this section: why did this prove not to be the case?

Several writers have claimed that Russia was exceptional in Europe, or at least different in degree. Michael Mann writes: 'In Germany, Austria, Hungary, and Italy after the first war, revolution failed because conditions present in Russia were more marginal there'.[132] What were these conditions? Following Trotsky, Tim McDaniel argues that there were four reasons why what he calls the 'autocratic capitalism' of Tsarist Russia tended to produce a revolutionary labour movement. First, it eliminated or reduced the distinction between economic and political issues. Second, it generated opposition for both traditional and modern reasons. Third, it reduced the fragmentation of the working class but also prevented the formation of a stable conservative bureaucracy, thus leading to more radical attitudes. Fourth, it forced a degree of interdependence between the mass of the working class, class-conscious workers and revolutionary intellectuals.[133] In addition to these factors, writers more committed to the Trotskyist tradition than McDaniel have tended to emphasise two other factors, which might be seen as the respective organisational expressions of McDaniel's third and fourth: workers' councils and the revolutionary party.

131 Trotsky 1977, p. 890.
132 Mann 2012, p. 206.
133 McDaniel 1988, pp. 41–7.

In the post-bourgeois revolutionary West, workers' councils – or at the very least, organisational forms wider and deeper than the existing trade unions – sprang up in the latter stages of the war in Britain, Italy and Germany as they had in Russia; revolutionary organisations of any size and implantation in the working class were however only established after the new revolutionary era signalled by October was underway.[134] Once the Hapsburg state had collapsed, Austria – or more precisely, Vienna – was in essentially the same situation as Glasgow, Turin or Berlin, with one additional aspect, suggested by Trotsky's comments about the 'centrifugal' nature of the belated bourgeois revolutions, which added another barrier to socialist revolution: nationalism. Hobsbawm has written of how, during the latter stages of the war, 'the dominant mood was a desire for peace and *social* transformation', but:

> Nationalism was victorious in the formerly independent nationalities of belligerent Europe, to the extent that the movements which reflected the real concerns of the poor people of Europe failed in 1918.... National independence without social revolution was, under the umbrella of Allied victory, a feasible fall-back position for those who had dreamed of a combination of both. In the major defeated or semi-defeated belligerent states there was no such fall-back position. There collapse led to social revolution.[135]

In fact, among the major defeated powers outside of Russia, Germany did not undergo a successful social revolution and in Austria it took bourgeois form – national independence and the granting of reformist demands. The role of Social Democracy was crucial here – not so much in holding back an otherwise insurgent proletariat, since only a minority were already committed to the complete overthrow of the state, but rather by convincing supporters that the arrival in office of the SPO itself signalled the triumph of socialism: 'Among the workers the feeling prevailed that power was already in their hands and that with the proclamation of the republic on 12 November 1918 the much dreamed-of "people's state", frequently embellished with the epithet "socialist", had been won'.[136] When revolutionary crisis re-emerged in the spring and summer of 1919, the Social Democrats were able to force through a series of reforms, including the eight hour day, unemployment benefit and disability compensation.

134 See, for example, Gluckstein 1985, pp. 233–40.

135 Hobsbawm 1990, pp. 127, 130.

136 Hautmann 1993, p. 97.

But if the Austrian and Czech states emerged as fully-formed and relatively developed capitalist states from the womb of the Hapsburg Empire, this was not the case further east. Here other factors came into play. Russia was defeated, but defeat did not have the same impact everywhere:

> While defeat drove some states towards social revolution, victory made others a reliable barrier against it. And victory meant infinitely more to the liberated nations of the east than to England [sic] and France. Here it only signified a narrow escape from disaster: there, the achievement of age-old hopes and dreams.[137]

The revolution in Russia had been waged in part to stop the war and radicalisation had increased as the Provisional Government had failed to do so. The first policy which Lenin proposed to Soviet delegates in the Smolny was, after all, a draft decree for a three-month armistice during which peace negotiations ('without annexations or indemnities') could be pursued by the belligerent states.[138] The Russian experience of mutiny and desertion, of soldiers retaining their weapons and forming soviets occurred during the war and signalled part of the revolutionary process. In Central Europe soldiers and sailors rebelled to prevent their lives being wasted in futile attempts to shift the military balance of forces and then from a desire to return to civilian life as soon as possible: surrender removed the threat of the former and demobilisation satisfied the latter.

But is a discussion of these factors even relevant? Is not the existence of the Bolshevik Party, a body unique among socialist organisations of the time, sufficient to explain Russian distinctiveness? Not necessarily. The Bolsheviks were still committed to achieving the bourgeois revolution in February 1917. 'After all', writes Tony Cliff, 'it is arguable that without Lenin – if he had not returned to Russia after the February Revolution – the reorientation of the Bolshevik Party towards the socialist revolution and the victory of October would not have happened'.[139] This was certainly Trotsky's position. In *The History of the Russian Revolution* he argues that the arrival of Lenin in Russia in April 1917 was decisive in pushing the Bolshevik Party towards the socialist revolution and the seizure of power:

137 Borkenau 1962, p. 99.
138 Lenin 1964a, pp. 249–53.
139 Cliff 1987, p. 440.

> Without Lenin the crisis, which the opportunistic leadership was inevitably bound to produce, would have assumed an extraordinarily sharp and protracted character. The conditions of war and revolution, however, would not allow the party a long period for fulfilling its mission. Thus it is by no means excluded that a disorientated and split party might have let slip the revolutionary opportunity for many years.

Trotsky is not saying that the Bolsheviks would never have arrived at the correct strategy without Lenin, or that the revolutionary opportunity would never have come again, simply that in revolutionary situations time is of the essence and that without Lenin – or, he added later in his diary, himself – it would have been allowed to pass. 'Lenin was not an accidental element in the historic development, but a product of the whole past of Russian history'.[140] Despite the objections of his greatest biographer, there is little doubt that Trotsky's judgement is correct on this point.[141] As we saw above, the Bolshevik Party were strongly resistant to Lenin's shift in position and internal disagreements continued up to and including the moment of insurrection itself. It is true that, unlike Trotsky, Lenin had a serious organisation which he could attempt to win over, and that once he had, the Bolshevik structures and previous implantation in the working class enabled it to carry its message more effectively than the other socialist parties; but even this can be exaggerated. In February 1917, the Bolsheviks were an illegal organisation of around 20,000 members, many of whom were either in external or internal exile, in jail, or in the army. By October it was virtually a different organisation, as Moshe Lewin notes:

> In 1917, the party underwent a rather astonishing change in structure and nature: the number of its cadres, which had not gone beyond 20,000, increased towards the end of the year to 300,000 or more, so that it became an authentic party of the urban masses, a legal, democratic party made up from diverse social strata and heterogeneous ideological horizons.

The party was 'better structured and better directed than all the others on the national scene, although strongly democratic, even factionalised, and accustomed to bitter political debates'.[142] In other words, the party that made the October Revolution was not built since 1898 or 1902, but in eight months preceding it in 1917. Any other conclusion involves the highly determinist and

---

140 Trotsky 1977, pp. 343–4. See also Trotsky 1958, pp. 53–4.

141 Deutscher 2003b, pp. 197–201.

142 Lewin 1985, p. 199.

fatalistic conclusion that all the other revolutions which followed in 1918/19 were doomed to fail or be restricted to bourgeois revolutions in advance because no revolutionary party pre-existed their occurrence.

The real difference between the Bolsheviks and other socialist parties has been explained by John Eric Marot, who points out, 'the election of solid Bolshevik majorities to virtually all the institutions of worker's power... happened not only or even primarily because of the organisational superiority of the Bolshevik Party, although its democratic cohesiveness was indispensable for it to fulfil its tasks... It happened because of Bolshevik *politics*'.[143] The point is of some significance in relation to the other parties of the revolutionary left in those areas of Eastern Europe where conditions were similar to those in Russia: Bulgaria and Hungary.

As Mann writes, there were parties with comparable revolutionary principles to those of the Bolsheviks, 'but only the Bolsheviks combined this with a short-term pragmatism attuned to the unpredictable flow of events'.[144] In particular, victory of the revolution on a socialist basis did not simply depend on winning over a majority of the working class, it meant gaining the support or – at the very least – neutralising the hostility of a peasantry which composed the vast majority of the population. Tibor Hajdu writes of the peasant attitude to revolution: 'When [land distribution] took place, they lost interest because they were satisfied; if the revolution did not distribute the latifundia, they grew disenchanted and became hostile'.[145] This again indicates the difference between Germany and the other states in Central and Eastern Europe: 'At one extreme, in Hungary, lack of peasant support was probably a sufficient cause of failure, as this was the most rural case. In industrial Germany, peasant support might conceivably have been dispensed with'.[146] Only the Bolsheviks were prepared to support and endorse peasant land seizures rather than attempting to oppose the peasants or impose nationalisation. In Bulgaria, the Tesnyaki ('the narrow socialists'), a party of similar vintage to the RSDLP and the one doctrinally closest to the Bolsheviks, refused to support peasant insurgency against the regime, first in 1918 and then, fatally for itself, again in 1923. This was not the only difficulty confronting the Tesnyaki; unlike Russia, there was no industrial working class of any size and consequently no possibility of workers' councils. In Hungary, however, there were both: the first war-time explosions of industrial class struggle actually began in the Manfred

143 Marot 2012, p. 164
144 Mann 2012, p. 206.
145 Hadju 1986, p. 109.
146 Mann 2012, p. 207.

Weiss munitions factory outside Budapest on 14 January 1918, before spreading to Austria and crossing to Berlin. The Hungarian Communist Party was formed in 1919 from an unprincipled fusion with former Social Democrats whose politics had not essentially changed, but nevertheless found itself in power in the spring and summer of 1919, during which time it attempted to nationalise the land which the peasants had only just seized from the nobles. Adopting a saner policy towards the peasantry would not of course have guaranteed the survival of the communist regime – any regime headed by the notoriously useless Béla Kun was obviously going to find itself in difficulties at some point – but it might have lasted long enough to establish a link to Central Europe for the embattled Russian state. But where communists did not make concessions to the peasantry, some of the more intelligent elements of the old regimes did, even to the point of carrying through agrarian reform. This occurred earliest and most decisively in the case of Romania, where the Boyars, under the impact of defeat at the hands of the German army in January 1917, enacted a law distributing some of the land to the peasants, who then mobilised in defence of the regime and the new settlement from attack by both Germany and the spread of the Russian Revolution: 'The agrarian reform in Romania was perhaps the strongest single obstacle that opposed the advance of Bolshevism towards the West'.[147]

But if socialist revolution had at least been conceivable in Central and Eastern Europe at the end of the war, in Turkey this was always a more remote possibility. Perry Anderson has identified the dual nature of the revolution of 1908:

> On the one hand, it was a genuine constitutional movement, arousing popular enthusiasm right across the different nationalities of the Empire, and electing an impressively inter-ethnic Parliament on a wide suffrage ... On the other hand, it was a military coup mounted by a secret organisation of junior officers and conspirators, which can claim to be the first of a long line of such episodes in the Third World in a later epoch.[148]

Yet, as Anderson also notes, this alliance was bound to be unstable, since the officers were interested in modernising Turkey to enable it to compete with the Western powers on their terms, not in opposing imperialism or in democracy. The quest for a nationalism capable of building a modern state, meant moving from public adherence to a civic variety to the actual assumption that citizens

147 Borkenau 1962, pp. 99–100. See also Stokes 1989, pp. 232–3.
148 Anderson 2009, p. 400.

had to be either Muslims or Turks. As the vast majority of the Empire's remaining European territories in Rumelia fell into the hands of the mainly Christian Balkan states, following the war of 1912, it appeared that uniformity of religion might not be sufficient, leading to the emphasis on Turkish ethnicity. The war and post-war imperialist attempts to dismember the Empire brought the implications of this shift to the fore in all their horror, first with the genocide against the Armenians in 1915, conducted in fear of their being used as an internal opposition by the Allies, then the expulsion – or 'population exchange' of the Greeks. Over a million Armenians were killed or allowed to die; 900,000 Greeks were expelled.[149] Ellen Kay Trimberger's explanation tends to underplay the horror of these events, but correctly identifies their relationship to the establishment of a bourgeois nation state:

> Economic development in Turkey necessitated the transformation of both external and internal constraints on the mobilisation of resources. Prior to World War 1, a large percentage of Turkish businesses and commercial enterprises were under direct foreign control.... Much of... productive and commercial enterprises was owned by Greeks, Armenians, and Jewish minorities. The latter problem was solved by an exchange of population with Greece after the War of Independence and by the free emigration of many other minority businessmen.[150]

Modern revolutionaries in Turkey have understandably reacted with incredulity to this description of the ethnic cleansing which accompanied the formation of the state: 'A Marxist who writes that ethnic cleansing is "solving" a "problem" is not thinking through the implications of what she is saying'.[151] Trimberger's formulations are indeed evasive, but this does not mean that ethnic cleansing was not necessary for the formation of a Turkish capitalist nation state. Anderson writes that the difference between the Jewish and Armenian genocides, 'lay essentially, not in scale or intent, but in the greater instrumental rationality, and civil participation, of the Unionist compared to the Nazi Genocide': 'The Turkish destruction of the Armenians, although fuelled by ethno-religious hatred, had more traditional economic and geopolitical motives'.[152]

149 Anderson 2009, pp. 405–12.

150 Trimberger 1978, p. 27.

151 Uzum 2004, p. 302.

152 Anderson 2009, p. 469. The irrational aspects of the Armenian genocide are discussed – and possibly over-stressed – in Sagall 2013, pp. 171–82.

The elevation of the events of 1908 over those of 1919–23 is partly a response to the way in which the latter are enshrined as 'the' revolution in the ideology of the Kemalist state which emerged from them:

> The revolution was made in 1908, not in 1923. This was when Turkish society took its leap forward and Turkey started out on the road to becoming a capitalist state. 1908 was a bourgeois revolution, but was made from below. Armenians and Greeks and Albanians and Turks made the revolution together.... What happened in 1919–1923 was a war of defence against ... imperialist invasion, not a war of liberation.[153]

The impulse behind this argument is understandable, even admirable – to foreground multi-ethnic popular involvement in the revolution and to undermine Kemalist nationalist ideology which is fixated on the later stages of the process. But this comes at a cost to historical understanding. The desire to place popular activity at the heart of bourgeois revolutions is misplaced: they are not dress rehearsals for socialist revolutions – which is why they can involve monstrous episodes of ethnic cleansing – but quite different types of event; in this case the most decisive moments in the creation of a functioning capitalist state occurred during and immediately after the war, not before it.

There was therefore a significant difference between Kemal and his superficially similar analogues in the West like Salazar in Portugal, Franco in Spain, even Metaxas in Greece, who had taken power in military coups with the intention of preserving the most conservative aspects of already backward capitalist states, against the emergent working-class threat.[154] Compared to them the actions of the CUP were closer to those of the original bourgeois revolutionaries. Take the 1916 decision to place Sharia courts under state jurisdiction of the Ministry of Justice. Sina Akşin writes: 'Born of the CUP's modern and bourgeois outlook, this was an important step towards secularism'. But as Akşin continues, 'it was also taken with a secondary consideration in mind, that of liberation from the system of Capitulations: the existence of religious courts had served Europe as a pretext for its objections to the authority of the Turkish judicial system'.[155] The reforms introduced by the CUP went further than the removal of Western interference in the functioning of the state:

153 Uzum 2004, p. [7].

154 Anderson 2009, p. 423.

155 Akşin 2007, p. 111.

> ... some ideologues among the Unionists understood that Turkish nationalism without strong socio-economic foundations would be a futile experiment.... towards the end of the war, thanks to a variety of wartime measures to encourage commercial and industrial activity, it was possible to observe the emergence of a 'national economy'. Not only was there a nascent Turkish bourgeoisie to compliment this development, but also a small working class.[156]

The smallness of that working class meant that it could not yet play the role that it had done in Russia. The Turkish Revolution is therefore of a different historical order from those which occurred within the same chronological time. Lukács wrote in 1923, as the final consolidation was taking place: 'Kemal Pasha may represent a revolutionary constellation of forces in certain circumstances whilst a great "workers' party" may be counter-revolutionary'.[157] The CUP could have achieved nothing other than a bourgeois revolution, but in doing so genuinely posed a challenge to imperialism; Austrian Social Democracy, at the other extreme, claimed to be for socialist revolution but merely inherited a bourgeois revolution in a context where the social forces already existed with which to transcend it.

Conclusion

Trotsky saw permanent revolution as a process that would enable the less developed countries to decisively break with feudal, tributary, or colonial rule under working-class leadership and move directly to socialism as components of an international revolutionary movement, without passing through a 'bourgeois' phase of development, as in Russia in 1917. In an important article first published in 1963, Tony Cliff argued that what had actually happened since then, particularly since the failure of the Chinese Revolution of the 1920s, was a process of what he called 'deflected' permanent revolution. Here, the working class is defeated, or is for other reasons either unable or unwilling to take power and another social force takes on the role of revolutionary leadership. On this basis the break with pre-capitalist or colonial states still takes place, but only in order for the countries in question to become independent parts of the world system, usually on a state-capitalist basis, as China did in

156 Ahmad 1988, p. 277.

157 Lukács 1971b, p. 311.

1949.[158] Although Cliff did not use the term 'bourgeois revolutions', he effectively treated deflected permanent revolutions as the modern version or functional equivalent. Both the original and the revised concept therefore involved fundamental social transformations leading to either socialism (permanent revolution) or some form of more-or-less complete state capitalism (deflected permanent revolution). These were alternative outcomes, which in every case resolved themselves in favour of the latter.

If the argument of this chapter is correct, however, then – with the exception of Turkey, where there was no working-class revolution to deflect – the process began much earlier than Cliff thought, with the first examples taking place in Europe itself at the end of the First World War, with the substitute forces for the revolutionary proletariat being either the reformist parties of the Second International which deliberately demobilised working-class self-organisation (Austria), bourgeois nationalist parties which temporarily won working-class support (Czechoslovakia) or, where the working class was defeated outright, by elements of the former regime, now forced reluctantly to accommodate to the modern world (Hungary). It was, however, the latter type which was to be the most common face of European capitalism, as the continent and the world slid towards another cataclysm. Mark Mazower writes of Hungary: 'At first, Horthy's right-wing regime – anti-communist, anti-democratic – seemed an anomaly in an era of growing democratisation, a last gasp of European feudalism. Time would show, however, that it was more than a relic from the past; it was also a vision of the future ...'[159]

The First World War had many unintended outcomes. One was to hasten the end of the pre-capitalist state system in Europe, to complete the bourgeois revolution, partly through the pressures of military emulation, partly through the social conflicts which the war produced among the defeated participants. The failure or refusal to go on to socialist outcomes except – temporarily – in Russia, meant that the system which emerged when the smoke of war had cleared now consisted of fully capitalist states still locked into imperialist competition that made a further war inescapable: cataclysm 1939.

158 Cliff 2003.

159 Mazower 1999, p. 11.

CHAPTER 13

'The New Era of War and Revolution': Lenin, Kautsky, Hegel and the Outbreak of World War I

Lars T. Lih

Introduction

In October 1914, shortly after the outbreak of World War I, Lenin wrote to his associate Aleksandr Shliapnikov: 'I hate and despise Kautsky now more than anyone, with his vile, dirty, self-satisfied hypocrisy'. This pungent summation of Lenin's attitude toward Kautsky – an attitude that remained unchanged for the rest of Lenin's life – is often cited. Ultimately more useful in understanding Lenin's outlook, however, is another comment, made four days later to the same correspondent: 'Obtain without fail and reread (or ask to have it translated for you) *Road to Power* by Kautsky [and see] what he writes there about the revolution of our time! And now, how he acts the toady and disavows all that!'[1]

Lenin took his own advice. He sat down in December, flipped through the pages of Kautsky's *Road to Power*, and came up with a page-and-a-half list of quotations that he inserted into an article entitled 'Dead Chauvinism and Living Socialism'. He then commented: 'This is how Kautsky wrote in times long, long past, fully five years ago. This is what German Social-Democracy was, or, more correctly, what it promised to be. This was the kind of Social-Democracy that could and had to be respected'.[2]

Three crucial implications about the impact of World War I on Lenin can be drawn from these comments. First, Lenin passionately *reaffirmed* the outlook of the wing of the Second International that he and others called 'revolutionary Social Democracy'. He did not reject it, he did not rethink it. Second, despite Lenin's fury at Kautsky's actions after the outbreak of war, he still considered the pre-war Kautsky the most insightful spokesman of revolutionary Social

1 Lenin 1960–8, Vol. 35, p. 167; Lenin, 1958–64, Vol. 49, p. 24 (letters of 27 October and 31 October 1914).

2 Lenin 1960–8, Vol. 21, pp. 94–101, 'Dead Chauvinism and Living Socialism' (December 1914). For more discussion see Lih 2009.

Democracy. Third, what was most important to Lenin at this crucial juncture was Kautsky's analysis of 'the revolution of our time' – or, in the more expressive formula also taken from Kautsky, 'the new era of war and revolution'.

According to the standard story, the sense of betrayal caused by the socialist parties' support for the war shocked Lenin to such an extent that he embarked on a radical rethinking that led him to reject 'the Marxism of the Second International', to renounce his earlier admiration for Kautsky, and to return to the original sources of the Marxist outlook. Lenin's rethinking is often tied to his intense study of Hegel's *Science of Logic* in autumn 1914. A series of innovative new positions found in Lenin's wartime writings reveal the impact of Lenin's new understanding of Marxism.[3]

The standard account we have just outlined gains its plausibility by overlooking two crucial things. First is Lenin's own rhetoric of aggressive unoriginality in the years 1914–16. Lenin insisted again and again with particular vehemence that he was merely repeating the pre-war consensus of revolutionary Social Democracy. Also overlooked is the actual content of the pre-war Marxist consensus, especially the part most crucial to Lenin, namely, Kautsky's analysis of 'the revolution of our time'. Recent scholarship has made it harder to ignore these issues.[4] The aim of this essay is to provide an alternative account that does not overlook the basic facts. My interpretation of events can be summarised as follows:

During the years from 1902 to 1909, Karl Kautsky put forth a scenario of the current state of the world that later had great influence on Lenin. The central theme of this scenario is that the world is entering a 'new era of war and revolution' that is characterised first and foremost by a *global* system of revolutionary interaction. In Lenin's view, this vision found practical expression in the Basel Manifesto of 1912, which he saw as a summary of the message of revolutionary Social Democracy. Kautsky's scenario and the mandates of the Basel Manifesto became integral parts of the Bolshevik outlook in the period

3 For a succinct statement of the standard story, see Peter Thomas's essay in this volume: 'Marxists found themselves unable to respond to the horrors of imperialist war with previously elaborated concepts;... the betrayals of the ostensibly "revolutionary" social democratic movement prompted a profound rethinking of the concept of revolution itself', a rethinking that included 'Lenin's return to Hegel in the early years of the war'. For a more detailed discussion, see the section on Lenin's notes on Hegel later in this essay.

4 See in particular the two volumes edited by Richard Day and Daniel Gaido (2009; 2012) and the Kautsky documents translated by Ben Lewis and Maciej Zurowski (Kautsky 2009/10 and Macnair 2013). Lenin's relations with Kautsky are a theme in all of my writings on Lenin; for the wartime years, see in particular Lih 2008, Lih 2009, and Lih 2011a.

immediately before the war, as shown in articles not only by Lenin but also by his lieutenants Zinoviev and Kamenev.

The outbreak of war caused Lenin to insist on the *continuity* between what he regarded as a pre-war consensus of revolutionary Marxism and the Bolshevik programme during 1914–16. This continuity explains why he *instantly* arrived at his basic programme, one that remained unchanged until early 1917. Throughout the war years 1914–16, he adopted a rhetorical stance of aggressive unoriginality and tied his own position as tightly as possible to Kautsky's pre-war scenario and to the Basel Manifesto. In his disputes with comrades on the left, it was they who were the innovators and Lenin who stoutly defended ideological continuity. Whatever originality and insight Lenin showed in his arguments and analyses, the positions he defended were in fact unoriginal – and he was proud of the fact.

Lenin's reaction to the outbreak of war cannot be understood without a solid grasp of the scenario of global revolutionary interaction set forth in Kautsky's writings and the first section of my essay is devoted to outlining Kautsky's vision of the new era of war and revolution. The section that follows analyses the Basel Manifesto of 1912 that Lenin saw as a fundamental expression of the pre-war consensus. The third section is devoted to articles written in 1910–13 by Bolshevik spokesman Lev Kamenev. Kamenev reprinted these articles in 1922 with the aim of documenting the continuity of Bolshevik positions before and during the war, and they accomplish this aim admirably.

These three sections lay the groundwork for my interpretation of Lenin's response to the outbreak of war and to the actions of the European Social Democratic parties. Before turning to a closer look at Lenin's response, I will outline a powerful alternative interpretation. One of the most intriguing and influential versions of the standard account of Lenin's radical rethinking points to his reading of Hegel's *Logic* and the more profound grasp of dialectics that proceeded from this reading. While I do not dispute the philosophical claims made by the authors who put forth this interpretation, I do not think their historical claims about Hegel's influence on Lenin's wartime political positions stand up to examination.

The Hegelist interpretation (as I will term it) paints a striking picture of Lenin during the first months of the war: finding himself in complete political isolation, Lenin retires from the hurly-burly of political activity, holes up in the Berne library with Hegel, and emerges only after a rethinking of the dialectical foundations of Marxism. His new outlook finds expression, among other places, in his writings on national self-determination from late 1916.

The last two sections of the essay are devoted to evaluating the two alternative interpretations in the light of the evidence. First I examine the seven months from the outbreak of war in August 1914 to the conference of émigré Bolsheviks in Berne in late February 1915, followed by a final section on Lenin's writings on national self-determination in late 1916. I conclude that Lenin was correct to stress the continuity between his wartime political platform and the pre-war consensus of 'revolutionary Social Democrats' about the fast-approaching new era of war and revolution.

Kautsky's Scenario of Global Revolutionary Interaction

> An era of revolutionary developments has begun. The age of slow, painful, almost imperceptible advances will give way to an epoch of revolutions, of sudden leaps forward, perhaps of occasional great defeats, but also – we must have such confidence in the cause of the proletariat – eventually of great victories.
>
> KARL KAUTSKY, 1905

Kautsky's *The Social Revolution* appeared in 1902, *Socialism and Colonial Policy* in 1907, and *Road to Power* in 1909.[5] In these three works, as well as many substantial and influential articles, Kautsky outlined a global view of the contemporary world. The key features of Kautsky's scenario are as follows:

1. After a generation of relative stability and only gradual progress, Europe and the world are entering upon a new era of war and revolutions that will be marked by profound conflicts and sharp shifts in power relations.[6]
2. The new era of war and revolution differs from the previous one, which lasted from 1789 to 1871, primarily by virtue of its global scope and of the new intensity of interaction made possible by growing ties among coun-

5 For English translations of these three works, see Kautsky 1902, Kautsky 1907, and Kautsky 1996; all three works are available online at the Marxists Internet Archive. The following discussion creates difficulties for a trope often found in writers in the Trotskyist tradition (for example, Neil Davidson in this volume) that claims that Kautsky was only radical circa 1905 when he 'temporarily fell under the influence of Luxemburg'.

6 Kautsky's outlook should be seen within the context of a 'widely shared awareness that great power competition had become radicalised, expanded in scope, and had taken on a new logic of life and death', as Adam Tooze puts it in this volume.

tries and in particular by new means of communication that allow accelerated access to modern ideas and techniques.[7]

3. The transition from a non-revolutionary situation to a revolutionary situation will require radically new tactics.
4. The revolutions that mark this new era fall into two broad categories: the socialist revolution that is on the agenda for Western Europe and North America; and the democratic revolutions that are on the agenda elsewhere in the world. The category of democratic revolutions can be further broken down into three main types: *political* revolutions to obtain political freedoms and overthrow absolutist oppression; revolutions of *self-determination* against national oppression; *anti-colonial* revolutions against foreign oppression.
5. One can no longer say that a socialist revolution is not yet 'mature' in Western Europe. A sharp growth of class antagonisms is one indication that we are on the eve of a socialist revolution. Anything less than a firm rejection of opportunism and its policy of class collaboration would be political suicide.[8]
6. The four types of revolutions overlap and interact with each other in ways that are unpredictable but that will certainly increase the overall intensity of the global revolutionary crisis. Thus any scenario of future developments must be extraordinarily open-ended.
7. Global interaction implies a rejection of simplistic models in which 'advanced' countries show 'backward' countries the image of their future. For example, in crucial respects Germany sees an image of its future in 'backward' Russia.[9]
8. The principal types of global interaction are: direct *intervention*, such as conquest, investments, and colonial domination; *observation* of the experience of other countries, allowing latecomers to swiftly catch up and overtake; and the direct *repercussions* of revolutionary events, due to the enthusiasm of some and the panic of others, the breaking of some ties and the creation of others.[10]

---

7 For reasons of space, I cannot give a full documentation of Kautsky's views. On issues not specifically discussed in this essay, I have provided references to illustrative remarks that can be found in Day and Gaido's *Witnesses to Permanent Revolution*: Day and Gaido 2009, pp. 183, 395–6 (on Japan), 640.

8 Day and Gaido 2009, p. 536.

9 Day and Gaido 2009, p. 219.

10 See in particular Kautsky 2009e ('Revolutionary Questions', 1904) and Kautsky 2009g ('The Consequences of the Japanese Victory and Social Democracy', 1905).

9. The capitalist world will try to preserve itself from revolutionary change in a variety of ways, and in particular, by imperialism, 'the last refuge of capitalism'.[11] Imperialist and militarist ideologies may stave off collapse by allowing the labour aristocracy to share in colonial profits and by presenting a plausible way out of the impending crisis. Nevertheless, these attempts will ultimately fail, if only because the world has already been divided up by the imperialist powers.[12]
10. Imperialism and militarism have greatly increased the chances of war, but the proletariat has no possible stake in wars between imperialist powers and will therefore not unite with the upper classes to fight one. The role of war as an incubator of revolution is likely to be extremely large, and there is a strong correlation between defeat in war and revolution.[13]
11. Only a resolutely anti-racist platform will permit Social Democracy to navigate the coming rapids of revolutionary change. Racist condescension prevents even some socialists from appreciating a basic fact about world politics: the colonies will demand, fight for and win their independence.
12. Russia occupies a crucial position in the process of global revolutionary situations. The triumphs and setbacks of the Russian revolution will therefore have an especially broad resonance in other countries.[14]

Such are the basic features of Kautsky's scenario of global revolutionary interaction. What remains to be brought out is the way in which these propositions cohere together as a system, since it was as a system that they were taken over by Lenin.[15]

Kautsky's vision of the current situation in Western Europe had been advanced by him at least since 1902 in polemics aimed at the 'opportunist' picture of class antagonisms melting away. Just the opposite, said Kautsky – class antagonisms were becoming sharper precisely because cartelisation at home and colonial policies abroad showed that capitalism was going through its final phase and that socialist revolution was on the agenda. 'The further cartels

11 Kautsky, 1996 (*Road to Power*, Chapter 9).
12 Day and Gaido 2009, p. 400.
13 Day and Gaido 2009, p. 386.
14 Day and Gaido 2009, p. 184.
15 György Lukács provides an excellent analysis of the systematic nature of Lenin's view of the global situation, although he shows no awareness of its roots in Kautsky and others (Lukács 1970).

develop and spread, the clearer the proof that the capitalist mode of production has passed beyond the stage when it was the most powerful agent for the development of the productive forces, and that it is ever more hindering this development and creating ever more unbearable conditions ... Socialism has already become an economic necessity today, only power determines when it will come'.[16]

In an effort to 'rub the rouge of health and youth into its wasted cheeks', bourgeois society was resorting to militarism and imperialism – as an economic imperative, as ideologies that promised a way out of the looming impasse of capitalist development, and as a means of bribing the upper reaches of the working class. As Kautsky observed in 1906, in England, as opposed to Russia or India, capitalist exploitation was 'a means of enriching the country, of accumulating a perpetually growing booty that was won through plundering the whole world. Even the propertyless classes benefit in many ways from this plunder'. This kind of explanation for the absence of worker militancy in the United Kingdom and elsewhere was commonplace in pre-war Social Democracy.[17]

Colonial expansion was only a short-term remedy for capitalist woes, since it would inevitably lead to heightened conflict at home and abroad. Since the world was almost completely divided up, colonial expansion could only result in armed conflict between the imperialist powers. Imperialist oppression was also leading to colonial revolts for national independence that, when (not if) successful, would destroy the imperialist system. 'English capitalism will suffer a frightful collapse when the oppressed lands rebel and refuse to continue paying tribute'.[18]

We now arrive at the second level of the system of global revolutionary interaction, namely, the democratic revolutions against absolutist, national and colonial oppression. Kautsky had much to say about each of these three types of democratic revolution. The principal revolutionary struggle for the destruction of absolutism and the establishment of political freedom was of course taking place in Russia. What needs to be stressed here is that Kautsky

---

16 Kautsky 1907.

17 Day and Gaido 2009, p. 631. In 1915, Lenin cited Kautsky, along with Marx and Engels, as an authority on British opportunism (Lenin 1960–8, Vol. 21, p. 154). In 1916, Karl Radek quoted a German Social Democratic supporter of the war, Paul Lensch, about the imperialist corruption of the English workers and comments: 'Lensch's view is not new. It is one of many he has borrowed from the radical Social Democrats. But it is doubtless correct' (Riddell 1984, pp. 461–2).

18 Day and Gaido 2009, p. 633; for a similar statement at the time of the Boer War, see Day and Gaido 2012, pp. 155–64.

offered an authoritative endorsement of the Bolshevik strategy for carrying out the anti-Tsarist revolution: a wager on the Russian peasant as a fighter for the democratic transformation of the country.[19] Kautsky could almost be called an honorary Bolshevik, and he was so regarded by all interested parties in Russia and German Social Democracy.

On the level of national revolutions for self-determination, Kautsky and Lenin shared a position that rejected both the over-estimation of the role of nationality by Austrian Social Democracy and its under-estimation by Rosa Luxemburg in Poland. The key commitment shared by the two men was the idea that 'the masses can only be filled with a durable enthusiasm for socialism where and insofar as the national question is solved'.[20] Following from this, both Kautsky and Lenin argued that the right of self-determination against national oppression must be respected, although Social Democracy did not necessarily advocate the use of this right in concrete cases; separatism in socialist and other worker organisations must be resisted; great power chauvinism (Germans vs. Poles in Kautsky's case, Russians vs. various national minorities in Lenin's case) must be opposed, even at the cost of bending over backwards to avoid offence; the ultimate solution to nationalism is to reassure national minorities that their democratic rights will be respected.[21]

Kautsky's attitude to national liberation movements in the colonies can best be seen in the response he made in 1907 to a group of Iranian Social Democrats who were unsure about the propriety of Social Democratic participation in the struggle against foreign capitalism.[22] Kautsky replied that 'socialist fighters cannot adopt an exclusively passive attitude towards the revolution and remain with their arms folded. And if the country is not sufficiently developed to have a modern proletariat, then only a [pre-socialist] democratic movement against foreign domination provides the possibility for socialists to participate in the revolutionary struggle'.

Kautsky went on to advise his Iranian correspondents that the Social Democrats may have to participate 'as simple democrats in the ranks of

19 Kautsky's classic statement of support for the Bolshevik position is 'The Driving Forces of the Russian Revolution and its Prospects' in 1906 (see Kautsky 2009e, which includes commentaries by Lenin and Trotsky; the young Stalin also wrote a commentary [Stalin 1953a]).

20 Jacobs 1992, p. 510, citing Kautsky in 1897. Jack Jacobs's study usefully compares Kautsky's attitudes toward the Jews and the Czechs.

21 For Kautsky's critique of the writings by Austrian Social Democrats on the nationality question, see Kautsky 2009/2010; also see Day and Gaido 2009, pp. 213–14.

22 'The Left in Iran, 1905–1940' 2010, pp. 123–8.

bourgeois and petit-bourgeois democrats'. They nevertheless will always have a wider perspective, since for them 'the victory of democracy is not the end of political struggle; rather, it is the beginning of the new unknown struggle which was practically impossible under the absolutist regime'. This new struggle required not only political freedom but national independence. The Social Democratic fight against capitalism in countries like Iran may not be able to put socialist revolution on the immediate agenda, but nevertheless such a struggle will 'weaken European capitalism and bestow greater strength on the European proletariat ... Persia and Turkey, by struggling for their own liberation, also fight for the liberation of the world proletariat'.

In 1909, Kautsky again stressed that the anti-colonial rebels were often supporters of capitalism. 'This does not in any way alter the fact that they are weakening European capitalism and its governments and introducing an element of political unrest into the whole world'.[23]

Kautsky's feelings about colonial liberation went deep. According to his biographer Gary Steenson, Kautsky had already predicted in articles he wrote in the 1880s that 'the all-too-gradual modernisation of the colonized countries would eventually yield native rebellion against domination by the Europeans'. He therefore emphasised 'the common interests of, and a possible coalition between, the industrial proletariat of the European nations and the natives of the colonies'.[24] Kautsky's attitude toward colonial independence movements was not just due to empirical observation and political strategy, but also to a visceral anti-racism:

> The colonial policy of imperialism is based on the assumption that only the peoples possessed of European civilization are capable of independent development. The men of other races are considered children, idiots, or beasts of burden, according to the degree of unfriendliness with which one treats them; in any case as beings having a lower level of development, who can be directed as one wishes. Even socialists proceed on this assumption as soon as they want to pursue a policy of colonial expansion, an ethical one, of course. But reality soon teaches them that our party's tenet that all men are equal is no mere figure of speech, but a very real force.[25]

---

23 Kautsky 1996, p. 83.

24 Steenson 1978, p. 75.

25 Kautsky 1996, pp. 80–1.

Kautsky's scenario of the new era of revolutions was a *global* system of revolutionary interaction primarily because of the role played in it by the national liberation movements. As he remarked in *Road to Power*: 'Today, the battles in the liberation struggle of labouring and exploited humanity are being fought not only at the Spree River and the Seine, but also at the Hudson and Mississippi, at the Neva and the Dardanelles, at the Ganges and the Hoangho'.[26]

The various types of revolution in Kautsky's scenario do not proceed along their own tracks in isolation, but are profoundly affected in every way by global interaction. Kautsky sets out with clarity the logic of what was later termed 'uneven and combined development', or, in Kautsky's words, 'the conjuncture of the most advanced with the most backward forms of societies and states':

> The backward nations have since time immemorial learned from the more advanced, and they have often therefore been capable of leaping with one bound over several stages of development which had been climbed wearily by their predecessors.
>
> In this way limitless variations arise in the historical path of development of nations ... And these variations increase the more the isolation of individual nations decreases, the more world trade develops, and thus the nearer we come to the modern era. This variation has become so great that many historians deny there are any historical laws. Marx and Engels succeeded in discovering the laws governing the variations, but they have only provided an Ariadne's thread for finding one's bearings in the historical labyrinth – they have definitely not transformed this labyrinth into a modern urban area with uniform, strictly parallel streets.[27]

I have outlined Kautsky's scenario of global revolutionary interaction. Before proceeding, we should note some implications Kautsky drew from this scenario about the coming era of war and revolution – implications that show up in Lenin's programme during the war. One such implication is the privileged position of Russia within the system. In 1902, Kautsky wrote an article for Lenin's underground newspaper *Iskra* entitled 'Slavs and Revolution' that asserted that 'the revolutionary centre is moving from the West to the East'. The 'revolutionising of minds' among the Russian people will lead to 'great deeds

26 Kautsky 1996, pp. 88–91.

27 Kautsky 1907. See also Day and Gaido, pp. 395–7. As Richard Day and Daniel Gaido well remark: 'Disputing the notion of any single pattern of capitalist development, Kautsky simultaneously rejected any idea of unilateral economic determinism' (Day and Gaido 2009, p. 617).

that cannot fail to influence Western Europe' and the blood of Russian revolutionary martyrs will 'fertilise the shoots of social revolution throughout the entire civilized world'.[28] Lenin was so fond of this article that he read lengthy excerpts of it in 1920 at the public celebration of his fiftieth birthday. Soon afterwards, he included these excerpts in his pamphlet *Left-Wing Communism*, commenting 'How well Karl Kautsky wrote eighteen years ago!'[29]

In the latter part of the decade, Kautsky often described 1905 as a turning point in world affairs that had inaugurated a 'period of continuous unrest throughout the Orient' (meaning both East Asia and the Islamic world).[30] For him, the event that started off the new era was not so much the Russian Revolution in itself as Japan's victory over Tsarist Russia, a victory which ended 'the illusion of inferiority' of non-Europeans and gave them self-confidence.[31] Nevertheless, the picture of Russia that emerges from Kautsky's extensive writings on the subject is a country whose revolutionary prowess had vast potential influence on socialist revolution in Western Europe, national revolution in Eastern Europe, and national liberation movements in 'the Orient'.[32]

Kautsky also argued that the revolutionary situation that was looming in the very near future would require a radical change of tactics. This was the point – widely misunderstood today – he was trying to make in 1910 with his famous distinction between a 'strategy of attrition' vs. a 'strategy of overthrow'. Kautsky explained that 'attrition' (the standard SPD activity of energetic socialist enlightenment and organisation) was appropriate to a normal, non-revolutionary situation, whereas 'overthrow' (mass political strikes and other non-parliamentary means of pressure) was appropriate to a genuinely revolutionary situation. Kautsky added that, while at present Germany was still in a non-revolutionary situation, nevertheless a revolutionary crisis could be expected very soon.[33]

Lenin took Kautsky at his word. Writing in 1910, he pointed out that 'Kautsky said clearly and directly that the transition [to a strategy of overthrow] is *inevitable* during the further development of the political crisis'.[34] Lenin there-

---

28 Day and Gaido 2009, pp. 61–5.

29 Lenin 1960–8, Vol. 40, pp. 325–7; Vol. 41, pp. 4–5.

30 Kautsky 1996, p. 83.

31 Kautsky 1907.

32 For an extended analysis of the differing impact of the Russian Revolution in the 'East' and in the 'West', see Dominico Losurdo's contribution in this volume.

33 Grunenberg 1970.

34 Lenin 1958–64, Vol. 19, pp. 367.

fore minimised the significance of the clash between the German Party's two honorary Bolsheviks: Kautsky and Luxemburg both believed that a fundamental turning point comparable to Bloody Sunday in January 1905 was in the works. The only disagreement was whether this turning-point would occur 'now or *not just yet*, this minute or *the next minute*'.[35]

A Polish Social Democrat close to the Bolsheviks, Julian Marchlewski, equated Lenin and Kautsky on exactly this point: Lenin 'recommends [in 1909], if you will, the same thing as did Kautsky [a year later]: application of the "strategy of overthrow" and the "strategy of attrition", each at the correct time'.[36]

As early as 1902, Kautsky had concluded that 'we must reckon on the possibility of a war within a perceptible time and therewith also the possibility of political convulsions that will end directly in proletarian uprisings or at least in opening the way toward them'.[37] In any such war between imperialist powers – as opposed to national and colonial independence movements – the proletariat had no cause to fight side by side with the bourgeoisie. As Kautsky put it in 1907:

> The bourgeoisie and the proletariat of a nation are equally interested in their national independence and self-determination, in the removal of all kinds of oppression and exploitation at the hands of a foreign nation. [But in the present era of imperialism,] a war in defence of national liberty in which bourgeois and proletarian may unite is nowhere to be expected ... At the present time the conflicts between states can bring no war that proletarian interests would not, as a matter of duty, energetically oppose.[38]

Looking back, Lenin insisted with great vehemence on the pre-war Marxist consensus that the outbreak of war would lead almost by definition to a revolutionary situation. The following statements, one from early 1916 and the other from late 1918, illustrate Lenin's rhetoric of aggressive unoriginality.

---

35 Lenin 1958–64, Vol. 20, p. 18.

36 Marchlewski 1910, p. 102 (July 1909). See Lenin 1960–8, Vol. 15, p. 458; Lenin 1958–64, Vol. 19, p. 50.

37 Kautsky 1902, pp. 96–7. For an extended analysis of the actual connection between the experience of war and social revolution, see Sandra Halperin in this volume.

38 As cited, with approval, by Rosa Luxemburg in the Junius pamphlet (Luxemburg 1970, pp. 424–6).

> The one now denying revolutionary action [Kautsky] is the very same authority of the Second International who in 1909 wrote a whole book, *Road to Power*, translated into practically all the major European languages and demonstrating the *link* between the future war and revolution.[39]
>
> Long before the war, all Marxists, all socialists were agreed that a European war would create a revolutionary situation ... So, the expectation of a revolutionary situation in Europe was not an infatuation of the Bolsheviks, but the *general opinion* of all Marxists.[40]

Lenin once stated that he had read practically everything by Kautsky, and indeed it is hard to believe that anyone in his generation knew the Kautsky corpus as well as he did.[41] Anything Lenin says about Kautsky should be taken very seriously indeed. Recent scholarship is beginning to catch up with Lenin's thesis that 'the new era of war and revolution' was a central theme in Kautsky's writings after the turn of the century. In this section, I have shown how this theme provides a dynamic unity to a wide range of Kautsky's positions and arguments.[42] In the next section, we will find out why Lenin thought the same basic theme was reflected in a solemn declaration of the united will of the entire Second International, the Basel Manifesto of 1912.

The Basel Manifesto

> The Basel Manifesto sums up the vast amount of propaganda and agitation material of the entire epoch of the Second International, namely, the period between 1889 and 1914. This Manifesto *summarises*, without any exaggeration, *millions upon millions* of leaflets, press articles, books, and speeches by socialists of all lands. To declare this Manifesto erroneous means declaring the entire Second International erroneous, the work done in decades and decades by all Social-Democratic parties. To brush aside the Basel Manifesto means brushing aside the entire history of socialism. The Basel Manifesto says nothing *unusual* or *out of the ordinary*.[43]

39 Lenin 1958–64, Vol. 27, pp. 109–10.

40 Lenin 1960–8, Vol. 28, pp. 289, 292.

41 Lenin 1960–8, Vol. 41, p. 468.

42 The closest thing to a statement of synthesis by Kautsky is the final chapter of *Road to Power* (Kautsky 1996).

43 Lenin 1958–64, Vol. 21, p. 44; Lenin 1960–8, Vol. 27, p. 102 (late 1915, unpublished).

Lenin's extravagant description of the Basel Manifesto of 1912 reflects the central place it occupied in his programme and rhetoric after 1914. As Lenin saw it, the Manifesto was a solemn commitment by Europe's Social Democratic parties to use the outbreak of war to engage in revolutionary action or at least work in that direction. Not to honour this commitment was a betrayal of everything that Social Democracy stood for.

In many ways, the Extraordinary International Socialist Congress held in Basel in November 1912 was the emotional highpoint of the entire era of the Second International, a fact that helps explain its far-reaching impact on the Bolsheviks. The congress was called at very short notice so that Europe's socialist proletariat could make its voice heard to prevent great power intervention in the armed conflict that had just broken out in the Balkans. The Congress was preceded by mass demonstrations throughout Europe culminating in Europe-wide synchronised rallies on 17 November. When representatives from all the European parties met in Basel on 24–5 November, the organisers pulled out all the stops, using all their accumulated experience of managing international conferences to make as impressive a display of socialist solidarity as possible.

The congress opened with a huge demonstration inside and out of the Basel Cathedral. 'Inside the cathedral, thousands of candles flickered in the wind, providing light to the dim and vast open spaces of the church. The church bells chimed for fifteen minutes, while militants methodically placed their red flags of the International in the nave of the cathedral ... It was a sacred celebration of the International's highest aspirations'.[44] One of the participants was the Russian Social Democrat Aleksandra Kollontai, who expressed her feelings in a letter:

> One felt the need to frighten Europe, to threaten it with the 'red spectre', in case the governments should risk a war. And standing on the table which served as a platform I did threaten Europe ... I am still dizzy with all I have lived through.[45]

The proposed Manifesto was long (four and a half pages) and made very concrete policy suggestions, but in line with the emphasis on solidarity, it was accepted unanimously by the congress. The Manifesto was important to the Bolsheviks not only because of its specific mandates but also its overall picture of the world and the current situation. Although it describes a world with

---

44 Callahan 2010, pp. 282–4. Callahan's chapter on the Basel Congress includes detailed tables that document the amazing scope of the Europe-wide demonstrations.

45 Haupt 1972, pp. 91–2.

different and interacting levels of revolutions, it does not invoke a truly global framework, since there is no mention of colonial resistance. Nevertheless, due to its origins in the Balkan Crisis, the resolution does endorse 'the right of democratic self-government' for Slavic nationalities, ties the struggle of the Slavs to the fight against 'imperialism' in Western Europe, and warns against 'the policy of conquest in Asia Minor, a policy which would inevitably lead directly to a world war'.

Within this system of revolutionary interaction, Russia occupies a privileged position. In the long paragraph devoted specifically to Russia, the resolution greets the recent strike movement in Russia and Poland 'with great joy', since 'tsarism is the hope of all the reactionary powers of Europe and the bitterest foe of the democracy of the peoples whom it dominates; to bring on the destruction of tsarism must, therefore, be viewed by the entire International as one of its foremost tasks'.

The threatened world war is seen as a product of 'capitalist imperialism' and therefore without 'even the slightest pretext of serving the people's interests... The proletarians consider it a crime to fire at each other for the benefit of the capitalist profits, the ambitions of dynasties, or the greater glory of secret diplomatic treaties'. Equally striking is the picture the Basel Manifesto paints of the International itself:

> Because the proletarians of all countries have risen simultaneously in a struggle against imperialism, and because each section of the International has opposed to the government of its own country the resistance of the proletariat and has mobilized the public opinion of its nation against all bellicose desires, there has resulted a splendid cooperation among the workers of all countries which has so far contributed a great deal toward saving the threatened peace of the world.

The 'unanimity' in the war against war allows the International to oppose to capitalist imperialism the power of the international solidarity of the proletariat and to 'assign a particular task to each socialist party'. Looking ahead, the Manifesto expresses the hope that, regardless of what may be the outcome of the crisis, the contacts between proletarian parties will grow stronger.

Given all of the above, what actions did the resolution mandate in case war did break out? The rhetorical aim of the Manifesto was to sound as threatening and scary as possible without committing sovereign national parties to specific courses of action. It begins by citing and endorsing the earlier Stuttgart resolution from 1907 that the working class in each country must 'take measures to bring about its early termination and strive with all their power to use the economic and political crises created by the war to arouse the masses politically and hasten the overthrow of capitalist class rule'. This language was included in the Stuttgart resolution due to the direct intervention of Rosa Luxemburg, Martov and Lenin himself.[46]

The Basel Manifesto contained additional strong language about the link between war and revolution, carefully presented as an objective warning rather than as a mandate to socialist action. Let the governments remember that, given the attitude of the working class, 'they cannot unleash war without danger to themselves'. Let them recall how the Franco-German War led to the Paris Commune, how the Russo-Japanese War led to the 1905 Revolution. Striking in these threats is the prominent role of the Russian Revolution of 1905 and also the strong implied link between defeat and revolution. Both these features showed up later in the Bolshevik wartime platform.

The Bolsheviks could make a good case that the International had solemnly committed itself to revolutionary action, but their case has the air of lawyerly parsing against the spirit of the document. The very use of revolution as a threat shows that the International was not particularly revolutionary. The Manifesto threatens the governments that if they 'cut off all possibility of normal progress and thereby drive the proletariat to desperate moves, they themselves must bear the entire responsibility for the consequences'. In other words: don't drive us to do something we will both regret. The Basel Manifesto did not aim at causing the outbreak of revolution: its aim was rather to prevent the outbreak of war and its attendant disasters, among which revolution seems to be included.

Nevertheless, the International had made a very serious and very public threat. Its failure to make good on this threat was evident to everybody, as shown by a comment made by the American socialist William Walling in early 1915. After quoting the 'formulation proposed by the Russian and Polish delegates, Rosa Luxemburg, Lenin, and Martoff' about hastening the overthrow of capitalist class rule, Walling goes on to observe that 'this threat and prediction of a revolution to follow the war was finally incorporated in the Stuttgart resolution and was adopted unanimously by the Congress of Basel in 1912. Naturally the time has not yet come for its discussion in connection with the present war – though evidently it has already been abandoned by the ultranationalist Socialists'.[47]

---

46 For background on the Stuttgart Congress, see Riddell 1984.

47 Walling 1972, p. 39. Toward the end of his book, Walling mentions the very day of writing one particular page: 20 April 1915 (Walling 1972, p. 431).

The Basel Manifesto deserves the central place it occupies in Lenin's rhetoric after 1914. It gave official sanction to the vision of a new era of war and revolution, and set forth the logic of revolutionary interaction, even if not on a fully global scale. It reflected the Second International's idealised and unrealistic self-image. When the Bolsheviks rejected the Second International, they did not reject this self-image, but rather set out to make it a reality in the form of a new and purified International. Their loyalty to the Manifesto reassured the Bolsheviks that they and they alone among the Social Democratic parties of Europe did not besmirch the banner of Social Democracy.

Kamenev on the New Era, 1910–1913

A large majority of the pre-war articles that Lev Kamenev republished in 1922 in his collection *Between Two Revolutions* deal with domestic Russian politics, both revolutionary and counter-revolutionary. At the end of the book, there is a short section of five articles published in the period 1910–13 that dealt with international issues. Kamenev introduced this section with the following comment: 'The goal of reprinting is to show that even in this area the Bolsheviks had before the war already set out the basic points that we needed only to develop further during the war and after it. Of course, at that time we could only *set out* these points, only *feel them out*'.[48]

Indeed, very little of Lenin's basic programme in 1914–16 is not foreshadowed in these articles. Along with Lenin and Zinoviev, Kamenev was a principal spokesman of Bolshevism before the war; we see in his writings the roots of the Third International in the Bolsheviks' dream of the Second International – what they fondly thought the International actually was. We also see the Bolsheviks setting themselves up for betrayal – so that when the betrayal came, they had a framework of interpretation ready and waiting.

Kamenev's pre-war writings deal with all four levels of Kautsky's global scenario. We hardly need to document his views about the first two levels – socialist revolution in Western Europe and the anti-Tsarist democratic revolution in Russia – so we will restrict our attention here to revolutions against national and colonial oppression. In a 1910 article on the 'Slavic question', Kamenev takes up the question of national self-determination and advances two concrete slogans: the demand for a democratic federal republic in the Balkans and 'the autonomy of Poland on the basis of the all-round democratization of

48 Kamenev 2003, p. 653 (Kamenev's emphasis). Note that all Kamenev's editorial notes from the 1922 edition were made during Lenin's lifetime.

Russia'. These two slogans stand in opposition to the imperialist nationalism of Russian liberals. Indeed, their realisation would not only lead to 'revolutionizing all the relations of capitalist Europe', but also remove nationality conflicts that stood in the way of proletarian struggle.[49]

Even more striking is Kamenev's exploration of the final level of revolution, the one most associated with Kautsky and that gave the Bolshevik scenario a truly global scope: the independence movement in the colonies and semi-colonies. In an article entitled 'Revolution in the East', Kamenev announced 'Asia has just entered into a long period of revolutionary transformations'.[50] The national independence movements in 'Asia' against European domination as well as against parasitic local elites – Kamenev names 'new Turkey', 'new Persia', 'new China', India and Egypt – represents an old type of revolution, but they are taking place in a fundamentally new context:

> The revolution of the nineteenth century is a bourgeois-democratic and national revolution, the revolution of the twentieth century is a proletarian and international revolution … The European tasks facing Asia are principally the same [as those facing the European revolutions of the nineteenth century] but they will be solved in a fundamentally altered environment … Revolutionary Asia sees alongside of it a European society that is vitally interested in its fate, a society split into two irreconcilable camps, a society that itself is living in the prospect of its own socialist revolution … Revolutionary Asia will find in Europe not only enemies, but also allies who have an interest in its progress.[51]

'Revolutionary Asia' and the socialist proletariat are natural allies, but not because there is anything socialist about the Asian revolutions. Despite the influence of European socialist ideas on the Asian intellectuals, 'the movement of the Asian democrats contains not a grain of socialism'. Kamenev sums up their programme concisely: 'overthrow of the old power [*vlast*], full rule by the people [*narodovlastie*], national independence'. In the new context of global interaction and revolutionary contagion, however, these national liberation

49 For the background in Kautsky's writings for Kamenev's scenario, see Day and Gaido 2009, pp. 216–18. In 1915, Kautsky quotes himself from 1904: 'A democratic Russia must tremendously rekindle the aspiration for national independence among the Slavs of Austria and Turkey'; Lenin, although denouncing Kautsky's 1915 argument in general, says about this assertion from 1904 'this is indisputable' (Lenin 1958–64, Vol. 21, p. 134).

50 Kamenev 2003, pp. 660–6.

51 Kamenev 2003, pp. 660–6.

movements have a huge impact directly on Europe. Kamenev quotes the Austrian Social Democrat Otto Bauer: 'The whole European economy is tied in the closest possible fashion with the East... The whole European system of states stands and falls with its domination over the Eastern countries'.[52] This is why (Kamenev states perhaps over-optimistically) the English, French and German workers follow Asian events with such attention: 'the socialist proletariat of Europe has long awaited the moment when the foundations of reaction in Asia begin to totter in order to strike their own decisive blow in Europe'.

Kamenev ends his article by asserting in very strong terms the privileged place of Russia in the system of global revolutionary interaction. The Revolution of 1905 was not only the 'immediate impulse' to the new awakening now taking place in Persia, Turkey, India and China, but it also had a powerful impact on the Western European Social Democratic movement. 'In the events that are now approaching, Russia is predestined to play a decisive role. It is the knot at which all the threads of the future meet'.[53]

The same central role is allotted to Russia in Kamenev's article on the Manifesto passed by the 1912 Congress at Basel.[54] According to Kamenev, the Manifesto asserted that overthrowing the Romanov dynasty is an 'international task' of the highest priority. And Russia's privileged position is understandable, because

> the relations that have been created in Europe and Asia in the second decade of the twentieth century are such that the proletariat of Russia is at the centre of international events. Much depends on what this proletariat says – its voice is listened to with great attention not only in proletarian Europe [but] in revolutionizing Asia... Revolution in Russia: this is the Achilles' heel of the whole system of relations in Europe and Asia. Only a new revolution in Russia can begin a new period of success for the proletarian cause in Europe and the democratic cause in Asia.[55]

---

52 Otto Bauer is often mentioned by Lenin after 1914 as one of the main spokesmen for prewar revolutionary Social Democracy; for writings by Bauer on international relations, see Day and Gaido 2012.

53 Such a view seems to have been a Bolshevik commonplace. See Stalin's remark in passing in 'Marxism and the National Question' (1913): 'Russia is situated between Europe and Asia, between Austria and China. The growth of democracy in Asia in inevitable. The growth of imperialism in Europe is not fortuitous' (Stalin 1953b).

54 Kamenev 2003, pp. 675–80 (for translated excerpts from this article, see Gankin and Fisher 1940, pp. 85–8 and Riddell 1984, pp. 90–2).

55 Kamenev 2003, pp. 675–80.

Kamenev himself was only one of the six Bolshevik delegates to the Basel Conference, but he was also the Bolshevik representative to the International Socialist Bureau and, as such, participated directly in working out the resolution's text.[56] Writing in January 1913, Kamenev already uses the language of 'civil war' adopted by the Bolsheviks a year and a half later:

> The basic point of view of the socialist International, as set forth and ratified in the Basel Manifesto, can be expressed as follows: given present circumstances, the only guarantee of peace between states consists in the intensification and sharpening of the civil war of the proletariat against the bourgeoisie inside each separate state ... The congress was imbued with the awareness that in its struggle against war, the proletariat had to develop its energy to the furthest limit, right up to the opening of civil war.[57]

The aim of this mandated civil war is not just peace, continues Kamenev, but 'the annihilation of the whole capitalist system', as proven by the language taken over from the 1907 Stuttgart resolution. For practical reasons, Kamenev approves of the resolution's lack of specificity about the actual tactics to be employed in each country. Still, he predicts that war would lead to a 'broad revolutionary movement' more quickly in Russia than in any other country.

For Kamenev, a resolution passed by an international Social Democratic congress was a very serious affair. He reacted with indignation to a cynical remark by the French loose cannon Gustave Hervé, who at this time (1912) was preaching the necessity of a bloc between socialists and liberals. But what about the resolution of the Amsterdam Congress (1904) prohibiting such blocs? Not important, replied Hervé – 'if a bloc (a long-lasting alliance) contradicts the bible, then call it a coalition or a cartel, you silly people'. Kamenev somewhat primly remarks that 'this tone of voice in relation to the mandates of international socialist congresses speaks for itself'.[58]

A very exalted view of the International manifests itself throughout Kamenev's articles. At Basel, he was much impressed (as were many other observers) by the unanimity and determination of the stand against war. He was proud of the way that the resolution set out very specific tasks to 'the national units of the international army of the socialist proletariat'. The Asian revolutions gave the International even more of a global presence: 'The

56 Kamenev 2003, p. 675.

57 Kamenev 2003, pp. 675–80.

58 Kamenev 2003, p. 674.

International Socialist Bureau has become almost the official institution to which the democrats of Asia direct their protests against the violently repressive actions of the European states'.

The Bolsheviks' high and unrealistic expectation meant that they were setting themselves up for a huge disappointment. As Kamenev bitterly remarked in 1922, apropos of the remark just quoted: 'The Second International betrayed the cause of the Asiatic and all other colonial revolutions in the same way as it betrayed the workers of Europe'. The mission of the Third International – founded in 1919 but a central goal of Lenin's from the outbreak of the war – was thus to become in reality what the Second International had been only in the exalted dreams of the Bolsheviks.

Kamenev also doomed himself to disappointment with his portrayal of German Social Democracy; we see the same combination of excessively high expectations with a ready-made explanation for betrayal when it came. In an article on the Chemnitz Party Congress of 1912, Kamenev sketched out the following map of the tendencies within the SPD. On one side were the opportunists, represented at the congress by Gerhard Hildebrand, who openly advocated acquiring colonies, by force if necessary, in order to win the confidence of the liberals. Hildebrand was essentially asking the party 'to cease being the party of the socialist proletariat'. Kamenev was reassured by the fact that Hildebrand was tossed out of the party by the congress.[59]

On the other side of Kamenev's map were 'the lefts', those who rejected Eduard Bernstein's theoretical revisions and Hildebrand's tactical opportunism. The Bolsheviks had always been extremely proud of the fact that 'in Russian affairs, all the outstanding theoreticians of German Social Democracy agree with the Bolshevik point of view'. But now a rift had opened up among the lefts, and in particular between Kautsky and Rosa Luxemburg, much to the glee of Russian opportunists and liquidators, as Kamenev noted in disgust.

Kamenev mentioned that the rift was not a profound one, but only 'a matter of timing'. As Kautsky said, sharpening class antagonisms meant that 'mighty battles' within Germany were inevitable in the near future. When this revolutionary situation arrived in the near future, then would be the time to apply radical, mass action tactics. Kamenev strongly agreed with Kautsky that different tactics were applicable depending on whether the existing situation

---

59 Kamenev 2003, pp. 667–71. Hildebrand was not the only party member to face party discipline for pro-colonial statements, as shown by Guettell 2012a, an excellent recent analysis that convincingly shows that German Social Democracy as a whole had a strong anti-colonial stand (in his introduction to this volume, Alexander Anievas somewhat one-sidedly emphasises the pro-colonialism in the SPD).

was revolutionary or not – although he also thought that the agitation of Luxemburg and her friends for more radical tactics was a necessary element of preparation for the 'mighty battles' soon to come.

Kamenev's map of German Social Democracy in 1912 can be summarised in his own words:

> On the right are the opportunists, heading straight for the liquidation of the party of the socialist proletariat. And on the left wing, we see on the one hand the advocates of a more active, mass tactic, who reflect the view of the masses, and on the other hand, the careful leaders [*vozhdi*] of the party, defending the old ways and not wishing to leave them until the transition to new rails is dictated by the enemies of the proletariat. Of course, the opportunists are always glad to support this 'centre' against those on the far left.[60]

As usual, bitter footnotes in the 1922 edition recorded Kamenev's sense of betrayal: 'Alas, they [the socialist *vozhdi*] didn't want to leave the old ways even when the class enemy threw down a direct challenge to the proletariat. We thought better of them than they deserved'. In August 1914, the German Party went the way of opportunism and *ipso facto* ceased to be a party of the socialist proletariat.[61]

Let us now ask ourselves: how would someone with Kamenev's views – his confidence in an imminent revolutionary situation at home and abroad, his high expectations of radical actions from the revolutionary Social Democrats of the International, his strong sense of global revolutionary interaction, and his map of political tendencies within German Social Democracy – how would such a person react to the events of August 1914? The following predictions seem plausible:

Our hypothetical Bolshevik would explain the debacle by means of his map of political tendencies. The same three forces are at work – opportunists, lefts and centre – but the balance between them has dramatically shifted. Opportunism has triumphed, the lefts are resisting, and the centre has revealed itself as unworthy of our trust. Our emotional attitude toward the opportunists and the lefts would not change much – we've always known who they were. But our fury against those whom we trusted and defended would be boundless. We were fooled once – we won't be fooled again.

---

60 Kamenev 2003, p. 671.

61 Kamenev 2003, pp. 668 and 672.

Our hypothetical Bolshevik would insist on carrying out what he saw as the sacred responsibility of fulfilling the mandate of the Basel Manifesto – in particular, turning the imperialist war into civil war.

Our hypothetical Bolshevik would continue to insist on the value of democratic revolutions in the global context against anyone tempted to downplay either national self-determination or national liberation struggles.

Our hypothetical Bolshevik would try to find some way of manifesting the privileged place of Russia in the new revolutionary situation created by the war.

Finally, our hypothetical Bolshevik would begin to work for an International that would live up to the exalted view of the old International – a new International that would really be militant and 'of one soul' in outlook, really accept the obligations mandated by international congresses, really be in a position to give tasks to 'national units of the army of the socialist proletariat', and really be a champion of national liberation, looked up to by revolutionary democrats all over the globe. And our map of Social Democratic tendencies shows us the pathway to achieving this new International: purge the opportunists, purge the centre with special vindictiveness, and leave only the revolutionary Social Democrats.

We will soon see whether any actual Bolsheviks resembled this hypothetical Bolshevik.

The Hegelist Alternative

In the last months of 1914, Lenin embarked on a reading of G.W.F. Hegel's *Science of Logic* and filled up over 150 pages with excerpts and comments (about three-fourths of the contents are excerpts).[62] His interest in reading Hegel was sparked off originally by a commission from a Russian encyclopaedia to write an extensive article on Karl Marx. The impact of his Hegel reading shows itself in the completed encyclopaedia article: Lenin preceded the discussion of Marx's economics and politics with sections on 'Philosophical Materialism' and 'Dialectics', an innovative procedure for the time (although Marx's economic doctrine still retains the central place). Lenin's reading of the *Logic* and his notebooks only became known to the public after his death.

So much is undisputed. Lenin's reading of Hegel has implications for a number of issues of philosophy and intellectual history: Hegel's conception of dialectics and its relations to Marxism, Lenin's own understanding of these issues,

62 Anderson 1995, p. 29.

and the impact of the notes on later Marxist intellectuals. These issues have given rise to lively disputes on which I make no comment, as they are outside my competence.

Recently, a strong case has been made that Lenin's reading of Hegel's *Logic* had a profound impact on the political programme he advanced after 1914. An early version of this contention was put forth by Raya Dunayevskaya in the 1950s.[63] In the mid-1990s, two book-length studies fleshed out the case, one from a perspective hostile to Lenin (*Leninism* by Neil Harding) and the other from a more sympathetic perspective (*Lenin, Hegel, and Western Marxism: A Critical Study* by Kevin Anderson).[64] In a collection of articles on Lenin published in 2007 three authors – Kevin Anderson, Stathis Kouvelakis and Etienne Balibar – also make the case for the crucial importance of the Hegel notes to Lenin's politics.[65] These two books from the 1990s and the three articles from 2007 are my source for what I call the Hegelist alternative to my hypothetical Bolshevik whose reaction to the outbreak of war was based on the pre-war scenario of the new era of war and revolution.

While the Hegelist authors disagree on a number of significant issues, they all present something like the following narrative: The radical intransigence of Lenin's reaction to the socialist betrayal in August 1914 led to his complete political isolation and an instinctive intuition on his part that Marxism had to be rethought, starting with its methodological foundations. So, despite the uproar around him, Lenin holed up in the Berne library during the last months of 1914 and studied Hegel's *Logic*. He arrived at a new understanding of dialectics that led him to reject 'the Marxism of the Second International' root and branch and to put forth innovative political positions in his writings of 1915–16. In particular, writings on the national question such as 'A Caricature of Marxism and Imperialist Economism' (late 1916) show the impact of his new dialectical thinking. All in all, Lenin's encounter with Hegel in the Berne library was a major event in twentieth-century political history.

Some representative comments will give the flavour of the Hegelist case. All of them evoke the image of Lenin withdrawing from the hurly-burly of politics to the quiet library in Berne. 'He spent long weeks in the library engaged in daily study of Hegel's writings'.[66] 'In the midst of unparalleled tumult he shut himself away in Berne public library with Hegel's *Logic*'.[67] 'Lenin withdrew into

63 Dunayevskaya 1988.
64 Harding 1996; Anderson 1995.
65 Anderson 2007; Kouvelakis 2007; Balibar 2007.
66 Anderson 1995, p. 4.
67 Harding 1996, p. 77.

the calm of a Berne library to plunge into his reading of Hegel ... Through these collages of quotations and notes taken in a Berne library, something began that would mark the twentieth century as a whole'.[68]

Consequently he had little time for political activity, so that his initial interventions after August 1914 were 'slow and rare'.[69] 'At the end of 1914 he took part in some meetings of refugees who were opposed to "social patriotism", finished writing an encyclopaedia article on Marx, and before anything else, *set himself to reading the metaphysicians*'.[70] Anderson makes the case by means of a page-number count: from August to December 1914, Lenin wrote 158 pages of Hegel notes, 19 pages of notes on other authors, 67 pages of letters, and 114 pages on other topics.[71]

One reason for his solitude was that he was 'totally isolated' politically.[72] 'His theses were uncompromisingly radical and so far out of joint with the all-pervading mood of patriotic jingoism that even his own comrades in arms doubted his grip on reality'.[73] But the basic motive for returning to Hegel was 'an evident attempt on his part to reconstitute Marxist theory after the betrayal of 1914'.[74] 'In the face of disaster it is a question of returning to the very basis, a theoretical refoundation of Marxism'.[75]

Lenin's reading of Hegel was 'a fundamental turning point in Lenin's political thought'.[76] It provided 'a philosophical anchorage for virtually all his principal political strategies'.[77] 'The new position that Lenin attained with his reading of Hegel is to be sought nowhere else than in his political and theoretical intervention in the years that followed the First World War'.[78]

When it comes to actually tracing connections between Lenin's notes on Hegel and specific political positions, we find considerable differences among the Hegelists. This is understandable: since Lenin himself made no explicit link

68 Kouvelakis 2007, pp. 167, 189.
69 Kouvelakis 2007, p. 166.
70 Balibar 2007, pp. 209–10.
71 Anderson 1995, pp. 108–9. Kouvelakis refers to these statistics to justify his statement that Hegel's *Logic* was Lenin's 'privileged and almost excusive terrain' for this decisive period (Kouvelakis 2007, p. 170). This description seems to go beyond what the page count implies. As we shall see, even in its own terms, Anderson's page count is misleading.
72 Balibar 2007, pp. 209–10.
73 Harding 2007, pp. 75–6.
74 Anderson 2007, p. 129.
75 Kouvelakis 2007, p. 168.
76 Balibar 2007, pp. 210–11.
77 Harding 1996, p. 237.
78 Kouvelakis 2007, pp. 194–5.

between his putative new understanding of the dialectic and any plank in his political platform, investigators must decide for themselves which of Lenin's policies are truly dialectical. Nevertheless, all of the Hegelists see the influence of Lenin's refurbished dialectical outlook in his polemics of late 1916 about national self-determination, in particular in articles such as 'A Caricature of Marxism and Imperialist Economism'.

Kevin Anderson's discussion of these writings is one of the more carefully worked-out accounts. Anderson thinks that Lenin was 'the first major political theorist, Marxist or non-Marxist, to grasp the importance that anti-imperialist national movements would have for global politics in the twentieth century'.[79] There are several reasons that lead Anderson to see the impact of Hegel's *Logic* on Lenin's discoveries. First, in Lenin's view, 'national liberation was the dialectical opposite of global imperialism, whereas the nationalism of the great powers of Europe, the United States, and Japan promoted and underpinned imperialism'.[80] Second, 'Lenin's 1915–16 arguments over national liberation hinge on how a particular, in this case a national movement, connects to a universal, in this case socialist internationalism'.[81] Finally, Lenin widened 'the orthodox Marxian notion of the revolutionary subject' to include national liberation movements.[82] Beyond these three specific links, Lenin's stand was influenced by a newly dialectical outlook that broke with the gradualistic 'evolutionism' allegedly characteristic of the Second International, a focus on 'self-movement' [*Selbstbewegung*], a readiness for leaps, catastrophes, and so forth.

All the Hegelist authors have important things to say about the theoretical issues raised by Lenin's notes, and I repeat that I am not concerned here about the nature of the dialectic or about twentieth-century Marxist theory. I dispute on historical grounds the case made for the influence of Lenin's reading of Hegel on his political programme from 1914 to 1916. In the final two sections of my essay, I will show first that the Hegelist picture of Lenin's activities in the first months of the war is seriously distorted, and second that Lenin's 1916 writings on national self-determination are evidence of continuity rather than rethinking. Before turning to this concrete case study, I will comment on a number of more general weaknesses in the Hegelist case.

In the first place, it operates with an increasingly out-of-date and desiccated picture of the so-called 'Marxism of the Second International'. The outlook of the Second International is pictured as a single whole, thus completely ignoring

79 Anderson 1995, p. 128. See also Anderson 2007, p. 146.
80 Anderson 2007, p. 131.
81 Anderson 1995, p. 34. See also Anderson 2007, p. 131.
82 Anderson 2007, p. 143.

the clash so crucial to Lenin between 'opportunism' and 'revolutionary Social Democracy'. The wealth of sophisticated debates in the decade before the war is reduced to vague labels such as 'evolutionism'. Again and again, claims are made for Lenin's originality that he himself never made – on the contrary! – and that do not hold up under examination.

The Hegelists do not inform the reader of the extreme paucity of Lenin's own claims for rethinking Marxist foundations. When we look through Lenin's notes, we are struck with an entire absence of any reference to concrete political issues: his excerpts and comments remain determinedly abstract. The Hegelists are constrained to build very large castles out of very little sand.

Take the case of the most famous passage from the Hegel notes: 'Aphorism: it is impossible fully to grasp Marx's *Capital*, and especially its first chapter, if you have not studied through and understood the whole of Hegel's *Logic*. Consequently, none of the Marxists for the past half century have understood Marx!'[83] This passage is always quoted for a very good reason: it is the *only* one anywhere in the notes that even suggests the need for a major rethinking of Marxism. Similar heavy weather is made in the philosophic sphere by a comment that Plekhanov's critique of Kantianism was from a 'vulgar materialist' standpoint. Despite his political disagreements with Plekhanov, Lenin had previously looked up to him as probably the premier Marxist philosopher in Europe and an inspiration for his own earlier foray into philosophy, *Materialism and Empirio-Criticism* (1908). Lenin's passing comment about Plekhanov in his unpublished notes is built up into a complete rejection of Plekhanov, of Lenin's own earlier philosophical writings, and of course 'the Marxism of the Second International'.[84]

Taken by themselves, these aphorisms *might* have the significance ascribed to them – or they might not. The *bon mot* about *Capital* might indeed be saying something like 'the entire Marxist movement of the last fifty years has been on the wrong track'. But it also might mean something like 'Marx is so deep and profound that we Marxists have not yet plumbed his depths'. Surely, one would think, if Lenin seriously meant the former, we would find explicit statements to that effect.

Instead, we find just the opposite. Lenin makes no public mention of his Hegel notes or of any new understanding of the dialectic. Instead, he arranges for the republication of *Materialism and Empirio-Criticism* in 1920. This occasion would have been a very good time to mention a new and more profound

83 Lenin 1958–60, Vol. 38, p. 180.

84 For a discussion of these passages, see Anderson 1995, pp. 64–6.

awareness of Hegel or his new rejection of Plekhanov as a vulgar materialist, but Lenin passed it up.

During the dispute over trade-union policy in 1920–1, Lenin unexpectedly made a short excursus on the philosophical meaning of the dialectic. Although he made no claims for originality, I think that we may properly see this comment as a manifestation of Lenin's heightened awareness of such issues. Lenin went immediately on to say: 'Let me add in parenthesis for the benefit of young Party members that you cannot hope to become a real intelligent Communist without making a study – and I mean study – of all of Plekhanov's philosophical writings, because nothing better has been written on Marxism anywhere in the world'.[85]

This unambiguous advice to young Communists would represent the height of irresponsibility if Lenin really believed that Plekhanov was a 'vulgar materialist' or that 'the Marxism of the Second International' was responsible for the disaster of 1914. In the three articles from 2007, no mention is made of these difficulties; Anderson and Harding do confront them in their longer treatments, but not very successfully. Taking a cue from Dunayevskaya, Anderson speaks of 'an ambivalent, secret Hegelianism' and tries to explain away Lenin's unqualified endorsement of Plekhanov.[86] Harding resorts to a notable understatement: 'There is something of a disparity between the burden that the dialectic was meant to bear as the foundational theory of knowledge of Marxism (and Leninism) and the meagre outline of its content that was publicly available to Lenin's supporters'.[87] The disparity is actually between the extravagant claims of the Hegelists and the lack of evidence for them.

Even Anderson and Harding do not confront all the contrary evidence. Consider the following comment from *Left-Wing Communism* (1920):

> What happened to such highly learned Marxists as Kautsky, Otto Bauer, and others – *vozhdi* of the Second International who are devoted to socialism – can (and should) serve as a useful lesson. They were completely aware of the necessity for flexible tactics, they studied and they taught Marxist dialectics to others (and much of what they did in this connection will forever remain a valuable acquisition of socialist literature), but in the *application* of this dialectic, they made such mistakes or showed themselves in practice *not* to be dialecticians, they turned out to be people who could not take into account the swift change of forms and

85 Lenin 1958–60, Vol. 32, p. 94.
86 Anderson 1995, pp. 114–6.
87 Harding 1996, p. 234.

> the swift filling of old forms with new content, that their fate is little more envious than the fate of Hyndman, Guesde, and Plekhanov.[88]

The basic weakness of the Hegelist account is one that it shares with all accounts that picture Lenin rethinking 'the Marxism of the Second International' rather than reaffirming revolutionary Social Democracy: it provides an ingenious explanation for something that needs no explanation, because it didn't happen. Lenin did not rethink Marxism or come up with a new programme. As we shall see, Lenin's reaction to the war is fully consonant with the reactions of the hypothetical Bolshevik mentioned earlier. He explicitly insisted over and over again that he was merely trying to apply the strong consensus of pre-war revolutionary Social Democracy to the new (but predictable and predicted) situation created by the war – and he was not at all secretive or ambivalent about this claim. Lenin aggressively insisted on his own unoriginality – and he was right.

Lenin: From the Outbreak of War to the Berne Conference

> I may testify that the fundamental slogans of Lenin's tactic in the imperialist war had been formulated by him in Austria during the first few days of the war, for he brought them to Berne completely formulated. And further! I have every reason for stating that this tactic had matured in Lenin's head probably on the first day of the war. My arrest on the third or fourth day of the war may serve as a proof of this statement.[89]

The Bolshevik G.L. Shklovsky goes on to relate ruefully that a telegram sent to him by Lenin asking him to organise anti-war protests was intercepted by the Swiss military authorities. This anecdote brings home how swift and how definite was Lenin's reaction to the outbreak of war. When hostilities broke out, Lenin was living in Poronin in Austrian Poland. He was quickly interned as an enemy alien under suspicion of spying, but after twelve days and the intervention of prominent Austrian Social Democrats, he was set free. He then had to pull up roots and move with his family (his wife and her mother) via Vienna to neutral Switzerland. Despite all this upheaval, he hit the ground running when he arrived in Berne on 5 September.

---

88 Lenin 1960–8, Vol. 41, pp. 87–8.

89 Gankin and Fisher 1940, p. 143 (originally 1925).

As soon as he got off the train, Lenin met with local Bolsheviks in Shklovsky's apartment to talk over the proper reaction to the war. At this meeting, Lenin quizzed his comrades about the reaction to the war by other Russian and European socialists. In the evening, he met with Robert Grimm, a leader of the Swiss Social Democrats, and talked with him about wartime tactics for the party. He then wrote down a draft of his theses about party tasks in relation to the war.

The next day, Lenin penned a letter to V.A. Karpinskii in Geneva and inquired if there was a Russian language printing press in Geneva that could print up leaflets against the war and its socialist supporters. He also wanted to know if there were any Bolsheviks leaving for Russia. Later that same day, a more formal conference of Berne Bolsheviks began and went on for a couple of days in a forest outside Berne. With a few changes, Lenin's theses were accepted by the group.

These first few days in Switzerland are emblematic of Lenin's activities until early 1915. He had definite aims which he pursued unremittingly:

- to get official party sanction for his views on the proper reaction to the war
- in pursuance of the above aim, to restore the various party institutions and replace the links shattered by the outbreak of hostilities
- in particular, to re-establish links with Russia
- to spread the word about the Bolshevik programme to a wider public by sending his theses to non-Bolshevik socialist conferences, reviving the party newspaper, and giving public lectures
- to inform himself of the socialist reaction to the war, mainly by devouring party newspapers from all over Europe.[90]

Lenin's first and overriding aim was to be in a position to advance his views as an official programme endorsed by Bolshevik Party institutions. His original theses from early September were reworked into a Manifesto entitled 'The War and Russian Social Democracy'. This was printed on 1 November in the first issue of the socialist party newspaper with the authority of the party's central

90 Owing to three first-rate documentary collections, from different times and political perspectives, the background context to Lenin's activities during 1914–16 is more accessible to those who rely on translations than for any other period in his career: Walling 1972 (originally published 1915), Gankin and Fisher 1940, and Riddell 1984. Krupskaya 1960 remains indispensable. I do not discuss the Left Zimmerwald movement in this essay; for this topic, see Nation 1989. For background on other Russian socialists during the war, see Thatcher 2000 and Melancon 1990.

committee. Lenin then concentrated on organising a wider conference of Bolshevik émigrés that eventually took place in Berne at the end of February 1915. He wanted to make this as representative and therefore authoritative as possible and went to great lengths to insist that Bolsheviks just coming from America and potential critics such as Nikolai Bukharin would be in attendance. The resolutions passed by the Berne Conference were essentially the latest version of the September theses and the November Manifesto.

The Berne Conference made Lenin's programme as official as it was going to get under wartime conditions. Lenin regarded the Berne resolution as the law and the prophets, and all the rest – for example, his 1915 treatise co-authored with Zinoviev, *Socialism and the War* – was commentary. The Berne Conference was a turning point in Lenin's wartime activities, so that it makes sense to regard the months from August 1914 through February 1915 as a single episode defined by Lenin's drive for official party sanction.

Official party endorsement could only come from official party institutions, so Lenin had to plunge into the task (in his own words) of 'overcoming tremendous difficulties in re-establishing organisational contacts broken by the war'.[91] Of special importance was getting the Bolshevik Party newspaper *Sotsial-Demokrat* up and running once more. The last issue had come out over a year earlier, and Lenin was very irritated that no one could even remember what number the last issue had been. It took a bit of digging around to ascertain that it had been No. 32. Thus on 1 November 1914, issue No. 33 of *Sotsial-Demokrat* rolled off the press containing the text of the Manifesto on the war. Lenin now had an official party newspaper that he could refer to as 'the Central Organ'.

Publishing this newspaper ran into all sorts of mundane difficulties, sometimes reaching comic-opera levels of absurdity. For the first issues, the only printer available with Russian fonts was a Ukrainian emigrant named Kuzma. Kuzma was an easy-going fellow who was happy to do jobs for fellow emigrants, but his wife wanted him to restrict himself to more lucrative work and therefore regarded the Bolsheviks almost as personal enemies. The Bolsheviks nicknamed her Kuzmikha, and Lenin's letters from this period contain frequent requests for 'a bulletin of Kuzmikha's moods': was she holding up the printing of the newspaper or not?[92]

The absence of *Sotsial-Demokrat* helps explain why Lenin wrote comparatively little for publication in September and October 1914: not for lack of something to say or desire to say it, but for lack of an outlet. As soon as *Sotsial-Demokrat* was up and running, Lenin wrote for it regularly: ten of his

---

91 Lenin 1958–64, Vol. 21, p. 37 (November 1914).

92 Karpinskii, 1969; Lenin 1960–8, Vol. 49, p. 136 (letter to Sophia Ravitch, August 1915).

articles appeared in the seven issues of the newspaper that came out in the four months before the Berne Conference in late February.

Another party task was re-establishing contact with the Bolsheviks in Russia, particularly in the city now known as Petrograd (a less German-sounding variant of Petersburg). Much of his correspondence with Aleksandr Shliapnikov in Stockholm is devoted to this topic. Lenin wanted to find out what was happening in Russia and also wanted to get party literature containing his own programme into Russia.

When he did find out what the Petrograd Bolsheviks and especially the six-person Duma Bolshevik faction were doing, he was pleased. The Duma members had sent off a strong rejoinder to the pro-war Belgian socialist Emile Vandervelde and distributed anti-war leaflets. The Petrograd Bolsheviks had reacted in this way without directives from abroad – or rather, if later memoirs tell us true, they followed the directives contained in the Basel Manifesto that also inspired Lenin.[93]

Lenin's theses and the Bolshevik Manifesto were not just academic exercises – in fact, they helped get the Duma faction arrested and put on trial, since a copy of Lenin's Manifesto was found in a police raid on a Bolshevik secret conference (Kamenev was at this meeting and stood trial with the Duma Bolsheviks). Thus Lenin's activist stand had the same effect on the Petrograd Bolsheviks as did his earlier telegram to Shklovsky.

Lenin also engaged in efforts to publicise what could now be called the official Bolshevik programme. He sent the Bolshevik Manifesto on the war to the International Socialist Bureau and to French, English and German Social Democratic newspapers. He arranged for the Bolshevik point of view to be presented in various socialist conferences in Stockholm, London and Lugano, Italy. He gave public lectures and showed up to heckle at the speeches by Russian socialists who supported the war. According to the invaluable reference source *Biokhronika*, he presented his position in public speeches in Berne on 11 October, in Lausanne on 14 October, in Geneva on 15 October, in Montreux on 26 October, and in Zurich on 27 October. He also showed up to wave the Bolshevik banner at speeches given by Russian Social Democrats with opposing views, including one by speakers from the Bund on 10 October, one by Plekhanov on 11 October, and one on 16 December by Martov.[94]

---

93 Badayev 1973.

94 *Vladimir Il'ich Lenin: Biograficheskaia khronika*, Vol. 3, 1912–1917, 1972. The multivolume *Biokhronika* provides exhaustive information about what Lenin was doing from day to day throughout his career.

These speeches were big affairs, with much attacking and counter-attacking. Krupskaya has a vivid account of Lenin's presence at Plekhanov's presentation in Lausanne, coming up nervously with a pot of beer in his hand to deliver his refutation.[95] Lenin's presentation of his own position at Zurich in late October was over two hours long, and the ensuing debate was continued the next evening. Lenin's Russian opponents attended in force. Trotsky, for example, aggressively attacked Lenin, asserting that dismissing Karl Kautsky as a traitor was absurd.

The *Biokhronika* for these months also informs us about Lenin's marginal notes on newspaper articles. Putting all these references together makes it abundantly clear that Lenin had embarked on an energetic research project into the socialist response to the outbreak of war. Archival evidence shows that Lenin consulted issues of the following newspapers and journals: *La Bataille Syndicaliste, Vorwärts, Die Neue Zeit, Avanti, Volksrecht, L'Humanité, Nashe delo, Arbeiter-Zeitung, Russkie vedomosti, Russkoe slovo, Sozialistische Monatshefte, Berner Tagwacht, Novyi mir, Leipziger Volkszeitung, Le Matin, Nashe slovo, Berliner Tageblatt und Handels-Zeitung, Nasha zaria, Den', Rech', Le Temps*. His correspondence also reveals his efforts to obtain Russian, Danish, and French newspapers. All this reading showed up in his later polemical pamphlets about the war and the collapse of the Second International.

On top of all this, Lenin wrote a fifty-page article on Karl Marx (one of the few ways he had of making money) and took extensive notes on Hegel's *Science of Logic*. His reading was not restricted to Hegel. Library records reveal that he checked out books on a variety of subjects, including the socialist response to the war, colonial policies, the Paris Commune, the American Civil War, a mathematics textbook on calculus, and a couple of books about the economic impact of electrification.

We will conclude this account of Lenin's activities with his own public description of them in early issues of the revived party newspaper:

> After overcoming tremendous difficulties in re-establishing organizational contacts broken by the war, a group of Party members first drew up 'theses' and on September 6–8 (New Style) had them circulated among the comrades. Then they were sent to two delegates to the Italo-Swiss Conference in Lugano (September 27), through Swiss Social-Democrats. It was only in mid-October that it became possible to re-establish contacts and formulate the viewpoint of the Party's Central Committee. The leading article in this issue represents the final wording of the 'theses'.[96]

95 Krupskaya 1960, pp. 286–8.

96 Lenin 1958–64, Vol. 21, p. 37 (first issue of *Sotsial-Demokrat*, 1 November 1914).

> We, who have established links with the Russian Bureau of the Central Committee and with the leading elements of the working-class movement in St. Petersburg, have exchanged opinions with them and become convinced that we are agreed on the main points, are in a position, as editors of the Central Organ, to declare in the name of our Party that only work conducted in this direction is Party work and Social-Democratic work.[97]

Lenin's hectic activities during the first seven months of the war bear little resemblance to the picture given to us by those defending the Hegelist interpretation. According to these writers, Lenin was utterly isolated politically, even from his closest allies; he retired for a space from political activity in order to rethink the foundations of Marxism; he then came up with his political programme only after reading Hegel's *Logic*. In reality, Lenin had his political programme ready literally from day one, and he immediately plunged into intense political activity to publicise his standpoint and to ensure official party support, which he received.

We earlier conjured up a hypothetical Bolshevik whose reaction to the war and Social Democratic apostasy corresponded both politically and emotionally to the worldview we found in Kamenev's pre-war articles. Let us now turn to the content of the programme Lenin so zealously propagated during the war years.

In the theses that Lenin wrote down immediately after arriving in Berne, we find the following basic points:

- The present war is an imperialist one and there is no reason to abandon 'the class struggle with its inevitable conversion at certain moments into civil war' (the canonical formula 'conversion of the present imperialist war into a civil war' occurs first in the Manifesto later in the fall)
- The actions of the leaders of the Second International constitute a betrayal of socialism and the ideological collapse of the International
- The culprit is Social Democracy's opportunist wing, 'the bourgeois nature and the danger of which have long been indicated by the finest representatives of the revolutionary proletariat of all countries'
- European Social Democracy's 'Centre' has capitulated to the opportunists
- A new, opportunism-free International must be established
- The nature of imperialist war makes it impossible to choose sides between the warring countries

97 Lenin 1958–64, Vol. 21, p. 100 (12 December 1914).

- Defeat of Tsarist Russia is 'the lesser evil'
- Democratic and national revolutions in Russia are still on the agenda
- Our campaign against chauvinism and 'social patriotism' (socialist support for the war effort) will 'in most cases' be supported by the workers[98]
- 'Illegal forms of organisation and agitation are imperative in times of crises'
- Pacifism is 'a sentimental and philistine point of view' that overlooks the necessity of armed conflict
- A republican United States of Europe should be a propaganda slogan.[99]

In the Manifesto worked out after further consultation and published in November in the first issue of the revived *Sotsial-Demokrat*, the following points are elaborated and clarified:

- The slogan 'conversion of the present imperialist war into a civil war' was unambiguously implied in the Basel Manifesto, yet the opportunists have refused to live up to it
- The Social Democratic workers in Russia have published illegal proclamations against the war, 'thus doing their duty to democracy and to the International'
- The second, non-socialist, level of revolution – 'genuine freedom for the nations' – is mentioned in a more general way, that is, it is not confined to Russia
- The slogan 'defeat of Russia is the lesser evil' should not be used as a justification by German social patriots
- The dominance of opportunism is explained by 'a now bygone (and so-called "peaceful") period of history'
- 'Revolutionary Social Democrats' feel 'a burning sense of shame' caused by the action of soi-disant Social Democratic leaders that 'dishonours the banner of the proletarian International'
- Kautsky is mentioned by name as an emblem of the Centre whose cover-up of opportunist sins is 'the most hypocritical, vulgar and smug sophistry'.[100]

---

98 The qualifying phrase 'in most cases' was not in Lenin's original draft and is evidently the result of consultation with Berne Bolsheviks.

99 Lenin 1958–64, Vol. 21, pp. 15–19; Gankin and Fisher 1940, pp. 140–3.

100 Lenin 1958–64, Vol. 21, pp. 25–34; Gankin and Fisher 1940, pp. 150–6.

The resolutions of the Berne Conference in February did not change anything of substance.[101] Of all the points listed here, the only one to disappear from view was the slogan about the United States of Europe. In the summer of 1915, Lenin came to the conclusion that this slogan, originally meant to call for democratic revolution against the crowned heads of Europe, gave too much aid and comfort to Kautsky's idea of 'super-imperialism', according to which capitalist countries might find it in their interest to join together to make money, not war. Lenin emphasised that as a *political* slogan – that is, as it appeared in the Manifesto and Berne resolutions – 'United States of Europe' still made sense.[102]

Otherwise, Lenin retracted nothing and added nothing to his basic platform in the years 1914–16. He spent these two years energetically propagating his original platform and defending it against all comers. We must now ask ourselves: is there something that ties all these particular points together, something that gives Lenin's programme a political and emotional unity? Yes, and it can be stated as follows: The era of war and revolution that was predicted by pre-war 'revolutionary Social Democracy' is now upon us, and we should act accordingly.[103]

As Lenin himself put it:

> It was none other than Kautsky who, in a series of articles and in his pamphlet *The Road to Power* (which appeared in 1909), outlined with full clarity the basic features of the third epoch that has set in, and who noted the fundamental differences between this epoch and the second (that of yesterday), and recognized the change in the immediate tasks as well as in the conditions and forms of struggle of present-day democracy, a change stemming from the changed objective historical conditions … (§)

101 Lenin 1958–64, Vol. 21, pp. 158–64; Gankin and Fisher 1940, pp. 173–91 (contains valuable memoir accounts and other material concerning the Berne Conference).

102 Lenin 1958–64, Vol. 21, p. 147. On Lenin's motivations for nixing the slogan of the United States of Europe, see Lenin 1958–64, Vol. 21, p. 344. Stathis Kouvelakis implies that this slogan was the sole content of Lenin's original theses of September 1914, thus overestimating both its role in Lenin's original programme and the significance of its removal (Kouvelakis 2007, pp. 166–7).

103 Two other candidates for a unifying theme are 'imperialism' and 'conversion of the imperialist war into a civil war'. As important as these themes are, they do not cover all four levels of the scenario of global revolutionary interaction. 'Revolutionary defeatism' is a non-starter as a candidate, if only because the phrase cannot be found in Lenin (see later discussion of 'defeatism').

> In the above-mentioned pamphlet, he spoke forthrightly of symptoms of an approaching war, and specifically of the kind of war that became a fact in 1914 ... (*)

The idea of a new era of war and revolution ties together the positive points of Lenin's programme: the two levels of revolution, socialist and democratic; the corresponding two kinds of war, unjustified imperialist war and justified national liberation war; the insistence on the type of tactics mandated by the Basel Manifesto; the targeting of opportunism as the main enemy. But the unifying principle also explains what is new about Lenin's wartime platform: the sense of betrayal because the representatives of socialism did not keep their promises, the insistence on a new International purged of opportunism, and the outrage directed so abundantly at the Centre and at Kautsky personally. Here is what the above passage contained hidden behind the ellipses (as marked by the symbols):

> (§) Kautsky is now burning that which he worshipped yesterday; his change of front is most incredible, most unbecoming and most shameless....
>
> (*) It would suffice simply to place side by side for comparison a number of passages from that pamphlet and from his present writings to show convincingly how Kautsky has betrayed his own convictions and solemn declarations. In this respect Kautsky is not an individual instance (or even a German instance); he is a typical representative of the entire upper crust of present-day democracy, which, at a moment of crisis, has deserted to the side of the bourgeoisie.

This passage shows how the image of Kautsky bifurcated in Lenin's mind into Kautsky 'when he was a Marxist' vs. Kautsky the Renegade. The earlier Kautsky was emblematic of 'revolutionary Social Democracy' whose principles were still valid and whose honour had still to be upheld. The present-day Kautsky was emblematic of a phenomenon for which Lenin coined the term *kautskianstvo*. This term is regularly translated 'Kautskyism', but this term is highly misleading, because it implies that Lenin rejected the views set forth by Kautsky in his pre-war writings. *Kautskianstvo* is not an 'ism' or a set of principles at all, but a type of political conduct: using revolutionary rhetoric to cover up the sins of opportunism. The paradigmatic example of *kautskianstvo* is Kautsky's own failure to live up to Kautskyism.

Although Lenin was stunned by what he considered to be the betrayal of the Social Democratic parties, not for a minute did he lack an explanation for what happened, because he applied the same map of intra-Social Democratic tendencies that we saw in Kamenev's pre-war articles. The cause of the betrayal was opportunism. Everyone (that is, all revolutionary Social Democrats) knew that opportunism was more bourgeois than socialist, everyone knew that it had grown more and more influential during the preceding era of peace and gradual reform – the only surprise was how far the rot had gone.

Craig Nation writes that among the left Social Democrats who opposed the war, 'it was axiomatic that after 4 August 1914 the Marxism of the Second International would have to be "purged of opportunism" '.[104] This is a standard formulation, but as a description of Lenin's outlook, it is highly misleading: Lenin did *not* reject the Marxism of the Second International. He rejected the Second International because it naïvely harboured a serpent within its bosom, opportunism, not realising how deadly its venom was. He nevertheless did not believe that opportunism had infected the actual ideology of pre-war 'revolutionary Social Democracy'. The prescribed remedy was to purge the projected new International of this venom so that the genuinely revolutionary Marxism of the old International could flourish. As Lenin put it in summer 1915:

> The old division of socialists into an opportunist trend and a revolutionary, which was characteristic of the period of the Second International (1889–1914) *corresponds*, by and large, to the new division into chauvinists and internationalists ... Social chauvinism is an opportunism that has matured to such a degree that the *continued* existence of this bourgeois abscess within the socialist parties has become impossible.[105]

Lenin's mobilisation of Kautsky's three-era framework reveals his attitude. In a polemic from early 1915 with Aleksandr Potresov, one of the most right-wing Russian Social Democrats, Lenin writes: 'The usual division into historical epochs, so often cited in Marxist literature and so many times repeated by Kautsky and adopted in Potresov's articles, is the following: (1) 1789–1871; (2) 1871–1914; (3) 1914–?' Lenin fully accepted this framework, but he objected to the way Potresov portrayed the second 'peaceful' period that was now coming to an end.

Potresov speaks of this era's 'talent for a smooth and cautious advance', its 'pronounced non-adaptability to any break in gradualness and to catastrophic phenomena of any kind', and its 'exceptional isolation within the sphere of national action'. This description of the era of the Second International is

104 Nation 1989, pp. 229.

105 Lenin 1958–64, Vol. 21, p. 244 (summer 1915).

completely standard today – but Lenin strongly objects to it, precisely because 'the impression is produced that [the socialism of the second epoch] remained a single whole, which, generally speaking, was pervaded with gradualism, turned nationalist, was by degrees weaned away from breaks in gradualness and from catastrophes'.[106]

Lenin protests that 'in reality this could not have happened' because class antagonisms were growing rapidly throughout the same period. As a result, 'none, literally not one, of the leading capitalist countries of Europe was spared the struggle between the two mutually opposed currents' within the socialist movement. Lenin makes no claim to be the first to grasp the danger of opportunism – on the contrary: 'There is hardly a single Marxist of note who has not recognised many times and on various occasions that the opportunists are in fact a non-proletarian element hostile to the socialist revolution'.[107]

Thus the Bolsheviks defended even their most radical-sounding and contentious slogans as based entirely on the pre-war Social Democratic consensus. As Zinoviev, Lenin's closest lieutenant during these years, wrote in February 1916:

> When the war started in 1914, our party announced the slogan: civil war! Transformation of the imperialist war into a civil war! In response, we became the object of numerous attacks, starting with those of the social chauvinist Eduard David and ending with the 'leftist' Russian Kautskyist, L. Trotsky. So what did we mean to say when we announced this slogan? We meant to say that the socialists of all countries, in the interest of the working class, were duty bound to fulfil honestly the obligation that they had undertaken at Stuttgart and at Basel. We meant to say what had been acknowledged hundreds of times by all the leaders of the Second International in the years preceding the war, to wit: that the *objective* conditions of our era established a *connection* between war and revolution. Nothing more!

Zinoviev reminded the reader that the essential language from the Stuttgart resolution, taken over by the Basel Manifesto, was adopted on the initiative of the Russian and Polish Social Democrats. 'On the question of the "civil war", the view of our party is essentially the same as it was in 1907'.[108]

---

106 Lenin 1958–64, Vol. 21, pp. 150–1.

107 Lenin 1958–64, Vol. 21, pp. 151, 109. Which of these descriptions of the Second International is closer to the standard description found in writers on the left: Lenin's or that of the 'liquidationist' Potresov?

108 Zinoviev 1970, pp. 54–5.

One theme in the pre-war scenario of global revolutionary interaction that we found in Kautsky and even more in Kamenev is the privileged position of Russia as a country that stood on the cusp between socialist revolution and democratic revolution, between twentieth-century revolution and nineteenth-century revolution, between Europe and Asia. This theme also finds expression in Lenin's wartime programme in the form of calls for Russia's defeat. In the words of the resolution passed by the Berne Conference: 'A victory for Russia will bring in its train a strengthening of reaction, both throughout the world and within the country ... In view of this, we consider the defeat of Russia the lesser evil in all conditions'.[109]

The 'Lesser evil' formulations appear in all three of the programmatic documents of the first months of the war: the theses written immediately after arriving in Berne, the Manifesto published in November, and the resolutions of the Berne Conference. Nevertheless, the call for Russia's defeat as a lesser evil never caught on, not even among the Bolsheviks. As noted by Hal Draper (to whose excellent analysis I am much indebted), 'outside of Lenin's immediate co-workers on the Central Organ in Berne, particularly Zinoviev in his own peculiar way, we cannot cite any known Bolshevik who defended it, or any section of the party which came to its defence against its critics'.[110]

The final clash between Lenin and the rest of the Bolsheviks over Russian defeat as the lesser evil came in Lenin's first 'Letter from Afar', written in immediate reaction to the fall of the Tsar in March 1917 and published in *Pravda* before Lenin's arrival in Russia. Lenin claimed that the February Revolution had justified the slogan of defeatism, but the *Pravda* editors in Petrograd simply removed this assertion. Just as in its first use in September 1914, so in its last use in March 1917, Lenin makes it clear that this slogan is referring to Russia's special position, about 'the defeat of the most backward and barbarous tsarist monarchy'. He also makes it clear he is not talking about defeat *by* the revolution, but defeat inflicted by German troops that *facilitated* the revolution. Since Lenin himself dropped any and all references to Russian defeat and defeatism after his return to Russia, he cannot have objected too strenuously. On this issue, Lenin joined the rest of the party and not the other way around.[111]

---

109 Lenin 1958–64, Vol. 21, p. 63.

110 Draper 1953–4.

111 Owing to the unavailability of Lenin's original draft of 'Letter from Afar' at the time of writing, Draper incorrectly locates the 'last gasp' of Lenin's defeatism in November 1916. In my forthcoming study of the reasons for the excisions made to Lenin's draft by the editors of *Pravda*, I argue that the removal of Lenin's reference to defeatism is the one clear case of actual censorship of Lenin's views. Draper convincingly shows that the claim that

The reason for the unpopularity of the Russian 'defeat as lesser evil' slogan is not far to seek: Russian defeat meant German victory. Lenin's slogan had Russian revolutionaries calling on the aid of German armies and justifying German 'social patriots' who used the evils of Tsarism as an excuse for their support of the war effort. This difficulty was immediately apparent to everybody.[112] Even Lenin penned an angry letter in November 1914 to German and Austrian Social Democratic newspapers protesting against the way they used his criticism of the evils of Russian Tsarism.[113] Faced with this difficulty, Lenin tried to generalise his slogan as a call for everyone's simultaneous defeat. As Draper well shows, the result was muddled and self-contradictory – and not the productive 'dialectic' sort of self-contradiction. Russia's special position could not be logically generalised.

Draper explains Lenin's insistence on Russia's special position as a clash between Lenin's new and original analysis of imperialist war vs. an unconscious hold-over from an earlier era when proletarian revolutionaries could still choose sides in a war between bourgeois states, depending on whose victory would be more progressive. This explanation is on the right track, once we realise that Lenin's analysis of imperialist war was not particularly original and that his insistence on the possibility of 'progressive' national war was not an unconscious hold-over but a central feature of his outlook. The scenario of global revolutionary interaction posited two levels of revolution: socialist ones against imperialist regimes and, democratic ones against both imperialist and traditional regimes. Proletarian revolutionaries could not choose sides in a war between imperialist powers, but they could and should choose sides in wars for national liberation, even when both sides were 'bourgeois'.[114]

In the next section, we will look at Lenin's insistence on this point. Here we observe that Russian Tsarism blurred the distinction between the levels of revolution. On the one hand, its participation in the European war made it a sort of honorary imperialist, although it was far from achieving 'the highest stage of capitalism'. On the other hand, it was a paradigm of an anti-democratic

---

'revolutionary defeatism' was the unifying principle of Lenin's wartime views was a post-Lenin invention made for political reasons.

112 For lucid analyses of some of the difficulties of the 'defeatism' slogan, see Gankin and Fisher 1940, pp. 146–9 (V.A. Karpinskii) and pp. 189–91 (Bukharin). In the November Manifesto itself, there is language that seems to have been inserted as a result of misgivings from Bolsheviks in Petrograd.

113 Lenin 1958–64, Vol. 21, p. 42.

114 Lenin 1958–64, Vol. 21, pp. 300–1.

ancien régime. When looking west, you couldn't choose sides between Russia and its foes. When looking east, you wanted to see Tsarism crumble.

Throughout the war years, Lenin presented himself not as a bold innovator or a fearless rethinker but as someone faithful to the old verities – as the socialist leader who kept his head while all about him were losing theirs. This is why he could walk off the train in Berne in September 1914 and start agitating that very day on the basis of a platform that remained unchanged until the fall of the Tsar. This is why he had the amazing self-assurance to defy the entire socialist establishment in the name of Marxist orthodoxy.

Debates over National Self-Determination, 1916

In the many polemical disputes conducted by Lenin in 1914–16, he always pictured himself as defending established consensus. In *Imperialism* (1916) and elsewhere, he attacked Kautsky's innovative idea of 'super-imperialism', first advanced in 1914.[115] His vociferous polemics with Trotsky were often tied to the clash between them just before the war over whether the opportunists should be purged from the party. National self-determination was another issue where Lenin saw himself as defending established positions. Not only was the right to national self-determination endorsed by the 1903 programme of Russian Social Democracy, but the legitimacy of wars of national liberation was an integral part of the 'new era of war and revolution' and the scenario of global revolutionary interaction.

In 1903, at the Second Party Congress, the main opponents of Point Nine of the party's 'minimum programme' – the recognition of the right of national determination – were Polish socialists who rejected the idea of separation from Russia as reactionary bourgeois nationalism. In 1913–14, the same dispute arose once again and Lenin waded in with a polemic aimed particularly at Rosa Luxemburg. Lenin repeated his basic point that

> if we do not put forth and emphasize in our agitation the slogan of the *right* to separation, we play into the hands not only of the bourgeoisie of *oppressing* nations, but also of its feudalists and its absolutism. Kautsky put forth this conclusion against Rosa Luxemburg a long time ago, and it cannot be disputed.[116]

115 For extensive selections from Kautsky's 1914 writings, see Walling 1972, pp. 218–33.

116 Lenin 1958–64, Vol. 25, p. 27.

In 1916, a group of Polish socialists returned to the attack. Their manifesto, drafted by Karl Radek, emphasised their *discontinuity* with the pre-war Second International: 'The self-determination formula was left to us as an inheritance from the Second International ... The policy of defence of the fatherland has brought results in the World War that very clearly show the counterrevolutionary nature of the self-determination formula'.[117]

In response, Lenin emphasised *continuity* with pre-war polemics. He argued that the critics of Point Nine in 1916 were making exactly the same mistake made by the critics back in 1903. In each case, the 'theoretical kernel' of the debate was that a dismissive attitude to the right of national self-determination was a form of 'economism', a Russian variety of opportunism that downgraded the urgency of democratic revolution.[118]

The legitimacy of wars of national liberation was also one of Lenin's major criticisms of Rosa Luxemburg's anti-war Junius pamphlet that appeared in 1916. In Luxemburg's pamphlet of over a hundred pages, the colonies and semi-colonies are viewed entirely passively. Either they are the occasion for conflict between the European great powers who seek to dominate them, or they are the victims of imperialist atrocities. The Junius pamphlet contains no hint that resistance by the colonies themselves was possible, much less headed for success.[119]

Lenin objected to Luxemburg's assertion that 'national wars are no longer possible'. But behind this theoretical issue was a passionate insistence on the scenario of global revolutionary interaction that he had shared with Kautsky. Lenin asserted that 'national wars waged by colonies and semi-colonies in the imperialist era are not only possible but *inevitable* ... progressive and revolutionary'. Lenin warned that the 'ludicrous and downright reactionary attitude of indifference to national movements' becomes 'chauvinism when members of the "great" European nations, that is, the nations which oppress the mass of small and colonial peoples, declare with a pseudoscientific air: "national wars are no longer possible"!'[120]

In autumn 1916, Lenin was forced to respond to yet another attack on Point Nine, this time from left-wing Bolsheviks such as Nikolai Bukharin and Iu. Piatakov. Again recalling the 1903 debates, Lenin called Piatakov's position 'imperialist economism'. In his long unpublished article 'A Caricature of Marxism and Imperialist Economism', Lenin carefully established the link between his

117 Riddell 1984, pp. 350–1.
118 Lenin 1960–8, Vol. 22, p. 326.
119 Luxemburg 1970, pp. 353–453 (this text does not contain Chapter Four).
120 Luxemburg 1970, pp. 590–2.

present argument and official party positions taken after the war broke out. He quoted the resolutions of the Berne conference of February 1915 and then noted that 'a commentary, or popular explanation, of our Party resolutions is given in the Lenin and Zinoviev pamphlet *Socialism and War*'.[121]

Just as with Luxemburg, Lenin bases his objection to Piatakov on the existence of two levels of revolution in the world. On the democratic level, 'the "defence of the fatherland" can *still* be defence of democracy, of one's native language, of political liberty against oppressor nations, against medievalism, whereas the English, French, Germans and Italians lie when they speak of defending their fatherland in the present war'.[122] This justified kind of war is not a thing of the past, as argued by Lenin's opponents. On the contrary, it is already on the agenda in Eastern Europe and will also be seen in the near future in the colonies and semi-colonies.

Having set up his two levels, Lenin then sets them in interactive motion, with each level taking advantage of the other:

> While the proletariat of the advanced countries is overthrowing the bourgeoisie and repelling its attempts at counter-revolution, the undeveloped and oppressed nations do not just wait, do not cease to exist, do not disappear. If they take advantage even of such a bourgeois imperialist crisis as the war of 1915–16 – a minor crisis compared with social revolution – to rise in revolt (the colonies, Ireland), there can be no doubt that they will all the more readily take advantage of the *great crisis* of civil war in the advanced countries to rise in revolt.[123]
>
> The social revolution can come only in the form of an epoch in which are combined civil war by the proletariat against the bourgeoisie in the advanced countries and a *whole series* of democratic and revolutionary movements, including the national liberation movement, in the undeveloped, backward and oppressed nations.
>
> Why? Because capitalism develops unevenly, and objective reality gives us highly developed capitalist nations side by side with a number of economically slightly developed, or totally undeveloped, nations.

A comparison of this passage with the corresponding passages by Kautsky in 1907 and Kamenev in 1912 (see respectively, pp. 373–4 and 383–4 above) will reveal that Lenin's claim of continuity with pre-war positions is not just rhetoric.

---

121 Lenin 1958–64, Vol. 23, p. 31.

122 Lenin 1958–64, Vol. 23, p. 39.

123 Lenin 1958–64, Vol. 23, p. 60.

Accordingly, even after two years of obsessive polemics directed against *kautskianstvo*, Lenin still has no compunction about associating his own position with 'Kautsky when he was a Marxist':

> Up to the 1914–1916 war, Karl Kautsky was a Marxist, and many of his major writings and statements will always remain models of Marxism. On August 26, 1910, he wrote in *Die Neue Zeit*, in reference to the imminent war: 'In war between Germany and England the issue is not democracy, but world domination, that is, exploitation of the world. That is not an issue on which Social-Democrats can side with the exploiters of their nation'.
>
> There you have an excellent Marxist formulation, one that fully coincides with our own and fully exposes the *present-day* Kautsky, who has turned from Marxism to defence of social chauvinism.[124]

Conclusion

The guiding principle of this chapter has been to take Lenin at his word. Lenin asserted as vehemently as he knew how that the Bolshevik programme was based on a pre-war consensus of revolutionary Social Democrats. He insisted that 'Kautsky when he was a Marxist' had provided the most cogent analysis of the new era of war and revolution. He denied that he had done any rethinking whatsoever: he was merely reasserting what the Basel Manifesto had laid down as the basic duty of every Social Democrat. After looking into the matter, I conclude that Lenin was right.

During the war years, Lenin adopted a rhetorical stance of aggressive unoriginality. This stance had a definite aim: to confer Social Democratic legitimacy on the Bolshevik programme. The fact that this stance served his rhetorical purposes in no way implies that Lenin secretly thought otherwise. In any event, what is historically important is the fact that he put forth a consistent platform, one that received official party endorsement by the Bolsheviks.

Many writers put great emphasis on Lenin's political isolation during this period. True, the anti-war position was shared by a small minority in European Social Democracy, especially at the beginning of the war. Also true is Lenin's failure to generate much enthusiasm from his comrades for some of the planks in his platform, in particular, his confused and confusing slogans about

124 Lenin 1960–8, Vol. 23, p. 35.

'defeatism'. Nevertheless, Lenin's political achievement in the period from the outbreak of war in August 1914 to the Bolshevik Berne Conference in February 1915 should not be underestimated: he kept his party united around an officially endorsed anti-war platform. The Bolsheviks were spared the deep splits over the war that afflicted the other European Social Democratic parties.

Lenin was able to accomplish this precisely because he did *not* have to rethink Marxism or to come up with an original new political platform. He was able to appeal to an outlook already widely shared within the party, as shown by Kamenev's pre-war articles and the independent anti-war actions of the Bolsheviks in Russia. These Bolsheviks did not need a directive from Lenin – they already had the mandates of the Basel Manifesto. The hypothetical Bolshevik constructed on the basis of Kamenev's articles fits a great many actual Bolsheviks.

Many people are very attracted to the idea that Lenin, shocked to the core by Social Democratic apostasy in 1914, embarked on a dramatic rethinking that led him to reject 'the Marxism of the Second International'. The Hegelist interpretation is one of the more documented and carefully argued versions of this scenario of rethinking. The Hegelist case rests on an undoubted fact: Lenin put a great deal of time and energy into reading and taking copious notes on Hegel's *Science of Logic* in the final months of 1914. Nevertheless, the claims made for the political importance of Lenin's encounter with Hegel do not stand up to examination.

Besides the general problems it shares with other versions of the rethinking scenario, the Hegelist case cannot account for the facts detailed in our investigation. At the outset, this interpretation faces a severe chronological challenge: Lenin came up with his wartime programme immediately after the outbreak of war, yet he did not get down to serious note-taking on Hegel until a few months later. The picture of Lenin holed up with Hegel in the Berne library, ignoring the hurly-burly of politics outside, is an arresting one, but it stands in stark contrast with the facts that show his energetic efforts to promote his programme. In the 1916 debates over national self-determination, Lenin is not promoting a new and more dialectical approach inspired by Hegel, but instead defending a traditional position enshrined already in the party programme of 1903.

In 1917, Lenin began to come up with genuinely new positions, reflected in the April Theses and *State and Revolution*. In the case of *State and Revolution*, we really do find Lenin going back to Marx on a particular issue and using his discoveries to critique the practice of the Second International – and we observe that Lenin was perfectly open about what he was doing and felt no need to resort to a stance of aggressive unoriginality.[125] An even more important source of new thinking was the fact that after his return to Russia, he was no longer a socialist intellectual arguing with other socialist intellectuals, but a leader of a political party vying for and then exercising power in an environment dominated by mass pressures. From 1914 to 1916 Lenin had the luxury of theorising and polemicising about the new era of war and revolution. From 1917 to the end of his life, he had to navigate his way, desperately trying to stay afloat, in the very midst of it.

125 For a more detailed discussion of the extent of Lenin's originality in these two cases, see Lih 2006 (*State and Revolution*) and Lih 2011b (April Theses).

Bibliography

Adas, Michael 2004, 'Contested Hegemony: The Great War and the Afro-Asian Assault on the Civilizing Mission Ideology', in *Decolonization: Perspectives from Now and Then*, edited by Prasenjit Duara, London: Routledge.

Afflerbach, Holger 1996 [1994], *Falkenhayn: Politisches Denken und Handeln im Kaiserreich*, 2nd ed., Munich: Oldenbourg.

Ahmad, Feroz 1988, 'War and Society under the Young Turks, 1908–18', *Review*, 11, 2: 265–86.

Akşin, Sina 2007 [1996], *Turkey from Empire to Revolutionary Republic: the Emergence of the Turkish Nation from 1789 to the Present*, London: Hurst.

Alberti, Rüdiger 1930, *Gott im Krieg. Erlebnisse an der Westfront*, Berlin: Acker.

Aldcroft, D.H. 1978, *The European Economy, 1914–1970*, London: Croom Helm.

Allen Jr., Ernest 1979, '"Close Ranks": Major Joel E. Springarn and the Two Souls of W.E.B. Du Bois', *Contributions in Black Studies* 3, 4: 25–38.

Allinson, Jamie C. and Alexander Anievas 2009, 'The Uses and Misuses of Uneven and Combined Development: An Anatomy of a Concept', *Cambridge Review of International Affairs*, 22, 1: 47–67.

——— 2010, 'The Uneven and Combined Development of the Meiji Restoration: A Passive Revolutionary Road to Capitalist Modernity', *Capital & Class*, 34, 3: 469–90.

d'Almeida, Patrice 2007, *Hakenkreuz und Kaviar: Das mondäne Leben im Nationalsozialismus*, translated by Harald Ehrhardt, Düsseldorf: Patmos.

Anderson, Kevin 1995, *Lenin, Hegel, and Western Marxism: A Critical Study*, Urbana, IL: University of Illinois Press.

——— 2007, 'The Rediscovery and Persistence of the Dialectic in Philosophy and in World Politics', in *Lenin Reloaded: Toward a Politics of Truth*, edited by Sebastian Budgen, Stathis Kouvelakis, and Slavoj Žižek, Durham, NC: Duke University Press.

——— 2010, *Marx at the Margins: On Nationalism, Ethnicity, and Non-Western Societies*, Chicago, IL: University of Chicago Press.

Anderson, M.S. 1966, *The Eastern Question, 1774–1923: A Study in International Relations*, London: Macmillan.

Anderson, Perry 1974, *Lineages of the Absolutist State*, London: NLB.

——— 1976, *Considerations on Western Marxism*, London: Verso.

——— 1992, *English Questions*, London: Verso.

——— 2009, 'Turkey', in *The New Old World*, London: Verso.

Anievas, Alexander 2011, 'The International Political Economy of Appeasement: The Social Sources of British Foreign Policy during the 1930s', *Review of International Studies*, 37, 2: 601–29.

——— 2013, '1914 in World Historical Perspective: The "Uneven" and "Combined" Origins of the First World War', *European Journal of International Relations*, 19, 4: 721–46.

——— 2014, *Capital, the State, and War: Class Conflict and Geopolitics in the Thirty Years' Crisis, 1914–1945*, Ann Arbor, MI: University of Michigan Press.

Anievas, Alexander, Nivi Manchanda, and Robbie Shilliam 2015, 'Confronting the Global Colour Line: An Introduction', in *Race and Racism in International Relations: Confronting the Global Colour Line*, edited by Alexander Anievas, Nivi Manchanda, and Robbie Shilliam, London: Routledge.

Aniya Masaaki 1977, 'Imin to Dekasegi', *Kindai Okinawa no Rekishi to Minshū*, Tokyo: Shigensha.

Arendt, Hannah 1951, *The Origins of Totalitarianism*, New York, NY: Harcourt, Brace.

——— 1973, *The Origins of Totalitarianism*, New York, NY: Harcourt & Brace.

Arnold, David 1979, 'European Orphans and Vagrants in India in the Nineteenth Century', *The Journal of Imperial and Commonwealth History*, 7, 2: 104–27.

Aron, Raymond 1950, 'Social Structure and the Ruling Class', *British Journal of Sociology*, 1, 2: 126–43.

Arrighi, Giovanni 1978, *The Geometry of Imperialism: The Limits of Hobson's Paradigm*, London: NLB.

Axelrod, Pavel 1976 [1906], 'Axelrod's Speech at the Fourth Party Congress', in *The Mensheviks and the Russian Revolution*, edited by Abraham Ascher, London: Thames and Hudson.

Ayala, Cesar 1999, *American Sugar Kingdom: The Plantation Economy of the Spanish Caribbean, 1898–1934*, Chapel Hill, NC: University of North Carolina Press.

Badayev, A. 1973 [1932], *The Bolsheviks in the Tsarist Duma*, New York, NY: Howard Fertig.

Bade, Klaus J. 1975, *Friedrich Fabri und der Imperialismus in der Bismarckzeit: Revolution–Depression–Expansion*, Freiburg: Atlantis Verlag.

——— 1988, 'Imperial Germany and West Africa: Colonial Movement, Business Interests, and Bismarck's "Colonial Policies"', in *Bismarck, Europe, and Africa: The Berlin Africa Conference 1884–1885 and the Onset of Partition*, edited by Stig Förster, Wolfgang J. Mommsen, and Ronald Robinson, Oxford: The German Historical Institute London and Oxford University Press.

Bairoch, Paul 1993, *Economics and World History: Myths and Paradoxes*, London: Harvester.

——— 1989a, 'European Trade Policy 1815–1914', in *Cambridge Economic History of Europe, Vol. XIII*, edited by P. Mathias and S. Pollard, Cambridge: Cambridge University Press.

——— 1989b, 'Les troisrévolutionsagricoles du monde développé: rendementsetproductivité de 1800 à 1985', *Annales*, E.S.C., 2: 317–53.

Baker, R.S. 1922, *Woodrow Wilson and World Settlement*, New York, NY: Doubleday.

Balibar, Étienne 2001, 'Outlines of a Topography of Cruelty: Citizenship and Civility in the Era of Global Violence', *Constellations* 8, 1: 15–29.

——— 2007, 'The Philosophical Moment in Politics Determined by War: Lenin 1914–16', in *Lenin Reloaded: Toward a Politics of Truth*, edited by Sebastian Budgen, Stathis Kouvelakis and Slavoj Žižek, Durham, NC: Duke University Press.

Banaji, Jairus 1976, 'Chayanov, Kautsky, Lenin: Considerations towards a Synthesis', *Economic and Political Weekly*, 11, 40: 1594–1607.

——— 2011, *Theory as History: Essays on Modes of Production and Exploitation*, Chicago, IL: Haymarket Books.

Baron, Samuel H. 1963, *Plekhanov: The Father of Russian Marxism*, Stanford, CA: Stanford University Press.

Barraclough, G. 1964, *An Introduction to Contemporary History*, Harmondsworth: Penguin Books.

Barratt Brown, Michael 1970, *After Imperialism*, 2nd ed., New York, NY: Humanities.

Barshay, Andrew 2007, *The Social Sciences in Modern Japan: The Marxian and Modernist Traditions*, Berkeley, CA: University of California Press.

Bauer, Otto 2000 [1907], *The Question of Nationalities and Social Democracy*, edited by Ephraim Nimni, Minneapolis, MN: University of Minnesota Press.

——— 2011a [1908], 'Austria and Imperialism', in *Discovering Imperialism: Social Democracy to World War I*, edited and translated by Richard B. Day and Daniel Gaido, Leiden: Brill.

——— 2011b [1910], '*Finance Capital*', in *Discovering Imperialism: Social Democracy to World War I*, edited and translated by Day, Richard B. and Daniel Gaido, Leiden: Brill.

Bayly, Christopher 2004, *The Birth of the Modern World, 1780–1914: Global Connections and Comparisons*, Oxford: Blackwell.

Beck, Hermann 2008, *The Fateful Alliance: German Conservatives and Nazis in 1933: The Machtergreifung in a New Light*, Oxford and New York: Berghahn.

Beck, Ulrich 1986, *Risikogesellschaft: Auf dem Weg in eine andere Moderne*, Frankfurt am Main: Suhrkamp.

Beck, Ulrich, Anthony Giddens and Scott Lash 1994, *Reflexive Modernization: Politics, Tradition and Aesthetics in the Modern Social Order*, Cambridge: Polity Press.

Beckett, I.F.W. 2007, *The Great War, 1914–1918*, New York, NY: Longman.

Behm, Erika and Jürgen Kuczynski 1970, 'Arthur Dix: Propagandist der wirtschaftlicher Vorbereitung des Ersten Weltkrieges', *Jahrbuch für Wirtschaftsgeschichte 1970, Teil II*, Berlin: Akademie-Verlag.

Bell, Duncan 2007, *The Idea of Greater Britain: Empire and the Future of World Order, 1860–1900*, Princeton, NJ: Princeton University Press.

Benjamin, Walter 1991a, *Gesammelte Schriften II.1*, Frankfurt am Main: Suhrkamp.
——— 1991b, *Gesammelte Schriften II.3*, Frankfurt am Main: Suhrkamp.
——— 1991c, *Gesammelte Schriften IV.1*, Frankfurt am Main: Suhrkamp.
——— 1991d, *Gesammelte Schriften IV.2*, Frankfurt am Main: Suhrkamp.
——— 1994, *The Correspondence of Walter Benjamin, 1910–1940*, Chicago, IL: University of Chicago Press.
——— 1996a, *Gesammelte Briefe, Band II*, Frankfurt/Main: Suhrkamp.
——— 1996b, *Selected Writings, Volume 1*, Cambridge, MA: Harvard University Press.
——— 1999, *Selected Writings, Volume 2.1*, Cambridge, MA: Harvard University Press.
——— 2002a, *Selected Writings, Volume 3*, Cambridge, MA: Harvard University Press.
——— 2002b, *Arcades Project*, Cambridge, MA: Harvard University Press.
——— 2003, *Selected Writings, Volume 4*, Cambridge, MA: Harvard University Press.
——— 2005, *Selected Writings, Volume 2.2*, Cambridge, MA: Harvard University Press.
——— 2007, *Illuminations: Essays and Reflections*, New York, NY: Schocken.
——— 2008, *The Work of Art in the Age of Its Technological Reproducibility, and Other Writings on Media*, Cambridge, MA: Harvard University Press.
Benhabib, Seyla (ed.) 2010, *Politics in Dark Times: Encounters with Hannah Arendt*, New York, NY: Cambridge University Press.
Benson, L. 1989, *The Working Class in Britain, 1850–1939*, London: Longman.
Berelowitch, Wladimir 2007, 'La révolution de 1905 dans l'opinion républicaine française', *Cahiers du monde russe*, 48, 2/3: 379–92.
Berger, Suzanne 2003, *Notre Première Mondialisation: Lecons d'un Echec Oublié*, Paris: Seuil.
Berghahn, Volker R. 1971, *Der Tirpitz-Plan: Genesis und Verfall einer innenpolitischen Krisenstrategie unter Wilhelm II*, Düsseldorf: Droste Verlag.
——— 1976, 'Naval Armaments and Social Crisis: Germany before 1914', in *War, Economy and the Military Mind*, edited by Geoffrey Best and Andrew Wheatcroft, London: Croom Helm.
——— 1993 [1973], *Germany and the Approach of War in 1914*, 2nd ed., London: Macmillan.
Berghahn, Volker R. and Martin Kitchen (eds.) 1981, *Germany in the Age of Total War*, London: Croom Helm.
Bernstein, Henry 1977, 'Notes on Capital and Peasantry', *Review of African Political Economy*, 10: 60–73.
Best, Geoffrey and Andrew Wheatcroft (eds.) 1976, *War, Economy and the Military Mind*, London: Croom Helm.
Bevan, G.P. 1880, 'On the Strikes of the Past Ten Years', *Journal of the Royal Statistical Society*, 43: 35–54.
Bianchi, Alvaro 2008, *O laboratório de Gramsci Filosofia, História e Política*, São Paulo: Alameda.

Bieber, Horst 1972, *Paul Rohrbach, ein konservativer Publizist und Kritiker der Weimarer Republik*, München-Pullach: Verlag Dokumentation.

Blackbourn, David 2003, *History of Germany, 1780–1918: The Long Nineteenth Century*, London: Blackwell.

Blackbourn, David and Geoff Eley 1984, *The Peculiarities of German History: Bourgeois Society and Politics in Nineteenth-Century Germany*, Oxford: Oxford University Press.

Blanke, Richard 1993, *Orphans of Versailles*, Lexington, KY: University of Kentucky Press.

Bley, Helmut 1975, *Bebel und die Strategie der Kriegsverhütung 1903–1913*, Göttingen: Vandenhoeck und Ruprecht.

Bloch, Ernst 1971 [1918], *Geist der Utopie*, Suhrkamp: Frankfurt a. M.

Blum, Jerome 1978, *The End of the Old Order in Rural Europe*, Princeton, NJ: Princeton University Press.

Bobbio, Norberto 1990, *Profilo ideologico del Novecento*, Milano: Garzanti.

Boggio Éwanjé-Épée, Félix and Stella Magliani-Belkacem 2013, 'Social Chauvinism as a Political Category in the French Metropolis', paper presented at the 2013 Historical Materialism Conference, London. Available at: http://www.leninology.com/2013/11/social-chauvinism-as-political-category.html.

Böhler, Jochen 2006, *Auftakt zur Vernichtungskrieg: Die Wehrmacht in Polen 1939*, Frankfurt am Main: Fischer.

Bordo, Michael D., Alan M. Taylor and Jeffrey G. Williamson (eds.) 2003, *Globalization in Historical Perspective*, Chicago, IL: University of Chicago Press.

Borkenau, Franz 1962 [1939], *World Communism: A History of the Communist International*, Ann Arbor, MI: University of Michigan Press.

Braunthal, J. 1967, *History of the International, Vol. 1: 1864–1914*, translated by H. Collins and K. Mitchell, New York, NY: Praeger.

Brecht, Bertolt 2003, *Poetry and Prose*, London: Continuum Press.

Breman, Jan 1987, *Taming the Coolie Beast: Plantation Society and the Colonial Order in Southeast Asia*, Delhi: Oxford University Press.

Breundel, Steffen 2003, *Volksgemeinschaft oder Volksstaat: Die 'Ideen von 1914' und die Neuordnung Deutschlands im Ersten Weltkrieg*, Berlin: Akadamie Verlag.

Brenner, Robert 1985, 'The Agrarian Roots of European Capitalism', in *The Brenner Debate: Agrarian Class Structure and Economic Development in Preindustrial Europe*, edited by T. Ashton and C. Philpin, Cambridge: Cambridge University Press.

——— 2006, 'What Is, and What Is Not, Imperialism?', *Historical Materialism*, 14: 79–105.

Brewer, Anthony 1990, *Marxist Theories of Imperialism: A Critical Survey*, 2nd ed., London: Routledge.

Bright, Charles and Michael Geyer 2002, 'Where in the World is America? The History of the United States in the Global Age', in *Rethinking American History in a Global Age*, edited by Thomas Bender, Berkeley, CA: University of California Press.

Bromley Simon 1994, *Rethinking Middle East Politics*, Austin, TX: University of Texas Press.

Broué, Pierre 2005 [1971], *The German Revolution, 1917–1923*, edited by Ian Birchall and Brian Pearce, Leiden: Brill.

Bukharin, Nikolai I. 1984, *Lo Stato Leviatano: Scritti sullo Stato e la guerra 1915–1917*, edited by Alberto Giasanti, Unicopli, Milano.

——— 1929 [1915], *Imperialism and World Economy*, London: Lawrence & Wishart.

——— 1972 [1915], *Imperialism and World Economy*, London: Merlin.

——— 1973 [1915], *Imperialism and World Economy*, New York, NY: Monthly Review Press.

Bull, Hedley 1966, 'Society and Anarchy in International Relations', in *Diplomatic Investigations*, edited by Herbert Butterfield and Martin Wight, London: Allen and Unwin.

Bullard, Dan 2012, ' "Vergiss nicht unsere Kolonien!" German Colonial Memory from 1919 to 1943', Ph.D. Diss: York University.

Bülow, Prince von 1932, *Memoirs, 1909–1919*, London: Putnam.

Burke, Edmund. 1991, 'Changing Patterns of Peasant Protest in the Middle East, 1750–1960', in *Peasants and Politics in the Modern Middle East*, edited by Farhad Kazemi and John Waterbury, Miami, FL: Florida International University Press.

Burleigh, Michael 1997, *Ethics and Extermination: Reflections of Nazi Genocide*, Cambridge: Cambridge University Press.

——— 2000, *The Third Reich: A New History*, New York, NY: Hill and Wang.

Bush, Ray 2011, 'Egypt: A Permanent Revolution?', *Review of African Political Economy*, 38, 128: 303–7.

Bush, Roderick 2009, *The End of White World Supremacy: Black Internationalism and the Problem of the Color Line*, Philadelphia, PA: Temple University Press.

Callahan, Kevin J. 2010, *Demonstration Culture: European Socialism and the Second International, 1889–1914*, Leicester: Troubador Publishing.

Callaway, Helen 1987, *Gender, Culture and Empire: European Women in Colonial Nigeria*, Oxford: Macmillan Press.

Calleo, David 1978, *The German Problem Reconsidered: Germany and the World Order, 1870 to the Present*, Cambridge: Cambridge University Press.

Callinicos, Alex 2007, 'Does Capitalism Need the State System?', *Cambridge Review of International* Affairs, 20, 4: 533–49.

——— 2009, *Imperialism and Global Political Economy*, Cambridge: Polity.

Candeias, Mario 2004, *Neoliberalismus: Hochtechnologie, Hegemonie. Grundrisse einer transnationalen Produktions- und Lebensweise*, Hamburg-Berlin: Argument.

Cannadine, David 1983, 'The Context, Performance and Meaning of Ritual: The British Monarchy and the "Invention of Tradition", c. 1820–1977', in *The Invention of Tradition*, edited by Eric J. Hobsbawm and Terence Ranger, Cambridge: Cambridge University Press.

Carr, Edward H. 1945, *The Soviet Impact on the Western World*, New York, NY: Macmillan.

——— 1952, *A History of Soviet Russia: The Bolshevik Revolution 1917–1923*, 3 Volumes, New York, NY: W.W. Norton & Co.

Carstern, F.L. 1972, *Revolution in Central Europe, 1918–1919*, London: Temple Smith.

——— 1982, *War against War: British and German Radical Movements in the First World War*, Berkeley, CA: University of California Press.

Chattopadhyay, S. 2006, 'The Bolshevik Menace: Colonial Surveillance and the Origins of Socialist Politics in Calcutta', *South Asia Research*, 26, 2: 165–79.

Chayanov, A.V. 1986 [1925], *Theory of Peasant Economy*, Madison, WI: University of Wisconsin Press.

Chickering, Roger 1993, *Karl Lamprecht: A German Academic Life (1856–1915)*, Atlantic Highlands, NJ: Humanities Press.

——— 1999, 'Total War: The Use and Abuses of a Concept', in *Anticipating Total War: The German and American Experiences 1871–1914*, edited by Manfred F. Boemecke, Roger Chickering, and Stig Förster, New York, NY: Cambridge University Press.

Childers, Thomas 1990, 'The Social Language of Politics in Germany: The Sociology of Political Discourse in the Weimar Republic', *American Historical Review*, 95, 2: 331–58.

Chu, Winston 2012, *The German Minority in Interwar Poland*, Cambridge: Cambridge University Press.

Chu, Winston, Jesse Kauffman and Michael Meng, 2013, 'A *Sonderweg* through Eastern Europe? The Varieties of German Rule in Poland during the Two World Wars', *German History*, 31, 3: 318–34.

Clark, Christopher 2012, *The Sleepwalkers: How Europe Went to War in 1914*, London: Penguin.

Claß, Heinrich 1914, *Deutsche Geschichte: mit 24 Vollbildern und unter bunten Karte des deutschen Siedlungsgebiets in Mitteleuropa*, Leipzig: Dieterich'sche Verlagsbuchhandlung.

Cliff, Tony 1987 [1979], *Revolution Besieged: Lenin, 1917–1923*, London: Bookmarks.

——— 2003 [1963], 'Permanent Revolution', in *Marxist Theory after Trotsky*, Volume 3 of *Selected Works*, London: Bookmarks.

Collins, H. and C. Abramsky, 1965, *Karl Marx and the British Labour Movement*, New York, NY: Macmillan.

Collotti Pischel, Enrica 1973, *Storia della rivoluzione cinese*, Editori Riuniti: Roma.

Comaroff, J. and J. Comaroff 1986, 'Christianity and Colonialism in South Africa', *American Ethnologist*, 13, 1: 1–22.

——— 1985, *Body of Power, Spirit of Resistance*, Chicago, IL: Chicago University Press.

Conrad, Sebastian 2008, *German Colonialism: A Short History*, translated by Sorcha O'Hagan, Cambridge: Cambridge University Press.

——— 2010, *Globalisation and the Nation in Imperial Germany*, Cambridge: Cambridge University Press.

Cooper, Frederick 1994, 'Conflict and Connection: Rethinking Colonial African History', *American Historical Review*, 99: 1516–1545.

Cooper, John M. 1983, *The Warrior and the Priest: Woodrow Wilson and Theodore Roosevelt*, Cambridge, MA: Belknap Press of Harvard University Press.

Cope, Zak 2012, *Divided World, Divided Class: Global Political Economy and the Stratification of Labour under Capitalism*, Montreal: Kersplebedeb.

Copeland Dale 2000, *The Origins of Major Wars*, Ithaca, NY: Cornell University Press.

Coutinho, Carlos Nelson 2012 [1999], *Gramsci's Political Thought*, Leiden: Brill.

Craig Gordon 1955, *The Politics of the Prussian Army 1640–1945*, Oxford: Clarendon Press.

Cronin, J.E. 1989, 'Strikes and Power in Britain, 1870–1920', in *Strikes, Wars, and Revolutions in an International Perspective: Strike Waves in the Late Nineteenth and Early Twentieth Centuries*, edited by L. Haimson and C. Tilly, Cambridge: Cambridge University Press.

Crouch, Mira 2008, *War Fare: Sustenance in Time of Fear and Want*, Belgrade: Fischer.

Dagen, Philippe 1996, *Le silence des peintres. Les artistes face à la Grande Guerre*, Paris: Fayard.

Daudin, Guillaume, Matthias Morys, and Kevin H. O'Rourke 2010, 'Globalization, 1870–1914', in *The Cambridge Economic History of Modern Europe, Vol. 2: 1870 to the Present*, edited by Stephen Broadberry and Kevin H. O'Rourke, Cambridge: Cambridge University Press.

Davidson, Neil 2003, *Discovering the Scottish Revolution, 1692–1746*, London: Pluto Press.

——— 2006, 'From Uneven to Combined Development', in *100 Years of Permanent Revolution: Results and Prospects*, edited by Bill Dunn and Hugo Radice, London: Pluto.

——— 2010, 'From Deflected Permanent Revolution to the Law of Uneven and Combined Development', *International Socialism*, 128: 167–202.

——— 2010a, 'Scotland: Birthplace of Passive Revolution?', *Capital and Class*, 34, 3: 343–359.

——— 2012, *How Revolutionary Were the Bourgeois Revolutions?*, Chicago, IL: Haymarket Books.

Davis, Mike 1986, *Prisoners of the American Dream: Politics and Economy in the History of the US Working Class*, London: Verso.

——— 2001, *Late Victorian Holocausts: El Niño Famines and the Making of the Third World*, London: Verso.

Davis, Ralph 1979, *The Industrial Revolution and British Overseas Trade*, Leicester: Leicester University Press.

Day, Richard B. and Daniel Gaido (eds. and trans.) 2009, *Witnesses to Permanent Revolution: The Documentary Record*, Leiden: Brill.

——— 2011 'Historical Scholarship on the Classical Marxist Theories of Imperialism', in *Discovering Imperialism: Social Democracy to World War I*, edited and translated by Richard B. Day and Daniel Gaido, Leiden: Brill.

——— (eds.) 2012 [2011] *Discovering Imperialism: Social Democracy to World War I*, Chicago, IL: Haymarket Books.

Deeb, Marius 1976, 'Bank Misr and the Emergence of the Local Bourgeoisie in Egypt', in *The Middle Eastern Economy: Studies in Economics and Economic History*, edited by Elie Kedourie, London: Frank Cass & Co.

Deng Xiaoping 1992–5, *Selected Works*, Beijing: Foreign Languages Press.

Deutscher, Isaac 2003a [1954], *The Prophet Armed: Trotsky, 1879–1921*, London: Verso.

——— 2003b [1963], *The Prophet Outcast: Trotsky, 1929–1940*, London: Verso.

Diner, Dan 2008, *Cataclysms: A History of the Twentieth Century from Europe's Edge*, Madison, WI: Wisconsin University Press.

Doyle, M.W. 1997, *Ways of War and Peace: Realism, Liberalism, and Socialism*, New York, NY: W.W. Norton & Co.

Draper, Hal 1953–4, *The Myth of Lenin's 'Revolutionary Defeatism'*: found at: https://www.marxists.org/archive/draper/1953/defeat/index.htm, accessed 21 October 2013.

——— 1978, *Karl Marx's Theory of Revolution, Volume II: The Politics of Social Classes*, New York, NY: Monthly Review Press.

Duara, Prasenjit (ed.) 2004, *Decolonization: Perspectives from Now and Then*, London: Routledge.

Du Bois, W.E.B. 1961 [1903], *The Souls of Black Folk*, New York, NY: Crest Books.

——— 1925, 'Worlds of Color', *Foreign Affairs*, 3, 3: 423–44.

——— 1970 [1910], 'The Souls of White Folk', in *W.E.B. Du Bois: A Reader*, edited by Meyer Weinberg, New York, NY: Harper & Row.

——— 1970 [1913], 'Socialism and the Negro Problem', in *W.E.B. Du Bois: A Reader*, edited by Meyer Weinberg, New York, NY: Harper & Row.

——— 1972 [1914], 'World War and the Color Line', in *The Emerging Thought of W.E.B. Du Bois: Essays and Editorials from* The Crisis, edited by Henry Lee Moon, New York, NY: Simon and Schuster.

——— 1970 [1915a], 'The African Roots of War', in *W.E.B. Du Bois: A Reader*, edited by Meyer Weinberg, New York, NY: Harper & Row.

——— 1972 [1915b], 'Hayti', in *The Emerging Thought of W.E.B. Du Bois: Essays and Editorials from* The Crisis, edited by Henry Lee Moon, New York, NY: Simon and Schuster.

——— 1972 [1916], 'The Battle of Europe', in *The Emerging Thought of W.E.B. Du Bois: Essays and Editorials from* The Crisis, edited by Henry Lee Moon, New York, NY: Simon and Schuster.

——— 1970 [1917a], 'Of the Culture of White Folk', in *W.E.B. Du Bois: A Reader*, edited by Meyer Weinberg, New York, NY: Harper & Row.

——— 1970 [1917b], 'The Problem of Problems', in *W.E.B. Du Bois Speaks: Speeches and Addresses, 1890–1919*, edited by Philip S. Foner, New York, NY: Pathfinder Press.

——— 1972 [1918], 'The Black Man and the Unions', in *The Emerging Thought of W.E.B. Du Bois: Essays and Editorials from* The Crisis, edited by Henry Lee Moon, New York, NY: Simon and Schuster.

——— 1919a, 'Returning Soldiers', *Crisis* 18 (May): 13, available at: http://www.library.umass.edu/spcoll/digital/dubois/WarRS.pdf

——— 1973 [1919b], 'The Black Man in the Revolution of 1914–1918', in *The Seventh Son: The Thought and Writings of W.E.B. Du Bois*, Volume 1, edited by Julius Lester, New York, NY: Vintage.

——— 1973 [1919c], 'An Essay Toward a History of the Black Man in the Great War', in *The Seventh Son: The Thought and Writings of W.E.B. Du Bois*, Volume 1, edited by Julius Lester, New York, NY: Vintage.

——— 1972 [1920], 'Dives, Mob and Scab, Limited', in *The Emerging Thought of W.E.B. Du Bois: Essays and Editorials from* The Crisis, edited by Henry Lee Moon, New York, NY: Simon and Schuster.

——— 1970 [1921a], 'The Class Struggle', in *W.E.B. Du Bois: A Reader*, edited by Meyer Weinberg, New York, NY: Harper & Row.

——— 1970 [1921b], 'Socialism and the Negro', in *W.E.B. Du Bois: A Reader*, edited by Meyer Weinberg, New York, NY: Harper & Row.

——— 1972 [1933], 'Marxism and the Negro Problem', in *The Emerging Thought of W.E.B. Du Bois: Essays and Editorials from* The Crisis, edited by Henry Lee Moon, New York, NY: Simon and Schuster.

——— 1998 [1935], *Black Reconstruction in America, 1860–1880*, New York, NY: The Free Press.

——— 1999 [1920], *Darkwater: Voices from within the Veil*, New York, NY: Dover.

Düllfer, Jost 2003, *Im Zeichen der Gewalt: Frieden und Krieg im 19. Und 20. Jahrhundert*, Cologne: Böhlau.

Dunayevskaya, Raya 1988 [1958], *Marxism and Freedom from 1776 until Today*, 4th ed., New York, NY: Columbia University Press.

Dunn, Bill and Hugo Radice (eds.) 2006, *100 Years of Permanent Revolution: Results and Prospects*, London: Pluto.

Eksteins, Modris 1989, *Rites of Spring: The Great War and the Birth of the Modern Age*, London: Bantam Press.

Elbow, Matthew H. 1953, *French Corporative Theory, 1789–1948*, New York, NY: Columbia University Press.

Eley, Geoff 1976, 'Defining Social Imperialism: Use and Abuse of an Idea', *Social History* 1, 3: 265–90.

——— 1986, *From Unification to Nazism: Reinterpreting the German Past*, London: Allen and Unwin.

——— 1991 [1980], *Reshaping the German Right: Radical Nationalism and Political Change after Bismarck*, Ann Arbor, MI: University of Michigan Press.

——— 2002, *Forging Democracy: The History of the Left in Europe, 1850–2000*, Oxford: Oxford University Press.

——— 2013, *Nazism as Fascism: Violence, Ideology, and the Ground of Consent in Germany 1930–1945*, London: Routledge.

Ellis, Marc 1992, ' "Closing Ranks" and "Seeking Honors": W.E.B. Du Bois in World War I', *The Journal of American History*, 79, 1: 96–124.

Eng, R.Y. 1990, 'Luddism and Labor Protest among Silk Artisans and Workers in Jiangnan and Guangdong, 1860–1930', *Late Imperial China*, 11, 2: 63–101.

Engels, Frederick 1884, 'Marx and the *Neue Rheinische Zeitung* (1848–49)', *Der Sozialdemokrat*, MECW, Vol. 26, 120; available at: http://www.marxists.org/archive/marx/works/1884/03/13.htm.

——— 1971, *Einleitung* [*zu Borkheims 'Zur Erinnerung für die deutschen Mordspatrioten'*], in *Marx Engels Werke*, Berlin: Dietz Verlag, Bd. 21.

——— 1975–2005, ' "Introduction" to Sigismund Borkheim's Pamphlet, *In Memory of the German Blood-and-Thunder Patriots* 1806–1807', in Karl Marx and Friedrich Engels, *Collected Works*, Volume 26, London: Lawrence & Wishart, London.

Etherington, Norman 1984, *Theories of Imperialism: War, Conquest, and Capital*, London: Croom Helm.

Evans, Richard J. 1985, 'The Myth of Germany's Missing Revolution', *New Left Review*, I, 149: 67–94.

——— 2004, *The Coming of the Third Reich*, New York, NY: Penguin.

——— 2005, *The Third Reich in Power*, New York, NY: Penguin.

Evans, R.J.W. and Hartmut Pogge von Strandmann (eds.) 1988, *The Coming of the First World War*, Oxford: Oxford University Press.

Fabri, Friedrich 1998 [1879], *Bedarf Deutschland der Colonien?/Does Germany Need Colonies? Eine politisch-ökonomische Betrachtung*, edited by E.C.M. Breuning and Muriel Chamberlain, Lampeter: Edwin Mellen Press.

Falter, Jürgen 1991, *Hitlers Wähler*, Munich: C.H. Beck.

Feis, Herbert 1930, *Europe, the World's Banker, 1870–1914: An Account of European Foreign Investment and the Connection of World Finance with Diplomacy before the War*, with an introduction by Charles P. Howland, New Haven, CT: Yale University Press.

Ferguson, Niall 1994, 'Public Finance and National Security: The Domestic Origins of the First World War Revisited', *Past and Present*, 142: 141–68.

——— 1999, *The Pity of War*, New York, NY: Basic Books.

Ferro, Marc 2002 [1973], *The Great War*, London: Routledge.

Field, Geoffrey G. 1981, *Evangelist of Race: The Germanic Vision of Houston Stewart Chamberlain*, New York, NY: Columbia University Press.

Figes, Orlando 1997, *A People's Tragedy: The Russian Revolution, 1891–1924*, London: Pimlico.

Fiori, Giuseppe, 1966, *Vita di Antonio Gramsci*, Laterza, Bari.

Fischer, Fritz 1961, *Griff nach der Weltmacht: Die Kriegszielpolitik des kaiserlichen Deutschland, 1914–1918*, Düsseldorf: Droste.

——— 1967, *Germany's Aims in the First World War*, London: Chatto & Windus.

——— 1969, *Krieg der Illusionen: Die deutsche Politik von 1911 bis 1914*, Düsseldorf: Droste.

——— 1974, *War of Illusions: German Policies from 1911 to 1914*, London: Chatto and Windus.

——— 1975, *World Power or Decline: The Controversy over Germany's Aims in the First World War*, London: Weidenfeld and Nicolson.

——— 1984, 'World Policy, World Power, and German War Aims', in *The Origins of the First World War: Great Power Rivalry and German War Aims*, edited by H.W. Koch, Basingstoke: Macmillan.

——— 1986, *From Kaiserreich to Third Reich: Elements of Continuity in German History 1871–1945*, London: Allen & Unwin.

Fisher, John 2009, 'A Call to Action: The Committee on British Communities Abroad, 1919–20', *Canadian Journal of History*, 44, 2: 261–86.

Fitzpatrick, Matthew P. 2008, *Liberal Imperialism in Germany: Expansionism and Nationalism, 1848–1884*, New York, NY: Berghahn Books.

De Felice, Renzo 1988, *Futurismo, cultura e politica*, Torino: Fondazione Giovanni Agnelli.

Flasch, Kurt 2000, *Die geistige Mobilmachung: Die deutsche Intellektuellen und der Erste Weltkrieg*, Berlin: Alexander Fest Verlag.

Fletcher, Roger 1984, *Revisionism and Empire: Socialist Imperialism in Germany 1897–1914*, London: George Allen and Unwin.

Fletcher, R.A. 1983, 'In the Interest of Peace and Progress: Eduard Bernstein's Socialist Foreign Policy', *Review of International Studies*, 9, 2: 79–93.

Föllmer, Moritz 2005, 'The Problem of National Solidarity in Interwar Germany', *German History*, 23, 2: 202–31.

Foner, Philip S. (ed.) 1970, *W.E.B. Du Bois Speaks: Speeches and Addresses, 1890–1919*, New York, NY: Pathfinder Press.

Förster, Stig 1999, 'Dreams and Nightmares: German Military Leadership and the Images of Future Warfare, 1871–1914', in *Anticipating Total War: The German and American Experiences, 1871–1914*, edited by M.F. Boemeke, R. Chickering, and S. Förster, Cambridge: Cambridge University Press.

Förster, Stig, Wolfgang J. Mommsen, and Ronald Robinson (eds.) 1988, *Bismarck, Europe, and Africa: The Berlin Africa Conference 1884–1885 and the Onset of Partition*, Oxford: Oxford University Press.

Foster, J. 1974, *Class Struggle and the Industrial Revolution*, London: Weidenfeld.

Foucault, Michel, 2003, *Society Must Be Defended: Lectures at the Collège de France, 1975–76*, translated by David Macey, New York, NY: Picador.

——— 2008, *The Birth of Biopolitics: Lectures at the Collège de France, 1978–79*, translated by Graham Burchell, New York, NY: Palgrave Macmillan.

Francioni, Gianni 1984, *L'officina gramsciana. Ipotesi sulla struttura dei 'Quaderni del carcere'*, Naples: Bibliopolis.

Francks, Penelope 2006, *Rural Economic Development in Japan: From the Nineteenth Century to the Pacific War*, New York, NY: Routledge.

Frech, Stefan 2009, *Wegbereiter Hitlers? Theodor Reismann-Grone: Ein völkischer Nationalist (1863–1949)*, Paderborn: Ferdinand Schöningh.

Fredrickson, George M. 1981, *White Supremacy: A Comparative Study in American and South African History*, Oxford: Oxford University Press.

Friedman, Thomas L. 2000, *The Lexus and the Olive Tree*, New York, NY: Anchor Books.

Fritzsche, Peter, 2008, *Life and Death in the Third Reich*, Cambridge, MA and London: Belknap Press at Harvard University Press.

Frosini, Fabio 2007, 'Beyond the Crisis of Marxism: Thirty Years Contesting Gramsci's Legacy', in *Critical Companion to Contemporary Marxism*, edited by Jacques Bidet and Stathis Kouvelakis, Leiden: Brill.

——— 2009, *Da Gramsci a Marx*, Rome: Deriveapprodi.

——— 2012, 'Reformation, Renaissance and the State: The Hegemonic Fabric of Modern Sovereignty', *Journal of Romance Studies*, 12, 3: 63–77.

Gall, Lothar 1986, *Bismarck: The White Revolutionary, 1851–1871*, Volume 1, London: Allen and Unwin.

Gankin, Olga Hess and H.H. Fisher 1940, *The Bolsheviks and the World War: The Origin of the Third International*, Stanford, CA: Stanford University Press.

Gartzke, Erik 2007, 'The Capitalist Peace', *American Journal of Political Science*, 51, 1: 166–91.

Gartzke, Erik and Yonatan Lupu 2012, 'Trading on Preconceptions: Why World War I Was Not a Failure of Economic Interdependence', *International Security*, 36, 4: 115–50.

Geary, Dick 1981, *European Labour Protest, 1848–1939*, London: Croom Helm.

——— 1987, *Karl Kautsky*, Manchester: Manchester University Press.

Geiss, Imanuel (ed.) 1967, *July 1914: Selected Documents*, London: Batsford.

——— 1976, *German Foreign Policy 1871–1914*, London: Routledge & Kegan.

Gerlach, Christian 1998, *Krieg, Ernährung, Völkermord: Deutsche Vernichtungspolitik im Zweiten Weltkrieg*, Zürich and Munich: Pendo.

——— 1999, *Kalkulierte Mord: Die Deutsche Wirtschafts-und Vernichtungspolitik in Weissrussland 1941 bis 1944*, Hamburg: Hamburger Edition.

Gerschenkron, Alexander 1962, *Economic Backwardness in Historical Perspective*, Cambridge, MA: Harvard University Press.

——— 1966, *Bread and Democracy in Germany*, New York, NY: Fertig.

Gerstenberger, Heide 1992, 'The Bourgeois State Form Revisited', in *Open Marxism: Dialectics and History*, Volume 1, edited by Werner Bonefeld, Richard Gunn and Kosmas Psychopedis, London: Pluto Press.

Gerwarth, Robert 2008, 'The Central European Counter-Revolution: Paramilitary Violence in Germany, Austria and Hungary after the Great War', *Past and Present*, 200: 175–209.

——— 2011, *Hitler's Hangman; The Life of Heydrich*, New Haven: Yale University Press.

Gessner, Dieter 1977, 'Agrarian Protectionism in the Weimar Republic', *Journal of Contemporary History*, 12, 4: 759–78.

Geyer, Dietrich 1987, *Russian Imperialism: The Interaction of Domestic and Foreign Policy, 1860–1914*, Leamington Spa: Berg.

Geyer, Michael 2001, 'Insurrectionary Warfare: The German Debate about a *Levée en masse* in October 1918', *The Journal of Modern History*, 73: 459–527.

Gillis, J.R. 1983, *The Development of European Society, 1770–1870*, Boston, MA: Houghton Mifflin.

Gillman, Susan 2003, *Blood Talk: American Race Melodrama and the Culture of the Occult*, Chicago, IL: University of Chicago Press.

Gilmartin, William and W.I. Ladejinsky 1948, 'The Promise of Agrarian Reform in Japan', *Foreign Affairs*, 26, 2: 312–24.

Gindin, Sam, and Leo Panitch 2004, *Global Capitalism and American Empire*, London: Merlin.

Gluckstein, Donny 1985, *The Western Soviets: Workers' Councils versus Parliament, 1915–1920*, London: Bookmarks.

Goda, Norman 1998, *Tomorrow the World: Hitler, Northwest Africa, and the Path toward America*, College Station, TX: Texas A&M University Press.

Goertz, Gary and Jack S. Levy 2005, 'Causal Explanations, Necessary Conditions, and Case Studies: World War I and the End of the Cold War', *COMPASSS WP Series*, 31. Published online 18 March 2005.

Göktürk, Denis, David Gramling, and Anton Kaes 2007, *Germany in Transit: Nation and Immigration 1955–2005*, Los Angeles, CA: University of California Press.

Goldstein, R.J. 1983, *Political Repression in Nineteenth Century Europe*, London: Croom Helm.

Good, David F. 1986, 'Uneven Development in the Nineteenth Century: A Comparison of the Habsburg Empire and the United States', *Journal of Economic History*, 46, 1: 137–51.

Gordon, Andrew 1988, 'The Crowd and Politics in Imperial Japan: Tokyo 1905–1918', *Past & Present*, 121: 141–70.

Gordon, Michael R. 1974, 'Domestic Conflict and the Origins of the First World War: The British and the German Cases', *Journal of Modern History*, 46, 2: 191–226.

Gordon, Robert, and Mervyn Meggitt 1985, 'The Decline of the Kipas', in *Law and Order in the New Guinea Highlands: Encounters with Enga*, edited by R. Gordon and M. Meggitt, Hanover, NH: University Press of New England.

Goswami, Omkar 1997, 'Jute Mill Strikes of 1929 and 1937 Seen through Other's Eyes', *Modern Asian Studies*, 21, 3: 547–83.

Gramsci, Antonio 1975, *Quaderni del carcere*, Turin: Einaudi.

——— 1980, *Cronache Torinesi 1913–1917*, edited by Sergio Caprioglio, Einaudi, Torino.

——— 1984, *Il nostro Marx 1918–9*, edited by Sergio Caprioglio, Einaudi, Torino.

——— 1987, *L'Ordine Nuovo 1919–1920*, edited by Valentino Gerratana and Antonio A. Santucci, Einaudi, Torino.

——— 1994, *Pre-Prison Writings*, Cambridge: Cambridge University Press.

Grant, Kevin, Philippa Levine, and Frank Trentmann (eds.) 2007, *Beyond Sovereignty: Britain, Empire and Transnationalism, c. 1880–1950*, Houndmills: Palgrave Macmillan.

Green, Jeremy 2012, 'Uneven and Combined Development and the Anglo-German Prelude to World War I', *European Journal of International Relations*, 18, 2: 345–68.

Grey of Fallodon, Edward, Viscount 1925, *Twenty-Five Years, 1892–1916*, Volume 2, New York, NY: Frederick A. Stokes.

Grimmer-Solem, Erik 2003a, *The Rise of Historical Economics and Social Reform in Germany 1864–1894*, Oxford: Oxford University Press.

——— 2003b, 'Imperialist Socialism of the Chair: Gustav Schmoller and German *Weltpolitik*, 1897–1905', in *Wilhelminism and its Legacies: German Modernities, Imperialism, and the Meanings of Reform, 1890–1930: Essays for Hartmut Pogge von Strandmann*, edited by Geoff Eley and James Retallack, New York, NY: Berghahn Books.

Gründel, Günther 1932, *Die Sendung der jungen Generation*, Munich: Beck.

Grunenberg, Antonia (ed.) 1970, *Die Massenstreikdebatte*, Frankfurt: Europäische Verlagsanstalt.

Guettel, Jens-Uwe 2012, *German Expansionism, Liberal Imperialism, and the United States, 1776–1945*, Cambridge: Cambridge University Press.

——— 2012a, 'The Myth of the Pro-Colonialist SPD: German Social Democracy and Imperialism before World War I', *Central European History*, 45: 452–84.

Hadju, Tibor 1986, 'Socialist Revolution in Central Europe, 1917–21', in *Revolution in History*, edited by Eric Hobsbawm and Milukas Teich, Cambridge: Cambridge University Press.

Hagen, Maximilian von 1955, 'Deutsche Weltpolitik und kein Krieg', *Historische Zeitschrift*, 179, 2: 297–307.

Hagen, William W. 2012, *German History in Modern Times: Four Lives of the Nation*, Cambridge: Cambridge University Press.

Hagenlücke, Heinz 1997, *Deutsche Vaterlandspartei: Die nationale Recht am Ende des Kaiserreichs*, Düsseldorf: Droste.

Hall, Stuart 1988, 'Gramsci and Us', in *The Hard Road to Renewal*, London: Verso.

Halliday Fred 1999, *Revolution and World Politics: The Rise and Fall of the Sixth Great Power*, Durham, NC: Duke University Press.

Halperin, Sandra 1997, *In the Mirror of the Third World: Capitalist Development in Modern Europe*, Ithaca, NY: Cornell University Press.

——— 2004, *War and Social Change in Modern Europe: The Great Transformation Revisited*, Cambridge: Cambridge University Press.

——— 2013, *Re-Envisioning Global Development*, London: Routledge.

Hamilton, Richard F. and Holger Herwig (eds.) 2003, *The Origins of World War I*, Cambridge: Cambridge University Press.

Hanna, Martha 1996, *The Mobilization of the Intellect: French Scholars and Writers During the Great War*, Cambridge, MA: Harvard University Press.

Hardach, Gerd 1977, *The First World War, 1914–1918*, Berkeley, CA: University of California Press.

Harding, Neil 1996, *Leninism*, Durham, NC: Duke University Press.

Harootunian, Harry 2000, *Overcome by Modernity: History, Culture, and Community in Interwar Japan*, Princeton, NJ: Princeton University Press.

Harvey, David 2001, *Spaces of Capital: Towards a Critical Geography*, New York, NY: Routledge.

——— 2003, *The New Imperialism*, Oxford: Oxford University Press.

——— 2007, *The Limits to Capital*, New York, NY: Verso.

Hasse, Ernst 1895, *Großdeutschland und Mitteleuropa um das Jahr 1950*, Berlin: Thormann & Goetsch.

Haug, Wolfgang Fritz 2006, *Philosophieren mit Brecht und Gramsci*, Hamburg-Berlin: Argument.

Haupt, George 1970, *Il fallimento della Seconda Internazionale*, Roma: Samonà e Savelli.

——— 1972, *Socialism and the Great War: The Collapse of the Second International*, Oxford: Clarendon Press.

Hautmann, Hans 1993, 'Vienna: A City in the Years of Radical Change', in *Challenges of Labour: Central and Western Europe, 1917–1920*, edited by Chris Wrigley, London: Routledge.

Hayashi, Yuichi 1981, 'Dokusen Shihonshugi Kakuritsuki–Daiichiji Taisen kara Shōwa Kyōkō Made', in *Nihon Nōgyōshi: Shihonshugi no Tenkai to Nōgyō Mondai*, edited by Teruoka Shūzō, Tokyo: Yūhikaku.

Heckart, Beverly 1974, *From Bassermann to Bebel: The Grand Bloc's Quest for Reform in the Kaiserreich, 1900–1914*, New Haven, CT: Yale University Press.

Heinemann, Isabel 2003, *'Rasse, Siedlung, deutsches Blut': Das Rasse- & Siedlungshauptamt der SS und die rassenpolitishe Neuordnung Europas*, Göttingen: Wallstein.

Herbert, Ulrich 2001, *Best: Biographische Studien über Radikalismus, Weltanschauung und Vernunft 1903–1989*, Bonn: J.H.W. Dietz.

Herf, Jeffrey 1984, *Reactionary Modernism: Technology, Culture, and Politics in Weimar and the Third Reich*, New York, NY: Cambridge University Press.

Hering, Rainer 2003, *Konstruierte Nation: Der Alldeutsche Verband 1890 bis 1939*, Hamburg: Hans Christians Verlag.

Herrmann, D.G. 1997, *The Arming of Europe and the Making of the First World War*, Princeton, NJ: Princeton University Press.

Hertslet, Sir Edward 1891, *The Map of Europe by Treaty*, London: Harrison and Sons.

Herwig, H.H. 1994, 'Strategic Uncertainties of a Nation-State: Prussia-Germany, 1871–1918', in *The Making of Strategy: Rulers, States, and War*, edited by W. Murray, M. Knox and A.H. Bernstein, Cambridge: Cambridge University Press.

Hewitson, Mark 2004, *Germany and the Causes of the First World War*, Oxford: Berg.

Heydecker, Joe and J. Johannes Leeb 1985 [1958], *Der Nürnberger Prozess*, Kiepenheuer & Witsch, Köln.

Hickman, Larry A. and Thomas M. Alexander (eds.) 1998, *The Essential Dewey*, Bloomington, IN: Indiana University Press.

Hildebrand, Klaus 2008 [1995], *Das Vergangene Reich: Deutsche Außenpolitik von Bismarck bis Hitler 1871–1945*, Munich: Oldenbourg.

——— 1989, *German Foreign Policy from Bismarck to Adenauer: The Limits of Statecraft*, London: Unwin Hyman.

Hilferding, Rudolf 1985 [1908], *Finance Capital: A Study in the Latest Phase of Capitalist Development*, Boston, MA: Routledge.

——— 2006 [1908], *Finance Capital: A Study in the Latest Phase of Capitalist Development*, London: Routledge.

——— 2011 [1907], 'German Imperialism and Domestic Politics', in *Discovering Imperialism: Social Democracy to World War I*, edited and translated by Richard B. Day and Daniel Gaido, Leiden: Brill.

Hitler, Adolf 1971, *Mein Kampf*, translated by Ralph Manheim, Boston, MA: Houghton Mifflin.

——— 2003, *Hitler's Second Book: The Unpublished Sequel to Mein Kampf by Adolf Hitler*, edited by Gerhard Weinberg and translated by Krista Smith, New York, NY: Enigma Books.

Ho Chi Minh, 1969, *Il Testamento*, pubblicato in appendice a Le Duan, *Rivoluzione d'Ottobre, rivoluzione d'Agosto*, Verona: E.D.B.

Hobsbawm, Eric J. 1968, *Industry and Empire*, London: Weidenfeld and Nicolson.

——— 1973, 'Lenin and the "Aristocracy of Labour"', in *Revolutionaries*, London: Weidenfeld and Nicolson.

——— 1975, *The Age of Capital, 1848–1875*, London: Weidenfeld and Nicolson.

——— 1987, *The Age of Empire, 1875–1914*, New York, NY: Pantheon Books.

——— 1990, *Nations and Nationalism since 1780: Programme, Myth, Reality*, Cambridge: Cambridge University Press.

——— 1994, *The Age of Extremes: The Short Twentieth Century, 1914–1991*, New York, NY: Pantheon Books.

Hobson, John Atkinson 1902, *Imperialism: A Study*, London: James Nisbet & Co.

Hofmeister, Bernd 2012, 'Between Monarchy and Dictatorship: Radical Nationalism and Social Mobilization of the Pan-German League, 1914–1939', Ph.D. Diss: Georgetown University.

Holloway, John 2002, *Change the World Without Taking Power: The Meaning of Revolution Today*, London: Pluto.

Holloway, Steven 1983, 'Relations among Core Capitalist States: The Kautsky-Lenin Debate Reconsidered', *Canadian Journal of Political Science / Revue canadienne de science politique*, 16, 2: 321–33.

Hoston, Germaine 1986, *Marxism and the Crisis of Development in Pre-War Japan*, Princeton, NJ: Princeton University Press.

Howard, Michael 1993, 'A Thirty Years' War? The Two World Wars in Historical Perspective', *Transactions of the Royal Historical Society*, 6, 3: 171–84.

Hudis, Peter and Kevin B. Anderson. (eds.) 2004, *The Rosa Luxemburg Reader*, New York, NY: The Monthly Review Press.

Hull, Isabel 2005, *Absolute Destruction: Military Culture and the Practices of War in Imperial Germany*, Ithaca, NY: Cornell University Press.

Hyrkkänen, Markku 1986, *Sozialistische Kolonialpolitik: Eduard Bernsteins Stellung zur Kolonialpolitik und zum Imperialismus 1882–1914 – Ein Beitrag zur Geschichte des Revisionismus*, Helsinki: Societas Historica Finlandiae.

Iba, Nantetsu 1927, *Nangoku no Shirayuri*, Tokyo: Shinoue Shuppanbu.

Iggers, Georg 1985, *The Social History of Politics: Critical Perspectives in West German Historical Writing since 1945*, New York, NY: St. Martin's Press.

Ingelson, John 1981, 'Bound Hand and Foot: Railway Workers and the 1923 Strike in Java', *Indonesia*, 31: 53–88.

Iritakenishi, Masaharu 1993, *Yaeyama Tōgyōshi*, Ishigaki: Ishigakijima Seitō.

Isnenghi, Mario 1970, *Il mito della Grande Guerra da Marinetti a Malaparte*, Roma: Bari-Roma.

Jackisch, Barry 2012, *The Pan-German League and Radical Nationalist Politics in Interwar Germany, 1918–1939*, Farnham, Surrey: Ashgate.

Jacobs, Jack 1992, 'Karl Kautsky: Between Baden and Luxemburg', in *On Socialists and 'The Jewish Question' after Marx*, New York, NY: New York University Press.

James, Clifford 1931, 'International Control of Raw Sugar Supplies', *The American Economic Review*, 21, 3: 481–97.

Jarausch, Konrad H. 1973, *The Enigmatic Chancellor: Bethmann Hollweg and the Hubris of Imperial Germany*, New Haven, CT: Yale University Press.

Jenkins, Jennifer 2013, 'Fritz Fischer's "Programme for Revolution": Implications for a Global History of Germany in the First World War', *Journal of Contemporary History*, 48, 2: 397–417.

Jochmann, Werner 1963, *Nationalsozialismus und Revolution: Ursprung und Geschichte der NSDAP in Hamburg 1922–1933: Dokumente*, Frankfurt am Main: Europäische Verlagsanstalt.

Joll, James 1961, *Three Intellectuals in Politics*, New York, NY: Harper and Row.

——— 1978, *The Unspoken Assumptions*, London: Weidenfeld and Nicolson.

——— 1992 [1984], *The Origins of the First World War*, 2nd ed., London: Longman.

Joll, James, and Gordon Martel 2007, *The Origins of the First World War*, 3rd ed., Harlow: Longman.

Jones, Larry Eugene 2006, 'Nationalists, Nazis, and the Assault against Weimar: Revisiting the Harzburg Rally of October 1931', *German Studies Review*, 29, 3: 483–94.

Jünger, Ernst 1922, *In Stahlgewittern: Aus dem Tagebuch eines Stoßtruppführers*, Berlin: Verlag von E.S. Mittler und Sohn.

——— 1926, *Der Kampf als inneres Erlebnis*, Berlin: Verlag von E.S. Mittler & Sohn.

Ka, Chih-Ming 1998, *Japanese Capitalism in Taiwan: Land Tenure, Development, and Dependency, 1895–1945*, Boulder, CO: Westview Press.

Kaes, Anton, Martin Jay and Edward Dimendberg (eds.) 1994, *The Weimar Republic Sourcebook*, Berkeley, CA: University of California Press.

Kafka, Franz 1949, *The Diaries of Franz Kafka*, New York, NY: Schocken.

Kamenev, Lev 2003 [1922], *Mezhdu dvumia revoliutsiiami*, Moscow: Tsentrpoligraf.

Kandal, Terry R. 1989, 'Marx and Engels on International Relations, Revolution, and Counterrevolution', in *Studies of Development and Change in the Modern World*, edited by M.T. Martin and T.R. Kandal, Oxford: Oxford University Press.

Kaneto Sachiko 2007, '1930-nen Zengo no Yaeyama Josei no Shokuminchi Taiwan e no Idō o Unagashita Puru Yōin: Taiwan ni Okeru Shokuminchiteki Kindai to Josei no Shokugyō no Kakudai o Megutte', *Immigration Studies*, 3: 1–26.

Kanoussi, Dora 2000, *Una introducción a los Cudernos de la Cárcel de Antonio Gramsci*, México D.F.: Benemerita Universidad Autonoma de Puebla/International Gramsci Society/Plaza y Valdez.

Kantorowicz, Ernst 1951, 'Pro Patria Mori in Medieval Political Thought', *American Historical Review*, 56, 3: 472–92.

Kasaba, R.S. 1988, *The Ottoman Empire and the World Economy: The Nineteenth Century*, Albany, NY: SUNY.

Kautsky, Karl 1902, *The Social Revolution*, Chicago, IL: Charles H. Kerr and Company.

——— 1907, *Socialism and Colonial Policy*, Marxists Internet Archive at: http://www.marxists.org/archive/kautsky/1907/colonial/index.htm.

——— 1919, *The Dictatorship of the Proletariat*, translated by H.J. Stennning, London: National Labour Press.

——— 1920, *Terrorism and Communism: A Contribution to the Natural History of Revolution*, translated by W.H. Kerridge, London: National Labour Press.

——— 1977 [1918], *Die Diktatur des Proletariats*, translated and edited by Luciano Pellicani, *La dittatura del proletariato*, 2nd ed., Milan: Sugarco.

——— 1996 [1909], *The Road to Power: Political Reflections on Growing into the Revolution*, translated by Raymond Meyer and edited by John Kautsky, Atlantic Highlands, NJ: Humanities Press.

——— 2009a [1902], 'The Slavs and Revolution', in *Witnesses to Permanent Revolution: The Documentary Record*, edited and translated by Richard B. Day and Daniel Gaido, Leiden: Brill.

——— 2009b [1903/1906], 'To What Extent Is the *Communist Manifesto* Obsolete?' in *Witnesses to Permanent Revolution: The Documentary Record*, edited and translated by Richard B. Day and Daniel Gaido, Leiden: Brill.

——— 2009c [1904], 'Revolutionary Questions', in *Witnesses to Permanent Revolution: The Documentary Record*, edited and translated by Richard B. Day and Daniel Gaido, Leiden: Brill.

——— 2009d [1905], 'Old and New Revolution', in *Witnesses to Permanent Revolution: The Documentary Record*, edited and translated by Richard B. Day and Daniel Gaido, Leiden: Brill.

——— 2009e [1906], 'The Driving Forces of the Russian Revolution and Its Prospects', in *Witnesses to Permanent Revolution: The Documentary Record*, edited and translated by Richard B. Day and Daniel Gaido, Leiden: Brill.

——— 2009f [1906], 'The American Worker', in *Witnesses to Permanent Revolution: The Documentary Record*, edited and translated by Richard B. Day and Daniel Gaido, Leiden: Brill.

——— 2009g [1905], 'The Consequences of the Japanese Victory and Social Democracy', in *Witnesses to Permanent Revolution: The Documentary Record*, edited and translated by Richard B. Day and Daniel Gaido, Leiden: Brill.

——— 2009/2010 [1907/08], 'Nationality and Internationality', *Critique*, 37, 3: 371–89 and 38, 1: 143–163.

Karpinskii, V.A. 1969, 'Stranichki proshlogo', in *Vospominaniia o Vladimire Il'iche Lenine*, Volume 2, Moscow: Politizdat.

Kehr, Eckart 1973 [1930], *Battleship Building and Party Politics in Germany 1894–1901: A Cross-Section of the Political, Social, and Ideological Preconditions of German Imperialism*, edited by Pauline R. Anderson and Eugene N. Anderson, Chicago, IL: University of Chicago Press.

——— 1977 [1965], *Economic Interest, Militarism, and Foreign Policy: Essays on German History*, edited by Gordon A. Craig, Berkeley, CA: University of California Press.

Kellogg, Michael 2005, *The Russian Roots of Nazism: White Émigrés and the Making of National Socialism, 1917–1945*, Cambridge: Cambridge University Press.

Kennedy, Dane 1987, *Islands of White: Settler Society and Culture in Kenya and Southern Rhodesia, 1890–1939*, Durham, NC: Duke University Press.

Kennedy, Paul M. 1980, *The Rise of the Anglo-German Antagonism, 1860–1914*, London: Allen & Unwin.

Kershaw, Ian 1987, *The 'Hitler Myth': Image and Reality in the Third Reich*, Oxford: Clarendon Press.

——— 1998, *Hitler 1889–1936: Hubris*, New York and London: W.W. Norton.

——— 2000 [1985], *The Nazi Dictatorship: Problems and Perspectives of Interpretation*, 4th ed., London: Arnold.

Kikekawa, Hiroshi 1967, *Meiji Chihō Seido Seiritsushi*, Tokyo: Gannandō Shoten.

King, Richard and Dan Stone 2007, *Hannah Arendt and the Uses of History: Imperialism, Nation, Race, and Genocide*, New York, NY: Berghahn Books.

Kinjō, Isao 1983, *Kindai Okinawa no Tetsudō to Kaiun*, Naha: Hirugisha.

——— 1985, *Kindai Okinawa no Tōgyō*, Naha: Hirugisha.

Kirshner, Jonathan 1998, 'Political Economy in Security Studies after the Cold War', *Review of International Political Economy*, 5, 1: 64–91.

Klemperer, Victor 2000, *The Language of the Third Reich: LTI-Lingua Tertii Imperii: A Philologist's Notebook*, translated by Martin Brady, London and New York: Continuum.

Knei-Paz, Baruch 1979, *The Social and Political Thought of Leon Trotsky*, Oxford: Oxford University Press.

Knight, G. Roger 2010, 'Exogenous Colonialism: Java Sugar between Nippon and Taikoo before and during the Interwar Depression, c. 1920–1940', *Modern Asian Studies*, 44, 3: 477–515.

Knox, MacGregor 1984, 'Conquest, Foreign and Domestic, in Fascist Italy and Nazi Germany', *Journal of Modern History*, 56: 1–57.

——— 1996, 'Expansionist Zeal, Fighting Power, and Staying Power in the Italian and German Dictatorships', in *Fascist Italy and Nazi Germany: Comparisons and Contrasts*, edited by Richard Bessel, Cambridge: Cambridge University Press.

——— 2000, *Common Destiny: Dictatorship, Foreign Policy, and War in Fascist Italy and Nazi Germany*, Cambridge: Cambridge University Press.

Koch, Hans W. (ed.) 1972, *The Origins of the First World War: Great Power Rivalry and German War Aims*, London: Macmillan.

Kocka, Jürgen 1999, *Industrial Culture and Bourgeois Society: Business, Labor, and Bureaucracy in Modern Germany*, New York, NY: Berghahn Books.

Komlos, J. 2000, 'The Industrial Revolution as the Escape from the Malthusian Trap', *Journal of European Economic History*, 29, 2–3: 307–31.

Kooiman, Dick 1980, 'Bombay Communists and the 1924 Textile Strike', *Economic and Political Weekly*, 15, 29: 1223–1236.

Koselleck, Reinhart 2002, 'War Memorials: Identity Formation of the Survivors', in *The Practice of Conceptual History: Timing History, Spacing Concepts*, Stanford, CA: Stanford University Press.

Kouvelakis, Stathis 2007a, 'Lenin as Reader of Hegel: Hypotheses for a Reading of Lenin's Notebooks on Hegel's *The Science of Logic*', in *Lenin Reloaded: Toward a Politics of Truth*, edited by Sebastian Budgen, Stathis Kouvelakis, and Slavoj Žižek, Durham, NC: Duke University Press.

——— 2007b, 'Marx's Critique of the Political: From the Revolutions of 1848 to the Paris Commune', *Situations*, 2, 24: 81–93.

Kramer, Paul A. 2006, *The Blood of Government: Race, Empire, the United States, and the Philippines*, Chapel Hill, NC: University of North Carolina Press.

Kraus, Karl 1974, *The Last Days of Mankind: A Tragedy in Five Acts*, New York, NY: F. Ungar.

——— 1990, *In These Great Times: A Karl Kraus Reader*, Chicago, IL: University of Chicago Press.

——— 1999, *Eine Ausstellung des Deutschen Literaturarchivs im Schiller-Nationalmuseum Marbach* (*Marbacher Kataloge*), Marbach: Deutsche Schillergesellschaft.

Krupskaya, Nadezhda 1960 [1933], *Reminiscences of Lenin*, New York, NY: International Publishers.

Kühlmann, Richard von 1931, *Gedanken über Deutschland*, Leipzig: Paul List Verlag.

Lacouture, Jean 1967, *Ho Chi Minh*, translated by Mario Rivoire, Milano: Il Saggiatore.

Lakatos, Imre 1970, *Criticism and the Growth of Knowledge*, edited by A. Musgrave, Cambridge: Cambridge University Press.

Lampe, J.R. and M.R. Jackson 1982, *Balkan Economic History, 1550–1950*, Bloomington, IN: Indiana University Press.
Laqueur, Walter 1992, *Europe in Our Time*, Harmondsworth: Penguin.
Larkin, John 1993, *Sugar and the Origins of Modern Philippine Society*, Berkeley, CA: University of California Press.
Larsson, Reidar 1970, *Theories of Revolution: From Marx to the First Russian Revolution*, Stockholm: Almqvist & Wiksell.
Lebzelter, Gisela 1985, 'Die "Schwarze Schmach": Vorurteile, Propaganda, Mythos', *Geschichte und Gesellschaft* 11, 1: 37–58.
'The Left in Iran, 1905–1940', 2010, special issue of *Revolutionary History*, 10: 2.
Léger, Fernand 1990, *Correspondance de guerre*, Paris: Cahiers du Musée National d'Art Moderne.
Leicht, Johannes 2012, *Heinrch Claß 1868–1953: Die politische Biographie eines Alldeutschen*, Paderborn: Ferdinand Schöningh.
Lenin Vladmir I. 1907, 'The International Socialist Congress in Stuttgart', in *Collected Works*, Volume 13, Moscow: Progress Publishers, 1972, 75–81. Available at: https://www.marxists.org/archive/lenin/works/1907/oct/20.htm.
——— 1955–1970, *Opere complete*, Editori Riuniti, Roma.
——— 1958–1964, *Polnoe sobranie sochinenii*, 5th ed., Moscow: Gosizdat.
——— 1960, *Collected Works*, 35 Volumes, Moscow: Foreign Languages Publishing House.
——— 1960 [1899], *The Development of Capitalism in Russia: The Process of the Formation of Home Market for Large Scale Industry*, in *Collected Works*, Volume 3, *1899*, Moscow: Foreign Languages Publishing House.
——— 1960–1968, *Collected Works*, New York, NY: Foreign Languages Press.
——— 1964 [1916b], 'A Caricature of Marxism and Imperialist Economism', in *Collected Works*, Volume 23, Moscow: Progress Publishers. Available at: http://www.marx2mao.com/Lenin/CM16.html
——— 1964a [1917], 'The Tasks of the Proletariat in Our Revolution (Draft Platform for the Proletarian Party)', *Collected Works*, Volume 24, Moscow: Progress Publishers.
——— 1962a [1905], 'The Fall of Port Arthur', in *Collected Works*, Volume 8, *January–July 1905*, Moscow: Foreign Languages Publishing House.
——— 1962b [1905], 'Two Tactics of Social-Democracy in the Democratic Revolution', in *Collected Works*, Volume 9, *June–November 1905*, Moscow: Foreign Languages Publishing House.
——— 1962c [1905], 'Social Democracy's Attitude towards the Peasant Movement', in *Collected Works*, Volume 9, *June–December 1905*, Moscow: Foreign Languages Publishing House.
——— 1962d [1905], 'Lessons of the Moscow Events', in *Collected Works*, Volume 9, *June– November 1905*, Moscow: Foreign Languages Publishing House.

——— 1962e [1905], 'The Socialist Party and Non-Party Revolutionism', in *Collected Works*, Volume 10, *November 1905–June 1906*, Moscow: Foreign Languages Publishing House.

——— 1962f [1906], 'Preface to the Russian Translation of K. Kautsky's Pamphlet *The Driving Forces and Prospects of the Russian Revolution*', in *Collected Works*, Volume 11, *June 1906–January 1907*, Moscow: Foreign Languages Publishing House.

——— 1962g [1907], 'The Agrarian Question and the Forces of the Revolution', in *Collected Works*, Volume 12, *January–June 1907*, Moscow: Foreign Languages Publishing House.

——— 1962f [1907], 'The Agrarian Programme of Social-Democracy in the First Russian Revolution, 1905–1907', in *Collected Works*, Volume 13, *June 1907–April 1908*, Moscow: Foreign Languages Publishing House.

——— 1963a [1908], 'The Assessment of the Russian Revolution', in *Collected Works*, Volume 15, *March 1908–August 1909*, Moscow: Foreign Languages Publishing House.

——— 1963b [1909], 'The Aim of the Proletarian Struggle in Our Revolution', in *Collected Works*, Volume 15, *March 1908–August 1909*, Moscow: Foreign Languages Publishing House.

——— 1963b [1911], 'The "Peasant Reform" and the Proletarian-Peasant Revolution', in *Collected Works*, Volume 17, *December 1910–April 1912*, Moscow: Foreign Languages Publishing House.

——— 1963b [1911], 'A Conversation between a Legalist and an Opponent of Liquidationism', in *Collected Works*, Volume 17, *December 1910–April 1912*, Moscow: Foreign Languages Publishing House.

——— 1963c [1911], 'Reformism in the Russian Social-Democratic Movement', in *Collected Works*, Volume 17, *December 1910–April 1912*, Moscow: Foreign Languages Publishing House.

——— 1963d [1912], 'Democracy and Narodism in China', in *Collected Works*, Volume 18, *April 1912–March 1913*, Moscow: Foreign Languages Publishing House.

——— 1963e [1913], 'The Historical Destiny of the Doctrine of Karl Marx', in *Collected Works*, Volume 18, *April 1912–March 1913*, Moscow: Foreign Languages Publishing House.

——— 1963f [1913], 'Backward Europe and Advanced Asia', in *Collected Works*, Volume 19, *March–December 1913*, Moscow: Foreign Languages Publishing House.

——— 1964a [1914], 'The Right of Nations to Self-Determination', in *Collected Works*, Volume 20, *December 1913–August 1914*, Moscow: Foreign Languages Publishing House.

——— 1964b [1914], 'The War and Russian Social-Democracy', in *Collected Works*, Volume 21, *August 1914–December 1915*, Moscow: Foreign Languages Publishing House.

——— 1964c [1916], 'Imperialism, the Highest Stage of Capitalism: A Popular Outline', in *Collected Works*, Volume 22, *December 1915–July 1916*, Moscow: Foreign Languages Publishing House.

——— 1964d [1917], 'Farewell Letter to Swiss Workers', in *Collected Works*, Volume 23, *August 1916–March 1917*, Moscow: Foreign Languages Publishing House.

——— 1964e [1917], 'The State and Revolution: The Marxist Theory of the State and the Tasks of the Proletariat in the Revolution', in *Collected Works*, Volume 25, *June–September 1917*, Moscow: Foreign Languages Publishing House.

——— 1964f [1917], 'Report on Peace, October 26 (November 8)', in *Collected Works*, Volume 26, *September 1917–February 1917*, Moscow: Foreign Languages Publishing House.

——— 1964g [1918], 'Report on the Activities of the Council of People's Commissars, January 11 (24)', in *Collected Works*, Volume 26, *September 1917–February 1918*, Moscow: Foreign Languages Publishing House.

——— 1966a [1920] '"Left-Wing" Communism–An Infantile Disorder', in *Collected Works*, Volume 31, *April–December 1920*, Moscow: Foreign Languages Publishing House.

——— 1966b [1921], 'Fourth Anniversary of the October Revolution', in *Collected Works*, Volume 33, *August 1921–March 1923*, Moscow: Foreign Languages Publishing House.

——— 1968, *Collected Works*, Volume 39, *Notebooks on Imperialism*, Moscow: Progress Publishers.

——— 1968 [1916], *Imperialism, The Highest Stage of Capitalism: A Popular Outline*, Moscow: Progress Publishers.

——— 1974 [1915], 'The Conference of the R.S.D.L.P. Groups Abroad', in *Collected Works*, Volume 21, Moscow: Progress Publishers.

——— 1976 [1914], 'Letter to A.G. Shlyapnikov, 17 October 1914', in *Collected Works*, Volume 35, Moscow: Progress Publishers.

——— 1984 [1912], 'To All the Citizens of Russia', in *Lenin's Struggle for a Revolutionary International: Documents: 1907–1916, the Preparatory Years*, edited by John Riddell, New York, NY: Monad Press.

——— 1999 [1916a], 'Imperialism and the Split in Socialism', in *Imperialism: The Highest Stage of Capitalism*, Sydney: Resistance Books.

Lewin, Moshe 1985, 'Leninism and Bolshevism: The Test of History and Power', in *The Making of the Soviet System: Essays in the Social History of Interwar Russia*, New York, NY: Pantheon Books.

Lewis, David Levering 2009, *W.E.B. Du Bois: A Biography*, New York, NY: Holt.

Lewis, W.A. 1978, *The Evolution of the International Economic Order*, Princeton, NJ: Princeton University Press.

Liebknecht, Karl 1986 [1918], 'The New "Civil Peace"', in *The German Revolution and the Debate on Soviet Power. Documents: 1918–1919, Preparing the Founding Congress*, edited by John Riddell, New York, NY: Pathfinder Press.

Lieven, D.C.B. 1983, *Russia and the Origins of the First World War*, London: Macmillan.

Liguori, Guido 2012, *Gramsci conteso: Interpretazioni, dibattiti e polemiche 1922–2012*, Rome: Editori Riuniti University Press.

Lih, Lars T. 2006, 'Review of Marc Angenot, *Jules Guesde, ou: Le Marxisme orthodoxe*', *Kritika* 7, 4: 905–18.

——— 2008, 'Lenin and Kautsky, The Final Chapter', *International Socialist Review*, 59, http://www.isreview.org/issues/59/feat-lenin.shtml.

——— 2009, 'Lenin's Aggressive Unoriginality, 1914–1916', *Socialist Studies: The Journal of the Society for Socialist Studies*, 5, 2: 90–112.

——— 2011a, 'Kautsky When He Was a Marxist (Database of post-1914 comments by Lenin)', *Historical Materialism*, http://www.historicalmaterialism.org/journal/online-articles/kautsky-as-marxist-data-base.

——— 2011b, 'The Ironic Triumph of Old Bolshevism: The Debates of April 1917 in Context', *Russian History*, 38: 199–242.

——— 2012, 'Democratic Revolution *in Permanenz*', *Science & Society*, 76, 4: 433–62.

Linne, Karsten 2002, *'Weisse Arbeitsführer' im 'Kolonialen Ergänzungsraum'*, Münster: Monsenstein & Vannerdat.

Liulevicius, Vejas Gabriel 2009, *The German Myth of the East: 1800 to the Present*, Oxford: Oxford University Press.

——— 2000, *War Land on the Eastern Front: Culture, National Identity and German Occupation in World War I*, Cambridge: Cambridge University Press.

Lockman, Zachary 1994, ' "Worker" and "Working Class" in pre-1914 Egypt: A Rereading', in *Workers and Working Classes in the Middle East: Struggles, Histories, Historiographies*, edited by Zachary Lochman, Albany. NY: State University of New York Press.

Lohalm, Uwe 1970, *Völkischer Radikalismus: Die Geschichte des Deutschvölkischen Schutz- und Trutz-Bundes 1919–1923*, Hamburg: Leibniz.

Long, David 1996, *Toward a New Liberal Internationalism: The International Theory of J.A. Hobson*, Cambridge and New York, NY: Cambridge University Press.

Long, James W. 1972, 'Russian Manipulation of the French Press, 1904–1906', *Slavic Review*, 31, 2: 343–54.

——— 1975, 'French Attempts at Constitutional Reform in Russia', *Jahrbücher für Geschichte Osteuropas*, Neue Folge, Bd. 23, H. 4: 496–503.

Longerich, Peter 2008, *Heinrich Himmler: Biographie*, Berlin: Siedler.

Losurdo, Domenico 2001, *Heidegger and the Ideology of War: Community, Death and the West*, Amherst, NY: Humanity Books.

——— 2008, *Stalin: Storia e critica di una leggenda nera*, Roma: Carocci.

——— 2011, *Liberalism: A Counter-History*, London: Verso.

Lower, Wendy 2005, *Empire Building and the Holocaust in the Ukraine*, Chapel Hill and London: University of North Carolina Press.

Löwy, Michael 1981, *The Politics of Combined and Uneven Development: The Theory of Permanent Revolution*, London: New Left Books.

——— 1992, *Rédemption et utopie: Le judaisme libértaire en Europe centrale: Une étude d'affinité élective*, translated by *Redenzione e utopia. Figure della cultura ebraica mitteleuropea*, Torino: Bollati Boringhieri.

——— 2006, 'The Marxism of Trotsky's "Results and Prospects": Permanent Revolution: A Decisive Break with the Mechanical Marxism of the 2nd International', *International Viewpoint*, available at: <http://internationalviewpoint.org/spip.php?article1118 >.

Lukács, György 1970 [1924], *Lenin: A Study in the Unity of His Thought*, London: New Left Books.

——— 1971 [1923], *History and Class Consciousness: Studies in Marxist Dialectics*, London: Merlin Press.

——— 1971a [1923], 'Critical Observations on Rosa Luxemburg's "Critique of the Russian Revolution"', in *History and Class Consciousness: Studies in Marxist Dialectics*, London: Merlin Press.

——— 1971b [1923], 'Towards a Methodology of the Problem of Organisation', in *History and Class Consciousness: Studies in Marxist Dialectics*, London: Merlin Press.

——— 1972 [1928], 'Blum Theses (Extracts)', in *Tactics and Ethics: Political Writings, 1919–1929*, edited by Rodney Livingstone, London: New Left Books.

——— 1983, *Gelebtes Leben, Pensiero vissuto: Autobiografia in forma di dialogo*, translated and edited by A. Scarponi, Roma: Editori Riuniti.

——— 1984, *Epistolario 1902–1917*, edited by É. Karádi and É. Fekete, Roma: Editori Riuniti.

——— 1988 [1922], *Geschichte und Klassenbewusstsein*, translated by Giovanni Piana, *Storia e coscienza di classe*, 7th ed., Milan: Sugarco.

Luxemburg, Rosa 1963 [1913], *The Accumulation of Capital*, London: Routledge and Kegan Paul.

——— 1969, *The Crisis in the German Social-Democracy*, New York, NY: Howard Fertig.

——— 1986 [1918], 'The Beginning', in *The German Revolution and the Debate on Soviet Power, Documents: 1918–1919, Preparing the Founding Congress*, edited by John Riddell, New York, NY: Pathfinder Press.

——— 1970, *Rosa Luxemburg Speaks*, edited by Mary-Alice Waters, New York, NY: Pathfinder Press.

——— 2003 [1896], 'Social Democracy and the National Struggles in Turkey', *Revolutionary History* 8, 3, *The Balkan Socialist Tradition and the Balkan Federation, 1871–1915*: 37–46.

——— 2009 [1905], 'The Russian Revolution', in *Witnesses to Permanent Revolution: The Documentary Record*, edited and translated by Richard B. Day and Daniel Gaido, Leiden: Brill.

Macnair, Mike (ed.) 2013, *Kautsky on Colonialism*, London: November Publications.

Macshane, D. 1992, *International Labour and the Origins of the Cold War*, Oxford: Clarendon Press.

Maddison, Angus 2001, *The World Economy: A Millennial Perspective*, Paris, France: Development Centre of the Organisation for Economic Co-operation and Development.

Maehl, William 1952, 'The Triumph of Nationalism in the German Socialist Party on the Eve of the First World War', *The Journal of Modern History*, 24, 1: 15–41.

Maier, Charles 1975, *Recasting Bourgeois Europe: Stabilization in France, Germany and Italy in the Decade after World War I*, Princeton, NJ: Princeton University Press.

Malinowski, Stephan 2004, *Vom König zum Führer: Deutscher Adel und Nationalsozialismus*, Frankfurt am Main: Fisher Taschenbuch.

Mandel, Ernest 1975, *Late Capitalism*, London: Verso.

Mann, Michael 1988, 'Ruling Class Strategies and Citizenship', in *States, Wars and Capitalism: Studies in Political Sociology*, Oxford: Oxford University Press.

——— 1993, *The Sources of Social Power, Volume II: The Rise of Classes and Nation-States, 1760–1914*, Cambridge: Cambridge University Press.

——— 2012, *The Sources of Social Power, Volume III: Global Empires and Revolution, 1890–1945*, Cambridge: Cambridge University Press.

Mann, Thomas 1983, *Reflections of a Nonpolitical Man*, New York, NY: F. Ungar.

Mao Zedong (Mao Tsetung), 1969–1975, *Opere scelte*, Pechino: Edizioni in lingue estere.

——— 1998, *On Diplomacy*, Beijing: Foreign Languages Press.

Marable, Manning 2005, *W.E.B. Du Bois: Black Radical Democrat*, Boulder, CO: Paradigm.

Marchlewski, Julian (J. Karski) 1910, 'Ein Missverständnis', *Die Neue Zeit*, 29, 1: 100–7.

Markov, Vladimir 1968, *Russian Futurism: A History*, Berkeley, CA: University of California Press.

Marks, Sally 2013, 'Mistakes and Myths: The Allies, Germany, and the Versailles Treaty, 1918–1921', *The Journal of Modern History* 85, 3: 632–59.

Marot, John Eric 2012 [1994], 'Class-Conflict, Political Competition and Social Transformation: Critical Perspectives on the Social History of the Russian Revolution', in *The October Revolution in Prospect and Retrospect: Interventions in Russian and Soviet History*, edited by John Eric Marot, Leiden: Brill.

Marx, Karl 1853, 'The Future of British Rule in India', *New York Daily Tribune*. Available at www.marxists.org/archive/marx/works/1853/07/22.htm.

——— 1981 [1894], *Capital: A Critique of Political Economy, Volume III*, London: Penguin.

——— 1993 [1894], *Capital: A Critique of Political Economy, Volume III*, translated by David Fernbach, New York, NY: Penguin.

Marx, Karl and Friedrich Engels 1975–2005, *Collected Works*, London: Lawrence and Wishart.

——— 1955–1989, *Werke* Berlin: Dietz.

——— 2002 [1848], *The Communist Manifesto*, Harmondsworth: Penguin.

Mason, Tim 1971, 'The Legacy of 1918 for National Socialism', in *German Democracy and the Triumph of Hitler*, edited by Anthony J. Nicholls and Erich Matthias, London: Macmillan.

——— 1989, 'Debate: Germany, "Domestic Crisis," and War in 1939', with a Reply by Richard J. Overy, *Past and Present*, 122: 205–40.

——— 1993, 'Domestic Crisis and War, 1939', in *Social Policy in the Third Reich: The Working Class and the "National Community"*, edited by Jane Caplan, Providence, RI: Berg.

——— 1995, 'Internal Crisis and War of Aggression, 1938–1939', and 'The Domestic Dynamics of Nazi Conquests: A Response to Critics', in *Nazism, Fascism, and the Working Class*, edited by Jane Caplan, Cambridge: Cambridge University Press.

Mass, Sandra 2006, *Weisse Helden, schwarzer Krieger: Zur Geschichte kolonialer Männlichkeit in Deutschland, 1918–1922*, Cologne: Böhlau.

Mastanduno, Michael 1998, 'Economics and Security in Statecraft and Scholarship', *International Organization*, 52, 4: 825–84.

Matayoshi, Morikiyo 1990, 'Okinawa Josei to Taiwan Shokuminchi Shihai', *Okinawa Bunka Kenkyū*, 16: 329–52.

Matsumoto, Hiroshi, *Mitsui Zaibatsu no Kenkyū*, Tokyo: Yoshikawa Kōbunkan.

Mayer, Arno J. 1959, *The Political Origins of the New Diplomacy, 1917–1918*, New York, NY: H. Fertig.

——— 1967, *Politics and Diplomacy of Peacemaking: Containment and Counterrevolution at Versailles, 1918–1919*, New York, NY: Alfred A. Knopf.

——— 1981, *The Persistence of the Old Regime: Europe to the Great War*, New York, NY: Pantheon Books.

——— 1990, *Why Did the Heavens Not Darken? The 'Final Solution' in History*, London: Verso.

Mazower, Mark 1999, *Dark Continent: Europe's Twentieth Century*, Harmondsworth: Penguin Books.

——— 2008, *Hitler's Empire*, London: Allen Lane.

Mazumdar, Sucheta 1998, *Sugar and Society in China: Peasants, Technology and the World Market*, Cambridge, MA: Harvard University Asia Center.

McDaniel, Tim 1988, *Autocracy, Capitalism, and Revolution in Russia*, Berkeley, CA: University of California Press.

McDonald, David MacLaren 1992, *United Government and Foreign Policy in Russia, 1900–1914*, Cambridge, MA: Harvard University Press.

McDonald, Patrick J., David M. Rowe and David H. Bearce 2002, 'Binding Prometheus: How the 19th Century Expansion of Trade Impeded Britain's Ability to Raise an Army', *International Studies Quarterly*, 46, 4: 551–78.

McDonald, Patrick J. 2009, *The Invisible Hand of Peace: Capitalism, the War Machine, and International Relations Theory*, Cambridge: Cambridge University Press.

——— 2011, 'Complicating Commitment: Free Resources, Power Shifts, and the Fiscal Politics of Preventive War', *International Studies Quarterly*, 55, 4: 1095–1120.

McDonald, Patrick J. and Kevin Sweeney 2007, 'The Achilles' Heel of Liberal IR Theory? Globalization and Conflict in the Pre-World War I', *World Politics*, 59, 3: 370–403.

McDonough, Frank 1997, *The Origins of the First and Second World Wars*, Cambridge: Cambridge University Press.

McGillivray, Gillian 2009, *Blazing Cane: Sugar Communities, Class, and State Formation in Cuba, 1868–1959*, Durham, NC: Duke University Press.

McGraw, Roger 1983, *France 1815–1914: The Bourgeois Century*, Oxford: Fontana.

McMeekin, Sean 2013, *July 1914: Countdown to War*, New York, NY: Basic Books.

McNeil, William. 2008, 'Globalization: Long Term Process or New Era in Human Affairs?', *New Global Studies*, 2, 1: 1–9.

Meade, Teresa. 1989, '"Living Worse and Costing More": Resistance and Riot in Rio de Janeiro, 1890–1917', *Journal of Latin American Studies*, 21: 241–66.

Meister, Robert 2011, *After Evil: A Politics of Human Rights*, New York, NY: Columbia University Press.

Melancon, Michael 1990, *The Socialist Revolutionaries and the Russian Anti-War Movement, 1914–1917*, Columbus, OH: Ohio State University Press.

Metzler, Mark 2006, *Lever of Empire: The International Gold Standard and the Crisis of Liberalism in Prewar Japan*, Berkeley, CA: University of California Press.

Meyer, Henry Cord 1955, *Mitteleuropa in German Thought and Action, 1815–1945*, The Hague: Martinus Nijhoff.

Michael-Matsas, Savas 2011, 'The Arab Spring: The Revolution at the Doors of Europe', *Critique*, 39, 3: 421–32.

Miki, Takeshi 1996, *Okinawa Iriomote Tankōshi*, Tokyo: Nihon Keizai Hyōronsha.

Milward, A.S. 1984, *The Reconstruction of Western Europe, 1945–1951*, Berkeley, CA: University of California Press.

Mintz, Sidney 1989, *Caribbean Transformations*, New York, NY: Columbia University Press.

Mishra, Pankaj 2012, *From the Ruins of Empire: The Revolt Against the West and the Remaking of Asia*, London: Penguin.

Mitzman, Arthur 1987, *Sociology and Estrangement: Three Sociologists of Imperial Germany*, New Brunswick, NJ: Transaction Books.

Mogk, Walter 1972, *Rohrbach und das 'Größere Deutschland': Ethischer Imperialismus im Wilhelminischen Zeitalter: Ein Beitrag zur Geschichte des Kulturprotestantismus*, Munich: Wilhelm Goldmann.

Mombauer Annika 2001, *Helmuth von Moltke and the Origins of the First World War*, Cambridge: Cambridge University Press.

——— 2002, *The Origins of the First World War: Controversies and Consensus*, London: Longman.

——— 2007, 'The First World War: Inevitable, Avoidable, Improbable, or Desirable? Recent Interpretations on War Guilt and the War's Origins', *German History*, 25, 1: 78–95.

——— 2013a, 'The Fischer Controversy 50 Years On', *Journal of Contemporary History*, 48, 2: 231–40.

——— (ed.) 2013b, *The Origins of the First World War: Diplomatic and Military Documents*, Manchester: Manchester University Press.

Mommsen, Wolfgang J. 1973, 'Domestic Factors in German Foreign Policy before 1914', *Central European History*, 6: 3–43.

——— 1980, *Theories of Imperialism*, Chicago, IL: The University of Chicago Press.

——— 1981, 'The *Topos* of Inevitable War in Germany in the Decade before 1914', in *Germany in the Age of Total War*, edited by Volker R. Berghahn and Martin Kitchen, London: Croom Helm.

——— 1996, *The Rise and Fall of Weimar Democracy*, translated by Elborg Forster and edited by Larry Eugene Jones, Chapel Hill: University of North Carolina Press.

Moon, Henry Lee (ed.) 1972, *The Emerging Thought of W.E.B. Du Bois: Essays and Editorials from* The Crisis, New York, NY: Simon and Schuster.

Mori, Takemaro 1971, 'Nihon Fashizumu no Keisei to Nōson Keizai Kōsei Undō', *Rekishigaku Kenkyū*, Special Edition, October: 135–52.

——— 2002, 'Continuity and Discontinuity between Prewar and Postwar: Issues in the Study of Modern Japanese History', *Hitotsubashi Ronsō*, 127, 5: 639–54.

Morikawa, Hidemasa 1970, 'The Organizational Structure of Mitsubishi and Mitsui Zaibatsu, 1868–1922: A Comparative Study', *The Business History Review*, 44, 1: 62–84.

Morita, Toshio 1973, 'Ōgimi Sonsei Kakushin Dōmei no Tatakai–Okinawa Ken ni Okeru Kakumeiteki Dentō no Hitotsu to Shite', *Bunka Hyōron* 147.

Morris-Suzuki, Tessa 1991, *History of Japanese Economic Thought*, New York, NY: Routledge.

Morton, Adam 2007, *Unravelling Gramsci: Hegemony and Passive Revolution in the Global Political Economy*, London: Pluto.

——— 2010, 'The Continuum of Passive Revolution', *Capital & Class*, 34, 3: 315–42.

Moses, John A. 1975, *The Politics of Illusion: The Fischer Controversy in German Historiography*, London: George Prior.

Mosse, George L. 1974, *The Nationalization of the Masses: Political Symbolism and Mass Movements in Germany from the Napoleonic Wars Through the Third Reich*, New York, NY: Howard Fertig.

Mukai, Kiyoshi 1983, 'Ryōtaisenkanki Okinawa ni Okeru Nōminsō Bunkai', *Nōgyō Keizai Kenkyū*, 55, 1: 11–18.

——— 1988, *Okinawa Kindai Keizaishi: Shihon Shugi no Hattatsu to Henkyōchi Nōgyō*, Tokyo: Nihon Keizai Hyōronsha.

Müller, Sven Oliver 2005, 'Nationalismus in der deutschen Kriegsgesellschaft 1939 bis 1945', in *Die Deutsche Kriegsgesellschaft 1939 bis 1945, Zweiter Halbband, Ausbeutung, Deutungen, Ausgrenzung*, edited by Jörg Echternkamp, Munich: Deutsche Verlags-Anstalt.

Mulligan, William 2010, *The Origins of the First World War*, Cambridge: Cambridge University Press.

Nagahara, Yutaka 1989, *Tennōsei Kokka to Nōmin–Gōi Keisei no Soshikiron*, Tokyo: Nihon Keizai Hyōronsha.

Nairn, Tom 1977, 'The Twilight of the British State', *New Left Review* I/101–2: 3–61.

Nakayoshi, Chōjo 1928, 'Ryūkyū no Jiwari Seido (3)', *Shigaku Zasshi* 39, 8.

Naranch, Bradley D. 2006, 'Beyond the Fatherland: Colonial Visions, Overseas Expansion, and German Nationalism, 1848–1885', Ph.D. Diss.: Johns Hopkins University.

Naranch, Bradley and Geoff Eley (eds.) 2014, *German Colonialism in a Global Age, 1884–1945*, Durham, NC: Duke University Press.

Nation, R. Craig 1989, *War on War: Lenin, the Zimmerwald Left, and the Origins of Communist Internationalism*, Chicago, IL: Haymarket.

——— 2009 [1989], *War on War: Lenin, the Zimmerwald Left, and the Origins of Communist Internationalism*, Chicago, IL: Haymarket.

Nettl, Peter 1966, *Rosa Luxemburg, Volume 2*, London: Oxford University Press.

Neumann, Franz 2009 [1944], *Behemoth: The Structure and Practice of National Socialism, 1933–1944*, Chicago, IL: Ivan R. Dee.

Nişancioğlu, Kerem 2013, 'The Ottomans in Europe: Uneven and Combined Development and Eurocentrism', Ph.D. Diss.: University of Sussex.

Noakes, Jeremy and Geoffrey Pridham (eds.) 1988, *Nazism 1919–1945, Volume 3: Foreign Policy, War, and Racial Extermination. A Documentary Reader*, Exeter: University of Exeter Press.

Noske, Gustav 1920, *Von Kiel bis Kapp: Zur Geschichte der deutschen Revolution*, Berlin: Verlag für Politik und Wirtschaft.

Noda, Kimio 1998, 'Sengo Tochi Kaikaku to Gendai: Nōchi Kaikaku no Rekishiteki Igi', *Nenpō Nihon Gendaishi*, edited by Akazawa Shirō, Tokyo: Gendai Shiryō Shuppan.

O'Donnell, Krista, Renate Bridenthal, and Nancy Reagin (eds.) 2005, *The Heimat Abroad: The Boundaries of Germanness*, Ann Arbor, MI: University of Michigan Press.

Ogg, F.A. 1930, *Economic Development of Modern Europe*, New York, NY: Macmillan.

Okihiro, Gary 1992, *Cane Fires: The Anti-Japanese Movement in Hawaii, 1865–1945*, Philadelphia, PA: Temple University Press.

Okinawa Kenshi 1968, Volume 17, Naha: Ryūkyū Seifu.

Okinawa Ken Kosaku ni Kansuru Chōsa 1930, Fukuoka: Fukuoka ken Naimubu.

Okinawaken, Yaeyama Shichō 1932, *Yaeyama Gunsei Yōran*, Yaeyama: Yaeyama Shichō.

Olson, Joel 2009, 'W.E.B. Du Bois and the Race Concept', in *Racially Writing the Republic: Racists, Race Rebels, and Transformations of American Identity*, edited by Bruce Baum and Duchess Harris, Durham, NC: Duke University Press.

Oltmar, Jochen 2005, *Migration und Politik in der Weimarer Republik*, Göttingen: Vandenhoeck & Ruprecht.

Olusoga, David and Casper W. Erichsen 2011, *The Kaiser's Holocaust: Germany's Forgotten Genocide*, London: Faber and Faber.

Oneal, John R. and Bruce Russett 2001, *Triangulating Peace: Democracy, Interdependence, and International Organizations*, New York, NY: W.W. Norton.

Onselen, Charles van 1982, *Studies in the Social and Economic History of the Witwatersrand 1886–1914*, Volume I. New York, NY: Longman.

O'Rourke, Kevin and Jeffrey G. Williamson 1994, 'Late Nineteenth-Century Anglo-American Factor-Price Convergence: Were Heckscher and Ohlin Right?' *The Journal of Economic History*, 54, 4: 892–916.

——— 1999, *Globalization and History: The Evolution of a Nineteenth-Century Atlantic Economy*, Cambridge, MA: MIT Press.

——— 2004, 'Once More: When did Globalisation Begin?', *European Review of Economic History*, 8, 1: 109–17.

Orr, Charles A. 1966, 'Trade Unionism in Colonial Africa', *The Journal of Modern African Studies*, 4, 1: 65–81.

Owen, Robert and Bob Sutcliffe (eds.) 1972, *Studies in the Theory of Imperialism*, London: Longman.

Pannekoek, Anton 2011 [1914], 'The Collapse of the International', in *Discovering Imperialism: Social Democracy to World War I*, edited and translated by Richard B. Day and Daniel Gaido, Leiden: Brill.

Papini, Giovanni 1913, 'La vita non è sacra', *Lacerba*, 1, 20.

Parvus [Alexander Helphand] 2009 [1905], 'What Was Accomplished on the 9th of January', in *Witnesses to Permanent Revolution: The Documentary Record*, edited and translated by Richard B. Day and Daniel Gaido, Leiden: Brill.

Peattie, Mark 1992, *Nanyō: The Rise and Fall of the Japanese in Micronesia, 1885–1945*, Honolulu, HI: University of Hawaii Press.

Perry, Jeffrey B. 2009, *Hubert Harrison: The Voice of Harlem Radicalism, 1883–1918*, New York, NY: Columbia University Press.

Peukert, Detlev J.K. 1991 [1987], *The Weimar Republic: The Crisis of Classical Modernity*, London: Allen Lane.

Pick, Daniel 1993, *War Machine: The Rationalization of Slaughter in the Modern Age*, New Haven, CT: Yale University Press.

Pitts, Jennifer 2005, *A Turn to Empire: The Rise of Imperial Liberalism in Britain and France*, Princeton, NJ: Princeton University Press.

Plekhanov, Georgy 1961 [1889], 'Speech at the International Worker's Socialist Congress in Paris (July, 14–21, 1889): Second Version', in *Selected Philosophical Works*, Volume 1, Moscow: Foreign Languages Publishing House.

Pogge von Strandmann, Hartmut (ed.) 1985, *Walther Rathenau: Industrialist, Banker, Intellectual, and Politician: Notes and Diaries 1907–1922*, Oxford: Oxford University Press.

Pogge von Strandmann, Hartmut 1988a, 'Germany and the Coming of War', in *The Coming of the First World War*, edited by R.J.W. Evans and Hartmut Pogge von Strandmann, Oxford: Oxford University Press.

——— 1988b, 'Consequences of the Foundation of the German Empire: Colonial Expansion and the Process of Political-Economic Rationalization', in *Bismarck, Europe, and Africa: The Berlin Africa Conference 1884–1885 and the Onset of Partition*, edited by Stig Förster, Wolfgang J. Mommsen, and Ronald Robinson, Oxford: Oxford University Press.

Poggi, Christine and Laura Wittman 2009, *Futurism: An Anthology*, New Haven, CT: Yale University Press.

Pohl, Dieter 2011, *Die Herrschaft der Wehrmacht: Deutsche Militärbesatzung und einheimische Bevölkerung in der Sowjetunion 1941–1944*, Frankfurt am Main: Fischer.

Polanyi, Karl 1944, *The Great Transformation: The Political and Economic Origins of Our Time*, Boston, MA: Beacon Press.

——— 1957 [1944], *The Great Transformation: The Political and Economic Origins of Our Time*, Boston, MA: Beacon Press.

Poley, Jared 2005, *Decolonization in Germany: Narratives of Colonial Loss and Foreign Occupation*, Bern: Peter Lang.

Portes, Alejandro, Manuel Castells, and Lauren Benton (eds.) 1989, *The Informal Economy: Studies in Advanced and Less Developed Countries*, Baltimore, MD: Johns Hopkins University Press.

Post, Charles 2010, 'Exploring Working-Class Consciousness: A Critique of the Theory of the "Labour-Aristocracy"', *Historical Materialism*, 18, 4: 3–38.

Potter, G. 1870, 'Strikes and Lockouts from the Workman's Point of View', *Contemporary Review*, 15: 525–39.

Pozo-Martin, Gonzalo 2007, 'Autonomous or Materialist Geopolitics?', *Cambridge Review of International Affairs*, 20, 4: 551–63.

Praclik, Gustav 1936, *Unter Stahlhelm und Fliegerhaube: Fronterlebnisse eines Kriegsfreiwilligen, 1914–1918*, Kassel: Oncken.

Prochasson, Christophe, and Anne Rasmussen 1990, *Au nom de la patrie: Les intellectuels et la Première Guerre Mondiale (1910–1919)*, Paris: La Découverte.

Proudhon, Pierre-Joseph 1969, *Selected Writings*, London: MacMillan.

Puchala, Donald J. and Raymond F. Hopkins 1983, 'International Regimes: Lessons from Inductive Research', in *International Regimes*, edited by Stephen Krasner, Ithaca, NY: Cornell University Press.

Puhle, Hans Jurgen. 1986, 'Lords and Peasants in the Kaiserreich', in *Peasants and Lords in Modern Germany*, edited by Robert G. Moeller, Boston, MA: Allen & Unwin.

Quataert, Donald 1986, 'Machine Breaking and the Changing Carpet Industry of Western Anatolia, 1860–1908', *Journal of Social History*, 13: 473–89.

Rapone, Leonardo 2011, *Cinque anni che paiono secoli: Antonio Gramsci dal socialism al comunismo*, Rome: Carocci.

Read, Jason 2000, 'A Universal History of Contingency: Deleuze and Guattari on the History of Capitalism', *Borderlands*.

——— 2003, *The Micropolitics of Capital: Marx and the Prehistory of the Present*, Albany, NY: State University of New York Press.

Reed Jr., Adolph L. 1999, *W.E.B. Du Bois and American Political Thought: Fabianism and the Color Line*, Oxford: Oxford University Press.

Reed, John 1977 [1919], *Ten Days That Shook the World*, Harmondsworth: Penguin Books.

Rehmann, Jan 1998, *Max Weber: Modernisierung als passive Revolution*, Hamburg-Berlin: Argument.

Reichert, R.W. 1969, *Crippled from Birth: German Social Democracy, 1844–1870*, Ames, IO: Iowa State University Press.

Reismann-Grone, Theodor and Eduard von Liebert 1905, *Überseepolitik oder Festlandspolitik?* Alldeutsche Flugschriften, No. 22, Munich: J.F. Lehmann Verlag.

Reiter, Dan 2003, 'Exploring the Bargaining Model of War', *Perspectives on Politics*, 1, 1: 27–43.

Renan, Ernest 1992, *Qu'est-ce qu'une nation?* Paris: Presses Pocket.

Ricossa, S. 1973, 'Italy 1920–1970', in *The Fontana Economic History of Europe: Contemporary Economies*, edited by C.M. Cipolla, Glasgow: William Collins Sons & Co.

Riddell, John (ed.) 1986, *The German Revolution and the Debate on Soviet Power, Documents: 1918–1919, Preparing the Founding Congress*, New York, NY: Pathfinder Press.

——— 1984, *Lenin's Struggle for a Revolutionary International*, New York, NY: Monad Press.

Riezler, Kurt 1972, *Tagebücher, Aufsätze, Dokumente*, edited by Karl Dietrich Erdmann, Göttingen: Vandenhoeck und Ruprecht.

Robinson, Cedric J. 1983, *Black Marxism: The Making of the Black Radical Tradition*, London: Zed Books.

Rock, David. 1975, *Politics in Argentina, 1890–1930: The Rise and Fall of Radicalism*, Cambridge: Cambridge University Press.

Roediger, David R. 2007, *The Wages of Whiteness: Race and the Making of the American Working Class*, new ed., London: Verso.

Röhl, John C.G. 1969, 'Admiral von Müller and the Approach of War, 1911–1914', *Historical Journal*, 12, 4: 651–673.

Rohrbach, Paul 1916, 'Das Kriegsziel im Schützengraben', *Deutsche Politik*, No. 6, 4 February.

——— 1926, *Deutschtum in Not! Die Schicksale der Deutschen in Europa ausserhalb des Reiches*, Berlin-Schmargendorf and Leipzig: Wilhelm Andermann.

Rolland, Romain 1916, *Above the Battle*, Chicago, IL: Open Court.

Romein, J. 1978, *The Watershed of Two Eras*, Middletown, CT: Wesleyan University Press.

Rosecrance, Richard N. 1985, *The Rise of the Trading State: Commerce and Conquest in the Modern World*, New York, NY: Basic Books.

Rosenberg, Hans 1943, 'Political and Social Consequences of the Great Depression of 1873–1896', *The Economic History Review*, 13, 1/2: 58–73.

Rosenberg, Justin 1994, *The Empire of Civil Society: A Critique of the Realist Theory of International Relations*, London: Verso.

——— 2000, *The Follies of Globalisation Theory: Polemical Essays*, London: Verso.

——— 2005, 'Globalisation Theory: A Post-Mortem', *International Politics*, 42, 1: 2–74.

——— 2006, 'Why Is There No International Historical Sociology?' *European Journal of International Relations* 12, 3: 307–40.

——— 2008, 'Anarchy in the Mirror of "Uneven and Combined Development": An Open Letter to Kenneth Waltz, paper presented at the *British-German IR Conference BISA/DVPW*, Arnoldshain: Germany.

——— 2013, 'Kenneth Waltz and Leon Trotsky: Anarchy in the Mirror of Uneven and Combined Development', *International Politics*, 50, 2: 183–230.

Rosengarten, Frank 1984–1985, 'The Gramsci-Trotsky Question (1922–1932)', *Social Text*, 11: 65–95.

Rosenthal, Sandra 1986, *Speculative Pragmatism*, Amherst, MA: University of Massachusetts Press.

Rossino, Alexander B. 2003, *Hitler Strikes Poland: Blitzkrieg, Ideology, and Atrocity*, Lawrence, Kansas, KS: University of Kansas Press.

Rothschild, Joseph and Nancy M. Wingfield 2000, *Return to Diversity: A Political History of East Central Europe since World War II*, New York and Oxford: Oxford University Press.

Rowe, David M. 2005, 'The Tragedy of Liberalism: How Globalization Caused the First World War', *Security Studies*, 14, 3: 407–47.

Royle, T. 1999, *Crimea: The Great Crimean War, 1854–1856*, Boston, MA: Little Brown and Company.

Russett, Bruce 1993, *Grasping the Democratic Peace: Principles for a Post-Cold War World*, Princeton, NJ: Princeton University Press.

Rutherford, Philip T. 2007, *Prelude to the Final Solution: The Nazi Program for Deporting Ethnic Poles, 1939–1941*, Lawrence, KS: University of Kansas Press.

Ryazanov, David 2009 [1903], 'The Draft Programme of "*Iskra*" and the Tasks of Russian Social Democrats', in *Witnesses to Permanent Revolution: The Documentary Record*, edited and translated by Richard B. Day and Daniel Gaido, Leiden: Brill.

Saccarelli, Emanuele 2007, *Gramsci and Trotsky in the Shadow of Stalinism: The Political Theory and Practice of Opposition*, New York, NY: Routledge.

Sagall, Sabby 2013, *Final Solutions: Human Nature, Capitalism and Genocide*, London: Pluto Press.

Saitō, Hitoshi 1989, *Nōgyō Mondai no Tenkai to Jichi Sonraku*, Tokyo: Nihon Keizai Hyōronsha.

Salvadori, Massimo 1979, *Karl Kautsky and the Socialist Revolution 1880–1938*, London: New Left Books.

Sassen, Saskia 1994, *Cities in a World Economy*, Thousand Oaks, CA: Pine Forge Press.

——— 1991, 'The Global City', in *Readings in Urban Theory*, edited by S.S. Fainstein and S. Campbell, Cambridge, MA: Blackwell.

Saul, Klaus 1974, *Staat, Industrie, Arbeiterbewegung im Kaiserreich: Zur Innen- und Außenpolitik des Wilhelminischen Deutschland 1903–1914*, Düsseldorf: Bertelsmann.

Saxton, Alexander 2003, *The Rise and Fall of the White Republic: Class Politics and Mass Culture in Nineteenth Century America*, new ed., London: Verso.

Scheerbart, Paul and Bruno Taut 1972, *Glass Architecture and Alpine Architecture*, New York: Praeger Publishers.

Scheler, Max 1915, *Der Genius der Krieges und der Deutsche Krieg*, Leipzig: Weissen Bücher.

Schmidt, Gustav 1990, 'Contradictory Postures and Conflicting Objectives: The July Crisis, 1914', in *Escape into War? The Foreign Policy of Imperial Germany*, edited by Gregor Schöllgen, Oxford: Berg.

Schmidt, Stefan 2009, *Frankreichs Außenpolitik in der Julikrise 1914: Ein Beitrag zur Geschichte des Ausbruchs der Ersten Weltkrieges*, Munich: Oldenbourg.

Schöllgen, Gregor 1980, 'Richard von Kühlmann und das deutsch-englische Verhältnis 1912–1914: Zur Bedeutung der Peripherie in der europäischen Vorkriegspolitik', *Historische Zeitschrift*, 230, 2: 293–337.

——— (ed.) 1990, *Escape into War? The Foreign Policy of Imperial Germany*, Oxford: Berg.

——— 1992, *Die Macht in der Mitte Europas: Stationen deutscher Außenpolitik von Friedrich dem Grossen bis zur Gegenwart*, Munich: Beck.

——— 1998, 'Kriegsgefahr und Krisenmanagement vor 1914: Zur Außenpolitik des kaiserlichen Deutschlands', *Historische Zeitschrift*, 267: 399–413.

Schlager, Neil (ed.) 2003, *St. James Encyclopaedia of Labor History Worldwide: Major Events in Labor History and Their Impact*, Volume 2., Farmington Hills, MI: St. James Press.

Schonfield, A. 1965, *Modern Capitalism: The Changing Balance of Public and Private Power*, Oxford: Oxford University Press.

Schröder, Hans-Christoph 1975, *Sozialismus und Imperialismus: Die Auseinandersetzung der deutschen Sozialdemokratie mit dem Imperialismusprobem und der 'Weltpolitik' vor 1914*, Bonn: Verlag J.H.W. Dietz Nachf.

——— 1979, *Gustav Noske und die Kolonialpolitik des Deutschen Kaiserreichs*, Bonn: Verlag J.H.W. Dietz Nachf.

Schroeder, Paul W. 2007, 'Stealing Horses to Great Applause: Austria-Hungary's decision in July 1914 in Systemic Perspective', in *An Improbable War?: The Outbreak of World War I and European Political Culture before 1914*, edited by Holger Afflerbach and David Stevenson, Oxford: Berghahn Books.

Schuman, F. 1942, *Europe on the Eve: The Crises of Diplomacy, 1933–1939*, New York, NY: Alfred A. Knopf.

Schumpeter, J.A. 1955, *Imperialism and Social Classes: Two Essays*, New York, NY: Meridian Books.

Schwarz, Bill 2011, *The White Man's World–Memories of Empire, Vol. 1*, Oxford: Oxford University Press.

Scott, James 2010, *The Art of Not Being Governed: An Anarchist History of Upland Southeast Asia*, New Haven, CT: Yale University Press.

Seligmann, M.S., and R.R. McLean 2000, *Germany from Reich to Republic, 1871–1918: Politics, Hierarchy, and Elites*, New York, NY: St. Martin's.

Selz, Peter Howard 1974, *German Expressionist Painting*, Berkeley, CA: University of California Press.

Semmel, Bernard 1968 [1960], *Imperialism and Social Reform: English Social-Imperial Thought, 1895–1914*, Garden City, NY: Anchor Books.

Sen, A.K. 2000, 'Capital, Labour, and the State: Eastern and Western India, 1918–1939', *Economic and Political Weekly*, 35: 2565–8.

Seton-Watson, R.W. 1914, *The War and Democracy*, London: Macmillan.

Sewell, William 1988, 'Le Citoyen/la Citoyenne: Activity, Passivity, and the Revolutionary Concept of Citizenship', in *The Political Culture of the French Revolution*, edited by Colin Lucas, Oxford: Pergamon Press.

Shanin, Teodor 1983, *Late Marx and the Russian Road: Marx and the 'Peripheries of Capitalism'*, New York, NY: Monthly Review Press.

Sheehan, James J. 1966, *The Career of Lujo Brentano: A Study of Liberalism and Social Reform in Imperial Germany*, Chicago, IL: University of Chicago Press.

——— 1968, 'The Primacy of Domestic Politics: Eckart Kehr's Essays on Modern German History', *Central European History*, 1: 166–74.

Simic, Andrei 1973, *Peasant Urbanites*, New York, NY: Seminar Press.

Shimizu, Hiroshi 1988, 'Dutch-Japanese Competition in the Shipping Trade on the Java-Japan Route in the Inter-war Period', *Southeast Asian Studies*, 26, 1: 3–23.

Shōji Shunsaku 2012, *Nihon no Sonraku to Shutai Keisei: Kyōdōtai to Jichi*, Tokyo: Nihon Keizai Hyōronsha.

Shōwa Seitō Kabushiki Gaisha 10 Nen Shi 2003 [1937], reprinted in *Shashi De Miru Nihon Keizaishi: Shokuminchi Hen*, Volume 16, Tokyo: Yumani Shobō.

Silver, Beverly J. 2003, *Forces of Labor: Workers' Movements and Globalization Since 1870*, Cambridge: Cambridge University Press.

Simms, Brendan 2003, 'The Return of the Primacy of Foreign Policy', *German History*, 21, 3: 275–91.

——— 2013, *Europe: The Struggle for Supremacy, 1453 to the Present: A History of the Continent since 1500*, London: Allen Lane.

Smith, Helmut 2008, *The Continuities of German History: Nation, Religion, and Race across the Long Nineteenth Century*, Cambridge: Cambridge University Press.

Smith, Neil 2003, *American Empire: Roosevelt's Geographer and the Prelude to Globalization*, Berkeley, CA: University of California Press.

Snow, Edgar 1967 [1938], *Red Star over China*, London: Victor Gollanz Ltd..

Sohrabi, Nader 1995, 'Historicizing Revolutions: Constitutional Revolutions in the Ottoman Empire, Iran, and Russia, 1905–1908', *American Journal of Sociology*, 100, 6: 1383–1447.

Sombart, Werner 1915, *Händler und Helden: Patriotische Besinnungen*, München-Leipzig: Düncker & Humblot.

Soutou, Georges-Henri 1998, *Le concert européen, de Vienne à Locarno*, in *L'ordre européen du XVIe au XXe siècle*, edited by Georges-Henri Soutou and Jean Bérenger, Paris: Presses universitaires de Paris-Sorbonne.

Spohn, Willfried 1977, *Weltmarktkonkurrenz und Industrialisierung Deutschlands 1870–1914: Eine Untersuchung zur nationalen und internationalen Geschichte der kapitalistischen Produktionsweise*, Berlin: Olle and Wolter.

Stalin, J.V. 1953a [1907], 'Preface to the Georgian Edition of K. Kautsky's Pamphlet *The Driving Forces and Prospects of the Russian Revolution*', in *Works*, Volume 2.

——— 1953b [1913], 'Marxism and the National Question', in *Works*, Volume 2.

Stedman Jones, Gareth 2007, 'Radicalism and the Extra-European World: The Case of Marx', in *Victorian Visions of Global Order: Empire and International Relations in Nineteenth Century Political Thought*, edited by Duncan Bell, Cambridge: Cambridge University Press.

Steenson, Gary 1978, *Karl Kautsky, 1854–1938: Marxism in the Classical Years*, Pittsburgh, PA: University of Pittsburgh Press.

Stegmann, Dirk 1970, *Die Erben Bismarcls: Parteien und Verbände in der Spätphase des Wilhelminischen Deutschlands. Sammlungspolitik 1897–1918*, Berlin: Kiepenheuer und Witsch.

Stern, Steve J. 1988, 'Feudalism, Capitalism, and the World-System in the Perspective of Latin America and the Caribbean', *American Historical Review*, 93: 829–97.

Stevenson, David 1995, *Cataclysm: The First World War as Political Tragedy*, New York, NY: Basic Books.

——— 1996, *Armaments and the Coming of War: Europe, 1904–1914*, Oxford: Oxford University Press.

——— 1999, 'War by Timetable? The Railway Race before 1914', *Past & Present*, 162: 163–94.

——— 2007, 'Was a Peaceful Outcome Thinkable? The European Land Armaments Race before 1914', in *An Improbable War?: The Outbreak of World War I and European Political Culture before 1914*, edited by Holger Afflerbach and David Stevenson, Oxford: Berghahn.

Stoddard, Lothrop 1920, *The Rising Tide of Color Against White World-Supremacy*, New York, NY: Charles Scribner's Sons.

Stokes, Gale 1989, 'The Social Origins of Eastern European Politics', in *The Origins of Backwardness in Easter Europe: Economics and Politics from the Middle Ages until the Early Twentieth Century*, edited by Daniel Chirot, Berkeley, CA: University of California Press.

Stoler, Ann Laura 1989, 'Rethinking Colonial Categories: European Communities and the Boundaries of Rule', *Comparative Studies in Society and History*, 31, 1: 134–61.

——— 2006, 'Degrees of Imperial Sovereignty', *Public Culture*, 18: 125–46.

Stoler, Ann Laura, Carole McGranahan, and Peter C. Perdue (eds.) 2007, *Imperial Formations*, Santa Fe, CA: School for Advanced Research Press.

Stolper, W.F. and Paul Samuelson 1941, 'Protection and Real Wages', *Review of Economic Studies*, 9, 1: 58–73.

Stone, Norman 1998 [1975], *The Eastern Front, 1914–1917*, Harmondsworth: Penguin Books.

——— 1983 *Europe Transformed, 1878–1919*, London: Fontana.

——— 2007, *World War One: A Short History*, London: Allen Lane.

Strachan, Hew 2001, *The First World War*, Oxford: Oxford University Press.

Stromberg, Roland B. 1982, *Redemption by War: The Intellectuals and 1914*, Lawrence, KS: The Regent Press of Kansas.

Struve, Peter 1983 [1898], 'Manifesto of the Russian Social Democratic Party (March 1898)', in *Marxism in Russia: Key Documents, 1879–1906*, edited by Neil Harding, Cambridge: Cambridge University Press.

Stürmer, Michael 1990, 'A Nation State against History and Geography: The German Dilemma', in *Escape into War? The Foreign Policy of Imperial Germany*, edited by Gregor Schöllgen, Oxford: Berg.

Sukhanov, Nikolai 1984 [1922], *The Russian Revolution 1917: A Personal Record*, edited by Joel Carmichael, Princeton, NJ: Princeton University Press.

Sun Yat-Sen 1976 [1924], *I tre principî del popolo*, translated by Settimio Severo Caruso, Turin: Einaudi.

Sweeney, Dennis 2014, 'Pan-German Conceptions of Colonial Empire', in *German Colonialism in a Global Age, 1884–1945*, edited by Bradley Naranch and Geoff Eley, Durham, NC: Duke University Press.

Taguieff, Pierre-André 2004, *Les Protocoles des sages de Sion: faux et usages d'un faux*, Paris: Berg International/Fayard.

Tainan Seitō Kabushiki Gaisha Hōkokusho 1918–1931, Okinawa Prefectural Archives, Document codes T00016044B–T00016058B.

Takagi, Shigeki 2008, 'Nanyō Kōhatsu no Zaisei Jyōkyō to Matsue Haruji no Nanshinron', *Ajia Keizai*, 49, 11: 26–46.

Tama, Shinnosuke 1995, 'Uno Kōzō no Nihon Nōgyōron', *Hirosaki Daigaku Nōgakubu Gakujutsu Hōkoku*, 58: 74–96.

Tamura, Hiroshi 1927, *Ryūkyū Kyosan Sonraku no Kenkyū*, Tokyo: Oka Shoin.

Taylor, Carol M. 1981, 'W.E.B. Du Bois: Challenge to Scientific Racism', *Journal of Black Studies*, 11, 4: 449–60.

Taylor, Keeanga-Yamahtta 2008, 'Classics of Marxism–W.E.B. Du Bois, *Black Reconstruction in America 1860–1880*', *International Socialist Review*, 57, available at: http://www.isreview.org/issues/57/feat-reconstruction.shtml.

Taylor, Kit Sims 1978, *Sugar and the Underdevelopment of Northeastern Brazil, 1500–1970*, Gainesville, FL: University Press of Florida.

Terada Michio 2008, *Yamada Moritarō: Marukusu Shugisha no Shirarezaru Sekai*, Tokyo: Nihon Keizai Hyōronsha.

Teschke, Benno, and Hannes Lacher 2007, 'The Changing "Logics" of Capitalist Competition', *Cambridge Review of International Affairs*, 20, 4: 565–80.

Thatcher, Ian D. 2000, *Leon Trotsky and World War One: August 1914 to February 1917*, Basingstoke: MacMillan Press Ltd.

Theweleit, Klaus 1977 and 1979, *Männerphantasien*, Volume 1, *Frauen, Flüten, Körper, Geschichte*, and Volume 2, *Männerkörper: Zur Psychoanalyse des Weissen Terrors*, Frankfurt am Main: Verlag Roter Stern.

Thomas, Peter 2009, *The Gramscian Moment: Philosophy, Hegemony, and Marxism*, Leiden: Brill.

Thompson, Willie 2004, 'Introduction: International, 1800–2000', in *St. James Encyclopaedia of Labor History Worldwide*, edited by Neil Schlager, London: St. James Press.

Tilly, C., L. Tilly and R. Tilly. 1975, *The Rebellious Century, 1830–1930*, Cambridge, MA: Harvard University Press.

Timms, Edward 1989, *Karl Kraus: Apocalyptic Satirist, Culture and Catastrophe in Hapsburg Vienna*, New Haven, CT: Yale University Press.

Tipton, F.B. and R. Aldrich. 1987a, *An Economic and Social History of Europe, 1890–1939*, Baltimore, MD: Johns Hopkins University Press.

——— 1987b, *An Economic and Social History of Europe, from 1939 to the Present*, Baltimore, MD: Johns Hopkins University Press.

Tombs, Robert 1981, *The War Against Paris 1871*, New York, NY: Cambridge University Press.

Tomiyama, Ichirō 1990, *Kindai Nihon Shakai to Okinawajin: Nihonjin ni Naru to Iu Koto*, Tokyo: Nihon Keizai Hyōronsha.

Tooze, Adam 2006, *Wages of Destruction: The Making and Breaking of the Nazi Economy*, London: Allen Lane.

——— 2014, *The Deluge: The Great War and the Remaking of the Global Order 1916–1931*, London: Penguin Press.

Tooze, Adam and Martin Ivanov 2011, 'Disciplining the "Black Sheep of the Balkans": Financial Supervision and Sovereignty in Bulgaria, 1902–39', *The Economic History Review*, 64, 1: 30–51.

Torp, Cornelius 2005, *Die Herausforderung der Globalisierung: Wirtschaft und Politik in Deutschland 1860–1914*, Göttingen: Vandenhoeck und Ruprecht.

Totman, Conrad 2007, *Japan's Imperial Forest Goryorin, 1899–1946: With a Supporting Study of the Kan/Min Division of Woodland in Early Meiji Japan, 1871–76*, Folkestone, Kent: Brill/Global Oriental.

Trachtenberg, Marc 1991, *History and Strategy*, Princeton, NJ: Princeton University Press.

Traverso, Enzo 2007, *A feu et à sang: la guerre civile européenne 1914–1945*, Paris: Stock.

Trebilcock, Clive 1981, *The Industrialization of the Continental Powers, 1780–1914*, London: Longman.

Trimberger, Ellen Kay 1978, *Revolution from Above: Military Bureaucrats and Development in Japan, Turkey, Egypt and Peru*, New Brunswick, NJ: Transaction Books.

Trotsky, Leon no publication date [1904], *Our Political Tasks*, London: New Park.

——— 1918, *The Bolsheviks and the World Peace*, New York, NY: Boni & Liveright.

——— 1929, 'Disarmament and the United States of Europe', first published in *Bulletin of the Russian Opposition*, No. 6, October 1929; English translation was published the same year in *The Militant*, New York, NY. Source: Fourth International, 6, 5, May 1945: 154–58. Available at: http://www.marxists.org/archive/trotsky/1929/10/disarm.htm.

——— 1938, 'Introduction to Harold R. Isaacs, *The Tragedy of the Chinese Revolution*', London. Source: Fourth International [New York, NY], 6, 10 (Whole No. 59), October 1945: 312–16.

——— 1945 [1921], *The First Five Years of the Communist International*, New York, NY: Pioneer.

——— 1958 [1935], *Trotsky's Diary in Exile 1935*, London: Faber and Faber.

——— 1959 [1930–1932], *History of the Russian Revolution*, Garden City, NY: Doubleday.

——— 1962 [1929/1906], *The Permanent Revolution and Results & Prospects*, London: Labor.

——— 1964 [1919], 'Trotsky to the Central Committee of the Russian Communist Party, 5 August 1919', in *The Trotsky Papers, 1917–1922, Vol. 1, 1917–1919*, edited by Jan M. Meijer, The Hague: Mouton.

——— 1969 [1908–1909/1922], *1905*, Paris: Éditions de Minuit.

——— 1969a [1929/1906], *The Permanent Revolution and Results and Prospects*, 3rd ed., New York, NY: Pathfinder Press.

——— 1969b [1906], *Results and Prospects*, in *The Permanent Revolution and Results and Prospects*, 3rd ed., New York, NY: Pathfinder Press.

——— 1969c [1919], 'Preface to the Re-Issue of This Work [*Results and Prospects*] Published in Moscow in 1919', in *The Permanent Revolution and Results and Prospects*, 3rd ed., New York, NY: Pathfinder Press.

——— 1969d [1929], 'Introduction to the First (Russian) Edition (Published in Berlin)', in *The Permanent Revolution* and *Results and Prospects*, 3rd ed., New York, NY: Pathfinder Press.

——— 1972a [1908–1909/1922], *1905*, Harmondsworth: Penguin Books.

——— 1972b, *Leon Trotsky Speaks*, New York, NY: Pathfinder.

——— 1973 [1939], 'Three Conceptions of the Russian Revolution', in *Writings of Leon Trotsky [1939–40]*, edited by Naomi Allen and George Breitman, 2nd ed., New York, NY: Pathfinder Press.

——— 1975 [1930], *My Life: an Attempt at an Autobiography*, Handsworth: Penguin Books.

——— 1977 [1930–2], *The History of the Russian Revolution*, London: Pluto Press.

——— 1980, *The Balkan Wars, 1912–1913*, edited by George Weissman and Duncan Williams, New York, NY: Monad Press.

——— 1980a [1908], 'The Turkish Revolution and the Tasks of the Proletariat', in *The Balkan Wars, 1912–1913*, edited by George Weissman and Duncan Williams, New York, NY: Monad Press.

——— 1980b [1909], 'The New Turkey', in *The Balkan Wars, 1912–1913*, edited by George Weissman and Duncan Williams, New York, NY: Monad Press.

——— 1980c [1912], 'In a Backward Country', in *The Balkan Wars, 1912–1913*, edited by George Weissman and Duncan Williams, New York, NY: Monad Press.

——— 1980d [1913], 'Stojan Novakovic', in *The Balkan Wars, 1912–1913*, edited by George Weissman and Duncan Williams, New York, NY: Monad Press.

——— 2009a [1905], 'Up to the Ninth of January', in *Witnesses to Permanent Revolution: The Documentary Record*, edited and translated by Richard B. Day and Daniel Gaido, Leiden: Brill.

——— 2009b [1905], 'Introduction to *Ferdinand Lassalle's Speech to the Jury*', in *Witnesses to Permanent Revolution: The Documentary Record*, edited and translated by Richard B. Day and Daniel Gaido, Leiden: Brill.

——— 2009c [1905], 'Social Democracy and Revolution', in *Witnesses to Permanent Revolution: The Documentary Record*, edited and translated by Richard B. Day and Daniel Gaido, Leiden: Brill.

Truong Chinh 1969 [1965], *Ho Chi Minh*, Rome: Editori Riuniti.

Turati, Filippo 1979a [1919], 'Leninismo e marxismo', in *Socialismo e riformismo nella storia d'Italia: Scritti politici 1878–1932*, edited by Franco Livorsi, Milan: Feltrinelli..

——— 1979b [1919], 'Socialismo e massimalismo', in *Socialismo e riformismo nella storia d'Italia: Scritti politici 1878–1932*, edited by Franco Livorsi, Milan: Feltrinelli.

Uechi, Ichirō 2003, 'Okinawa Meijiki no Kyūkan Onzon Seisaku ni Kansuru Ichi Kōsatsu', *Waseda Hōgakkaishi*, 53: 1–46.

Ulam, Adam 1969 [1965], *Lenin and the Bolsheviks: The Intellectual and Political History of the Triumph of Communism in Russia*, London: Fontana Library.

Uno, Kōzō 1973–1974, *Uno Kōzō Chosakushū*, 11 Volumes, Tokyo: Iwanami Shoten.

Uzum, Cem 2004, *Making the Turkish Revolutio*, Istanbul: Antikapitalist.

Valéry, Paul 1957, 'La crise de l'esprit', in *Œuvres*, Volume 2, Paris: Gallimard.

Van der Linden, Marcel 2007, 'The "Law" of Uneven and Combined Development: Some Underdeveloped Thoughts', *Historical Materialism*, 15, 1: 145–65.

Van Laak, Dirk 2004, *Imperiale Infrastruktur: Deutsche Planungen für eine Erschließung Afrikas 1880 bis 1960*, Paderborn: Ferdinand Schöningh.

Van Ree, Erik 2013, 'Marxism as Permanent Revolution', *History of Political Thought*, 34, 3: 540–63.

Vatter, Sherry 1994, 'Militant Journeyman in Nineteenth Century Damascus: Implications for the Middle Eastern Labor History Agenda', in *Workers and Working Classes in the Middle East: Struggles, Histories, Historiographies*, edited by Zachary Lockman, Albany, NY: State University of New York Press.

Veblen, Thorstein 1915, *Imperial Germany and the Industrial Revolution*, New York, NY: Macmillan Company.

Vladimir Il'ich Lenin: Biograficheskaia khronika, Vol. 3, 1912–1917, 1972, Moscow: Politizdat.

Volkov, Shulamit 2012, *Walther Rathenau: Weimar's Fallen Statesman*, New Haven, CT: Yale University Press.

Vom Bruch, Rüdiger 1982, *Weltpolitik als Kulturmission: Auswärtige Kulturpolitik und Bildungsbürgertum in Deutschland am Vorabend des Ersten Weltkrieges*, Paderborn: Schöningh.

Von Liebert, Eduard 1925, *Aus einem bewegten Leben: Erinnerungen*, Munich: J.F. Lehmann Verlag.

Wade, Wyn Craig 1997, *The Fiery Cross: The Ku Klux Klan in America*, New York, NY: Oxford University Press.

Walkenhorst, Peter 2007, *Nation-Volk-Rasse: Radikaler Nationalismus im Deutschen Kaiserreich 1890–1914*, Göttingen: Vandenhoeck & Ruprecht.

Walker, Gavin 2011, 'Postcoloniality and the National Question in Marxist Historiography', *Interventions: International Journal of Postcolonial Studies*, 13, 1: 120–37.

Walling, William 1972 [1915], *The Socialists and the War*, New York, NY: Garland Publishing Inc.

Waltz, Kenneth N. 1979, *Theory of International Politics*, Reading, MA: Addison-Wesley.

Watson, David Robin 1974, *Georges Clemenceau: A Political Biography*, London: Eyre Methuen.

Weaver Frederick Stirton 1974, 'Relative Backwardness and Cumulative Change: A Comparative Approach to European Industrialization', *Studies in Comparative International Development*, 9: 70–97.

Weber, Thomas 2008, *Our Friend 'The Enemy': Elite Education in Britain and Germany before World War I*, Stanford, CA: Stanford University Press.

——— 2010, *Hitler's First War: Adolf Hitler, the Men of the First List Regiment, and the First World War*, Oxford: Oxford University Press.

Weber, Max 1995, 'Zwischenbetrachtung', *Schriften zur Soziologie*, Leipzig: Reclam.

——— 2004, 'Intermediate Reflections on the Economic Ethics of World Religions', in *The Essential Weber: A Reader*, edited by Sam Whimster, London: Routledge.

Wehler, Hans-Ulrich 1969, *Bismarck und der Imperialismus*, Cologne: Kiepenheuer und Witsch.

——— 1970a, 'Bismarcks Imperialismus 1862–1890' and 'Probleme des Imperialismus', in *Krisenherde des Kaiserreichs 1871–1918. Studien zur deutschen Sozial- und Verfassungsgeschichte*, Göttingen: Vandenhoeck & Ruprecht.

——— 1970b, 'Bismarck's Imperialism, 1862–1890', *Past and Present*, 48: 119–5.

——— 1972, 'Industrial Growth and Early German Imperialism', in *Studies in the Theory of Imperialism*, edited by Roger Owen and Bob Sutcliffe, London: Longman.

——— 1985, *The German Empire, 1871–1918*, Leamington Spa, NY: Berg Publishers.

——— 1995, *Deutsche Gesellschaftsgeschichte, Dritter Band: Von der 'Deutschen Doppelrevolution' bis zum Beginn des Ersten Weltkrieges 1849–1914*, Munich: Beck.

Weinberg, Meyer (ed.) 1970, *W.E.B. Du Bois: A Reader*, New York, NY: Harper & Row.

Weitz, Eric D. 2007, *Weimar Germany: Promise and Tragedy*, Princeton, NJ: Princeton University Press.

Wells, H.G. 1960, *The War of the Worlds*, New York, NY: Random House.

Wernecke, Klaus 1970, *Der Wille zur Weltgeltung: Außenpolitik und Öffentlichkeit im Kaiserrecih am Vorabend des Ersten Weltkrieges*, Düsseldorf: Droste Verlag.

Wheeler, Douglas 1972, 'The Portuguese Revolution of 1910', *Journal of Modern History*, 44, 2: 172–94.

Wildt, Michael 2002, *Generation des Unbedingten: Das Führungskorps des Reichssicherheitshauptamt*, Hamburg: Hamburger Edition HIS Verlag.

——— 2006, '"Eine neue Ordnung der ethnographischen Verhältnisse": Hitlers Rede vom 6. Oktober 1939', *Zeithistorische Forschungen/Studies in Contemporary History* 3, available at: http://zeithistorische-forshungen,de/16126041-Wildt.

——— 2007, *Volksgemeinschaft als Selbstermächtigung: Gewalt gegen Juden in der deutschen Provinz 1919 bis 1939*, Hamburg: Hamburger Edition.

——— 2009, *An Uncompromising Generation: The Nazi Leadership of the Reich Security Main Office*, Madison, WI: University of Wisconsin Press.

Williams, William Appleman 1959, *The Tragedy of American Diplomacy*, Cleveland, OH: World Publishing Company.

Williamson, S.R. 1991, *Austria-Hungary and the Origins of the First World War*, London: Macmillan.

Winter, Jay 1995, *Sites of Memory, Sites of Mourning: The Great War in European Cultural History*, New York, NY: Cambridge University Press.

Winzen, Peter 1977, *Bülow's Weltmachtkonzept: Untersuchungen zur Frühphase seiner Außenpolitik 1897–1901*, Boppard: Boldt.

Witt, Peter-Christian 1970, *Die Finanzpolitik des Deutschen Reiches von 1903 bis 1913: Eine Studie zur Innenpolitik des Wilhelminischen Deutschland*, Lübeck: Matthiesen Verlag.

Wohl, Robert 1979, *The Generation of 1914*, Cambridge, MA: Harvard University Press.

Wolfe, Patrick 1997, 'History and Imperialism: A Century of Theory, from Marx to Postcolonialism', *The American Historical Review*, 102, 2: 388–420.

Wrigley, C. 1990, *Lloyd George and the Challenge of Labour*, London: Harvester Wheatsheaf.

Yamazaki, Ryūzō 1978, *Ryotaisenkanki no Nihon Shihonshugi (jyō)*, Tokyo: Ōtsuki Shoten.

Yamazaki, Shirō 1996, 'Senji Kokōgyō Dōin Taisei no Seiritsu to Tenkai', *Tochi Seido Shigaku*, 38, 3: 4–17.

Yanaihara, Tadao 1988 [1929], *Teikokushugika no Taiwan*, Tokyo: Iwanami Shoten.

Yasui, Kunio 1978, 'Daiichiji Taisengo ni Okeru Jyūkagaku Kōgyō no Tenkai' in *Ryotaisenkanki no Nihon Shihonshugi (jyō)*, edited by Yamazaki Ryūzō, Tokyo: Ōtsuki Shoten.

Yasuoka, Shigeaki 1982, *Mitsui Zaibatsu*, Tokyo: Nihon Keizai Shimbunsha.

Young, Louise 2013, *Beyond the Metropolis: Second Cities and Modern Life in Interwar Japan*, Berkeley, CA: University of California Press.

Ziemann, Benjamin and Claus-Christian W. Szejnmann 2003, '"Machtergreifung": The Nazi Seizure of Power in 1933', *Politics, Religion & Ideology* 14, 3: 321–37.

Zilliacus, K. 1946, *Mirror of the Past: A History of Secret Diplomacy*, New York, NY: A.A. Wyn.

Zimmerer, Jürgen 2003, 'Holocaust und Kolonialismus: Beitrag zu einer Archäologie des genozidalen Gedenkens', *Zeitschrift für Geschichtswissenschaft*, 51, 12: 1098–1119.

——— 2004, 'Colonialism and the Holocaust: Towards an Archeology of Genocide', in *Genocide and Settler Society: Frontier Violence and Stolen Indigenous Children in Australian History*, edited by A. Dirk Moses, New York and Oxford: Berghahn.

——— 2004, 'Die Geburt des "Ostlandes" aus dem Geiste des Kolonialismus. Ein postkolonialer Blick auf die NS–Eroberungs- und Vernichtungspolitik', *Sozial Geschichte. Zeitschrift für die historische Analyse des 20. und 21. Jahrhunderts*, 1: 10–43.

——— 2011, *Von Windhuk nach Auschwitz: Beiträge zum Verhältnis von Kolonialismus und Holocaust*, Münster: LTI.

Zinoviev, G. 1970 [1916], 'Encore au sujet de la guerre civile', in *Contre le Courant*, Paris: Maspero.

Žižek, Slavoj 2009, 'De la démocratie à la violence divine', in *Démocratie, dans qel état?*, Paris: La Fabrique.

Zola, Emile 1996, *La Bête Humaine*, New York, NY: Oxford University Press.

Zweig, Stefan 1964, *The World of Yesterday: An Autobiography*, Lincoln, NE: University of Nebraska Press.

Index

Printed in the USA
CPSIA information can be obtained
at www.ICGtesting.com
LVHW022347040124
768229LV00039B/974

9 781608 466344